75   70   65   55

Frobisher Bay

H u d s o n   S t r a i t

tenholme

C. Chudleigh
(C. Chidley)

U n g a v a
B a y

Chimo

L A B R A D O R

C. Mugford (Grimmington I.)

55

George R.

Whale R.

Koksoak or Kaniapiskau R.

Clearwater L.

Richmond
G.

Little Whale   R.
Great Whale   R.

Kaniapiskau L.

Hamilton   R.

nrietta
ria
. Jones

Nichikun
L. & Ho.

a m e s

B a y

R.

East Main
East Main Ft.

Ruperts Ho.
Ruperts   R.

Lake
Mistassini

A

D

A

Mingan

Seven Isds

50

Albany
Ft.

Charlton I.

Moose Ft.

N

R.

Nottaway R.

Waswanapy
L. & Ho.

L. St. John

River   St. Lawrence

NEW
BRUNSWICK

Tadoussac

Abitibi R.

Frederick Ho.

Ho. &
L. Abitibi

Kinoogoomisee L.

Height of Land

St. Maurice R.

Quebec

Fredericton

45

chipicpton Co.
coton

L. Timiskaming
& Ho.

Three Rivers

L. St. Peter

Sault St. Marie

L. Nipissing

Ottawa

Coulonge Ft.

Sable L.

R.

Grand

Two Mts L.

Montreal

Lachine

Boundary 1818 & 1846

L. Champlain

5   80   75   70

HUDSON'S BAY COMPANY
1670-1870

Volume I: 1670-1763

PRINCE RUPERT, THE COMPANY'S FIRST GOVERNOR

from a portrait by Lely in the Company's possession

HUDSON'S BAY COMPANY

1670-1870

Volume I: 1670-1763

BY

E. E. RICH, M.A.

Master of St. Catharine's College, Cambridge
Vere Harmsworth Professor of Imperial and Naval History

WITH A FOREWORD BY THE RIGHT HONOURABLE
SIR WINSTON CHURCHILL, K.G., O.M., C.H., F.R.S., M.P.
Grand Seigneur of the Company of Adventurers of England
trading into Hudson's Bay

TORONTO
McCLELLAND AND STEWART LIMITED
1960

Printed by Robert MacLehose & Company Limited
The University Press
Glasgow, Scotland

© Hudson's Bay Company, 1958

First Trade Edition, 1960
Published by McClelland and Stewart Limited

FOREWORD

MANY great merchant expeditions set out in the last four centuries from the shores of these Islands and materially altered the history of the lands to which they sailed. Of these, none was more prominent than the Hudson's Bay Company. Its resounding title, 'The Adventurers of England Trading into Hudson's Bay', aptly conveys the spirit which has imbued it from its Royal origins in the 17th century to the present day. Its interests have swelled from the early trading posts, where furs were the principal article of trade, to the vast commercial undertakings of the 20th century, when the Company is active in so many spheres of exploration and development in every Province of Canada. It is most fitting that the story of this epic of British enterprise, interwoven with the growth of the great country that Canada has become, should now be written.

Winston S. Churchill

Chartwell,
Westerham,
Kent

September, 1957

PREFACE

FROM THE BEGINNING of its history the Hudson's Bay Company has always shewn great care for the preservation of its documents, and though it has not managed to achieve complete documentation of every phase of its history it has come very near to doing so. It has preserved a unique and magnificently full series of documents which take the story back even to before the Charter of 2nd May, 1670, and with great cost and sense of purpose it has assembled its archives, sorted and catalogued them, and prepared them for the use of the historian. Then the Hudson's Bay Record Society was established, to publish the actual documents in full, with fair comment and criticism by way of introduction and notes. In due course, a generation later, the Company has passed from the publication of its documents to a full and official History, down to 1870. The History has been issued to members of the Hudson's Bay Record Society in two volumes, in 1958 and 1959; this seems appropriate, for the History was very much in mind when the Record Society was founded some twenty years ago and the value for the History of the volumes already published by the Society must immediately be obvious to the reader.

Such a History has been a stimulating and absorbing task. There is nothing impersonal about the story of the Company. At every stage the characters of the men, of the officers and of the committee-men, must be assessed and there are few indeed on whom the archives throw no light. The writing of such history becomes no less difficult because it is absorbing, and at every stage as the History has taken shape I have found the encouragement and advice of the Chairman and the Committee of the Record Society invaluable.

The Record Society in its turn has had behind it the support of the Governor and Committee of the Hudson's Bay Company, and this also I have enjoyed in full measure. At the heart of the matter lie the magnificent archives and the meticulous and devoted staff who care for them and who make them available to the historian. As Archivist of the Hudson's Bay Company and Assistant Editor of the Record Society, Miss Johnson has contributed greatly to this History, and the ability to give to the History the same care which Miss Johnson and her staff bestow on the Record Society's volumes has been one of the great advantages of publishing the History by means of the Record Society.

The end-date of the History, stopping in 1870, conforms to the Company's normal practice in allowing access to its archives, and it has proved entirely acceptable. A neat two centuries of history have an attraction of their own, especially when the period is marked by so great an event as the Deed of Surrender. After 1870 both Canada and the Company were different; a further History to deal with the later period will surely be written, but not for the moment. The limits set, moreover, have proved to contain the substance for two bulky volumes. It could not well be otherwise; but to alleviate the bulk, notes have been almost completely excluded. For the most part such notes could only be citations of documents, almost all of them in the Company's Archives but some of them in the Public Record Office, the British Museum, the Bibliothèque Nationale, the Archives Nationales and in private collections. Citations of this kind the ordinary reader would find valueless, and they have been omitted. But, for those near enough to the documents for such citations to have a meaning, special copies of the History have been given to the Library of the British Museum, to the University Libraries of Oxford and Cambridge, and to the Public Archives of Canada; further annotated copies may be examined in the Company's offices in London and in Winnipeg. My hope is that in this way scholars may use the notes but the general reader, who could not in any case get at the documents, will not find himself burdened with them. He may, however, refer to the suggestions for further reading at the end of the chapters; they are not meant to be exhaustive.

My debt to the Record Society's Committee, and to the Company and its officers, is so clear that it almost needs no expression. Equally valuable has been the harmony with the University Press, Glasgow, which twenty volumes of Record Society publication have left intact; and to me the tolerance and interest of the other Fellows of St. Catharine's and of my wife and family (as I seemed in danger of immersion in so large and so detailed a subject) have been inestimable, and quite essential. But with so much of goodwill and assistance I must nevertheless come to the point at which I confess that the errors are mine alone.

E. E. RICH

St. Catharine's College
Cambridge

CONTENTS

BOOK THREE

From Utrecht to Paris, 1713-1763

ILLUSTRATIONS

MAP

BOOK ONE

The Fur Trade and the Charter

CHAPTER I

THE FUR TRADE AND THE NEW WORLD

In medieval England, as in the rest of western Europe in the middle ages, common furs of local origin were among the normal commodities of everyday life. Goat-skins and sheep-skins, an occasional deer-skin, dogs, cats, hares, and above all conies, were in common use and denoted neither rank nor wealth in the wearer. Fine furs came from the Scandinavian or Russian outskirts of the medieval world, and they were prized and priced according to the beauty and quality which the arctic or semi-arctic conditions of growth gave to the pelts, and according to the cost and difficulty of the trade-route along which they had reached the market. Such furs —foxes, bears, beaver, sable and ermine—were in constant demand and sure of a steady market as insignia of rank and wealth. They formed one of the main commodities of the trade of northern Europe, and the two great terminal points of this trade predominated over all intermediaries, the 'factories' at Novgorod and at Bruges.

London's fourteenth-century trade with Bruges was in itself of vital importance to the clothing industry of Flanders, and in addition the Teutonic Hansard merchants had from the twelfth century onwards enjoyed their own privileges and developed their corporate unity in the Steelyard of London. London therefore had two means of access to the fine furs of the North and the Baltic—direct trade with the Hansards in London, or indirect trade through Bruges. Although the right to wear furs was strictly regulated in England by a series of sumptuary laws from 1337 onwards, yet there was an active market in fine furs and the very frequency of the enactments indicates that such furs were in constant demand.

Such a trade gave occasion in London for regulation by a Skinners' Company. The skinners were certainly so organised by 1319, and they received a charter from Edward III in 1327. With their market in the region of St. Mary Axe they flourished and took their fair share in the disputes of precedence and privilege which marked the history of London in the fifteenth century. They split into two, re-united in a single company, and retained both their civic status and their trade privileges by numerous re-affirmations of their charters. Thereby they maintained control not only over the sale and working of furs in London but also over such trade and work elsewhere in England. Struggles between the artisan furriers and tawyers and the Masters of the Company were almost inevitable, especially as the development of fine woven fabrics in the fifteenth and sixteenth centuries did not produce any decline in the demand for furs but rather, by playing its part in a general development of choice garments, led to wide use of furs as trimmings and decorations.

In the sixteenth and seventeenth centuries, when American furs began to affect the European market, therefore, the fur trade in London and throughout England had behind it a long history, an important and privileged controlling company, and a skilled and independent body of artisans. All of this served to supply a luxury demand for furs used in the skin. As yet the practice of felting fur was little used, and the beaver, the fur *par excellence* for felting, was not available in quantity. Such beaver as was used seems to have come, like other furs, from the Baltic trade, often by way of Bruges (though some beaver are reputed to have been taken even in England), and the beaver was not broken up and felted but was used in the skin, like other furs. The 'Flaundrisch bevere' hat of Chaucer's merchant was either a very early and remarkable felt or was a skin hat, not felted. The normal tradition is that felt hats were first made on the continent in 1456 and that they were first made in London in 1510. Even so, the feltmakers did not develop any great importance or achieve the status of a company to control their craft until the time of Charles I.

Such a tardy development of the fur-felting industry in England was of a piece with the slow English approach to the fur-bearing areas of the New World. These were, in any case, areas which attracted little attention until the more promising routes to the East and to the West Indies had been developed, exploited and monopolised, and even then England was a slow starter. For zeal to discover and settle in the New World took but little hold of statesmen, merchants, or seamen in England during the Tudor period. Whilst some few notable experiments were indeed made and some pioneer tracts were written, it remains true that England did not stake a serious claim to trade or to settle in the New World until the Stuart period.

In Elizabethan England the emphasis, particularly as far as the fur trade was concerned, lay not in the direction of the Americas but in trade to the Baltic and eastern Europe. For this trade the first great English joint-stock company was founded. Later to be known as the Muscovy Company, it took as its original title 'The mysterie and companie of the Merchants adventurers for the discoverie of regions, dominions, islands and places unknown'. Its first voyage in 1553 derived from a conviction that the way to Cathay could be found by means of a North-east Passage, but although it was led by Richard Chancellor, who combined in his person the tough seamanship of the Bristol school and an outstanding mathematical ability, two of the Company's ill-fated ships were lost in the ice with all hands. The third, under Chancellor, made land near Archangel and secured from Czar Ivan trade concessions which were reinforced, on Chancellor's return to England in 1555, by a royal charter giving the monopoly of the trade to Russia. It was envisaged that this would make the Muscovy Company the intermediary for the whole of Europe in the important commodities of hemp, wax, train-oil, tallow, furs and (significantly) felt. Meanwhile the Hansard merchants had lost their privileges in England in 1565 and the strongly nationalistic Company of Merchant Adventurers of England dominated our trade to the Low Countries and there, based upon the rapidly rising town of Antwerp, bought for import the infinite variety of goods demanded by the eclectic taste of Elizabethan England. These goods included furs and the whole range of Baltic produce formerly brought to England by the Hansards.

So, between the Muscovy Company and the Merchant Adventurers of England, the trade in furs of Baltic origin was strengthened and organised during the years of discovery. This was natural, for the great English trading companies were normally interested not in ocean voyages but in continental trade (for which, indeed, they were founded and organised). But although Tudor England was thus preoccupied with the European continent there were both theorists and practical men who were looking across the Atlantic. The great companies might be tied to European trade, but individual merchants could be got to support ocean ventures, especially in the western ports. This spirit predominated in particular at Bristol, where the Bristol Society of Merchant Venturers showed an enterprise in marked contrast with the apathy of the London merchants. In Bristol, Plymouth, Dartmouth and the other western ports a vital and increasing school of seamen learned, in the tradition of John and Sebastian Cabot, to cross the North Atlantic; and there ship-owners, merchants, ships-captains and the enterprising men of the countryside, pooled their ideas about North America.

These were ideas in which fishing, trade, discovery and settlement, all had their place. Bristol was the centre of the movement, and the practical knowledge of the Bristol men was brought into closer contact with the small school of Elizabethan imperial planners when in 1584 the Younger Hakluyt was promised the next vacant prebend at Bristol. The promise was won when he presented his *Discourse of Western Planting* to Elizabeth, and was a most apt reward for that treatise. For the *Discourse* marked a new approach to the Atlantic, to America and to the fur trade, by the courtly theorists. Largely economic in its approach, it emphasised the decay of our European markets, the need to find fresh outlets for our produce and for our redundant population, and the need to find fresh sources of the commodities which we brought from Europe. The English title northward from Florida to 67° was claimed as deriving from the Cabot voyages. Within this vast area Hakluyt was able to quote reports for most of the goods required, from silkworms to ships' masts. Among other matters he quoted Stephen Gomez' 1524 account of 'Norumbega' with its excellent martens, sables and other furs, and followed it with the Frenchman Stephen Bellinger's recent report on the coast south from Cape Breton, with its beaver, otter, marten, seal and other skins, and with 'a kynde of muske called Castor'. Jacques Cartier's account of the furs of the St. Lawrence was included, and the *Discourse's* section on commodities concluded with the account that there were 'upp within the graunde baye exceedinge quantitie of all kyndes of precious furres (whereof I sawe twentie thousande frenche Crownes worthe the laste yere broughte to Paris to Valeron Perosse and Mathewe Grainer the kinges skynners) also suche aboundaunce of trayne oile to make sope, and of fishe as a third parte of Europe ys furnished therewith'.

Richard Hakluyt was bringing the furs of North America into his planning of a British Empire. In this he had the French for an example. The French fishermen who frequented the Banks of Newfoundland and the mainland coasts had during the middle years of the sixteenth century developed a constant and lucrative fur trade with the Indians with whom they came in contact, and as a result of his experience and his conversations in Paris, Hakluyt was now, at a formative moment, including fur in the list of goods which England might derive from American settlements instead of from doubtful friends and possible enemies among her neighbours.

Fur, however, normally played but a small part in the plans of the Elizabethans. Virginia, with a climate similar to that of Spain or Italy, seemed to most Elizabethan planners and pamphleteers the ideal counterpart to England. The Elder Hakluyt's *Pamphlet for the Virginia Enterprise* agreed that a settlement there could make us independent alike of the Mediterranean and Spanish trades and of the Baltic, and to Virginia Raleigh directed the first English colonising voyages of 1584 and 1585. Raleigh's settlements failed; but from the project came a succession of expeditions and of royal grants which culminated in the charter of the Virginia Company in 1606 and in the settlement of Jamestown in 1609. Furs were not one of the prime commodities which occupied the planners and pamphleteers or which were sought in the Virginia ventures; emphasis was upon the essentials of a national economy, upon grain, wine, metals, timber, hemp and flax. But furs soon proved to be a valuable trade for the Virginia settlers, and the great charter of the Virginia Company, revised in 1609, proved to be adequate cover for settlement much further north. Sub-dividing the vast grant, a Corporation of New England set up a series of subordinate undertakings, not all successful but which included New Plymouth and Massachusetts Bay. So the Virginia project in its turn led to the New England settlements; there also furs soon proved to be the chief commodity in which the settlers could win a market. The Elizabethan preoccupation with the southern produce of Virginia had within a generation come round to the point which the Younger Hakluyt had made in his *Discourse*, the value of the northern fur trade.

Meanwhile the Virginia Company's charter had been used as cover not only for the New England colonies but also for an abortive fur-trading company and, in 1627, for a Canada Company. Interest in Canada was not a novelty in 1627. England had turned in that direction with Frobisher's attempts to discover a North-west Passage in 1576, 1577 and 1578, under the charter to the Company of Adventurers to the Northwest, and with the last voyage, of 1582, made by that Company. Frobisher had certainly penetrated as far as Hudson Strait and Baffin Land in 1576, but his ventures bore little promise of establishing settlements, and Humphrey Gilbert by 1578 had managed to secure to himself and his associates the task of planting Newfoundland. Gilbert's death at sea ended this episode, but the search for the North-west Passage was still pursued by his brother Adrian who, in 1583, secured a charter for all places discovered between the equinoctial line and the North Pole for the attractively-named 'Colleges for the Discovery of the North-West Passage'. The projects for a North-west Passage and for settlement in Newfoundland therefore lingered on, and in 1610 the Bristol merchants managed to secure a new charter to settle Newfoundland, under which they sent out several voyages. At the same time, from 1622 onwards, attempts were in hand to settle Nova Scotia under the terms of a charter granting all lands between New England and the St. Lawrence. This brought opposition to French settlement into the open, for the French post at Port Royal had already been destroyed in 1613 by the New Englanders and, despite its re-settlement by the French, it was the site chosen for the settlement of the Nova Scotia Company.

But rivalry with the French, and desire for the fur trade which they enjoyed and which by 1627 was already the main support of their Canadian settlement, was made more clear by the charter to the Canada Company. This body set out to trade and plant in the region of the St. Lawrence itself. It was chartered for this purpose, and to dispossess the French there. The first expedition of 1627, under David Kirke, conquered all Canada except Quebec, traded with the Indians, and brought home a considerable cargo of furs. In the following year Quebec itself was taken and the great Champlain and his garrison were brought to England with their furs. The Admiralty Court decided that the furs should not be sold until the disputes with the French had been settled, but they were nevertheless put on the market (it was alleged that the Adventurers broke open the ware-house) and made a very good price. Though many of them went to a French buyer (for France was more used to the fur trade than England and had wider markets ready to absorb the produce) peace with France brought a series of claims and counter-claims. The lands of Canada were restored to the French, but Kirke and his Adventurers probably made handsome profits and knew the value of the fur trade of Canada, so that English interlopers began to frequent the St. Lawrence in search of furs, and in 1633 Kirke and his company secured a patent for a monopoly of the trade of the river and gulf of Canada, in beaver and all other skins and wool, for thirty-one years.

The Canada Company did not conduct any continuous trade in furs—or in anything else—but it whetted the appetites of Englishmen for the profits of the fur trade and it also coincided with further and more purposeful attempts at the discovery of the North-west Passage. Henry Hudson had made two voyages for this purpose before he deserted the English and made his 1609 voyage in the service of the Dutch East India Company. This took him to the Hudson River, and so gave to the Dutch that river's approach to the furs of Canada. Next year he set out on his last tragic voyage, once more in English employ, and in the service of several members of the Muscovy Company took his ship the *Discovery* through Hudson

Strait and down to James Bay in the 'Bottom' of Hudson Bay. There he wintered, and on his return voyage in 1611 he was cast adrift, to perish, by his mutinous and starving crew.

Hudson's last voyage brought little encouragement for a fur trade, for he wintered at a summer hunting-ground of the Indians and saw only one Indian and traded only two beaver. But it gave a great impetus to renewed efforts at a North-west Passage, and in 1612 he was followed into the Bay by Thomas Button, sent out with two ships by a new 'Company of Merchants, Discoverers of the North-West Passage'. Button made land on the western shore of Hudson Bay and worked his way south to Nelson River, which he named and took in possession. Here he wintered and got fresh provisions from the partridges of the place. But he, like Hudson, saw no Indians and did nothing to stimulate any hopes of a fur trade.

The search for a North-west Passage nevertheless continued, and steadily added to British knowledge of the seas which would ulti-mately give a maritime approach to the fur-bearing lands of the far north. Nor were the English the only explorers in this field; voyages by Bylot and Baffin in 1615 and 1616, and by Hawkridge in 1617, were supplemented by the Danish expedition of Jens Munck to Churchill River in 1619–20. Then further English voyagers pene-trated to the Bay when in 1630 the Bristol Merchant Venturers fitted out Captain Thomas James, and a body of London merchants sent Captain Luke Fox. Both men explored the southern coast of Hudson Bay between Port Nelson and Cape Henrietta Maria, and James and his crew wintered in huts in a bay of Charlton Island before hazarding the return voyage in the following year.

Whilst such voyages kept alive the desire for the North-west Pass-age, and gave English mariners an important tradition of arctic navigation and a fair knowledge of the shores of the southern parts of Hudson Bay, genuine colonisation had also taken place on a scale not hitherto contemplated. Stirred in part by the religious troubles of seventeenth-century England, in part by the economic troubles of Europe and the lack of markets and employment, English families had moved across the Atlantic in increasing numbers as the century wore on. This was something quite different from the predominantly anti-Spanish moves of the courtiers and gallants of the early years of the century, moves which had always been liable to slide away from settlement into commerce-raiding and piracy, in which a search for bullion was always apt to upset the plans for agriculture. These were moves by very mixed cross-sections of England's population (a pop-ulation more used to changing its abode in search of work than would be imagined) and they were by no means all reputable married citizens. But they, especially the New England settlers, were dominated by the sober, largely Non-conformist, family settler. Here, therefore, there was place for that outward expansion in search of political, religious and economic opportunity which has driven the frontier of settlement across the plains and over the mountains of America. But there was not place for any abandonment of agriculture as the basis of society. Such purchases as the infant colonies needed to make in England therefore had to be made, once the early capital of the ventures was exhausted, by sale in England of a cash-crop. For the southern colonies tobacco for a time supplied this cash-crop. But for the northern settlements no such agricultural crop was available. Furs supplied the place.

BOOKS FOR REFERENCE

BODILLY, R. B.—*The Voyage of Captain Thomas James for the Discovery of the North-West Passage, 1631* (London, 1928).

COLE, C. Woolsey—*Colbert and a Century of French Mercantilism* (New York, 1939), 2 vols.

FISKE, J.—*The Dutch and Quaker Colonies in America* (London, 1899), 2 vols.

HECKSCHER, E. F.—*Mercantilism*; authorised translation by M. Shapiro (prepared from the German edition and revised by the author), revised (2nd) edition edited by E. F. Söderlund (London, 1955), 2 vols.

INNIS, H. A.—*The Fur Trade in Canada* (revised edition, Toronto, 1956).

KIRKE, H.—*The First English Conquest of Canada* (London, 1908).

McGRATH, P. (ed.)—*Records relating to the Society of Merchant Venturers of the City of Bristol in the seventeenth century* (Bristol, Bristol Record Society, 1952).

MacINNES, C. M.—*A Gateway of Empire* (Bristol, 1939).

SCOTT, W. R.—*The Constitution and Finance of English, Scottish and Irish Joint-Stock Companies to 1720* (Cambridge, 1910–12), 3 vols.

TAYLOR, E. G. R.—*Tudor Geography 1485–1583* (London, 1930).

TAYLOR, E. G. R.—*Late Tudor and Early Stuart Geography 1583–1650. A sequel to Tudor Geography, 1485–1583* (London, 1934).

TAYLOR, E. G. R. (ed.)—*The original writings & correspondence of the two Richard Hakluyts* (London, The Hakluyt Society, 1935), 2 vols.

TEMPLE, Sir William—*Observations upon the United Provinces of the Netherlands*. With an Introduction by G. N. Clark (Cambridge, 1932).

UNWIN, G.—*Industrial Organization in the Sixteenth and Seventeenth Centuries* (Oxford, 1904).

WHEELER, John—*A Treatise of Commerce*. Reproduced from the London edition of 1610. With a bibliographical note by George Burton Hotchkiss. (New York, Facsimile Text Society, 1931), Series 5, Vol. 2.

WILLIAMSON, J. A.—*Maritime Enterprise 1485–1558* (Oxford, 1913).

ARTICLES

TAYLOR, E. G. R.—'Richard Hakluyt'. See *The Geographical Journal* (London, The Royal Geographical Society, 1947).

TAYLOR, E. G. R.—'The English Worldmakers of the Seventeenth Century and their Influence on the Earth Sciences'. See *The Geographical Journal* (London, The Royal Geographical Society, 1948).

CHAPTER II

CHARTERED COMPANIES

Puritan rule and Dutch rivalry greatly hardened and strengthened England's concepts of Empire in the middle years of the seventeenth century. Settlement and the clear subordination of the colonies to the mother country, combined with emphasis on navigation and the West India trade, were then worked into a policy and embodied in statute. In this England was not alone. The second half of the seventeenth century saw all the states of western Europe looking across the Atlantic in a newly purposeful mood from which the semi-piratical exuberance of the sixteenth century was missing.

Spain, despite her defeats at sea, had vindicated her grasp of Central and South America; the coastal fringes of North America had been settled by English and Dutch colonists in their temperate regions, whilst further north New France boasted some three thousand *habitans* by 1663. The West Indies were still in dispute, but the rising emphasis on those islands reveals the importance being given to navigation as a source of income and as a defence in war; it reveals, too, emphasis on trade as a source of balanced payments rather than on bullion as a product of mineral wealth and exploitation. Colonies would bring commodities which must otherwise be bought from foreign countries; or they might bring commodities which could be sold to foreign countries. In either case the balance of trade, the balance of foreign payments, would be strengthened and the mother country would be placed in a less precarious position, less liable to be milked of her bullion for payment, less liable to be influenced by trade embargoes.

This change of emphasis, with the accent increasingly on trade and farming rather than on mines or commerce-raiding, left the normal machinery for the acquisition and the settlement of colonies unaltered. The period saw some experiments both by the English and by the French in 'Crown Colony' administration, but they were ill-starred and unpopular; the normal method of acquisition, administration and settlement, remained a chartered company. The pattern varied in detail but the principles remained constant; there was a hard core of common practice arising from common views and common needs, for the chartered company had behind it both a tradition of usefulness and a capacity for action in the difficult circumstances of seventeenth-century colonial expansion. Those circumstances demanded that the incentives for expansion and settlement should arise from private desires and be supported by private capital; but they also demanded that such desires should be regimented in the interests of the state. For this reconciliation of private incentive and state interest the chartered company seemed invaluable.

The companies were always private in that much (though not always all) of the capital required for planting and trading came from private purses. But they were public in that they required some sort of a charter to give them their claims to lands and trade, to promise them support against foreign rivals and to grant them monopoly against rivals of their own nation. Without such a charter and promise of support they could not get the financial backing necessary for such speculative ventures as overseas settlements. The companies were public, too, in that they were saddled with public or quasi-public duties—the defence of the lands to be occupied, care for law and good governance, for religion, for relations with native princes and peoples—and with the regulation of the expected trade in such a way as to conform to the national interests. This last function was a quite normal feature of those attempts to regulate trade so as to secure that over-all balance of foreign payments which, in one form or another, dominated the economic policies of every European state of that day.

The chartered company was by no means above reproof. Its ideals were at best a curious medley of private profit and national service; and it seldom fulfilled its ideals to the letter. But attempts at alternatives were not encouraging—as when Jamaica was directed by the English government, or when the Casa da Contratation organised the trade of the Spanish colonies, or alternatively when the East India trade was thrown to the disorganised practices of English interlopers under Charles I. For the seventeenth century the chartered company was appropriate both in its ability to raise finance and in its ability to win the support of government; the criticisms which contemporaries hurled at it were either due to its abuses but not to its principles, or they came from rivals who accepted the underlying concepts but wished to set up their own corporations, to enjoy in their own right the privileges which they condemned in others. Attacks on the chartered company certainly abounded, and the freedom of subjects to trade unless excluded by Act of Parliament was freely alleged. A restive Governor of Barbados could complain that nobles and gentry ventured no more than they would throw away at dice and that merchants hoped only for extraordinary gains, while both withdrew their support when the colony most needed it. But serious, and by no means biased, government enquiries sought the views of the merchants in their companies, and it was accepted that the forts and factories needed for 'Traffique with infidels and Barbarous nations' could only be established and maintained by companies. There was very little criticism which was based on a genuine belief in free trade in colonial produce or which traversed the basic concept of the chartered company for this purpose.

If the chartered company was the accepted form of organisation for colonial settlement and trade, some hope of profit was an essential feature, without which the company would fail to raise capital and so would fail to carry out its task. The insistence varied with circumstances and personalities, but it was always there. With the French it was an accepted weakness that they wished always to have their profits before their ventures had been given time to take roots. The English were, on the whole, more patient; they accepted the dictum of Bacon that in planting a colony we must reckon as we do in planting an orchard, and count on losing the first twenty years, to come to fruition in the end. Yet even so the Virginia settlers were told that unless they produced some sort of return cargo to offset the capital costs they 'were like to remain as banished men'. Failing profits, the chartered company showed that 'private purses be but cowld comforters to poor settlers', and all settlements under this system were therefore bound to seek some easily obtainable cash-crop. Despite early hopes, the northern colonies of New England had no such resource. There, interest had always been in homestead subsistence farming rather than in plantation production of an export staple crop. The New Englanders might reluctantly produce an occasional shipment of wood-ashes for soap-making, or a little corn, but on the whole their colonies were void of produce which could easily be made into shipments to pay a dividend to projectors or proprietors—except for furs.

The New England settlers, moreover, were sturdy individualists, as averse from twisting their lives for the interests of absentee proprietors as their soil was barren of export commodities. But they could not deny outright the claims of the Virginia Company through whose charter they derived their right to the soil, and so they were forced to buy their freeholds and freedoms. They agreed to pay, in the only commodity which they could produce and which was acceptable to the Company. This was fur, the cash-crop of the northern colonies. The fur trade of New Plymouth was reserved for the joint stock of the Company and it was for an annual payment of fur that the Pilgrim Fathers bought out the rights of the Plymouth Company and secured the ownership of their lands, and the southern colonies also found furs a valuable export.

Shipments of furs, especially of elks[1] and beaver, with marten, otter, fisher, and 'small furs' as supplements, early began to be consigned from the colonists to London, there to be sold to the skinners and to the rising felt-making industry. London was at this time developing a new activity in the fur trade, largely stimulated by the ease with which it could be supplied with furs from the North American colonies. The active artisan skinners had rebelled against the 'City Company' elements in their trade in 1606 and had secured a Privy Council order (subsequently annulled) giving them a place in the management of their trade. Other signs of activity in the fur trade may be seen in the organisation of the Feltmakers' Company in 1629, and in its attempts to regulate its trade. English shipments of furs bore no comparison with those from New France; nor did their importance challenge comparison in the colonies from which they came. Furs were supplements to an increasingly settled agriculture, not the mainstay of the colonial economy. But they played a valuable part in the economy, they stimulated an English interest in American trade, and they bore such promise of great wealth that they might at any moment seize men's imaginations and provide that flux of fortune-seeking which would run together the elements of arctic discovery, settlement, trade and navigation, which were all in men's minds at the middle of the seventeenth century. For shipments of furs came regularly from Maryland, Virginia and Carolina, and the proprietors of the last colony (who included the Earl of Shaftesbury, later a founder-member of the Hudson's Bay Company) managed to get beaver, cats and foxes from its trade and fully understood the part which fur would play in any American settlement.

For similar reasons, but with markedly different emphasis, the French settlers further north also attempted to buy their freedom from metropolitan projectors by annual payments of furs. Here, from the start of settlement, there had been a danger that the ease with which furs could be got, by trade with the Indians or by trapping, would divert the energy of the settlers and the enthusiasm of their backers from agriculture and the heavy work of clearing the ground for crops.

---

[1] The Canadian Moose was not known to European heralds, merchants or lawyers, who therefore wrote of elks, a European animal and known to them, when they meant 'moose'. See Ramsay Traquair, 'The Coat of Arms', *The Beaver* (Winnipeg, Hudson's Bay Company), June 1945, p. 44.

Any examination of the story of the early fur trade of Canada is bound to give the impression that the fur trade of the St. Lawrence completely dominated French settlement in the New World. This is only partly true; it is clear that while the fur trade ran through a series of crises and exhausted the capital of a series of companies without bringing any great profits, the growth and economic stability of the French settlements continued slowly but surely, and that the emphasis on fur must be placed in its right proportion as the emphasis on a cash-crop in a peasant society.

From the first, a monopoly of the fur trade had been an important feature of French attempts to settle and to govern Canada. Early in the seventeenth century, while the English colonies were just getting established, the great financier William de Caen had underwritten the Compagnie de Montmorency in 1620 and then, in 1628, the Compagnie de la Nouvelle France (also called the Compagnie des Cent Associez) on condition of getting control of the trade in furs from Canada to France. Although de Caen's efforts coincided with Kirke's attempts to set up an English Canada Company and to stake England's claims to the furs brought down the St. Lawrence, and the claims of the Compagnie de Montmorency and of the Compagnie de la Nouvelle France were under severe dispute, the weight attached to the fur trade stands out clearly.

The Compagnie de la Nouvelle France won its case against the Compagnie de Montmorency in 1634, and the Cent Associez who formed the victorious *compagnie* were given control of the trade on condition that they recompensed William de Caen and the Compagnie de Montmorency. But neither by general participation in the fur trade nor by setting up an internal syndicate to run the trade (a *compagnie particulière*) could the Associez make profits. So in 1645 they were happy to make an arrangement which was similar to that between the English settlers and their companies. There was, however, the vital difference that whereas the English settlers bought their lands for payment in beaver the French *habitans* bought the right to participation in the fur trade. For a thousand beaver a year, payable in Paris, the *habitans* got their freedom to share in the trade.

At the same time they achieved a measure of civic independence, with the establishment of their own Council at Quebec, with a tax on the beaver and fur trade to pay the costs of administration—the *Droit du Quatre*, payment of every fourth beaver and every tenth elk skin, which imposed such hardships on the French fur-trader. The trade, however, fell into the hands of five or six families who found it only too easy to buy food and goods at La Rochelle on the credit inspired by the wealth of beaver, and who then, having over-spent their credit, transferred their custom to Le Havre, pleading the usurious rates charged by the Rochelle merchants.

By 1656, the *habitans* were ready to surrender the trade back to a company. The outcry resulted in a royal commission, of which the dominant member was the future Governor of Canada, de Lauzon. The conclusion was to set aside the fur trade of Tadoussac as a *Ferme* to pay the administrative costs of the colony, while the *habitans* were to cease paying their annual tribute to the Company. De Lauzon's successor, d'Argenson, then granted out the *Ferme* of the trade of Tadoussac to a small group of local *habitans*. La Rochelle continued to supply the merchandise for Canada under this arrangement—at profits varying from sixty per cent. on dry goods to a hundred per cent. on brandy, part of which was to go towards paying off the £10,000 of debts to the Rochelle merchants which the previous period of trade had piled up.

This was arranged in 1660; but already missionary feeling was running high against the predominance of brandy in the French fur trade, and the arrangement was soon upset, so that in 1663 the Crown took over the colony as its own property and formed the new *Compagnie des Indes Occidentales* for the combined trade of the West Indies and of Canada, to supply goods and to take the beaver of the colony in return. The *Compagnie des Indes Occidentales* soon failed; among other difficulties which it had to encounter was the suspicion of the great Intendant of Canada, Talon, 'qui ne voulait point de Compagnie', who used his privileged position to engage in the fur trade (as it was alleged), and sent voyages into the interior, encouraging the over-development of the trade.

This brought on the scene Aubert de la Chesnay, who was to become the most persistent and effective advocate for developing the fur trade of Canada under controls (by which he meant a company) which would yield profits, but with such enterprise as would exclude other nations from the trade. He arrived in Canada as the agent of the French merchant-outfitters, especially those of Rouen, who were anxious to collect the advances which they had made to the Canadians, and found, as he was to find throughout his career, that although there could be no doubt that beaver was the only hope of the Canadian colony, the only means of purchasing its wants in Europe, yet the organisation of that vital trade was fraught with extreme difficulty, especially for a man whose main task was to collect debts and to represent French merchants.

Thus, although it was universally accepted that the fur trade was

the only strength and salvation of the colony, the abuses and privileges with which it was enmeshed, and the duty which it bore of
paying the costs of administration of the colony, meant that by the
time Charles II was restored to the throne of Great Britain even the
habitans were unwilling to undertake its responsibilities, much
though they wished to enjoy its profits. The *Compagnie de la Nouvelle
France* was no more confident. In 1663 it gladly surrendered its
privileges to the Crown, but its position had by then become so complicated that no simple arrangement could be made either with the
Crown or with the *Compagnie des Indes Occidentales*, which was soon
chartered by the Crown to undertake the affairs of Canada. It was
reckoned that the *Compagnie de la Nouvelle France* had spent over a
million livres and had accumulated debts of four hundred thousand
livres. The *Compagnie des Indes Occidentales* could make nothing of
such a position, and in 1665 the *habitans* once more took over the
fur trade of the colony. The *Compagnie* kept its rights to the territories as specified in the grant of 1628, but the peltry 'de laquelle
seule provient l'utilité qui se retire dudit pays' was surrendered to
the *habitans*, except for the privileged area of Miskou and the coast
of Acadia and Cape Breton, in return for their undertaking to pay
the clergy and the civil officers, including the Governor.

While the fur trade of Canada was thus encumbered with debts,
enmeshed with privileges, and ensnared with duties, it also found
that it had serious rivals, immune from these handicaps, to dispute
the markets of Europe, and even of France. The importations from
the New England settlers have already been noted, and they were a
steady stream—perhaps of indifferent southern pelts—during the
second half of the seventeenth century. Moreover, the Dutch settlements in North America were not different in this matter from the
French and the English. They had in the Hudson River a good
route to the Great Lakes, they had contacts with Indian tribes who
brought down furs (especially with the Iroquois) and they valued the
trade so brought. When the Dutch West India Company (under
which the settlements at Orange, Manhattan and New Amsterdam
were established) wished to press its claims for chartered rights it
did so largely on the basis of its fur trade, and to encourage settlement the States General broadcast the information that 'Furs were
to be had of the natives very reasonably'. The Dutch reckoned that
their trade was highly profitable and was capable of yielding, one
year with another, a profit of six hundred thousand guilders.

In this emphasis on fur, therefore, lay the germ of international
rivalry. For all of the countries concerned part of the incentive to

North American settlement lay in the hope of finding alternative sources of Baltic products, and although furs did not rank in this context as highly as pitch, tar, timber and naval stores, they were nevertheless the one commodity which could in fact be easily got from North America. They could moreover be used for a trade to the Russian fur market which allowed the purchase there of the hemp, tar and other commodities required.[1]

The French, heavily dependent on furs, therefore saw a double threat in the English actions during the second Dutch War, in 1665–6. Their own situation was in any case unsatisfactory; the *Compagnie de la Nouvelle France* had ceded its rights to the Crown in 1663, and the *Compagnie des Indes Occidentales* had been set up in 1664 to take over control, with the Carignan-Salières regiment to give strength to the colony and with de Tracy as a roving administrator for the interim period, followed by Jean Talon as Intendant and de Courcelles as Governor. Difficulties abounded; it was not until 1666 that the fur trade was completely disembarrassed of the claims of the *Compagnie de la Nouvelle France*, while at the same time the inroads of the Iroquois caused such grave misgivings that early in 1666 de Courcelles led an expedition to bring them to order. He failed disastrously and it was not until September of that year that de Tracy repeated the attack successfully.

In the meantime Kirke and the English Canada Company revived their claims under war conditions. They petitioned for the enforcement of their chartered rights to Nova Scotia, Canada and the valley of the St. Lawrence in 1660, with emphasis on the hope of supplying Baltic goods—all the produce of the Sound of Denmark. Then, in 1666, the year of the French disaster against the Iroquois, they again raised the question of their charter and Kirke led an expedition which made a deep inroad into Canada, bringing out at least one cargo of beaver. The French hoped that the war might not spread to the colonies and instructed the Canadians to preserve peace overseas if possible, but the British Canada Company hoped that the government might be persuaded into maintaining the claim to Canada and vindicating it at the peace.

Kirke was to be disappointed, for the Treaty of Breda, in 1667, restored to the two kingdoms their possessions as they held them on 1st January, 1665, and British claims to Canada were thereby denied. But at the same time as this threat to the French position and trade developed, the Hudson River saw another and more successful English attempt at expansion in North America and at better

[1] For this trade system cf. Ch. V.

supplies of furs. Talon had written already to Colbert to urge that the French attempts to bring the Iroquois to order should also aim at the conquest of the Dutch settlements and the securing of a monopoly of furs for Canada—which would also entail the restraint of New Sweden and of New England. Talon had a personal knowledge of the fur trade; he reckoned that when the English, instead of the French, captured the Dutch posts and thereby united the fur out-puts of Boston, Manhattan and Orange, they secured over a million pounds of beaver a year. Thereby, he thought, they got quantities which made them very serious competitors for the supply of the European market. Though his estimate of the produce of New England and New York was certainly an exaggeration as far as quantity was concerned, the basic fact remained that, as a result of the second Dutch War and the capture of the Dutch North American colonies, England had developed a lively interest in the North American fur trade and was henceforth a serious rival to the French.

The rivalry, however, was only incipient by 1667. Neither London nor the English merchants were as yet competent even to handle the fur trade of New York, and when the terms of the Treaty of Breda made it clear that the Dutch settlement would pass to England, to the Duke of York in full possession, the Dutch colonists petitioned that 'the trade of beaver (the most desirable commodity for Europe) has always been purchased by commodities brought from Holland, as camper duffles, hatchets and other ironworks made at Utrecht, etc., much esteemed of by the natives, and if these fail the very trade itself would fail, and the French of Canada (now encroached to be but half a day's journey from the Mohawks) supplying them may totally divert the beaver trade'. The inability of England to enter into this trade, and the danger of seeing it slip into French hands, was such that the Committee for Foreign Plantations gave the Dutch the right to trade to the extent of three ships a year for the next seven years. Such a breach in the all-important Navigation Acts underlined both the importance of the fur trade and England's in-ability to engage profitably in that trade.

Canada was therefore, for the moment, still supreme in the fur trade of the New World, and there were good reasons for this. The nearer the English settlers moved towards the fur-bearing lands of the far north the more deeply they committed themselves to fishing and to subsistence farming, whereas the nearer the French got to the beaver the more they succumbed to the lure of the woods and forsook the plough for the canoe, the trap and the gun.

There seemed little serious reason for French fears that England would supplant them as the bulk-providers of furs for the European market, for there were geographical and national causes for their obsession and their predominance. The French settlements in the lower St. Lawrence, attractive in many ways, were inhospitable in comparison with New England. The rivers and lakes, too, were natural highways into the interior whereas the Alleghanies tended to restrict English settlement to the coastal areas. The French were few in numbers—only about two hundred *habitans* by 1642 and only about three thousand after serious efforts at organised emigration, by 1663—they were partly military and largely adventurous, and they were predominantly male in a way in which the family groups of New Englanders were not. They were more of a garrison than a colony, and they required steady encouragement of female emigration to enable them to balance their lives and set up families in the New World. The English had emigrated with their wives and families, their household goods, farm stock and cattle; they were in every way a more settled and less adventurous, if equally determined, community.

Moreover, the French priests led one of the most magnificent examples of penetrative missionary endeavour which the modern world has seen. They journeyed thousands of miles into the hinterland of the St. Lawrence whereas the New Englanders, intolerant in their Puritanical self-righteousness, ignored and increasingly abhorred the heathen and certainly projected no serious plans for their conversion to Christianity. French policy, too, was strongly influenced by the legend of an 'Inland Sea' which could be reached by river and lake and which would then lead by easy water-routes to the Pacific and so to the trade of the Far East.

Not least among the causes of the different reactions to the fur trade was the fact that New France lay contiguous to magnificent fur-country, and that farming there could often only be engaged in for six months of the year, whereas New England furs were often inferior since they were grown in less rigorous conditions, they came through the medium of a long and vulnerable Indian trade route, and the pursuit of furs took time which could more profitably be spent on agriculture.

The result of the contrast was that by 1665 the French colony had to be taken over by the Crown, it was insecure in every sense, economic and military, and the fur trade had to be curtailed by a system of licences. In contrast, the English colonists were so well established and so independent that the Cromwellian government was forced to insist on their allegiance to England. The chartered companies had produced widely different results in the different circumstances, and although the union of New England and New York produced a very respectable volume of furs, and frightened the French, there seemed little likelihood that circumstances as they existed at the signing of the Treaty of Breda in 1667 could produce effective rivalry for the European fur-market.

But already a train of events had been started which brought about precisely that consequence.

BOOKS FOR REFERENCE

BIGGAR, H. P.—*The Early Trading Companies of New France* (Toronto, 1901).

BONASSIEUX, P.—*Les Grandes Compagnies de Commerce* (Paris, 1892).

BRADFORD, A.—*History of Massachusetts, from 1764 to 1820* (Boston, 1822–29), 3 vols.

BROWN, L. Fargo—*The First Earl of Shaftesbury* (New York, 1933).

MARGRY, P.—*Rélations et mémoires inédits pour servir à l'histoire de la France dans les pays d'outremer, tirés des archives de la Ministère de la marine et des colonies* (Paris, 1867).

MARGRY, P. (ed.)—*Découvertes et Etablissements des Français Dans l'Ouest et Dans le Sud de l'Amérique Septentrionale* (Paris, 1879–88), 6 vols.

WADMORE, J. F.—*Some Account of the Worshipful Company of Skinners of London . . .* (London, 1902).

WRONG, G. M.—*The Rise and Fall of New France* (London, 1928), 2 vols.

CHAPTER III

GROSEILLIERS, RADISSON AND THEIR SUPPORTERS

The Treaty of Breda left in British hands that substantial part of the fur trade which came from New England and New Netherland, and since the general theories of navigation and the balance of imperial trade were against the concession which allowed the Dutch colonists to continue their fur trade, within a year of the Treaty it was revoked. It would leave a 'way for fforrainers to trade with the rest of his Majestys Plantations, and preventing the Exportation of the Manufactures of England, and shall thereby destroy His Majestys Customes and the Trade of this Kingdome, which is in a great measure upheld by the Plantations'. This was bringing the heavy guns of the trade theory to bear on the small target of the Hudson River fur trade. But it shows the importance which could be attached to that trade, and the threat implied to Canadian dominance and solvency if the Dutch posts should be fully exploited. It showed, too, the attraction of the fur trade to the individual settler, for every man was left free to trade in furs, on request. The English-American fur trade was developing fast, and shipments of furs from New England soon became more regular in the mixed cargoes of the period.

This threat to the Canadian economy was realised in France. But the inherent difficulties of regulating and taxing a trade which depended on the adventurous spirit of its participants led the French to present to the British an even more dangerous opportunity, a chance to add to the already threatening bulk of the furs of New England and New Netherland those of New Wales, for so the British called the lands surrounding Hudson Bay. Such an opportunity might very easily have been mis-handled in the busy and venal London of the Restored Stuarts, but it was not likely to be overlooked. In such a Court and City it could be sure of arousing interest; the question was whether it would meet the necessary practical support.

The Restoration policy in imperial trade was a close-knit and purposeful policy, not to be cried down because it was often achieved by intrigues and often entrusted to fortune-seekers. Based upon the Cromwellian Navigation Acts, it accepted the integration of domestic

and colonial trade into one over-all balance, and it aimed at supplementing the economy of Britain by that of her colonies, who
would provide markets for her manufactures, raw materials for her
industries, and a transport system which would give a reserve of
ships and seamen for wars. So integrated, the imperial economy
would become increasingly independent of alien supplies or markets
and stronger because, as an imperial unit, it would achieve a balance
of exports over imports. Any colonial trade that would supply goods
which must otherwise be bought outside the empire, or which could
be sold on the European market, would meet favour, and any project
which showed promise of such a reaction would be sure of discussion
and of favourable reception.

It was a truculently nationalistic concept, and it was a concept
which was under constant revision to bring it into line with the facts
of the world situation, to combat the power and wealth of the state or
states which seemed to offer the gravest threat to our national economy. Here policy slowly but surely shifted from rivalry with the
Dutch to hostility to the French.

This was a period in which the spirit of adventure moved along
with sophisticated manners, elaborate dress, scientific enquiry and
financial acumen. This was the land of both the Royal Society and of
the Bank of England—and of many projects akin to both—the land
of Robert Boyle, the 'father of chemistry' (and uncle of the Duke of
Cork) and also of Robert Vyner, the father of Exchequer Bills; both
of them were to become Adventurers of the Hudson's Bay Company.

The scientific enthusiasms of the period, the desire for a balanced
imperial trade, the opposition to the Dutch, and later to the French,
the wish to make fortunes for courtiers who had shared the royal
exile—these things mingled, and grew by mixture, with the chance
to get the furs of Hudson Bay because that chance brought them all
into relation with one of the oldest and strongest of British traditions
in the story of exploration.

This was the tradition of the North-west Passage to Cathay, a
tradition as inherent and as important in the British approach as the
tradition of the Inland Sea was in the French. Despite a century and
a half of disasters the idea still ruled men's minds; it had never become a mere convention to which lip-service must be paid before
more practicable projects were broached. It was a seriously held and
warmly supported concept, and any project which embodied a further
attempt to discover the North-west Passage was certain of influential
support in Restoration England. It would be backed by the scientists, the Admiralty, and the vast financial and political interests. It

would claim support from all who were filling the debates in Parliament, the pamphleteering press and the coffee-house gossip, with discussions of the best methods of organising our trade on a balanced imperial basis.

The rich mixture was fertilised by the voyage to England of two French-Canadian adventurers. The strange pair, Médard Chouart and Pierre Esprit Radisson, brought both the knowledge and enthusiasm of the Canadian *coureur de bois*, the wood-runner at home with the Indian and content to winter in the woods, and some fixed and pertinent geographical notions of their own, to London.

The story is confused and romantic. In 1664, before the Treaty of Breda had stimulated English interest in the fur trade, among the commissioners sent out to America to settle the boundaries of the British possessions, to adjudicate on the disputes between the colonies and to bring them to loyalty to the restored monarchy, was Colonel George Cartwright. The commissioners had been chosen by the Duke of York, and such 'frivolous placemen' could do little to win the loyalty of the New Englanders to the restored monarchy. As far as the British colonists were concerned their record was to a large extent one of ineptitude and prevarication. But they were not without capacity of a sort, as George Cartwright was to show.

Cartwright was alleged to be a Papist, but this seems to have won him less hostility from the Puritans of New England than did the misbehaviour of his fellow-commissioner, Sir Robert Carr, who was suspected of keeping a 'naughty woman' in America during his stay there. Between the two there is nevertheless some cause for confusion, for the findings of the commissioners were sent home to England in 1665 by the hand of Cartwright. Yet the report of his voyage is attributed to 'George Carr'—a mixture of the names which creates a mythical person and which is almost certainly a mistake for George Cartwright. The report certainly did not come from George Carteret nor from Sir Robert Carr, who returned in 1667. Cartwright was captured on his voyage home by a Dutch ship, his papers were thrown overboard—this was a relief since he had with him detailed reports of all the colonies, and maps, which would have been dangerous in Dutch hands—and he and his companions were landed in Spain, to make their own way to England. It was when he got to England in December 1665, that 'George Carr' made his report, probably to Arlington, a powerful member of the Cabal.

Most of this report was a routine account of the achievements of the commissioners and of the misfortunes of the voyage home. The significant addition came at the end, when 'George Carr' added that

'Hearing also some Frenchmen discourse in New England of a passage from the West Sea to the South Sea, and of a great trade of beaver in that passage, and afterwards meeting with sufficient proof of the truth of what they had said, and knowing what great endeavours have been made for the finding out of a north-west passage, he thought them the best present he could possibly make His Majesty, and persuaded them to come to England'.

So Médard Chouart, Sieur des Groseilliers, and his brother-in-law, Pierre Esprit Radisson, came to London in the Plague Year. Between them they probably possessed more experience and knowledge of the French-Canadian system of fur-trading than any other two men could claim, and their experiences had left with them a deep conviction that the best approach to the furs of the far north was not by the normal Canadian route of the St. Lawrence and the Great Lakes, but by a sea voyage to Hudson Bay and so to the northern outlets of the fur areas instead of to their southern approaches.

The weight of experience which the two men brought, coupled with their bizarre and forceful personalities, were to count for much in launching the British on a new attempt to get the furs of the north, and in sustaining them in those attempts. The geographical conviction which they brought was not a whit less important. It introduced a fundamental difference in concept, a difference which was to persist when the colourful personalities of its original advocates had been largely forgotten. It brought into existence a rivalry which was not only between French and British but was also between two different routes, the one dependent on sea-going ships and seaboard posts to which bulk cargoes could be shipped direct from Europe, the other dependent on approaches by canoe through the waterways of Canada with a consequent emphasis on Canada as an entrepôt, and on light and easily transportable goods.

The two men were fully aware of the significance of the new view to which they hoped to rally the English court, for they had arrived at their conviction by hard experience. They had even left New France rather than see such dearly-won conclusions stifled because the needs of Canada demanded that the fur trade should take the St. Lawrence route, and should be taxed in the process. Their experience had taught them that any advocacy of a fur-route other than the St. Lawrence would be opposed because it threatened the revenues of the colony; and since it proved true that the full exploitation of the Bay route entailed direct access to European shipping, their proposals were not merely in extension of current trade practices—they implied a fundamental challenge.

Such a challenge as Groseilliers and Radisson embodied was almost certain of support in London. Courtiers, financiers, administrators and scientists, equally anxious to make their own fortunes, to strike a blow at French trade and to probe the mysteries of the Arctic, were all bound to be interested. So it proved. Their journey from Spain brought them to a London ridden by the plague. The Court had moved to Oxford, and the first news of their arrival in England comes, significantly enough, in a letter from the Secretary of the Royal Society to Robert Boyle, telling of the Frenchmen's great journeys and of the hopes of a North-west Passage. The Royal Society was just beginning to organise the collection of maritime and geographical data and to publish its 'Directions for Sea-men bound for far Voyages' with an insistence on the keeping of ships' logs, while Robert Boyle, perhaps the most distinguished physicist of the early days of the Society, was particularly interested in problems of heat and frost and in arctic phenomena. He was also something of an imperialist, the first President of the New England Company when it was revived in 1660 and a privileged member of the Hudson's Bay Company when it was founded; his interests then were not financial but scientific and he was allowed to buy a share for only £100, being 'left a Liberty to adventure one or two hundred pounds' and deciding to stick at the minimum £100 which gave him access to the information which he sought.

It was probably Boyle and the scientists who arranged for the Frenchmen to go to Oxford. There they began easily and successfully to move in the courtly circles. They were taken in hand at this stage by Sir George Carteret—Radisson later said that it was he who had been responsible for bringing them from America, but he here confused Carteret and Cartwright. Sir George was an important member of the newly-founded Royal African Company, and he epitomised in his character and career that many-sided interest in naval, commercial and colonial projects which marked so many of the shrewd and purposeful courtiers of the Restoration period. He stood firmly behind Groseilliers and Radisson for many years.

With such influence behind them the Frenchmen received an audience from King Charles himself. He listened with interest and enjoyment, gave the Frenchmen small tokens of his pleasure, asked for a written account of the land and peoples of Hudson Bay, and retained the explorers with a small pension of forty shillings a week. Their story was worth this much attention even if it were merely treated as a romance, especially so when it was seen against the characters of the men.

Of the two Frenchmen, Groseilliers can be assessed from the brief and formal evidence of the courts of Canada as a bluff, rather truculent wanderer, incurably adventurous and incurably litigious; solid, slow, but determined. In contrast, Radisson emerges from one contemporary description as 'ce fripon de Radisson'. Most of the evidence of the careers of the two men comes in the form of accounts given by Radisson, and it is clear that he was boastful and egotistic. Between them they made a colourful pair, and they had a colourful story, full of purpose and of promise, to tell.

Groseilliers, migrating to Canada from Charly-sur-Marne as a boy, perhaps in 1641, had moved inland from the Lower St. Lawrence and was serving with the Jesuit missions in Huronia by 1646. Here he had personal contact both with the influences which were driving the French inland towards Lake Winnipeg (their 'Inland Sea') and thence to the south and the west, and also with the reaction which was evident in Iroquois attacks on the Hurons and which was driving the French away from Lake Huron and Lake Michigan to seek their pelts elsewhere. So real had this Iroquois threat to the Canadian fur trade become that not a beaver skin was brought to Montreal in the year 1652–3. In such circumstances adventurous and active Canadians could hardly be prevented from going ever further into the woods to seek and trade furs.

The *coureur de bois* was the essential answer to Iroquois encirclement; if Canada was to get the furs on which she depended, the *habitan* would have to go and fetch them however much he might be legislated against in the interests of settlement and agriculture. Such a way of life came easily to the young *habitan*, though not all were so adventurous or so purposeful as Groseilliers. Marriage did little to tie him to his home and his farm at Trois Rivières, and from 1654 to 1656 he was absent as emissary from the Governor of New France to the western tribes, to get them to break through the Iroquois cordons and to bring their furs to Montreal again. With one French companion (Radisson later claimed that it was he, but this is most improbable) Groseilliers accompanied on their return journey the few Indians who had come down to Montreal despite the Iroquois. With them he went up the Ottawa, through Lake Nipissing, down French River to Georgian Bay in Lake Huron, and thence south, probably as far as Lake Michigan, the Straits of Mackinac and Green Bay. His precise route is largely a matter for conjecture, but the certainty is that Groseilliers and his unknown companion journeyed far into the interior of North America, almost certainly as far as the Straits of Mackinac.

They were most favourably impressed with what they saw, and they brought down to Quebec with them in 1656 a fortune of fourteen to fifteen thousand *livres* in furs for themselves, and a flotilla of about thirty Indian canoes laden with skins which revived the economy of the French colony. Perhaps even more important, they met the Illinois, the Sioux and above all the Christinos or Crees. The Cree lands reached 'as far as the North Sea' and the Crees gave Groseilliers accounts of the 'Bay of the North' and of the possibility of access to that bay by sea-going ships. There was much here that was as important for the future as Groseillier's argosy of furs was vital for the present, especially since he found on his return that his new wealth could not be exempted from the tax of the '*Quart*', despite his plea that he had brought down the Indians to enrich the colony. He emerged from this experience a man with unrivalled knowledge, with considerable wealth, with a grievance, and with a great idea.

While Groseilliers had been gaining his experience, and his conviction about the 'Bay of the North', as the companion of missionaries or of trading Indians, Radisson had undergone a quite different training. A half-brother of Groseilliers' second wife, and so a brother-in-law of his friend, he had been brought from France as a boy. It was later to be a matter of controversy whether he was born in France or in Papal territory at Avignon, and he is even described at times as an Italian. During a Mohawk raid on Trois Rivières the lad was captured in 1651, and was carried off to live for some time as an adopted member of a Mohawk family. An attempt at escape was followed by severe torture, and his life was only saved by the intervention of his adopted Indian family. He relapsed into Indian habits, spent a period on the war-path, and then successfully escaped in 1653 to the Dutch settlement at Orange. Thence he returned to France, travelling via Holland, and so back to his family at Quebec in 1654. The whole adventure, from start to finish, apparently took only three years—but chronology is always difficult to ascertain where Radisson was concerned.

At Quebec he found that peace between the French and the Iroquois made it possible for the Jesuits to begin a mission to the south. Radisson now spent an adventurous couple of years, in 1657 and 1658, accompanying a Jesuit voyage to Onondaga, and it was largely due to his knowledge and ingenuity that the party escaped with their lives and found their way back to Quebec in April 1658.

The two relatives, unique in their knowledge and experience, and now co-operating for the first time, then set out in the summer of

1659 for the north. They had to evade the ban of the Governor on journeys into the woods, and they had to avoid the solicitations of the Jesuits. They took with them one un-named French companion, who soon turned back, and they went in company with a flotilla of Indian canoes returning from trade. Their purpose was to contact the Crees once more and to probe the rumours of the great wealth in furs which could be got from the 'Bay of the North'. Travelling through Lake Superior, they reached the forests of Wisconsin and there spent the winter with the Sioux, returning to Lake Superior in the early spring of 1660. There they met the assembled Cree nation and, according to Radisson, they journeyed northwards with them down a river to Hudson Bay. This journey to the Bay was practically impossible in the time available, for Groseilliers and Radisson were back in Montreal in the summer of 1660 and a sworn account of a voyage of 1663 by the Saguenay River to Nemiskau and the great river which falls into the 'mer du Nord' (presumably Rupert River) said that the Indians there had never seen white men. But they had convinced themselves of the wealth of the northern fur areas and of the need to approach them through the 'Bay of the North', and even if they had not themselves reached the sea there was other evidence to support their convictions; for an Indian made such a journey during the years 1658–60 and the Jesuit Father Druillettes got an account of it from him.

Their own success and the general rumours of the riches of the northern lands left no doubts in the minds of Groseilliers and Radisson that a new and fundamentally different approach to the fur trade was required. They returned with large private fortunes in prime furs, and accompanied by sixty Indian canoes, but it was a singular misfortune for France that two such men, enthusiastic for their new idea, should have been badly mis-handled on their return to Canada. On their own furs they were certainly made to pay the heavy tax of the '*Quart*', and they probably had to pay fines and further exactions as well. They later claimed that Groseilliers was imprisoned for illicit trading and that they were fined four thousand *livres* towards the cost of building a new fort at Trois Rivières, with a further fine of six thousand *livres* for general purposes. Whatever the details of their treatment, there can be no doubt that it left them with a strong sense of injustice. They had brought a stream of life-giving furs to the colony; they had proved the wealth of the north and they had pioneered a new and efficient approach to it. Their reward was fines, imprisonment and abuse.

To seek redress and to solicit financial backing for the exploitation of the sea-route to the Bay, Groseilliers went to France in 1661; possibly Radisson followed him. But they failed to get either redress or support although one merchant seems to have promised the use of a ship. Returning to Canada therefore, they began to prepare a sea voyage to the Bay, there to meet the Northern Crees and to trade with them. The plan miscarried, but it brought the two men to the coast, to the world of ships and seamen. In their disappointment they journeyed on from Isle Percée to Cape Breton, determined to continue even to Port Royal and New England to get ships and support if they could not find them in Canada. They found the merchants of Boston more enterprising than those of Canada, and in 1663 a ship was fitted out and set forth; but it was so late in the year before they started that the captain decided to put back when he was faced with the hazards of Hudson Strait. The failure of the voyage resulted in prolonged legal disputes as to the responsibility for the failure, and though during this period half-hearted preparations for a further voyage from Boston were under way, it was at this time that the two adventurers were enticed to England. 'In the meantime,' wrote Radisson later, 'the Commissioners of the King of Great Britain arrived in that place, and one of them would have us to come to New York, and the other advised us to come to England and offer ourselves to the King, which wee did'.

Ending with the adventure of the fight at sea with the Dutch caper, and with the landing in Spain and journey thence to England, this was a story adventurous and purposeful enough to capture the imaginations of less impressionable men than the courtiers and the King. They listened and promised support. When the Court moved from Oxford to Windsor, Groseilliers and Radisson moved too, and in 1666 they accompanied the Court back to London, with a promise of a ship to prosecute their designs. Then, on their return to London, they were put in the care of Sir Peter Colleton.

Colleton, like Carteret, was a member of the group of courtiers who were most deeply and actively concerned with the problems of setting up a balanced imperial economy. As a younger member of that group he was the natural choice for the task of taking care of the Frenchmen. For it was a closely-knit group to whom the story of the 'Bay of the North' and of the furs and the passage to the Pacific to be found there, made an appeal—closely-knit although informal. The patronage of James Duke of York and of Prince Rupert, brother and cousin of the monarch, was reasonably assured; but, as was natural, they were more taken up with affairs of state than with private ventures. Behind them, already recognisable as a group, stood about six men with many interests and deep convictions. If the Frenchmen's story did not appeal to these men, then it would appeal to nobody in England, for the group had experience and judgment, and a vision of the integration of the parts of an empire into a whole. Actuated in part by personal interests, they also aimed at unifying the trade of all the parts of the empire so 'that they may be most serviceable one unto another, and as the whole unto these our King-domes, so these our kingdomes unto them'.

Chief in the group stood Anthony Ashley Cooper, later first Earl of Shaftesbury. In close and constant association with him were the two Colletons (Sir John and Sir Peter), Carteret, the Duke of Albe-marle, Lord Arlington and Lord John Berkeley. In 1663, these men (in company with Clarendon and Sir William Berkeley, but without Peter Colleton) had been given a charter for the development of the land then known as South Virginia (it was called Florida by the Spanish and the French), and in 1665 this charter was renewed and amended, to become the foundation of the colony of Carolina. The land was inauspicious for the kind of settlement which the pro-prietors had in mind, and a previous grant by Charles I also stood in their way, but their care for colonisation is clear and purposeful. The moving spirit was Shaftesbury, with his secretary John Locke close behind him and drafting the Fundamental Constitutions for Caro-lina. Their interest, and the interest of the half-dozen men who thought as they did, gave consistence and continuity even when it became certain that Carolina could not produce any such returns on investment as would make it an attractive speculation. In 1669 each proprietor was ordered to pay in the sum of five hundred pounds to the banker John Portman, and was allowed to invest up to a further two hundred pounds in each of the four succeeding years, and in 1670 the charter for Carolina was again renewed. Carolina was not a speculation which attracted investors; it was a venture by the small group of men, led by Shaftesbury, who believed in such things. In 1670 the same group (allowing for deaths and suc-cessions) were given a charter for the development of the Bahamas, Providence Island, and other lands in the West Indies, and the most cursory glance at the records of the Council for Trade and Plantations makes it abundantly clear that Shaftesbury was the lead-ing spirit in colonial matters, that there was much purposeful plan-ning mingled with the speculative charter-seeking of the 'frivolous placemen' at the Court, and that behind Shaftesbury were about half a dozen men whose approval or disapproval would settle the fate of the French-Canadian adventurers.

Radisson and Groseilliers made their appeal, in fact, not to a haphazard and spontaneous group of men who were attracted by the romance of their story, but to a co-ordinated group with great interests in the colonial field, with considerable experience, and with a definite purpose. Shaftesbury, Craven, Carteret, Peter Colleton, and Albemarle (Christopher), the men who were granted the Bahamas in 1670 and who had undertaken the planting of Carolina in 1666, with their banker John Portman, were the men who took up the project put forward by the two French-Canadians. That Peter Colleton should have been given the task of supplying the out-of-pocket needs of the two wanderers was the sign that they might count on the support of Shaftesbury and his group. This was evidence of serious interest rather than anything else, for by December 1667, Colleton had only expended £96 6s. 2d. on his charges.

But although they had the ear of the King and the support of this group of courtiers, Groseilliers and Radisson were destined to meet many disappointments. The Dutch dominated the Narrow Seas in 1666, and no voyage could be set forth from the Thames in that year. In 1667 more serious preparations were undertaken, but the voyage was muddled because, once more, the best of the summer weather was allowed to pass before the outfit was ready.

Even such ineffective support meant that the Frenchmen's friends were no longer merely a group which happened to hold ideas in common; they were knit together in common action and investment. Exactly how far such co-ordination had gone by 1667 it is difficult to establish. Contemporary report spoke of a belief that the King had granted his royal commission and the 'sole trade of what Countryes they shall discover' to a group of adventurers who would undertake this voyage to the Bay in 1667. It was a most probable grant to have been sought and given, for such charters were the commonplace spur to exploration and the enlargement of colonial trade in that period. At a later period the Hudson's Bay Company stated that the two Frenchmen were credited with 'eight yeares and ½ service at home and abroad in the Companyes employment'; this was the reckoning in October 1675, and it would mean that the Company accepted responsibility for the two men as from the spring months of 1667. In fact the supporters of the idea of a maritime approach to the furs of the north were in 1667 loosely organised into an informal group which was sufficiently coherent to be given the royal grant (of which no copy has yet been found) and to give the confidence necessary for them to provide from their private means for the costs of maintaining the Frenchmen and fitting them out for a voyage. Sir

Peter Colleton shouldered the costs of keeping Groseilliers and Radisson in London up to December 1667, and after that the general funds of the supporters gave them two or three pounds every four or five days until they were at last sent to sea.

Such a loose organisation inevitably had its disadvantages in bad control and ill-considered action, and the muddle of the 1667 voyage shows this to the full. Sir George Carteret seems to have undertaken the responsibility of purchasing a ship for the voyage in that year, but his purchase proved quite unsuitable. The first Ledger of the Hudson's Bay Company, recording the absorption of these dis-organised and largely personal expenses into the common stock when it had been formed, reports that on 4th January, 1668, Carteret was credited 'By cash paid for the *Discovery* ketch (which was bought for the Companyes use and Sold by their Order) more then she pro-duced upon Sale £70'.

It is clear from such subsequent entries that during 1667 and 1668 the informal group which was prepared to back the projected voyage was being drawn into a closer organisation as demands for money and for the acceptance of responsibility began to accumulate with the launching of an actual voyage. As yet there was no formal organisation, but individuals advanced the necessary funds, and something of the process can be gathered from the records of later years when the advances so made were accepted by the Hudson's Bay Company. The foolish purchase of the *Discovery*, or the costs of maintaining Groseilliers and Radisson, were by no means the only such charges carried forward from the informal into the formal organisation. In October 1667, Francis Millington, a Customs Com-missioner of London, connected by blood and interest with the bank-ing circles of the City, began to advance small sums which were later credited towards the cost of a share. So did his wife's uncle, the greatest banker of the London of that day, Sir Robert Vyner; and John Fenn, Paymaster of the Admiralty, always on the look-out for a shrewd investment for the funds which passed through his hands, began to advance cash for working expenses in December 1667.

Here was the beginning of support from financiers, standing behind the courtiers and scientists, who themselves do not seem to have made any great advances of money at this time except for Colleton and Carteret. Millington, Vyner and Fenn were indeed financiers who were deeply engaged in the administration of public funds, but the great private banking interests were also represented at this time by John Portman, who began to make advances towards a voyage: he was at the same time acting as banker for the proprietors of Carolina. And although the great courtiers seem to have done their share more by winning royal approval than by advancing cash, one who was very near to them began at this time to lend his own money. This was James Hayes, private secretary to Prince Rupert, the King's cousin, an expert in finance and thoroughly at home in the profitable border-territory between private trade and government concession. He paid from his private purse £20 in December 1667, and he now began to give a coherence and a purpose which they obviously needed to the scattered interests involved.

In fact, the financial support which was forthcoming for a voyage to the Bay was negligible. The sums advanced did not exceed £200 for any one man, and for the kind of supporter involved this was nothing; the process showed how the sharing of such risks on some sort of joint-stock system enabled wealthy men to experiment in highly risky ventures without prejudicing their fortunes.

But although the courtiers produced little money, and the City men nothing which could damage them, the determination of Hayes counted for much, and so did the interest of John Kirke. The fourth son of Gervase Kirke, an English merchant resident in Dieppe, he had taken part with his brothers in the capture of Quebec and in the attempts to win the French fur trade. With him came the tradition of the Canada Company, with its still undisputed royal charter and legal title, its long-standing feud with the French of Canada and its wistful knowledge of the potential wealth to be got from furs. John Kirke brought these factors to the group which was forming to support the project, and he brought, too, some real knowledge of the fur trade and of French methods. He was allotted an active part in supervising the two Frenchmen and in purchasing supplies for the proposed expedition. It was accepted that the Cree Indians would probably have become accustomed to French goods, so that the preparations for the voyage included the purchase by Kirke from France of a consignment of brandy and of a further assortment of French goods from a Mrs. Katherine Rose. Tobacco, however, was bought from a London tradesman.

In all this business of preparation much depended on the expert knowledge of Groseilliers and Radisson, and John Kirke was the obvious man to bring them into line with British conditions and with the possibilities of the situation. They needed some sort of watch-dog at this time, too, for an attempt was afoot to entice them into Dutch service and the French were also watching them closely and were anxious to anticipate the plans for a voyage to the Bay, about which no secret had been made. As events were to prove, there was no

B

loyalty which would tie the two Frenchmen to their English patrons; they were bound chiefly by the frustration which they had met in France and when, as in 1667–8, they had behind them three years of waiting in England, culminating in the purchase of a useless ship and a further period of delay, it is not to be wondered at that they should at least have been willing to keep open their contacts with France. Radisson certainly did so, and there is on record a slightly later offer by him (2nd May, 1670) to put the French in possession of the lands to be discovered. Yet the formation of something like a unified body of supporters, able to put up some money and to get something in the nature of a royal grant, and even to seek the loan of a naval vessel, boded well. Even the abortive voyage of 1667 was at least a sign of practical support. Groseilliers and Radisson therefore remained in London, and serious and active preparations for a voyage went forward during the winter 1667–8.

Commonplace enough in many ways, the small speculative advances of money by wealthy and powerful men who could well afford the losses involved nevertheless mark a vital mingling of personalities between the adventurous and purposeful French-Canadians, now for ten years set on their concept of the 'Bay of the North', and the hardening group of their patrons—wealthy, powerful men, comparatively enlightened, and convinced imperialists. They were ready to take a modest chance, as much in the wider interests involved as in the hope of making their own fortunes, but they were not prepared to undertake great risks. Their influence, as much as their personal help, produced the voyage of the *Eaglet* and the *Nonsuch* in June 1668.

BOOKS FOR REFERENCE

BRYCE, George—*The Remarkable History of the Hudson's Bay Company including that of the French Traders of North-Western Canada and of the North-West, XY, and Astor Fur Companies* (London, 1910).

CLAPHAM, Sir John—Introduction to *Minutes of the Hudson's Bay Company 1671–1674* (Toronto, The Champlain Society, 1942, and London, The Hudson's Bay Record Society, 1942), Vol. V.

EGERTON, H. E.—*A Short history of British Colonial Policy* (London, 1897).

MacKAY, Douglas (revised to 1949 by Alice MacKay)—*The Honourable Company. A History of the Hudson's Bay Company* (Toronto, 1949).

NUTE, Grace Lee—*Caesars of the Wilderness. Médard Chouart, Sieur des Groseilliers and Pierre Esprit Radisson, 1618–1710* (New York, 1943).

RADISSON, Pierre Esprit—*Voyages of Peter Esprit Radisson, Being an Account of his Travels and Experiences among the North American Indians, from 1652 to 1684,* edited by Gideon D. Scull (Boston, The Prince Society, 1885).

THWAITES, R. G.—*Black Gown and Redskins, adventures and travels of the early Jesuit missionaries in North America*, with a new preface by D. B. Quinn, selected and edited by E. Kenton, with an introduction by R. G. Thwaites (London, 1956).

THWAITES, R. G.—*The Jesuit relations and allied documents. Travels and explorations of the Jesuit Missionaries in New France, 1610–1791* (Cleveland, 1896–1901), 73 vols.

WILLSON, Beckles—*The Great Company (1667–1871) Being a History of the Honourable Company of Merchant-Adventurers Trading into Hudson's Bay* (London, 1900), 2 vols.

ARTICLES

NUTE, Grace Lee (ed.)—'Radisson and Groseilliers' Contribution to Geography'. See *Minnesota History* (Saint Paul, 1935), Vol. XVI.

NUTE, Grace Lee (ed.)—'Two Documents from Radisson's Suit Against the Company'. See *The Beaver* (Winnipeg, Hudson's Bay Company, December 1935).

CHAPTER IV

THE *EAGLET* AND THE *NONSUCH*

The conjunction of the ideas and of the persistence of the two romantic realists from Canada with the courtiers and financiers from London bore fruit when, on 5th June, 1668, two small vessels dropped down the Thames under pilotage, ready for one of the most momentous voyages in the history of the North. The *Eaglet* ketch[1] with her captain, William Stannard, had been lent for the voyage by Charles II. She was one of the 'small vessels' of the Royal Navy, of fifty-four tons burthen, sixteen feet beam and forty feet length. Aboard her sailed Radisson. The other ship was the *Nonsuch*, also a ketch, of forty-three tons, fifteen feet beam and thirty-six feet length. She had been a naval craft, but had been sold in 1667 to Sir William Warren, who made her available for the voyage. The bluff Groseilliers was aboard, and the ship was commanded by Captain Zachariah Gillam, the New Englander who had sailed with the Frenchmen on the expedition which had been fitted out in Boston in 1663.

The captains were most emphatically left in command of their vessels, as sailors must always be. The Frenchmen were super-cargoes only, to be treated with the greatest respect, but also with a certain amount of suspicion. The captains were to 'use the said Mr. Gooseberry and Mr. Radisson with all manner of civility and courtesy' since they were 'the persons upon whose Credit wee have undertaken this expedition'. The trade goods (including 'wampume-age'[2] bought from the Frenchmen) were nevertheless under the control of the captains, who were to hand them out only in lots of fifty pounds value each.

[1] The company's documents, and indeed most contemporaries, are usually careful to specify the kind of vessel mentioned—ketch, dogger, pink, or ship. The ketch normally had only two masts, a main and a mizzen; the main almost amidships and carrying a square sail, with a foresail and a jib, the mizzen at the stern with a lateen sail. A dogger was also two-masted but was more blunt at the bows; her mainsail and topsail would be square, her foresail triangular, and she would have no jib. Her mizzen would be square. A pink carried three masts and was square-rigged on her main-mast and fore-mast while she carried a lateen sail on her mizzen. A ship was a full-rigged three-master. Cf. Clapham, *H.B.R.S.*, IV, xxi–xxx, iv.

[2] *Wampum* was the standard currency of the early fur trade. It consisted of small white shells which could best be got from Long Island, and was in universal demand by the Indians of North America.

Trade was placed before discovery—as it tended to remain. But the passage to the South Sea was to be sought if occasion offered and it is clear from the instructions to the captains that such discovery was a definite factor in the incentives for the voyage. Support was being given to the Frenchmen, they 'having told us that it is but 7 daies padling or sailing from the River where they intend to trade unto the Stinking Lake [the Lac des Puants, or Lake Winnipeg] and not above 7 daies more to the streight which leads into that sea they call the South Sea and from thence but forty or fifty leagues to the sea itself in all which streight it Ebbs and flowes by meanes whereof the passage up and downe will be quicke'. Yet for this first voyage the possibilities of trade, with copper and other minerals as supplements to furs, stood foremost. If preliminary reports seemed to justify it, a separate vessel would be sent for the purposes of discovery in 1670.

It was intended in 1668 that both ships should winter in the Bay. In the spring of 1669 such returns as might have been traded were then to be put aboard the *Nonsuch* and brought home. The captains were, however, to change ships; Stannard and Groseilliers were to come home on the *Nonsuch* while Radisson and Gillam were to stay for a second winter with the *Eaglet*.

Finally, both captains were instructed to keep accurate logs of their voyage. In this they were almost for a certainty instructed in recording the data which the Royal Society wished to accumulate, and which were tabulated in its 'Directions for Seamen' issued at this time.

From the *Instructions* to the captains it is evident that the Frenchmen had muddled the chronology of their previous journeys and had taken to speaking with personal conviction of matters which they only knew by Indian report. So they convinced their backers that they had in fact (though they most probably had not) paddled down a river northwards to the shores of Hudson Bay in 1659–60, and that the same area could better be approached by sea. Such a notion in effect denied the geographical concept that the fur trade of North America found its best natural outlet by the St. Lawrence. This challenge to the accepted concepts of geography and economy lay at the roots of the 1668 voyage. It was on the vindication of this fundamental idea that the backers staked their modest subscriptions, and it was in the vindication of this idea that the voyage began a new era in the history of the fur trade and of Canada.

For despite an early set-back the 1668 voyage was a convincing success. Early misfortune placed the whole responsibility on the

Nonsuch and on Gillam and Groseilliers, for the *Eaglet* proved 'by reason of the deepness of her Wast unable to endure the Violent Stormes they mett with all', and she was back in Plymouth 'with some losse', by August 1668. She was re-fitted in the naval dock-yards and later served in the West Indies, but in the meantime she had taken Radisson and half of the equipment out of the Hudson Bay venture. The *Nonsuch* however sailed on, wintered in the Bay, and returned with a full vindication of the basic concept of the voyage in the shape of a good cargo of prime furs.

But during the summer and winter of 1668–9 this was not to be anticipated with any certainty. All that was known was that the *Nonsuch* had sailed on through weather which had defeated the *Eaglet*. This did not in any way detract from the growing volume of sup-port. The Adventurers showed the greatest confidence and purpose-fulness, and as soon as the *Eaglet* had returned they began to plan a further voyage. They stated that they would venture again as soon as the weather permitted, and they begged the use of the *Hadarine*, a pink, 'shee being a Vessell of less worth to His Majesty and much more fitt then the other for the said Expedition'. Though they were disappointed in this request—for James Duke of York refused to release the *Hadarine*—yet during this winter of disappointment and surmise the remarkable fact is that support for the project was in-creasingly marked by an organisation which betokened confidence in a long-term future. Stability and the permanence of the finance re-quired for an assured trade replaced the rather haphazard personal subscriptions for a single voyage, so that by the time the *Nonsuch* returned to London with proof of the soundness of the underlying idea there was already in existence a corporate body of 'Adventurers' with a definite legal position, ready to finance and control the trade now made possible.

Here two elements were involved, the financial and the legal, and they lent each other mutual support. It was not until October 1669 that the *Nonsuch* returned, sailing from Plymouth for the Downs on 8th October. But it was during the latter half of 1668 and the early months of 1669 that most of the 'Founder's Shares' of the embryonic company were subscribed for. The full share seems to have been taken as £300, but there were many variations and the loose arrange-ments which had yet to be transformed into something of the formalities of a company allowed considerable latitude. Seldom did a subscriber pay his full due in one payment either. Nevertheless finance accumulated, support was being organised, personalities were getting committed to the project.

Prince Rupert himself began to pay for a full share in June 1668, and by May 1669 he had subscribed £270. Other members of the Court made equally important but equally modest subscriptions at this time. The great Henry, Earl of Arlington, paid £200 in July 1668, while Anthony Ashley Cooper, later first Earl of Shaftesbury, advanced £200 in August 1668, and increased this to £300 in 1669. The intermediary between Court and City, James Hayes, made small payments over a considerable period—£20 in December 1667; £55 in April and £125 in June 1668; £50 in February 1669; £20 in May of that year—these were sums which he produced from his pocket to meet immediate requirements, as in all probability were the advances made by other supporters.

Following Hayes came his brother-in-law, Sir Edward Hungerford, who began to make advances in December 1668; behind him came an influential number of city financiers and officials. Sir John Robinson, Lieutenant of the Tower of London, had apparently already paid something towards the expenses of the *Nonsuch* before he brought his subscription up to £400 in April 1668. William Pretyman, merchant adventurer to India and Remembrancer of the Exchequer, began to pay in during February 1668, as did John Portman, goldsmith, banker and Treasurer of the Carolina Company. Sir John Griffith, a great city magnate, took over more than £200 of the cash advanced by Sir Peter Colleton, and finally Sir Robert Vyner, the King's principal banker and at certain stages of his career the dominant financier of Restoration London, steadily advanced necessary small sums and brought his holding up to £200 by August 1668.

Such payments are not large, either by modern standards or when considered against the sums which these men were prepared to invest in the royal debt, in land, or in other securities. Shaftesbury's contribution of £300, for example, is negligible when put against his annual income of about £23,000. But it must be remembered that they were cash advances for a particular venture rather than investments in an established concern, and that the adventure was highly speculative. The amounts would best be measured against the scale of investment in similar projects; and here it should be considered that the proprietors of the Providence Company reported that their shares cost £600 each, and that they thought such a sum should entitle them to some respect since in other companies a man was accounted a patriot if he adventured £100 before the company had declared a dividend.

The financial process remained nebulous and uncertain; cash

advances were merged with advances in kind and there appears the inclusive item of 'Remains of a former cargo' in the books of the Hudson's Bay Company—but whether the 'former cargo' was held to be that of the *Eaglet* and *Nonsuch* voyage of 1668, or the abortive *Discovery* affair of 1667 is not clear. The absorption of the 'former cargo' brought into the concern a further list of significant persons —Albemarle, the General Monk who had restored the Monarch, was credited with £82 5s. 3d.; Sir George Carteret with £208 16s. 8d.; Sir Peter Colleton with £181 11s. 10d.; William, Earl of Craven with £82 5s. 3d.; and Alderman Sir John Robinson with £170 18s. 4d. under this heading.

Among the elusive arrangements it is significant that Prince Rupert should have sold £100 of the £270 which he had advanced and that then he should have paid in a further £30 to bring his payment up to a round £200 in 1670, while his secretary James Hayes, the active organiser of the affair, should likewise have made a payment of £30, to bring him up to a round £300, in May 1670. For May 1670 was the month in which the other development, the achievement of legal status, reached its consummation alongside the building up of financial stability. The two sides of the development had probably started together, when the rumour of some sort of royal grant of trade and propriety had accompanied the subscriptions towards the purchase of the *Discovery* and the financing of the preparations for a voyage in 1667. Such a grant, though its precise terms have never been discovered, would be in the ordinary nature of such ventures as they were arranged in that time. This would be merely an overseas application of the normal British patent law, whereby a person or a corporation who brought a new invention or a new trade into production was granted the sole right to enjoy the profits for a period of years. There had been many heated discussions over such patents in the Tudor and early Stuart reigns, and although abuses of such a system were universally decried and widely disliked, yet a general agreement was current that such grants for new-found trades, overseas or domestic, provided a proper stimulus and repaid initiative.

Some such grant would probably be required, too, to stimulate investment in the new approach to the fur trade and to elicit the subscriptions which financed the purchase of the *Discovery* and the setting out of the *Eaglet* and the *Nonsuch*. Though it may not have been a full legal commission from the Crown, some such grant almost certainly was made, perhaps only verbally; and certainly one item in the rumour was carried out to the letter. For with the loan of the *Eaglet* it became clear that His Majesty 'lends them a small Fregate into the Bargain'.

The next, more ascertainable, step was taken in June 1669, when Radisson had spent a disappointed winter and spring in London, and when Groseilliers and Gillam were still lost to their supporters. This was a period when confidence and purpose might well have been low. But in just the same way as this was a period in which purposeful subscriptions began to accumulate, so it was a period in which the legal position was strengthened and clarified. On 23rd June, 1669, a royal grant gave the sole trade of the northern parts of America to a group of men who were in fact the City element, as distinct from the courtiers and the scientists, within the loose body which was taking shape to support the project. They were named as Hungerford, Robinson, Vyner, Colleton, Hayes and Kirke. Sir Peter Colleton may perhaps seem a stranger among these men, a courtier rather than a financier, but he was anxious about his money and he soon sold the rights acquired by his payments. The others were all primarily interested in a profitable trade. They were ready to support the venture and they had all actually subscribed towards the cost of further development. But to elicit their full support they required some form of guarantee that the profits would be theirs.

There is no record of any kind of a rift between these City men, with their grant now made, and the rest of the members of the group. The City men were at this very time rallying to the support of the general project, and it is not to be supposed that James Hayes, for one, would have made any attempt to deceive or anticipate Rupert in such a matter. For the whole idea was still most speculative, Rupert was Hayes' patron and employer, and his influence would quickly secure the annulment of such a grant if it smelled as though the secretary were betraying his master's interests. The grant therefore cannot be taken as evidence of a rift among the supporters, but simply as a sign of their power and of the fact that one group, the financiers, wanted and got assurance on this particular point.

Four months after this grant the *Nonsuch* came to port and spread a great confidence that a profitable trade would be forthcoming. This confidence did not derive from any estimate of the actual profits of her voyage, for no such estimate was then made. Nor can it be attempted now. The costs of the voyage can only be pieced incompletely together from the items entered in the Ledger of the Hudson's Bay Company when it later took over the liability for such charges.

Payments made over the years to the Frenchmen would have to be carried into such an account, as well as later payments for damages to the two ships; and though detailed costs of some of the trade goods are ascertainable it is impossible to find the charges for others, such as the *wampum* bought from the Frenchmen, and still more impossible to be certain that all such charges have been included. The 'incident charges' too, for customs payments, dinners, 'Secret Service' money to steer the project through the Court and to secure the use of the *Eaglet*, are all muddled since the first statement of such charges covers the years from 1667 to 1670. So although some items are quite definite—the wages in the *Nonsuch*, for example, cost £535 5s. 11d.—the real costs of the voyage cannot be ascertained; and without the costs any attempt at a profit-and-loss statement must be abandoned.

On the voyage itself, too, no satisfactory accounts were kept. The backers had sent Thomas Gorst to look after their interests and to make an account to them. Fortunately he went on the *Nonsuch*, so that he completed the voyage. But his statement of the disbursements made on board the *Nonsuch* is quite unsatisfactory. He recorded expenditure of £179 8s. 6d. between March 1668 and June 1672, a long period, for which he entered no details, and he concluded with the lame statement 'By Cash disbursed whereof I cannot find the particulars £19 4s. 9d.'.

It is in any case almost certain that the returns on board the *Nonsuch* would not have been a very generous recompense for the outlay of the previous four years, including the costs of setting out three ships. The customs payments came to £33 5s. 10d., and the furs were sold with little delay or trouble for £1,379 6s. 10d., the bulk of them going to one prominent London furrier, Thomas Glover. At prices varying from 7s. 8d. to 10s. 6d. a pound he bought £1,233 worth. He was to play a great part in the early history of the Hudson's Bay Company, and his purchase of these first skins from Hudson Bay was as important as anything he later managed, for it made it clear to the supporters, who had no expert knowledge, that the furs from Hudson Bay were of a quality and condition which ensured ready sale in competition with those of Canada or the New England colonies. The safe return of the *Nonsuch* and the easy sale of her cargo therefore turned the whole project from a speculation, almost an act of faith, into a reasonable commercial venture which only required effective organisation and stable trading conditions to be certain of success.

BOOKS FOR REFERENCE

BRYCE, George—*The Remarkable History of the Hudson's Bay Company* (London, 1910).

CLAPHAM, Sir John—Introduction to Hudson's Bay Record Society, Vol. V.

MACKAY, Douglas (revised to 1949 by Alice MacKay)—*The Honourable Company* (Toronto, 1949).

NUTE, Grace Lee—*Caesars of the Wilderness* (New York, 1943).

RADISSON, Pierre Esprit—*Voyages of Peter Esprit Radisson . . . 1652 to 1684*, edited by Gideon D. Scull (Boston, The Prince Society, 1885).

WILLSON, Beckles—*The Great Company (1667–1871)* . . . (London, 1900), 2 vols.

ARTICLES

MOOD, Fulmer—'The London Background of the Radisson Problem'. See *Minnesota History* (Saint Paul, 1935).

MOOD, Fulmer—'Hudson's Bay Company Started as a Syndicate'. See *The Beaver* (Winnipeg, Hudson's Bay Company, March 1938).

CHAPTER V

THE EUROPEAN FUR-MARKET

In common with the rest of Europe, the England of the Restoration had moved from an obsession with the power of Spain to jealous admiration of the Dutch. The Dutch Wars showed the world that the sea-power of the United Netherlands could dominate the narrow seas, and their land forces also proved their worth in the major struggles of the century. But it was their merchant skill rather than their military or naval strength which roused the opposition of other powers.

Antwerp had 'engrossed' to itself the spice trade of Portugal before the Dutch had themselves financed voyages to the Far East, and the mart at Amsterdam became the great bourse through which the treasure of the New World found its way, in large part, into the economy of western Europe. The stupendous prosperity which resulted allowed the Dutch to venture most purposefully into the colonial field themselves, and their East India Company soon controlled the Eastern spice trade (driving the British East India Company out from the islands) while their West India Company seized possession of Brazil, founded the West Indian colonies of Surinam and Curaçao, and set up the New Netherland settlements of New Amsterdam, Manhattan and Orange, on the most eligible sites on the North American coast.

All of this was cause for emulation, and one after the other the Dutch were despoiled of their assets. But the deepest cause for anxiety in England lay not in their colonial power but in their Baltic trade. Here the Dutch were profiting from their medieval heritage. Bruges and Antwerp had been the great marts through which the Hansard merchants had circulated the products of the Baltic through western and southern Europe; they had their Kontors in other places (especially in London) but the Low Countries were the sites of the markets in which the main currents of trade met. Much of this Baltic produce was in non-essential goods—honey, furs, linens—and at times corn was shipped, but its great importance lay in the fact that the Baltic was the source of naval supplies. Apart from clap-boards, there was tar, hemp, spars and masts, and rope. All western countries were dependent on the Baltic trade for these essential munitions of war—and indeed they remained so dependent until the advent of the iron ship. Therefore they were dependent on the Dutch, as on the Danes who controlled the Sound. Throughout the discussions on colonial problems in the sixteenth and seventeenth centuries the possibility of finding sources of these naval stores in the New World held a prominent place.

The Dutch mastered the Baltic trade partly because of their geographical situation, partly because of the traditional pre-occupation therewith, partly by reason of their habit of granting commercial freedom in their cities; but mostly because they were able to supply the produce of the New World to the Baltic cities and powers. Their own herrings played a part; spices, tobacco, sugar and tea were also shipped. But furs too were a prime commodity for shipment into the Baltic, and in their consideration of the fur trade and its possible enlargement the English courtiers, statesmen, and financiers of the Plague and Fire years were aware that they were dealing with a trade which might interrupt some of the flow of Dutch shipping into the Baltic and so help to redress the all-important Balance of Trade while at the same time it gave to England its own independent access to Baltic supplies.

There was at the back of this an acceptance of a great change in the flow of the fur trade, for whereas the medieval fur trade had brought furs (among other commodities) from Russia to the West, the trade of the seventeenth century took the furs to Russia. This reversal of trade was one of the consequences of the opening up of the New World, for the Americas rapidly revealed that they contained inexhaustible reserves of valuable furs.

From the first report sent home by Henry Hudson in 1610 the Dutch had accepted the value of the furs to which their settlements gave them access; Manhattan was an admirable centre for the trade, and Long Island was the source of much of the *wampum* which was the universal small currency for the Indian trade.[1]

While the fur trade was a valuable adjunct to settlement for the Dutch, the economy of French Canada rested on the broad back of the beaver. This was accepted as a most dangerous dependence on a single trade and on a commodity which might easily suffer from a glutted market. Canada in the 1670's produced in a normal year, in which the trade was not interrupted by wars or lack of goods, something like sixty to eighty thousand beaver; and this was a supply of fur which tended to increase rather than to decrease, so that before the end of the century the annual returns were nearer a hundred-and-fifty thousand. The fate of Canada clearly depended on finding

[1] For *wampum* cf. p. 36, n. 2 *supra*.

a market in Europe for such quantities of furs. It was self-evident that there was a limit to the quantities which could be absorbed, for fur was not like sugar, capable of creating greatly expanding markets in France. The power of the colony to buy its necessities from France would be cut by half if the beaver trade were trimmed to the capacity of the fur-market in France.

Less dependent on the fur trade than New France, the New England colonies nevertheless found therein an essential source of purchasing power. The Pilgrim Fathers had early challenged Dutch interest in the beaver trade, they paid for their freedom from the English Adventurers who had official title to the ownership of their lands in shipments of beaver, and both they and the other English colonists found in furs the best means of guaranteeing the payment of their officials. From New England, Virginia, and Maryland came constant shipments of furs to London, and the annual average at the end of the seventeenth century was over 8,000 skins. The trade in skins was, as the pioneers had foreseen and as New Plymouth protested, 'one of the greatest supports of their plantation'.

The colonies thereby produced enough furs to leave no great and obvious market in England for such quantities of furs as Radisson and Groseilliers promised. Indeed, the prospects of uniting the furs of both the English and the Dutch colonies which were opened up by the capture of New Netherland were such that the French took alarm. Intendant Talon urged Colbert straightaway to secure the Dutch colonies from England, and so to get a monopoly of the fur trade; and as the English developed the resources of their captures the French even claimed that they got as much fur from 'Nouvelle Hiorck' as was produced by the whole of Canada—from which they concluded that they must seize New York if Canada were to be made solvent.

Yet France could not herself absorb the furs produced from Canada. Whereas in the period before the Hudson Bay trade was opened up there are no records of shipment of furs from England to the continent, from France there was a regular and important export trade. In Russia the French found the outlet which they needed; but they found also that they were forced to reach this market through the intermediary trade-system of the Dutch.

The furs which their West India Company had brought to Europe from New Netherland had been in part consumed by the Dutch themselves. But in part they had been caught up in the important trade which the Dutch conducted with the Baltic. Not only did the Dutch ship through the Sound to the Baltic ports but they also established a considerable trade round the North Cape with Archangel. Here, like the English, they were enjoying a side-issue of their attempts to discover a North-east Passage to the Pacific. At Archangel they traded under such favourable terms that from sixty to eighty ships a year were required, and from Archangel they worked inland to Novgorod and the other great towns of Muscovy. They brought back from this trade the fine furs of Russia, now to be sold in competition with those of the New World. But the competition between the two streams of fur was not so serious as might appear, for while the Russian furs were fine furs, to be used in the pelt, those from the New World were predominantly beaver and were destined to be broken and felted.

Beaver was admirably adapted for felting, since the hairs of beaver fur are barbed and a beaver felt had unique qualities of cohesion. It could be worked more strenuously and would wear better than a felt made of any other fur. The fur, torn from the pelt, was pounded and mashed together, soaked, and perhaps impregnated with a mixture of an adhesive and a stiffener such as shellac. It was then rolled and pressed into a sort of cloth (felt) which could be given a fine pile surface. Felt could be shaped and moulded in a way which a woven fabric could not, but it had not the strength of woven cloth unless the adhesive were of a particularly fine quality, or unless the fur itself aided the process, as beaver fur did. The better the fur used, the less important were glue and shellac, and consequently the more pliant and weatherproof was the felt.

That an important trade should develop in shipping the beaver of the New World to Russia was due to the fact that the Russians, with their age-old experience of the fur trade behind them, had mastered a peculiar trade secret. They alone, in the seventeenth century, knew how to extract the 'beaver wool' from the pelt to the best advantage. Good prime beaver, taken in the winter, carried two kinds of fur, the long guard hairs and an undercoat of matted velvet fur. This the French called the 'duvet', and it was this 'beaver wool' which was of most value for felting. The Russian skill was to comb out the beaver wool in such a way as to leave behind a fine pelt consisting of the guard hairs, and such combed pelts were of greater value for use by furriers 'in the skin' than were the original pelts before they had been combed. So the Russian trade passed the beaver in both directions—as uncombed pelts going in to Archangel and the Baltic, and as separate consignments of beaver wool and of combed pelts coming back again to the West.

For a generation the Russians maintained their secret, until towards the end of the seventeenth century. During that time two or three thousand combed skins a year came back to Hamburg, which was the chief mart for such fine skins. Quantities also came to other ports, including Amsterdam. This city was the unchallenged centre of the trade to Archangel, and each year some fifteen or twenty ships sailed thence in May, so as to arrive in time for the Archangel fair, while a similar flotilla set out in June. So much was it accepted that Russia was the ultimate destination of much of their prime beaver that 'castor de moscovie' was a trade term in common use in Canada and France. It denoted a prime *castor sec*, a winter skin in good condition, not worn or processed at all by the Indians but simply dried, so that it carried both its guard hairs and its '*duvet*'; and since it had been stretched and dried it was known by the English as '*parchment*'. In distinction from the *castor sec* or *parchment*, of which the best qualities were 'castor de moscovie', stood the *castor gras*, which the English called '*coat beaver*'. The *coat beaver* was a skin which the Indians had themselves worn for a time after preparing it. This treatment greased and softened the skin but robbed it of its guard hairs and left only the wool or '*duvet*', so that the resultant pelt was ready for English or French felters to shave off the wool, without invoking the Russian skill. Both *parchment* and *coat beaver* had their subdivisions, especially among the French. But the main distinction held, between *coat beaver* already fit for use and that 'propre à envoyer en Moscovie'.

Felted beaver hats had been an innovation in fifteenth-century Europe. In sixteenth-century England they had been something of an imported foppish outrage, figuring in Peter Stubbes' *Anatomie of Abuses* in 1583 as hats 'of a certain kind of fine hair . . . these are called bever hats, of xx, xxx or xl shillings price, fetched from beyond the sea'. They took hold, however, and soon began to be made in England also. In the first half of the seventeenth century the commercial possibilities were such that a Beavermakers' Company tried to set up a monopoly in the process, only to have its royal charter annulled in 1640 because the Haberdashers' Company and the Feltmakers' Company also wanted to share in the trade. By the Restoration the Feltmakers' Company of London was vigorously confiscating and burning imported hats, while hats in which beaver was mixed with wool or coarser fur were forbidden by law. The Restoration gallant wore his high-crowned beaver with an air, as did his lady; and he was even prepared to buy a beaver at second-hand, to borrow an unbecoming hat so as to save his beaver from the rain, or to purloin his friend's beaver and leave a cheap hat in exchange. In all of this England was but keeping pace with continental fashion. In the last quarter of the seventeenth century the beaver hat was a social necessity.

As the fashion of the great fur-felted hat spread through Europe, the demand for beaver wool for felting increased and became a steady factor in international trade. The Dutch had been deprived of their own fur-bearing colony when the British took New Netherland, but they continued to act as the essential shippers in the Russian trade, and in addition to their annual argosies to Archangel they may also be seen from 1667 onwards shipping from fifty to eighty thousand skins a year to the Baltic ports of Riga, Dantzig, or Konigsberg, to Denmark and Livonia. This was at a time when the Dutch had no direct access to the fur trade. The furs which they shipped must have come either from France or from England, and since the British fur trade at that time was in no position to re-export anything like this quantity from the produce of the British colonies it is clear that these large consignments must have been the onward shipment from France of Canadian furs—as in fact they were.

It is significant that at this time Colbert was setting up the French *Compagnie du Nord* with the object of encouraging French shipping in the Baltic trade, and that one of the clauses on which he agreed with that *Compagnie* was that it should buy the *castor sec* from Canada, should ship it to Muscovy and should be obliged to take in return the beaver wool, of which the Russians held the secret and whose best market was in Paris. The French *Compagnie du Nord* failed to capture this trade from the Dutch—indeed, it failed in most things and its last ship was sold in 1684—but the trade persisted none-the-less. Plans were discussed for establishing direct trade between Canada and Russia or (since the interests of metropolitan France made that impossible) for direct trade between France and Russia. But both projects fell through. Even had they succeeded they would only have underlined the importance of Russia as the reserve market for the bulk of the furs of North America at this time.

So large and obvious a trade-system cannot have escaped the attention of the men who were discussing the fur-trade possibilities offered by Groseilliers and Radisson. The Port Books in which the shipments from London and the other ports were recorded for purposes of customs payments show that at this time there were occasional shipments from England to Russia of hides, rabbit and hare skins; but no beaver. Then, in 1669, there is record that thirty beaver skins were shipped from England to Dantzig, and ten to

Narva. These minute consignments went through the Sound into the Baltic, and paid the Sound Tolls—hence the record. They give no evidence as to whether similar shipments went to Archangel and so by the more normal route to Russia, but minute though they may be, they are evidence that in England there were at least some furriers who were interested in the great Baltic market for beaver and who were trying to see whether English furs could compete with the French there. It is even possible—and indeed probable— that these beaver were part of the cargo which the *Nonsuch* brought to London in 1669.

That any trade which might be got from Hudson Bay would find its way into the European trade-system, though perhaps with London developing as a major consumer, was emphasised by two incidents which occurred soon after this exploratory shipment to the Baltic in 1669. The first was that in 1670, when a further voyage had been sent out from London, some of the furs were quite certainly sold on to the European market; this time they went to Genoa. Beaver wool also began to be exported to the continent, to Rouen and to Antwerp.

The second indication of the ideas which men had in their minds at this time comes from the motto chosen by the Hudson's Bay Company. The exact date at which the motto and the Company's arms were adopted is not definite. But it was in the early formative days, for the first seal was cut in 1671 and the Company's arms, though apparently without authority from the College of Arms, were in use by 1678. So it is a fair assumption that the motto, if it is at all relevant, can be taken as a sign of the approach to the 'Bay of the North' which the pioneers of the Company adopted. The words 'Pro pelle cutem' have proved difficult to translate and still more difficult to interpret.[1] But they have a direct and simple relevance to the trade of *parchment beaver* to Russia and the combing there of the beaver wool from the skin. The Company from the start of its career set out to get skins ('Cutem') in order that the wool ('Pellis') might be combed from them. It wanted beaver not for use in the skin but as a basis for fur-felting, and its motto is a clear sign of acceptance that this business of felting was what men had in mind. Perhaps some skins might be ready for felting without Russian

---

[1] Cf. *The Beaver*, September 1924, p. 430, in which appears an attempt to link the motto either with Juvenal's 'Pro cute pellem' (Satire X, 192) or with Job, ch. 2, v. 4 (Vulgate ed.) 'Pellem pro pelle'. As a literary derivation either might suffice, but as an indication of a line of thought the motto is singularly appropriate to the process of extracting beaver wool.

intervention, for the *coat beaver*, or *castor gras* had been worn by the Indians till there was nothing but the under-fur left on the soft and greasy skin, and one of the great merits of the approach to the beaver lands through Hudson Bay was that the furs got there were mostly prime *coat beaver* which allowed English and French felters to shear off the '*duvet*' and get to work without Russian help. But it was necessarily the Baltic which would have to handle any *parchment* skins.

The fact that a fur trade from Hudson Bay would involve trade with Russia, and would probably involve severe competition with the Dutch, was rather an additional argument for the trade than a deterrent to the group of courtiers who were ranged behind Shaftesbury and Colleton. For as they saw things, the dependence of England upon Dutch intermediaries for naval supplies from the Baltic was one of the greatest weaknesses of England. The return of the *Nonsuch* with furs which were acceptable in the Baltic would seem to them to fit the fur trade from Hudson Bay into their over-all concepts of an imperial trade.

BOOKS FOR REFERENCE

Bang, Nina—*Tabeller over Skibsfart, 1661–1783* (Copenhagen, 1939).
Boissonade, P. et Charliat, P.—*Colbert et la Compagnie de Commerce du Nord (1661–1689)* (Paris, 1930).
Denys, Nicholas—*The Description and Natural History of the Coasts of North America (Acadia)*, edited by William F. Ganong (Toronto, The Champlain Society, 1908).

ARTICLES

'Armorial Bearings'. See *The Beaver* (Winnipeg, Hudson's Bay Company, June 1924).
Rich, E. E.—'Russia and the Colonial Fur Trade'. See *Economic History Review* (Cambridge, 1955), Vol. VII.

CHAPTER VI

THE CHARTER

Two days after the *Nonsuch* paid the customs due on her beaver in London, on 21st October, 1669, the City men obtained a renewal of the promise of the sole trade which they had obtained on 23rd June. Though shrouded in some slight mystery since it does not mention by name all of those who were clearly implicated in the grant, the reiteration must have given to these men confidence that the profits to be won would be theirs; it would give cohesion, would have a stabilising effect, and would give the feeling that in such a grant they now had something more than vague hopes to enjoy in common. It made inevitable the emergence of a closer legal unity, the development of a permanent body of men who would maintain this privilege. The mineral rights were granted, with the propriety of the seas, straits and lands, as well as the sole commerce, within the entrance to Hudson Strait, to be held in free socage, on the same terms as the Manor of East Greenwich (the standard prototype of such tenure) on payment of two elks and two black beaver a year to the Crown 'whensoever and as often as Wee Our heirs and Successors shall happen to enter into the said Countries . . .'. In view of the fact that the *Nonsuch*, whatever her returns on her cost, had shown that 'even those who carried out no venture' had brought home ten or twelve pounds' worth of beaver by bartering their small possessions, this was a grant which demanded serious implementation. It went further than the grant of the previous June, and it followed after the return of the *Nonsuch*, which made a great difference. But it was not yet the definitive Charter of the Hudson's Bay Company.

Possession and privilege would, however, inevitably breed coherence, and the unity and purpose which such a grant would give when combined with such prospects of trade, the lack of any rift between Court and City, can clearly be seen in the story of the winning of the Royal Charter of the Hudson's Bay Company.

Here it was James Hayes, moving between the Court and the City, who was the schemer and organiser. He was close to Rupert, ready with answers and reasons, and anxious to drive the matter to a conclusion. He it was who found from his own pocket (later to be charged to the Company!) the necessary £169 14s. 6d. for 'taking

KING CHARLES II WHO GAVE THE COMPANY ITS CHARTER

from a portrait by Lely in the Company's possession

out the Patent with the whole Charge of the same and the Duplicate', and he also produced the £20 5s. 6d. 'other money expended about the publicke business of the Company' at this time. With his secretary thus deeply involved, and with such a promising scheme already largely vindicated in practice and privileged in theory, with firm support already pledged, Rupert followed up his interest (he had by now subscribed £200) and in April 1670 put forward to the Council a draft charter on behalf of all the adventurers. The Prince's 'docket on Hudson's Bay' went to the Privy Council on 13th of that month, and received the Privy Seal on the 18th.

From this move came the Charter under the Great Seal of England, granted on 2nd May, 1670. This gave the Adventurers all that they could have hoped for, or that Rupert could have asked. It bore a close relation in some details to the earlier grants of privilege of June and October 1669, but it was more carefully and explicitly worked out and phrased.

The eighteen Adventurers—not merely the 'City' men who had previously sought reassurance—who had by May 1670 subscribed to support the voyages were, firstly, incorporated by the name of the 'Governor and Company of Adventurers of England tradeing into Hudson's Bay', with a common seal and with full legal rights as a corporation to sue and be sued, to hold land and to dispose of it. Their affairs were to be managed by a Governor and a Committee of seven, with a Deputy Governor to act for the Governor. Rupert was nominated Governor in the Charter, and the Committee were also nominated, to hold office until 10th November, 1670, after which they were to be elected annually. Oaths of loyalty were to be exacted from newly-elected Governors, Deputy Governors, Committee-men and even from all members of the Company, and any officer could be removed by a General Court of the Company for 'not demeaning himself well' in his office.

Thus organised, the Company was granted the 'sole Trade and Commerce of all those Seas Streightes Bayes Rivers Lakes Creekes and Soundes in whatsoever Latitude they shall bee that lye within the entrance of the Streightes commonly called Hudsons Streightes together with all the Landes and Territoryes upon the Countryes Coastes and confynes of the Seas Bayes Lakes Rivers Creekes and Soundes aforesaid that are not actually possessed by or granted to any of our Subjectes or possessed by the Subjectes of any other Christian Prince or State'. They were to be the 'true and absolute Lordes and Proprietors' of this vast territory, and they were to hold it, as had been envisaged in the grant of October 1669, in free and common socage, on the same terms as the Manor of East Greenwich, paying yearly to the Crown two elks and two black beaver whenever the King, his heirs and successors, should enter the territories so granted.

These lands were to be reckoned as a plantation or colony, and were to be known as Rupert's Land; and the Company was to own the mineral and fishing rights there as well as the exclusive trade and the land itself. With the example of the way in which previous colonising companies had seen the settlers predominate over, and break loose from, London control (and in particular the way in which the Massachusetts Company had transplanted overseas its central direction—the core of the Company itself) the Hudson's Bay Company's Charter made allowance for such a tendency. It was expressly stipulated that the Governor and Company might transfer themselves overseas. They might hold their meetings 'in any place or places for the same convenient within our Dominions or elsewhere'. Further to make the setting up of a colony possible, the Company was given the right to make 'Lawes Constitucions Orders and Ordinances' and to enforce them with penalties and punishments. It was to appoint Governors and Councils in its territories, with powers to examine upon oath and to judge all residents in both civil and criminal cases. Local 'Factors' were to transfer those awaiting trial to the post at which the Governor and Council should be in residence or (if it should be more convenient) to Great Britain itself, while it was settled that appeals should lie to the law courts in the United Kingdom.

The right of exclusive trade was most exactly detailed and was extended to waters and lands to which access lay through the Company's waters and territories. Any trader infringing this grant of exclusive trade was to incur the King's displeasure and was to forfeit both his merchandise and his ship, the Crown taking half of the forfeit and the Company the other half. The interloper was also to remain in custody until he had given bail of £1,000 not to repeat his offence. Even apart from trade, access to Rupert's Land was forbidden except to those approved by the Company, which was given permission to deport to the United Kingdom any person infringing this clause.

So vast a grant was comprehensive and perpetual beyond the scope of normal patents granted to those who founded or introduced new trades and industries. But it was not peculiar when compared with other grants to colonising companies, and it is against such grants that it should rightly be considered. Later development threw the emphasis so much more on trade than on settlement that the clauses giving the exclusive right of trade tend to receive undue attention. But the Charter in itself must, from an analysis of its terms, be considered as the charter of a colony, Rupert's Land, as much as the charter of a trading company. As such, it ran true to form and bore a close resemblance, for example, to the outstanding charter to the Virginia Company. The possibility that the whole direction of the Company might migrate to the colony was taken into account, whilst the further possibility that the trade would fall into the hands of the settlers (as in other colonies) was also allowed for.

It was equally possible that the Company might develop either on a perpetual joint stock, trading continuously as a unified body (as the East India Company had ultimately done) or by a system of calls and subscriptions for each voyage, dividing the returns from each voyage among those individuals who had subscribed to that voyage. It was therefore ordained in the Charter that each member who had promised a subscription for a voyage must pay according to his promise. It was further left open for the Company to adopt the 'Cape merchant' system of colonial trade into which most colonising companies fell. In this system the settler conducted the local trade and collected the goods for shipment across the Atlantic; the company supplied the 'Magazeen Ship' and reserved to itself the business of the 'Cape merchant' in shipping the produce home and in supplying the wants of the settlers from home. The Charter left it open for the Hudson's Bay Company to adopt this device, and a system of licences for conducting the local trade was explicitly mentioned, while it was also contemplated that an individual shareholder might be allowed 'to trade or traffique as a freeman of the said Company'— a possibility which would have turned the Company away from a joint-stock trade into a Regulated Company in which individual members traded under rules laid down by the Company.

Indeed, the Company only stumbled into its firm adherence to close control and to joint-stock trade as circumstances made opposition to private trade possible and necessary. There was nothing in the Charter, or in the minds of the men who drew up the terms of the Charter, to indicate that this was thought inevitable or even desirable in 1670. In particular, the increasing resistance to private trade by ships' captains and other servants of the Company only developed as the trade expanded. The Instructions for the pioneer voyage of the *Eaglet* and the *Nonsuch* had accepted the probability that some private trade would be carried. The Adventurers thought that 'some small private adventures may be also carryed by you and your men which wee doe not refuse to allow but doe absolutely restraine all persons from tradeing themselves with the Indians because thereby our Trade may be distroyed and the said Mr. Gooseberry and Mr. Radisson loose theire credit with the Indians'. Private ventures were therefore to be 'disposed of in a like manner as our owne goods are'.

Later challenges to the Charter obscure these important clauses and tend to falsify our views of what was in the minds of the men of 1670, to give to them a clear and purposeful ambition for a trade monopoly instead of an undefined and uncertain possibility of a colony with all sorts of potential developments. These developments included the possibility of a controlled trade, but that was only one possibility among others. The opposition which the Charter met also tended to make men read into it ideas which were not there. It was, for example, clear that settlement was envisaged as one possibility; but there is no word in the Charter which lays the fostering of settle- ment on the Company as a duty. Further, although the preamble to the Charter recited that the Adventurers had undertaken a voyage (that of the *Eaglet* and the *Nonsuch*) 'for the discovery of a new Pass- age into the South Sea', yet there was no word in the Charter which in any way obliged them to continue such exploration.

The whole Charter was, in fact, a magnificent grant of rights and privileges, not a specification of duties. The only duty laid upon the Company was the payment of two elks and two black beavers in the then unlikely event of the King or his heirs or successors setting foot in Rupert's Land. It was fluid enough, and generous enough, to furnish conditions in which a closely-controlled joint-stock trade could develop in a region in which normal colonial settlement soon proved impossible, and the Charter slid naturally into position as the warrant for such a trade system. The change of emphasis, from pos- sible settlement to probable trade, was early and easy. Indeed, much of the change in emphasis had already been achieved before the Charter was granted, and it is possible even to take the clauses em- powering settlement as mere formalities. Certainly, from the start of the chartered Company's operations, trade predominated. So the Charter achieved a unique position in that it became the only charter for a colony which was used to cover not settlement but a trade. Thus interpreted, it furnished the conditions of the Company's trade for two centuries. It furnished, too, the basis of most of the criticism from which the Company suffered during that time.

In truth, the magnificent Charter has always been something of an enigma in the history of the Company, and has deluded both its supporters and its opponents. From the set phrases of the grant has risen an inevitable tendency to treat the history of the Company and of its trade as a study in the exercise of monopoly; and it is true that the Charter went far to prevent English interlopers from challenging the Company in its control of the trade of the Bay-posts themselves. But the Company never had a monopoly in any sense which would allow it to exploit lack of competition, to dictate prices and conditions either of purchase or of sale. At the posts by the Bay the Company's men had always to meet competition from the South—from Canada and the St. Lawrence basin and later from the United States. In the markets of London the furs from this competitive trade had to be sold in competition with furs, often of equal quality and greater in quantity, from the New England and southern states and (after 1763) from Canada; and in the markets of Europe the Company's furs had to meet the same competition again.

Whether competition came from the French of Canada, from English subjects trading from Canada, from English colonists in New York, Albany, Virginia or Maryland, or from independent citizens of the United States, the result was the same. The Indians had competitors for the purchase of their furs, and the furriers and the felters had alternative sources of supply. So the Company had always to buy and to sell in competition with active rivals. Its survival was due to its mastery of the essentials of its trade as much as to the privileges which it enjoyed; and even in the exclusion of English rivals from its barren and inhospitable domain the Company owed its immunity as much to the difficulty of navigation as to its chartered rights. For the first two English ships to attempt an interloping voyage were both wrecked (the *Expectation* in 1683 and the *Mary* in 1688) the French found lack of Bay-pilots a constant handicap, the attempts at discovery of a North-west Passage and at unseating the Company which culminated in the Parliamentary enquiry of 1749 depended on former employees of the Company and were forced to seek the shelter of the Company's posts, and the Company's policy of avoiding publication makes it clear that a monopoly of knowledge and experience was its greatest asset.

The Charter, moreover, was granted in a period when 'the prerogative was high'. Even within the Committee there were always those whose political convictions would not support so strong a claim, and the Company throughout its history showed a canny reluctance to bring the Charter to the challenge of a test-case in the courts of law. Circumstances being favourable, the chance to get the Charter confirmed in Parliament was taken in 1690. But the Parliamentary confirmation was for seven years only, and an attempt to secure a renewal in 1697 lapsed unaccountably during the second reading in the House of Commons. Thenceforth the Company always knew that its unconfirmed Charter was suspect; it might perhaps have been in a stronger position had it never sought Parliamentary sanction, and the next legal challenge to the Charter, in 1749, found the Law Officers of the Crown in some doubt and anxious that a test-case might be brought so that the position might be clarified. The episode was passed off, largely because there was not enough confidence that the Company could be challenged commercially to make a legal challenge worth-while. Yet when the next challenge came, from the North-westers of Montreal, it was still doubtful what importance could be attached to the Charter, and the North-westers secured important legal opinions to support their contention that it had no validity. While anxious not to nullify it completely, in case they might secure enjoyment of its privileges for themselves, they defied it in practice even to the extent of sending a ship to the Bay and of establishing a post on Charlton Island. It was certainly not because it enjoyed chartered privileges that the Company came precariously intact through its struggle with the North-westers, nor were those privileges of any value in the subsequent competition with American trappers and settlers.

The Charter gave form and continuity, dignity and confidence, to the Company. But its survival as a trading corporation was due to the sound trading practices which it developed within its chartered domain. The history of the Company nevertheless falls naturally into four periods, each marked by a distinct challenge to the Charter.

From 1670 to 1713 the challenge came from the French of Canada, roused from an early tolerance which had arisen partly from their own difficulties, partly from the Bourbon support for the House of Stuart. Until the Treaty of Utrecht confirmed the British in possession of the Bay, the Company was always liable to find its posts captured, even in times of peace, and at the end of the period the biggest book-asset it possessed was the large claim for damages due from the French. This was a period in which the Company had first to establish its trade, to set up its posts, to defend them, and to get some elementary knowledge both of its territories and of the fur trade. It is a period marked by one-sided documentation; the London records are full, but little or nothing comes from the Bay. The formative development is that, one after the other, strangers and newcomers to the fur trade—courtiers, bankers, politicians, diplomats or merchants—slowly establish sound practices of administration and accountancy, face the everlasting problems of financing the voyages on credit when the first small subscribed capital has been dissipated, and emerge from a long war with something which bears promise of becoming a national asset.

In contrast with the financial stringency of the first period, the period from 1713 to 1763 is marked by solvency and even prosperity, by a constant succession of dividends and by the accumulation of a substantial reserve of invested capital. This was a period in which the Committee were perhaps lucky to come scatheless through the South Sea Bubble, but in which they showed a genuine capacity for organising the trade and in which their success stirred up the challenge of English rivals which culminated in a Parliamentary enquiry in 1749. At the same time the French of Canada penetrated to the prairies and probably as far west as the Elbow of the Saskatchewan, and the Company had to face opposition both in the hinterland of its posts and in the markets of Europe. Conservative, perhaps unenterprising, in its reaction, the Company nevertheless survived all the challenges. For it was in competent control of a flourishing trade, and when the period ended with the British conquest of Canada the Company was master of an experienced and enterprising school of inland voyagers who were bringing down the trade of the Rockies, the Prairies, Athabaska and the Winnipeg area, to the posts by the Bay, while the initial steps had been taken in setting up posts inland up the rivers.

The conquest of Canada ushered in the third period in the history of the Company, a period dominated by the challenge of British traders working from Montreal. The organisation and the enterprise of the North-westers led the fur-trade frontier to the Pacific and to the Arctic; but although they traded furs far in excess of those handled by the Company, and although their preponderance in the trade must stand unquestioned, they failed to disrupt or supersede the Company and the challenge ended in a coalition in which the staid Hudson's Bay management, reinvigorated by some North-westers, remained in control. This was a period in which the Company was brought into sore straits, for Napoleon dominated Europe and markets were upset, dividends ceased and reserves were spent. But sound and reliable habits of trade proved more enduring than the flamboyant extravagance of the North-westers, and after its coalition with the North West Company, the Hudson's Bay Committee started on the fourth period of its history (from 1821 to 1870) with something nearer to a practical monopoly of the fur trade than it had ever hitherto enjoyed.

Yet the Americans had followed closely on the heels of the North-

westers in their passage to the Pacific coast, and they had got before-
hand in the development of a sound overland route, so that in its
fourth period the Company stands as the exponent of British claims
to the Pacific slope (and to its fur trade) at a time when British official
opinion is behind the advance of settlement into the prairies but is
reluctant to challenge American claims to Oregon. So although the
Company starts this period with a practical monopoly and with a
Parliamentary confirmation of its exclusive trade, it is left without
governmental or popular support in facing two contestants against
whom trading competence can achieve nothing more than delay.
For a profitable trade in furs could not be driven where the settler
had replaced the trapper, nor where American markets, prices and
practices bid up costs, fostered discontent and provoked governmental intervention at a level where the Hudson's Bay men could
not be sure of support from politicians who wanted no more imperial
commitments.

The personality and achievements of George Simpson stamp the
first half of this period with a character of its own. The 'Little
Emperor' as Governor of Rupert's Land moulded the coalition of
the two companies into a fascinatingly efficient business management
which controlled life, trade and settlement, from coast to coast and
which produced unexampled prosperity for the Company and, indeed, for its servants. But even George Simpson could only use the
commercial efficiency of which he was master to achieve delay, and
he knew it. The contested border areas were trapped bare while
systematic recuperation was encouraged elsewhere. So when, eventually, Oregon went to the United States and the settlers moved into
the prairies, the Company yielded up its territories and many of its
privileges and embarked on a fifth period in its history (as yet un-
written).

The history of the Charter had come full circle by the end of the
fourth period in 1870, for colonisation again dominated men's minds
as it had done in the original phrases of the grant of 1670, two full
centuries earlier.

BOOKS FOR REFERENCE

Hudson's Bay Company—*Charters, Statutes, Orders in Council, &c. Relating to the
Hudson's Bay Company* (London, Hudson's Bay Company, 1949).

BOOK TWO

From Charter to Utrecht, 1670-1713

CHAPTER VII

THE ESTABLISHMENT OF THE BOTTOM
OF THE BAY

With Rupert in a clear and legal position as Governor, and with a full and perpetual title to its lands and trade, the new Company had every cause for self-congratulation in 1670, every reason to organise itself so as to exploit the trade and wealth delivered to it. Confidence in the value of the sea-approach to the Bay must have been high, for the furs brought by the *Nonsuch* could not be counted as a satisfactory yield on the cash laid out. The real yield lay in the proof that the sea-approach to the Crees was justified, and in the reports brought back by Gillam and Groseilliers.

Of these two, Groseilliers must obviously have talked on his return to London, but he has left nothing on record; Gillam is far from eloquent in his testimony but at least four summaries of his evidence have survived. He was interviewed before the Royal Society and his answers were recorded; a 'Breviate' of his log was published about 1675 in John Seller's *English Pilot*; in 1683 James Hayes submitted to the Council a Memorandum of the Company's history in which Gillam's voyage was summarised; and the State Papers, Domestic Series, also contain brief and formal mentions of his return and of the prospects of the trade which he had opened up. From the last source came the main facts—that Gillam was 'environed with ice' for six months, that his men hauled the ketch on shore and built a 'house' to winter in, that they found the natives civil and beaver in plenty. Radisson later declared that Gillam had built his 'house' (which was called Charles Fort) on the ruins of an English house built sixty years previously. This attempt to vindicate the continuity of English settlement and title, linking the *Nonsuch* voyage with that of Captain James depends, however, only on the statement of Radisson and he, of course, was not present in James Bay in 1668.

The 'Breviate' of Gillam's log is mainly concerned with navigation at sea and adds few details of the winter's residence ashore, or of the trade conducted. The *Nonsuch* had passed Hudson Strait and sighted Digges Island by 11th August. Gillam then worked his way down south into the great bay, made friendly contact with Indians from the mainland, and was by them conducted into the mouth of Rupert River. The river was frozen by 9th December and (to take up the evidence from the Royal Society Papers) Gillam and his men built a wooden house ashore. They dug a cellar twelve feet deep in which they successfully preserved their sea-beer all through the winter whilst they lived on ships' provisions supplemented by deer and fowl which they shot, and on small beer brewed from malt which they had brought. Though friendly, the Indians were inclined to pilfer. Game and fish were abundant, especially partridges and 'brave pikes', and they found that the Indians followed the game in a nomadic way of life.

With spring weather some three hundred Indians came in to trade, and the party found that a winter by the Bay had not been so terrible as had been feared. Gillam lost not a single man 'only on returning they found some trouble of Scurvy in their mouths'.

The friendliness with which the Indians met Gillam and Groseilliers (whose ability and experience probably go far to explain that friendliness) were confirmed in a treaty of amity which Gillam made with them. He was also alleged to have 'purchased' their lands from them. Their nomadic way of life, with its ignorance of ownership of the soil in a European sense, would make such a treaty probable enough, but largely meaningless. It would, however, lend support to the claims of the Company as against any other European claimant. This treaty of purchase, in fact, was not vouched until other Europeans challenged the Company's chartered rights to the soil. Then, in 1683, James Hayes maintained that Gillam 'discovered a River in the bottome of the said Bay upon the East Maine, where he mett with the native Indians, And having made a League of Friendship with the Captain of the said River and formally purchased both the River itself and the Lands thereabouts, he gave it the name of Rupert River'.

Such 'purchases' were not normally parts of European approaches to non-European lands in the seventeenth century. True, the Dutch had 'purchased' New Netherland, and on occasions the English also made such a bargain. The eighteen original settlers of Rhode Island, for example, claimed that they had bought the island from the Chief Sachem of Narragansett country. But even when such a bargain was made it could do no more than underline the disparity between the two societies represented, the lack of economic values or of legal concepts in common between the two parties.

Gillam's 'Treaty' with the Indians was indeed to be quoted in arguments as to title, but the true estimate which the Company itself placed on it can be judged by the fact that when French claims based on such treaties were put forward, the Company refused to attach serious weight to them. As for the Indians, said the Company, 'noe Action or Resolution of those Savages can alter an establisht Right.' Radisson, in 1699 writing as a strong partisan of the Company, explained further that 'for the presents they have need of they would give themselves up this Day to God if they had knowledge of him and tomorrow they would give themselves to the Devil for a pipe of Tobacco and they would even deliver up their In heritance for the like things. And they received at each place where the English have been Settled theire presents for takeing Possession whosoever hath known those Savage Nations doth understand the Same things'.

Gillam's 'Treaty' therefore was a gesture, but a gesture which gave the Company an additional title to Rupert's Land. Yet its titles, however they might be derived, would need effective vindication to carry any weight. France, England and Holland, were all in their different ways basing their designs for overseas expansion on a denial of Spanish and Portuguese claims to divide the world between them by virtue of a legal title derived from the Papal Bull *Regnans in Excelsis*. Each nation produced its own form of rebuttal, but between them all there was little to choose, and the essence of the argument had been tersely put by the Elizabethans who had told the Spaniards that 'Prescription without possession availeth nothing'. The seventeenth century had not departed from this doctrine, nor could it do so without surrendering everything to the King of Spain, who could claim any part of the non-European world 'by colour of a donation from the Pope when at any time he shall have leisure to look that way'. There was no urgency as far as Spain was concerned, but it was common doctrine that neither charter from the English Crown nor treaty with native captains would be valid title if they were not supported by effective occupation. Even then, the question of first discovery might complicate the issue, for statesmen were liable to claim by effective occupation or by first discovery according to which gave them the stronger position.

The legal subtleties lay in the future; in 1670 the immediate and obvious fact was that the newly-chartered Company must settle its lands in order to support its claims, and must grasp the trading possibilities in order to recover its outlay and to make some profit—for the *Nonsuch* had done none of these things.

The Hudson's Bay Company Charter was the achievement of a small and closely-connected group of men, rallying behind Rupert, stimulated by Shaftesbury, and organised by James Hayes. The business of the newly-chartered Company, and its small subscribed capital, were necessarily in the hands of this small group and of their personal friends; and whatever the Charter's wider significance and more lasting influence may be, it must not be forgotten that its first result was to give this small group legal claims, continuity of interest and purpose, and a corporate legal personality. It was in accordance with this new legal status that James Hayes early undertook to get a seal cut for the Company.

This closely-knit group was essentially metropolitan in organisation and interest. True, some measure of success by the sailors and traders in the Bay was necessary to evoke the support of London, and some measure of instruction from the Bay was necessary to educate London in the difficulties and advantages of the position. But, provided it was so stimulated and advised, it was the London Committee which dictated that mild and benevolent approach to the Indians, that insistence on conservative and consistent methods of trading, that constant financial backing and that endless confidence, which made long-term policy the hall-mark and short-term exploitation the exception in the Company's history.

The ebb and flow of dominance between London and the Bay were, of course, affected by knowledge and personalities, but in 1670 there were no Bay-side establishments, and London clearly controlled the situation. Yet Groseilliers, Radisson and Gillam, with Gorst to support them and to add detail, were certainly not overlooked by the Committee which was set up by the Charter. Nevertheless, it is the London Committee which claims attention in 1670, and which provides the information for the story, too. The Minutes Books of the Company begin in 1671, mingling the constant Minutes of the active Committee with those of the very occasional General Courts of all the Adventurers. In the cryptic manner of business minutes, they often fail to record the reasons for decisions taken, and they omit much which was discussed without a vote. But within such limitations they give a guide to the decisions taken by the London Committee from the start of the Chartered Company and even earlier, for they reveal that one of the first decisions taken by the Committee was to appoint a Governor for their overseas territories. This, like so many things in the early days, was a sequel to action taken before the Charter was secured, for the problem had been faced and the choice of a man made in the period when the prospects of winning the Charter were still uncertain.

As early as December 1669, the Quaker Charles Bayly was released from the Tower of London on the surety of the Governor of the Tower, John Robinson. Robinson was one of those who had subscribed to send the *Nonsuch* to the Bay, and he guaranteed that Bayly should betake himself to the navigation of Hudson Bay and the places discovered there. Little is known of Bayly's previous history and the reasons for his appointment remain a mystery, as does so much of his career as a servant of the Company. He had at some time been a resident of Maryland, he had gone to Rome in an attempt to convert the Pope to Protestantism, and he had been imprisoned in Rome, in France and in England. Of a piece with his attempt to convert the Pope was a special personal reproof addressed to Charles II by Bayly. He must have had either influence or a most striking and attractive personality, for he was released on parole from six years' imprisonment in 1669 in order that he might go on a special mission to France and when, on his return, he was again released for service in Hudson Bay the order for his release stipulated that he must be assured of such conditions and allowances as should be agreeable to reason and the nature of his employment. He joined the Company not only as an employee but as a stockholder, with a full share of £300 to his credit.

The Adventurers, having covenanted with Bayly, set to work to prepare that effective occupation of their territories of which his appointment was the symbol. This was the period, in 1669, when the 'City' men were both seeking a reassurance as to the grant of exclusive trade and pledging their support to the enterprise. It was at this time that the Adventurers paid for a translation of Radisson's account of his previous voyages and also set to work to fit him out for a further voyage after his disappointment in the *Eaglet*. For this purpose Hayes had secured from the Admiralty the loan of the *Hadarine* pink, and when this permit was rescinded Radisson was sent off, again with Captain Stannard, on the *Wivenhoe*, a naval pink, in May 1669. Again Radisson failed, though on this occasion he and Stannard probably got as far as Hudson Strait.

It argues much for the confidence and purpose of the Adventurers that in the midst of such disappointments, with the *Nonsuch* out of contact, they should not only have made their agreement with Bayly and have continued their pressure for a charter, but should have begun to build a vessel especially for the trade. Their finances were

c

by no means adequate for their needs, and the *Wivenhoe* voyage of 1669 had to be partly fitted out on credit, for it carried an item in the accounts of £20 for interest on 'severall summes of money'. Nevertheless the *Prince Rupert* was built for the Adventurers during the year 1669–70 and was ready to set out on the first voyage to be made under the Charter, in June 1670. Classed as a frigate, she was of 75½ tons burthen, twice the size of the *Nonsuch*, and her hull at five guineas a ton cost the Adventurers £396 7s. 0d., which, with other work, running rigging, decoration and guns, brought her first cost up to over £600. The *Wivenhoe* was once more borrowed and she and the *Rupert* sailed together from Ratcliffe Wharf on 31st May, 1670. Aboard the *Rupert* was Zachariah Gillam in command, with Groseilliers to direct trade and contacts with the Indians. With them went Thomas Gorst, who had gone as supercargo on the *Nonsuch* in 1668. Master of the *Wivenhoe* was Captain Robert Newland, and with him sailed Radisson, Governor Bayly, Nehemiah Walker (son of a stockholder, himself a stockholder, and later a ship's captain) with others.

The fact that this voyage was intended to be more than another exploration, or even a successful trading venture, was emphasised not only by the presence of Bayly as Governor but also by the shipping of bricks and building materials, powder, shot and 'great Gunns to be left in the Bay'. The intention to start settlement and governance was obvious.

Bayly presented to the Company the original books which he kept in the country, and they have disappeared; he should officially also have delivered a report, and the ships' logs should have been handed in too. But none of this evidence has survived. Instead, we have to be grateful that Thomas Gorst was aboard, for from his diary comes the only account of the venture. At Digges Island the two ships separated, the *Wivenhoe* taking Radisson and Bayly westwards to found a post on the Nelson River. This was to be the Company's main post, and the Nelson or the Hayes River was regarded as being more likely to lead to the rich beaver territory to the northwards of the Great Lakes than was Rupert River or any of the rivers of the East Main.

Gillam took the *Rupert* south-east to Charles Fort, which he and Groseilliers had built the previous year. They arrived on 8th September and repeated their precautions of 1668–9; the ship's beer was buried for the homeward voyage, fresh supplies were brewed, game was killed, the ship was docked and a house was built—this time of two storeys and with a brick chimney. Indians came in freely to trade.

Then, in mid-October, Radisson came over to them in the boat from the *Wivenhoe* with the news that the ship had been almost wrecked on Mansel Island but had been got to Nelson River, where Bayly and others (Nehemiah Walker being his assistant) had gone ashore and had taken formal possession of all the lands and territories of 'Port Nelson' in the name of the King, nailing up the King's arms on a tree. No Indians had been met in Nelson River, but the natural resources of the district were most attractive; there was plenty of game, fruit and wood. Then a storm took the *Wivenhoe* out of the river and she could not be got back again, the weather turned bitterly cold, two men died and Captain Newland and others were desperately sick. In a general atmosphere of discouragement they decided to leave Nelson River and to join the *Rupert* at Charles Fort, but Captain Newland died on 13th October, and Gillam brought the *Wivenhoe* in to Rupert River, where she also was duly docked for the winter.

In the New Year Radisson went off for a two months' journey to Moose River. A later expedition followed him to trade beaver there, and in March and April garden seeds were sown and reaped at Charles Fort, the hogs and hens which had been taken out and which had survived the winter were killed and eaten, and a small 'shallop' which had been taken out in plank was launched and used for coastal work.

The Company had sent him out to found a permanent settlement, but Bayly could not get enough volunteers to stay in the country with him. Gorst thought he could have had the men if he had given firm orders and a definite lead, but the whole expedition started for England on 1st July, 1671, with Bayly navigating the *Wivenhoe* since her mate had died as well as her Captain.

On the homeward voyage the shallops were sent off on tours to explore the coast, and they found the remains of several former British expeditions. It is even possible that they found the remains of Henry Hudson himself, near Point Comfort, and they were confident that they discovered the remains of Captain James' expedition on Charlton Island. Having thus gathered much information of the coast of the Bay, Bayly started for the open sea on 24th July, 1671, and on 26th October it was reported from Plymouth that the 'missing ship' from Hudson Bay had arrived there. This was the *Wivenhoe*, the *Rupert* being already safe in port.

Bayly's return was too late for another voyage to be set forth in 1671, and in any case the Committee had made no preparations. Bayly had been expected to winter in the Bay, and to be there ready to receive whatever shipping might be sent out to him in 1672, so his return with all his men was the first and most obvious disappointment which the Committee had to face. Against this they could indeed set the fact that he and his crews had spent a winter in the Bay, that they had made a reasonable trade, had built a substantial post on Rupert River and had opened up Moose River for trade. But they had met with disaster in their voyage to Nelson River and their failure to set up a post there—the first of several failures—was to prove a great source of weakness in the future.

The returns in beaver on the *Rupert* and *Wivenhoe* were nevertheless really satisfactory. Customs on the *Rupert*'s cargo amounted to £69 6s. 7d. and on the *Wivenhoe*'s to £52 13s. 0d. The skins were looked over by Thomas Glover, the great furrier, but he obviously did not make a satisfactory bid for them, so they were put up for public auction. When put into lots for sale they amounted to twenty-seven lots, which were sold in the New Year 'by the candle' at Garraway's Coffee-house, the most famous London business rendezvous of the period. Sale 'by the candle' was a system in which an 'upset price' was called as the candle was lit and bids were made as the candle burned. Whoever had made the highest bid when the candle guttered out was the purchaser. The Company 'set up' 3,000 lbs. of beaver at seven shillings the pound and a little later, in April, set up a further 8,000 lbs. at the same price after an attempt to get eight shillings.

They sold the whole of this second parcel to the brothers Joseph and Louis Deluvrier—a pair of rather elusive merchants with French connections as well as French names. The Deluvriers also bought a parcel of otter and moose for £10 and paid part of their bill of £2,810 by selling 834 gallons of brandy to the Company for its next voyage, for the French background to the fur trade had from the start made brandy one of the prime articles of trade; £25 worth of brandy had been part of the cargo of the 1668 voyage and a further consignment of 236 gallons had been aboard the *Wivenhoe* in 1669.

With or without the Deluvriers' brandy, the 1672 sales were most encouraging and produced a gross revenue of £3,860. This seems an extravagant return on one year's trading for a company whose full authorised capital, not yet fully paid in, was as yet only £8,720. But already a distinction between share subscriptions and working capital must be taken into account, and though these fur sales of 1672 seem to yield an exorbitant interest on share subscriptions, the cash taken should be set, not against share subscriptions but against the actual costs of the voyage. These costs had been largely met by credit. Most of the Adventurers had lent money to set out the 1670 voyage, and in January 1672, for example, James Hayes had to step in and lend the Company a further £50 of his own money free of interest, a loan which had not been repaid as late as 1675. Not all the loans were so cheap, and as the voyages became more regular this feature of the Company's finances became perpetuated. The working capital for each voyage was almost entirely borrowed, either from tradesmen whose accounts were paid in arrears but with interest, or in direct loans from members of the Company and their friends. Such loans bore a fixed and agreed interest, and they formed a first charge on the proceeds from a year's trading. They performed the function and had many of the features of a debenture share, and they were often repaid with interest at the end of a fur sale which marked the end of one year's trade, only to be immediately renewed to provide the cash for the outfit of the next year.

In 1672, therefore, although the Adventurers had reason to congratulate themselves on their fur sale and to look forward to a prosperous future, they could not give themselves a dividend—nor were they able to do so until 1684, a record of fourteen years' trade since the Charter or of sixteen years' since the *Nonsuch* sailed, without dividend.

The fur sale itself was a little disquieting too, for it revealed a danger that the Company might fall into the hands of a small number of furriers who would be able to hold it to ransom. At some stage in the marketing of small furs it is essential that they should be handled in bulk, so that the furs may be matched for colour and quality and so reach the public in graded lots. Already the Company was aware of this problem, and it hired skilled London furriers to lot its furs before sale. There was therefore no satisfaction, but only a concealed threat to the Company, when it saw its beaver bought complete by an 'engrosser', a large furrier who took the whole consignment, as Thomas Glover took the *Nonsuch*'s cargo in 1669 or as the brothers Deluvrier took the April consignment in 1672. Efforts to spread the market and to popularise the use of beaver were necessary, and they were undertaken. John Kirke had already been credited with $98\frac{3}{4}$ lbs. of beaver to be 'made into Hatts and presented to Severall persons according to Orders of the Committee', and this genteel form of advertising was to be repeated several times in the next few years.

Another disconcerting fact was that the voyage had not accomplished either of its basic purposes—the settlement of the country

in general terms, or the opening up of the Nelson and Hayes River
territories as the main settlements. Bayly was himself home again,
and none of the Company's employees had remained out to perpetuate its title; the official occupation and the nailing up of tokens
were still empty formalities.

If the Committee were disappointed in some matters and in difficulties in others, they did not falter. Influenced by Radisson, by
Bayly, and by the furs which had been traded there, they took an
early decision to make their chief post at Moose River, and they
pressed on with sensible preparations for a voyage in 1672. Here
they used the knowledge and experience of Groseilliers, Radisson,
Gillam and Bayly to guide them in their purchases, and a further
increase in shipping was also planned. In addition to the *Rupert* the
Company bought the 'Barke called the *Employ*' for £126 in May
1672. She was to winter in the Bay while the *Rupert* brought the
cargo of the year home. Hayes, the 'contact man' *par excellence*, was
also empowered to organise a dozen carpenters to prepare the ships
and to seek from the Navy some more suitable vessel in place of the
Wivenhoe, and although the Committee had at one time resolved to
send only two ships that year, the *Messenger*, a 'dogger', was borrowed
and prepared for the voyage.

The three ships left London together in June 1672, once more
with Bayly aboard and charged to carry out effective occupation of
the chartered lands. Bricks and mortar for building the 'Fort' at
Moose were shipped, and about half of the thirty or forty men taken
had contracted to stay in the country. The trade goods showed a
preponderance of guns, knives, hatchets, powder and shot, brass
kettles and fowling pieces; tobacco and brandy also figured.

The important problem of 'private trade' was now dealt with
firmly but not, as it proved, finally. The first two voyages had already
shewn the need for a firm stand on this matter. The *Eaglet* and the
Nonsuch had been sent out with no certain knowledge of the trading
possibilities involved and with the loose instruction that 'some small
private adventures may be also carryed by you and your men'. All
private ventures were to be sold with the Company's furs on the
return to London. But in 1670 the two Frenchmen and Gillam were
definitely of opinion that they might conduct their own trade as well
as that of the Company, and so must Bayly have been. Captain
Newland, too, had shared a 'cargason of goods' valued at £65 which
went aboard the *Wivenhoe* and was taken over for the Company
when Newland died; and when the *Rupert* and the *Wivenhoe* returned to London in 1671 the Committee had to be careful to

specify in its orders that it was dealing with the 'returned cargo *belonging to the Company*'. Bayly was allowed two lots of beaver each of £30 value, presumably as his private trade, whilst Groseilliers and Radisson also had £162 15*s*. 0*d*. credited to them 'for beaver'. Now, with the trading possibilities taking more definite shape, this aspect needed attention, and it was ordered that for 1672 no one should be employed to stay in the country except by the Committee, and that no goods should be shipped without their consent 'to the ende the Ships bee not hereafter pestered as they were the Last voyage'. All employees were to oblige themselves not to trade in beaver on pain of forfeiture of their goods and wages.

On their return in 1673 Gillam was again questioned by the Royal Society, but once more it was Thomas Gorst who left the account from which narratives of the venture have to be compiled. He was appointed by Bayly to keep a Journal, which later found its way into the hands of John Oldmixon and was used by him to write the Hudson Bay part of his 'British Empire in America'. As Oldmixon not unjustly remarked, although 'the Events it contains are too trivial to be remembered . . . They serve to give . . . an Idea of an Infant Colony, in one of the rudest Parts of the World'.

The expedition made for Rupert River, and there from the start was manifested one of the permanent features of the Company's trade; the local chief and two friendly Indians came to Bayly to beg for subsistence. This was given them, and they were sent fishing. Here already was shown the marked tendency for the Indians to become dependent on the traders, and the danger threatening the trader and the Indian alike if shipping failed and they became completely dependent on the resources of the country.

Governor Bayly and his men stayed the winter of 1672–3 at Rupert River, doing nothing of note but yet clearing a good trade, for when in 1673 Gillam brought the *Rupert* back to England with the *Messenger* both ships were well laden. Radisson had come home with Gillam, and the *Rupert* brought 7,044 lbs. and the *Messenger* 7,064 lbs.; the whole cargoes were sold to Thomas Glover at 7*s*. 6*d*. a pound, and the sale gave the Committee over £5,000 with which to carry on its business.

The *Employ*, as the Committee had intended, remained in the country with Bayly, Groseilliers, Gorst and its captain, Samuel Cole. Bayly sent the sloop to kill seals at Point Comfort, to get oil; he traded with a few Indians (including one who alleged that he came from Quebec), shot geese and other game, and got his men over mild attacks of scurvy in the spring. Then, in July 1673, Bayly sent

Groseilliers in the *Employ* to make a further attempt at settling 'Port Nelson'. Groseilliers arrived in August in Nelson River, but at that time of year could find no Indians, nor could he find Severn River though it was marked on the charts. But at Nelson he found relics of Sir Thomas Button's visit and brought them back to England. Meanwhile, in March 1673, Bayly had himself gone to Point Comfort in search of fresh meat, and during his absence the post prepared to meet trouble from the Indians of Nottaway River, and also received a deputation from the local chief 'Cuscididahs' who was in fear of an attack from these Indians, stimulated by the Jesuits from Canada.

In both the visit of the Indian from Quebec and in the fears of 'Cuscididahs' were to be seen signs that the British challenge to the fur trade was not passing without notice in Canada, nor even in France itself. Bayly was soon faced with more weighty evidence of the new French interest, roused by the success which the Company's ventures had so far achieved.

It is certain that some of the furs which the Company sold in London had already found their ultimate market in Europe. Some were reported as having been sold in Genoa; Thomas Glover traded to the great European fur-centres and England was beginning to export beaver wool; it is most probable too that the great purchase made by the brothers Deluvrier in 1672 was at least in part re-sold in Europe. French and Canadian profits were under threat.

In any case the France of Louis XIV and Colbert was not a land to stand idly by whilst her claims were ignored, her trade was disorganised and the financial stability of her chief colony was disrupted. True, she had many preoccupations, and it did not follow that she would always see eye to eye with the fur-traders. But Colbert had long been attracted by the Arctic, and as early as 1664 he had received envoys from Amsterdam who wanted him to take up the Dutch ambitions of discovering a 'Chemin des Indes par la mer du Nord'. The project appealed to Colbert, but for many years he was unable to pursue it. He knew that the English colonists could easily over-run Canada—as in fact they captured Acadia—and he strove to preserve peace in America despite the battles in Europe. Then, when peace with England came in 1667, the Treaty of Breda brought not only an end to hostilities but an active naval alliance between France and England against the Dutch, with James Duke of York as commander of the combined fleet. So Colbert was still unable to oppose British projects for Hudson Bay.

But though he was thus prevented by diplomatic reasons from

taking a firm stand against the English patronage of Groseilliers, Radisson and their project, Colbert was alive to the potential value of the scheme. He paid due attention when, early in 1670, the Dutchman Van Heemskerk, who had sailed with Radisson and Stannard in the *Wivenhoe* on the abortive voyage of 1669, began to report on the English plans. Van Heemskerk was taken under French protection and given a grant of 'all the lands which have been and shall be discovered by him in all North America entered from above Canada towards the North Pole and extending to the South Sea and as far as he can reach'. He had been told of a land which he called 'La Floride du Nord', a land of good rivers and safe anchorages, and from London he wrote to Paris asking to be out-fitted for a voyage of discovery, and to be given a monopoly of the trade.

Colbert, dominating French commercial and diplomatic affairs, firmly supported Van Heemskerk and was at this time, in 1669, most anxious that a French voyage should forestall any British attempt. Canada was much in his mind, with plans for stimulting emigration of both men and women, for encouraging the Indian trade (even by permitting the sale of brandy in 1668) and for allowing the over-numerous nobility to take part in trade. Van Heemskerk himself was equally urgent, prepared to sail under British colours if the French would not grant his terms, and Colbert anxiously enquired of his ambassador at the Court of St. James whether Groseilliers and Radisson had already succeeded in opening up a sea-route to the Bay under British auspices 'being sure that the King of England ... will grant them what they demand'.

By September 1670 the French government was informed that the *Nonsuch* had brought such fine furs from the 'Floride du Nord' that two London bankers had formed a company in which 'Prince Robert' was interested and to which the King lent his support. French information was that two small merchantmen and a royal frigate had been sent out to the Bay, and there were fears that Van Heemskerk might run into opposition. Van Heemskerk had in fact been called to Paris from Dunkirk, fitted out with an expedition of three ships in 1670, and had set forth on his voyage in August. He completely failed to make the Bay, but he represents a lively interest in the Bay project and he was ready to set forth again (in winter!) if his backers would provide shipping. He might easily have faced the Company with an active French challenge before it had established any claim by discovery, trade, treaty or settlement. Though he failed to make such a challenge his voyage was the cause of a diplomatic incident, an English protest to which Colbert smoothly replied that if it should prove that the lands which Van Heemskerk was seeking were already in British occupation, then the French King would withdraw his protection. In fact, the diplomatic alliance between the Courts of England and France during the period following the Treaty of Dover was such that French-Canadians could not be allowed to provoke any serious dispute with the English notwithstanding Colbert's interest in the fur trade, in shipping, and in a passage to the Pacific. Even Colbert warmly agreed that there should be 'a good intelligence' between the two countries on colonial problems.

But New France was in a different position. There the vigorous Intendant Talon was devoting himself to attempts to increase the population and to stabilise the economy. By 1670 he was already complaining that the beaver trade to Russia was ruined because of the vast quantities of furs which the English got from their captured Dutch colonies through Orange and Manhattan, in addition to those got from Boston. He reported, in addition, that two British ships and three barques had wintered in the 'Bay of the North' and had made a great trade; this was the Company's charter voyage of 1670–1 as reported at Quebec by Indian rumour. Talon decided to counter this threat to the trade of his colony by sending some 'man of resolution' overland from Canada to the Bay, to persuade the Crees to come down to Canada to trade.

In the fall of 1671, therefore, Talon sent to the Bay a party consisting of eight Indians, a man named Sebastien Pennara, Paul Denis Sieur de St. Simon, and the Jesuit Father Albanel. St. Simon was a young man of twenty-three, Albanel 'a little old man' toughened in many a northern winter. The young soldier and the old priest were to travel right to the coast of the Bay, they were to trade in furs there, to find out whether a ship could winter and whether a factory could be established and maintained. They were to take possession of the territories in the name of the King of France, and they were told that a barque of sixty tons would probably be sent to the Bay, ostensibly to seek for a North-west Passage but really to trade with the Indians. They were to examine the English post at Charles Fort, and they were to restate the claims of the French to the land there 'as those countries have been long ago originally discovered by the French'.

They found Charles Fort empty, since Bayly and his whole complement had returned to England in the fall of 1671. St. Simon later gave evidence that they had found two Hudson's Bay Company's houses, both deserted, and that they had never heard of anyone wintering there—there were no doors or windows on the houses. Albanel baptised some Indians, the party exchanged presents with the Indians, they explored for some distance along the shores of the Bay, and they formally took possession of the country in the name of the King of France and nailed up the French royal arms as a token which would be appreciated by the Indians and would be a formal act in substantiating French claims.

It was therefore a real physical threat and challenge which Bayly faced on his return to the Bay in 1672. The practicability of overland trade with Canada had been demonstrated, personal contacts had been made, the English right to the territories had been denied in a way which was clear to the Indians. From now on, to quote Gorst, 'The French us'd many Artifices to hinder the Natives trading with the English; they gave them great Rates for their Goods, and oblig'd Mr. Baily to lower the prices of his, to oblige the Indians, who dwelt about Moose River, with whom they drove the greatest Trade'.

The commercial rivalry of the St. Lawrence and the Bay for dominance of the fur trade of the north was afoot, marked from the start by the struggle to maintain the 'Standard of Trade', the formalised price-list for furs in terms of European goods.

For the English traders a formal 'Standard' in which the value in trade of each item of goods was rigidly stated was an essential part of the system. It emphasised the fact that the traders were only employees with little or no latitude in their trade; it left no open scope for the giving of presents, the adjustment of prices according to personalities and opportunities, or the chances of a successful haggle. Certainly it left no room for the sort of practice in which a trader purposely left small articles, such as needles or thimbles, where the Indian might steal them, in the confidence that this opportunity would draw the Indians to him and so he would get a good trade. Such rigidity contrasted with the suppleness of the French, whose traders were always far more independent, and who could make a generous bargain in order to attract trade and then drive hard terms to take advantage of opportunities. They were more free with presents, too, and they would give good prices for some furs (for example martens) in order to get the Indians to bring them their whole catch.

The rigidity of the English 'Standard' was without doubt a handicap, and as time passed the Committee discovered that the traders found their own means to adjust the 'Standard' and to give it the necessary variability, as Bayly was obviously doing. But a rigid standard was necessary if the Company was to avoid competition between its own posts, or extravagant expenditure of its goods. Moreover, it gave to the Indian a certainty of the rewards which he would get, and since the Company's purpose was to develop a pattern of Indian life in which fur-hunting and an annual journey to the Bay to trade the furs were essential parts, certainty of trade conditions was a necessary part of the system.

So, although its rigidity was a defect and there can be no doubt that the 'Standard' was an indirect result of the Company's feeling that it should enjoy an absence of competition and so should not create that element itself, there were reasons and even advantages in the 'Standard'. It reveals that beaver was the only fur to which the Company paid serious attention, for the 'Standard' worked by stating the value in beaver of each item of goods and then by stating the value in beaver of all other kinds of furs. So in the Company's fur accounts the beaver is the term of accountancy, and the goods in the posts and the fur-returns for which they were traded were alike kept in terms of 'Made-beaver'—the prime winter beaver skin taken in good condition.

Rigid though the 'Standard' appeared, Bayly managed to modify it in the face of French rivalry; and he needed flexible control of his trade, for Albanel had accomplished much. Like every resident in New France he was convinced that Groseilliers and Radisson had been the key to the British effort (as indeed they were) and he had left with the Indians a letter for delivery to Radisson on his next visit to the Bay. There is no evidence that Bayly knew of this when Radisson came out with him in the autumn of 1672, and there is no evidence that Albanel's solicitations affected Radisson at this time. His return to England with Gillam in 1673 was in accord with former arrangements, and in London he showed no sign of readiness to forsake the English. He was given a medal by the Company and was accorded a salary of £100 a year, he married a daughter of Sir John Kirke, and he took an active part in the preparations which the Committee made for further trade, especially in the purchase of 'Biscay hatchets' such as the French used. But although there is no reason to suppose that Radisson parted from Bayly on bad terms, he was probably largely responsible for the decision to recall its Governor which the Committee made on 24th February, 1674. No reason for the decision is recorded, but it was probably due to private trade, for the precautions of the previous year proved ineffective. Gillam was dismissed for private trade on his return in

1673, and later events were to prove that Bayly was capable of serious mismanagement and that he misapplied £828 15s. 6d. worth of the Company's goods during his tenure of office.

The Company in 1673 was in no position to afford even the smallest peculation. Bayly appears not to have expected a shipment in that year; indeed, the Company would have been very hard put to it to send an outfit in 1673 after the three-vessel expenses of 1672. The furs from the *Rupert* and the *Messenger* were not sold until January 1674, and funds were very low indeed—so low that to set out the 1672 ships the Company had already found it necessary to make a 'call' on each of its stockholders of £50 for each full £300 share (the 'call' to be repaid out of the first trading profits) and had then had to borrow to pay its debts. When the two ships arrived in port a further £3,500 had to be borrowed to pay off the seamen and to square creditors, and in February 1673 the Committee decided to increase the capital of the Company by a further £1,500 if subscribers could be found. Then, towards the end of the year, when preparations were being made for a voyage in 1674, they decided that first they required a statement of the Company's finances, 'of the whole Stocke by way of Credit, and by way of debt how it hath bin disposed of, in as cleare a way as can be'. The account, if it was rendered, has not survived, but forthwith came a resolution that the Company needed a 'husband' to superintend the purchase, storing and shipment of goods, and that two committee-men should be appointed to examine all tradesmen's accounts and to countersign all bills.

The general financial stringency and the charges against himself were alike unknown to Bayly. The opposition of the French was what troubled him. Traders from Quebec had followed after St. Simon and Albanel and had built a post only about a week's paddling up Rupert River, intercepting many Indians on their way to trade with the English. Bayly held a council to discuss the problem and to decide whether to move his own post from Rupert River to Moose River, a course which he favoured himself as a means of evading French interference and which would conform to the Committee's instructions to make Moose the chief post. But Groseilliers was in favour of merely making a trade trip to Moose in the shallop, and in May 1674 Bayly took this course, sending Groseilliers, Gorst and others. They drove a very poor trade at Moose, however, not because they met with rivalry from the French, but because Groseilliers had by now begun to get such a reputation for hard dealing that the Indians would not come down to trade with him.

During the absence of this party the 'Nodways' created a scare but did not in fact attack Charles Fort and 'this fright being over' Bayly himself sailed to Moose, traded 1,500 skins from Albany Indians who had come in to trade, and then sailed on to Albany River, where he found little or no beaver. He did, however, treat with the 'King and his Son' and promised to come with a ship to trade at Albany in 1675. The Indians in turn promised to have beaver ready and to bring the upland Indians down to trade. Bayly then sailed on towards Cape Henrietta Maria, made contact with the Indians of New Severn River and heard from them that there was little beaver there. So, having suffered great hardships, he put back and reached Charles Fort at the end of August 1674, after a two months' voyage.

There he found that Gorst had explored up the Nottaway River as high as the Falls, and that Père Albanel was once more on the shores of the Bay. The Jesuit had been sent north again by Frontenac, successor to de Courcelles as Governor of New France, and his express object now was to seduce Groseilliers from his British allegiance. The priest had wanted to take Groseilliers' son on the journey, but this Frontenac had vetoed; Albanel had however brought a letter to Groseilliers and a further letter from Frontenac commending the priest to Bayly—which was just as well, for he arrived by canoe in a sad state, having been delayed and robbed by Indians. Bayly took him in and treated him well. But food was running short and the outlook was so precarious by mid-September 1674 that Bayly resolved that he would have to return the whole establishment to England in the little *Employ* if no ship from England arrived by the 17th of the month, although it was most doubtful by then whether he had enough provisions left for the voyage.

Then, dramatically, on the 15th September seven great guns were heard at sea, and in the next two days they welcomed in the *Rupert*, (once more under the command of Gillam, who had made his peace with the Committee) and the *Messenger*, now turned into a pink (a three-masted vessel) instead of the two-masted dogger which she had been on her former voyage; she had also been re-named the *Shaftesbury*. Gillam had survived his troubles over private trade, and had been paid in full though the Company in its determination to fight private trade had gone so far as to order a Chancery prosecution against him. But if Gillam had convinced the Committee, Bayly had suffered in his absence. Aboard the *Rupert* was a new Governor with orders that Bayly should hand over all goods, stores, papers and books, should assist his successor in discovering and preventing private trade, and should come home with the ships.

William Lydall had been chosen as Governor because he had considerable experience in the Russian fur trade. A surety of £1,000 had been taken of him—a very considerable sum in 1674—and he had been most strictly bound to suppress private trade, although the Committee was still in a fairly open mind and prepared to allow private trade in other goods than beaver so long as the commerce was conducted openly. He was sent out with great expectations, but his actual period of service was short and negligible.

Bayly, the good Quaker, handed over his charge and ceased to be called Governor. This was a humiliation tolerable only if he were to leave the scene immediately, but after several councils it was decided that the ships had arrived too late in the season for them to attempt a return journey and that they must winter in the country. With the ships' crews to feed it was obviously going to be a winter of short commons, and Gorst as storekeeper began straightaway to ration the flour. But Lydall stepped in to decree that 'If we starve we'll starve together', and by the lavish use of provisions in the early days brought them all very near to doing so.

At this point Oldmixon ceases to write from Gorst's Journal and there is no further record of that winter by the Bay. The party probably split up for ease of accommodation. But in any case it was an explosive mixture of personalities which was there congregated— the old Quaker Governor curtly superseded by a man who clearly had no touch with the realities of life by the Bay; the new Governor largely responsible for the scarcity of food which became increasingly ominous as the winter wore on; the Jesuit watching, listening and planning; Groseilliers touched by the Jesuit and secretly ready to desert the British; and Gorst recording it all and exasperated at the frustration which had followed the veto on his sane precautions. Small wonder that at the end of the winter Lydall decided to relinquish his post.

The whole establishment save four men sailed for England when the ice broke in 1675. That was the extent of the Company's grip on its lands after five years of chartered trade. But one of the four who remained was Charles Bayly, who stayed on to resume the command of which he had been deprived but in which Lydall had failed.

Bayly now remained as Governor in the Bay until the summer of 1679, when he was called home to answer charges which had been made against him, probably on the old grounds of private trade but perhaps also on grounds of general mismanagement and lack of discipline. There was a good deal of evidence for such charges, and clearly his residence by the Bay took the edge off Bayly's Quakerism. But it was also alleged that much of the evidence was perjured.

The period is marked by a gap in both the Minutes and the Correspondence Books kept by the Company, and only oblique references from other dates throw light on Bayly's work, his merits and his defects. It is clear nevertheless that during this time the old Quaker did much to establish the Company's posts and practices, but that he did so in a slipshod and unbusiness-like way, with much kindliness but without any great driving force of personality or conviction to make up for his lack of attention to detail.

After the experience with Lydall the Company seems to have been content with Bayly, and his recall in 1679 must have been a sudden move, for the Committee had just the previous year sent out his viol to solace him and had raised his salary from a mere £50 a year to £200.

These signs of appreciation were merited, for Bayly drove a good trade. His relations with the Indians appear to have been friendly and successful, for the Company always alleged that he confirmed Gillam's treaty of friendship and purchase, and there is no record of trouble with Indians during his period although Gorst leaves no doubt that the 'Nodways' were threatening during the early years. Bayly further agreed with the Indians on a 'Standard of Trade' which may easily be that which Oldmixon printed, he having copied it from Gorst's Journal. If so, the 'Standard' was soon driven down by Bayly in response to French pressure, so that the prices paid to the Indians were better than could appear, with ten good skins for a gun (for which the Company paid about one pound) as the basis of the tariff.

Furs were not Bayly's only concern; he bore in mind the possibility of other commerce, and even of minerals, and he strongly advocated the development of a deposit of 'isinglass' (the mica or 'female' type) which he had found in 'Slood River' on the Eastmain near Rupert River. He was not so confident about the 'male' type (the true isinglass derived from sturgeons' bladders) though he reported that even this could be got in large quantities in Moose River. As for the mica, this was almost certainly what he had in mind when he boasted that he had a good fur trade and had discovered 'even something which would make this establishment more important in the future, without explaining what this might be'.

Following his instructions of 1672, Bayly during his second period in command developed a post at Moose River, where the 'grand Factory' was kept up at Hayes Island. The post there, near to the western end of the island, was in use in 1673 and was in constant occupation from 1674, when Bayly possibly wintered there so as to be away from Lydall; after Lydall's departure he made Moose his chief post. In addition he had built at Albany (Chichewan River as the Company called it until 1683). He had visited the river in 1674 and had promised to return to trade in 1675. Before he left the country in 1679 he had established a 'house of some strength' there, on Bayly Island, and had put John Bridgar in charge. True, the trade at Albany was not yet established by the time Bayly was recalled, but he assured the Committee that it would be 'very extraordinary'. He had also declared his intention of settling a post at New Severn, and had even stated that he had done so. But this project merely diverted his attention and resources from the Committee's order to settle Nelson River, and in fact neither Nelson nor Severn was settled in his time. The omission at Nelson was a serious lapse from the long-term policy which the Committee had adopted for very good reason, but it does not seem to have rankled with them.

Bayly's successor, John Nixon, on his arrival in 1679, reported that he found everything in disorder, with the servants living licentiously, spending and 'imbazling' goods, and the fact that until his last year in office the Committee kept Bayly on the pittance of £50 a year may both explain and be explained by this lack of control. Yet the trade returns during Bayly's period of office were on the whole very satisfactory.

When the *Rupert* and the *Shaftesbury* had returned to London in 1675, leaving Bayly and his four companions to carry on the trade at Charles Fort, they brought furs, including moose skins, which sold for £4,715. This was a welcome return, without doubt, but even this was not enough for the Company's needs. At this juncture Hayes himself lent £1,500 and was the intermediary for the borrowing of a further £200 to pay the customs on the returns of furs, and large loans were needed for the preparation of the 1675 outfit.

Next year, in 1676, the *Rupert* wasted her voyage on a search for Busse Island. This island had been glimpsed off the coast of Labrador on many occasions from 1578 onwards, and Gillam was reported to have sighted it several times on his voyages. It was reputed to be rich in whales 'easie to be struck, Sea-Horse, Seal and Codd in abundance', and the Company began to seek possession of it in 1673 and finally got a charter granting the island in 1675, at a cost of £65. The *Rupert*, however, failed to discover any trace of the island in 1676, though it was marked on maps; and it has never been seen since. The result was that only one ship, the *Shaftesbury*, made the voyage in 1676, returning with furs which sold for £1,972—a meagre sum compared with the sales of 1675, but yet the Committee rewarded the ship's captain, Joseph Thompson, with a handsome chain and medal.

In 1677 the *Shaftesbury* again sailed alone, but her returns were then more promising and realised £4,831 17s. 8d. at the sale in December of that year. The *Rupert* was the Company's own ship, and it is unlikely that she should have been idle for the season between her return from the Busse Island expedition and 1678. But there is no record of her employment during that period, and she certainly did not trade with Bayly. In 1678 she was fitted out to sail with the *Shaftesbury*, and an important innovation was that the *Rupert* was to winter in the country whilst the *Shaftesbury* brought home the returns. This arrangement resulted in a standstill in the trade, for the *Shaftesbury* was wrecked off the Scillies on her homeward voyage, and although some of her guns were salvaged the Company had no furs to sell during that year.

This lack of trade, for which Bayly was in no way to blame, coincided with a crisis in the affairs of the Company, a crisis of which the wintering of the *Rupert* and the recall of Bayly were both symptoms. For the *Rupert*, at 75 tons, was really too large to be left in the Bay for coastal work or intercommunication between the posts. The purpose must have been to use her as a guard-ship with her twelve pieces of cannon to guard the coast. She was a sign that fears of the French were rising in London, and that the fears were for a seaborne rival rather than for overland voyageurs. Bayly's recall in the next year, 1679, was another sign of this rising fear and of the changes of personality and influence which accompanied it.

To replace Bayly as Governor the Committee chose John Nixon, about whom very little is known save that he himself later stated that he had served in the East Indies. He was possibly a Scot, for some of his spellings suggest that he pronounced his words with a Scots accent and he certainly advocated the employment of Scots in the Bay in place of the 'London childring' whom the Committee recruited. He was certainly a tetchy fellow. Despite the fact that he was the protégé of Shaftesbury and Colleton the Committee demanded from him the enormous surety of £5,000. Such a precaution denotes a general uneasiness, for in 1679 the diplomatic and political situation was such that the support of the group of courtier-statesmen ranged behind Shaftesbury, which had been so largely responsible for the founding of the Company, and which had now given Bayly's post to Nixon, might easily become a handicap.

BOOKS FOR REFERENCE

CLAPHAM, Sir John—Introduction to Hudson's Bay Record Society, Vol. V.

CLARK, G. N.—Introduction to *Minutes of the Hudson's Bay Company 1679–84* (Toronto, The Champlain Society, 1945–46, and London, The Hudson's Bay Record Society, 1945–46), Vols. VIII and IX.

NUTE, Grace Lee—*Caesars of the Wilderness* (New York, 1943).

OLDMIXON, J.—*The British Empire in America, containing the history of the discovery, settlement, progress and state of the British colonies on the continent and islands of America* (London, 1741), second edition, 2 vols.

OLDMIXON, J.—'The History of Hudson's-Bay . . . Being the last chapter of volume I of *The British Empire in America* . . . (London, 1708)' edited by J. B. Tyrrell in *Documents Relating to the Early History of Hudson Bay* (Toronto, The Champlain Society, 1931).

TAYLOR, E. G. R.—Introduction to *Copy-Book of Letters Outward &c Begins 29th May, 1680 Ends 5 July, 1687* (Toronto, The Champlain Society, 1948 and London, The Hudson's Bay Record Society, 1948), Vol. XI.

ARTICLES

JOHNSON, Alice M.—'The Mythical Land of Buss'. See *The Beaver* (Winnipeg, Hudson's Bay Company, December 1942).

JOHNSON, Alice M.—'First Governor on the Bay'. See *The Beaver* (Winnipeg, Hudson's Bay Company, June 1945).

ROUSSEAU, Jacques—'Les Voyages du Père Albanel au Lac Mistassini et à la Baie James'. See *Revue d'Histoire de l'Amérique Française* (Montreal 1950), Vol. III.

CHAPTER VIII

THE COMPANY UNDER CITY INFLUENCE, 1679–1682

The shipments of the years immediately following the Charter-voyage made it clear to the Company that, whatever the defects of their Quaker Governor as a man of business, he had nevertheless stabilised a trade of the greatest potential value. The greater their suspicion that Bayly was lax and unbusiness-like, the greater the prospects of the trade, for it was flourishing even under his régime, and he was emphatic that a start had barely been made.

What had become clear to the Company during Bayly's period in command was equally clear to the French of Canada. To the extent to which the English Company was gaining experience and confidence the fur trade of Canada was under threat. The counter-check had begun to show both in Hudson Bay and in Europe before the first Governor was recalled. Moreover, the years of joint warfare against the Dutch which had followed after the Treaty of Dover had worn thin the sympathy between the French and English peoples; and by 1676 it had also become possible for French statesmen to draw a clear line between support for the English Crown and acceptance of the English people. For the major issue in English politics was the religious one, and the struggles between Court and Parliament over the Test Act and the Declaration of Indulgence in 1672 and 1673 had made the alignment of personalities clear, so that French feeling became noticeably anti-English even if it remained to some extent pro-Stuart.

As the religious question again arose over the Second Test Act in 1674 this differentiation between Court and people became even more clear, and it was projected into the Committee-meetings of the Company, where it revolved round a deep cleavage between James Duke of York and Anthony Cooper, Earl of Shaftesbury.

Of the two, Shaftesbury was by far the more active in the Company's affairs. He had been the dominant member of the Council for Trade and Plantations at the time when Groseilliers and Radisson were brought to England and when the Hudson Bay project secured royal favour and its Charter, and in 1672 he became President of a revised Council and also Lord Chancellor. His was the predominant voice, in those years, in discussions of trade and colonies and it is certain that without his support the Hudson's Bay Company would not so easily have won its privileges. Carolina and the Bahamas were the main overseas ventures to which his personal finances were committed, and he was quite devoted to his 'darling Carolina'. For those colonies he nourished plans for trade and settlement, and for the establishment of an over-all balance within an imperial economy. Hudson Bay figures very little in his voluminous personal correspondence and accounts. But yet at one time he held over a thousand pounds' worth of stock; he was Deputy Governor in 1673–4 and a member of the Committee in 1675–6. During the attack on private trade he played an active part, and his hostility to Zachariah Gillam over that matter led the New Englander to take part in a gun-running expedition to Carolina, to stir up trouble in Shaftesbury's other colonial venture.

Shaftesbury's attention to the business of the Company throughout was remarkable. It was he who vouched for John Nixon as a successor to Bayly as Governor. But already by the time he put forward Nixon in 1679 Shaftesbury was beginning to lose both his influence and his interest in the Company. It must be remembered that 1678 was the year of the Popish Plot, of Titus Oates, and of the great movement to exclude James Duke of York from the throne and to support the claims of Monmouth. Shaftesbury led the Parliamentary opposition to the Court and its policy. He had been dismissed from the Lord Chancellorship in 1673. He was dismissed from the Privy Council in 1674 and was also committed to the Tower in that year. He was an active and leading opponent of Popery and a supporter of the Exclusion Bills during the troubles of 1678–80, and his support of Monmouth in the end led to his flight from the country and death in exile in 1682.

James Duke of York had by contrast merely been given a full £300 share in the Company in 1672, in the exuberant period following the return of the *Rupert* and the *Wivenhoe*. He made no payment, and he took no active part in the affairs of the Company. But he was later elected Governor on Rupert's death, and the decision to offer him a share and to solicit his interest was a wise one. Opinionated, bitter and stubborn, the last male Stuart to occupy the British throne was nevertheless a firm believer in the British Navy, in imperial projects of all kinds, and in the forwarding of imperial trade. His sympathies for the Hudson Bay venture were in any case assured. It was but politic to give him a share in the Company, especially in 1672 when the Dutch War had brought national unity, when James was popular, and when the Popery disputes were not yet at a head.

By 1678–9, however, the position was vastly different. The English political situation was in such turmoil that James was watching events from the comparative security of Scotland; and the affairs of the Company were equally involved. Here the ship *Shaftesbury* and the Earl of the same name each played an important part. The wreck of the ship added something of a financial crisis to the political and personal storm within the Company. She had been insured for £2,252 (a strangely accurate sum), but it was to be several years before the underwriters (many of whom were members of the Company) paid in full, and even so the sum would have been inadequate for the Company's expenses. To the loss of confidence inevitable in such a blank year the great lord after whom the ship had been named now contributed his personal and political share. Having lost the Lord Chancellorship, his membership of the Privy Council, his personal freedom and royal favour, for his opposition to the Court and its policy, he cannot be blamed for losing also his enthusiasm for a company whose future seemed to depend on a French acquiescence which was in any case declining and which in its turn depended on the British Court maintaining views which Shaftesbury deplored. He sold the last of his stock in July 1679.

At about the same time as Shaftesbury went, the Company lost many more of that type of Restoration courtier stockholder. No dividend had yet been paid, the voyages were normally financed on a credit system which would be hard hit by the lack of a fur sale in 1678, French opposition was being unmuzzled, and the domestic scene was clouded and revolutionary. The shrewd and knowledgeable Sir Peter Colleton sold out his holding soon after Shaftesbury, in December 1678, and the great Henry Bennet, Earl of Arlington, sold out in November. Already Sir George Carteret had sold out in May 1678, and Sir John Kirke in February.

This was an almost complete defection of the surviving 'foundation members' of the Company. Of them all only Rupert and Craven, each with £200 invested, Hungerford with a full £300, and his brother-in-law Hayes stood with the Company throughout.

But Hayes now had a dominant holding of £1,500, and it is clear that the split within the Company was in effect the triumph of the Hayes faction over the Shaftesbury faction. This meant that the Company now became a trading concern and little more. The notions of possible settlement which had been written into the Charter, and which conformed to the notions which, under Shaftesbury, dominated the Council of Trade and Plantations, drifted into the background. Experience had already shown that the shores of the Bay were inhospitable and that settlement would probably be impossible, or nearly so. Although Quaker Bayly had established the Company's trade, yet the posts were barely adequate for that purpose and could not in any sense be considered as settlements. It may therefore seem that such an outcome was inevitable from the start. But the terms of the Charter had implied settlement and Shaftesbury and the courtiers who went with him stood for settlement. Their continued influence might well have brought greater insistence on that aspect of the Charter; but Hayes gathered round him, to replace the courtiers, a group of City financiers whose weight and competence were invaluable but whose interests were more closely confined to the trading possibilities.

The issue was shrouded at the time, and the Company's papers at this juncture are quite inadequate and throw no light on the changes or their causes. Shaftesbury's papers, too, are almost wholly silent on his relations with the Company; but they reveal a malevolent mistrust of Hayes, whom he accused of being a secret Papist, a vice-sodden profligate who had killed his first wife with disease and had run through the fortune of his second wife, a pander who for a mere five shillings would supply 'pretty women' to chance acquaintances—a mean and dishonest rogue. These were notes prepared for use in court in case Hayes should be called as a witness against Shaftesbury at his trial, so presumably the former Lord Chancellor was prepared to substantiate such charges. They certainly make one wonder what kind of man James Hayes was, and they make it clear that the withdrawal of Shaftesbury and the predominance of Hayes within the Company were two aspects of the same problem.

But if Hayes represented to Shaftesbury the triumph of a despicable Roman Catholicism, and adulation of James Duke of York, there was solid City backing for the new management. This had been building up within the Company for some years before the crisis of 1679. Perhaps the most important single instance of its growth is that the great Sir Robert Vyner had again bought a share in 1676. He had lost over £400,000 by the stop of the Exchequer in 1672, and he had sold his share in the Company in 1675. Now he began to take an active part in the Company's business, though hampered by illness.

The sale of shares by the courtly 'foundation members' made it possible for many of Vyner's complexion to find their way into the Company. William Walker, banker and goldsmith, held a steady and businesslike stake of £200 from 1674 onwards and he also was an active committee-man and executive of the Company. Richard

Cradock, merchant of London, came into the Company only during the crisis period of 1679, but he also proved a most active member of committee. John Letten came into the Company at much the same time; he was prepared to invest up to £1,000 during the next year, to allow his house to be used as an office and to give generously of his services. Colonel Henry Meese of London, merchant, was another who rallied to the Company at this time; he had behind him a career as a settler and administrator in Virginia and a connection with the tobacco trade which was put to good account. Interesting among the Company's supporters was Lady Margaret Drax, the first woman to hold stock in the Company. Hayes advised this widow of a colonial governor to put in £300 as early as 1670, and he now persuaded her to double her holding, in 1677. The many-sided genius Sir Christopher Wren also began to buy stock in 1679. It must not be forgotten that his brother was secretary to James Duke of York, but Wren brought to the Company not only a readiness to advance money at difficult times but a shrewd and active judgment, assiduous attention as a committee-man, and willingness to serve on the committee for trade and as Vice-Deputy Governor.

Most important after Hayes, who stood in the midst of this change-over to City financiers and merchants, and for whom it was to a large extent the creation of a 'Hayes caucus', was Sir Robert Clayton, former Sheriff of the City, and Lord Mayor of London. A scrivener and banker (scriveners with their special knowledge of title deeds and mortgages were often but little removed from money-lenders), one of the wealthiest citizens, Clayton rivalled Sir Robert Vyner in financial importance. He was a Director of the Bank of England in later years and was a strong supporter of the Whig and Orange interests. Clayton's first contact with the Company was when he and his partner John Morris began to act as bankers for the Committee in 1675. Times were already hard, and Hayes had then to lend the considerable sum of £1,500 to steady the Company's finances. Clayton and Morris lent a further £500 in June 1676, and Clayton then bought a full £300 share in February 1678, a further £300 share in March and another £100 of stock in May; they received, and later disbursed, the £4,715 13s. 9d. from the December fur sale of 1675 and the £1,972 1s. 7d. from the sale of January 1676. They paid off the £1,500 which Hayes had lent to the Company and also settled the account of John Lindsay, former Treasurer, paying out £3,305 13s. 7d. to William Walker, who acted as Treasurer in 1676–8 and therewith paid some of the Company's accounts. By the time of the general defection of the courtly members in 1679, Clayton's holding stood at only £700, but it is not surprising that with his talents, his wealth and his obvious interest in the Company, he should have been elected Treasurer of the Company in 1679.

Clayton's membership and support must have meant a very great deal to the Company in finance and credit, and in general prestige. By June 1679 he had negotiated a loan of £3,200 for the Company on the security of the Charter and the common seal, and he produced the cash in hand for paying off the seamen on their return from the Bay in 1679. But although he was a shareholder and an office-holder, Clayton kept his relations with the Company on a strictly business footing which certainly helped the Company to improve its hitherto casual business technique. A list of stockholders had been printed in 1675, when it had been resolved that every adventurer should have one vote for each hundred pounds of stock which he held, that three out of the seven members of the Committee should be freshly elected each year, and that each committee-member must have at least two hundred pounds of stock. Now the list of stock-holders was formally entered into the ledger and the clerk, account-ant and secretary (John Stone was all three), was ordered to prepare a 'perfect and compleat State of the Accompts of the Company'. He was also ordered to see that no books or papers should be removed from the committee-room without order.

Too much of this rising spirit of efficiency must not be ascribed to Clayton alone, for the unmistakable trend of the share-dealings of the 1678–79 period was to replace the earlier 'gentry' type of stock-holder who had been the core of the 'foundation-members' by a much harder core of financiers and merchants, of whom Clayton was but one among others, albeit a powerful and wealthy member of the City.

This is the period at which the gap in the Company's Minutes Books and Letter Books ends. The break in continuous documenta-tion may be due to the fact that the outgoing courtier stockholders took their records with them when they went, leaving their succes-sors to find their own way. More probably it was due to one man only, James Hayes. He, with Rupert, was the chief survivor from the earlier régime, and he almost certainly had in his possession all of the documents which mattered. He treated the Company's docu-ments very largely as his own personal property—and he later caused a great deal of trouble by so doing and had to be forced to return important papers to the Company. He was in control of the books of the Company during the transition period, and the Com-pany never recovered possession. It cannot be doubted that the

Company, however haphazardly, kept some sort of records for the blank period, and whether Hayes or some other member of the Committee took them in custody, it was possible for them to disappear. After 1679 such cavalier treatment of papers was no longer easy. Not only was there a rule against it, but the Company was increasingly dominated by a group of exceedingly competent business men. Whilst the tide of French opposition was rising both in Europe and in Canada its affairs were organised by an assiduous Committee composed of such men; they were not only stockholders but committee-members.

Rivalry with the French was the accepted condition of the trade which the new Committee took over in 1679, despite the fact that their advent meant a triumph within the Company for the supporters of the Stuarts and Roman Catholicism. But rivalry with the French in itself would not have caused the defection of the old courtier-members, though opposition to James as heir to the throne and to Hayes as his underling might have made them desert a company which seemed tied to such views. Trade prospects probably mattered little to them, though they were by no means averse from making their fortunes; and the chance that the French might contest the trade, as such, should not be over-stressed in this affair. For men of their stature their stakes in the Company were small in the extreme. Yet those who were left in control alleged that the cause of the defection was the fact that the Company's trade stood low and that the courtiers who sold their shares did so for financial reasons as well as for personal and political causes. The Committee explained the departure of Shaftesbury and Colleton as being due to the reason that 'the interest of the Company looked with so ill an aspect untill the arrival of the *John and Alexander* [in December 1679] that those worthy persons and severall others were discouraged to continue longer in the bottome where they were'.

But finance alone does not explain the changes, for Bayly's trade returns had always been satisfying, and his last shipment, on the *John and Alexander*, gave the Company badly-needed credit. The cargo sold well; the *parchment* especially was bought up by the 'Engrossers' (for export), and so the arrangements which the Committee had begun, to prepare it for Russia, were cancelled. But even so encouraging a sale was, in the existing difficulties, 'scarce enough to make us just to our Creditors and to provide supplies' for a new expedition in 1680, although it raised the considerable sum of £8,131 6s. 7d. with a further sum of £141 7s. 3d., in addition to money raised by furs other than beaver.

As serious French opposition became inevitable, and the Company's financial commitments mounted, the new London Committee's chief contribution, perhaps more important than the financial backing which it brought, was the persistent confidence with which it pursued the Company's aims. True, this confidence was in 1679 very largely due to the changes in control, but it none the less gave purpose, direction and financial support, to action by the Bay.

Governor John Nixon had been sent out in 1679 with two vessels, the *John and Alexander* of a hundred and seventy-eight tons, borrowed from the Navy and placed under Captain Nehemiah Walker, and the *Colleton* yacht of about forty tons, built to the Company's orders and launched in May 1679. The voyage was not an entire success, and it added in many ways to the Company's difficulties.

The *Colleton* put back in a storm before leaving the Channel, and underlined a permanent difficulty. The Committee later, on enquiry, held that the mate and crew of the *Colleton* had 'forsook the Voyage when there was no necessity for it, staved the Bulkhead of the Vessell, and pretended the storm had done it'. But Nixon as a passenger on the *John and Alexander* was a witness to the fact that the yacht was separated in storm and fog from her larger consort, leaving her master, two of her crew, her boat and some of her provisions, with the *John and Alexander* because Captain Nehemiah Walker had invited them aboard but carried too much sail in drunken over-confidence in a heavy sea and made Captain Tatnam of the *Colleton* so drunk that he could not return aboard his own ship.

Since its whole position rested on its sea-approach, the Company was utterly dependent on its ships' masters and on the weather for the voyage out and home. Experience had already taught that if the ships left London later than 25th May they would be too late for the return voyage to be made in the same year, there would be no furs for sale, and captains and crews would have to be paid for the whole year. Bad weather or bad seamanship would have much the same effect as a late start—perhaps worse since they might cause trouble on the outward voyage and rob the posts of their provisions, their goods and the prestige, on which the whole trade rested.

But the Company at this time was most indifferently served by the ships' masters on whom so much depended. Gillam for example was without doubt a good navigator and a sturdy servant; but he was wedded to private trade and was not amenable to discipline. Radisson said of him that since he was sure of his wages he was quite indifferent to the value of the trade which he brought home. Draper,

who was appointed to succeed Gillam, was dismissed before he ever
sailed, although he was later employed. Stannard twice failed to
reach the Bay. Captain Morris of the *Messenger* had undoubtedly
traded for himself and landed his furs at Plymouth on his return,
whilst William Bond at first put such a value on himself that he was
refused employment, and he later insisted on his right to private
trade. Captain Newland had traded; Shepard 'behaved himself ill'.
It was a sorry list, and in 1679 the Company was forced to admit that
one of its captains, Nehemiah Walker, son of a prominent stockholder and official of the Company, was a truculent fellow, given to
drink and ready to take quite unnecessary risks with his ship and the
Company's cargo—or with his consort—in his 'drunken pranks',
whilst Tatnam of the *Colleton* was a feeble creature who could not
resist a drink and could not hold it either. In the Bay the *Rupert* was
under the command of Powers, and he also showed that he was
easily capable of coming aboard 'so drunk as beasts' and flouting the
authority of the Company as represented in the person of its
Governor.

Governor Nixon found that Walker, by causing the return of the
Colleton, had caused 'above £500 loss to your Honours, and a great
discomfort to me', yet the *John and Alexander* was so large by comparison with the *Colleton* that he had adequate goods for his trade,
and next year the Committee could tell him that they knew he had 'a
large proportion of all sorts of goods' left over from this 1679 outfit.

Nixon's first year in office, however, produced nothing worthy of
record, no news of any fresh establishment nor any comment on his
performance save that the Committee raised his salary from £100 to
£200 a year whilst remarking that his report was chiefly taken up
with underlining the chaos which he had inherited.

While Nixon was thus settling himself into his post, the *John and
Alexander* was making her way homewards. She made a long and
unhappy voyage, for aboard was Bayly, abused and mocked by
Walker till he was often reduced to tears; and she met head winds
and did not arrive in London till December 1679. Her cargo, as has
been seen, gave the Committee a most welcome respite from pressing
tradesmen. The Feltmakers' Company of London were large buyers
and the greater furriers such as Thomas Glover also made considerable purchases. But the cargo also gave rise to some discussion and
difficulty. The problem was whether the furs should be sold in lots
by auction or should be sold in bulk at a contract price, and whether
they should be kept for the London furriers and felters or should be
sold for export. The Committee decided to rely completely on

auction sales 'by the candle', and although on the second issue they made a decision to sort out the *parchment* beaver suitable for the Russian market, no action was taken, probably because it became clear that the London buyers would buy the whole consignment at reasonable prices.

When the *John and Alexander* had been returned to the Admiralty and her ship's company had been paid off, the Committee turned with stubborn and unfaltering confidence to prepare an outfit for 1680. Their feelings when Bayly died shortly after his arrival home were not such matters as they wrote into their formal and terse Minutes. But they gave him a good funeral; and then they turned to impress the Indians with their acceptance of the goodwill which Bayly had earned for the Company. They sent out a plaque to be set up in his memory, while at the same time they embarked on a long and tortuous attempt to draw up a proper account with his widow.

Their first 'Bay-Governor' had left the Company a promising heritage. Uncouth as his posts might appear, they were adequate protection for his men. The Indians had got used to the constant presence of the Englishmen and had begun to regulate their lives to a pattern in which annual ship-times and a permanent garrison were controlling features. A mixture of realism and kindliness clearly was his, and although he may have left his accounts with the Company in a muddle, he had about him that simple shrewdness which would not easily be over-reached in the Indian trade. Not least among the benefits which he conferred on his employers was the opportune arrival in London of his last cargo of furs, in the *John and Alexander* in 1679.

The returns in the *John and Alexander*, although they left the Committee still with 'no great reason to boast', sold for nearly nine thousand pounds, a sale which left the Company 'more considerable in the opinion of the world'. Two problems immediately arose. The new Committee of business men had recently decided that 'If it please God the stock shall be Augmented Fifty p. Cent a Dividend of 20 p. Cent shall forthwith be made to the Adventurers', and that thenceforth half of any annual profits should be allotted to dividends. A revenue of nine thousand pounds on a stock of ten thousand five hundred should surely have raised this issue. Yet although it has been stated that a dividend of twenty per cent. was paid in this year, there is no evidence that anything of the kind was even discussed, such was the low state of the Company's affairs and the swift absorption of sales-money into the payment of debts.

The second problem was clearer. The Company after its sale was in a position to pay off the large loan of £3,200 which it had negotiated in the previous June through its Treasurer the Lord Mayor, Sir John Clayton. He, however, resolutely refused to touch the Company's money. He insisted that he had arranged the loan for a year and that he would require a full year's interest. He won his point, and so saved the unravelling of a complex business network, for most of the sum was actually advanced by the Adventurers themselves in their private capacities. They lent about half of the sum involved to two London merchants, John Wyse and William Couldesdon; Clayton and his banking partner Morris made up the rest of the sum, and the Company then mortgaged the Charter to this group of investors (including Rupert the Governor and several other Adventurers) in return for working cash to carry on its trade. The Adventurers freely sold among themselves their shares in this loan, with its fixed interest at five per cent., and the whole incident provides an admirable example of the way in which working capital could be provided by such a joint-stock company. It might have been expected that in such circumstances the Company would have made a 'call' on its proprietors for the money required. Instead, it answered its needs by a fixed-interest loan, ostensibly from an outside source but really from a body of the proprietors. The negotiation resulted in a complicated series of assignments, and Clayton obviously had good reason for wishing the arrangement to run its full course. He may have had reason on his side, but he was not re-elected Treasurer of the Company.

For its next voyage, of 1680, therefore, the Company turned directly to its members for loans. In direct negotiation enough Adventurers could be found who were prepared to advance money at six per cent. (the legal maximum) and the Committee hoped that the ships would be home, the furs sold, the voyage 'wound up' and the loans repaid before Christmas. Many of the members (including Christopher Wren) simply lent again the money which they had just received from the repayment of the loan of the previous year.

Thus financed, the Committee decided that the best course would be to hire a large vessel for the Atlantic crossing, and for several years it pursued this course (not without criticism), keeping its own smaller shipping for use in the Bay itself. Accordingly the *Prudent Mary* of about a hundred and forty tons was hired by charter-party, with her part-owner and captain, Richard Greenway, to sail her out and back. After some discussion the Committee also sent out a forty-ton frigate, the *Albemarle*, built to their orders, together with the yacht *Colleton*, now re-equipped and under a new captain, Walsall Cobbie.

A last-minute letter, sent from Gravesend as the Committee despatched the ships, emphasised that 'we shall not think our Interest in the Bay so well secured As it ought to be untill we have made a Settlement to the Northward of Cape Henrietta Maria'. Fears of encroachment were obviously rising, not only from rival English merchants and from the French but also from within the Company itself. At the last moment, at Gravesend, the Committee's suspicions had been aroused and the private letters to servants in the Bay had been opened. From these it proved that Thomas Phipps, a committee-man himself, and one whose cousin and namesake held the important position of warehousekeeper at Moose Factory, had been working against his colleagues. He was 'Obnoxiouse to just excepcion' and was suspended from the Committee, whilst Nixon was warned that all letters homewards should pass through his hands, so that no private correspondence either way would be possible. The urgency to settle the key points of the Company's domain and to forestall possible rivals is therefore easily understandable.

Such short-term urgency is important and worth noting. More important, these instructions of the reorganised Committee of 1679–80 breathe an unmistakable spirit of kindly shrewdness, of enterprise, and above all of confidence—and in 1680 confidence in the future of the Company was the Committee's most valuable attribute. For there were no furs for sale in London in that year after the February sale of the remains of the 1679 shipment. Following his orders to load the returns into the hired ship and to keep the Company's vessels in the country, Nixon had sent the *Prudent Mary* off well loaded—but, fortunately as it proved, not with his total returns. She was the only ship sent home that year, and when she was wrecked in the Bay itself off Tetherley's Island, the Company was left in London 'totally in the Darke as to all our concernes'. The only news of any kind was a Canadian rumour that none of the ships of the expensive 1680 outfit had arrived in the Bay, and the Committee were forced to contemplate not only the loss of the returns for a single year, but of the trade-goods on which the whole position depended. In due course much of the *Prudent Mary*'s furs and even some isinglass, with some of her fittings, were salved; her Captain and crew got away safely; and she had been insured for £5,650. But none of these future consolations was any help to the Committee who had strained their credit to send the 1680 voyage and which all London now knew had no trade available for the current year.

Nevertheless, there was no halting or delay in preparing a voyage for 1681. The first problem was to raise credit, and here the Company's former Treasurer, Sir John Clayton, proved a sore disappointment. He stuck out for eight per cent. interest, a rate higher than the legal maximum which other members of the Company enjoyed for their loans, and he refused to confuse his two businesses, as banker and as potential Treasurer of the Company. In the hope that the *Prudent Mary* might arrive and ease the situation, the Committee delayed the election of a Treasurer; but there was no arrival, the money had to be raised, and rather than elect a Treasurer who would not oblige it in its difficulties the Company left the office vacant.

The Committee reckoned that to pay creditors and outfit a new voyage would need £4,200, equivalent to forty per cent. of the Company's stock. Members were therefore allowed to advance as much as forty per cent. of their holdings. They had produced the large sum of £3,200 in June 1679 and this seems to have been about the limit of their resources. But James Hayes introduced to the Company a City merchant, Walter Tindall, and from him a further £2,000 was borrowed. The cash was produced by Clayton's partner Morris, and that firm once more took the Charter into its custody as security and acted as banker, combining this new borrowing with the loan which had been raised from stockholders. Morris and his backer (a Mr. Webb) therefore ostensibly advanced 'the whole summe of Five thousand one hundred and twenty pounds though in truth they have advanced Two thousand pounds only and the rest is advanced by severall of the Members of the Company'. The debt was greater than had at first been thought necessary, and the Company had to pay eight per cent. But it had ample funds for its immediate needs, and its creditors were for the most part easy men who had deep confidence in the Company.

Thus able to satisfy its creditors, the Company hired the ship *Diligence*, of about a hundred and fifty tons, and put her under command of Captain Nehemiah Walker. His terms had been too high in 1680, and he had been 'destitute of all employment by our having entertayned and hired another ship and commander'. He was glad to get the *Diligence*, and set forth in June 1681, loaded with trade goods, with a cask of 'Norembergh Toyes', with a billy goat and two nannies, a sow with pig, duplicates of the Instructions of 1680, and further brief reminders of the chief points involved.

'Amongst them all wee judge *none of greater moment then the speedy settlement of Port Nelson*' wrote the Committee.

Rupert River might indeed be the most obvious scene of French encroachment, the Nemiskau might be the route by which Albanel and overland Frenchmen had hitherto approached the Bay. But at the heart of the situation lay the fact that Rupert and Moose Rivers did not completely fulfil the ideas which Groseilliers and Radisson, and their British supporters, had held in 1667–70. Hayes River or the Nelson River would come nearer to their plans, as providing a sea-and-river route to the hinterland of the Great Lakes, the true source of the beaver of the north. Hence the early attempts at 'Port Nelson', the disappointment at the failure of the *Wivenhoe* to make a settlement there in 1670, the voyage thither of Groseilliers in 1673, and Bayly's own attempt in 1674.

Governor Nixon, to whom these instructions were directed, seems to have spent winter 1680–1 largely in attempts to turn Charlton Island into a suitable entrepôt for the trade, at which the 'country shipping' from the posts could meet the great ship from England, load the furs aboard and take the cargo from her. He managed to build a warehouse twenty feet square and '2 stories and a half high' at Charlton, and the Company later alleged that he also sent the *Albemarle* to Nelson River in 1680, to carry out the most weighty of his Instructions. But no proof of the statement has ever come to light. In any case, no settlement was made, even if the ship was sent, and it may be said that Nixon failed to carry out this order. But at Charlton Island, knowing the shifts to which the non-arrival of the wrecked *Prudent Mary* would put the Committee, and anxious also to get the ship-wrecked seamen on their way, he had set about sending the *Rupert* home early in 1681. This was in accordance with his emergency Instruction that 'if it should please God at any time our ships from hence should miscarry, shee might come home upon such an exigence with what goods you have ready', and the precaution proved invaluable although it took away the guard-ship from the Bay at a time when it seemed as though it might be needed.

The ice was clear, and the *Rupert* was got off from the island, with the *Albemarle* in convoy, on 9th August, 1681. They arrived at Falmouth early in October, and the Committee immediately met to dispose of their cargoes. These were very considerable, 24,123 beaver, more than twice the amount reckoned on in a normal good year at this time, and they proved most welcome to the Committee. They showed, too, that although Nixon might have failed to carry out his Instructions for settlement in Nelson River, he had inherited

D

a lively trading system from Bayly, and had done much to organise and exploit it.

The Committee had had no business to transact between the despatch of the *Diligence* in June 1681 and the return of the *Rupert* and *Albemarle* in October, and held no meetings during that time. Then the furs were sold for the magnificent sum of £15,721 4s. 9d., a total greater by half than the fully-paid-up capital of the Company. But welcome though this cash undoubtedly was, there were signs that the Company would soon have to choose between throttling down its trade or actively seeking new markets for disposing of it. Following hard after this sale the Committee began to make applications that beaver wool might be exported free of duty to the continent. This would be the beaver wool shorn from the *coat* beaver, not that combed from the *parchment*, for the Russians still held the secret of the latter process, and the meaning of the petition was that there was more *coat* beaver now coming from the Bay than the English felters could absorb. It would have to be processed and the beaver wool then sold on the continent in rivalry with the combed variety coming from Russia. Nothing seems to have come of the proposal, for the great cargo of 1681 was safely sold in London and the Committee were in funds again. But it was becoming probable that before very long, given continuous success, French and English beaver would be selling in constant rivalry on the continent. Indeed, it is clear that this had already happened but that the London market had been sufficiently active for the Committee not to worry about the European sales which would follow on purchase in London. But a great cargo such as that of 1681 could threaten congestion and demanded care for the secondary disposal of the product.

The £2,000 borrowed through Walter Tindall was now repaid, as were the loans made by members of the Company, and most generous preparations were made for the next voyage. The pattern of the Company's finances was becoming more settled. A good sale enabled the tradesmen to be satisfied and the loans, with their interest, to be paid off. Thus the financiers, many of them shareholders, who supplied the Company with working capital and credit, drew their fixed 'debenture-type' interest as the first call on the trade of the year. But when they had been satisfied and the tradesmen paid, the Company, even in 1681, had immediately to borrow again and to buy the trade goods for its next voyage on credit. The credit, however, was good. Terms were generous and expansive plans could be contemplated when such success had been achieved.

The result of this financial system was that the profits of the trade were being distributed in a far wider circle than the limited number of official shareholders. The Adventurers were almost in the position of being guarantors of each voyage while the outfits were actually financed, under this guarantee, by those who lent at fixed interest for short periods. The short-term loan, however, was very often renewed as soon as it had been paid off. Walter Tindall, for example, having been for the moment paid off following the sale of 1681, was immediately asked to lend afresh, and he provided the Committee with a further £1,000 of working capital.

This financial system proved sufficiently flexible for the Committee to get the *Diligence* off to the Bay in June 1681, after an autumn and winter in which there were no furs to sell. After wintering in the Bay, she arrived in the Downs in September 1682 with a fine cargo of 18,680 beaver, in addition to other furs. The hired ships *Lucy* and *Friendship* soon followed; they brought no furs, yet they brought peace of mind to men who must have been full of doubts since their ships had sailed in the previous June and July. But they left much room for uneasy speculation also. The lack of dividend for so many years, and the costs of ship-hire, trade-goods and wages, must have weighed heavy on the Committee too, and they had strained their credit to the utmost to send out the voyage of 1682. Moreover, the Committee must have been doubtful if dividends would ever reward them, for it seemed more than likely that any quantity of furs which would promise a dividend would only produce a glutted market.

At the end of October 1682 the Committee decided to put up for sale the skins which the *Diligence* had brought. The starting-price was to be twelve shillings and sixpence the pound for *coat* and eight shillings for *parchment*. To steady the buyers they found it necessary before the sale to declare that they expected no further shipment that year and that they would not in any case put any more furs on the market before the end of September 1683, and then not at lower prices than they were now offering. Nevertheless at the sale on 15th November, 1682, only sixteen lots of the *coat* beaver were sold and the Company was left with thirty-six lots on its hands. This was a very heavy proportion of the most profitable furs, all the more disquietening in the face of possible rival shipments to introduce serious competition to the London fur-market. In fact the *coat* beaver of 1682 stuck with the Company until 1684, and it was possibly the feeling of relief which their sale then brought that led the Committee to declare the long-expected first dividend in that year.

In 1682, however, the sign was most ominous, and although the sale brought in the handsome sum of £6,028 15s. 7d. the worries of the Committee are best reflected, not in the persistent confidence with which they faced their major problems but in the unfair pettiness with which they rounded on the clerk, Mr. Stone, and refused to give him a testimonial on his departure 'which this Committee does so ill resent at this time when they had most need of his service That they doe according to his desire dismiss him the Company's service and refuse to signe the said certiphycate'. It was an ungenerous touch in men who normally dealt with their employees fairly if meticulously, and it is an indication of the exasperation and worry which beset the Committee in that year. Their troubles were to some extent alleviated by the fur sale and by the fact that in Stephen Evans or Evance (later Sir Stephen and Governor of the Company) they had found a banker whose conduct contrasted strongly with the strict correctness of Sir Robert Clayton. Evans had a long acquaintance with some of the members, and at this time he was financing a partnership between Rupert and Shaftesbury for steel-making and gun foundries. Before the sale was held in November 1682, the Committee resolved that 'by reason Mr. Evans and Company has bin ready to supply the Company with severall summs of mony for their necessary occasions before the sale of their beavor' the whole proceeds of the sale should be handled by Evans. But Stephen Evans and Company were not by any means the only bankers with whom the Company dealt at this time. Much of the Company's business went to Thomas Cook and Company, and at times John Temple and Company also handled the Company's affairs. Yet the backing of Stephen Evans was a source of great confidence, and of financial strength.

For in 1682, with grave fears that a French expedition, or an English rival, might invade the Bay, the Company had ventured as never before. In that year they had overhauled and repaired the *Rupert* after her two years in the Bay, the *Albemarle* also was set in order and a new ship of forty tons, the *Craven*, was launched and put in commission in June. In addition, two further ships were hired for the voyage, the *Friendship* and the *Lucy* both of a hundred and twenty tons burthen. A 'Greenland shallop' for use in the country was also ordered, and was delivered in May 1682.

The arrangements for preparing these ships for the 1682 voyage showed increased vigilance, and probably increased efficiency. Members of the Committee who sold goods to the Company had already been ordered to declare their interests—a significant and salutary rule—and now the Secretary-Treasurer of the Company,

Onesiphorous Albin, was nominated 'Husband' to see to the purchase and stowage of goods. In particular, he was to be 'buying in all good pennyworths he can meet with in the woollen manufactory'. Enquiries were made about the prices of French blankets, but ultimately the posts were supplied with Cotswold blankets from the Witney area, a type of goods which later became a staple of the trade.

Lists of trade goods were prepared as early as December, and James Knight (who had served as shipwright in the Bay) and John Bridgar (who had commanded the post which Bayly set up at Albany) were freely consulted and asked to advise on goods which their experience made them think appropriate. They proved 'very ingenious and knowing men in the business of our trade', but when the cargoes were assembled emphasis was on the stock goods already in use—guns, powder and shot, tobacco, hatchets and awls, brass kettles, woollens and knives. The only articles which compare for novelty with the 'Norembergh Toyes' of the previous year were an assortment of 'painted looking-glasses'. But the weather to be expected at Nelson River led also to the inclusion of snow-shoes and snow-glasses. Two hundred and fifty-seven gallons of rum and two hundred and sixty-two gallons of brandy were also included.

To Albany was to go three times the quantity of blankets allotted to any of the other posts. Here, probably, can be seen the influence of James Knight, the shipwright who ended his career as a member of the Committee and Governor of all the posts in the Bay. On his return to London in 1681 he was appointed Chief at Albany in succession to Bridgar and was given a gratuity of £16 for 'all his good service at Hudson Bay'. He certainly was, as the Committee found him, 'able and dexterous in their business', and as the years passed he won an increasingly dominant position in the Company; by some happy chance he seemed more able than anyone else at this time to bring practical experience of Bay-side conditions into real co-operation with London managerial and financial control. At Albany he was to act as Deputy to Nixon; a special 'deputation' to confirm his appointment was drawn up, but he received his instructions orally and they are not among those preserved in the Company's archives.

While the influence of Knight can be seen in the care taken for development of the trade of Albany under Nixon, the influence of Bridgar can be seen in the fact that the *Rupert* and the *Albemarle* were ordered to sail direct to Nelson River and to set up a post there. Thwarted for so many years, the Committee had decided in 1682 to take the settlement of Nelson River into its own hands.

The general instructions of 1682, however, differed in but little from those of previous years. Prudence, integrity, and industry were emphasised; justice towards Indians and towards those under command went with this general approach. Treaties of amity were to be made with the Indians, but Indian women were to be rigorously excluded from the posts, both because they debauched the Company's servants and because they used provisions and embezzled goods. Those whom 'neither the Lawes of God or Man can restraine from Wickedness' were to be sent home. The isinglass trade was to be worked on, and George Geyer (with previous experience in the Bay, and later to be a Governor there) was now sent out especially for that purpose. Nixon was further instructed to emulate the industry of the French and to send men 'up into the Countrey', to meet the Indians, make treaties with them, and persuade them to come down to trade at the coast. Here the Committee was formulating the ideas which Bayly had put forward. But the Governor was given no men or equipment to carry out the instruction.

The most pressing matter in these instructions of 1682 was the insistence on preventing private trade and on guarding against interlopers. Infringement of the right of sole trade had been reported aboard the *Albemarle* in 1681, and Nixon had commented in his 'report' of that year on the losses caused by servants who persisted in trading. Ships' captains were undoubtedly among the offenders, and Nehemiah Walker among others had to be pardoned for trespassing on his employers' preserves. During the previous winter Nixon had apparently run out of trade goods, and the servants had been allowed to trade their own blankets and other property rather than send the Indians away unsatisfied, perhaps never to come down to trade again. With the generous cargoes sent in 1682, and with double the quantities of normal provisions, the Committee insisted that there was to be no repetition even of such trade, though it condoned the expedient of 1681 and made generous allowance to the men involved.

The firm ruling by the Committee served to mask serious doubts. The French were not the only rivals whom the Committee feared. The feeling that the Company's Charter might be challenged had been rising for some time, and James Hayes stood at the centre of the Company's defence here, as against the French. He had secured a copy of the Tudor Charter to the Muscovy Company as early as 1671, in order to make sure that that early grant had not been so vaguely expressed as to include the Bay. In 1680 when Thomas Phipps' conspiracy had been discovered, Hayes had dispensed £10

'Secret Service' money; now in 1682, in view of a wide feeling that a challenge was imminent, the Instructions and General Letter Outwards were carefully submitted to him for scrutiny.

On the very eve of the departure of the ships these misgivings came to a head, and the Committee must have had the most serious doubts about the faithfulness of the men into whose hands they were committing this important and expensive outfit.

First, the general system for the conduct of business came under fire. The Committee had moved into their first permanent quarters at Scriveners' Hall during the year. Hitherto they had met in the house or office of one or other of the members, and in such conditions organisation, despite the changes of 1679, must have been at least a little haphazard, and had probably suffered from lack of access to essential papers. Now, with a carefully-chosen Secretary and Treasurer appointed to act as 'husband' for the cargoes, and with rules for checks on payments and the filing of vouchers for purchases, a 'Faire Booke of Orders' to record decisions, and renewed care to keep all books available for consultation in the office, the business should have got on to a more regular footing. But when the Committee went to see the ships off at Gravesend they found that, despite orders to stow the cargo so as to help unloading on arrival in the Bay, everything was in disorder. The *Rupert* and the *Albemarle* were both badly loaded; 'parcels' of goods were lying about the decks and both ships had to be re-stowed, with some of the ships' provisions transferred to the hired ships which were bound for Charlton Island, not for Nelson River as the two Company ships were.

Also on the eve of departure, the behaviour of the ships' captains suddenly became most ominous. The Committee were aware that some servants were ready to cross the narrow line separating private trade as Company employees from the outfit of an interloping expedition. Nixon, too, had heard the possibilities discussed from the 'Mouth of one who is not unlikely to enterprise it', and the Committee had both warned the governors of such a possibility and had devised an oath for servants against private trade. The Committee's worst fears must have seemed confirmed when, at the last moment, Captain Bond refused to take the oath, Knight developed a quarrel which has not been explained but which caused him to be suspended from his appointment until it was cleared up, and Gillam, suddenly 'absenting himselfe to the neglect and prejudice of the Company's affaires', threw everything into consternation. Within the few days left, Knight and the Committee were reconciled, Gillam was back upon his ship and the 'young blade' Bond had complied 'with abundance of difficulty' and was sent off in command of the *Craven*, but with the suspicion that if the Committee had had time they could have found the goods for private trade on board his ship.

It must have been with the greatest misgivings that the Committee returned to London, there soon to learn that their New England rivals, still shipping New York beaver into London, were on the move and that Zachariah Gillam's son Benjamin, like his father a New England sea captain, had been in England on the eve of his father's departure. As yet, in 1682, the Committee had nothing but suspicion of the New Englanders, of their own servants or of the French, to go upon. But shortly after the ships had sailed came definite news of a totally different sort.

The ketch *Expectation* had sailed from Dartmouth bearing four former employees, and was clearly designed as an interloper. Of the renegades Richard Lucas had been mate of the *Prudent Mary* when she ran aground, and he was suspected not only of going now to trade against the Company's chartered rights, but also of aiming to pick up some of the beaver from the *Prudent Mary* which he had hidden on Tetherley's Island. Moreover the former committee-man Phipps was found to be the 'chief contriver' of the whole affair, so that the Committee saw the Company beset by treachery in high and low places, and rivalled from both sides of the Atlantic whilst its own servants, even when loyal, served but indifferently. Suspicion was everywhere, for the *Expectation* was obviously depending on being able to 'debauch and draw from their Fidelity some of those who now serve us'.

In fact, the *Expectation* put back quickly into the westerly haven of Dartmouth and there spent the winter 1682–3. But the Committee had taken immediate action which could not be revoked when this news filtered up to London from Devon. A petition to the King, and so to the Council and the Law Officers, to establish the Company's chartered rights, promised delay. A fifty-ton ketch was therefore to be sent in pursuit. Then a committee-meeting, held under the chairmanship of Christopher Wren in the absence of Sir James Hayes, decided that the season was too far advanced for such a voyage to be warranted, and postponed action. It was the lateness of the season which had, in the meantime, caused the *Expectation* to put back to Dartmouth. But James Hayes carried the Committee with him at a meeting on 14th July; the *James* ketch was bought, Captain Maximilian Keech of the Royal Navy was given command, six guns were mounted, Keech was given a special permit from Rupert in his capacity as Vice-Admiral of England allowing him to fly the King's Jack within the Bay, and at the end of July 1682 he sailed by the North Sea and the Orkneys, to intercept the *Expectation* if possible and to capture her in the Bay if necessary.

The 'long and Serious Debate' which had produced the decision that it was too late in the season, but which Hayes had over-ridden, proved only too well justified. The *James* was never seen again after her departure from Tynemouth, and must have sunk in the North Sea. In view of the haste and lack of inspection with which she had been bought, she may well have been rotten and have foundered.

The tragic fiasco over the *Expectation* interrupted the Committee in the midst of the settlement of bills which normally (by this time) followed after the dispatch of the ships. Among other overdue business was the settlement of the account of Bayly's widow, who disputed the Company's reckoning, and settlement of the charter-party of the *Prudent Mary*, payment being disputed since Captain Greenway had not fulfilled his contract. The *James* cost the Company over £793 which it could ill afford at this time, and the unhappy affair was rendered even more unfortunate in that it was the last occasion on which Rupert gave the Company effective service, for he died in November 1682, to be replaced as Governor by his cousin James Duke of York. James was unanimously elected, but the election cannot have been smooth, for it did not go through until the sixth meeting after Rupert's death, and the crisis had arisen just at the time when the political struggle over the exclusion of James from the throne had reached its climax with his return from Scotland, the trial of Shaftesbury for High Treason, and his flight into Holland. The need to elect a Governor gave the Company a chance to show its political allegiance and to dissociate itself from Shaftesbury and his views. In some ways it was a great opportunity, but it was certainly not an easy one.

The Company in 1682 was, therefore, beset by both English and New England rivals, unsure of its trade, unsure of its sea-captains, uneasy at its new Governor and insecure in its political and diplomatic position. Doubts and difficulties there must have been, and even recriminations after the bitter episode of the ill-fated *James* ketch. But the Company's records contain no note of anything but serene and almost unimaginative attention to routine business, even when it became clear that Radisson had completely ruined the costly attempt to establish a post in Nelson River.

BOOKS FOR REFERENCE

HUDSON'S BAY RECORD SOCIETY—Vols. V, VIII, IX, XI.
BROWN, L. Fargo—*The First Earl of Shaftesbury* (New York, 1933).
RADISSON, Pierre Esprit—'Relations des Voyages de Pierre Esprit Radisson, dans les Années 1682, 3 et 4'. See *Report on Canadian Archives, 1895* (Ottawa, 1896).

CHAPTER IX

GOVERNOR JOHN NIXON, 1679–1683

The mounting threat of rivalry, from French-Canadians, from English interlopers and perhaps from rivals in New England, was due to the fact that with Bayly as its Bayside Governor the Company had established a trade which bore promise of great profits. Its history was still essentially the history of a small company with inadequate capital, financing each annual voyage on credit, and the interest of the documents lies in their revelation of the means by which this was accomplished. The Company had not yet paid a dividend; but it had aroused both fear and emulation. The maritime approach to the fur trade was one in which many, both French and English, now wished to share.

This result had been achieved because the long-sighted purposefulness of the London Committee had not been altered by the change in its construction in 1679. The old courtiers and the new financiers were alike willing to support a Company which for ten years had paid no dividend. Equally important was the choice of the first two effective Bay-side Governors (the intervening Lydall excepted). Bayly and Nixon both had their defects; but the friendly Quaker had taught the Indians to trust him and to expect steady terms of trade, while the morose John Nixon had brought a shrewd mind to the assessment of the Company's problems and had in his turn improved the trade relations which Bayly had established. Despite the financial stringency of the period he received generous—almost too generous—support from the Committee.

Nixon had sailed out to take up his appointment in 1679 in the borrowed *John and Alexander* and had seen the little *Colleton* turn back on the voyage. In 1680 he got the substantial reinforcement of the *Prudent Mary*, the *Colleton* and the *Albemarle*. So generous an outfit was perhaps most remarkable in that it ascribed three of his ships, the *Colleton*, the *Albemarle* and the *Rupert* (which was already there) for retention and use in the Bay. The two small vessels were to stay in the country for two years 'absolute' and for more if it seemed desirable, so with the *Rupert* Nixon would have three ships for guard duties and coastal trade and communications. He reckoned the cost of such arrangements at about £2,500 for shipping alone, and probably he was not far out in his guess.

Such evidence of the determination and confidence of the Committee is underlined by the detailed Instructions which they then sent to Nixon. These are the first detailed instructions available since the Company had taken up its Charter and sent Bayly out to settle and trade. They show no intimate knowledge either of the possibilities or of the difficulties of the Bay. They warrant Governor Nixon's complaint (in 1682) that 'it is not possible for your Honours to knowe in England by guess what is most convenient for your interest, as it is for me to knowe heere by experiance'. The instructions reveal a ripening suspicion that Bayly had been a lax disciplinarian and a careless trader, a feeling which Nixon confirmed with his reports of idleness and incapacity; but the general approach was kindly and generous, even moral in tone. Prayers and homilies and readings from the Bible were to be held regularly, and Bayly was censured for neglecting instructions of this nature—a strange omission in a Quaker. The men were to be assured of promotion and security.

The most significant feature was the clear apprehension of French advances and the need for haste in settling posts other than Rupert River and Moose. 'Port Nelson' and New Severn were not only planned, but instructions were given direct to the ships' captains, and they were supplied with materials for building, since the Committee wrote under fears of designs for interloping and judged it necessary that settlement should be *suddenly put in execution*.

Much was made of reliance upon Nixon's judgment as the man on the spot—'When wee have said all, wee must leave much to your prudent conduct'—but he was given very little latitude on the location and arrangement of his posts. The chief factory was to remain on Hayes Island in Moose River. But Gillam's old Charles Fort in Rupert River was also to be kept up, since Bayly had reported workable isinglass near at hand. The house which Bayly had set up at Albany, and which Nixon in his first year had developed into 'a house of some strength' under the command of John Bridgar, was approved and he was also told to set up posts at New Severn and Nelson. These establishments were to be achieved without delay, for the Committee were feeling a new urgency in staking their claims to these rivers.

Nixon was also told that Charlton Island had been selected as the rendezvous for the ships from England and the sloops from the several factories, and he was ordered to build a large warehouse there and to use it to assemble the furs in readiness for swift loading and shipment home. Not only Charlton Island but each post was to be provided with a good waterproof warehouse, and Nixon was urged to handle his trade-goods systematically, to send home defective or unattractive goods, and to see that his warehousekeeper sent home annual lists of the stock on hand at the end of each season. Further, Nixon was to economise European provisions and to encourage the use and growth of local supplies. Here was one of the eternal problems for a Company which always found the shipment of European food expensive and unsatisfactory, for a winter on nothing but 'hard tack' was almost bound to result in scurvy. As early as the 1670 voyage, peas and mustard had been planted and reaped; and under the influence of Groseilliers and Radisson the English had managed to keep hens and hogs through that first winter at Charles Fort. Radisson had goats and hogs shipped out for him, and garden seeds had formed part of the 1674 outfit. Now Nixon was supplied with seeds and urged to garden with them, and to grow fresh meat by keeping hogs, especially on Charlton Island where they might easily be protected from wild beasts.

Nixon was also pressed to diversify the Company's trade and to develop alternatives to beaver by sending home small furs such as martens. Feathers were also to be collected and sent home, the Committee estimating that there must be plenty of this commodity available where so many geese and other fowl were killed every year. But the chief alternative to beaver, in the hopes of the Committee, was to be the isinglass-mica of which Bayly had written and spoken. During the preparation of the 1680 outfit the Committee had recruited a couple of miners to help this development, and although these technicians withdrew from their engagements before the ships sailed, Nixon was still urged to develop this possible source of wealth.

Much of these Instructions, with emphasis on siting posts and developing trade in an orderly manner, was natural and well reasoned. But yet there was in the Committee's orders something of urgency, especially when the need to anticipate the French and to win over the Indians to the English posts was dealt with. The memorial-plaque to Bayly was designed to let the Indians know that he was dead and that the Company had used him well. His policy, inherited from Gillam, of making treaties with the Indians was to be pursued. The treaties were to be so made that 'it might be understood by them that you had purchased both the lands and rivers of them, and that they had transferred the absolute propriety to you, or at least the only freedom of trade'. In a postscript Hayes, who had been empowered so to do by the rest of the Committee, told Nixon to brand wooden tallies with the Union Flag as a means of impressing the Indians and sealing the bargains. Nixon was also to forestall the French by taking possession of any other rivers or harbours which might seem desirable.

The wreck of the *Prudent Mary* prevented Nixon from getting his returns home in 1680, and left him with the ship's captain and crew to feed and house through the winter. It left him, too, with problems of discipline and loyalty, for the *Prudent Mary*'s officers discussed with him the chances of an interloping voyage. The Committee, however, were able to raise enough loans to get the *Diligence* hired and despatched, under Captain Nehemiah Walker, in 1681, after a winter in which there were no furs to sell, and Nixon was there at Charlton Island ready to meet her on her arrival in September. His warehouse was ready for the unloading, his sloops had brought the furs in and were ready to take the trade goods to his posts on the mainland. But at the moment when the organisation should have slipped into a working routine Nixon saw everything fall into confusion and folly.

He had already formed an adverse opinion of Nehemiah Walker, both as a seaman and as a man, for he had himself made the outward voyage with him in 1679 and had seen his drunken pranks, his great self-confidence, and the irresponsible way in which he failed to realise that the wreck or loss of a ship was more than a maritime affair; it robbed the trade of its goods and supplies and imperilled the whole situation of those left by the Bay. In 1681, as Walker came in to Charlton Island, Nixon's worst opinions were confirmed. For the over-confident Walker came in carrying too much sail, struck on a shoal, and lost his rudder. Nixon had to steer the *Diligence* to her moorings by towing a 'coyl of junk'—otherwise he stood to have another wreck on his hands, to set alongside that of the *Prudent Mary*, and to see all his provisions and trade-goods spoiled and delayed.

As it was, Nixon was delayed on the island until it was too late in the season for him to be able to get away to the mainland and to winter at Moose. In order to meet the ship he had left his post just when the Indians were coming down to trade, and when there was a great deal to do about the fort, and he found himself, and the thirteen Company servants whom he had taken to the island with him, isolated from the main problems of his command at a vital time. Eventually he was forced to spend the whole winter on the island, with his band of useless servants, living in close proximity to Walker and his crew of twenty-two seamen—for the *Diligence* could not possibly be loaded, repaired and despatched in time to have any reasonable prospect of a safe passage out through the Strait.

It was not a pleasant winter, and the immediate discomforts and personal affronts which Nixon suffered obviously affected the composition of the 'Report', which he wrote during the winter and spring and sent home in 1682. It has survived, significantly enough, among the papers of the Hon. Robert Boyle at the Royal Society, the first detailed and substantial account of conditions by the Bay.

The immediate shipping difficulties, which had led Nixon to be shut up out of touch with his posts, naturally take a large part of his Report, and here his comments fall, with considerable reiteration, under three heads. He thought a small ship of about ninety tons, properly loaded, would serve the Company better than a 'great ship' such as the *Diligence*, would be handier in ice and fog and would arrive more punctually, so that goods could be distributed to the posts in good time and without pressure. It was because the *Diligence* was a 'great ship' that Nixon had landed in his 'laberinth of troubles'. Secondly, he thought the 'great ship' too expensive. The *Diligence* actually cost the Company £2,118 for this voyage, but Nixon did not know this and was to a great extent merely guessing at costs. He was on surer ground when he said that the 'great ship' either had to be loaded in a hurry, or get caught in the ice, or spend the winter in the Bay. Hurried loading meant taking men off from other necessary work, whilst wintering in the country meant paying the captain and crew a whole year's wages for one month's work. Thirdly, the 'great ship' would be hired and not the Company's property. Consequently her captain would seldom be really co-operative; he would stand only to the terms of his charter-party, would often defy the authority and diminish the prestige of the Governor, and by bringing in seamen at better wages would breed dissatisfaction and insolence among the Company's servants. All of this general criticism was loaded with many instances from the dark winter of 1681–2, when Nixon had not managed to get the sloop and the yacht away to supply the factories until mid-October, and when both had lost their rudders on their return to Charlton Island. By that time the ice was driving at sea and it was not until 5th November that Phipps the warehousekeeper was able to get to the mainland after a second attempt and a most dangerous journey, leaving the Governor in ignorance until the following March.

Much of Nixon's criticism of the 'great ship' was bound in with his refusal to accept Charlton Island as a suitable rendezvous. A smaller vessel could winter without danger at Moose, where the

Governor could both be at hand at ship-time and yet be near his Indians and his factory at that important time when all efforts should be directed to the Indian trade, to the goose-hunt, to developing his garden and to getting in wood. Charlton Island was remote from the Indians, as much out of touch with the mainland as 'from East-india to London', and difficult for navigation. It was, moreover, ice-bound far later in the spring than the mainland, so that the small sloops and yachts destined for country use could work along the coast from Moose whilst Charlton Island was still unsafe for shipping; for the rivers carried the ice straight out to sea from the coast, whereas at the island it drove up and down with the tide and took till the middle of June to clear. Lastly, Charlton Island could easily be captured from sea, especially with a discontented servant to pilot a man-of-war. And although Nixon was emphatic that the mainland posts needed to be made strong, warm and tight, and to be put in a 'postour of defence' in case of Indian affronts, he regarded the defence of Charlton Island as more difficult and more important. A concentration of trade-goods there would be open to European attack, not to petty Indian affronts, and would be impossible to defend. In any case it would deflect defensive effort from the posts on the mainland.

Nixon, if allowed a free hand, thought he might have made Albany the chief post. He had already developed a 'Fort' there and he took great care with it; in 1681 he had sent over all the provisions he could spare from Moose. He then arrived himself at Albany just in time to stop the departure of 4,000 skins which were going away for lack of goods, and he there met an old Indian who had never seen Europeans before, 'the discreetest salvage that ever I heard'. The 'salvage' had promised to come down in 1682 with a hundred canoes, and Nixon grieved sore to be kept at the island, putting such trade in jeopardy. He sent off a sloop from the island to Albany as soon as ice permitted in 1682, and he was most relieved to find that the efficient Phipps had also sent a boat from Moose River, proving himself 'much of a man in time of need'. Nixon himself took the sloop to Albany in July and there found all in better order than he expected save that the men, many of whom were due to end their contracts, were not satisfied with their pay and were uneasy that some to whom Nixon had previously promised better terms had been refused by the Committee. He concluded that Albany was the best post for trade but difficult for navigation, and that therefore he would cancel his first desire, and would not make it his chief post.

As far as the balance of control between London and the Bay

went, Nixon was to some extent on the defensive; but yet he made many shrewd suggestions. He was bound to feel that the Committee would always be influenced by those near at hand, that they would be (as he plainly said they had been) acting in ignorance and accepting bad advice. They must trust their Governor, must leave him room to exercise his judgment, and must strengthen his authority, perhaps by giving him powers of summary jurisdiction according to martial law. They must, too, listen to his advice about trade-goods and shipments of stores; no planks or building materials were needed, but good tradesmen in the country would be well worth while—smiths, carpenters, sawyers, coopers, tailors, edge-tool makers. In all of these matters he held (probably with justification) that the Company was losing money by inefficient work done in England and shipped out.

Given such support and the provisions and goods which he required, the Governor would be able to plant and reap turnips and colewort, and probably buck-wheat. He would require to have two years' provisions on hand, but he should make his own bread instead of having it shipped out. He would not breed goats and hogs, for they ate too much to make them worth while, but he would experiment with either Shetland or Orkney sheep.

The *Diligence* on her departure in 1682 left but thirty men in the country, but Nixon reckoned that there ought to be at least fifty in permanent residence. These ought to be country lads, or better still Scots, instead of the 'London childring' who pestered him. Even so the Governor would need to be kept supplied with more liquor, butter and cheese, than the Committee had given to Nixon, for the men would need to be 'encouraged with drams', and the Governor would need to be in a position to make small presents and to entertain, especially if the Committee intended to continue such costly argosies as it had sent out in 1682. 'When I beheld 5 Captains in the sound all with their cullers flying it was a lovely sight to see in the Northwest' but 'my poore quarter cask of sack knew it full well'.

In all of this Nixon was shrewd if perhaps a little petulant. He is the necessary corrective to the predominantly London origin of the bulk of the evidence available, and he makes it clear that, with all their desire for efficiency and order, the Committee were still capable of sending out shoes which would not wear, edge-tools which would not stand the climate, woollen garments badly made and guns which endangered the life of the Indian.

But Nixon was not only critical and corrective. He was constructive on the major problem of the period, and indeed of the whole of the Company's history. He thought it necessary (as Bayly had done) to send men inland to trade. Such enterprise should follow after the setting of the factories in order and the improvement in the quality of the trade-goods. First the Company must entice the Indians down to trade and ensure that they behaved with respect on their arrival. Then Nixon would imitate the French in establishing posts 'in the rivers, that goe doun into Kennedy'. The 'Poyets' of far Athabaska too, should be got down to trade at the Bay by the Company persuading their neighbours not to kill them, but to make them prisoners so that the Company might take care of them and rear them up as ambassadors to send inland to their own people. Here was a pointer to two important concepts later adopted by the Company when it pushed into the interior; then the importance of maintaining some measure of peace between the different Indian tribes and confederacies became a constant theme, and the training of Indians to act as ambassadors to their own peoples also became constant practice.

Here, however, in advocating penetration into the hinterland in somewhat more practical terms than Bayly had used, Nixon felt that the Company might not be completely covered by its Charter. In his accurate, rather cold and sententious way, he pointed out to the Committee that as far as inland trade went its 'patant is verry darke' in that it did not define the Company's domain by lines of latitude or longitude; nor did it (as was later alleged) specify possession of the basins of all rivers, creeks and lakes falling into the Bay. It merely gave possession of islands, lakes and creeks *within* the Bay, which left the hinterland wide open to doubt.

Finally Nixon concluded his suggestion that he should be supplied with 'extraordinaries' such as Nantes brandy, Westphalia hams, cheese, sugar, sherry and a butt of malt ('that the men may see you have respect to me'), with the rather truculent statement that 'I am antiant and water doth not agree with me'. He was then foolish enough to speak freely of his own willingness to retire and of a possible successor, and the Committee lost no time in appointing Henry Sergeant to the post, on 3rd January, 1683. Little compassion need be wasted over Nixon in his dismissal, for he was by his own confession 'antiant' in 1683. But apart from his shrewd criticisms he had done well for the Company. He had profited from the good reputation left by Quaker Bayly and had made the most of it; trade was good, as were prices in London. The Company by 1683 could claim that it had arrived at a very considerable trade and that the profit to the whole nation as well as to His Majesty's customs revenue was not inconsiderable—this was in asking for intervention against a rumoured fur-trading company from Brandenburg—and its stock stood at a thirty-three per cent. premium on the London Exchange. Shipments of furs from New York still influenced prices in London considerably, but the Company was accepted as well established and as controlling an as-yet-unexploited source of magnificent beaver. The French knew that 'Their country is the only place for fine Beaver and other small peltries. There is no doubt that if they are left in the Bay they will render themselves masters of all the trade of Canada inside six years'. It was a tempting and profitable trade which was rousing the French of Canada to challenge the Company.

BOOKS FOR REFERENCE

HUDSON'S BAY RECORD SOCIETY—Vols. V, VIII, IX, XI.

CHAPTER X

FRENCH RIVALRY, 1675–1682

Although the changes in the Committee of the Hudson's Bay Company in 1679 were so clearly due to hostility between the supporters of James Duke of York and supporters of Shaftesbury, with the former organised behind James Hayes, yet it is noteworthy that the circumstances in which Hayes and his supporters took control were marked by ever more open rivalry from the French of Canada. Here the Jesuits played their part, and Albanel in particular played an important role.

After the winter of 1674–5 at Moose Fort, with its starvation, caballing and suspicion, only the discredited Governor Bayly and three men stayed behind to perpetuate English claims to the Bay. Governor Lydall, Groseilliers, Gorst and all the other men sailed in spring with the ships, and Albanel sailed with the rest for England. There 'by the connivance of some who favoured the Papists' he was allowed to journey into France and ultimately was to succeed in winning back to France the renegades Groseilliers and Radisson.

The welcome which he managed to get for these two men in France was due to a feeling that French and English interests must lead to a clash despite the desire for amity. The conditions in which the Treaty of Dover had been signed, in the same year as the Company's Charter had been granted, had changed. Joint rivalry with the Dutch had then been the cause for the open clauses of the Treaty and had been reason enough for the suppression of minor rivalries; and support for the Roman Catholic projects of the Stuart monarchs had been reason for the secret clauses of the Treaty and for tolerance of ventures in which they were personally concerned.

But from about 1674 onwards signs of change were clear. Albanel's second voyage to the Bay, his semi-official luring away of Groseilliers and Radisson, both by the shores of the Bay and later in London, and their ultimate journey to France, told much to those who were in close touch with courtly and diplomatic circles, and the outlook in 1676 must have been threatening. For although Colbert was himself still in favour of restraining the Canadian fur-traders in the interests of farming-settlement, and Frontenac as Governor was apathetic towards the Jesuits and the problems of the Bay, yet commercial relations had begun to deteriorate. Colbert's tariffs, designed largely to curb the Dutch, put so many restraints on English trade that they almost led to an Anglo-French war, as they did in fact lead to a renewal of the Franco-Dutch war, and Albanel and the Jesuits had substantial backing in France in 1676.

When Rupert succeeded James Duke of York as commander of the combined fleets, the French failure to support him in battle against the Dutch left him by 1673 convinced that he must take the British ships back to the Thames and disarm them. His charges in Parliament against the conduct of the French fleet caused the greatest ill-feeling in France, and when the English made a separate peace with the Dutch in 1674, leaving the French to fight on alone until 1678, the cleavage between the two countries stood out undisguised. This coincided with a revival in French imperial and mercantilist interests, for in 1673 Colbert sent the Sieur de Patoulet to Canada to organise the trade of the colony, with special instructions to encourage the growing of flax and of masts for naval stores.

Already, in Canada, Talon had drawn up his plan for stabilising the economy of the French Empire. Religious missions and trade together were to enlarge the bounds of the colony, and its population was to be strong alike for war or work, with Canada and the Antilles supplementing each other. Flax and timber grown in Canada were to give to France the supplies which she normally drew from the Baltic, and furs and skins were to provide the chief source of customs revenue.

Louis de Buade, Comte de Frontenac, coming in as Governor of Canada at this juncture, brought to these problems his own personal contribution. He was anxious to mingle the French and the Indians so as to make a single race; he urged the use of French as a *lingua franca*, and that Indian children should be schooled with French children. In 1673 he made his celebrated voyage to Lake Ontario, there to hold a *pow-wow* with the Iroquois and other tribes. At the focal point of that lake he established Fort Frontenac, and he looked favourably on a proposal from the merchants of Quebec that they should make themselves responsible for the upkeep of the post. A little later he accepted a proposal from the Chevalier de la Salle that he should be responsible for inducing settlement and colonisation in the region of the fort. Frontenac, in all of this, was more inclined to foster the southward and westward expansion and trade of New France than he was to indulge in northern ventures. He was, how-ever, in difficulty because of the official policy for restraining and regulating the penetration of the *coureurs de bois* into the hinterland of the colony. In 1672, 1673, and again in 1674, the *coureurs* were forbidden to be absent in the woods for more than twenty-four hours without a licence; but Frontenac found that the officials connived at their trade and that when he took effective action he became the butt of endless abuse. So, although he was clear in his intentions for the restriction of the Indian trade within organised markets, and the spread of Canada to the south and west, his actual policy could not be so clear and simple. Although on the whole he accepted the order that he should conciliate the English, yet he also realised that there must in any case be rivalry for the Indians' trade between Montreal and the former Dutch posts at Orange and Manhattan, and he was further reminded (by the Jesuit Father Nouvel) that the establishment of English trade in the 'grande baye du nord' had already, by 1673, diverted numbers of the Crees from Lake Superior, and so had diminished the number of canoes which came down to Canada to trade.

Frontenac's main purpose was represented by the establishment of Fort Frontenac, the settlement projects of La Salle, and the voyage of Louis Jolliet from Lake Ontario to the Gulf of Mexico (all by easy water, it was said, with only one 'décharge', where Lake Ontario falls into Lake Erie). Yet he ran into criticism for not sufficiently restraining the *coureurs*, and for not cutting down the use of brandy in the Indian trade. He could not, in fact, overlook the potential development of the normal *coureur's* trade, expanding to the north, nor the potential threat of the Hudson Bay posts. He therefore sent Albanel north on his second journey in 1674, encouraging the little Jesuit in some points, restraining him in others. For Frontenac had been instructed to watch Jesuit plans and pretensions with care. Their Indian policy was suspect and they were also Ultramontanists, supporting the fullest pretensions of the Papacy in rejecting Louis XIV's efforts to establish a pragmatic Gallican authority over the Church in France. Frontenac not only favoured other missions as against the Jesuits (particularly the Recollects) but he was also in favour of the Recollect-La Salle plans for opening the Mississippi valley rather than of Jesuit designs for expansion northwards to Hudson Bay, with their consequent emphasis on fur instead of settlement.

A letter from Frontenac which Albanel brought to Bayly in 1674 was taken by the good Quaker as a sign of a kindly spirit, and the Jesuit was well treated and given an equal share of the short commons and meagre amenities of the English post. This letter was freely quoted in later disputes as evidence that Bayly and Frontenac 'did conciliate a good Intelligence and amity without complaineing of any Injury done by the Company in building Forts and makeing Settlements and commerce there or without makeing any pretence to the Land thereabouts'. In an unofficial and somewhat negative way this was perhaps true, for Frontenac did not issue any formal challenge to the English posts or trade.

Nevertheless the French were creeping up towards the Bay from the south. They advanced from eight days' to one day's journey from the Company's post at Charles Fort, and Bayly and Frontenac, despite their friendly correspondence, were both feeling for an opening. Bayly saw the remedy to the French outposts in sending men inland to draw the Indians down to trade by the Bay. It proved the right and inevitable solution; but it took the Company the best part of a century to carry it out effectively and Bayly, like so many of his successors, was prevented by lack of men and goods from pursuing this course. Yet he managed to detach a couple of Frenchmen from their allegiance and sent them, Eustache Prevost and Thomas Leclerc, to England, with the beaver which they had traded.

Frontenac, on his side, followed up Albanel's venture by a special mission to the Bay to report on the English posts and to persuade the Indians not to trade with them. Under his instructions the brothers Louis and Zacharie Jolliet (already experienced travellers and geographers, with a voyage down the Mississippi to their credit) left Quebec in May 1679, and travelled via the Saguenay, Lake Mistassini and the Marten and Rupert Rivers to the Bay. Louis Jolliet must have reached Charles Fort early in June 1679, for he left a missionary and some of the party (probably including his brother) at Lake Nemiskau at the end of May, and the ships from England had not yet arrived when he reached the Bay. There Louis Jolliet wrote to Bayly to say that he would be glad to be allowed to purchase provisions, and Bayly hastened ashore from the *Rupert* to profer a sincere greeting. 'You are here in peace', said the Quaker, 'and have nothing to fear. You may stay as long as you please'.

But whilst Bayly told the French that they had nothing to fear, he also made it clear that he thought the English had nothing to fear either. He told Jolliet that he had a ship of twelve guns (the *Rupert*) for defence, and that though he had lost a barque of forty tons in the spring floods he had another of the same size, one of fifteen tons and three boats, all designed for the coastal trade within the Bay. He had under his command three forts (Moose, Rupert and Albany) rather far distant from each other but each prosperous. He alleged that he also had a post at New Severn, and he said he proposed to build in the spring at the mouth of the rivers which ran up to Lake Superior—probably he meant at the mouth of the Hayes and Nelson Rivers. His strength, he said, was sixty men; he had all the beaver trade he could handle, and he had hopes of developing other commodities also. He added, perhaps not quite logically, that he had sent presents up to the Assiniboines, from whom alone prime beaver could be got, and that he would have their trade under control within six years.

Undoubtedly Bayly was to some extent trying to impress Jolliet, but it is evident that neither he nor the London Committee had been idle in the period between 1675 and 1679, although there are no records to give details of their operations.

Jolliet spent two days at Charles Fort, during which Bayly offered him ten thousand francs down and a thousand livres a year if he would enter the English service, and Jolliet carefully noted the strength and weakness of the English position, and he reported that 'Whenever it shall please His Majesty to wish to expel the English from this Bay in order to be Master of all the country and the Beaver trade, it will be Easy to provide the means and put them into Execution. The forts at present have but the name of Fort. They are small squares of pickets which enclose their houses. They build to resist the cold and not the arms of those who might attack from the land'.

So, with some suspicion but in outward amity, Jolliet's visit to the Bay ended. In the meantime the Jesuit Albanel had worked in London to take Radisson and Groseilliers back to a welcome in France in 1676. The rising impression that the French government would support Albanel's moves instead of suppressing him was such that at this time the Company pleaded for diplomatic intervention, to get the French government to forbid its subjects to encroach.

But Albanel met a willing response from Radisson and Groseilliers. They were without doubt in a disgruntled mood, feeling that the English Company, now that it was established, was neglecting their advice in favour of ignorant Englishmen, such as Bayly, or of New Englanders such as Zachariah Gillam. So much Radisson himself admitted. More to the point, Radisson was putting on paper his thoughts on the means by which the fur trade could become an important monopoly for French Canada. He compiled a memorandum on the French fur trade in its widest implications in which he pointed out that the St. Lawrence and the Great Lakes gave the French an incomparable advantage for the penetration of the country. Further, the voyage of La Salle down the Mississippi, opening up the south from Lake Erie, ought to be linked up with an attempt to reach the Western Sea via 'Freshwater Lake', whilst a North-west Passage should be sought by sea through Hudson Bay. This venture should be outfitted with a 'double chaloupe'—a double-skinned shallop for use in the ice—and a brigantine of from twelve to fifteen tons. It would take two or three years to accomplish, and would be the means of fulfilling a permanent French ambition. It would complete the quartering of North America by the French, and exclude the English of Hudson Bay from the lucrative fur trade.

Radisson then seized on the obvious point that there were only three outlets for the furs of the north—the St. Lawrence, New York (the Hudson) and Hudson Bay. Having made his proposal for closing Hudson Bay to the English by an expedition which would also seek for the North-west Passage, he next developed an idea for stifling the trade of New York by French settlement on the north shore of Lake Ontario and at the entry to Lake Erie, with two forts in the area. The New York furs were traded in the north by the Iroquois and their traffic would be cut by French settlement as out-lined by Radisson.

Radisson was here co-ordinating both Frontenac's plans (for settlement with a fortified post near Fort Frontenac together with penetration down the Mississippi) and those of the northern school. His memorandum is unfinished and undated, but it occurs in con-junction with a copy of the pardon for Radisson's offences against France which was granted in December 1675. It was clearly a part of the development of the French approach to the fur trade at this time, and it shows the part played by Radisson in developing a spirit of rivalry and hostility. He alleged that he was solicited to come from London by Colbert, who promised him, besides a pardon, four hundred louis in gold, payment of all his debts and suitable employ-ment, and it is clear that his experience and his ideas made him invaluable to both sides if the French and the English were to challenge each other in the Bay.

The existence of Radisson's anti-English memorandum and the details of his negotiations with the French government would, of course, be unknown in London. But the fact that late in 1675 both he and Groseilliers slipped across the Channel to join Albanel (who had been willingly allowed to depart) could not be overlooked. The pardon and the welcome extended to them were evidence of the influence of the Jesuit element in France and they also showed that the friendly atmosphere of the Treaty of Dover was evaporating and the Hudson's Bay Company could no longer count on the French government curbing those fur-trade and Jesuit elements which advocated rivalry and opposition in the north.

As yet, however, Radisson and his plans had not been firmly accepted in France. Although he had been cut off from his pension of £200 a year by his father-in-law Kirke, he was unable to get his English wife to France and was regarded with deep suspicion at Paris. In 1679 he was encouraged to come to England in an effort to get his wife to follow him back, while Groseilliers had gone to Canada, despairing of getting the French to undertake an effective attack on the English in the Bay. Signs of the changing times were to be seen, however, when even Frontenac wrote in 1678 that it was essential to push towards Hudson Bay so as to be in a position to dispute possession with the English.

With the defection of Groseilliers and Radisson the danger that French traders might anticipate British settlement had clearly been increased. Nixon's hint that the Charter was 'very darke' as to boundaries was therefore most pertinent. But so far, up to 1681, the French government had only temporised with the problem. Groseilliers and Radisson had been given a patent for white porpoise fishing in the St. Lawrence and for sea-otter trading at Anticosti, they had been sent to Canada and there they had been taken in hand by Frontenac in 1676 and had met a body of the Canadian fur-traders to discuss their plans, and to assess the prices at which Canadian beaver should be sold. But Frontenac still looked on them, the Jesuits and northern projects in general, with suspicion, and no help was forthcoming from the fur-traders. So Groseilliers went back to his family at Trois Rivières and Radisson sailed once more for France, to seek employment and to serve at sea for some years. His futile voyage to Canada had, he alleged, cost him four thousand livres, and his service at sea ended in a shipwreck in which he lost all his goods, to the value of a further £2,000. He was even forced to sell a miniature of Charles II which the King himself had presented to him, together with the gold chain to hang it round his neck. He was eager for employment and for action, and when paid £1,000 for the expenses involved was ready to prove his good faith by a further journey to England to bring over his English wife to France.

The Hudson's Bay Company was now fully aware of Radisson's moves, and as early as 1676 the Committee had sent in a petition asking for the help of the King against the plots to ruin the 'Colony and Trade in Hudson's Bay'. But there had been little urgency in the matter until the two kings began to drift apart, in the years 1679–81. Charles still proved willing to accept the subsidies which

Louis showered upon him, as a means of evading the control of Parliament with its clamour against Popery, but he proved astute and obstinate in his refusal to sell the interests of England or to allow France to dominate the continent of Europe. Louis was dissatisfied alike with the part which Charles played as intermediary for concluding the Treaty of Nymwegen, to end the war between France and Holland, and with the marriage between Charles's niece Mary and the Dutch Stadtholder William. So by 1679 the potential rivalry of the Canadian fur-traders and the Hudson's Bay Company was beginning to be reviewed. The tension which followed the failure to make joint war on the Dutch was rising from about 1674 onwards, but it was still restrained from reaction on the Hudson Bay trade by the peculiar condition of Canada itself.

The whole economy of Canada was at a standstill in these years because the furs could not find a market at prices which enabled the colony to pay its way. The *Compagnie des Indes Occidentales* which had taken over the fur trade when the colony had reverted to the French Crown in 1663 had failed to satisfy either the *habitans*, the government, or its own proprietors; its charter was revoked in 1674 and the monopoly of the fur trade of Tadoussac was then sold for seven years (he actually held it for ten) to Jean Oudiette, who also bought the control of the sugar dues from the French West Indies and all other rights of the *Compagnie*. Oudiette acquired not only the monopoly of the fur trade but also the farm of the *Quart* of beaver and of the tenth of elk skins, and all other dues in Canada; he also undertook to defray the costs of administering the colony.

But the year 1675 was most unfortunate for such a speculation because it was just at that time becoming obvious that the increase in the quantities of furs, which was almost inevitable as more and more Indians became accustomed to and dependent upon European trade, would prove an embarrassment. Already in 1675 the produce was 61,000 pounds of beaver; next year it was up to 70,000 pounds, and in 1677 to 92,000. There followed something of a decline, to 80,000 pounds in 1678, to 68,000 in 1679 and to 69,000 in 1680, and the decline was of as great importance in stimulating rivalry as the previous increase had been in repressing it. For Oudiette found that the effective French market was limited to a demand for about 60,000 skins a year. These, however, were wanted in qualities which accorded badly with the production of Canada; the hatters wanted about one third of their skins as *parchment* and the rest as *coat*. So Oudiette had ready sales for about forty thousand *coat* beaver a year and for about twenty thousand *parchment*; anything above these quantities in either kind of skin would have to be sold, probably to Russia via Holland, at surplus disposal prices. But from the start of his contract Oudiette found that from the Canadian trade he was unable to secure more than four thousand *coat* skins a year, whereas he was overflown with shoddy *parchment*. This was merely the reflection, in terms of beaver-quality, of the way in which French expansion in the fur trade had tended under Frontenac towards the Mississippi and the south; it was in itself an argument for redressing the balance and meeting the needs of the French market by expanding into the north, the area which produced the prime *coat* beaver, for the Iroquois did not even know how to 'engraisser' their beaver.

Oudiette's solution to this serious and fundamental problem was put before the meeting of the Council of Quebec at which both Groseilliers and Radisson were present, in October 1676. The establishment of the Council was another feature of the failure of the *Compagnie des Indes Occidentales* and, as on this occasion, it gave opportunity for the expression of the feelings and desires of the colonists in matters which affected them. The solution which they were now asked to consider was that the prices of beaver should be graded so as to stimulate the trade in *coat* and to discourage *parchment*. Oudiette had taken on his contract on the basis of a uniform price of four and a half livres the pound for all qualities, payable in cash, in bills of exchange on France, or in merchandise; he was then allowed to exploit his monopoly and make his profit by selling in France at a maximum price of ten livres the pound. This had been the proposal put forward in 1674 by the *habitans*, hard hit by the previous variable prices which had dropped from eight livres down to less than three, at which they found they could not buy their necessary European supplies. Oudiette's proposal that prices should be graded so as to stimulate the production of *coat* naturally met opposition from those who were well content with the trade as it stood—as long as the excessive *parchment* could be passed on to him. But his new scheme was promulgated by Edict in May 1677, with a range from five livres and ten sous the pound for *coat* down to three livres and ten sous the pound for *parchment*.

This could only, at best, be a long-term solution for Canada, for it would not be operative until the hunting Indians had felt the reactions of the prices, and had altered their methods of hunting and of preparing the skins. Moreover the Indians' reaction would vary according to the method of trade and the availability of an alternative market for the furs which they produced.

As far as methods of trade went, the Canadian system was at that time in the throes of two bitter arguments. The system of taking the trade to the Indian 'in his habitation' by allowing the *coureur de bois* to travel about and live with the Indians was under the gravest criticism; and so was the basis of the *coureurs'* trade, the habit of trading brandy to the Indians. The new Intendant, Duchesnau, was fully convinced that the great need of Canada was an increase in population. 'Le pays souffre si fort de la disette de monde que beaucoup de terres demeurent incultes', he proclaimed. In this he had Governor Frontenac behind him with a policy of subsidies for large families, and Colbert with a veto on new discoveries save under grave necessity or in circumstances of great advantage. But Duchesnau quarrelled fiercely with Frontenac over the extent to which this need for an agricultural population should lead to suppression of the *coureurs*. Frontenac's submission was that it was almost impossible for him to carry out the Ordinance (of 1672) forbidding trade in the habitations of the Indians because of the connivance of Intendant Duchesnau and of the *habitans*. But he was himself accused of such connivance, and especially of allowing westwards expansion under Daniel Greysolon, Sieur Dulhut ('irretrievably Anglicised as Duluth'), who in the fall of 1678 led an expedition to the west aimed at extending French control beyond Lake Superior and setting up for himself a trade there. Duluth was working towards the Western Sea with the purpose of controlling the Indians of the western Lake Superior area (the Sioux, Crees, Assiniboines and Saulteurs) who formed the background for the trade which found its way down to the posts on Hudson Bay. He reached 'the extremity of Lake Superior', where the city of his name now stands, but he was then diverted southwards to the Mississippi. Duluth was in this the counterpart of Frontenac's plans for developing the trade of the Fort Frontenac area under La Salle and for exploring southwards under Louis Jolliet. For despite his protestations, his suspicions of the Jesuits, and his amity towards the English, Frontenac had definite ambitions for the expansion of Canada and there was weight in the charge when Duchesnau accused him of receiving bribes from Duluth, and said that there were five or six hundred *coureurs* in the woods with the Governor's knowledge despite the veto.

Apart from the question of the *coureurs*, the two great officials also differed on the question of trading brandy to the Indians. Here also a royal decree was involved. The trouble was of long standing, and the Bishop of Quebec had challenged the traders on the subject before ever the English began to offer rivalry. In 1678 the Intendant was ordered to call an assembly of twenty *habitans* and to get their views on this vexed subject; some were in favour of the punishment of drunken Indians, some in favour of restraints on the traders, but with very few exceptions (of whom Jolliet was one) the assembly was convinced that brandy was absolutely necessary if the Indians were to be brought to the French posts to trade. But though La Salle and others insisted that brandy was the essential element of the fur trade and that the Indians did not get enough of it to do them any serious harm, the use of brandy for trade to Indians was forbidden in May 1678.

But the veto was as difficult to enforce as the veto on the *coureurs*, and like it it brought Frontenac into conflict with his Intendant. Here Colbert took the Governor's part and administered a severe reproof to the Intendant for the vigour of his charges, for by 1678–9 part of the argument about these problems of the *coureurs* and about the use of brandy was beginning to turn on the nature of the English opposition in the fur trade. Those *habitans* who most vigorously advocated the use of brandy argued that without it the Indians would take their trade to Orange and Manhattan. Duluth's voyage was also regarded as a means of countering the drift of furs to the former Dutch posts, and part of the move against the *coureurs* was due to the allegation that they sold their furs to the English. Impossible as it seemed to the French administration, Duchesnau alleged that since the English fur-traders did not have to pay the heavy taxes borne by the French, English colonists could pay twice the price for beaver that the French could afford. He said that above £60,000 worth of furs went to the English colonies from Canada yearly, and he developed a theory that the salvation of the trade of Canada could only be secured if a company could be formed to buy Orange and Manhattan from the Duke of York, whatever the cost.

While Duchesnau thus saw the rivalry of the English colonies as a dominant factor in the Canadian trade, he also accepted the new posts on Hudson Bay as worthy of attention; and while he urged that New Netherland should be bought from the English he felt (by 1681) that the posts on the Bay should either be destroyed by force or should be stifled of trade by the French building posts on the rivers that ran down to the Bay. Frontenac, too, was thinking and acting somewhat along these lines, for he was excused from the charge of having allowed evasion of the veto on *coureurs* because the voyage (of Duluth) which he was alleged to have licenced was towards Hudson Bay, and it was of service to the French Crown to contest English claims there. Jolliet's journey to the Bay in 1679 **therefore** falls into the general picture of the development of the

Canadian fur trade, and the diplomatic and personal cross-currents of that development.

But although Louis Jolliet's overland journey was thus organised by Frontenac and approved by Colbert, a contemporary voyage by his brother Zacharie was neither sponsored nor approved. Little is known of the voyage—merely the statement from Frontenac that Jolliet and a kinsman named la Lande had taken a ship under pretence of fishing near Anticosti, and had been convicted on their return to Quebec in March 1680 of having traded with Indians and of having taken their furs to the English, making a treaty and exchanging presents with the Governor of Hudson Bay. This is an incident in the tenure of Governor Bayly of which there is no other record save this meagre statement. But there can be little doubt of the incident. The two men were fined two thousand livres and their ship was confiscated, to be subsequently released again for fishing. It was held that they had damaged the trade of Tadoussac to the extent of ten thousand livres.

The two young kinsmen were described, Jolliet as the nephew and la Lande as the half-brother, of Aubert de la Chesnay, who had provided their outfit and who rescued their ship after confiscation. De la Chesnay was at that time in Canada as the representative of Oudiette and the farmers of the customs, and it was even reported that the farmers had outfitted the voyage. An able merchant, a vivid and realistic trader, de la Chesnay was convinced that the way to redress the balance of the types of fur required by the French hatters was to invade the trade of the north, there to get the *coat* beaver required. Already in 1676 he had been once convicted of sending a shallop on a trading voyage, to the detriment of the trade of Tadoussac. But the way in which his ship traded with Governor Bayly in 1680 shows him as a man more concerned with trade than with patriotism, as his flouting of the interests of those whom he was supposed to represent shows him as more concerned with profits than with loyalty. Yet de la Chesnay combined knowledge, wealth, influence and determination to a remarkable degree, and it was his lively purpose to contest the trade of the Bay which gave point and effect to the plans of Albanel and to the desertion of Radisson and Groseilliers from the English service.

After a further venture, which brought back a ship-load of furs and merchandise to Quebec, de la Chesnay went to France to secure permission to make a maritime approach to the fur trade. This was fundamental. De la Chesnay wanted to take ships into the Bay, not to approach overland from Canada. In this he was thinking along the same lines as Radisson and Groseilliers, and he was, despite his early history of trade with Bayly, shaping for clear and purposeful rivalry with the Hudson's Bay Company. It would be rivalry of a dangerous sort, dependent on ships, on their bulk cargoes and on the great impression which they made on Indians. This was the time, in the years following on the Treaty of Nymwegen, in 1679–81, when the English and French courts were drifting apart, and the appearance in Paris of such a man, convinced that the salvation of Canadian trade lay not in further restrictions but in a maritime approach and in increases in the quantities of *coat* beaver, brought action. While in Canada both Frontenac and Duchesnau were incurring censure for laxity in enforcing the vetoes on the fur trade, in France de la Chesnay managed to secure a charter for the *Compagnie de la Baie d'Hudson* in 1682.

Colbert, with all his restraints on precocious expansion of the French colony, had always been interested in the possibilities of navigation to the north, and had been restrained in part by the needs of diplomacy, in part by the troubles of the Canadian fur trade, as well as by his desire to maintain a concentrated agricultural population. He had long had in his possession a copy of the English company's Charter (perhaps obtained at about the time when it was granted, when he had failed to anticipate the English Adventurers by his support of Van Heemskerk's voyage), and in 1680 two further copies, translated into French, also were in circulation in Paris. Radisson at this time was called upon to prove his good faith by bringing his English wife over to France, and he was even allowed to visit England to do so. But fickle as ever, he warned the English of the rising urgency in the French threats, and a postscript to the Instructions of 1681 carried the warning to Governor Nixon and ordered him to fortify his posts.

As yet, in 1681, no official recognition seems to have been accorded to the plan which de la Chesnay was putting forward. But he and Radisson came together in Paris, as was almost inevitable, and in 1681 they both returned to Canada, reasonably sure that de la Chesnay's proposal for a *Compagnie de la Baie d'Hudson* would be accepted—as it was in the following year—and ready to equip ships to carry out their purpose by conducting a trade voyage in the Bay.

Warned by Radisson, and with other sources of information at their disposal, the Committee of the Hudson's Bay Company could not fail to note the increase in French activity. The trade which was just beginning to bear fruit seemed liable to many challenges, and the warning sent to Governor Nixon was part of a general awareness that it would need to be defended. For the moment, in 1681, although it was ominous that Radisson had gone to Canada once more, the threat hung fire. But only for the moment.

In Canada de la Chesnay had assembled in his support a body of merchant opinion to press Governor Frontenac for permission to fish and trade along the coast to the northwards of the mouth of the St. Lawrence. This Frontenac refused to allow, partly because such a permit would interfere with the establishment of the French customs-farmers at Tadoussac but also because it would contravene his policy of amicable relations with the English in the Bay. Eventually, however, de la Chesnay secured a permit for fishing on the coast of Anticosti, persuading Frontenac that such a permit did not contravene his policy of abstaining from contest with the English for possession of the Bay. Frontenac, nevertheless, did not acknowledge the English claims to ownership; he merely thought it inopportune to contest them. So licenced, de la Chesnay and his associates fitted out Radisson and Groseilliers for an expedition which enormously exceeded their permit.

Whilst this practical threat was developing, a theoretical challenge was also launched. Early in January 1683 the Hudson's Bay Committee were asked to consider and comment on a note sent in to Paris by de la Barre, the new Governor of Canada who had succeeded Frontenac in May 1682. The French had sent the note to their Ambassador in London to find out the English reaction, and in due course it found its way to the Committee for comment. De la Barre had written in November 1682, and he had plainly intimated to his government that a challenge to the British by the Bay was due, was justifiable, and was in fact under way. His claim was that the English were making settlements in lands which the King of France had taken into his possession over twenty years ago. His intention, so he said, was to leave the sea-trade to the Company but to prevent English expansion inland from the Bay. 'Sils avancent comme ils font de méchants petits forts dans les terres du Roy pour débaucher nos Indiens ie les en fairay chasser ce qui me sera aisé estants forts foibles.'

De la Barre was a man of purpose, known to British imperialists for his uncompromising hostility in the West Indies. His actual period as Governor of Canada, it is true, was short and ineffective, dominated by the need to rehabilitate Quebec after the fire of 1682 and by the quarrels between fur-traders and priests over the use of spirits in the Indian trade. His instructions as he took office, moreover, were most directly favourable to the English. He was warned

E

of the *habitans'* tendency to rely on the fur trade rather than on agriculture, and he was told that any expansion which might result from voyages of trade and discovery would not be advantageous. It would therefore be better to develop agriculture in the areas which had already been cleared of forest, and he was specifically told to refuse permits for voyages and to make one exception only, in favour of La Salle's voyage to the south, if he thought that voyage likely to be useful.

The Committee of the Hudson's Bay Company could not know of this instruction; nor could they see into the future and envisage the difficulties in which de la Barre's régime was to be involved. For them the present was made menacing by the arrival of such a man, with undisguised northern ambitions and a deliberately hostile spirit, in place of the conciliatory and south-facing Frontenac. The Committee therefore gave de la Barre's note the most serious attention, and instructed James Hayes to draw up the answer.

It was significant that de la Barre had suggested to his sovereign that he would not dispute the English right to the maritime approach and the sea-trade; his objection was to inland penetration. In actual fact, by 1682 the Company had not yet penetrated inland at all; its posts were almost lamentably maritime in their siting. Nevertheless Bayly had suggested some sort of penetration and so had Nixon, and the Committee itself was even on the point of ordering some such penetration in the instructions of June 1683. But nothing had been accomplished by November 1682, the date of de la Barre's memorial, or by January 1683, when Hayes made his reply.

The reply took the form, very largely, of an historical account in general terms, in which it was alleged that British subjects had frequented the Bay for over a hundred years and had taken possession of several places there, whilst no French had ever been known to sail or traffic within the Bay. Gillam's voyage in 1667 (no mention was made of Groseilliers and, of course, the date should have been 1668), his treaty with the Indians and his taking possession of the land, were emphasised, as were the Royal Charter, the confirmation of Gillam's treaty by Bayly and the acceptance of the situation by Frontenac. As the French were later to point out, it was stretching terms widely to call such voyages as those of Button and Fox, or the earlier ventures of Frobisher, Davis and Hudson, 'frequenting' the Bay. But the essence of the Company's case lay in its Charter, in Gillam's voyage and the subsequent founding of posts, and in the absence of French opposition until de la Barre's letter. Hayes insisted that the delay in the French opposition was due to lack of

French claims, not to the poverty of the trade, for 'The possession of this Trade is of too great a Consequence to have been passed in Silence upon any such Account for soe long an Interval of time as Twelve Yeares'.

It was a reasonable case, especially for a Company which had just elected the heir to the throne as its Governor. Much discussion must have gone on behind the scenes in the preparation of the answer to the French ambassador, of which the official reply of the Company, delivered by Hayes, was but a part. For when in March 1682 Sir Leoline Jenkins, Secretary of State, finally delivered his answer it contained not only all the points made by Hayes but the further (and as it proved vitally important) claim that although the Company had so far only found it convenient to build by the shores of the Bay, nevertheless it claimed the right to extend inland by virtue of its Charter, its treaties with the Indians, and the British right of first occupation of the Bay and its surrounding lands.

This was a necessary statement if the Company were not to accept the solution premised by de la Barre—that the British should be tolerated in their coastal posts but forbidden to advance inland. The insistence on such a claim must have been the result of a suggestion by someone near to the heart of the matter. It proved to be essential to the development of the Company, and to the vindication of the Bay-side approach to furs. But it was not a product of the collective wisdom of the Committee, for the Committee officially made no such claim at this time. Perhaps they were still musing over Nixon's dictum that such penetration was essential but that the Patent was 'verry Darke' as to the Company's rights in the interior. Whether the suggestion sprang from James the new Governor, from Hayes in unofficial discussions, or from a more lawyerly and official appreciation of the need to controvert the implication of the French memorial, is unknown. The French did not take up the challenge and the episode of de la Barre's letter may seem insignificant; but once the point had been made for it, the Company henceforth never hesitated to assert its right to penetrate inland, wherever its men and posts might be actually disposed.

BOOKS FOR REFERENCE

HUDSON'S BAY RECORD SOCIETY—Vols. V, VIII, IX, XI.

BREBNER, J. B.—*The Explorers of North America 1492–1806* (second edition, London, 1955).

Nute, Grace Lee—*Caesars of the Wilderness* (New York, 1943).

ARTICLES

Burgesse, J. A.—'Jolliet on James Bay'. See *The Beaver* (Winnipeg, Hudson's Bay Company, December 1947).

Rich, E. E.—'Which Jolliet?'. See *The Beaver* (Winnipeg, Hudson's Bay Company, Autumn 1956).

CHAPTER XI

THE SETTLEMENT OF NELSON RIVER, 1682

The challenge of the French had led to a full and formal enunciation of the Company's claims in January 1683. They were logically formulated in such a way as to imply the sovereignty of the British Crown to the hinterland of the Bay and the Company's right, derived from the Crown, to penetrate inland and not to be confined merely to the shores of the Bay. This (as it proved) was a far-reaching claim. But, as ever, 'prescription without possession availeth nothing', and the formal claim needed the sanction of actual occupation. The legal assertion therefore had to be supported by the setting up of posts, and in this the Committee showed a serene purposefulness which overrode lack of cash and the many difficulties of the trade.

The instructions of 1681 had insisted on the settlement of Nelson River, and those of 1682 had taken the matter out of the hands of Governor John Nixon and had directed John Bridgar independently to that project, with the *Rupert* and *Albemarle* under command, while the *Craven*, the *Friendship*, the *Lucy* and the Greenland shallop also made the voyage. Knowing something of the plans of Radisson, de la Chesnay and Albanel, the Committee realised the importance of being before-hand with their own moves. Dependent as they were upon the sea-approach, the English found that ships' captains were one of the keys to the problem—and just at this time ships' captains seemed even more unreliable than ever.

Old Zachariah Gillam, the independent New Englander, lost sight of since his troubles over private trade ten years previously, now reappeared and asked for employment. He had actually spent some of the intervening time in an attempt to upset Shaftesbury's control of the trade of Carolina and it is possible that this was some sort of recommendation to the anti-Shaftesbury Committee; but it argued that the old man had not mended his ways. He was, however, given command of the *Rupert* at the perhaps rather ungenerous salary of £100 a year (Walker was paid £200 with a gratuity) since he 'has bin an old servant and done the Company formerly good service'. He was to sail the *Rupert* direct to Port Nelson and to remain and help establish the long-sought post there before going on to winter at Rupert River. With him was to sail his kinsman and former mate, now also seeking re-employment, Ezbon Sandford, who was given command of the *Albemarle*. Sandford was to stay and winter at Port Nelson. The two hired ships *Friendship* and *Lucy* were to go to Charlton Island, to complete their unloading and loading there within twenty days and to return (with or without the furs of the year) according to their charter-parties. The last small company vessel, the *Craven*, 'the best and Strongest barke was ever sent into those parts', was designed for Albany but was to go first to Charlton Island. In effect, therefore, the Committee was devoting its own shipping, the *Rupert*, the *Albemarle* and the *Craven*, to the establishment of the country and was committed to hiring larger vessels for the ocean voyage.

This policy was directed most purposefully at the establishment of 'Port Nelson'—for so the Committee referred to the post planned for Nelson River or Hayes River. For this John Bridgar, who had come home from Albany and had gone on leave to Dublin, was re-engaged for three years. He was to be Governor at Nelson and was to be independent of Nixon at Moose. A separate seal was cut for the use of the establishment at Nelson and the situation was tactfully explained to Nixon as being due to the fact that 'wee can Expect but small or no assistance from you in the makeing of a settlement there, by reasons of your greate distance from thence'. Bridgar was given a regular commission as Governor, the *Rupert* and the *Albemarle* were loaded with the particular object of a new establishment in view, and Ezbon Sandford was nominated Deputy to him. Ten 'honest and able Fellows batchelors' from building trades were sought, and some half-dozen were actually engaged.

For the Committee the position, as known during the winter of 1682–3, was that the *Expectation* had sailed from Dartmouth to challenge the Charter and perhaps to bring out some of the Company's own furs hidden from the wreck of the *Prudent Mary* on Tetherley's Island. The *James* had been sent after her and (though this was not yet known) had been lost at sea; and during the winter it had been discovered that the *Expectation* had put back to England after all. Rumours of a challenge from New England were also abundant, and several of the Company's servants were under grave suspicion. Radisson and Groseilliers had also moved from France to Canada; but whether the Committee knew this does not appear. By January 1683, this was still the extent of the Committee's knowledge, and the answer to de la Barre's memorandum made no mention of any specific interruption to trade. But during the winter and early summer, whilst the legal and diplomatic challenge of the French was met in London, a three-fold challenge was manifest on the Bay.

First to arrive was a vessel from Boston, the appropriately-named *Bachelor's Delight*. As the Committee reported the matter 'one Benjamin Gillam, sonne of Zachariah Gillam sayled from Boston in New England in July was a 12 m. [actually June 1682] in a ship called the *Bachelor's Delight* burthen about 50 Tons 10 guns and 14 men all Bachelors and very resolute Fellowes'. Young Benjamin Gillam had been in London earlier in the year, as the Committee discovered. He had for a certainty talked with his father, newly reappointed to command the *Rupert*, and had probably talked with his relation Ezbon Sandford, with other New Englanders in the Company's employ, and with James Knight.

It is not clear when, or how, the Committee first heard of the *Bachelor's Delight*. They later alleged that their information came from one of their own ships, but they had no ship from the Bay between the arrival of the *Diligence* (with Nixon's report) in October 1682, and the return of the *Diligence* once more in October 1683. The *Diligence* certainly did not bring the news in 1682, and the way in which the expedition is first described by the Committee deals only with the departure of the *Bachelor's Delight*, not with her voyage, so that the source of the information was probably a shipping report from Boston. At any rate, the Committee knew of her departure by April 1683.

The actual course of events in Nelson River in 1682 seems to have been that eventually recounted by the Hudson's Bay Company. But since in the end the whole story hinged on a few vital days it was almost inevitable that in the early stages all parties should have claimed that their ships arrived a day or so in advance of their rivals. Ultimately the Company's case was that the *Bachelor's Delight* had left New England on 21st June, 1682. She had arrived in Nelson River on 18th or 19th August and had moved some twenty-six miles up a 'Breach to the Northward' to settle on 'Bachelor's Island' in Nelson River.

Meanwhile Radisson and Groseilliers had left Quebec with two small ships, the *St. Pierre* and the *Ste. Anne*, fitted out by de la Chesnay and his associates. They had twenty-nine men, and apparently de la Chesnay himself accompanied them, although there is no mention of his taking any active part in the expedition. Their own original account was that they had arrived on 20th August, but later in argument they said that their arrival in the Ste. Theresa River (the Hayes River, separated from the Nelson by a low marshy point at its mouth) was a day earlier, 19th August. Radisson himself (at a later date, when he was once more in the service of the Hudson's

Bay Company) admitted that he had arrived after Gillam, whilst the surgeon and several members of the crew of the *Rupert* swore that the French from Canada did not arrive until 'about the one and Twentieth day of August 1682'. This, however, could only have been hearsay evidence, for it is certain that the *Rupert* was the last arrival and could not have witnessed the arrivals of the other two vessels. The French moved about ten miles up the Hayes River, and Radisson lost no time in visiting the Indians of the neighbourhood, to persuade them to come down and trade with the French, whilst Groseilliers busied himself with the construction of a house, or perhaps two houses, on the south bank of the Hayes.

The first knowledge which the French had of the presence of young Gillam and the New Englanders was when Radisson heard gun-fire on his return from visiting the Indians. This would be about 26th August. He found Gillam and his crew burying one of their company and approached in his canoe with such care, giving the appearance of Indians, that it was not until he had actually been allowed aboard the *Bachelor's Delight* that his identity and purpose were discovered. The details of this strange encounter in the Nelson River are, like so much of the career and achievements of Radisson, obscured by time and partisan evidence. Radisson contrives to give the impression that he almost alone was deluding the New Englanders, whilst Gillam said Radisson had seven canoes with fourteen 'savages' in company, and Gillam's mate, John Outlaw, said that Groseilliers also was present on this occasion.

The accounts all carry an air of naive surprise, but it is most likely that the only matter for surprise as between these two parties of interlopers, the New Englanders and the French, was the time and place of the encounter, for it is most probable that each knew of the other's intention to venture to Nelson River. Radisson alleged that his own backer, de la Chesnay, had offered the large reward of £1,000 to young Gillam to take part in the French expedition, whilst the members of the Hudson's Bay Committee who disliked Radisson later alleged that it was he who had first conceived the idea of a rival post in Nelson River, and that he had spoken of it to young Gillam when the latter was in London and had then sent him to New England, whence he arrived in Nelson River ahead of his father and the Company's ship *Rupert*. These are admittedly unsubstantiated charges, but they make it probable that the surprise was not quite so complete as Radisson pretended.

Having been identified, and having discovered that the *Bachelor's Delight* was herself an interloper and not in a position to quibble,

Radisson told Gillam that he and Groseilliers had fifty Frenchmen and a commission from the French crown to build a post and to forbid trade to aliens. Apparently there was a show of producing an imposing document of some kind, and the question later arose as to whether the French had in fact any such authority or whether their presence without warrant could be construed as simple piracy.

Then, when he continued his journey from Bachelor's Island to his own ships in the Hayes River, Radisson met the *Rupert* under old Zachariah Gillam coming in to land. Aboard was John Bridgar with his instructions to establish a post at Port Nelson, and with full equipment for so doing. Radisson, having spied out their strength, challenged their right. He assured them that he and Groseilliers had already built a fort, that they already had two ships and a numerous company of men, and that they expected the arrival of a third vessel. He even went so far as to say that the French had already been in residence for a year, and that they had over three hundred men there. There is no reason to suppose that Bridgar suspected Radisson at this point, or that he had any notion that there was any third party in the neighbourhood. It was in any case too late in the season for him to take the *Rupert* elsewhere, out of reach of French rivalry and out of the area of which Radisson maintained he had taken possession for France, so he tried to bring the *Rupert*, despite the French, into Nelson River. Even for this he was tragically late, for the *Rupert* was driven off-shore by ice on 21st October and was lost at sea with Zachariah Gillam and about nine of her crew.

The *Albemarle* had also been ordered to Nelson River in 1682, and Ezbon Sandford had been nominated second-in-command to Bridgar at the new post. But he had died on 6th October. The circumstances are not known, but it later became clear that his ship had not got to Port Nelson but wintered at Rupert River and went to the Nelson in the following summer, 1683. So when he had lost the *Rupert* Bridgar was left ship-less, defenceless and short of supplies, and he was henceforth utterly dependent on Radisson. The French appear to have succoured the fifteen or so men left from the English expedition and to have treated both them and the New Englanders amicably until the early spring. Then Radisson captured the bachelors' post, and their ship, in February. Gillam said this was effected after Radisson and a party of Frenchmen had stayed with him as guests for a fortnight, but Radisson said that it was after Gillam had stayed with the French. Thenceforth the New Englanders were closely guarded, their house was burned down, and their six guns were removed by Groseilliers.

Bridgar, at this time, was in difficulties in his post for lack of the cargo of the *Rupert*, especially for lack of powder to kill fresh provisions, and he did not know about the New Englanders until one of them escaped to give him the news of the capture of the bachelors' post. Then, to quote Groseilliers' rather incoherent account, 'having learned that there was yet another vessel, he felt obliged to oppose us.' He and some of his men visited the French post, stayed about three weeks, and were declared prisoners when they wished to depart. This made the capture and destruction of the post which Bridgar had built an easy matter, which Radisson soon accomplished.

The Hudson's Bay men place the capture of their post in June 1683, by which time the French, who had been very ill provided by their sponsors, with 'a very bad Barke ill maned and Worse Furnished with Necessaries laden with sorry refuge Goods that had been for the Most part of them in the ware houses above 20 years which barke was Accompanied by another Barke Much Worse then the first', were making preparations for leaving the scene of their exploits.

The French ships *St. Pierre* and the *Ste. Anne* had been sheered off as the ice rose in the rivers with the spring floods, and the French decided to 'cannibalise' the *St. Pierre* in order to make the *Ste. Anne* navigable. Then the Hudson's Bay men were to be sent to Rupert River at the Bottom of the Bay in the *Ste. Anne* whilst the New Englanders and most of the French were to sail to Quebec in the *Bachelor's Delight*. Jean Baptiste Chouart, son of Groseilliers, with seven men, was to stay behind to trade at Nelson River and was to receive a ship during the coming year.

At the last moment fears of conspiracy made the French take Bridgar to Quebec instead of sending him to the Bottom of the Bay, and twelve men on a leaky and ill-found *Ste. Anne* ultimately reached the Company's posts there, whilst the overburdened *Bachelor's Delight* brought her prisoners and cargo to Quebec on 20th October. There the New Englanders and their ship were released by Governor de la Barre, and so was Bridgar.

This colourful episode then became the subject of a long and obscure series of diplomatic interchanges and claims, not least of which was a claim for £5,000 damages from the French on account of the *Bachelor's Delight* herself. It was the Company's case that the *St. Pierre* and the *Ste. Anne* had, in fact, left Quebec before the warning note from Governor de la Barre had been sent in November 1682, and still more before it had come to the Company's attention in January 1683. Further, the note itself was without any foundation.

The British denial of de la Barre's claims was tacitly accepted and it was never claimed that Radisson and Groseilliers had any warrant from the French king. It was even doubtful if they had any from the Governor of Canada. Their expedition was, in fact, a 'private Piraticall Expedition against the Order and Prohibition of the Governour of Canada and was disowned afterwards by his most Christian Majesty and satisfaction directed'.

Further, the Company alleged that the English had 'frequented' Nelson River ever since Cabot's voyage in 1497, and that formal possession had been taken ever since Button's voyage. In the Company's own time, they came to insist that in 1669 [1670] Captain Newland had entered the Nelson River in the *Wivenhoe*, had 'settled' there and had nailed up the arms of the King of England. Nehemiah Walker came forward to swear that in 1670 he had gone ashore with Bayly on the north bank of the river, had stayed there in an Indian tent and had formally taken possession, nailing up the King's arms in brass. The Company made much, too, of Gillam's 'Treaty' with the Indians at this juncture, maintaining that it had bought the land from the Indians 'pour des considerations vallables', and they maintained that Groseilliers, in the Company's pay, had taken possession of Nelson River in the *Employ* in 1672 (though they quoted the date as 1662) when he had spent ten days there and had left presents for the Indians.

In answer to the French claim that Groseilliers and Radisson were Frenchmen and therefore no English claim could be based on their voyages, the Company replied that they had been merely super-cargoes, employed to direct trade with the Indians, and that the actual voyages were made by Englishmen. The French were 'no navigators or Skilled in Sailing to make a Discovery but only Usefull when we should arrive there having the Language of the Savages and so capable to Invite them Downe to Trade but the Voyages were Conducted by English Seamen and English Pilotts'. With this statement, when he had made his peace with the Company, Radisson agreed, saying that on the *Nonsuch* voyage of 1668 Groseilliers had served only as 'Interpreter amongst the Savages'.

Having made its replies on grounds of first discovery, the Groseilliers-Radisson-Gillam settlements, and subsequent trade, the Company came to the events of 1682–3. Here they avowed that de la Barre's note was the first challenge to their title and that, apart from the fact that the French irruption of that year was unsponsored and piratical, it was 'the First Time that ever the French did Sail a Vessell in Hudson Bay since the beginning of the World let them prove otherwise if they can'. After some early attempts to gloss over the fact that Benjamin Gillam was an interloper, who 'did not own the English Company', they established that the order of arrival in that decisive year at 'Port Nelson' was, first Benjamin Gillam, second Radisson, and third Bridgar. They saw in the late arrival of Bridgar (who had left London in May) signs of the treachery of Zachariah Gillam and piously felt that his inability to move to safe quarters, and his death with the loss of his ship, was a 'Just Reward of his perjury and perfidiousness'—but since they found the loss of the *Rupert* a severe blow to their own plans we may wonder how they finally reconciled their concepts of divine rewards and punishments to the facts.

In insisting that Benjamin Gillam arrived ahead of Radisson the Company may perhaps seem to have taken advantage of the ten days' discrepancy between French and English calendars at that time. But this is improbable since the evidence came from Gillam himself, his mate John Outlaw, several members of the crew of the *Rupert*, and ultimately Radisson himself. Of these all but Radisson used English dates alone; Radisson used no accurate dates and his testimony is hard to follow, but he clearly said that the New Englanders had already put in to the 'Branch to the Southward' before the arrival of the French. John Calvert, surgeon of the *Rupert*, carefully took the discrepancy in calendars into account; and he swore that the New Englanders arrived four days before the French.

The French case, apart from assertions that they had frequented the Bay since the early sixteenth century and that they had sent a ship to Nelson River in 1675, rested on the assertion that the English voyages were only in search of a North-west Passage, and that they made no settlements or trade and so could not establish a right to the territories. For this, said the French, ancient possession, or continual habitation, or trade, were needed. They, in their turn, claimed first settlement because Groseilliers and Radisson were French subjects, and they asserted that whereas they had long conducted an overland commerce with the Indians of the Nelson River area the English had never had a settlement there until 1682, in which year the order of arrival gave priority to the French since Radisson arrived (as they said) ahead of Bridgar and still more ahead of Benjamin Gillam. In another version they placed the arrival of Radisson three days ahead of Gillam and a further four days ahead of Bridgar, but they did not modify the claim that Radisson was first on the scene.

In all of this diplomatic interchange, which lasted till the end of the century, there is much evidence that the documents which have survived are the results of the 'briefing' of diplomats by the interested parties, so that quite untenable statements creep in since the diplomats who penned the letters were dealing merely with a routine matter. This explains the French assertion, at one stage, that the *Bachelor's Delight* had been lost in the ice as well as the *Rupert*. It explains too the statement that Bridgar had arrived before Benjamin Gillam. Anxious as the Company was to maintain the earliest possible arrival of Bridgar, no English claim was made that he had beaten Gillam; in fact if the Company intended to claim that anyone had arrived ahead of Radisson it would have to be the New England interlopers. Accordingly the (probably justifiable) priority of the *Bachelor's Delight* was insisted on throughout, and the Company alleged that Benjamin Gillam was under His Majesty's Protection though 'he did not owne the English Company'.

The self-confident knavery with which Radisson tricked both the New England and the Old England party, and the irony of the arrival of the four ships within a few days of each other after so many years of delay, give to the episode a vitality which the muddled accounts and the endless claims and counter-claims never quite disperse. The net outcome was that a French outpost was left at Nelson, to trade largely with goods taken from the English Company, and that the Company was left with a large outstanding claim for damages at a time when its prime need was for furs and for cash in hand.

Whether the loss of the *Rupert* could rightly be attributed to the presence of the French, and their veto on old Gillam's entry into the safety of Nelson River, is an open question. The Company always asserted that a claim lay, but the size of the claim varied with the years. By 1713, at the time of the negotiations for the Treaty of Utrecht, the *Rupert* was reckoned at £3,760 14s. 11d. and a detailed list of her cargo was submitted to prove the claim. By that time, however, interest (if it could be got) exceeded the original sum, and at £7,013 9s. 10d. made the total claim for the *Rupert* up to £10,774 4s. 9d. A more 'modest computation', as the Company itself described it, placed the loss of the *Rupert* at £6,000 in 1699, whilst the capture of Bridgar, his post and his men, was estimated at a round £25,000 and the goods taken and traded by Radisson at £3,500.

Although a precise account of the cost and cargo of the *Rupert* was in the end submitted, and interest was accurately worked out, these claims were not, and could not be, accurate. The gravest result from the episode was that the Company's trade had been interrupted, its basic titles had been challenged, and the confidence of the Indians had been seriously undermined. Such items could not figure in any estimate of damages, but they were well appreciated by the Committee of the Company, and they were probably used as a multiplying factor to raise the actual losses to the total of the mighty damages claimed.

Just as the claims for damages are almost a screen for the vindication of the Company's wider claims, so the endless disputes as to priority of days in 1682 cover a major dispute as to title. Here again, as in the claim for cash compensation, the dispute dragged on and merged with later quarrels in which the same fundamental problem was involved, and both sides were tempted into declarations of the absolute legal and ethical position for European countries taking possession of overseas territories.

The French claimed that their charter to the Canada Company of 1627 had granted to that company New France up to the Arctic Circle, and that this had followed after the Commission of 1540 to Roberval to take over the lands discovered by Verezzano in 1525 and by Cartier in 1534 and 1535, including the 'Baye du Nord'. Under charter of the Compagnie de la Nouvelle France, they maintained that Jean Bourdon had sailed into the Bay in 1656 and that in 1661 and again in 1663 mission voyages accompanied by a few soldiers had gone overland, in response to Indian pleas, to the Bottom of the Bay, where the Sieur Couture planted a cross and copper and lead plaques 'au pied d'un grand Arbre' in 1663. Despite Bourdon's voyage, the French had found it better to approach the Bay overland, and they founded a post at Nemiskau, two or three leagues from Rupert River, in 1661. They were building up a claim by prior discovery and subsequent trade, to give title to the French King which could then be passed to French companies. Such a title could, they asserted, also be supported by treaties with the Indians, in this case by the fact that the Iroquois had made formal submission to the French in 1665, and that de Lauzon, acting on behalf of the French King, had formally accepted the submission of each of the seventeen nations of the confederacy at Sault Ste. Marie in 1671. They denied that the exploring voyages of the English could give title, and they maintained that 'for Establishing the Right upon the possession of a Country is not sufficient to have Discovered the Same and to have Lived there some time but there must be an Ancient possession and a Continued habitation or at least a Trade maintained'.

With this the English agreed—but with a difference. Their view was that 'Whatever Chance Voyage may have been made or missions sent for the sake of Religion with soldiers to protect the Missionaries, the same could not bring any prejudice to the Right of His Majesties Subjects', which was deduced from first discovery. They gave themselves the advantage of speaking in round figures and alleged that they had been trading to the Bay for twenty years before the French challenged them, and thought it unreasonable to vouch French treaties and charters which would give them rights to the whole of North America. It was 'much most just and reasonable to rely upon Actuall discoveries and upon possession taken in view of all the world'.

Here the basic problems give point to this argument over an episode which did not involve more than sixty rather undistinguished men from all three parties to the dispute. For the French the treaties, rights and charters, applicable to Canada, the St. Lawrence basin, the Great Lakes and southwards, were also applicable to the north and the 'Baye du Nord'. For the English this was not acceptable, and the Company raised the fundamental issue when it claimed that the 'Country of Canada and that of Hudson's Bay are two different Provinces and have no Relation but that of Neighbourhood'. Hudson Bay was not a 'Dependance of Canada'.

Here, in the form of a dogmatic legal dictum, was posed the problem which Groseilliers and Radisson had posed as a practical economic problem—the rivalry of the Bay and St. Lawrence, the question whether the fur lands of the north were dependencies of Canada or not.

BOOKS FOR REFERENCE

HUDSON'S BAY RECORD SOCIETY—Vols. VIII, IX, XI.
NUTE, Grace Lee—*Caesars of the Wilderness* (New York, 1943).

CHAPTER XII

THE CHARTER VINDICATED AND THE FIRST
DIVIDEND PAID, 1683–1684

Whilst the Committee entered into this long argument they did not neglect the more immediate problems of organising and pursuing their trade. Foreseeing that the French had opened an issue which would not quickly be ended, the Committee requested that, pending the end of the dispute, the French King should be asked to issue injunctions to the Canadians forbidding further incursions and ordering immediate restitution. No such immediate safeguard could reasonably be expected although the government in France was by no means pleased by the filibustering enterprise of the Canadians. But the Committee continued nevertheless with their trade arrangements.

The election of the Duke of York as Governor in the midst of these troubles, in January 1683, promised well. He sent for the Company's Charter and seemed likely to take an active interest in the trade. But as the year wore on he proved a disappointment, more discriminating and aloof, less of a partisan, than the Company had expected. When he was asked to sign the instructions of the year, to Governor Sergeant, to Bridgar and to Captain Nehemiah Walker, he told Hayes 'that he did never signe any Orders or papers of any Company he was Governor of'. There was nothing in the Instructions which should have caused difficulty, especially in the light of his known views and enthusiasms.

Interlopers, whether foreigners or subjects of the British Crown, were to be seized, and the 'unfaithful servants' of the Company, with their incorrigible lapses into private trade, were to be closely watched. All officers were to take an oath, whilst officers and men alike were to enter into obligations for fidelity and good behaviour. As a further precaution they were to be warned that their baggage would be searched when they arrived back in England; the Committee were not prepared to accept any theoretical right to private trade in beaver, although in practice they were very reasonable. Further, Sergeant was told that the Company's trade had roused the hostility of the French of Canada (not necessarily those of Europe) and that he must look upon them as 'a standing enemy from whome you are never to expect any Friendship or faire Dealeing'. Rupert

River and Moose (Hayes Island) were therefore to be most alert, as the places of nearest settlement to the French.

Simple assertion of rights and attention to honesty was, however, by no means all that the Committee had in mind in 1683. Sergeant was told that since Chichewan (now renamed Albany in honour of the new Governor of the Company) was, on Nixon's showing, the place of the greatest trade it must be his own residence and the chief post. This was contrary to Nixon's advice, for he had found the Albany post at Bayly's Island difficult of access; and in fact Sergeant did not carry out this order until 1684, by which time the post had been moved to the south bank of the river. Charlton Island was still, despite Nixon's complaints, to be the rendezvous for the ships and the country trade, and the Governor was to leave his post every spring and settle himself at Charlton Island to organise his trade ready for the arrival of the ships.

But the Bay-side posts were not to occupy all of Sergeant's attention. He was firmly instructed to choose out strong and active servants who knew the Indian tongues and to send them inland to 'Draw downe the Indians by fayre and gentle meanes to trade with us'. Should this succeed in bringing large numbers to the posts it would entail a care that they did not overwhelm the Company's servants, and, both at the established posts and in the new areas to be opened up, the former practice of making treaties was to be pursued, so that the Company's 'right and propriety' and its 'sole freedome of Trade' might be recognised and affirmed. But Sergeant was not to depart from the Standard of Trade which Bayly had laid down.

Once more, the Governor was exhorted to do his utmost to grow as much provender as possible and was supplied with seeds for that purpose. He was encouraged, too, in the development of any new trade—fishing, making oil, or the working of isinglass. This side of his Instructions was accompanied by the trenchant warning that Charlton Island must be kept constantly occupied and fortified 'we intending as soone as may be to plant a Colloney there'. But there is no mention in the Minutes or in any other extant correspondence of this proposal and it is impossible to know how seriously we ought to take this isolated statement. Certainly it was an ambition which bore little fruit. If, indeed, it was a serious ambition it ended with the inauspicious experiment of allowing Governor Sergeant to take his family to the Bay.

For the rest, Sergeant's Instructions were taken up with news of the interlopers, and with quite unexceptionable moral counsels. In particular, he was to be careful that no Indian women were allowed within the Company's posts. The general tone was that of the shrewd but kindly men who, in the previous year, had directed that the officers of the interloper *Expectation* should be sent home for trial but that the common men, having been deluded, might be taken into the Company's service if they wished.

There was no reason why the Duke of York should not have subscribed such instructions, which were a fair enough reflection of the character and mood of the Company, and his refusal must be taken as a refusal to embroil himself in the Company's affairs. Despite this discouragement, preparations for another voyage were pushed on rapidly, and by April 1683 the Committee had again hired the *Diligence*, under Nehemiah Walker, and the *George* ketch of about sixty tons under John Abraham, former mate to Walker, whom the Committee appointed despite Nixon's poor opinion of him. Abraham was to sail to Port Nelson, to supply Bridgar there, for the Committee fondly expected Bridgar to have set up a post. The cargo was carefully bought, and much of Nixon's advice had been taken; there was a supply of buckwheat; bricks and building materials were cancelled at the last moment; and several Scots had been recruited. Besides their cargo the ships carried strict instructions to the Company's officers to seize all interlopers, and information of the sailing of the *Bachelor's Delight*. James Knight, although apparently in sympathy with the New Englanders, was left undisturbed in his post at Albany, but the other appointments of the previous year were all revoked except for Bridgar. Nixon himself was superseded by Henry Sergeant as Governor, and Gillam, Bond and Sandford, were all ordered home on the understanding that if they proved to have no connection with the New England venture or the *Expectation* the Company would continue to employ them, but that the Company could not trust them further until their loyalty had been investigated.

The instructions to the Company's employees were followed by an injunction to the Governor of Massachusetts bidding him impound the *Bachelor's Delight* and her cargo until the rights of her voyage could be settled legally. Here James Hayes was once more the prime mover in asserting the Company's rights, and the injunction was followed by the grant of a power of attorney from the Company, first to seize the *Bachelor's Delight* and then the Company's ships the *Rupert* and the *Albemarle* if they should break 'their Faith and great trust with us' and bring any contraband trade to New England. Finally, Hayes secured a royal warrant directed to the Governor and Council of Massachusetts, telling them to seize any interloping vessels and to prosecute their crews according to the law.

In the midst of all this stern writing of chartered rights, royal injunctions and powers of attorney, it is difficult to remember that the Company was still but a young and almost private venture, using at the utmost two or three ships a year, keeping at most fifty men overseas (Nixon put this figure as a maximum), working in the gravest difficulties and not yet able to pay a dividend. The sense of proportion, and of the direct personal relations involved, is restored when we find even the efficient Hayes writing to the Governor of Massachusetts that 'We had a List of the Names of the Owners but have lost it', or when the new Governor Sergeant is told to treat the Indians with justice and humanity, to punish and discourage all dissolute and profane persons, and to see to it that Common Prayer be daily read and the Lord's Day observed. The close personal activity and attention to detail of those who might seem to be fully occupied with high policy is shown when 'Mr. Frampton' claimed a three-years'-old account for tobacco supplied. No entry to cover his claim could be found in the books, but he supported his case by saying that Sir James Hayes knew all about it.

Such incidents restore the intimacy and close personal relations of this young Company at a time when its public correspondence tends to give the impression of something resembling a great, and rather pompous, government department at work.

It was a sombre and purposeful mood, nevertheless, in which the Committee dealt with these matters, for this was a time, in 1683, when the March fur sale failed. Almost half of the furs shipped in 1682 were inferior in quality (probably the result of trading with new Indians who had not yet been trained to prepare their skins properly) and the *coat* beaver left over from 1682 still found no buyers in 1683. The Committee also feared with reason the invasion of their English markets and pleaded that the Navigation Acts be enforced so as to exclude beaver which came from intermediate traders, not from the country of origin.

Though sufficiently established to rouse the French, the Company was yet far from solvent, and Committee members had to lend money to pay the tradesmen in July—Christopher Wren lent £200. Yet the servants were given advances of pay before they sailed, the Governors were not stinted in their presents of casks of canary, Sergeant was given a gratuity to help him get together his outfit, Nehemiah Walker was given a gratuity of £80 for his past good services, and smaller gratuities were given to some common servants.

The fact that the Company, despite all its difficulties, never ceased to aim at modest expansion, can be seen not only in the

unrealistic order to send men inland, but also in the permission given
to Governor Sergeant to take his family, and in the recruitment of
'Mr. John French, M.A.' as Minister of the Bay. The Committee
paid £5 6s. 0d. for his Bibles, prayer books and homilies. Sergeant's
'parcell of Women' (as the Committee later described his establishment) consisted of his wife and her companion Mrs. Maurice, the
first white women to winter by the Bay. He also had his son with
him. So domesticated a Governor inevitably suffered disrespect from
the outrageous Captain Nehemiah Walker on the outward voyage
in the *Diligence*, and if the womenfolk and the priest were meant
to be the start of settlement by the Bay, the Company chose an
inauspicious conductor for them.

In all of this the Committee were acting with a confidence which
was in complete contrast with their knowledge of the situation, for
Governor Sergeant and his family were sent off in the early summer
of 1683 while the Committee were still uncertain of the details of
events in Nelson River in 1682, of the fate of the *James* ketch, or the
exploits of the interloper *Expectation* which Maximilian Keech had
been sent to capture.

It was not until the ships returned to London in the fall of 1683
that the Committee had to consider the first authentic reports of the
events and the situation in Nelson River. This information was
brought by the *George*, a small ship which had been sent out to
reinforce the post which Bridgar was supposed to have established
in 1682. Although there is no clear account of the news which the
George now brought, the position was that the *Albemarle*, which
should have accompanied Bridgar and the *Rupert* on their ill-fated
journey in 1682, had instead put into Rupert River after the death
of her master, Ezbon Sandford. There she had spent the winter. In
the early summer of 1683 John Abraham sailed her from Rupert
River to Nelson River, arriving after the departure of Radisson and
his prisoners, to find young Chouart and his small party of seven
Frenchmen in possession.

Abraham built some sort of a post, which the Committee accepted
as being on the south side of Nelson River; in fact it was probably
on the north shore of Sir Edward Dering's Island. This post of the
Company at Nelson River was named Fort Hayes, and there the
George joined Abraham and the *Albemarle*, bringing James Walker,
who had been appointed warehousekeeper to assist Bridgar. It was
Walker's letter, dated from Hayes Fort, which gave the Committee
an authentic account of the events of the previous year and of the
existing situation. Still, as news began to come through, the Com-

mittee were better informed of the disasters of the previous year than of the steps which had been taken to remedy the situation. It was, however, certain that some sort of post had been established to dispute Nelson River with the French.

The *George* was by far the smaller of the two ships sent out in 1683. The main outfit of the year had been carried once more in the hired ship *Diligence*, in which Captain Nehemiah Walker had taken out Governor Sergeant and the bulk of the trade goods, destined for the Bottom of the Bay. Walker now brought home from Moose not only a superfluity of furs but momentous tidings and a party of highly controversial prisoners.

The interloper *Expectation*, rumours of whose departure for the Bay had caused the Committee (under Hayes' dominance) to take the precipitate action which resulted in the loss of the *James* ketch in 1682, had spent the winter in Dartmouth harbour and emerged renamed the *Charles* in April or May 1683. She was laden with woollens and other trade goods, with guns, powder, shot, kettles and the like, to the value of about £1,400, and her course had crossed Walker's on his outward voyage (exactly where was a point which was hotly discussed but was never clearly determined) and acting on his orders he had taken her prisoner. He had put some of his own crew aboard and had later wrecked his prize on Charlton Island in an attempt to sail her down to the Bottom of the Bay.

The *Expectation* appears to have been a well-found ship. Her cargo had cost a considerable sum and had been got together with knowledge and skill. The heavy expenses involved in preparing and maintaining ship and cargo had been paid by a syndicate of four, of whom one was Charles Boone, at one time a Member of Parliament, and another 'John Phipps . . . now in America'. About him his relation (probably his brother), the Thomas Phipps of whom the Committee had held such well-founded suspicions the previous year, gave evidence that he had been informed of the whole project and had been entrusted with the management of his relation's share of the venture. The project was apparently well known in City circles, and the four partners were offered tempting prices for some of their share, for it was expected that the profit would be at least a hundred per cent.

The management of the ship and trade was confided to Richard Lucas, a former servant of the Company who had sailed as mate on several voyages and had been wrecked in the *Prudent Mary* in 1680. The Company had not treated him hardly and had given him two gratuities for his work over the wreck, but probably the factor which led him to take employment under the interlopers was that he was allowed by them to carry goods to trade on his own account, whereas the Company's attitude towards private trade was steadily hardening. A similar temptation had led Daniel Lane, a foremast hand who was under engagement to the Company, to desert and sail with Lucas. His desertion enabled the Company to sue him for £3,000 and to get him thrown into the Poultry debtors' prison, from which he wrote offering to give evidence on the Company's behalf if they would release him. His offer was accepted.

The capture of the *Expectation*, alias the *Charles*, and the return of her captain and some of her crew as prisoners, immediately led the Company into a long law suit in the Admiralty Courts. The opening 'Libel' was filed in December 1683, and the final judgment was not given until December 1684. The suit revealed that Walker had carried through the affair with much of his habitual bravado; he had tried to lure Lucas aboard his ship by an invitation to dine and had then boarded the *Expectation*. Lucas, having failed to escape by sailing into the ice, tried to resist the boarders and 'made a pase' at the first man on deck. But he was knocked down before he could do anything. Walker then helped himself to the choicer parts of the *Expectation*'s cargo, eight or ten gallons of brandy, half a hundred-weight of sugar and about six gallons of sherry and, it was alleged, declared that he was acting by authority from the King and the Duke of York, that he was now master of the *Expectation* and would sink her if he wished.

It is difficult to see that in his major actions Walker was doing more than carry out his instructions to seize any interloper with all goods on board, although the minor oppressions could not be so supported by authority and gave grounds for counter-accusations of piracy, especially when the Hudson's Bay men finished the voyage by needlessly wrecking the ship. Much turned upon the place where the *Expectation* was taken, and about this there was a good deal of hard swearing on both sides, the Company's witnesses stating that she was taken near Cape Charles within Hudson Strait, and was clearly covered by the Company's Charter, whereas the interlopers maintained that she was taken on the high seas, at least a hundred leagues from Hudson Bay, before she had traded or could possibly have traded with any place covered by the Charter.

As the case proceeded Lucas, like Lane, made his peace with the Company and was admitted once more to their employment. His evidence, as sworn earlier in the suit, could not alter significantly, but probably the fact that he was known to have changed allegiance would prevent his being relied on, and as he was a material witness it is not surprising that judgment was given for the Company and all concerned, from the Committee down to the owners of the *Diligence*, were absolved from any claim by the interlopers. Even so, the case rumbled on for years before the Company could be sure that it had heard the last of the *Expectation*, and even though it appeared to be vindicated at law—which was in itself a most valuable point for the Company—it was to discover that law was an expensive commodity. The charges of the case came to £549 2s. 5d., and of this only £39 was 'recovered at law' as costs. 'Profit and Loss' had to bear the remaining £510 2s. 5d. Against this might perhaps be set the jack-knives, fowling-guns, pistols, duffles, red broadcloth, shot and brandy, which had been rescued from the wreck of the *Expectation*. But they were valued only at £76 19s. 7d., and the Company was a clear loser in the episode, even if the cost of the *James* in the previous year is left out of the account.

For Nehemiah Walker the outcome was still more unfortunate. The evidence given in the trial left on the Committee an impression which, added to Nixon's denunciations and the reports of Walker's ill-conduct towards Governor Sergeant, led to a resolution never to employ him again. This was harsh treatment for one who in this matter had merely carried out his instructions with a vigour which proved most salutory. But Walker's defects were glaring, and the Committee could not afford unreliable sea-captains.

The legal action, unsatisfactory as it might have seemed, had at least given a clear vindication of the Company's chartered rights, and the costs must be reckoned as money well spent on this account. Less clear, but equally important, was the fact that the action convinced the City of London that the Company was well-connected at Court and could defend its privileges. This aspect was revealed when, some fifteen years later, the Company itself referred to this verdict 'which they [its rivals] would insinuate was because the Prerogative was High in those days'.

The *Diligence* had not only brought the prisoners from the *Expectation* home in 1683. She had brought a good cargo too.

Despite the failures to settle and trade at Nelson River, the Company's posts at Moose and Albany—the Bottom of the Bay—had continued a profitable trade during 1682-3, and in October of 1683 the *Diligence* and the *George* brought the produce of the year to London. The *George* brought a mere hundred and eighty beaver, but the *Diligence* brought 20,175 beaver of different kinds, together with a proportion of other furs, fox, otter, musquash, fisher and elk.

This compared reasonably with the returns of previous years, 24,123 beaver in 1681 or 18,680 in 1682. But those years had brought to the Company more peltry than the London market could absorb, and the cargo of 1683 again proved excessive. The sale in November 1683 produced only £4,536 6s. 8d., and once more the *coat* beaver proved unsaleable. The Company had over 7,000 *coat* beaver on its hands. Fortunately it now had its own warehouse, having moved into Scriveners' Hall as a permanent office and taken over the warehouse there. But although the problem of storage space was thus dealt with, the Committee had to face new problems raised by this continuity of stock-in-hand. It became necessary to employ a permanent warehousekeeper, to keep moths out of the skins and to keep them in condition pending sale, matters which had not arisen in the days when a temporary warehouse could be hired on the safe assumption that the furs would be sold as soon as they could be sorted and lotted. The piling up of the *coat* beaver therefore cut the Company's cash-in-hand in two ways and in itself went far to make a more continuous system of accountancy inevitable.

All of this made the provision of an outfit for 1684 more difficult. But £4,000 odd, the produce of the sale of November 1683, was enough for immediate needs. The Committee had at last succeeded in getting back from Sir Robert Clayton the Charter, pledged to him in 1679, redeemed in 1680, but somehow or other returning to his possession in the negotiations over the loan of 1682 although Clayton's terms were rejected in that loan. He seems to have had an obsession with the Charter, and the Company had to make many applications before it could get it from him. It is quite possible that the terms of the mortgage in which the 1682 loan was negotiated were accepted by Clayton as an opening for taking possession of the actual territories of the Company, whereas to the Committee the mortgage was nothing but a formality, a legal form of words giving security for a loan, which was never contemplated as a possible threat to title. At least it is clear that the Committee had been foolish enough to take money on mortgage, that Sir Robert was strangely constant in his desire to keep the Charter in his possession, and that the Committee realised that something was afoot and proved equally persistent in getting the Charter into its own 'black box'. It must have been a relief to those members who had any suspicions of the hard-dealing former Treasurer when this was accomplished. For the rest, the produce of the 1683 sale could not be considered satisfactory, but it gave enough funds to allow the preparation of the 1684 voyage.

For this, the sub-committee for trade was ordered to meet daily, and the usual care went into the purchases. Nixon was on hand, to advise if needed, for he had come home in the *Diligence*, once more the guest of the unpredictable Nehemiah Walker, and now with the added slight that he had been recalled 'in regard of your great age and disability to travaile and endure the Hardship'—which was an ignominious adaptation of his own truculent 'I am antient and water doeth not agree with me!'

Moreover, the return of defective goods from the Bay had begun to be a very salutory reminder of the need for care in purchasing goods. The return of 12,000 long knives in 1682 had been a serious warning; and defects had also been reported in about a thousand other knives, 141 guns, 740 powder horns, 720 scrapers and 346 sword blades. These were all goods on which an Indian's life might depend and in which the Company could not afford to make mistakes. Other goods, copper lace, women's stockings, knitted caps and brass wire, would not have such disastrous effects, but they would destroy confidence and prevent a return of Indians in future years. The returned goods were partly repaired and put in good order, partly sold at auction; the Committee began early to prepare a 'Sheame of what goods are necessary to buy against the next Shipping'. Now, too, workmanlike attempts were made to bring data derived from accounts of stock in hand and goods traded into the plan of purchases, and a sign of the inevitable effect of European trade on the habits and economy of the Indians was shown when the Committee resolved that for 1684 two years' provisions of flour, oatmeal and pease, should be provided 'in Regard the Natives Shall be Supplyed with some as they have need by way of trade'.

With all their insistence on the discovery of new trades, and the suggestions which they put to their Governors for developing isinglass, feathers and minerals, the Company had so far achieved nothing but an experimental shipment of isinglass. Now came a new possibility, for their surgeon brought home on the *Diligence* a box of castor, or castoreum, the gland secretion from 'beaver stones' which had considerable value as a medicament and later as a base for perfumes. Dr. Kerr was allowed to keep his box of castoreum, but the Committee realised that here was a commodity which was being wasted, and henceforth encouragements to the Indians to bring in castoreum as well as skins form a regular feature of the Committee's instructions.

As the Admiralty action over the *Expectation* ran its course, and the disputes with the French drew to no very clear conclusion, the

Committee pushed ahead with normal business. After a careful survey of the proposed cargo they decided early in 1684 that the Bottom of the Bay would require sixty-four tons of goods and Fort Hayes (Nelson River) fifty-three tons. But they decided also that the establishments must be considerably increased for purposes of defence, and that there should be two posts in the Nelson, one in the 'North River' (the Nelson) and the other in the 'South River' (the Hayes). Nine men had been left in Fort Hayes in 1683, and they were now to be reinforced by a further thirty-one.

The Committee therefore decided to hire two ships for 1684, and though originally they thought that eighty tons burthen would be ample, they settled on the *Happy Return* of a hundred tons, and on the pink *Lucy*. Both were loaded with guns, 'petteroes', halberds, swords, ammunition, grenades, pikes and drums, in addition to the normal trade cargo; and both were placed under men with experience of the Bay. The *Happy Return* was to sail under William Bond, and the *Lucy* under John Outlaw, former mate to Benjamin Gillam on the *Bachelor's Delight*. Both men had a background of opposition to the Company; and both had come to accept the Company's terms.

The hiring of the *Happy Return*, despite the fact that she was a little larger than was ideal, may have been accepted because she was the property of the Company's Treasurer and Banker, Stephen Evans. There was nothing at all reprehensible in this, and it was common for members of the Company, and of the Committee, to provide shipping and goods and to undertake the insurance of the voyages both as individuals and in combinations or syndicates. Indeed, as early as 1676 William White, a factory hand, had his arrears of wages made up to £50 by a gratuity and put this into the general stock, becoming a shareholder while he remained an employee. He also supplied brass-ware to the Company and acted as a general factotum, buying and selling for his fellow-servants and even lending money to the ships' captains. Gerrard Weymans also, a member of the Committee, was the owner of the *Diligence*, which had been many times hired for the Company; and Samuel Ongley, a shareholder, was a haberdasher who sold the shirts which the Company required. Innumerable examples of this sort could be quoted, and the only check which had been thought necessary was the resolution of 1681 which enjoined that 'Every Member haveing share or part in any Goods to be sould to the Company, or Shipp to be Fraited for the Companies use, shall if he be then present or in any waies privy to any such Bargaine declare his Interest to the

Company and cause the same to be Recorded otherwise on discovery to be made thereof it shall be Deemed fraud in the Company and every such Member shall forfeit his whole stock or submitt to such Mulct as a Generall Court shall Impose'.

The practice of allowing members to undertake lucrative business leading to a contract with the Company meant that the Company achieved some indirect control over the subsidiary businesses of its trade. But it also had the result of allowing individual members who so speculated to reap a profit from the trade before the general trade itself was in a position to pay a dividend, in the same way as the pseudo-debenture borrowings allowed interest to be paid on such loans before the general stock had earned a share-out. Thence, probably, derived some of the steady support which the Company enjoyed during its long probation period before the first dividend was declared.

But that period was now, in 1684, drawing to a close. Throughout the winter the unsaleable *coat* beaver had been carefully looked after and divided into lots. The Committee now decided to mix it with the newly-arrived furs from 'Port Nelson' and the Bottom of the Bay and to offer the mixed lots for sale in February 1684. Knowing that ultimately their furs must in part at least be bought for the European market, they asked one of their number to discover from his trade connections on the continent whether the 'Canada Company' had brought good cargoes to the French sales. But the weather then broke, in February 1684, and no news could be got from the continent for nearly eight weeks. Thus isolated from the continent, the Committee postponed the sale until 12th March, then to 19th, and then, starting at the unambitious 'upset price' of eight shillings a pound, sold all the furs at prices varying from 8s. 2d. up to 9s. 2d. The total realised was £8,575 2s. 9d. to which one buyer, Peter Barr, contributed over half (£5,086 13s. 3d.).

The Committee's relief at getting rid of the stock of *coat* beaver was such that a week after the sale, on 25th March, 1684, they voted themselves and their fellow stockholders their first dividend—of fifty per cent! To make the gesture more notable still, they resolved to pay their Governor, His Royal Highness James, Duke of York, in gold; the rest were to be paid in warrants on the goldsmiths, that is by cheques drawn on Stephen Evans and Company or on Thomas Cook and Company.

It was a heady moment. The Committee further resolved to hire a third ship, the *John and Thomas* of 120 tons, for the 1684 voyage, the Governor's dividend was made up to guineas instead of pounds and was presented to him 'in Gold in a faire imbrodered purse', and the small band of thirty-seven stockholders got their dividends. These varied from £450 paid to William Yonge, and £350 to Sir Robert Clayton and Sir Edward Dering, down to several sums of £25 to holders of a mere £50. Sir James Hayes though still Deputy Governor had by this time let his holding dwindle to £300 and he only got a dividend of £150.

Goodwill was so general that Mate Lucas was given a post on the newly-hired ship despite his past history; Edward Randolph was voted a piece of plate of £10 value for acting as the Company's agent at Boston in the affair of the *Bachelor's Delight,* and even Nehemiah Walker was given a loan of £50 'Considering he has Beene and Old Servant of the Company'.

On some things, however, the Committee would not relax; the old Standard of Trade was to be insisted on and sent out to 'Port Nelson', and Nixon (still on hand in London and still not completely paid) was given a very long cross-questioning on the reasons why he had lowered it—so long that the Committee wearied and adjourned the sessions. In the end he was paid the arrears of his salary in full although the Deputy Governor (by then Sir Edward Dering) 'Declared his Dislike' since Nixon had lowered the Standard. In the letter outwards to Governor Sergeant of this year, 1684, the Committee were still quite convinced that Nixon had been wrong to act as he had done; they found his reasons, mustered 'in his Councell booke as he calls it', slender and weak, and they insisted that Sergeant should undo the damage. He was to try to get nine beaver for the $3\frac{1}{2}$ foot guns, ten skins for the 4 foot guns, eleven for the $4\frac{1}{2}$ foot and twelve for the 5 foot guns. Further, he was to restore the martens to eight for a beaver, since they were becoming the Company's best furs and Nixon had changed the ratio to four for a beaver; moose were to be restored from one to two for a beaver, and the greatest change was to be in musquash, where Nixon had established the rate as twelve to a beaver and the Committee wanted fifty, since they sold in London for only $2\frac{1}{2}d.$ each.

Experience in trade was giving the Committee a more authoritative and less fussy tone in its correspondence. Experience was teaching other things too. Forty guns 'such fashion as the Interloping guns but far surpasses them in goodness' were sent out, and the indents for goods were compared with the year's trade and the amount of stock on hand at the different posts. This showed that the Governors were ordering goods recklessly; there should have been 962 guns remaining in the country (though the Committee's accounts made the total 991) and the annual trade was something less than four hundred. Yet the Governors ordered a further 1,150 regardless of the fact that they had over two years' supplies on hand, many of them beginning to suffer from rust.

Experience showed, too, that Governor Sergeant's womenfolk had caused a great deal of trouble, and although the Committee at one time consented that Hugh Verner's wife should go out to join him at Rupert River (provided he paid her passage and allowed the Company £12 a year for her 'diet') the decision was later revoked 'upon divers good considerations' and the Committee resolved that neither she nor any other woman should go out. So, in effect, ended the Committee's project for establishing a colony in Rupert's Land.

The preparations for this 1684 voyage reveal several minor points of interest, such as the first employment of Henry Kelsey, later to distinguish himself so signally as an explorer and a trader. He was taken on as an apprentice, in itself a significant demonstration of the Committee's acceptance of the need to train up skilled personnel. The only reference to anyone else of his name in the Company's books is to a 'Captain Kelsey' who had supplied the Company with a dinner as part of the preparations for Gillam's second voyage in 1670. The two may have been related, for some sort of personal contact must have preceded young Kelsey's start on so adventurous a career, but the connection has never been proved.

Other significant developments were the employment of more Scots, the building of two Greenland shallops, 'the fittest boates to make discoveries', and the reiterated decision to make a settlement in 'Slood River' (Eastmain). The settlement was to be made by Brian Norbury, one of two brothers engaged on Nixon's recommendation, whose parents were 'persons of good value' and who might have made a good surveyor, for he had been 'entred in the Mathematicks, and hath a peculiar Genius for making of Landskips'. The isinglass mine was the chief objective here, and men and equipment were sent out for the purpose.

The successful sale of 1684, and the issue of the Company's first dividend, fitted into a period in which the Company was gathering its knowledge to organise and develop its trade. Of all its actions in that year none is more significant than the determination to train the Company's own officers by an apprentice system.

BOOKS FOR REFERENCE

Hudson's Bay Record Society—Vols. VIII, IX, XI.

CHAPTER XIII

RADISSON RECAPTURES NELSON RIVER

More important than the instructions, or than anything else connected with the 1684 voyage, was the fact that at the last possible moment the Committee suddenly admitted Radisson once more to the Company's service. On the eve of the departure of the ships they were told by Sir James Hayes and William Yonge that Radisson was again in England, and was protesting his fidelity to the Company. Hayes and Yonge were clearly summing up previous negotiations of which the rest of the Committee were already informed, for they announced straight away that they had made an agreement with him for £50 a year and a £200 share of the stock—which now at last had paid a dividend. He was to hold the stock during his life and good behaviour. All of the Committee agreed except Gerrard Weymans; he was a merchant with trade connections in France and elsewhere on the continent, importing Baltic hemp and pipe staves, timber, honey, bay rum, Mediterranean marbles, and furs, and exporting cloths, and was probably better informed about conditions in France than most of the Committee. But there seems no reason to believe that he had any particular information about Radisson and he was, in any case, over-ruled. Radisson's services were accepted and warmly welcomed, and he was given a silver tankard.

Behind this acceptance of the renegade lay a very considerable story. There was undoubtedly a widespread 'official' French wish not to antagonise England at this time, and consequently a fear that de la Chesnay, Radisson and the Canadian merchants engaged in the 1682 voyage to Nelson River, might find no official support and might even be made the scapegoats of the diplomatists. There was also a great deal of personal ambition and of personal hostility involved. Out of it arose the belief that Radisson had been 'debauched' by Gideon Godet, French Protestant servant of the British Ambassador to Paris, Lord Preston. Godet, it was said, promised Radisson that he should be made perpetual secretary to Preston and that, since his English wife, daughter of Sir John Kirke, had now died, he should marry Margaret Godet, daughter of the intermediary. Gideon Godet without any doubt played an important part in smuggling Radisson to London at this time, and Radisson certainly married Godet's daughter Margaret, but the rest is surmise. Radisson himself later swore that on his return to France in 1683–4 he had been called into consultation by Colbert's son, de Seignelay, who had succeeded his greater father as Minister of the Marine. Also involved was Callières, later to be one of the French plenipotentiaries at the Treaty of Ryswick. The two statesmen reasoned with Radisson and Callières dictated to him a memorandum 'pour terminer les differends' with England and then instructed Radisson to get a pass from Lord Preston which would allow him to sail under English auspices to Nelson River, there to withdraw young Chouart and the other Frenchmen whom he had left there, and thus to undo the work of his 1682 expedition and leave the English in sole possession.

Such an account fits in well with the later statements of the Hudson's Bay Committee, who said that Radisson came to them in 1684 at the orders of 'a great minister of France' and that he set out for the Bay, once more a servant of the Company 'by concert of the Ministers of France'. Much the same story, too, was given in James Hayes' later account of the affair. Hayes then reported to the King that 'two *Gentlemen* very well knowne to his Lordship' brought to Lord Preston a written proposal that Radisson and Groseilliers should go to Port Nelson 'under the Passport of the Hudson's Bay Company' and should bring out the French whom they had left behind there.

There was certainly some sort of official French connivance at the back of Radisson's return to the English Company in 1684. But his second desertion from France was not without danger to himself, as appears from a memorandum about an 'officier français du détachement de la Marine qui revient du Canada à qui l'on fait injuste demande. Si les Anglais veuillent il leur remettra la Baie d'Hudson. ... Il scait toutes choses'. The memorandum was endorsed 'Faire arrester le faire mettre à la Bastille'. But Radisson seems never to have suspected how near he was to imprisonment, nor to have had any compunction about the part he proposed to play. He seems to have sailed through the whole affair with the utmost self-confidence, and indeed the business was being managed by personages in whom he should surely have placed his trust. On his arrival in England he presented himself to Charles II and to the Duke of York, and their recommendation went far to reconcile the Committee of the Hudson's Bay Company to him.

Already there was within the Committee a powerful group which had begun to work for Radisson's return to England, and which appears to have been the first to make a move. It was alleged that William Yonge, an old and reputable member of the Company, who had paid his £300 for a full share as early as July 1670, was the prime mover. Inspired by genuine confidence in the man, and mindful of the origins of the British approach to the Bay, Yonge sent '3 or four Insinuating Letters' to Radisson in Paris. James Hayes was also involved with Yonge, and when it began to appear that Radisson might respond to the overtures a small private sub-committee of the Company was set up which 'for more privacy' held its meetings at the Half Moon Tavern in Cheapside—a tavern reputed to be the centre of much crypto-papist pro-French caballing.

This 'Half Moon' Committee had considerable influence and knowledge, and although William Yonge seems to have been the first to make contact with Radisson himself, it was Hayes who carried the greater weight once the project was launched. It had been Hayes who had first heard that Radisson was back in France fresh from the capture of Bridgar and the English expedition to Nelson River, in 1683, with the detail that he had reached La Rochelle in a French frigate. Hayes had thereupon written from his country house at Great Tew in Oxfordshire to the Duke of York's secretary (a brother of Christopher Wren) to explain that Radisson had gone post-haste to Paris to explain the great value of the Bay. Hayes hoped that influence might be brought to bear to get the British ambassador, Lord Preston, to press the French King for examplary justice. So the Company might be rescued out of the 'Jawes of the French Leviathan'. If the French could be diverted from Nelson River for but one year, wrote Hayes, the Company would then be 'so well provided by the next yeare after that they shall find it a very difficult thing to make any future attempts with successe'.

Preston was therefore instructed to press the Company's complaint, and he put forward several memorials to de Seignelay, to whom the French deputed the problem. Preston found that the French did not at this time deny the Company's case. At the utmost they deferred action until reports from Canada should have stated the Canadian side of the affair. But even in this there was no real enthusiasm to support Radisson and de la Chesnay. These two were involved in an inevitable quarrel with the farmers of the French dues over the *Quart* of the beaver taken in Nelson River, and they were also involved in a back-scenes struggle between the supporters of Frontenac, La Salle and southern expansion by the Mississippi on the one hand, and the supporters of de la Barre, the Jesuits and expansion to the northward, on the other. Moreover James Duke of York was the chief hope of the French diplomats who wished to reintroduce Roman Catholicism as the state religion into Great Britain; but he was also the Governor of the Hudson's Bay Company and (despite his refusal to countersign the 1683 orders for Governor Sergeant) was a firm exponent of British claims.

So Radisson and Groseilliers were of only secondary importance in French eyes in 1684; the major issues were the security of the English alliance and the dominance at that time of the La Salle-Mississippi group led by Callières and the Abbés Bernou and Renaudot. It was not, however, until late in April 1684 that any kind of policy began to emerge from the confusion of plans and personalities at Paris. Until then Radisson and Groseilliers were riding high, and the Company and its Committee, and the British Ambassador acting on their behalf, were tormented by doubts and fears. Then a royal ordinance decreed that the furs brought out from Nelson River must be subject to the usual tax of one-fourth levied on all furs in Canada. This meant that the profits hoped for by de la Chesnay and his syndicate would disappear in taxes and that Radisson and Groseilliers had very little hope of getting their promised reward; it was a sign, too, of the decline of de la Barre's influence, for he openly supported de la Chesnay. Towards the end of the month came the second indication that official French opinion had turned against the Port Nelson venture when Lord Preston was informed that the Governor of Canada had been ordered to 'restore the possession of Port Nelson, and of all which they had violently taken, to the English'.

This was indeed a happy issue for the Company, but even so it was by no means clear that such an order could reach Canada in time to take effect in 1684, and in the meantime the Company had been faced with the duty of preparing and sending out Governor Sergeant and the 1683 outfit, grappling with the failures of the fur sales, submitting to the shrewd censures of the returned Nixon, vindicating the Charter in the Admiralty Courts against the claims of the interloper *Expectation*, and preparing the cargoes for the outfit of 1684. The successful sale of March 1684 must have come just as the first inklings of the official French attitude were coming through, and the combined success in the Admiralty Court, in the London fur market and in the Paris salons might well have gone to the heads of less distracted men. Whilst the first dividend was still a bare week old the news of the French decisions began to arrive; but no firm order could yet be depended on. So the currents leading to the recall of Radisson began to work.

F

Preston 'durst not write it positively' until he had been directly informed by a minister of the order to restore Port Nelson, and it was clear that the French were anxious to combine placation with the maximum delay. It was therefore a shrewd move of James Hayes, William Yonge and their 'Half Moon party' to entice back Radisson into the Company's service, to play upon his rising conviction that the French would not in any case support his settlement or grant him his furs, and to send him out to uproot his own post. That de Seignelay and Callières should have intervened to persuade Radisson to accept the English offers, and that the latter should actually have dictated to Radisson the terms of his acceptance (as Radisson alleged) must have been due to their desire to find a solution which would quiet the English without formally abandoning the French-Canadian claims.

Provision was also made for Groseilliers to come over to England, and the Company would have welcomed him. But prime reliance was placed on Radisson—and that must have been little comfort to a Committee which, despite the fact that he had been forced to take an oath and to give security in gold (he pretended that he had left the money with the Committee so that a monument might be raised to his memory should he die on the expedition!) knew only too well how doubtful was his loyalty. In fact, their best insurance against renewed treachery was Radisson's knowledge that he could not hope to get full protection, or even a free market for his furs, in France even although he was sponsored unofficially by two great French ministers. Gerrard Weymans cannot have been alone in thinking that Radisson could not be trusted. Nevertheless he was perforce welcomed and was sent forthwith to the Bay, with special poultry and fresh provisions aboard the *Happy Return* for his personal use, and with instructions to the Company's servants to treat him with all respect 'as one in whome we have entire confidence and trust', whose advice was to be followed in reducing the French factory and in making the Company's settlement 'in and aboute Port Nelson'.

The slim confidence in Radisson's loyalty must have given the Committee many uneasy hours during his absence in 1684, for until his return in the autumn there could be no proof that confidence had not been once more misplaced, and soon after Radisson's departure the Committee received John Bridgar and got from him a written account of the duplicity by which Radisson had captured him and his men in 1682-3 and caused the loss of the *Rupert* in the ice. Bridgar had returned to London by way of Quebec and New

England, and he had obviously brooded on his story and prepared his narrative in advance, for he delivered it to the Committee within a week of their demand for it. No copy of the narrative has survived; but clearly it placed Bridgar in a reasonably favourable light and therefore blackened Radisson, for although the Committee refused to pay Bridgar's salary as Governor of Port Nelson except for the time during which he had actually exercised that office, from 17th September, 1682, to 6th June, 1683, they gave him a gratuity of £68 17s. 11d. to meet the bills which he had drawn and they paid the 'Charges' which he had incurred in his stay in Canada and New England.

But the Committee were already beginning to wonder if the magnificent dividend of late March 1684 was justified. The case of the interloper *Expectation* was dragging on in the Admiralty Courts; Nehemiah Walker had been arrested by the opposition, and the Committee, mistrustful of Walker though they might be, felt forced to bail him out, 'upon proofe of the matter that it is really the Company's concern and ought to affect them'. The Secretary and members of the Committee also had to be bailed. Uncertainty of the outcome was increased by financial troubles, for the Committee, having dispersed the produce of the sale in the dividend and in the 1684 outfit, were soon looking round for a loan of £1,000 to meet immediate demands, refusing the Secretary an advance in salary and driving him to seek dismissal, and making a serious attempt to strike a balance in the books and to discover what the actual financial position was.

It was uncertainty rather than actual difficulty which inhibited the Committee. The refusal of the Secretary's claim, for example, was made in the form that the Committee did not think it fit 'considering the present condition of the Company'. Yet he was given a gratuity (non-recurrent) of £100—a large sum when considered against his salary of £80 a year—and his claim for more permanent recognition was accepted and his annual salary was raised to £180 at the end of the year, on 19th December. This was four days after the action against the interloper had ended and the Company's status had thereby been substantiated, and a week after the fur sale which followed Radisson's return to London with proof that, this time, the Committee had not misplaced their trust.

But although Radisson vindicated their trust, fulfilled his mission and was back in the Thames by October 1684, the Committee could not even then feel entirely easy about the French opposition. Still less could suspicion be lulled before Radisson's return; and fear of the French was the greatest cause of the Committee's uneasiness, and of the difficulties in raising money, during the summer of that year.

The expedient of sending out Radisson to undo his own work, if it proved justifiable, left untouched the ultimate decision on rights. Lord Preston's claims that an official restoration should be made had not been met by the French, and once the Company had realised the point involved it showed itself quite unwilling to accept the back-door expedient of Radisson's services as a substitute for an open acknowledgment of right. Pressure for a more satisfactory settlement continued, all the more so since the Committee were informed that the French of Canada were by no means of one mind with those in France who were disposed to placate the English, and that an expedition from Canada to the Bay was in hand. There was truth in these rumours, though the details were not known. But it was known officially that Governor de la Barre had himself written to Governor Bradstreet of New England to tell him that he was resolved to support the French post at Nelson River by land and by sea. He wrote in similar terms to Boston, and the Company feared that unless it got government support this determination to oust the English 'both by force and by fraud' would surely succeed.

As might be expected, it was Sir James Hayes who was foremost in pressing the Company's case after the departure of the ships with Radisson, and it was the new Governor, His Royal Highness James, Duke of York, whom Hayes and the working members of the Committee strove to interest in the Company's case. Towards the end of August the Committee noted that Hayes had exchanged several letters on the Company's affairs with Lord Preston's secretary, and asked him to prepare a memorial of the matter and to present it in person to His Royal Highness, soliciting 'some suitable Resentment'. This was to be done without delay since the outcome of Radisson's expedition was so uncertain, for the Committee feared 'a deplorable account of our affaires when our shipps are expected home', and they wished to get the English Court involved on their side before the position began to appear hopeless.

It was nevertheless late in September 1684 before Hayes presented his 'Narrative of the French Action at Port Nelson' to the Court at Winchester. This was cutting things fine, perhaps too fine, if news of Radisson's expedition had been as bad as the Committee feared, for the interest of the Court had not been secured before the Company's ships had again dropped anchor in the Thames. The *John and Thomas* from Charlton Island, and the *Happy Return* and the *Lucy* from Port Nelson were all back by 24th October. Fortunately their news was good, and confidence boomed once more and met answering support. The Company then sent in a firm petition, which was sent on to Lord Preston without delay. It was alleged that the Company had been 'Damnified to the vallew of at least £10,000' by the events at Port Nelson, and it was requested that de la Chesnay and his partners should be made to pay damages by the Governor of Canada, who should also be given 'absolute Commands' not to allow any further ships to sail from Canada to the Bay.

This was an attempt to complete the picture and to confirm an inclusive claim to the Company's chartered rights. Lest anything should be left to chance the Committee also spent £7 15s. 0d. on an 'entertainment at Fontacks house' for Lord Preston and gave him a bedcover made of black beaver. Already the Governor of New York, Colonel Thomas Dongan, had written to assure the Company that no further interlopers should be allowed to set forth from that port. This, with the decision of the Admiralty Court case against the interloper *Expectation*, closed the possibility of rivalry from Great Britain or from New England, and Radisson's 1684 expedition left no doubt that he had effectively cleaned up the French outpost in the Hayes River. It remained only to confirm that fact in theory and, with the Duke of York crowned as James II early in 1685, the Company would be well assured of its claims.

In all of this, the success of Radisson was the trigger which set off the train of confident negotiation. He had not only cleared up the French post but had brought back the Frenchmen and their peltry with him to London. This was a most real achievement to set against the unconfirmed rumours of further French-Canadian expeditions. Radisson had met little difficulty in accomplishing his objective, since there were only seven Frenchmen in their post (although the French later alleged that they were thirty), and they had spent an uneasy winter alongside the new English post which Abraham had established in the Nelson River. To secure themselves the French had withdrawn up the Hayes River (to Rainbow Island) and had set up some sort of post there; but it can have been little more than a hut, 'a place meerely to sleepe in' as the Company later described it.

In the spring the French drove a successful trade with friendly Indians, including some Assiniboines and some Crees. The English protested that this trade was the outcome of the trade-goods which Radisson had taken out of the *Rupert*, and this is quite probable in view of the poor outfit with which the *St. Pierre* and the *Ste. Anne* had been sent out. Certainly by the spring of 1684 the Frenchmen

were looking anxiously for the reinforcements which had been promised them when Radisson and Groseilliers had sailed away, and
when Radisson came back in English employ he had a quick success
in persuading them, like himself, to desert to the Hudson's Bay
Company.

At this stage Governor Abraham seems to have stepped in and
insisted that the Frenchmen must be shipped to England, and in
September the return voyage began. Aboard the *Happy Return* with
Radisson were his 'nephew' Jean Baptiste Chouart or Goslier
(Grosseilliers' son) and four other Frenchmen; three more were
aboard the *Lucy*. Almost equally important were their furs, which
far outnumbered those traded by Abraham at the English post.
Aboard the *Happy Return* were 3,070 *coat* beaver and 3,204 *parchment* taken by the French as against 1,445 *coat* and 1,825 *parchment*
taken by the English, whilst aboard the *Lucy* were 3,271 *coat* and
3,195 *parchment* taken by the French as against 1,826 *coat* and 1,169
parchment from the English.

Altogether the returns exceeded 18,000 skins, a figure certainly
comparable with the 14,700 got from the posts in the Bay in 1682.
It was alleged that the French beaver sold for £7,000, and at the
end of the year the 'Voyage to Port Nelson' account carried a credit
balance of £6,479 14s. 10d. This was, of course, a purely paper
figure, for the Company kept its beaver accounts in the *Trade
Account* in which the furs at nominal value were set against the cost
of the outfit in actual figures. At that nominal value they were then
transferred to the *Sales Account*, and the profits showed in that
account, not in the *Trade Account*, as the difference between the
arbitrary figure at which the furs were assigned to *Sales* and
the actual prices which they realised from the buyers. So when the
average skin weighed a little more than a pound and the actual
selling prices varied from about fourteen shillings down to about
seven shillings the pound, the *Sales Account* contained an element of
profit of ten shillings (more or less) for each skin which was transferred to that account at an alleged price of two shillings and threepence a skin. These were the figures current at this time. But the
skins taken from the French were put into the 'Voyage to Port
Nelson' account at no cost, presumably because they were set against
losses to the French; the total returns on the *Lucy* (9,461 skins) were
costed at only £224 12s. 6d. and those on the *Happy Return* (9,544
skins) at only £245 5s. 0d., whilst an equivalent quantity of 18,912
skins from the Bottom of the Bay was costed at £1,949 4s. 8d. This
was a method of accountancy which, as the Committee discovered,

did not lend itself to close analysis, and little can be gathered from such accounts save the fact that the Committee convinced themselves that their trade was sound and profitable.

The General Court of the Company shared the Committee's confidence. Radisson was paid a gratuity of a hundred guineas and the General Court confirmed the arrangement that he should get a salary of £50 and the benefit of a share of £200 in the stock for life 'while he continue faithfull in the Companies service', and also recommended that the other Frenchmen should be taken on at favourable terms. The business of preparing the outward cargo for the 1685 voyage was put in hand even before the furs of 1684 were sold, and Radisson was asked to prepare a list of goods which would be required. Captain Bond of the *Happy Return* and Captain Outlaw of the *Lucy* were again taken into employment, and Captain Outlaw was also given a gratuity of £25 for his services at Port Nelson. He also reported that at the request of the Royal Society he had taken with him a 'brass log' which he had found useful in navigation, and the Company bought the log from him.

Meanwhile two other matters were engaging the attention of the Committee. Of these a minor but important problem was to find some increase in the uses to which beaver was put. Interesting here are the attempts to spread the use of beaver stockings during this year. To popularise the fashion a pair of stockings was given to the Duke of York; but it was a fashion which never took hold. At the same time two beaver hats were made, one for the King and one for the Duke of York; the hats cost £5, but since Charles II was dead before they were ready one was given to James II (by Hayes) and the other was taken by Richard Cradock, a member of the Committee, in lieu of several pairs of snow-shoes with which he had supplied Bridgar when he set off for Port Nelson in 1682.

Such means of seeking publicity were signs of the times; there was a serious danger of repeating the glut of skins which had caused the *coat* beaver to stick so badly from 1682 to 1684. The sale was not held immediately the cargoes of 1684 had been cleared through the customs but was delayed until the end of the year, and even then it was decided that no attempt should be made to sell the *coat* beaver. *Parchment* and small furs were apparently still in demand, and the Committee now began its steady and long-continued drive to improve the trade in small furs, especially in martens (which it managed to get the customs officers to treat as fisher at a lower rate for payment). Martens were now 'our best furs and turnes best to accounte'; they were 'mightily requested' in London, and the Company's employees were pressed to increase their returns, though without altering the Standard of Trade from eight for one Made-beaver.

A further minor matter which the Company took up with the Customs Officers, who seem to have been very friendly—what with their exclusion of Dutch and French beaver under the Navigation Acts, and their preferential rating of marten as fisher—was a two-fold attempt, to be allowed to 'draw-back' the customs payments on their tobacco when it was re-exported, and a more comprehensive effort to secure the 'Like privilege that the East India Company and the Royal African Company and other Companies of merchants have, by their Charter, for the shipping out, customs free, of the clothes, provisions, victuals, arms, ammunition, implements and materials or provisions necessary for the maintaining and defence of their forts, colonies and factories'.

BOOKS FOR REFERENCE

Hudson's Bay Record Society—Vols. VIII, IX, XI.
Evelyn, John—*The Diary of John Evelyn*, edited by E. S. de Beer (Oxford, 1955), 6 vols.
Nute, Grace Lee—*Caesars of the Wilderness* (New York, 1943).

CHAPTER XIV

ADMINISTRATIVE REFORM AND A NEW
GOVERNOR, JOHN CHURCHILL

The business of preparing the outfits and of trying to secure a market for the furs was by 1684 accepted as the essence of the Company's existence, and the purpose of colonisation and settlement was well in the background. From the point of view of the trade accounts the 1684 dividend was, it seemed, a slightly unwarranted piece of exuberance, and even with the successful venture to Nelson River and the capture of the French furs behind them, the Committee could not regard their trade with any great confidence. But although organisation of the trade was a necessary duty, upon which everything ultimately hung, yet markets and supplies seemed in 1684 to be of only secondary importance when compared with the task of vindicating the Company's case against the French of Canada. If this should fail, then no amount of competent trade-organisation would avail. Accordingly not only was the policy of the previous year pursued, in petitions to the Crown and in representations to Lord Preston at Paris, but the organisation of the Company was modified so as to secure the secrecy and effective action which such quasi-diplomatic negotiations required.

Hitherto the Company had developed very little in its organisation beyond the Governor, the Deputy Governor and the Committee of seven, which the Charter had set up. Sub-committees for trade had come into existence and had disappeared from the Minutes when the immediate urgency had passed. There had indeed been a secretary, Thomas Rastell, from the start in 1670, and an accountant, Richard Beane, had been paid for 'setting and stating the several accounts' from time to time, from 1674 onwards. In the early days, too, there had been a treasurer, Richard Hawkins, to whom payments were made in 1673 and 1674. He was followed by John Portman, who handled the business of receiving and disbursing the Company's money, and who was in turn followed in 1675 by John Lindsay, a purely business man with no pretensions to gentility. The infiltration of business men in the 1679–80 period had brought a closer attention to book-keeping, the appointment of a 'husband' to care for the Company's property, and of a secretary to keep the books (they were both posts filled by the same man, Onesiphorous

Albin). In 1679, too, came the business of the appointment and the non-renewal of Sir Robert Clayton as treasurer, at the end of which the two great banking houses of Thomas Cook and Company and Stephen Evans and Company began to handle the finances of the trade.

Evans, in particular, became very deeply involved in Company affairs and ultimately became Governor. But both he and Cook acted rather as bankers than as treasurers. That is to say, they received the cash from fur sales or other sources and then advanced it to the treasurer or the secretary to meet bills, or even paid bills themselves (as they paid the 1684 dividend). But they acted in these matters only on instructions from the Committee; they did not engage in day-to-day routine administration of the Company's funds. Of the two, Thomas Cook seems to have handled the larger sums, but neither of these bankers ran any danger of confusing his private business with that of the Company.

The accounts of the bankers give a rough idea of the solvency of the Company if it had been called on to meet a sudden demand for cash. Cook received a little over £5,000 in November 1681 and had only disbursed about £3,600 by the following June. Evans, meantime, had received over £6,000 in December 1681 and had disbursed about £100 more than he had received by the following June. From the end of 1683 to the end of 1684 Cook had taken in almost £9,000 on behalf of the Company; but he had paid out over £1,000 more than he had received. During the year 1681–2 Evans handled about £6,500 of the Company's money and left himself with a balance in hand, on behalf of the Company, of over £500. He received a further £1,600 in November 1682 and almost £7,000 in the following March. But he was called on for most of it and when his account was checked in July 1683 he had paid out a mere £2 6s. 2d. more than he had received. Similar was the experience of a third banker, John Temple and Company, who received the large sum of £6,630 10s. 6d. at the end of 1681 and had been drawn on for exactly that sum by September 1682. The bankers' accounts therefore show that at this time the Company could just about make revenue (including loans) meet expenditure, but that there were certainly no surpluses accumulating in the bankers' hands.

The expeditions of 1684 and 1685, and above all the great dividend of 1684, absorbing £5,100, upset this equable arrangement. For even behind these apparently balanced figures lay a great deal of borrowing, and the fact that the bankers' accounts were kept almost even merely meant that the Company borrowed privately rather than from professional bankers. The interest account at this time shows steady payments which indicate that the debts of the Company were never cleared off and that they sometimes exceeded the paid-up capital (as when £966 1s. 0d. was paid in interest for the period November 1689 to July 1690, a sum which included some arrears of payments but which shows that the Company had borrowed at that time something in the neighbourhood of £20,000.

Apart from interest and repayment of loans, most of the sums paid out by the bankers went to members of the Committee, who then spent the money on the Company's business. Such payments went especially to Gerrard Weymans and to William Walker, who were made responsible (apparently without payment) for settling tradesmen's accounts, preparing ships, and paying wages.

The introduction of this much method, most of it due to the need to borrow from those who required at least a minimum of order in the management of the Company's business, came about for the most part in the 1679–80 period. It was at that time, too, that it was decided that membership of the all-important Committee must depend, in the first place, on the holding of at least £200 in the stock of the Company.

But though committee-men were thus forced to qualify for their office in 1679 it was decided that though any member of the Company might attend a meeting of the Committee, he could merely listen to the discussions there and could not vote; at the same time all members of the Committee were required to take a special oath, not to divulge the business of the Company to those who were not of the Committee. The books of the Company were not to be removed from the Committee-room without special order, and shortly afterwards the Secretary was ordered never to deliver any books or papers relating to the Company without leave of the Committee to anyone who was not a member of the Committee. The oath of faithfulness for the servants of the Company was also revised, by no less a person than Christopher Wren, at this time, and the Committee also took power to carry on with the Company's business even if the Governor or Deputy Governor should be absent.

So by the end of 1683 the Company had a simple but effective system for the conduct of its business, with a secretary-husband, a series of bankers, and a treasurer or team of *ad hoc* treasurers drawn from the Committee. The general stockholders indeed still had their right to attend meetings of the Committee, but they were not allowed to consult the papers under discussion, and the actual conduct of business was firmly in the hands of the Committee.

The delicate negotiations against the French, and the need for constant representations at Court, inevitably increased the Committee's control of business, and at the turn of the year, 1684–5, led even to a reversal of the policy of allowing ordinary members to attend Committee meetings. In the midst of the attempts to enlist Lord Preston on the side of the Company it was agreed, in January 1685, that it was 'inconvenient that any member of the Company should heare the Debates of the Committee'; so the by-law giving that right was suspended. True, the suspension did not last long, the business with Preston was soon over, and within the month 'The cause being taken away which at that time gave occation for the makeing thereof', the arbitrary rule was revoked. Yet here was evidence of the way in which the Committee could control even its own position within the Company when it so wished.

That such authority in the hands of a small caucus did not lead to abuse was due to the genuine interest in the long-term well-being of the Company which the Committee consistently showed. At this time, whilst they thought it necessary to place the conduct of business closely in their own hands, they also disciplined themselves and took stock of their position. Counsel's opinion was taken as to whether a vacancy on the Committee must be immediately filled, to bring the numbers up to those specified in the Charter, and the system of payment for committee-attendance was also revised. Instead of the payment of a noble (worth about ten shillings at that time) for each attendance, it was decided that the Committee should merely divide up £200 a year between them as 'Attendance-money'. Prompt attendance at committee meetings was to be enforced; all members were to attend within half an hour of the time set! Before long important members, such as John Letten, were deprived of their committee-money for departing from the meetings before the business was concluded, and at the same time members were again ordered not to show any letters, books, accounts or papers to anyone without the permission of the Committee.

With all of this emphasis on the Committee and their rights and duties it is noteworthy that the vacancy in the Governorship caused by the coronation of James II was filled at a General Meeting of all shareholders, not (officially) by Committee nomination. But the influence of the Committee was obvious and weighty. The Company's interests would probably have been best served if James had been willing to retain his position as Governor, and nothing was done until Hayes had sought advice as to whether a new Governor need be chosen 'seeing our Governour is now our Sovereigne Lord the King'.

JAMES, DUKE OF YORK, THE COMPANY'S SECOND GOVERNOR

from a portrait by Huysmans in the Company's possession

This was the year of Monmouth's rebellion, of the Bloody Assizes in the West, and of John Churchill's demonstration both of his ability in the field and of his weight in politics. He not only defeated Monmouth's forces, he also carried to James the loyalty of the preponderant Whig elements in the kingdom, making it known that he would not compromise his allegiance to the Protestant faith but that he would nevertheless support James. For a Company in the peculiar position of the Hudson's Bay Company, seeking a successor to the reigning monarch as Governor and needing all the political and diplomatic support it could get, Churchill was the obvious first choice in 1685.

It says much for the place achieved by the Company, despite the fact that so far it had paid but a solitary dividend and its chartered rights were challenged, that such a man should have accepted the Governorship. Yet he seems to have shown little or no hesitation. He had 'bought' a share of £300 in March 1684 and he 'bought' a further £100 in May 1685. It is, indeed, open to some doubt whether Churchill actually paid cash for these shares. They may well have been presented to him by William Yonge, the prominent Committee-member who had been instrumental in bringing Radisson back into the Company's service and who always acted in close co-operation with Churchill in the Company's affairs. Or they may even have remained Yonge's property and have been transferred only nominally to Churchill in order to give him a qualification. But at least officially the shares were Churchill's, so that his capital interest was considerable in those days of small individual holdings, when even James Hayes held only £150.

It was on 1st April, 1685, that Churchill was nominated, unopposed, as Governor at the General Meeting of the Company which had been specially called. He was then invited to dinner on the following day, when he was formally elected. A new form of oath was then administered to him, in which a strange precaution was taken. In addition to requiring him to swear that he would not disclose the Company's secrets, the Committee exacted an oath that 'Dureing the present Joynt Stock of the said Company I will not trade in any private way to any of the Lymits of the said Company's Charter'. After this straightening of the ways, the newly-elected Governor was taken by James Hayes, the organiser, to dinner at the Rummer Tavern in Queen Street.

Having got their man, the Committee set to work to embroil him in the Company's affairs, to maintain his interest and to retain his goodwill. He was to be summoned to all Committee-meetings—an indication that he might be expected to be something more active than either Rupert or James had been—and he was presented both with an address of congratulations on his success against the rebels in the West and with a cat-skin counterpane. The latter cost only £8 16s. 0d. for the skins plus £5 8s. 3d. for 'dressing', but Churchill 'took it very kindly and thanks the Company for so noble a Guift'.

BOOKS FOR REFERENCE

HUDSON's BAY RECORD SOCIETY—Vols. V, XI.
NUTE, Grace Lee—*Caesars of the Wilderness* (New York, 1943).

CHAPTER XV

THE INFLUENCE OF THE BAY ON LONDON, RADISSON AND JAMES KNIGHT

Already, before Churchill's sympathies were so firmly enlisted, the formal contest with the French was well in hand. An address of congratulation to the King on his accession was approved and despatched in February 1685, including the hint that the Company doubted not 'of your Majestyes gratious and powerful Protection'. The Company was gathering its forces to rebut the French claims, and in the process, in the early months of this year, commissioned the celebrated map-maker Thornton to draw a most topical map of the Bay, with large-scale insets of the various harbours, and particularly of Nelson River. Here the details of Bridgar's abortive settlement of 1682; of Gillam and the *Bachelor's* intrusion, and Radisson's dominance in that year, are all commemorated, although perhaps a trifle obliquely, as in the naming of the 'Prisoners Islands', where the English were presumably confined. Thornton had already done work for the Company; his maps were of undoubted practical use, and the ships' captains were provided with them, as with the 'Instructions' drawn up by Zachariah Gillam, to aid them in their navigation. But the 1685 map was too apposite to be entirely due to a wish to clarify the problems of navigation. It aimed to show, and was later adduced as showing, that the names used in and around Nelson River were entirely English or Indian, and that therefore the French had not preceded the English there.

The first move, however, came from the French, who in April 1685 presented a memorial complaining of Radisson's depredations. This was a garbled account in which the French, perhaps to allow some scope for English delicacy if a withdrawal should be contemplated, placed responsibility for Radisson's recapture of Nelson River on orders which he was supposed to have received from Thomas Dongan, Governor of New York, rather than on direct orders from London.

Radisson had, of course, arrived so hurriedly in England and had departed so precipitately that there could not possibly have been time for him to have received instructions from New York, and the English sources contain no reference to Dongan as the inspirer of this move. Yet this was the charge which the French were repeating among themselves, not merely something cooked up in order to accuse the English. They were urging their diplomats to secure from the English a promise that 'D'unguen' should be commanded to set out no further raids such as Radisson had perpetrated in 1684, and the introduction of Dongan's name into the affair serves to place the whole incident of Radisson's return to the English service in its proper context.

The edge of colonial rivalry between England and France, shown despite the European interdependence of the royal houses, was clearly visible in the major policy of James II and of his advisers for colonial defence. Here the plan was at once to reduce the small English static garrisons (ineffective, like the Hudson Bay forts, against European attack though valuable against Indian raids), and to centralise and co-ordinate the defence arrangements of the North American and the West Indian settlements. New York was the key position, and Dongan the most active and effective governor. Under him the military strength of New York was doubled; he set forth proposals for a forward line of defence in the Indian country, with posts on Lake Ontario, Lake Champlain, Salmon River and at Niagara, and with smaller posts between Lake Ontario and Schenectady to secure passage for the fur-traders into the Indian lands. Although he never quite won support from London for his plans, at the end of his régime Canada found herself faced with a reasonably united 'Dominion of New England' commanding a permanent military force of about two hundred men and with a reserve of registered militiamen amounting to over fifteen thousand.

This was the major problem of colonial rivalry which the French administration faced in these years, and as the discussions developed at a high diplomatic level it became increasingly obvious that the New England colonies and the West Indies dominated the statesmen's minds, and the obscure affair of Radisson's raid on Nelson River was a confused and subordinate problem. Almost it may be said that the Nelson River affair can only be treated seriously if it can be linked to the more important developments of which Dongan was the chief protagonist.

Dongan therefore, a most colourful and outspoken individual who would in any case have attracted much attention to himself and who posed a serious threat to the French position in North America, was worked into the French reaction to Radisson's latest exploit as the originator of the plan for the recovery of Nelson River. This merely emphasises the extent to which events in Nelson River were removed from the front rank of diplomatic incidents, and by the time that Radisson's exploit had reached the terms of a diplomatic memorandum it had passed through so complicated a channel of information that there can be no cause for surprise that the account was garbled and unreliable.

Twisted though it might be, the French memorandum of April 1685 was more than the Lords of Trade and Plantations could rebut from their own knowledge. For them also Hudson Bay was not a major issue, and the French protest was sent to the Committee of the Hudson's Bay Company. As might be expected, it was Sir James Hayes who brought it forward for consideration, but the Committee had their own narrative ready and within ten days the Company's answer was ready for submission to Churchill and to Sunderland, the Principal Secretary of State who had originally sent the French memorial to the Company and who had also in the meantime been given a copy of the Company's Charter in so far as it granted the sole trade to the Company. The answer, with Hayes once more as the intermediary, was that the French were 'notoriously mistaken'; the errors in fact were underlined, perhaps a little sarcastically, while the Company also entered a forthright denial 'that the French have any colour of pretence to the River of Port Nellson'.

As against the inaccuracy of the French statements, the position of the Company was so strong, and it also coincided with such strength in the British national position vis-à-vis the French, that Sunderland duly told the French ambassador that the Company's claims both to Nelson River and to the whole of the Bay were clear and that there could be no question of any arrangement by which English and French each remained in possession of areas under occupation. In all of this Sunderland was closely following his brief from the Company, but his rebuff of the French memorial had a vigour of its own, indicating something more than a mere official substantiation of the Company's claims.

With Sunderland's reply to the French, the diplomatic problems of title fall into the background for a period of the six summer months, during which the 1685 outfit occupied the attention of the Committee. Here Radisson naturally found his experience called upon, his advice was taken in ordering trade guns from Holland (which turned out a bad bargain, not up to the sample), and his influence was also to be seen when two goats from Norway were sent over to the Bay, and the food problem in general was taken in hand on the lines which he advocated and practised. Indian corn was ordered from Virginia, and the men's rations were ordained at five pounds of flour a week, five pounds of meat a week and forty gallons

of malt a year, an approach to the problem which was in part dependent on 'every ones Industrey to get Provissions of fowle and fish'.
Too heavy a dependence on imported provisions was to prove an
expensive luxury which the Company for many years tried to prune
down, and Radisson also knew the value of fresh food and the overwhelming danger of scurvy.

In one of the prime articles of trade, too, French practices were
this year adopted and adapted. After many years' trial of 'Engelish
Tobacco', that is to say, West Indian or Virginian tobacco made up
in England, the Committee had grown tired of constant complaints
and in October 1684 had ordered Brazil tobacco. To this item of
trade our stable relations with Portugal gave us ready access, and it
was to prove a great asset. The price was indeed three times that of
the English tobacco, so that the traders were ordered to adjust their
prices accordingly; but the Company, having 'made search, what
Tobacco the French vends to the Indians' was henceforth firmly
wedded to the Brazilian product, which became a staple of the trade.

Radisson was not only providing the main arguments for the
Company to conduct its case against the French—his Journals of his
voyages of 1682 and of 1684 were delivered into the Company's
care, and copies and translations were made—but he was also making
a valuable contribution to the practical business of preparing a cargo
for trade and, perhaps with less justification, was intervening in vital
problems of personnel and appointment. Bridgar, his victim in
Nelson River in 1682, was once more in the Company's employment; and he was, after a full debate in 1685, chosen Governor of
Port Nelson for three years at a salary of £100 a year, with Radisson
to go as Superintendent and Director of Trade. But after their
experiences in rivalry the two men had little respect for each other,
and Radisson protested so vigorously against the prospect of serving
under Bridgar that he secured the reversal of the appointment and a
promise that Bridgar should not go to Port Nelson. Bridgar was
offered instead the post of Deputy Governor of the Bottom of the
Bay at the same salary, with his tenure extended from three to four
years, and he accepted.

But though Radisson got the Committee to agree with him over
Bridgar, they were more obstinate over other conditions. They
allowed him fresh provisions for the voyage, and a hogshead of
claret 'such as Mr. Radisson shall like and approve of', but after a
long debate they refused to agree to the terms of employment which
he proposed. He was allowed no concession in the way of private
trade and he finally agreed for a hundred pounds a year while he

should be out of the country on the Company's service, with a promise that the Company would take generous account of any extraordinary service; his wife was first offered a cash settlement of three hundred pounds 'in case he dyed in this Expedition' and then, by Churchill's intervention, was promised a life interest in a hundred pounds stock in the Company instead.

It is worth noting that it was Churchill, attending Committee meetings, who proposed both the compromise over Bridgar and over Radisson's wife. But the other Frenchmen proved as difficult to agree with as their leader. They could not be entirely relied on (and they were in fact at this time in correspondence with France) but they had a knowledge and a confidence which could not be found in English servants, and the Committee were prepared to take some chance with them. In this the Committee were supported by a General Court of the Company, to which the question was put. The Frenchmen were kept in London at the Company's costs, and Hayes was called in to decide on the proposals to be agreed with them, but they all refused to take an oath of fidelity which would also have precluded them from private trade, and their contracts were declared void. So it was not until the middle of April that they were agreed, Chouart for £80 for his past services and £80 a year, and the others for proportionate gratuities and wages. They were all compelled to take an oath of fidelity, to sign a contract 'done into French', and to give security for their good behaviour. Radisson went bail for the others and he also gave a bond for £300 that he would make the voyage, and a further bond for £2,000 that he would fulfil his covenant with the Company, whilst the other Frenchmen were required to put in bonds for £500.

Under these conditions Radisson went as Superintendent and Chief Director of Trade to Port Nelson, and he was pointedly warned that 'as we have placed you in a Post of Eminency, so we expect extraordinary performance from you'. He was to exercise his genius alongside a Governor and Council appointed for Port Nelson, but his exact relations with these officers were left obscure. He was to 'enterprize nothing, without the Knowlidge and allowance of the Governor and Councell', though it is not clear whether this gave them a veto since he himself was only told that he must 'communicate' all his plans to them and 'advice with them' on all occasions.

In his account of his actions in 1684 Radisson had underlined his fixing of an economic Standard of Trade, and his Instructions for 1685 emphasised the need to set such a Standard as would bring the Indians down to trade. The Indians had told him in 1684 that the

English at the Head of the Bay were giving three axes for a beaver, and they wanted the same terms at Port Nelson. Radisson had refused presents except to the Captains; had, indeed, insisted that they must give him presents instead, and had set the Standard at ten knives for a beaver and one musket for twelve beaver, only to find Abraham intervene and set the Standard at seven to ten beaver for the musket, and so in proportion. Radisson was now made immune from such interference, was given complete control of the Standard, and was given easy colleagues. On the withdrawal of Bridgar's appointment, Thomas Phipps, warehousekeeper at Albany and an experienced trader, was made Governor at Nelson with orders to ship himself thither in a sloop to be provided by Governor Sergeant from Albany. Phipps might well look forward to a difficult command, for not only had he got Radisson and the Frenchmen to keep in their proper places, whatever those might be; he also had 'Mr. Sam Missenden' as warehousekeeper, 'a Gentleman very well recommended to' the Committee and a man to be treated with kindness, but a troublesome fellow as it turned out. In addition John Abraham, the former Governor, was relieved of his command for deserting his post but was kept on at Nelson River as second-in-command, to receive the ships and bestow the trade-goods until Phipps should arrive from the Bottom of the Bay.

If the personnel attached to Phipps at Nelson River gave promise of a difficult winter, his trading instructions were simple—indeed the burden was thrown so much on Radisson that the Governor's instructions hardly dealt with trade at all. Phipps was, however, urged to press on with the settlement of New Severn, if it had not already been accomplished, 'that no Enemy to the Company may get a footeing there before us'. The Company had explored this region in Bayly's time, and the Quaker had even told Louis Jolliet that a post had been established there. But in 1680 Nixon was still being pressed to make a settlement, and the *Albemarle* was loaded with deals and nails for building there. Again nothing had been done. Nor had Bridgar been in any position to carry out the Instructions of 1683, to settle New Severn, and John Abraham, who brought out six extra men for the purpose in 1683, also found full occupation in re-settling Nelson and Hayes Rivers, and nothing was done at New Severn. Still the Committee persisted, and in 1684 George Geyer had been sent out to Governor Sergeant at Albany principally with the object of making this settlement. It was to this last project that the Committee referred in 1685, telling Phipps that 'We hope you will finde New Severne to be already settled'. In fact Geyer replied that the river was 'well settled', and even this problem was removed from the sphere of Phipps.

Whilst Phipps was virtually nominated Governor to provide a channel of administration for Radisson at Port Nelson, Henry Sergeant at the Bottom of the Bay received a far more traditional set of Instructions. He was reproved for the extravagance of his indents, for his demands bore no relation to the volume of the trade which he conducted; yet the Committee made a push to provide him with 'all things necessary for one yeare, and a good overplus for Increase of Trade'. Emphasis was on the Dutch guns, the Brazil tobacco, the provisions for the men, and the number of men necessary for trade and defence; but personalities included the appointment of Thomas Gorst 'without wages or advance money, but only what the Company will please to give him at the End' of his four years' contract, the recall of Sergeant's Deputy Governor, James Knight, and the demand of her father for the return of Mrs. Maurice, companion to Mrs. Sergeant.

The serious trade matters under discussion for the Bottom of the Bay were the habit of private trading in which the ships' captains persisted, the need to encourage the taking of small furs, especially ermine, and the need to push penetration into the hinterland. Here the Company tried to overcome the reluctance of its servants by promising rewards to those who brought down Indians to the factories to trade, and named three men 'haveing the Lingua, and understanding the Trade of the Countrey' who had been chosen for this purpose. Even these men, however, refused to venture, and Sergeant was forced to report that despite his pressure none of the servants would travel inland.

Closely akin to the old problems of settling New Severn and of sending men up-country was the other old plan for developing isinglass. Here it was reported that Sergeant had discovered a new mine, which he was urged to test. On the other hand, it was clear that he had delayed action upon the resolution of 1684, when Brian Norbury had been sent out especially to settle Slude River. The Committee continued to press for action; it was ready to send out men if the new vein proved profitable, and during the summer it even discussed a plan for sending out a Russian 'upon the Slood Design'. Search for commodities other than beaver was clearly in evidence, and isinglass seemed the most probable.

While the influence of Radisson, with his bias against Bridgar and his overwhelming knowledge of Indian character and of the resources of the arctic, is clear in the Instructions sent out in 1685, those of 1686 are stamped by the personality of a native English servant of the Company—the Deptford shipwright James Knight. Knight, though suspect of New England sympathies when young Gillam had challenged the Charter in the *Bachelor's Delight* in 1684, vindicated his character. He had already served in the Bay and won a gratuity of £50 for his good service before he was taken on as Chief at Albany in 1682. 'Able and dexterouse' in business, he then advised on the purchase of trade goods in London, and before he sailed he was made Deputy Governor of the Bay. But he was obviously very much of an individualist and clearly addicted to private trade, for he almost forfeited his appointment in 1682 and was at one time forbidden to board any of the Company's ships.

The troubles were solved in time for Knight to sail, and he ultimately took out his brother Richard to the Bay as a private passenger, paying his fare since he was not a servant of the Company. Knight seems not to have forfeited the respect of his employers, and not to have fallen under any serious suspicion of entertaining any interloping ideas. He served as Chief at Albany and as Deputy Governor of the Bay for his full period of three years and was then brought home since his time was expired in 1685. It is, however, clear that his conduct in office had not been altogether above suspicion and he was called on to answer 'severe charges' made by Governor Sergeant. He had without doubt indulged in some trifling trade in beaver and in fact he continued throughout his career so to do. But the Committee accepted his rebuttal, refrained from dismissing him, and gave him a certificate of honesty and fidelity although when Sergeant appeared against him in person Knight's answer was found unsatisfactory.

With the Frenchmen brought home by Radisson firmly committed to their inborn ideas on private trade, the Committee was at this time unable to be as dogmatic as it could wish, and a plan of encouraging servants to trade and to trap so long as they declared their takings and shipped them home openly was proceeded with. The pelts were then to be sold by the Company at its open sales, so that there would be no rivalry in price or quality for the London furriers' custom, and the servants were given 'so much money as the Company shall think fitt'. Above all the Company wanted to retain its control of the London market, and decided that servants' pelts should never again be handed over to them 'in specie'.

Although he may perhaps have been under a slight cloud during the winter of 1685–6, Knight emerged during that time as a native Englishman with experience of the Bay, clear-headed, courageous and attractive to the Committee, able to analyse a situation but not so offensively pedantic as Governor Nixon had been. In comparison with Radisson and the Frenchmen he won the support of several members of the Committee; and at worst his habits of private trade were no worse than those of the French. We therefore find that during the winter his ideas occur on several occasions. He started by proposing economies, both on general lines and especially in reduction of staff at the posts and in the abandonment of Charlton Island. Told to 'digest his thoughts in writing', he suggested that the total of 89 men at the factories should be reduced to a mere 36—18 at Albany, 12 at Moose and 6 at Rupert River. He appears to have left Nelson River out of his calculations, perhaps treating it as a separate problem; but in leaving out Charlton Island he was certainly acting of set purpose, for he argued that the depot there weakened the other posts, could be easily captured by an enemy, involved heavy wear and tear on the shipping, and entailed the subsequent re-shipment of all trade-goods.

On what was perhaps a more fundamental point, Knight was less progressive but no less shrewd, for he argued that in the circumstances there was no possibility of sending Englishmen to the heads of the rivers, to rival the French there. According to Knight, the threat foreshadowed by Duluth, cutting off the Indians from the Bay-side posts, could be met only by getting the Indian captains themselves to persuade their tribes to come down to trade. For this purpose he advocated sending out a barrel of oatmeal every year to Albany, since he said that the Indians would certainly come down to trade when they knew that food for their return journey was there ready for them.

In this matter Knight was putting forward a strange mixture of timid conservatism and of shrewd realism, for the English were indeed not as yet fit to travel to the headwaters of the rivers and to rival the French there. One of the touches in Radisson's *Rélation* of his 1682 voyage to Port Nelson which carries most conviction is the purely incidental mention of the fact that young Gillam was astonished at the strength of a canoe, and as yet the situation in the Bay had not developed beyond the point at which the French hada virtual monopoly of river travel whilst the English had a virtual monopoly of the sea-route. For this the reasons were partly historical and partly geographical. The natural French approach was overland, and their history had also bred a succession of tireless canoe voyageurs; the English neither needed the land-approach nor had mastered the craft. Nor had they the raw materials for canoe-building, for the birch does not grow by the shores of the Bay. The

English, on the other hand, seldom felt any lack of competent pilots either for bringing their large ships to the Bay or for the important boat-work in shallops along the coast during the summer months. Allowing for the circumstances of his discourse, Radisson had been justified when he explained to the Indians in 1684 that 'les françois n'estoient point des bons hommes de mer qu'ilz apprehendoient les glaces au travers desquelles il falloit passer pour venir apporter des marchandises d'ailleurs que leurs vaisseaux estoient foibles et Incapables de resister dans les mers du nord mais que pour les anglois ilz estoient robustes hardis et entreprenans, qu'ilz avoient la cognoisance de toutes les mers Et des grandz Et fortz vaisseaux'.

Knight was therefore in the genuine tradition of the conflict as far as it had developed by 1686 when he gave his advice. He was more conservative than the Committee, which in any case knew better than he did the weight behind the French threat to cut off the Bayside posts by picketing the headwaters of the rivers. But although the Committee realised the peril, it could not provide the remedy, for it proved impossible to get Englishmen to go up-country. Robert Sandford had been specifically named for this assignment in 1685, but he and the other men named preferred to return to England rather than to travel inland, and Knight was only accepting the facts when he advised against such inland penetration. Indeed, his advice was virtually adopted, for the only point in the Instructions of the year which could be construed as persistence by the Committee in a policy of sending men into the hinterland was a personal note advising Samuel Missenden, now appointed Chief at New Severn and Deputy Governor to Phipps at Nelson, that he was wise to apply himself diligently to 'the attaineing of the Indian Lingua'.

For the rest, the Instructions demanded that a Council should deliberate the abandonment of Charlton Island and should report its opinion, whilst economies in establishment were to be pursued and the men were to be reduced, as proposed by Knight, to a total of thirty-six as against the fifty-six actually employed. The practice of making gifts of beaver coats to the ships' captains was frowned on, as was the custom of private trapping and trading—'what ever comes to our servants hands, whither by the one way or the other, it ought to be esteemed as our owne, for we are at great and vast charges there'.

Two 'great guns' firing a nine-pound shot, nine feet long and each with its own carriage, were sent out to defend the post in Hayes River against the French, and John Abraham was recalled; he was already suspect as 'timerous and imprudent' for having allowed the French ships to settle in the Gargousse River in 1684 when (as the

Committee thought) he might by stratagem or by open hostility have dispersed and taken their men and seized their trade. Thomas Phipps had in fact been ordered to succeed Abraham at Port Nelson in the previous year, but it was not yet clear in London whether he had done so, and since he had demanded an increase in salary from £100 to £200 a year Phipps was given the chance of continuing on his old terms or of coming home.

As for Radisson himself, he appears to have remained at Nelson River during the winter 1685–6, but to have sent his nephew, young Chouart, on a voyage into the interior to bring the Indians down to trade. No record of this voyage survives, and for many reasons it must be doubtful if it was ever made (for Chouart planned to desert to the French if he got a chance), but Radisson without doubt exercised considerable skill in arranging the Standard of Trade in Nelson River and was largely responsible for the satisfactory returns of 1685, so that in the Instructions of 1686 the Committee, with 'intire confidence in his Integrity and faithfullness', ordered that the trade at Nelson River should be left entirely to him. He was again given sole control of the setting of the Standard of Trade, with emphasis on inviting down the 'great Nations' who had the best furs, and the possibility of sending Frenchmen into the interior was further promoted by orders (at Radisson's request) for birch bark to be sent from the Bottom of the Bay to Nelson.

Radisson without doubt was still the main source of the Committee's hopes after sixteen years of trade. He was assured that his interests were in good hands, and although James Hayes had been one of the chief sponsors who had managed his return from France in 1682, yet the fact that Hayes now resigned his active interest in the Company and was replaced as Deputy Governor by Sir Edward Dering was held out to Radisson (though the names were not mentioned) as proof that 'our Committee & Government now is so constituted that you must doe your Faith great violence if you beleeve that there is any one but who is intirely your friend'. But heavily as the Committee leaned on him, he was no longer irreplaceable, or even indispensable. A native English tradition, backed by knowledge and experience in the Bay, had developed and had been accepted.

BOOKS FOR REFERENCE

HUDSON'S BAY RECORD SOCIETY—Vol. XI.
CHANNING, E.—*History of the United States* (New York, 1905–32), 6 vols.

CHAPTER XVI

THE FINANCING OF THE TRADE, 1685–1686

As the Company approaches its twentieth year of trade it is tempting to allow the high lights to dominate the scene, to concentrate on the character and achievements of the heroic Governor, on the bizarre personality of Radisson, the subtle diplomatic exchanges with the French, the magnificent dividend of 1684, and the growing certainty with which the Committee handled the Company's affairs. These are indeed elements which must not be forgotten. But the real reason for the survival of the Company lay in the annual miracle by which it conjured up sufficient credit to outfit a voyage. The Instructions repay detailed study; but the cargoes of trade goods which accompanied the Instructions strained the Company's resources to the point at which, in June 1685, it was agreed that no more money should be paid to any person whatsoever until all the accounts of the tradesmen had been cast up and the Company knew how much it owed, whilst Stephen Evans the banker was asked to continue a loan of £1,600 for a further six months and members of the Committee were urged to press their acquaintance to lend to the Company. Evans agreed for only £1,000, not the full £1,600, but Committee-men and their friends were responsive and produced over £3,000 in loans at six per cent., so that, when it had been ascertained that the pressing debts of the Company stood at about £4,000, the new loans, with £3,649 19s. 1d. from an extra fur-sale in April, enabled the Committee to satisfy creditors. An earlier sale had brought in about £12,000, and the Committee, dealing with an annual turnover which exceeded its total nominal capital, was able to carry on. But it had been a near thing, and a sub-committee on accounts was in constant sessions during the summer of 1685. Its labours were not made easier by the practice of carrying share purchases into the accounts, so that a profit-and-loss appreciation of the trading position was confused by share transfers, yet by September 1685 the sub-committee had arrived at £13,815 9s. 7d. as the 'amount of the last Cargo and what money and for what account has been paid out of the proceeds of the last sales and moneys borrowed this yeare'. This certainly did not represent the true trading expenditure for a year. It included repayments of the short-term fixed-interest loans which virtually provided the Company with its debenture capital, and the actual trade turnover was a much less sum, in this as in most years—how much less is not clear.

The cargo items in any one year naturally varied with the projects in hand, and in a year such as 1682, when the settlement of Port Nelson was provided for, extra expenses were necessarily incurred. Merchandise, with considerable fluctuations, cost about £2,500 to £3,500 in most years, and the costs of 1685 come within such a wide generalisation. Merchandise for Port Nelson then ran to £1,675 8s. 9d., whilst goods for the Bottom of the Bay cost £784 4s. 8d. This was, in fact, a year marked by quite a modest outfit, and though merchandise was only one of the items which went to make up the costs for any year, it was on the whole the controlling factor on which customs, 'charges' for wharfage, lighterage and porterage depended, and to which the amount and cost of shipping hired, with wages for seamen, had to be adjusted.

The only important item which was not directly controlled by the size of the cargo was the cost of the establishments in the Bay. At this date the Company's accounts were not kept in such a form as to make any comparison between the costs of shipping and the costs of the posts easy, because analysis is upset by the sudden intrusion of large and undifferentiated items such as the entry for 30th August, 1683—'Sundry accounts £932 2s. 2d. Ditto £1,766 2s. 2d.' Even less enlightening is the entry of £6,086 3s. 3d. as Sundry Accounts in 1684. But in general there can be little doubt that at this time the costs of shipping, normally dependent on the amount of cargo, equalled or outweighed the costs of the land posts. When ships were hired, the wages of seamen, their provisions and the ships' stores, were all included in the cost of the charter-party, and the cost of hired shipping in a normal year came to about £3,000 or a little less. When the Company's ships were employed for the Atlantic crossing the costs are elusive, for no account was made for the depreciation of the ships; but the Committee seems never to have doubted that it was cheaper to hire rather than to own the ships for the long voyage.

For the voyage of 1685 shipping costs came to £500 for the hire of the *Owner's Goodwill*, £700 for the *Happy Return*, £650 for the *Success*, and £420 for the *Perpetuana Merchant*—a total of £2,270. Of these four ships only the *Owner's Goodwill* was independently owned. Of the others the *Happy Return* belonged to Stephen Evans, the *Success* had been bought by 'some members of the Company' on the understanding that the Committee would then hire her, and the *Perpetuana Merchant* was owned by a similar syndicate. Samuel Clarke, a prominent member of the Committee, owned a quarter share in the *Success* and an eighth share in the *Perpetuana Merchant*. These arrangements reveal the way in which members of the Company, and even of the Committee (provided they declared their interest) sub-contracted the business of the Company and made profits, or perhaps losses, even when the general concern could not pay dividends. Samuel Clarke's example as a ship-owner in 1685 is particularly apt. It shows the wisdom of the Committee in hiring its shipping, for both of the ships in which Clarke held interests came to grief on the voyage.

For the Committee one of the great advantages of hired shipping was, of course, that it made it unnecessary to lay out large sums of money on this item before the ships sailed; the owners would need to be paid a portion of their agreed terms as 'imprest', and there would be miscellaneous expenses involved. But the outlay came within the hundreds instead of within the thousands of pounds at the outset, and the item for 'charges' would not fall due until the voyage had been completed, the furs sold and the cash paid in. Against this must be set the fact that the 'charges' for the voyage of a previous year fell due just before preparations for the next voyage began to be put in hand, so that the result of the system of hiring was that there was a year's delay in meeting the bills for shipping—which meant that the habit was in any case difficult to break since change would involve meeting double the expense in a single year.

In 1685 the 'charges' for 1684, amounting to £1,011 14s. 2d. had fallen to be paid just as the outfit for the year began to assemble, and in the stringency of that year there was no question that all the ships should be hired. Against the liability for £2,400 for merchandise and £2,270 for shipping, the costs of the land posts were mounting and had reached a comparable sum by 1685. In the early years after the Charter the posts had cost between £300 and £200 a year under Governors Bayly and Lydall, but the policy of increasing the number of posts, and the need to increase the number of men in each post as a guard against French moves, brought landsmen's wages up to £1,222 14s. 6d. by 1682, while landsmen's provisions came to something near £450 for each post. In 1685 provisions for the posts came to £2,983 14s. 3d. 'Stores' for the posts varied greatly according to the projects which were in hand at each place, so that, for example, in one year Hayes Island might absorb £429 16s. 0d. of stores while Rupert River got only £39 18s. 10d.

Too close an analysis of such figures is obviously not warranted, but it appears that out of an annual expenditure of about £7,000 on trade the Committee would allocate about £2,500 to freight charges, about £2,500 to merchandise and about £2,000 to wages, provisions and costs of the posts. The 1685 outfit, with its merchandise costs of £2,459 13s. 5d. its shipping cost of £2,270 and its provisions item of £2,983 14s. 3d., fits reasonably into such a general assessment and must have involved the Company in a total expenditure on overseas account of more than £7,000, a total which might well cause the Committee qualms since interest charges and post-dated costs for earlier voyages had also to be met. Though by borrowing or buying goods on credit to the amount of about £4,000, and by raising over £15,000 by fur sales the Committee just about managed the necessary expenditure in 1685, they must have wondered many times if the magnificent dividend of 1684 had been entirely justified.

Normally the Committee went almost into recess between the despatch of the ships from Gravesend in late May and their return in September or early in October. Then would follow all the business of putting 'waiters' on board to prevent pilfering and private trade and to preserve the Company's interests, the ships would be searched both for the Company's needs and for the Customs requirements, the letters from the Bay would be read and analysed, the captains and any returned officers would be interviewed by the Committee. And when the returns had been warehoused and viewed, perhaps by a professional skinner or furrier called in to advise both on the quality of the pelts and on the state of the market, arrangements for a sale would be put in hand. The business of disposing of the returns of the voyage would then run the Committee on until preparations for the shipment of the next year began again.

In 1685, however, there was no recess between the despatch of the ships in late May and their return in the autumn. The financial difficulties were such, the threat of French action and the certainty of French claims against the Company were so serious, that the Committee were forced to spend the summer months in close investigation. The two dominant factors were the great outpouring of resources which the 1684 dividend of fifty per cent. had involved, and the virtual certainty that French inroads would soon be renewed, with a consequent threat to trade.

Whatever the possibilities of French opposition might be, when the ships of 1685 were safely despatched the main problem of the year was that of finance. The close scrutiny of the accounts in which the summer of 1685 was occupied could not in itself produce either cash or credit. At best it might ensure better expenditure when cash or credit had been obtained. For the moment its results were disconcerting, for even James Hayes had his accounts returned to him with a request for further details of the expenditures which he claimed, as did William Walker, another important Committee-man. It was not until early in October of 1685 that the Secretary and Husband, Onesiphorous Albin, got his accounts cleared, and even then much muddle was condoned for the sake of getting something accepted. The sum of £573 11s. 0d. paid out for customs due on the shipments home of 1684 was inserted as 'omitted to be entered till now', and as late as 1694 accounts to a total of £2,030 19s. 3d. 'which ought to have been Ballanced formerly by Mr. Albin' were admitted. As a measure of expediency his accounts were neverthe-less accepted with 'all things Right from and to that tyme' on 5th October 1685, a new ledger was started, and it was acknowledged that the general accounts of the Company had been balanced up to 24th November, 1684.

Albin was soon to abscond from the Company's service and was to appeal, unsuccessfully, to the King in Council. In the meantime, he was available, with a show of new-found efficiency and probity, to act as Husband in the preparation of the outfit for 1686. For this the basis was the fur brought home in 1685. In October of that year the *Happy Return* had brought from Port Nelson 7,833 Made-beaver, costed at eighteen pence each, at £587 9s. 6d., while the *Owner's Goodwill* brought from the Bottom of the Bay (Albany) a further 7,117 skins costed at £800 13s. 4d. These were not great returns, but they were as good as could be expected when it is considered that the outward bound *Perpetuana Merchant* had been taken by the French, and the *Success* had been lost in December on her return journey, and the cash got from selling these furs enabled the Com-mittee to face the 1686 outfit with no great qualms.

As early as the previous December they had begun to purchase 'Toys' from the Nuremberg area for the trade, and to arrange for the direct purchase of Brazil tobacco from Portugal, while in the end-ess struggle against pilfering and private trade they had decided on Trade-mark with which all their goods were to be stamped. The Dutch guns upon whose superiority Radisson had insisted in 1684 had been found defective, and British workmanship was now pre-ferred. The Dutch were 'very bad guns', which did not agree with the samples; their bridging was defective and needed close inspec-tion and repair, and moreover they were liable for an import duty unless the Company registered them for re-export, as the Royal African Company registered its imports—a complication with the customs authorities which was obviously not worth while.

The Happy Return was again chartered for the 1686 voyage, as was a larger ship, the *Abraham and Robert*, the latter for £950 plus a gratuity to the captain. Both captains were instructed to seize any English interlopers under the terms of the Charter, and any foreigners under the terms of the Navigation Acts. The cargoes for the Bottom of the Bay were charged at a little over a thousand pounds and the provisions shipped out cost almost five hundred pounds and were chiefly remarkable in that for the first time they included some Indian corn ordered on Radisson's advice in 1685 and now bought from Boston and taken out for the consumption of the Indians. Though the 1686 outfit for the Bottom of the Bay was meagre, for Port Nelson a lavish outfit was sent. Here, to set against the freight charge of £978 1s. 6d. for the *Happy Return*, there was shipped £1,513 9s. 0d. goods for Port Nelson and £944 5s. 11d. for New Severn. With land provisions and charges, the cost of this outfit for Port Nelson was entered at £4,185 5s. 10d.

Such sums are, of course, minute in comparison with the grandiloquence of the Charter, the as-yet unknown extent and wealth of the lands then granted, or the commitments of comparable companies for foreign or colonial trade at that time. But they were adequate to bring to England as much of the peltry of the Bay as the English market could absorb or could forward to Europe; and they were enough to tax the resources and ingenuity of the Committee to the utmost. It was with justification that in all of their Instructions the Committee wrote of the cost of the cargo sent and of the quandary into which the trade had fallen. In 1686, when the ships had cleared from Gravesend, a stock-taking revealed that the Company's debts were almost equal to the capital which had been subscribed. The Secretary reported that on 16th June, 1686, the Company owed £4,250 to tradesmen, a further £3,650 to 'debenture' loans by bonds under the Company's seal, and £2,035 7s. 0d. to Stephen Evans. A good year's trade was urgently needed.

CHAPTER XVII

THE FRENCH *COMPAGNIE DE LA BAIE D'HUDSON,* 1684–1685, AND THE CAPTURE OF THE *PERPETUANA MERCHANT*

Given any choice between action or litigation, the Committee in 1685 would undoubtedly have chosen litigation against the French, for although they challenged the very foundations of the Company's trade yet they did allow that trade to continue in some form, and the flow of furs was the essential requisite for any further activity. But on Christmas Eve, 1685, came the first news of the course which the French had taken, news that the *Perpetuana Merchant* had been captured on her outward voyage and that the supplies which she was carrying for the trade were taken. This report originally came to London as a merchants' rumour from La Rochelle, but it proved true, and it proved the key to much involved and threatening activity in Canada, and was followed by a further rumour that the Canadians were setting out an expedition with canoes, to seize the English and all their effects in the north-west.

The two reports, of French maritime activity in the Bay and of an overland threat to the English posts, between them show the re-actions of Governor de la Barre and his Council to the English. De la Barre was in many ways the French counterpart to Colonel Dongan, taken up by the plan to unite the English colonies for military purposes, the importance for controlling the Iroquois, and the threat to Canada implicit in such a plan. De la Barre was convinced that Dongan had plans for fomenting wars between the Iroquois and the tribes in the French alliance, and of getting control of the vast hinterland of North America and ousting the French from trade there. The rumbling hostility between the two Governors not only reveals the deep clash between French and English ambitions on the American continent but it also shows strong personal antipathies between the two men. The Frenchman held that Dongan was extremely provocative and was only prevented from planting arms among the Iroquois by fear of touching off a major European war, while Dongan (lapsing from English to French or Latin according to his mood) felt that de la Barre 'est un très honeste Gentilhomme, mais ne m'a pas Escrit dans une manière Civile et Convenable'.

Governor de la Barre, therefore, saw the rivalry for the fur trade and Hudson Bay as part of a wider rivalry between French and English, and his reactions were complicated by such an appreciation. He was nevertheless deeply imbued with the needs of his colony and was not prepared to subordinate the American problems, involved enough in themselves, to the greater complications of an overall Franco-British settlement, as the European diplomats tended to do. For him the difficulty was to pursue French plans in the Bay at the same time as he thwarted English plans to the south—and to make both gambits acceptable in France.

For de la Barre and his Councillors opposition to the English had a unity which derived from an economic approach. They were convinced that it was necessary for the Canadian economy that the English should be driven from the fur trade, both by the conquest of the Iroquois and the consequent stifling of the fur trade of New York and Manhattan, and by the suppression of the English posts on Hudson Bay. Both programmes could be forwarded by supporting the designs of Daniel Greysolon, Sieur Duluth, whose ideas centred round the exploitation of the natural advantages of the Lake Superior area. Development there would at the same time threaten the traffic in furs to Albany and New York and would also lead to control of the headwaters of the rivers which ran down to the Bay. By 1684 Duluth had accomplished a great deal, he was writing to de la Barre from the Cree territory, was in correspondence with the French post which Radisson had left in Hayes River, and had begun to work for the interruption of the flow of furs down the rivers to the Company's posts. With an establishment in 'Mandan River' he was confident that the Indians trusted him, and he was ready to stake his life that, given two years to further his plans, he could starve the Bay posts of their trade. This, clearly, was a plan of attack which de la Barre could not ignore, and in fact he shared Duluth's confidence and wrote to France in 1683 that he could by this means completely stop the Company's trade without any cost, and that he would report his success later.

Duluth, however, brought to light some of the many difficulties implicit in any expansion of the French fur trade by overland expeditions. Such ventures were not quite attuned to the ideas which dominated the French administration and which formed the basis of the colonial policy of Colbert. There was more at issue here than the fairly simple problem of appeasing the English and making life easy for their Stuart kings, though that also was a factor which should not be overlooked. Colbert had for long thought that the chief danger to the establishment of a stable French colony in Canada was

G

diffusion of effort—'Qu'il vaut beaucoup mieux occuper moins de pays et le bien peupler que de l'étendre d'advantage et avoir des Colonies faibles'—and he had forbidden discoveries and expansion save under grave necessity or when great advantages seemed certain. For this reason he had refused Jolliet permission to settle among the Iroquois, and for this reason he showed the gravest suspicion of de la Barre's determination to enter upon a war with them. This was to be undertaken only if the Governor was certain of complete and rapid success, despite the arguments that the English were stirring up the Iroquois against Canada and her allies, for Colbert was convinced that a long period of peace and consolidation was essential for Canada. Moreover, Colbert was convinced that the fur trade ought to be in many hands but controlled by a system of licences. In general he insisted that overseas trade and the economic strength and independence which were the mercantilist ideal should be organised in great companies (and pleas against such concepts were safer when they were anonymous) but Colbert fought strongly for the participation of the *habitans* in the fur trade so that economic stability might be wide-based. Such a system, organised by distribution of twenty licences a year, had been set up in 1681, and de la Barre had even been told to try to devise some means of freeing this important trade from the crippling taxation necessary for revenue purposes, while the possibility of abolishing the monopoly of transport to Europe had also been put to him. But de la Barre pushed his threat against the English at Albany by giving Duluth a permit for many canoes for a whole year—a fact which led to the suspicion that he had a share in their trade, and which led to a severe reprimand. On the other hand, freedom to trade brandy with the Indians was restored to all merchants, and the general attempt to foster a widespread trade whilst yet restraining far-flung adventures was shown in a decree which allowed the nobles and gentry of New France to engage in wholesale or retail trade without derogating from their title of nobility.

De la Barre's plans to follow up his support for French settlement in Nelson River by attacking the Iroquois and by supporting Duluth were therefore highly controversial. Moreover Duluth was not the only protagonist of plans to nip out the trade which went down the rivers to the Bay; he was merely the most prominent in 1684 and the subsequent years. The idea had been a constant theme for many years; it was, indeed, inseparable from the basic French doctrine that Rupert's Land was an inseparable part of Canada. The notion had been expressed by Louis Jolliet when he reported on his visit to the Bay in 1679 that French posts could easily starve the English of trade and that 'il sera facile quand il plaira à sa Majeste l'ordonner de les empescher de s'establir plus loin sans les chasser ni sans rompre avec eux'. A detailed proposal for an overland journey, designed to 'couper aux Anglais le commerce des castors par les terres', was sent to France with an explanatory map in November 1684, and the Intendant de Meulles then asked for permission to send off twenty canoes to make posts in the rivers above the English, to oblige them without violence to give up their trade.

This was the proposal of which the English Committee got news from La Rochelle, and it had come to early fruition. In March 1684 Zacharie Jolliet, brother of the more famous Louis but himself already widely experienced in the fur trade of the Bay, was sent off by de la Barre, along with Ignace Denis, to take possession of Nemiskau, and to interfere as much as possible with the trade which passed there on its way to the English. Eventually a copy of de la Barre's order to Zacharie Jolliet came into English hands, and the Company realised that he was instructed to build a post at Nemiskau, and to declare that, acting under orders, he intended to prevent the English from passing him in order to trade with the Indians, and that he was to regard as an enemy of France any one who opposed him.

For the time being, in 1684 and 1685, this overland threat bulked less in the discussions of the English Committee than did the maritime ventures, and even the Governors by the Bay treated it with scant respect, so that it got very little attention until Jolliet's work at Nemiskau had been absorbed into the overwhelming overland attack conducted in 1686 under de Troyes and Iberville. Zacharie Jolliet, however, was by no means unsuccessful, little though the London Committee knew about him. From his earlier venture to the Bay and his contacts with Quaker Bayly he had a background of friendship with the English, and from his outpost he wrote to Hugh Verner at Rupert River, sending him a copy of his orders and 'as a good friend' advising him to clear out with all his people, since reinforcements for the French were due and Jolliet, having memories of the hospitality which in the past he had enjoyed, would be sad to have to fight to win the English posts. He protested his personal friendship and offered his good offices when the fight should come. Enclosed in his letter to Verner, Jolliet also sent a warning to Governor Sergeant at Albany, but the latter considered the warning merely as a 'french trick' and took no action.

Altogether, therefore, Jolliet's establishment was overlooked, and when the major overland threat developed in 1686 the English were left wondering why they had not had better information and made better preparations. But the episode in itself is part of the native French-Canadian approach to the problems of the Bay, as of de la Barre's struggle with the English, and when the details of Jolliet's penetration and of his orders came to be known in London they made it clear that French overland opposition had a core of clear and purposeful thought.

For the moment, however, the overland threat was obscure and lightly dealt with. Radisson's every thought was bound up with the advantages of a sea-approach to the Bay, and Radisson was in the ascendant in London in 1685. Moreover, it appeared as if de la Barre and the Canadian opposition were also dominated at that time by the maritime approach. Here the chief protagonist, the counterpart to Duluth with his insistence on Lake Superior and the overland approach, was that Aubert de la Chesnay who had organised the 1682 voyage of Radisson and Groseilliers. Deeply involved in the consequences of that voyage and in the furs which had been brought to Quebec in the *Bachelor's Delight* in 1683, de la Chesnay had become so wealthy and important a citizen that he was held to dominate Quebec (he helped substantially to meet the consequences of the great fire of 1684 there), and his rivals reported to France that he was the only Councillor to whom Governor de la Barre ever listened.

But even to so great, wealthy, and determined a man, all was not plain sailing. There hung over him the evil repute that on his maritime venture to the Bay in 1679 he had been convicted in open court of having traded to Governor Bayly the furs which he then took (or at least of allowing his subordinates to do so). Such action threw doubts on his patriotism and showed his willingness to defraud the Farmers of the dues. He was accused, on these lines, of a plan to smuggle the furs brought back by Radisson and Groseilliers direct to Europe, and such a plan would be of a part with his habitual approach to the fur trade.

Over the fate of the *Bachelor's Delight* and her cargo, therefore, de la Chesnay came into conflict with the Canadian administration. In the end the Intendant, de Meulles, ordered that the Farmers of the Customs should give letters of exchange for the full value of the cargo of the *Bachelor's Delight*, but that the letters covering the amount due for the *quart* should not be negotiated until the problem had been referred to France; for it was open to doubt whether furs got from so far afield as the Bay would be subject to the customs system of Canada. De la Barre as Governor then stepped in (under de la Chesnay's influence) to exempt the furs from the *quart* as coming from districts not covered by the Farmers' patents. In this de la Barre was running counter to Colbertist policy, for Colbert ordered the furs to go to Quebec and pay the *quart*. De Seignelay, who was 'chargé de tout ce qui concerne le commerce' in 1683, was also inclined to the Farmers; and in 1684 Oudiette was renewed in his monopoly of buying beaver in Canada and selling it in France, while a veto was put on direct shipment to Europe of furs got from Hudson Bay.

Having incurred reprimand for acting independently over the cargo of the *Bachelor's Delight*, de la Barre ran into further trouble for his complaisance in dealing with the ship herself. Since Colbert's first reaction to the whole story of the events at Nelson River in 1682 was that he must not rouse the hostility of the King of England and de la Barre was in very grave doubt as to what sort of case Radisson could make for the possession of the ship (or of her cargo), he released the ship to young Gillam, hoping thereby to avoid a major dispute. As Governor, though strongly in favour of de la Chesnay and of the maritime approach to the Bay, de la Barre could not take a very rosy view of the affair of the *Bachelor's Delight*; he looked on Radisson and Groseilliers as merely two 'malheureux' who had brought in a few thousand pelts for the customs-farmers to squabble over. But his action brought a sharp rebuke and he was told that whether the ship had been captured justly or unjustly she should have been considered as a prize and her fate should have been settled by the Sovereign Council of Quebec, not merely as an administrative act by the Governor. He was also told, perhaps with more point, that the release of the ship would be construed as an admission that the French were in the wrong and that the English had taken possession of Nelson River before the arrival of the French. This plea was in fact put forward by the English, while the owners of the ship also pleaded for £5,000 damages.

The rebukes which followed on the freeing of the *Bachelor's Delight* were perhaps unmerited, for de la Barre's trouble really arose because both the overland and the maritime approach to the Bay held promise of consequences, economic, military and diplomatic, which Colbertist France was not ready to face. But although both France and Canada were obviously eager to placate the English over the 1682 affair, and Intendant de Meulles had by 1683 summarised it by saying that Radisson had gone to Nelson River 'sans congé ny passeport de personne', yet the expedition had achieved a remarkable and provoking success; and Aubert de la Chesnay was in favour of following it up with further shipments. The danger of a head-on clash with the English Company was appreciated; de Meulles accepted that he must either abandon the trade of the Bay or drive the English completely out, and to sway his decision he argued that, as a consequence of the 1682 voyage, the French had in Nelson River a small garrison of men whom they must either support or withdraw.

Appeals to France for direction in this quandary met only with delay and mixed counsels, for in France not only was Colbert more deeply concerned with the European situation than with the American problems, but even his overseas plans hinged more on the West Indies and the New England colonies than on Hudson Bay. There was indeed in France an active and well-informed body of men eager to pursue the concepts of a Western Sea route to the Pacific, and therefore to push French exploration into the lands to the north and west of the Great Lakes. But to these men, especially to Abbé Bernou and his correspondent Cabaert de Villarmont, the last exploit of Radisson and Groseilliers at Port Nelson was not a source of pride but merely the last culminating proof of the folly and danger of their activities. They had started the English off on their approach to the Bay, had given them a title to that area by leading them through Hudson Strait before the French had been able to establish themselves, and now they had brought the whole issue to the level of a diplomatic incident which would be considered as part of the general Franco-British rivalry instead of being left to settle itself in an obscurity where the simple fact of French possession would clinch the matter. To this school of French geographers and humanists therefore, Radisson and Groseilliers were traitors, and the argument was produced that they could not have given any title to the English since treason could not bestow a title. Their actions at Port Nelson in 1682 were merely an added embarrassment, about which the least said the better. Their capture of the English expedition was as bad a betrayal of French interests as their original desertion to England. For while the maintenance of any kind of French post in Nelson River would eventually have squeezed out the English by the sheer pressure of competition, the interruption of the English voyage brought all sorts of other factors into play. 'Ils gâtèrent tout en pillant les habitations angloises' wrote these convinced and subtle schemers.

It need not necessarily have followed that French interests would suffer because the dispute for the possession of Nelson River was removed into the European arena. But there was too good reason to fear that at the French Court Canadian problems would be subordinated to European interests, and the pro-Canadian savants saw the whole history of the problem in the light of the indifference with which the claims of such men as Radisson and Groseilliers had been met in the past. They argued that, given enthusiasm and the right use of the undoubted talent which was available, France could easily have captured the whole fur trade, and it would have been worth at least three million crowns a year to that country.

Governor de la Barre, therefore, was left to decide what to do about the post in Nelson River in the light of his own enthusiasms and the promptings of de la Chesnay. The decision to support or to withdraw had to be made, and it had to be followed by a choice between support by land or by sea. In view of the characters and convictions involved, there could be little doubt of the course which would be followed, and in 1683 an attempt was made to reinforce the Frenchmen in the Bay by sea. Despite the opposition of the Farmers of the *quart*, two ships were fitted out in Quebec and sent into the Bay.

It is a commentary on the apparent ease and confidence with which the English year by year sent their ships to the posts in the Bay that the two French captains returned to Quebec without managing to reach Nelson River or to make any contact with the small French garrison left there, though they brought back with them garbled and tantalising accounts of a great river in the west, in 58°, where the natives had never before seen white men and where there was such plenty of everything that they did not bother to keep the beaver skins, but ate the flesh and burned the skins.

Such a voyage, unproductive though it was, inevitably stimulated hopes, and de la Barre was here, as ever, strongly under the influence of de la Chesnay. There was a rising feeling, too, among the *habitans* that de la Chesnay had hit on the right method to counteract the English, for when they were mobilised in 1684 for de la Barre's war on the Iroquois the *habitans* grumbled mightily and protested that it would be far better to fit out a couple more ships, manned by thirty or forty young and unmarried men, rather than to drag the householders away from their families. De la Chesnay was therefore able to prevail on the Governor to establish the *Compagnie du Nord* in March of 1684. It was sometimes called the *Compagnie de la Baie du Nord*, or even the *Compagnie de la Baie d'Hudson*, and although Intendant de Meulles complained that the Governor had set up this company without consulting either his Intendant or the Farmers of the Custom, and that it might cause the ruin of Canada by diverting the trade of furs away from the colony, to the profit of a small minority, yet it met with general approval.

The establishment of the *Compagnie du Nord* reflected the views of the maritime element, for which de la Chesnay stood above all others. Difficulties with the Farmers of the *quart* had yet to be settled, and the implication of determined rivalry with the English Company had yet to be faced. But for the moment, in 1684 in Quebec, de la Chesnay was in the ascendant and the *Compagnie du Nord* set to work to build two vessels for the vindication of its maritime approach to the Bay, while at the same time it petitioned hard for the loan of a naval vessel for the same purpose.

Such a determination to go by sea, however, brought into discussion one of the basic problems of the French-Canadian fur trade. If the Bay was to be approached by sea, why should Quebec, or French Canada as a whole, come into the trade at all? Would not the more sensible and economic route be that of direct trade between Europe and the Bay? Those who were certainly no friends of de la Chesnay gave their opinions that it would be difficult and dangerous to make the *Compagnie* ship its furs into Quebec merely in order that they might pay customs there. The furs should go direct to France since by the time they had completed their voyage to the Bay they could only get to the St. Lawrence at the very end of open water, some time in October when the river was dangerous in the extreme. Here was a clear statement of one of the basic factors of the situation, with the disconcerting conclusion that although Canada depended on the fur trade yet if that trade was to be conducted with maximum efficiency, by sea, then Canada brought little but difficulties to the trade and entailed an extra year's delay between outfitting and sale.

This was a problem, not always so clearly stated or so honestly faced, which remained throughout the history of the North American fur trade. The French government called for a detailed memorandum on the claims and the alleged advantages of the *Compagnie du Nord*, while that *Compagnie* went ahead with its plans, secure in the support of Governor de la Barre.

The Governor, however deeply imbued he might be with de la Chesnay's doctrine, was equally alive to the threat which Thomas Dongan and his Iroquois policy seemed to point at Canada, and his sense of the urgency of Dongan's threat drove de la Barre in 1684 to interfere with the *Compagnie du Nord*. Obsessed by the need to subdue the Iroquois, and by the dangers of a war with them, he requisitioned the smaller of the two ships which the *Compagnie* had built (a vessel of fifty tons) and sent it off to France with an urgent plea for reinforcements. This left only one small ship at the disposal of the *Compagnie*, and though it may have made an ineffective voyage more probably it waited till its consort had returned from France and then, late in 1684, the two ships set out from Quebec to seek the small post which Radisson had left behind, which had been left unsupported for almost two years and which had just been closed down by Radisson himself, now in English pay. In command of the expedition was the Sieur de la Martinière, a Councillor of Quebec who thereby incurred a double reproof—for neglecting his duties as Councillor and for demeaning his position by taking orders from merchants. Aboard as Chaplain was the Jesuit Father Silvy, and he has left the best account of the expedition.

The French ships arrived in Hayes River on 22nd September, 1684 (French style), only a week after Radisson and his English companions had departed for London with the young Frenchmen and all the furs which they had traded. The delay in the French arrival does not entail the conclusion that a few days might easily have changed the story of the Bay, for Radisson and the English from London were not the first on the scene in 1684. Abraham had come from England in the *George* in 1683, had arrived in the Nelson River after Radisson had departed for Quebec with his prisoners, and had settled a small post on the south bank of the river. His presence forced young Chouart and his small party to retire to Rainbow Island in Hayes River, so that they were already feeling deserted and out-manoeuvred when Radisson arrived in 1684. This made it all the easier for him to persuade them that they had been abandoned.

But although Radisson found it easy to persuade young Chouart to accept the Company's service, with the result that de la Martinière found no French post on his arrival, he found no very formidable English opposition either. Abraham was building a new post, to be called York Fort, on the north shore of Hayes River, but his men were still living in tents while the post was under construction. The English, however, had their cannon ashore and a night attack by the French was driven off, after which the two parties agreed to spend the winter, 1684–5, in 'amity and tolerance'. The French were certainly in the weaker position and they retired to Gargousse River (French Creek) on the south side of Hayes River and some distance from the English post. Both Abraham and de la Martinière were later reproached for their apathy during this winter, but each had been sent out in the expectation that he would meet no opposition and neither had the force or the authority to deal with the situation which he found. De la Martinière had set off from Quebec at a time when Governor de la Barre was still groping for firm instructions from France; but after he had departed the Governor had received a brief summary of the English complaints, followed by instructions that he was to avoid giving further offence to the English. He was also, however, to prevent them from establishing themselves in Nelson River, and to further this object he was to propose that neither side should make any new posts and that each should acknowledge the other in the posts which they already had. This, said de la Barre's instructions, the English would certainly concede since they could not possibly be in any position to resist French attacks.

These instructions were belied by the facts as de la Martinière found them, but in general he carried out the intention of the French Court although the instructions arrived after his departure. The significant change arose not from the actions of de la Martinière but from the situation which he found; whereas the French post had been abandoned, the English were indeed able to resist. They had sent out armaments for their post at 'Port Nelson', and in due course the French government learned with alarm that Radisson on his arrival had, with John Abraham, begun another English post at the most advantageous place on Hayes River and that it was a proper fort with four bastions and a ten-foot moat, well supplied and properly manned. The French could no longer be so confident that the English would accept a truce which would give the advantages of possession to the French, and de la Martinière's acquiescence was well warranted by the situation into which he had stumbled.

He spent a quiet winter alongside Abraham and then, as he was returning to Quebec with a cargo estimated to be worth ten thousand crowns, de la Martinière met the *Perpetuana Merchant* outward bound as part of the 1685 outfit.

The English captain, Edward Hume, was summoned aboard the Frenchman and his ship was then ignominiously taken without resistance. The surprise seems to have been complete, but two days later, when the French met the *Owner's Goodwill*, her captain, Richard Lucas, proved more wary than Hume. He refused to come alongside, stood off, and escaped although fired on. Hume was taken to Quebec and thence sent to France. He was in England by February 1686, ready to give a sworn account of the capture of his ship in time of peace, but the Company had not waited for his arrival before taking action. Already, in November 1685, they had put in a plea that the King should send a memorial to the French setting out the way in which they had further violated the Company's territories instead of making amends for the damages done in 1682. Although the cargo of the *Perpetuana Merchant* was assessed in Quebec at £1,000 (as the mate was informed) and the actual cost was somewhere in the region of £1,400, yet the Company computed its loss by the capture at between £5,000 and £7,000 without reckoning any interest for delayed payment, and ultimately the claim on this account rose to £10,000.

In due course a further narrative of the capture came in from Bridgar, for he also had met the French, with the *Perpetuana Merchant* in their custody. He had been unable to rescue her, since Captain Outlaw in the *Success* was not strong enough, and though Outlaw's evasion was accepted as all that he could reasonably have accomplished, the Committee concluded that Hume had been a poor cowardly fellow who had surrendered at the first call.

The *Perpetuana Merchant*, with her swollen account for damages, was perforce added to the list of the claims against the French—claims whose sum already overtopped the complete paid-up capital and the entire assets of the English Company. An attempt to recover some of the loss by impounding a French ship which took refuge from the weather in Milford Haven came to nothing, but the Committee showed no relaxation in their attempts to get remedy by diplomatic means. Yet the capture of the English ship soon became merely one minor incident in the wider conflict of English and French on the American continent, a conflict whose shape and purpose were emerging from behind the screen of European alliances, with rising emphasis on the economic importance of the fur trade both in the Bay and in the New England colonies.

Governor de la Barre had been superseded in 1685, brusquely told that his age prevented him from being effective. His conduct of the Iroquois war, upon which he had embarked despite the warnings from Paris, had proved disastrous. However much truth there may have been in his contention that such a war was preventive, anticipating Dongan's purpose of arming the Iroquois for an attack on the French and their allies, it was de la Barre who had begun the campaign, only to find himself beset by so many difficulties that he had not been able to exploit the successes achieved by the *habitans* and to end with a truce which was in stark contrast with Colbert's order that a war should only be entered on if it promised easy and complete victory, the final solution of the Iroquois problem. Colbert characterised the peace as shameful and de la Barre was relieved by the Marquis de Denonville, appointed to be Governor in January 1685.

But although the maritime approach had suffered something of a set-back with the supersession of de la Barre, the comparative failure of de la Martinière's expedition, and the addition of another petty squabble over the *Perpetuana Merchant* to the already complicated story, French plans were now more coherent than they had formerly appeared, for the *Compagnie du Nord* was there to give continuity and to stress the Hudson Bay aspects of the differences between the two countries.

The establishment of the *Compagnie* by de la Barre had roused criticism and some opposition, as against which it had gained strength because it represented the maritime approach to the Bay. Once established, it attracted considerable support and Denonville was even told, before he left to take up his office, that he was not to prevent the Canadians from trading to the Bay by insisting on the theoretical duty that all furs should pass through Quebec. He was, on the contrary, to do his best to prevent furs from going down the rivers to the English post on Nelson River, and he was to regard the whole matter as still open, to discuss the Bay-trade with his Intendant de Meulles and the principal *habitans*, and to make a report to France.

At the same time the *Compagnie du Nord* broadened its bases and, stressing the importance of the trade rather than of any one particular means of winning it, enlarged its purpose so as to include an approach by land as well as by sea. This made a strong appeal in France, and the *Compagnie* submitted a plea for possession of the territory of Hudson Bay and of the French post there, with a right to send north by river twenty canoes charged with men, munitions and merchandise, with the object of making further establishments above the English and of preventing them, without any use of force, from trading with the Indians. Thus the English would be forced to withdraw from the trade and the territory. The project, said the French company, could easily be accomplished, but they also asked for rights of reprisal against the English and for permission to continue their trade by sea as well as by land, saying they would arrange it with the Farmers of the custom at Tadoussac.

These far-reaching demands were accorded by the French government, and the *Compagnie du Nord* (*de la Baie d'Hudson*) was granted the monopoly of the trade of the Bay for twenty years, with permission to set up two posts, one to be on Lake Abitibi or thereabouts and the other at Lake Nemiskau. They were to send their furs to Quebec and to pay the proper dues to the Farmers of the customs or make suitable arrangements with them. In accordance with such a recognition of the French *Compagnie*, Denonville was instructed to try to assess the quality and value of the Bay peltries, to discuss with the *habitans* all possible means of keeping this trade from the English, and to support the Canadian company.

Denonville was, in fact, not far removed from his predecessor in his approach to the problems which faced him. He also was quite convinced that the Iroquois attacked the French and the Hurons at the instigation of the English (and any reading of the correspondence of Thomas Dongan makes it clear that this was true) and that they must be put down by the use of regular troops. He was also as much alive to the possibilities of attacking the English in the Bay by an overland expedition as by sea and was in a quandary between the two—as de la Barre had been with both Duluth and de la Chesnay spurring him on. Although the *Compagnie du Nord* had got its concession confirmed and had also been granted the possession of the small post left by de la Martiniére in Gargousse River, an arrangement with the Farmers of the *quart* was not achieved until November 1686, and by that time it was reckoned that de la Chesnay owed the Farmers two hundred and thirteen thousand *livres*; he agreed to pay by handing over a consignment of corn, the canoes and trade goods which he had 'in the woods', and by giving to Oudiette a share in the *Compagnie du Nord* valued at ninety thousand *livres*. Thus the interests of the Farmers of the customs, with their monopoly of the fur trade of Canada, and those of the *Compagnie du Nord* were amalgamated and the Farmers got a heavy interest in preserving and expanding the *Compagnie*.

For the moment, however, in 1685, this matter of the interests of the Farmers, and the chance that sea-borne furs would evade the Quebec entrepôt, only served as arguments for delay in embarking on any further sea-borne ventures to the Bay. Attention therefore turned to overland expansion and to projects for cutting the Bayside posts off from the interior. Much of the background of such an attack can be seen in the correspondence conducted while the renegade Frenchmen were in England, bickering about terms, standing out for their right of private trade, and making difficulties about their oath of loyalty before they sailed on the 1685 voyage.

From the English accounts of these episodes it would be difficult to imagine that any deep problem was at issue, and indeed it is most probable that the Company and even Radisson were ignorant, but from the correspondence preserved in France there emerges a deep plan to exploit the overland approach from Canada, and to make use of young Chouart for the purpose.

His nephew reported to Paris all of Radisson's plans, together with his own intention to accompany Radisson in 1685 and then to

flee overland to Quebec. De la Chesnay, pushing the claims of the
Compagnie du Nord in Paris, managed to visit London in 1685, and
young Chouart was in touch with him. The young man resisted the
temptations of an English bride (a lure which had undoubtedly done
a great deal to tie Radisson to the English interest and to make him
eternally suspect to the French) and de la Chesnay wrote to Denonville, Governor-Designate, putting forward the proposals of young
Chouart, stressing his importance and the possibility of using his
proposed overland journey to Canada from the Bay to make contact
with the Indians and to persuade them not to take their furs to the
Bay. Denonville was empowered to check the fidelity of the young
man, to decide whether the project would work out, and to take
action. He settled on an offer of rewards to any of the French who
might desert back to France, and of a price of fifty pistolets to be put
on Radisson's head.

This projected desertion of young Chouart makes one wonder
what happened during the winter in which Radisson kept him in
the woods, 1685–6; for this was exactly the opportunity for which
Chouart must have longed, admirable for allowing him to make his
way to Quebec and to persuade the Indians, with whom he had the
same sort of adoptive relationships as had Radisson, not to come
down to trade with the English. There is no account extant of his
journey, and it must be doubted if he ever went, for in 1687 the
Committee protested that the Frenchmen employed at Port Nelson
by Radisson's intercession refused to travel inland or to do anything
more than the other hands although they were paid from £30 to £80
a year as against the other hands' £10 to £12. Whatever the reasons
or the personalities involved, the plan to use young Chouart to iso-
late the English posts from the Indians of the interior came to nothing. But although young Chouart failed, the other aspects of the
plan had too much weight behind them to be overlooked merely
because he could not be utilised. The plan represented the most
active thought and enterprise of a vital element in Canadian society.

BOOKS FOR REFERENCE

Hudson's Bay Record Society—Vol. XI.

Cole, C. Woolsey—*Colbert and a Century of French Mercantilism* (New York, 1939).

O'Callaghan, E. B. and Farrow, F. (eds.)—*Documents Relative to the Colonial History of the State of New-York* (Albany, 1856–87), 12 vols.

Tyrrell, J. B. (ed.)—*Documents Relating to the Early History of Hudson Bay* (Toronto, The Champlain Society, 1931).

CHAPTER XVIII

DIPLOMATIC DISCUSSIONS; DE TROYES AND
IBERVILLE CAPTURE THE BAY POSTS, 1686–1687.
THE TREATY OF 1686 AND THE TRUCE OF 1687

While the English Company had been preparing its outfits for 1685 and 1686, and while the French *compagnie* had been winning recognition and sending out its first ships, the statesmen had been trying to integrate the claims of the two companies into a settlement of the outstanding differences between the two countries, both in Europe and in America.

The French *compagnie* had effective leadership and considerable influence, and the French envoys found themselves served with memoirs and passed them on to the English diplomats, who in turn passed them for reply to the Committee of the Hudson's Bay Company. So much, in fact, did the negotiations assume the character of a dispute between the two companies, rather than between the two kingdoms, that at some stage Lord Preston was reported to have said that the whole thing 'n'était qu'une affaire de marchands'. The French gloss on this rather cavalier utterance was 'que cette affaire ne regardait point le Roy son Maistre ne s'agissant que de l'intereste des marchands', with the inference that the two companies should settle their disputes among themselves.

Negotiations in 1684 had achieved only a promise that the French would ask for a report from the Governor of Canada, followed by the reluctant concession that Port Nelson should be restored to the English. They dragged through 1685 against a background of the obvious indifference of James II but with no slackening of the Company's pressure, and it was at this juncture that the name of Sir William Trumbull first began to appear in the Company's books. Although he later became Governor of the Company (at the instigation of Marlborough), he was never active in the Company's business even in that high capacity, and in 1685 he appeared merely as a diplomatic envoy whose good offices were invoked to support the Company's claims.

Trumbull, a Fellow of All Souls College, Oxford since 1657, a Bachelor of Laws in 1659 and a Doctor of Laws in 1667, with a prosperous practice in Doctors' Commons and as Judge Advocate of the Fleet, had entered into public employment in 1683 when he had been sent to Tangier to settle a number of legal problems between the King and the inhabitants of that possession. His heart was not in the 'dismantling' of the city, and on his return he refused the office of Secretary of War in Ireland but was made Clerk to the Deliveries of the Ordnance Stores in 1684, and was then, in October 1685, appointed Envoy Extraordinary to France.

This appointment was against Trumbull's wish, but the King insisted, though Trumbull's Protestantism and his legal background made him not altogether acceptable to the French court. He had many difficulties to meet in Paris, ameliorating attacks on English Protestants and pressing the claims of English merchants. It was in this capacity that the Hudson's Bay Company first took notice of him, for not only was he their obvious representative in their disputes with the French (as his predecessor Lord Preston had been) but his legal knowledge made him an admirable exponent of the problems involved in the claims and counter-claims of right and priority. This, indeed, led Louis XIV to complain that a training in English law was not the best preparation for an intermediary between the English and French courts; on the contrary, it often produced difficulties where none really existed. The lawyer was, however, just the character whom the Company would have chosen to expound its case, with insistence on chartered rights and legal niceties rather than on the general aims of a diplomacy in which a Roman Catholic monarchy in England tended to become the pensioner of the French king. The Governor, Churchill, suggested that the Committee should dine the envoy to France at the Swan Tavern in Old Fish Street on 29th October, 1685, and the suggestion was accepted.

What passed at the dinner, or even what the entertainment cost, is not minuted. But Trumbull was won over. The Company's affairs did not figure in his original official Instructions, although French encroachments in the West Indies did; and his first care after appointment would obviously have to be the consequences of the Revocation of the Edict of Nantes, which Louis had signed whilst Trumbull was awaiting transport and which placed the important community of Protestant English merchants resident in France in the gravest danger. Nevertheless, on the evening of his first public audience with the French king, Trumbull reported that he was at work preparing a memorial 'Concerning the Company of Hudsons Bay'.

The Committee had not only dined the Envoy Extraordinary, it had also put in a formal petition to the Crown; and Sunderland,

Principal Secretary of State and Lord President of the Privy Council, had instructed Trumbull to make a formal protest about the
seizure of the *Perpetuana Merchant*. Accordingly he put forward his
memorial early in December—a straightforward and brief account
of the French incursions of 1682 and 1684, with the capture of the
Perpetuana Merchant, all based on an unequivocal English claim to
Nelson River.

In this Trumbull was emphasising what was to be the traditional,
almost monotonous, theme of the Company's complaints against the
French of Canada—and the answer did not greatly differ from the
French tradition either. Early in January 1686 the French reply
emphasised that in 1682 Radisson and Groseilliers had been first
on the scene in Nelson River, that Radisson in 1684 had led the
English to pillage the rightful possessions of the French, that the
French ships of late 1684 had left the English, re-established by
Radisson, in peace while they set up a French post in the Gargousse
(or French Creek), that enquiries would be made about the subsequent capture of the 'petit vaisseau', the *Perpetuana Merchant*.

The Company, not unnaturally, could find small comfort in this,
and the Committee immediately submitted a reply insisting on
English priority at Port Nelson and on the rights of the Company
under its Charter. Emphasis was upon the complete dominance of
the British Crown—'his Majesty of England hath Long since the
whole undoubted Right of those Seas, Streights, Bayes, Rivers,
Lakes, Creeks and sounds, in whatsoever Latitude, with all the
Lands, countryes, & Territories, upon the Coasts and Confines'.
This rebuttal was soon followed by a petition, in February 1686, in
which can plainly be seen a fear that the French were determined to
exterminate the Company. The Committee were by now haunted by
fear that another ship, the *Success*, might have been taken by the
French, since she had not returned in the fall of 1685. Actually she
had been 'cast away' in December 1685, in the Bay; but her non-
return was not only a loss but also a threat to the Committee.
Furthermore, it fitted in with the fact that three French 'spies' had
been captured near Albany River and sent to England, and that the
French were reputed to be fitting out a further expedition against
the Company's posts (as indeed they were).

The French threat was so real that the Committee could well
include in their memorandum a cry that 'your Petitioners at their
owne great charge have enountered with Interlopers of old England
and New England, but the power of Canada, they cannot withstand,
without your Majestyes Royall Assistance'. They therefore asked

for a frigate from the Royal Navy as convoy and for the exaction from Louis of a veto on further expeditions from Canada, and that the Company's ships might, if this were refused, be granted 'Letters of reprizall'. The estimate of the total damages already suffered, which accompanied this petition, amounted to the enormous sum of £60,000, beginning with a 'modest computation' of £25,000 for the loss of the *Rupert* and the interruption of the settlement at Port Nelson in 1682. The interception of trade by the French post in the Gargousse in 1684 was computed at £10,000, the loss of the *Perpetuana Merchant* at £5,000, while Duluth's interruption of trade was held to have cost the Company a further £20,000.

For the moment, and indeed for the remainder of the year, to the end of Sir William Trumbull's period of service in Paris, no satisfactory response could be got from the French largely because the French embassy in London was able to report that James II had been shewn the temporising answer of January 1686. This had promised enquiries in Canada, and the French ambassador reported that James was content to await the result. Such stagnation, and pre-occupation with domestic problems in Europe, was not, however, matched in Canada, nor could the Hudson's Bay Company derive any comfort from the delays and evasions. An enquiry in Canada would take time, and it was also clear that there was in France a strong and organised group which would spin out the negotiations and deny the Company's claims at every turn. The fundamental question of the title to the lands round Nelson River had not even been debated despite the legalistic approach of Trumbull, and discussions had centred round the minor matter of the capture of the *Perpetuana Merchant*.

Such tactics promised no final and definite settlement, on which the English Company could base its trade policy, and they gave opportunity for further moves by the French which would still more prejudice the English case. In the early days of 1686 the rumour was that such moves would take the form of an overland expedition to attack the English posts; for the *Compagnie du Nord* was in fact at that time preparing the magnificent exploit which came to be known as the de Troyes expedition.

De la Chesnay had warned his colleagues from London that the English posts were well manned and that the ships of 1685 had taken out sixty men, so that considerable force would be required if an attack were to succeed. A major military exploit was therefore planned, to go overland from Canada by canoe. The hazards of such a venture needed no emphasis, but the skill of the Canadian *voya-*

geurs would offset most of the dangers and difficulties, and there were already posts established on the route which would be followed. Some chances, moreover, had to be taken, for the fate of the Canadian fur trade seemed to be at stake, caught between the threat from Hudson Bay and that from New York. Of the two, New York must be allotted at least an equal share in the assessment, for whereas Hudson Bay merely seemed likely to put upon the market better skins, perhaps at cheaper prices, from a hitherto untapped source, New York threatened to rob the French of the skins upon which the Canadian trade had always depended. The French sensed a vital danger when they learned that from their New England settlements 'the English were making Preparations to transport to their villages in Missilimakinac better and cheaper Commodities than those they had from the French'. They were convinced that 'if the English should put such a Design in execution, the whole Country would suffer by it', since the rivalry of New York was to them as vital as that of the Bay. It was, according to a memorandum of this period, almost indispensable that the French should make themselves masters of 'Nouvelle Hiork' if the colony of Canada were ever to thrive, for the English got as much peltry from that source as the French got from the whole of Canada. Denonville urged Louis to buy New York from the English and thus to settle the problem without a war, and it was even proposed to exchange the treasured Antilles islands for this key colony.

But while there were weighty arguments behind the French obsession with New York, there were equally important considerations on the other side. The Colbertist concept that a settled agricultural population must be the ultimate aim for Canada, and that fur-trading expeditions, especially to the north-west, should be regarded as a dangerous extension of the frontier of settlement, was of the utmost importance. This was a view held in high places, it conformed to the general theories of colonial settlement—and in the end it seems to be fully illustrated by the history of Canada. But yet in the sixteenth and seventeenth centuries views on emigration were far less swayed by the need to find homes and good living conditions for European subjects than by the need to keep important overseas areas under loyal inhabitants. Control of commodities which were necessary supplements to those of the mother country was the aim of the economist-imperialists of those days, and colonies which produced raw materials which did not supplement those of the mother country might indeed be held for a variety of military, diplomatic, or personal reasons, but they were always subject to acute criticism.

A breath of this air of contemporary criticism helped to divert French effort from New York and the Iroquois and to launch the northern expedition of the *Compagnie du Nord (de la Baie d'Hudson)* in 1686, when the Intendant de Meulles wrote that the fur trade was the only trade which promised to give France commodities from Canada which would supplement her own produce instead of rivalling it. This meant, as de Meulles said, that if the French conquered the Iroquois they would merely win lands capable of yielding wine and grain, and the Canadian economy would develop on lines which would render the colony independent of French produce and not capable of supplying France's wants. The only conclusion would be that the colony would have to conduct its trade with France's rivals. This was shrewd, almost prophetic, reasoning by the Intendant; it put in a short paragraph the whole problem of north American colonies in a mercantilist empire. More to the immediate purpose, perhaps, was the attitude of the new Governor, Denonville.

Although de la Barre's handling of the French attempt to get the fur trade of Nelson River was one of the chief reasons for his recall, yet Denonville was by no means precluded from fostering a similar venture. He wanted to send ships once more to the Bay, and the *Compagnie* sought the loan of a frigate from the French navy for the purpose. No frigate was available, and indeed Denonville was appalled at the low standard of arctic navigation of the French; their captains were dependent on Dutch charts even of the St. Lawrence, and the Governor was emphatic that a school of navigation for Canada must be set up immediately. But although a maritime approach was out of the question, the claims of the *Compagnie* were on the whole well received in 1685, and the trade of Nelson River for thirty years was granted to it in return for supporting an overland expedition from Quebec to the Bay and for defending the trade to be got.

Soldiers and an overland approach were therefore the French answer to the recapture of Nelson River by Radisson and the English, and Governor Denonville was in full agreement with the plan. He knew of the probability that young Chouart would desert from the English, he was engaged in trying to get hold of Radisson again, he had brought troops with him from France to end the Iroquois war; and for his own purpose he singled out from among the officers who had arrived in Canada with him the young Chevalier de Troyes, recently given command of a company of infantry. To him Denonville gave his instructions in February 1686; he was to set up French posts on the 'Baie du Nord' and at the mouths of the rivers there, and he was to seize any interlopers, particularly Radisson and his adherents.

De Troyes set off from Montreal at the end of March 1686, with a detachment of a hundred men in thirty-five canoes, five officers and a chaplain. Of his officers three were brothers; le Sieur de Ste. Hélène, le Sieur de Maricourt and le Sieur d'Iberville were three of the eleven sons of Charles Lemoyne, seigneur de Longeuil et de Chateaugay, a Canadian who had trained all his sons as sea-captains and who was to see them all take active and effective parts in the Canadian wars against the English. Of them all Pierre Lemoyne d'Iberville, third son, was to become the most famous; he was twenty-five in 1686 and was to spend the rest of his life in opposition to the English. In addition, De la Noue, Aide-Major, was a brother-in-law of the three Lemoyne brothers; Pierre Allemand, the quarter-master, had been to Port Nelson with Radisson in 1682 and had gone again on the 1684 expedition with de la Martinière. The chaplain Père Silvy, a Jesuit, was also making his third voyage to the Bay. He had gone overland to the Bay in or about the year 1678; he had gone again, by sea, on the 1684 expedition, and he was now to prove a useful *voyageur*, capable of playing an active part in the expedition. De Troyes was therefore the only one of the officers to whom the conditions presented any novelty. The rest were fully confident in their powers to make the journey by canoe and to pacify the Indians as they went. The men, too, were at home on the journey, for only thirty were professional troops and the rest were Canadian *voyageurs*.

The professional soldier in de Troyes found Canadian insouciance trying, but as the journey proceeded he managed to get them to stand guard and to accept some discipline and so when he began to approach the English posts he retained the advantage of surprise. By 18th May (French style) he had reached the French post in Lake Timiskaming, where fourteen Frenchmen were engaged in trade, and where Iberville and his brother Ste. Hélène reorganised the post in the interests of the new *Compagnie du Nord* which had paid most of the expenses of the expedition. Escaping from a forest fire which they had themselves started, they arrived at Lake Abitibi on 2nd June and there built a post and conducted a mock attack by way of training. An officer and three men were left in the post when the expedition moved on, to reach the forks of Moose River on 19th June and then to move into a carefully-prepared attack against Moose Factory on Hayes Island.

They found the Indians ready to welcome them since there was a general report that the Governor of Albany (Sergeant) had flogged an Indian, and they were able to get a clear idea of the post at Moose both from Indian report and from their own careful reconnaissance before they attacked on 21st June. The Company's ship, the *Craven*, had set her sails the previous day and was moored a league and a half below the post, of which de Troyes gives a far better description than can be found in the Company's own documents. It was square, each side a hundred and thirty feet long and protected by palisades from sixteen to eighteen feet high; the palisades were flanked by bastions of soil kept in place by stone-work, and the two bastions facing the river mounted three cannon each while the two bastions facing the 'desert' mounted two cannon each. The post was well set out and solidly constructed, and de Troyes was obviously impressed with its design and defensibility.

The action at dawn on 21st June was a lively one, and it loses nothing in de Troyes' account. There were two feints to cover the main attack on the great door facing the river, a mêlée between two parties of French who took each other for English, the smashing down of the main door and the entry of Iberville with gun in one hand and sword in the other, firing his gun up a stair and cutting down the English with his sword until the door was rushed by the remainder of the French and the post surrendered. There were seventeen English, who had fought for half-an-hour but were still in their shirts when they surrendered, and de Troyes was astonished at their laxity. Their cannon were not supplied with powder and shot, and they mounted no guard save in the mornings and took no notice of dogs barking, Indians passing or other strangers, so that Ste. Hélène, spying out the defences, had been able to push his ram-rod down the cannon before the action and assure himself that they were not loaded. All of which served to convince de Troyes that the English were most cowardly unless they happened to be at war! They were imprisoned on the old French hulk, the *Ste. Anne*, rotting in the river after bringing the English from Port Nelson in 1683. The garrison might well have been stronger, for Bridgar and his officers had departed from Moose the day before the French attack, going to Fort Charles (Rupert River) and leaving in command an ordinary hand, Anthony Dowrage, of whom there is no other mention though Governor Sergeant reported that of the two Indian women whom the French discovered in the fort one was in his cabin.

De Troyes spent four days at Moose, making up his mind whether to go next for Albany where he would find plenty of food which he badly needed (for Moose was ill supplied) or whether to go for 'Fort Rupert' (Fort Charles, Rupert River), which would be easier to take but where there would be few victuals and to which the *Craven* had sailed from Moose. He decided in favour of Fort Charles since he thought it could be taken without cannon, and accordingly he set off in canoes on the difficult journey, taking with him the two smallest cannon from Moose, on 25th June.

Arriving off Rupert River on 30th June, he found the *Craven* off Point Masakonam, working up to the post; the canoes shadowed the ship through the ice till night-fall, when the French camped on Point Comfort. Next day de Troyes' party worked their way carefully to a small river while Iberville's brother, Ste. Hélène, was sent ahead with two Frenchmen and an Indian to reconnoitre the fort. On the 2nd July he came in to report that the *Craven* was moored just below the post and that the post itself was a square with four bastions, not unlike that at Moose River, but that there seemed to be no cannon except two pieces in each bastion and that the redoubt was not in the middle of the fort and had a flat roof instead of a sloping one. The bastions also were more insignificant, being made only of soil held in by planks. The general impression confirmed reports that the fortifications were designed rather against Indians than against European attack, and there was no guard mounted either in the post or on the ship.

Iberville was given command of thirteen men and ordered to capture the *Craven*, using two canoes to reach the ship while a covering party from the shore fired on all who showed their heads on board. Ste. Hélène was to attack the fort by destroying the main gate, when de Troyes and the rest would assault, aided by the two small cannon.

Positions were taken up during the short summer night, and the attacks started at dawn on 3rd July. The attack on the fort was diversified by firing through all the windows, by throwing grenades, and by sending a man up a convenient ladder to throw more grenades down the chimneys. This last operation brought out into the open a wounded Englishwoman, Mrs. Maurice, companion to Governor Sergeant's wife. She had been on her way home in 1685 on board the *Success*, under Captain Outlaw, an eight-gun ship (the French reported her as twelve-gun) which had been lost off Point Comfort on her return voyage, so that Outlaw and his crew, and Mrs. Maurice, were still in Fort Charles when de Troyes arrived.

The noise and confusion, with the two small cannon playing bass (as de Troyes said) must have been most alarming, and the English soon surrendered. There were some thirty of them, including the crew of the *Success*. Once again the English were imprisoned aboard a hulk, this time a 'jak' or yacht, the *Colleton*, which had foundered near the post.

The two canoes under Iberville, meanwhile, had taken the *Craven* with all the éclat of a cutting-out expedition. They found but one man on deck, snugly wrapped in his blanket; the rest of the crew were so fast asleep below decks that the French had to stamp on the deck to waken them. The deck-watch hand tried to resist and had to be shot; the rest put up some fight but soon gave in. Among the captives on board were Bridgar himself and Outlaw. Ashore, the prisoners included two carpenters who were there to repair the *Colleton*, and whom de Troyes commanded to proceed with that operation. He destroyed the post, leaving only the cook-house, and loaded all the contents into the *Craven*, which he ordered Outlaw to bring over to him at Moose as soon as possible. He intended to use the ship for the capture of Albany, and he put aboard five iron cannon from Rupert; the other three cannon, rather surprisingly, were made only of wood and were burned with the rest of the post. After taking Albany, de Troyes intended to send food and gear for the *Colleton* to bring out the prisoners from Rupert River.

On 9th July de Troyes set off from Rupert River in his canoes, taking Bridgar with him, to return to Moose and prepare for his attack on Albany. Iberville and his brother Ste. Hélène contrived to remain on board the *Craven* for the voyage instead of going by canoe, and the canoe flotilla, lacking their knowledge, almost got lost at sea in a fog, wrecked by sailing in too high a wind, and ruined by sheer starvation and ignorance of the route. They eventually arrived at Moose on 17th July, to find the *Craven* already there, ready to be discharged of her cargo and to take on board the heavy cannon from Moose.

De Troyes and the bulk of his party then set out once more in their canoes for Albany, experiencing the difficulties and dangers of this sort of navigation in Hudson Bay to the full. They were not certain of the exact location of the post and had no guide save an Indian who made it quite plain that he understood nothing at all. But they were rescued from their dilemma by the English at Albany firing off seven or eight cannon as a welcoming signal. Surprise was the great advantage which de Troyes possessed; the English were quite unaware of the approach of the French expedition, and presumably the Albany men thought the French canoes were Indians coming to trade.

Landing unopposed, the Canadians approached the post through the marshes, and Ste. Hélène was again sent off to spy out the strength of the English before the *Craven* under Iberville's command hove in sight, wearing the ensigns of the English Company and bringing with him Bridgar, Outlaw and Mrs. Maurice. From their hiding-place de Troyes and his men watched the ship come in and anchor at the mouth of the river on the morning of the 23rd July, after which de Troyes decided on an emplacement for his siege cannon but, before setting his famished and weary men to work on the heavy task of building a battery, he summoned the English to surrender.

Sergeant's reply was in such terms as to leave the impression that what he needed was a few cannon-shot so as to allow him to surrender with good grace. But de Troyes' battery proved most difficult to erect, what with the ground being so frozen that it could only be dug with axes and the terrain being so marshy that the diggings had to be drained. The work could not have gone on but for the inactivity of the garrison, who made no attempt to interrupt it. But although spasmodic fire had kept the English from interference, the cannon could not be got from the ship until the wind changed and allowed her to come up to land. The intervention of Ste. Anne, to whom each Frenchman promised forty sous for the repair of the church at Beaupré and the dedication of the English flag after the capture of the post, achieved the change of wind, and on the 25th the cannon were mounted, ready for use and aimed at the Governor's house. The first salvo was fired as Sergeant was at supper with his wife and the minister (Mr. French). Mrs. Sergeant fainted as two shot passed, one in front of her face and the other under the arm of a servant who was pouring the wine.

Next morning, the 26th, the battery was aimed at the fortifications and, after a mass said by Père Silvy, a heavy cannonade of over a hundred and forty shots in less than an hour was rained on the fort. By the end of this time shot were scarce, the French raised a great cry of 'Vive le Roy' and judged that the English reply, muffled because it came from a cellar, was lacking in vigour and really meant that they were ready to surrender—as indeed they were, for soon a small boat with a white flag appeared. It was the minister, to act as intermediary. De Troyes cut brusquely through his compliments and arranged to meet Sergeant, taking good care not to let the English see the famished state of his men.

The surrender was given aboard two shallops in mid-stream, with Sergeant making a great deal of ceremonial and offering wines and hospitality and de Troyes anxious to get the business over before the poor state of his men became apparent. Sergeant made no difficulty so long as seemly Articles of Surrender were accorded to him, and he yielded the fort and all its contents on condition that the personal property of the servants of the Company and of the Governor should be left to them, that they should be sent to Charlton Island to await shipping for England, and that they should be provided with food until shipping came.

Iberville was then sent to Charlton with the English and twenty Frenchmen, while de Troyes gave orders for the defences of Albany to be destroyed. The defences of Charlton were also to be dismantled in case the English might cause trouble when the two ships which were expected arrived from England. Bridgar went back from Albany to Moose with de Troyes; he was then to join the other English at Point Comfort, where Outlaw was to meet them with the reconditioned yacht from Rupert River and all the English from that post, and where those from Albany and Moose were also to assemble for what promised to be a very crowded voyage to England.

Having made these arrangements to interrupt the English trade and to leave the English ships no establishments or men with whom to deal (except at Port Nelson) de Troyes set off for a further canoe journey, back to Quebec, on the 19th August. Iberville, left behind as Governor with forty men and his brother Ste. Hélène under his command, changed the plan for sending the prisoners to England and was responsible for sending the fifty-two English in the *Colleton* to Port Nelson instead. This was a sign of Iberville's quality, for conditions were shocking and supplies clearly inadequate even for so limited a journey; the Company alleged that twenty of the English died, 'frozen and Starved and some faine to bee Eaten up by the rest of the Company'.

The damages inflicted by de Troyes and his truly remarkable expedition were estimated by the Hudson's Bay Company at £50,000; the actual loss in shipping and goods was put at £5,562 12s. 0d. shipping and £17,550 goods, and although any exact account of such an interruption cannot be expected there can be no doubt that it was a most serious blow both to trade and to reputation. It left the English with no post save Port Nelson, with little reputation among the Indians, and with the cavalier brothers Iberville and Ste. Hélène in charge of French posts where the British should be—the post of Ste. Anne at Albany, St. Louis at Moose and St. Jacques at Rupert. Sorry as the immediate loss undoubtedly was, the most serious damage was probably due to the fact that determined Frenchmen were henceforth in command of the very places on the Bay to which the English had habituated the Indians to come for trade, a situation which entailed an annual loss of about £20,000.

The contrast between the activity of the French and the in-activity of the English was marked and shameful. De Troyes was with reason delighted at the hardihood and courage of his men, their endurance on the difficult journeys and the bravado with which they attacked the posts. The English, on the other hand, were not only unprepared—for they seem to have expected no attack save at Port Nelson—but had little heart for the battle. The Company later sued Governor Sergeant for failing in his duty at Albany, and the Governor in his defence gave evidence of a spirit of mutiny among his men and satisfactorily explained the facile surrender. The law-suit was 'arrested', Sergeant was paid an agreed sum in lieu of wages (which he would have forfeited if cowardice had been proved) but he was held up as an example to later Governors as one who had 'extraordinary tainted' the 'antient bravery' of the English by his negligence and cowardice. Despite the recriminations of the Gover-nor and his men, and their attempts to lay the blame on each other, the Committee thought them all almost equally at fault and had no doubt that the surrender was due to the 'ill Conduct perfidious-nesse and Cowardize of Mr. Sergeant and most of his men, whose behaviour was little better when they came to Port Nelson'.

Of all this story the London Committee remained dangerously uninformed. The *Abraham and Robert* had returned from Port Nelson in October of 1686, but she brought no news of the Bottom of the Bay except that the *Happy Return*, which had been designed to take the outfit for the year to Charlton Island, had never got there. Actually, she had been 'bulged with a large peace of ice' thirty leagues inside the Strait early in July and had sunk in three-quarters of an hour. Captain Bond and his crew had managed to get to Port Nelson, probably taken off from the wreck by the *Abraham and Robert*, but the loss of the ship meant that the French in the Company's posts at the Bottom of the Bay did not get the trade goods which they had expected. It also meant that the Committee had no direct contact with their ill-fated posts during 1686.

De Troyes, in the meantime, arrived back in Quebec early in October 1686, to be met with the warmest acclamations. To Governor Denonville he became 'the most intelligent and effective of our captains'. But Denonville hastened to add, in his official report, that his Instructions had not bidden de Troyes to take the English posts but only to capture that one in which Radisson commanded. Since the only appointment which Radisson held was that of chief trader at York Fort, Hayes River, he was nowhere in command; and de Troyes was unable to get to Hayes or Nelson River, so that Denonville's Instructions were not of much relevance. Moreover, the fear which Denonville was obliquely expressing, that high diplomacy might cancel out the results of de Troyes' exploits and even blame those responsible, was unnecessary. The magnificent exploit fitted admirably into the diplomatic situation in Europe as it was developing in the fall of 1686.

News of the affair reached Paris just in time to be sent to Barillon, the French envoy extraordinary in London, as he concluded a Treaty on November 8/19th, 1686. The Treaty was 'for the quieting and determining all Controversies and Disputes that have arisen or may hereafter arise betweene the Subjects of both Crowns in America'. James and his Councillors were negotiating under a fear that unless the talks were kept secret English Parliamentary opposition would prevent agreement; a general neutrality was eagerly sought, and on the English side there was no statesman, not even James himself by this time, alive to the imperial problems involved. The Treaty of neutrality therefore almost inevitably embodied a diplomatic triumph for the French. No mention was made of the English claims to sovereignty over the Iroquois and each king agreed to refrain from giving assistance to the 'wild Indians' with whom the other monarch might be at war. This was a virtual abandonment of the Iroquois to French attacks (which Denonville speedily put in train), a reversal of Thomas Dongan's policy which might well have proved fatal to the English position in North America.

The Treaty was equally a triumph for the French as far as Hudson Bay was concerned. Barillon was expressly forbidden to talk of de Troyes' exploit, and by the time that the Treaty was ratified in December 1686, the English still did not know that the three posts at the Bottom of the Bay were in French hands. The French knew full well, and they hurried on the negotiations for ratification with the intention that the Treaty should become effective before the news got out, for the Treaty was based on the maintenance of the *status quo*. All territories were to remain in the hands of their present possessors while commissioners settled the disputed boundaries between Canada and Rupert's Land. The result was to stabilise the French possession of the posts which they had so recently won, and of whose loss the English had purposely been kept ignorant at the time of signing. Small wonder that when news of de Troyes' success came it caused a great murmuring against the

King in London, and that the loss of the posts on the Bay added to the volume of resentment which finally drove him from the throne.

As yet, however, throughout 1686 ignorance reigned. The Committee had heard rumours of the French intention, but not of the outcome. Indeed, as late as the following June they were still guessing about the fate of their posts, and were forced to depart from their normal custom and to leave wide discretionary powers to the Governor at York Fort. Forced by their doubts to make no consignment to Moose or the other posts at the Bottom of the Bay, they wrote to Geyer, now Governor at York Fort, that so far their information of what had happened came partly from New York, but mostly from La Rochelle 'from the French themselves which makes us unwilling to beleeve all wee heare to be true but are in some Small hopes that One place or other at the Bottom of the Bay may still hold out'. Should this prove so, then Geyer was to send help and supplies from his post.

These were the highest hopes which the Committee could permit themselves, and the rumours floating in London were cause for serious alarm. First news, apparently, had come from Edward Randolph. He had served the Company in New York over young Gillam's voyage in 1682, had been thanked and rewarded, and was still in correspondence with James Hayes. He now wrote from Boston, giving the New York report of the capture of the three posts, and adding that the reason for the affair was that the previous French exploits in the Bay seemed to have gone unpunished. Other reports from France were gathered together and made into a dossier which is in itself a significant example of the way in which mercantile news travelled and was confirmed in the late seventeenth century. The dossier was prepared for Governor Churchill and was approved by him. By the end of the year the Company had the original New York-Boston rumour and three French reports. Here facts were mixed with opinions and, for example, an English merchant writing from La Rochelle gave it as his opinion that 'for a freind I can tell you that 100 french that Lives their can doe more in the woods than 500 that the English can send out of England against them', while an anonymous French report added that even the one remaining post at York Fort could now easily be starved of furs by the French 'fixing in the Passages of the Rivers which come downe to the said fort'.

So far, however, there was little which could be authenticated, and when in November 1686 the Company returned to its diplomatic attack on the French on the occasion of the appointment of a new envoy, Bevil Skelton, to replace Sir William Trumbull at Paris, the subject of complaint was still only the delays in settlement for the 1682 affair and the capture of the *Perpetuana Merchant*. It was not until Richard Smithsend, former mate of the *Perpetuana Merchant*, arrived in London in February 1687 that any new information became available. Smithsend had been taken with the ship and the rest of the crew to Quebec, where the *Perpetuana Merchant* had been declared a prize of war and her crew kept in prison; he had therefore been in Quebec when de Troyes set forth, and he had heard the first news of his success, with the perhaps pardonable addition that Bridgar had been clapped in irons, hand and feet. Smithsend and others were ordered to Martinique, where they were to remain until it became clear whether the action of the French in Canada would produce a war with England or not, but they missed the island, landed at Guadeloupe and were there discharged and made their way to England either by way of Barbados or Nevis; but before they had sailed for the West Indies the captured ships from the Bay (presumably the *Craven*, though Smithsend thought it was the *Success*) came into the St. Lawrence with the furs there taken.

A special General Court of the Company was ordered to consider this positive evidence of de Troyes' depredations, and on 17th February, 1687, Lord Churchill as Governor, the Earl of Craven, Sir Edward Dering as Deputy Governor, and several other members of the Committee presented their petition for redress to the King at Whitehall. After reciting earlier grievances, the petition came to Smithsend's evidence, of which an affidavit was annexed. Previous damages were assessed at £60,000 and the losses by de Troyes at 50,000 beaver and a great quantity of provisions and stores. The plea was for securing from the French King a definite veto on further hostilities, the return of captured posts, and a confirmation of the Company's grant of the sole trade of the Bay according to the Charter.

The last plea was directed against possible English interlopers, but the rest of the petition was against the French, and was rightly set in terms which emphasised the delays and uncertainties imposed by the French government. The need was for 'Effectuall Comande' from Louis to his Governor of Canada, and it was evident that all previous remonstrances had failed because promises made in Paris were not observed in Quebec. The petition in itself was so damning a recital, the position of Churchill in those troubled days was so strong, and the general dissatisfaction in Court and City with the conduct of affairs was such, that even James was unequivocal in his reply. 'Gentlemen', he answered, 'I understand your businesse, my honour and your money are concerned, I assure you I will take a particular care in it and see you righted'.

Skelton in Paris was immediately instructed to be very earnest and pressing in his insistence, and instructions from Sunderland, Lord President of the Council, were aided by the fact that Skelton was well known to Sir Edward Dering, Deputy Governor of the Company, and that a certain Captain Slater, a member of Skelton's suite, was also solicited to be a 'remembrancer' to the Envoy Extraordinary. Early in March Skelton delivered a strong remonstrance to the French court, with a plea for restoration and immunity, but Captain Slater passed the private intelligence to his friends that delay was once more the French reaction, and a further petition was sent early in April 1687, asking for a 'verry positive' remonstrance and for strong pressure for an immediate order from the French King. The Company pointed out that James' promise of support had encouraged them to embark on a fresh outfit but that their ships must depart before the end of May 1687 (the charter-parties for the ships stipulated departure before 25th of May) and that if the ships were to carry the required mandate from the French King no delay was possible. It would certainly take too long to attempt to settle the intricate problems of boundaries and damages.

This was quite true, for the French reply to the urgent protestations was to agree rather sardonically that the two companies should cease their rivalry, which merely enriched the Indians, and to appoint plenipotentiaries to negotiate and settle the disputes in London. The appointment was accompanied with a not altogether unjustified reference to the large number of complaints, petitions and counter-petitions which had piled up over the affairs of the fur-posts, and a suggestion that the emissaries should get back from memoranda to the original documents on which the case rested. The Sieur de Bonrepaus was appointed special envoy to work on the affair with M. Barillon, French ambassador in London, with full powers to examine and adjust the differences, while the English were represented by Sunderland, Lord President of the Council, by Middleton, Principal Secretary of State, and by Godolphin. They were well briefed by the Company, for whom William Yonge prepared a paper on the 'Case of the Adventurers of England tradeing into Hudson's Bay in Refference to the French'.

This is probably the most logical and compelling document in the whole long series, and it speaks much for the capacity of 'Esquire Yonge' that he should have been deputed to draw it up and should have succeeded so admirably. The 'Case' briefly alleged the right of prior discovery as belonging to the English, passed to the Company's Charter as giving the King's right, thus derived, to the Company, and then set out the story of the French attacks from 1682 onwards. The French claims were rebutted in detail and it was alleged that the English had possessed the Bay for a hundred years, and the Company had traded there for twenty years, before Radisson interrupted the trade by his 1682 venture to Port Nelson. Logical as the 'Case' might be, it was nevertheless straining points when it alleged that the English were already settled in Nelson River when Radisson arrived in 1682, and in maintaining that anything done by Radisson could give no claim to France since he was, alternatively, an Italian or a native of Avignon and so a subject of the Pope, not of France, whereas his actions could not detract from the English claims since he had been naturalised, he had acted merely as an interpreter when in the English service, and he had admitted that he was acting as a pirate when he went back to the French.

Each of the English Commissioners was given a copy of the 'Case', together with a 'Deduction of the Companies Dammages' amounting to £110,000, and they were further pressed and coached, to make an early settlement and to make it in favour of the Company. William Yonge was the Company's intermediary with Lord Churchill (for he had private connections with him and perhaps even owned the stock in the Company which stood in the Governor's name) and the same arguments were reiterated with little change. The Company and its influential Governor were insisting on their twenty years' of uninterrupted trade and on the fact that they had spent about £200,000 during that time. As a national interest they therefore began to put forward claims for Letters of Marque to enable their own ships' captains to take reprisals against French shipping, while they also suggested that the King might 'lett loose your Majesties Subjects of New England and your other Plantations upon the French in America'.

While the main problem was under such pressure the minor matters of evidence were not neglected. The Committee set to work to get the sworn testimony of two or three men who could prove the Company's right of possession at Port Nelson, and that Gillam was there before the French in 1682; and William Bond came forward to swear that he had spent fifteen days there with Bayly in the *Imploy* in 1673 and had returned again in 1674. It was probably with this in mind that Iberville himself wrote that the English could prove by good evidence that they had been in the Bottom of the Bay before the French came, and that he had himself seen the spot to the east of Charlton Island where they had wintered long before the French appeared, and had been shown by the Indians at Nelson River the place on the coast to the north where two English ships had wintered and a great ship had stayed, the crew being dead; the wreck, he said, was still there.

Evidence was also sought from the French correspondents of the members of the Committee, but little was forthcoming except that the Company employed an eminent civil lawyer, Thomas Pinfold, Judge-Advocate-General of the High Court of Admiralty, to stress the legal maxims involved in the 'Case of the Company' which William Yonge had prepared.

Whether this was merely taken as 'Counsel's Opinion' or whether it was submitted to the emissaries is not clear. It would only have been one more memorandum in the barrage to which the diplomats had been subjected when they held their first meeting in London on 18th May, 1687. The French commissioners had been pressed to establish the claims of the French company just as strongly as the English pressed their claims. Port Nelson, in particular, was to be insisted on since it was the most important and since the *Compagnie du Nord* had embarked on a programme of shipbuilding expressly for the purpose of trading to Nelson River. Accordingly the English claims for restitution and for damages up to £111,255 16s. 3d. were rebutted and the damages denied. The French answers were passed on to the Company on 5th June and a reply was drawn up by 10th.

Apart from the wider argument that the trade of the Bay was now so important to England that it was 'a valuable Jewell in your Majesties Imperiall Crowne', the English case was coming to rest on a firm claim to title by first discovery and actual possession, while the French (as in their second memorial, delivered in July) argued that 'Tis well knowne that Collony's cannot bee wholly established but by time and the Care and paines of those whoe have the management of it'. They argued that their missionary ventures, their early knowledge and their gradual spread from the St. Lawrence, gave them good title since they had 'Solidly established their Commerce towards the Land'.

A further series of letters followed, Lord Preston was called in to deny that the French had ever demanded any satisfaction for English raids from him while he was in Paris, the cartographical evidence was scrutinised, and in May 1687 the Commissioners appointed a conference at Whitehall.

The French were then asked to make a proposition, and there

H

emerged, early in August 1687, what the English Company called the 'expedients proposed by the French Commissioners'—a proposal that the three posts in the Bottom of the Bay should be restored to the English and that Port Nelson should be handed over to the French. Some such partition seemed necessary since each King refused to admit the other's right to the whole of the Bay, but the complete exchange of existing possessions which the French proposed aroused severe comment. Having made such protracted efforts to establish themselves at Port Nelson, the English were not likely to cede it now; they found 'neither Justice, Reason nor Equity' in the French expedient, and did not think it should be dignified by a formal answer. Both the posts at the Bottom of the Bay which the French proposed to cede and that at Port Nelson which they hoped to acquire were English by ancient right and (a more doubtful point) has been in English possession at the time of the treaty of November 1686; they rejected the suggestion that the French should reap where the English had sown and urged that if the French got any share of the Bay the English trade in furs would be undermined and the Company would have to dissolve.

The French, too, were not entirely satisfied with such a proposal. Late in May they had written to tell the French in Canada to hold their hands since they hoped to arrange that both nations should be allowed posts at Port Nelson, and they would then also keep the Bottom of the Bay. The French of Canada, however, thought that the root of the trouble was the fact that the English could always offer better and cheaper trade-goods and that if they remained in Nelson River they would be immune from French encirclement by land whereas if they could be got to exchange Nelson for the Bottom of the Bay the French could then cut off their trade at leisure.

As the dispute dragged on, the Company failed to enlist the support of its ex-Governor James II. The Secretary and the Deputy-Governor Sir Edward Dering went down to Windsor to put the Company's answer to the French before His Majesty early in September but 'his Majesty was pleased to declare that hee was then goeing upon his progresse and therefore had noe time to enter upon the whole matter, but at his returne hee would have the papers read to himselfe and would take it into his owne Cognizance and would take care to protect the Companie'. So although, when the Commissioners returned to their disputes in November 1687, the English insisted on their right to the whole of the Bay, to the sole trade and to full satisfaction, the utmost which could be achieved was a truce, and it was agreed that no further hostilities were to be undertaken by either side until further information could be got from America to help settle boundaries.

The truce was agreed on 1st December, 1687, and was to last till 1st January, 1689, and thereafter until orders to the contrary should be sent. This 'Instrument' was communicated to Churchill and it was agreed that instructions to preserve the peace should be sent to the local Governors of each nation, but in effect nothing had been accomplished by the lengthy discussions of 1687. True, the English Crown, even in its desperate weakness of that year, had at last supported the Company's widest claims in the widest terms. Further, the vital importance of Nelson River had been accepted by both sides to the dispute, and French appeals to vague geographical factors had been rebutted along with a claim, which appeared at this time, that the Treaty of Breda of 1667 had given them propriety since it was before the English voyage under Gillam and gave to each country the territories which it then possessed.

The legal and historical claims of the Company were weakest at Port Nelson, but Port Nelson (York Fort) was in actual English possession. At the Bottom of the Bay the French were indeed in possession, but the Company's rights there were indisputable on any realistic basis of settlement and possession, and of prior discovery too.

BOOKS FOR REFERENCE

Hudson's Bay Record Society—Vol. XI.
Clark, Ruth—Sir William Trumbull in Paris, 1685–1686 (Cambridge, 1938).
Lahontan, Baron de—New Voyages to North-America. Reprinted from the English edition of 1703 and edited by Reuben Gold Thwaites (Chicago, 1905), 2 vols.

CHAPTER XIX

TRADE, POLITICS AND DIPLOMACY, 1686–1688

The Committee had reserved its case for the future, but for the present it alleged that it had but the one post at Port Nelson in effective occupation. Although the discussions of 1687 reiterated this claim it was not entirely true, for 1685 produced a repetition of the instruction to settle a post at New Severn River, and in 1686 Governor Geyer was congratulated upon having accomplished this, and a further shipment of £900 goods was sent. So, with Samuel Missenden in command, the new post, known as Fort Churchill, augmented the Company's grasp on its territories even if it did not as yet augment the returns. Fort Churchill in New Severn River was never to become a major establishment, never to rival the later Fort Prince of Wales in Churchill River (with which it can easily be confused), but in 1687–8 it was a significant addition to the British posts.

The returns from the Bottom of the Bay for 1686 had, of course, been taken to Quebec by the French. Estimated at 50,000 skins, they inevitably cut the Company's trade by more than half, and no beaver were brought to London from the Bottom of the Bay between the shipment received in November 1685 and that of November 1693. The *Abraham and Robert* however brought over 20,000 skins from Port Nelson in 1686, and although this seemed little enough to the Committee it was in itself enough to see the 1687 voyage launched, with three ships, the *Dering*, the *Huband* and the *John and Thomas*, all consigned to Governor Geyer at Port Nelson.

Of these the *Dering* and the *Huband* belonged to the Company but the *John and Thomas* was chartered at a cost of £550. This, with wages and a supply of 'Large Quantityes of all Sorts of Goods for Trade' (carefully selected because Geyer had returned a wide assortment as unsaleable in the previous year, including some 'Old Dutch guns') and with wages and stores for the ships and for maintaining and building posts, together made a heavy commitment for the Company. Nevertheless, confidence that the King was resolved that the boundaries would be settled and that 'noe Forreigner shall upon any pretence molest us in our rightfull possessions any more' produced the necessary effort and the ships were despatched early in June 1687—a departure from the rule of sailing in May which speaks much for the desire to get a warrant from the Commissioners if possible.

At this time Stephen Evans as banker stood the Company in good stead. Some small debts, about £500, were paid off early in the year, but this did not denote anything like balanced finances, and by December an attempt to balance the books to Michaelmas had failed by £204 13s. 3d. unaccounted for. By the end of the year even Stephen Evans had called a halt. In December the Committee noted that they had drawn upon him for considerable sums beyond what he had received and that he had requested that they 'would not att present drawe any more'. They were forced to borrow from themselves in their private capacities to pay the wages due and to raise a further £2,000 on the Company's bond towards paying off Evans' overdraft. Actually, during the year from January to December 1687 Evans had received £5,411 12s. 0d. and had been drawn on for £10,510 5s. 8d.

Some of the difficulties in finance and administration at this time can be traced to the departure of Sir James Hayes. He had preserved his dominant position in the Company, and apparently his influence at Court, since the fall of Shaftesbury. But the rift which had then been revealed must have remained. Hayes certainly took a deep interest in the fate of 'The little man in the Tower', and he cannot afterwards have been accepted on easy and friendly terms by the other members of the Committee. He and his ideas were unacceptable to Churchill, under whose Governorship Hayes began to lose his dominance, and when in 1687 and 1688 the cause of James II and Popery was obviously losing ground in England, the flaws in Hayes' character were accentuated and his value to the Company declined rapidly. But it was not to be expected that Hayes would make an easy or graceful departure; his accounts had to be checked over, and when he sold his last £100 of stock in January 1688 the Committee ordered that the money should not be paid until Hayes had settled his account with the Company, to which he at that time owed 'a Considerable Summe of money'. Hayes brought an action in the King's Bench, and though Counsel's opinion was that payment for the stock could not be prevented, the Committee decided on a Chancery action 'to cause him to give an accompt of the severall moneys hee has received from this Company'.

As recently as 1684 Hayes had been the acknowledged leader in the Company's moves against the French, petitioning the English Court, corresponding with New York, and largely responsible for bringing Radisson back from France in that year. He was again elected Deputy Governor in 1684 and was paid his Committee-money on account of the time he had put in at Court and in travelling, although he had not actually attended the Committee-meetings. But with the election of Churchill as Governor in 1685, and the financial enquiry which ensued, Hayes began to lose his dominance in the Committee and he was replaced as Deputy Governor by Sir Edward Dering at the election of November 1685, after which he took little active part in the Company's affairs and was chiefly concerned to evade demands for detailed accounts of his expenditure and for the return of papers which the new Committee thought necessary for the conduct of the Company's business. He eventually returned the originals of Benjamin Gillam's Journal (presumably for the *Bachelor's Delight*) and of Radisson's 'Narrative', but there remained a suspicion that he could have been more helpful if he had wished, and he was invited to accompany the Committee to wait upon Lord Sunderland in May 1687, to present the Company's case to the Commissioners, and to bring with him 'what papers you may thinke usefull (if you have any such)'. His answer is not known; but he sold the remainder of his stock, and had not cleared his accounts with the Company by the time of his death in 1693.

Such an embittered parting from the most active of the 'founder-members' of the Company would go far to explain the apparent confusion of the Company's affairs in 1686–7. The troubles were made worse because the Secretary and Husband of the Company, Onesiphorous Albin, was under grave suspicion at this time, and his mismanagement was clear. The last item recorded in the Company's books on Hayes' account is for £136 14s. 9d. which Hayes had paid out on merchandise, which Albin ought to have repaid him. Albin had produced an acceptable set of accounts up to November 1685, but although his requests for an increase in salary were met by the Committee (with an increase from £80 to £180, plus a gratuity of £50 for past services) he absconded from the service of the Company in October 1686. Unknown to the Company, he was at this time in correspondence with the French court, and a coded letter from him survives, in which he offered to betray the Company's secrets. The Committee could not have known of this treachery, but they discovered that Albin was embroiled in all sorts of troubles and debts, and he was discharged. His account was not finally balanced until 1697, by which time it had become clear that £412 19s. 2d. was outstanding. This was not written off as a bad debt until 1713 and in the meantime, in the midst of the troubles of 1686, the Committee were faced with a petition to the King from their absconded and dismissed secretary. They rebutted his claims, alleging they had just discovered that he had for some years been an undischarged bankrupt, and so Albin's petition was dismissed and the Company was vindicated.

The Albin affair, seen in perspective, is a minor one concerned with the discharge of an unsatisfactory servant. But it involved Hayes and the major difficulties of parting from that dominant man during a time of acute diplomatic pressure; it was conducted at a level on which appeals to the King himself, and an investigation by the Privy Council, were considered reasonable; and it could have left an impression on the statesmen whose goodwill the Company needed that the fur trade of Hudson Bay was in the hands of a small group of mean traders who underpaid and overworked their servants and whose whole business was in inextricable muddle. Not less important was the result that at this time of stress the new accountant could not find his way about the Company's books and needed to be 'put into a method' by members of the Committee.

The fur trade in general was in the 1680's going through a period which seems inevitable in any colonial trade, particularly when that trade is in luxury goods for which there is no irreducible minimum demand. Gluts in supply, economies in consumption, interruptions for political reasons, and changes in public taste, all easily affected the beaver trade. But the trade could not react to economic conditions by varying the quantity and quality of its products, partly because those products were not under control. They were the result of natural causes and cycles, and they were harvested by Indians who could not conceive of the ultimate destination of their produce and who could only be remotely influenced by traders who were themselves removed from the pressure of the European market by a lengthy trade-routine. Some four years of trans-oceanic correspondence were required for a European situation to be knit into the processes of the fur trade, for the consequent orders to be formulated and conveyed to the trapping areas, and for the modified catch (if indeed modification were possible) to find its way to Europe. Normally the cycle would be nearer to six years before any fluctuations in European conditions could have any effect on the pelts delivered in Europe; and modification even then seldom proved possible.

Moreover, the fur trade was not susceptible to pure economic influences even to this very limited extent, for the French trade was in the hands of the customs-farmers and was bound to produce the revenues on which the public administration and the religious endowments of Canada depended. This meant that French furs had to be produced and sold, whatever the state of the market, and the prices and quantities of furs delivered on the European market by the French affected the prices at which the Hudson's Bay Company could sell its wares in London. Normally, restrictive tariffs and difficulties of shipping and currency combined to make the English and the European markets almost self-contained, but in 1686 the state of the European market was such that despite the Navigation Acts, and their veto on the introduction into England of colonial goods in any shipping save that of the country of origin or that of English owners, the Company was alarmed to find that the London market was being upset by the importation of considerable quantities of beaver wool. French successes, and their relaxations in the laws governing their own trade, had given them greatly increased quantities to dispose of, and the Skinners of London, whose interests would be served by reasonable price-cutting but who could not afford to see the whole fur trade in a turmoil, joined the Company in a petition against the foreign imports, while the Company began the slow process of trying to modify its trade to meet the threat of a glutted market. 'Beevor grows lower and lower in price here every Day' they wrote to John Bridgar in 1686; martens and small furs were therefore to be traded as much as possible, and the Indians were to be encouraged to trade them 'for they turne to better account than Beavor and are mightily requested here'.

Despite this, and the general uneasiness, the fur sales in London were not going too badly. Port Nelson was bringing in some 20,000 skins a year (20,152 in 1686; 20,485 in 1687; 20,928 in 1688; 27,201 in 1689) and the big London furriers were buying briskly. Such men as Thomas Glover, who had bought so largely in the 1670's, were still in the market, and Richard Gawthorne, who had bought as much as £7,355 worth in 1681 and £5,997 worth in 1682, was buying both beaver and small skins. The Committee, in fact, thought it 'A Tollerable Trade', and even though Port Nelson was the only post (with New Severn) the returns in 1687 were such that they decided not to throw all the furs on the market. Instead, after postponing the sale until 23rd November, they decided then to offer only forty lots of old *coat* beaver and all the small skins of the current shipment.

Such a decision showed worldly wisdom when the market was weak and when so many disputes were on hand, all owing their origin to the general feeling (in England as in France) that the fur trade was a limitless source of wealth. The Commissioners on the Nelson River affair were still in session, the political situation in

England was coming to a boil with Churchill deeply involved in the maturing plot to oust James from the throne and with the Seven Bishops on trial; and trade was jumpy in London.

The Committee had to watch this complicated situation most carefully, and the Governor's inside knowledge of the intrigues at Court was here of the greatest value. Late in September 1687 Sir Edward Dering as Deputy Governor prepared a paper to give to Churchill for use 'as a handle to bring on the Companies businesse', having heard of a convenient Sunday occasion when Lord President Sunderland might be approached at Windsor. Churchill, however, advised delay and secured from Sunderland a postponement until the Company's ships should be back from the Bay. The letters were then combed for details of de Troyes' capture of the posts and of the insolence and inhumanity of the French, while further details of the already-known French incursions were gathered. Bridgar himself had been brought home in the *John and Thomas* after his winter at Port Nelson, and he now appeared before the Committee, while Governor Sergeant also was home with his 'whole parcell of women', to submit his own version of the capture of the posts and of the mutinous conduct of his men, together with Hugh Verner, who had been in command at Rupert River when de Troyes captured Fort Charles there.

Verner not only brought authentic news of the capture of Fort Charles but also of the attempt which had preceded de Troyes, when in 1684 de la Barre had sent Zacharie Jolliet to set up a post at Nemiskau, there to cut off the English posts from the Indians. Apparently this was the first news which the Committee had of this effort, which was completely eclipsed by de Troyes; but Verner brought home both a warning letter which Jolliet had sent him, and a copy of the actual order which de la Barre had issued. The steadiness of the French threat was thereby underlined, as well as the military inefficiency of the English traders. This evidence, arriving in London in 1687, must have added greatly to the Committee's troubles, for Verner made it clear that any interim arrangement for pacification of the shores of the Bay would always be subject to overland threats and to intimidation of the Indians of the interior, of which news would arrive very slowly in London, and which would prove most difficult to control.

The French affair was moving towards its interim solution, in the Truce of December 1687, while these troubles mounted against a background of a sadly divided English Court and Parliament. But the French were not the only rivals to the Company. At last, in

1686, John Abraham had concluded a long and stormy career as a servant of the Company by being recalled in disgrace to London. He had gone out with Governor Bayly as early as 1674, had sworn false witness (according to Nixon) against Bayly and had taken sides with Nehemiah Walker against Nixon in his turn. In 1683 he had been sent out as Governor of Port Nelson but had arrived to find that Bridgar had himself been captured by Radisson in 1683 and had failed to establish such a post. Abraham had wintered 1683–4 in the Nelson River in opposition to young Chouart and the Frenchmen left behind by Radisson, and he had then built Hayes Fort, Nelson River, on the south shore. In 1684 he had been given a commission as Governor of Port Nelson, but he had deserted his post and was on his way home before his commission arrived; fortunately he met the ship of the year at the mouth of the Bay and returned to take up his command and to witness the subjugation of the French post by Radisson. He was then in charge of the building of a new post, York Fort on the north shore of Hayes River, with George Geyer in immediate command. Here he met the French maritime reinforcements under de la Martinière, sent out to reinforce young Chouart in 1684, and he spent the winter 1684–5 opposite the French post in the Gargousse River, an acquiescence for which he was severely taken to task. The Committee, who had deemed that he had forfeited his commission when he started for home in 1684, and who in 1685 made him only Deputy Governor of Port Nelson under command of Thomas Phipps, now, in 1686, called him home.

On his return Abraham appeared before the Committee and told them how he and Michael Grimington had sailed in the *Hayes* sloop from Nelson River in spring 1686 and had gone about fifty leagues to the north. There they found 'a faire River' which seemed to them admirable for trade. The Committee were so struck by Abraham's description that in June 1687 the settlement of Churchill River (for that was the name of the discovery) was ordered without loss of time and the *Huband*, now sent out for the first time, was recommended for the task.

Abraham had submitted a set of proposals for Churchill River, and although the Committee refused to take him back into employment the proposals were kept and were sent out to York Fort. Whaling was almost certainly a major incentive from the start, for the orders to make a settlement contained the phrase that 'what things may be wanting to Carry on the Fishing Trade or any other designe shall certainly be sent', and the sailors who had been with

Abraham said that in sailing up the river 'wee saw many 1000ds of white whales and soe tame that they were continually sporting round the sloope, and when wee went ashoare in our Canoe wee found them very Troublesome, and dangerous, neare over setting the Canoe'. At a time when it was estimated that England imported about £26,000 worth of whale oil or whalebone a year from Holland and Germany, there was an obvious attraction in the 'little New Factorey begun detached from Port Nellson'.

But the little new factory was not yet a reality despite orders for the *Huband* to be so employed, the Churchill River post was not settled in 1687, and in February 1688 the Committee firmly resolved that it should be settled that year, with a good ship, an adequate cargo, and materials for white whale fishing. The *Dering* was then instructed to sail for Port Nelson, load building materials for Churchill there, and return to Nelson for the winter after unloading at the proposed post. The *Colleton* yacht was to accompany the *Dering* from Nelson to Churchill, and was to winter at Churchill, where Thomas Savage was to be chief with eight men under him. The stores shipped included two shallops, boats for whale fishing, and a sow for the use of the factory; whale-fishing material was also included, and a harpooner, Edward Mills, bred in the Greenland whaling industry, was 'entertained' despite the fact that the Committee had, on the whole, now decided against whaling. They had debated the matter at great length, considering its uncertainty and great charge, and had decided not to proceed with it but to send a small cargo merely for a trade post. On this basis the 1688 orders to Governor Geyer at Port Nelson were most emphatic that the new post must be founded.

Abraham's plan (for there can be little doubt that the idea arose from his voyage of 1686 and from his pleadings before the Committee) succeeded so well that by 1690 the Committee were 'well pleased with the beginnings made in the Whale Fishing'. Nine tons of white whale blubber were shipped home in 1689, the first year; they were costed at £1 a ton and after some discussion as to whether the upset price should be £24 a ton they were set up at £18 a ton. The Committee had good reason to be satisfied and to encourage Port Nelson to seek similar new products, seal skins, drugs and dyes, whalebone, seahorse teeth and so on. But Abraham himself had not been accepted by the Committee and, full of enthusiasm for his discovery, he was a potentially dangerous rival. He had got financial support and a ship for an interloping voyage to the Bay, and he soon had with him another renegade from the Company's service in John

Outlaw. The latter had sailed as mate to Benjamin Gillam on the *Bachelor's Delight*, had been captured by Radisson and on his release had given valuable evidence for the Hudson's Bay Company, who in return had given him a post as a ship's captain. He had, however, wrecked his ship, the *Success*, on her homeward voyage in December 1685 (a crazy time of year to be at sea in the Bay), and had spent most of the winter at Rupert River. There he had been captured by the French for a second time when de Troyes stormed the post in 1686, and he had ultimately found his way with Bridgar, Sergeant and the other prisoners, to the English post in Hayes River, where Geyer had the unsatisfactory Abraham under command. Outlaw could not, of course, have been on the pioneer voyage which Abraham and Grimington had made to Churchill River in 1686, but when he got back to England in 1687, and he and his crew were refused their pay by the Company, he threw in his lot with Abraham. He was obviously a restless unsatisfied kind of man and in 1687 he had a real grievance. He finished his career in French pay, preying on English commerce in the St. Lawrence; Abraham ultimately took similar employment.

The Committee knew their danger, and whereas the instructions of previous years had carried the standard warning to traders and ships' captains to capture interlopers, those of 1687 were far more explicit. Abraham and his plan for Churchill River were detailed— 'hee makes great Braggs that wilbee a better Settlement then any has yett been found'—and his ship the *Mary* was named. Captain Groves, her commander, had been stayed by Royal warrant until he had taken oath that neither he nor his ship were bound for Hudson Bay, but Abraham had kept out of the way and avoided such an oath, so that the Committee were still afraid that his design to interlope was afoot. There was also a rumour of an interloper being fitted out at Boston.

The petition which the Company had put in, largely against the French, in February 1687, had also borne in mind the possibility of English interlopers and had included a phrase asking 'that the Petrs. may have the Sole Trade of Hudson's Bay according to the Purport and gratious intencion of your Maties Royall Charter'. As news of Abraham became more positive, this general move also became more pointed, with an action against Captain Groves of the *Mary* in May–June 1687, a decision to petition again in February 1688, the sending in of a petition in March 1688, and at last, on 31st March, 1688, a Royal Proclamation against interlopers. This proclamation forbidding anyone but the Company shipping to Hudson

Bay or Hudson Strait was given the fullest publicity and was printed and published at the Royal Exchange and also in Middlesex, while both the ships' captains and the Governors of posts were once more warned of the dangers.

But although the Committee could only warn in general terms of projects of which rumours came from Holland and from Ireland, there was at hand a firm report from Cork, written in May 1688 and telling of Abraham again. The *Mary* of London had come into port; Captain Zachary Bardon master. After being held up by the Company in English ports, he had shipped for Cork and had taken thence a cargo of tallow for Holland, where he traded for eight guns, ten peteroes and an abundance of small arms, and signed on thirty men. Thus equipped, he sailed back to 'Ballymore' (really Baltimore) in Ireland where he bought the *Humphrey and Thomas* of forty tons alias the *Rainbow* of Cork, and entered out for Newfoundland. The latter was 'laden as deep as she could swim' with provisions, liquor, a malt mill and a brewing pan.

The interloping argosy sailed in the summer of 1688, a further trouble to be faced by the Committee at a time of Revolution at home and uncertainty abroad. But the next news was that Abraham and Outlaw were both prisoners of the Company. They were both aboard the *Mary* when she was sighted by the Company's ship *Churchill* in August, in the middle of Hudson Strait, in a sinking condition. The *Mary* sank the next day, and Outlaw and Abraham were taken to the Company's new little re-founded post at Albany. After that they sink from view save as a moral to point the difficulties of the fur trade, for they were the scapegoats of the story urged by the Company to prove that the voyage was 'extream hazardous through the Mountains of Ice which must be passed'; theirs was 'the English Ship Interloping there, and in distress in the Ice just ready to sink, the Companies Ship seasonably (by God's Providence) saved all the Mens lives and the Ship sunk immediately'.

BOOKS FOR REFERENCE

HUDSON'S BAY RECORD SOCIETY—Vols. VIII, IX, XI.

DAVIES, K. G.—Introduction to *Hudson's Bay Copy Booke of Letters Commissions Instructions Outward 1688–1696* (London, The Hudson's Bay Record Society, 1957), Vol. XX.

CHAPTER XX

IBERVILLE RULES AT THE BOTTOM OF THE BAY

The fact that the crew of the interloping *Mary* should have been rescued by the *Churchill* was in itself a sign of the confidence, and indeed of the prosperity, of the Company in these apparently desperate years, for the *Churchill* was one of four ships sent out in 1688, of which two were to re-settle the Bottom of the Bay. Here was evidence that, difficult and troublesome though these years undoubtedly were for a body with such close political and diplomatic connections as the Hudson's Bay Company, they were nevertheless years of unexampled prosperity. Despite the loss of its posts, the political uncertainty, the glut of beaver, the challenges of interlopers and French opposition, the Company declared a dividend of fifty per cent. in 1688, a further twenty-five per cent. in 1689, and in 1690 it trebled its stock and then declared a dividend of twenty-five per cent. on the increased stock after a long debate as to whether it might not well rise to thirty per cent.

Such buoyancy seems completely out of phase with the general position of the Company's affairs, and each of these acts requires comment and explanation, the more so since the 1690 dividend on the trebled stock was the last to be paid for almost twenty years, until payments were resumed in 1718.

The 1688 dividend may be to some extent explained by the confidence induced by the end of negotiations with the French. The agreement for peace in North America, concluded in December 1687, at the end of the long discussions in London, augured well. The Committee fully accepted this treaty and rather trustingly expected the French to do the same, for it had been the French who had put forward the plea that each side should restrain its agents to its own posts and should avoid competition. To avoid dispute the Committee now decided to make Radisson and the other Frenchmen in the Company's employ into English citizens at the Company's expense, and accompanied a decision to send what it hoped would prove an inoffensive expedition to re-found Albany in 1688 with a petition that the French should also avoid provocation by agreeing not to send any ship to the Bay but to supply their posts and men there by the overland route. This Lord President Sutherland thought would not be to the Company's interest (presumably because the inference would be that the French claims to the hinterland might be implicitly acknowledged by such an arrangement) and the proposal was withdrawn. It is true that the Committee were trying to recruit some military men at this time, but it is obvious that they thought an arrangement might be acceptable, and that they imagined the French were in as complaisant a mood as themselves.

This, if true, was an opportunity which demanded great efforts, and after a good sale in May 1688 had brought in £9,238 the Committee were in a confident mood—confident enough to spend £5,100 on a dividend, and confident enough to send a generous and purposeful outfit to the Bay. The *John and Thomas* and the *Dering* were ordered to the post which was developing an identity as 'York Fort in Hayes River of Port Nelson River', where George Geyer was to remain as Governor and Chief, with Churchill River and New Severn under him; and to strengthen his resolution he was given not only a commission from the Company but 'in a way which was never before practiced' he was also given a Royal Commission with power to make Indian treaties and to seize French ships. He was outfitted with care, was told that he should never again be troubled with Dutch guns, but was warned not to depart from the Standard of Trade set up by Radisson. Yet he was to leave the Indians satisfied and, above all, was to undersell the French in some goods, though not in all; trade should be so conducted that the Indians would come again 'and not for Once and never seen them more'—a sound maxim for any merchant at any time. Castoreum—Beaver Cods—was to be declared a 'Company's Commodity' in which servants would be forbidden to trade, and Geyer was to extend and increase trade as best he could, for 'as Wee see our Trade increase and a larger Cargoe Come home every yeare, soe you shall find our Favour and kindnesse increase towards you'.

But instructions for developing the trade of York Fort and for strengthening the new post at Churchill were only part of the Committee's projects in 1688. In addition to the two ships sent to York Fort the outfit for the year included the *Churchill* and the *Yonge* designed for the re-settlement of a post at the Bottom of the Bay—for even at the Bottom of the Bay the Committee thought it possible to establish trade within the framework of agreement with the French. In this, as it proved, the Committee were pathetically ignorant and over-confident. As for the Frenchmen left in the Bay, they thought them in a poor way and ready to yield easily. They wrote that Geyer might easily have re-established the Bottom of the Bay in 1687 if he had been sent there, that there were only about fifteen Frenchmen in

Moose, and 'they in a Despaireing perishing Condition', and that
Geyer was to drive out the French of Canada by enticing to York
Fort the trade of the 'straggling French that pick up Beaver from
the Indians'. The instructions for the Bottom of the Bay were couched
in similar terms; the English could not be too jealous of the French,
but they were told that there were 'many Discontents of that Nation'
from whom they were to buy furs either by barter or by bills of exchange, offering at the same time to give them passages home.

This was a complete mis-reading of the general French attitude,
for the Canadians were quite convinced that, whatever the outcome
of the London negotiations, ultimate French domination of the Bay
was certain; the *coureurs* would soon strangle English trade without
touching the persons of the Englishmen. In France itself confidence
was equally high, and Governor Denonville was ordered to prepare
a map as a basis for discussions and was told that King Louis intended to take such lands as were thought necessary for French trade
and the preservation of Canada.

If they erred in underestimating French and Canadian determination, the members of the Hudson's Bay Committee were guilty
of a still more serious mis-reading of the character and intentions of
Pierre Lemoyne d'Iberville and his brothers, whom de Troyes had
left behind in command, and whom Colbert had confirmed in this
arduous position.

But the purposes, and even the actions, of the Frenchmen in the
Bay were as yet unknown to the London Committee in 1688, and
they placed complete confidence in two soldiers, Captain John
Marsh and Captain Andrew Hamilton, whom Churchill as Governor
had brought forward for appointment. A certain Captain Bushell,
nominated by Sir John Huband, was dismissed with twenty guineas
'travel money' after he had been rather precipitately appointed, and
Marsh and Hamilton were given Royal Commissions in the same
terms as Geyer. Marsh was to be Governor in the Bottom of the Bay,
with Hamilton as Second in Command and with Captain Bond of
the *Churchill* as 'Admirall att Sea' and third in Council. They were
provided with mortars and other arms, but their purpose was not to
attack the French—merely to defend themselves if it should prove
necessary. Marsh was to build a new post at Albany 'without annoying the French, or Disturbeing them, unless they Assault him', but
he was given considerable latitude in interpreting his instructions.
In general he was encouraged to act 'for the Honour of the Nation
and for the interests profitt and benefitt of the Company', but he and
the rest of his officers were told in set terms that 'It is impossible

for us at this Distance to give you exact directions in every particular how to manage our affaires'. In addition to his supplies and trade goods, Marsh had at his disposal the *Churchill* and the *Yonge* frigates. Both ships were to winter with him, to add their man-power and their fire-power to his defensive strength.

The whole project speaks of a great confidence in a peaceful arrangement with the French, and of hopes for a quiet and prosperous trade. On those lines it accorded well with the dividend of 1688. But it was to prove entirely at variance with the actual situation by the Bay. Yet Marsh and his two ships made a prosperous voyage and arrived in good heart after meeting Abraham's interloping ship, the *Mary*, in a sinking condition in the Strait. Abraham and Outlaw and most of their crew were taken aboard the *Churchill*, and with these additions to his numbers (if not to his strength) Marsh began his task of re-creating an English settlement at Albany. He moved from Bayly's Island, the site of the Company's old post (which had been occupied by the French and which they called Ste. Anne) to a nearby island which he called Churchill Island. There he began to build, and there he met the opposition of Pierre Lemoyne d'Iberville.

Iberville, the 'Jean Bart Canadien', must be accepted as one of the most colourful and effective personalities of this period. But he struck even Frenchmen in widely different ways. To de Troyes he was all that a subordinate should be; Governor Denonville confirmed him in his command of all the posts of the Bay and wrote of him as 'un très sage garçon entreprenant et qui sait ce qu'il fait'. But Denonville in 1688 was nearing the end of his period in office, he was to be superseded by Frontenac, appointed for the second time in May 1689, and to Frontenac Iberville was merely another of the excitable, boastful and troublesome Canadians who so embroiled his policies. 'C'est un homme qui se vante beaucoup, qui crève de présumption, et qui a beaucoup plus en vue ses intérêts et son commerce que le service du Roy'. Iberville was, said Frontenac, nothing but 'un babillard et un petit présomptueux'.

Such widely different appreciations of the character of Iberville need not astonish us; there was without doubt in him both the hardihood and the clarity which attracted Denonville and the rashness and egotism which repelled Frontenac. That so forceful an individualist, so self-confident a commander, so successful a soldier of fortune, should have roused both loyalty and opposition was almost inevitable. More important than his personal character were the views for which he stood, for Iberville was first and foremost a sailor, as were his brothers, with a career to make in the French navy and with long periods of effective service afloat. He brought to the problems of the Canadian fur trade his experience and his convictions as a sailor. Over a long and spectacular period he achieved magnificent results by the mingling of his two interests, the sea-approach and the fur-trader's knowledge, and the fact that Iberville's first contact with the Bay came as second-in-command of de Troyes' land attack should never obscure the clarity of his views on maritime strategy. Nor should the chance that his most spectacular *coups* were achieved with slight resources hide the fact that his projects were vast and fundamental, nor detract from the persistence with which he advocated his views over long years, to gain only spasmodic support. Iberville's period in command in the Bay is marked by bizarre exploits, by his tremendous personality, and also by the impact of his dominant theory of the need for a French maritime approach. For the ten years of his command he never ceased to press for action on these lines; he secured only such meagre and haphazard support that his successes are taken as the triumphs of his leadership in the field. But his views transcended the local tactical problems in which he nevertheless revelled; they were held over a long period, and they involved the fundamental concept of a French rivalry conducted by sea instead of over land.

Circumstances had already given Iberville a chance of shewing (if there were any need) the uncompromising spirit of opposition with which he was animated; for Iberville was not such an opponent as preserved many of the amenities of hostilities. In the capture of the English posts by de Troyes he had greatly distinguished himself; the rapid action of the dawn assaults inspired him, and his skill at arms was great. But even his companion Allemand admitted that as soon as Iberville was put in command of the captured post at Rupert River he 'ne suivait pas les articles de la capitulation, de quoi se sont plaint les Anglais'. He took command of the English posts and prisoners in the fall of 1686, and began to disperse the English. Those at Charlton Island who could not get aboard the *Colleton* and sail to Port Nelson made some sort of a shallop from the wreckage of the *Success*, off Albany, and set sail for Moose in September 1686. They were wrecked off Point Comfort but eventually reached Moose overland at the beginning of October, to find a 'very Cold Recepcion' from the French there. Iberville would do nothing more than supply them with guns, shot, nets, and turn them loose to hunt and fish their way through the winter. When appealed to, he merely told them that they must separate or starve each other—an intransigence which by the end of the winter had (according to the English) developed into 'if wee Could not gett to keepe us alive wee must bury one another'. It is a harsh and bitter story, but Iberville's men were near to starvation themselves.

The English survived the winter 1686–7, though with some casualties, and in June of 1687 were ordered aboard the *Craven* for Rupert River. Meanwhile Iberville had also captured the *Hayes* sloop which Michael Grimington was bringing down from Nelson River to the Bottom of the Bay in the autumn of 1686. This was a course of which the Committee approved when they heard of it, but their apprehensions that 'the Vessell goods provissions and men are all Fallen into the Hands of the French', proved only too well founded. The *Hayes* was apparently caught in the ice near Charlton Island, and Iberville sent five men from Moose to take her; two of these returned sick, and the remaining three were captured by the English crew. But they eventually made themselves masters of the vessel when the 'Captain' was drowned, and the pilot (Grimington) was ashore 'Cutting a peece of Timber to mend his Rudder'. Two men were killed and the third was forced to sail the vessel at the orders of the French. Grimington was eventually also taken on board and the *Hayes* sailed off in company with the *Craven* to Rupert River, with Grimington a prisoner aboard the *Hayes* and about ten English aboard the *Craven*.

At Rupert River they remained until a flotilla of French had arrived from Canada by canoe in July 1687. Iberville's own account of his deeds says that he then, in summer 1687, took the English prize and his beaver to Quebec; other accounts allege that he went overland by canoe. The English prisoners certainly were taken by canoe—suffering considerably on the way—and arrived in Quebec early in September.

There Iberville emphasised his views on the need for sea-transport to the Bay to such effect that, although ordered back to the Bay, he was sent in the autumn to France, specially commissioned by Denonville to present his plans to de Seignelay, son of Colbert and Intendant de la Marine. The difficulties of the canoe approach were emphasised, for the rivers had been so low in 1687 that even victuals could not be got in to Iberville's garrisons. A ship full of trade-goods was the great need, and the lack of such shipment reflected badly on French prestige in the eyes of the Indians and drove them to trade at Port Nelson. A naval approach was essential, and it needed Royal support to maintain the efforts of the *Compagnie du Nord*, for already the beaver argosies were becoming the prey of pirates in the

St. Lawrence. At least one naval vessel was needed to supplement any ships which the *Compagnie* might fit out.

But emphasis on the maritime approach brought doubts about the relative value of the Bottom of the Bay and of Nelson River (doubts which were to remain constant features in French policy). The *Compagnie* was suggesting in 1687 that with a ship it could retake its post in Nelson River, and that then it would be able to afford to abandon the Bottom of the Bay. Denonville followed this up with a plea that if it should prove impossible to secure the whole of the Bay then at least 'Rivière Bourbon' (Nelson River) should be secured to the French, since it had better communications than the Ste. Thérèse (the Hayes) on which lay York Fort. Whether for the Bottom of the Bay or for Nelson River, naval support was held to be absolutely necessary. Without a man-of-war the *Compagnie* would be ruined, for 'il n'est pas possible de pouvoir soutenir l'enterprise de cette baie autrement que par mer'.

Here was a deep and deliberate challenge to the Hudson's Bay Company, couched in terms of serious understanding. The plan which Iberville took to France (dragging Michael Grimington with him, since the rest of the English had already been sent to La Rochelle and had found their way thence to England) was that two *Compagnie* ships should be escorted by one royal vessel. He succeeded in his plea and in April 1688 set out on his return journey to Quebec in the best sailing vessel of the French navy, the *Soleil d'Afrique*.

Before he sailed for France in 1687 Iberville had arranged that overland reinforcements should be sent for the minute and starving garrisons which he had left behind, six men each in Fort St. Louis (Moose) and Fort Ste. Anne (Albany) supporting life on a meagre ration of Indian corn. Some sixty men were therefore sent by river to their relief, and of this James Hayes' old correspondent Edward Randolph gave early news, in January 1688 from New York; though he had to confess he had 'forgott' the name of the 'Great River' up which the French party journeyed to the Bay.

Iberville and the *Soleil d'Afrique* therefore left Quebec in company with two small ships equipped by the *Compagnie de la Baie d'Hudson* (as the *Compagnie du Nord* was now generally called) in June 1688, and arrived in the Bay in August, at just about the same time as the 1688 outfit of the Hudson's Bay Company destined for a new settlement at Albany, with Abraham and the other interlopers saved from the *Mary*, also sailed into the Bay. From the capture of the *Hayes* sloop Iberville had become possessed of the Company's Letter Outwards to Bridgar of 1685, and here, in phrases describing the 'French pirates' who had taken the *Perpetuana Merchant*, were hopes that 'there may come a time of Retaliation'. This was enough to warrant suspicion of any English ships seen in the Bay, especially as Iberville's view of the Truce of December 1687 seems to have been that it should preclude the English from any attempt to re-establish the posts which had been captured by de Troyes and himself while the negotiations were in progress.

His rate of sailing was so held up by one of the small ships provided by the *Compagnie* that in the end Iberville left her to come on alone and sailed straight for Charlton Island, where he arrived on 9th September, 1688. It was then already so late in the season that the shallop which should have met him there, loaded with furs (it is most interesting to find the French, like the English, using Charlton Island as a depôt at which their peltry could be assembled to meet the sea-going ships), had been sent back to Fort St. Louis (Moose). Leaving his ships to unload at Charlton, Iberville immediately followed in a canoe to Moose and brought back the shallop loaded with 34 to 35,000 beaver, thirteen packs of marten and ten of otter. They were put aboard the *Soleil d'Afrique*, which was to sail for Quebec as soon as the wind abated, while Iberville went to Albany and the Bottom of the Bay. Here there were reported to be about 15,000 pounds of beaver which it would clearly be impossible to ship out to Quebec that year (1688).

After a rapid voyage Iberville arrived at Albany and there discharged his shallop and loaded the furs. It was not, apparently, until he was on the point of leaving the river to sail back to Charlton that he became aware that the *Churchill* and the *Yonge* had also arrived. This seemed to Iberville a manifest breach of the treaty terms, and he lost no time in opening hostilities.

Of the subsequent events perhaps the most notable feature is the marked contrast between the joyful and self-satisfied spirit of the French accounts and the quiet and almost timorous voice of the English. Iberville immediately sent out a couple of canoes to take up the buoys in the river; the English fired on the buoy-lifting parties, but their navigation was nevertheless ruined and both English ships went aground in attempting to get up the river. The *Yonge*, however, was warped off and landed her men by night. This brought a French attack by land, but in the course of the next fortnight the English, using the *Yonge* as a tender for the *Churchill*, landed their goods and men despite sniping from the French, pitched their tents and got the lightened *Churchill* also in. The captain of the *Mary* was killed in a night ambush during this period.

Of events up to the middle of October Iberville sent accounts to Quebec by his cousin Martigny, an overland winter journey to Canada which was an epic in itself. With broken guns and deserted by their Indian guides, Martigny and his French companion were forced to follow the lakes in order to fish, and they did not get to Sault Ste. Marie until the following May. Here Father Albanel once more comes into the picture, at the Sault, comforting and advising the *voyageurs* and informing them of the intricacies of the wars of the Indians through whose lands they would have to pass.

Iberville's news, when it arrived at Quebec in early July 1689, was typical of the man and of his purpose. He reported that the English had close on a hundred men under command, that he had only seventeen, but that he hoped to make himself master of his enemies. A further message, sent off in April 1689, arrived not long after that of the previous October which had been so long on the way. Iberville had decided that if he made Albany River too unpleasant for the English he would only drive them out of the river to Charlton Island, where they would fall upon the goods which he had landed from the *Soleil d'Afrique*, guarded by only six Frenchmen. He therefore relaxed his pressure until the English ships had been firmly gripped by the ice; then (as the English also related) he captured Captain Bond and his pilot when they were out hunting partridges, and the next day captured eight men who had gone to the woods to seek their officers, not knowing they were captured.

The English declared that they sought only to live at peace, for that was the English interpretation of the way in which the Truce of December 1687 should have worked, and their own instructions were to settle without annoying the French. They even offered to trade their merchandise with the French for beaver at four shillings and sixpence each and so to live side by side until further orders should arrive from Europe or from Canada. Iberville agreed to this, provided the English promised not to go beyond the small island on which they were tented (Churchill Island) whilst he had complete liberty of passage. The English thereupon brought their goods to barter in the middle of the river, and thenceforth for some time the two parties lived 'en bons amis'. But Iberville feared treachery and captured from among the English party an Irish Catholic who had already approached him and who now, as a prisoner, assured him that none of the English promises could be depended on.

If Iberville needed any assurance that he might break the truce and attack the English it was given when Governor Marsh, protesting his good faith, sent Abraham over to the French as a hostage for the good behaviour of the English. Abraham lost no time in declaring that he himself was nothing but an interloper captured by Marsh and that he did not trust the English. This appeared to justify a breach of the truce, and Iberville cunningly enticed the four senior English hands into his post with a promise of fresh meat; then a sledge party of seventeen was enticed over as porters for the prisoner Captain Bond's luggage, and the English surgeon was invited to go shooting and was then captured. Even the English took alarm when, on the heels of this, they were called on to give up all the goods in their hands; they replied that they still had forty men and 'que ce n'était pas une proposition'.

Towards the end of December Governor Marsh died, and Andrew Hamilton took command. Sniping and hostilities continued, and soon he had to surrender, having only eight sound men at his disposal. Iberville eventually agreed that he should pay the salaries of the officers up to £2,500 and that he should give the English a ship and victuals to find their way to England.

There then remained only the two ships in English hands. But the *Churchill* and the *Yonge* had been robbed of their guns for the defence of the post ashore and they were easily taken in the spring of 1689. Of the original complement of eighty-five men brought out by the English ships three had been killed in action but twenty-five, including Governor Marsh, had died of scurvy and hardship. The prisoners were confined to the ships (from which the arms were taken ashore) and to the old French fort, while the French moved in to the newly-built English post on Churchill Island.

Having accomplished the absorption of Marsh's attempt to re-establish Albany, Iberville then sent to Charlton Island, where he found his minute garrison was still in possession of the goods landed from the *Soleil d'Afrique* and four of the six were taken over the ice to add to the inadequate guards on the captured English ships and men at Albany. At the same time the French in Canada, learning of Iberville's success, decided in the early summer of 1689 to reinforce him and sent his brother Ste. Hélène overland with an expedition of fifty men, including some sailors who would be useful in bringing the English ships and their furs to Quebec.

The two brothers met at Fort Ste. Anne (Albany) in August 1689, when Iberville not only received his reinforcements but also got orders to sail one of the English ships to Quebec. He was in a good position and a good mood to do this, for although he had not taken the English post in Hayes River (had not even attacked it) he had carried out most of his other plans. After his success at Albany he heard that there had been an English shallop investigating the post at Moose (Fort St. Louis), and that it had then sailed on to Fort St. Jacques at Rupert River. He therefore sailed the captured *Churchill* to Rupert River as soon as he had put affairs in order at Charlton, and easily secured the surrender both of the shallop and of a ship which he found there. This was the *Huband*, sent down from York Fort by Governor Geyer.

Iberville had therefore captured the *Hayes* sloop, a shallop, the *Churchill*, the *Yonge* and the *Huband*, had confirmed his hold on the Bottom of the Bay and had completely broken up the English attempt to re-settle. He sent his brother Ste. Hélène back to Canada overland with Captain Bond and several English prisoners; the other English survivors were put aboard the *Huband* and left to make their way to England or to New England, and in September Iberville himself sailed for Quebec in the *Churchill*.

On his voyage he almost completed his work of destruction, for he fell in with the Company's ship the *Dering*, homewards bound from York Fort. Captain Young had spent the winter at York Fort according to his instructions of 1688, and now, in 1689, was bringing home a fine cargo of 27,201 beaver. He seems to have been completely taken in by Iberville, who was flying the King's Jack and the Company's flag on the *Churchill* and who spoke to him in English. The two ships sailed in company for a hundred and twenty leagues, during which Iberville never got a chance of inviting Young on board and so weakening the *Dering*. He dared not make a direct attack since part of his crew on the *Churchill* were English prisoners, and so the *Dering* escaped to arrive safe in the Thames with news that all was not well, and that at least the *Churchill* was in French hands.

More definite news had to wait until Captain Hamilton and the English who had been put aboard the *Huband* brought it. About thirty of the English, including some of Abraham's interloping crew, had been set on board the *Huband* and ordered to New England by Iberville. The ship's company, however, were 'resolved for England'. They set course to cross the Atlantic and at last the *Huband* was driven by contrary winds and lack of stores to Limerick. There Hamilton sold the ship for £100, of which he kept £40 himself and paid off his crew with the remainder. The great venture of 1688 was ended, but it was late in 1689 or early in 1690 before definite news of the disasters at the Bottom of the Bay began to trickle through to London from this source.

BOOKS FOR REFERENCE

HUDSON'S BAY RECORD SOCIETY—Vols. XI, XX.

CARON, I.—*Journal de l'expédition du Chevalier de Troyes à la Baie d'Hudson en 1686* (Beauceville, 1918).

CROUSE, Nellis M.—*Lemoyne d'Iberville: Soldier of New France* (Ithaca, New York, 1954).

FRÉGAULT, G.—*Iberville le Conquérant* (Montreal, 1944).

LE JEUNE, L.—*Le Chevalier Pierre le Moyne, Sieur d'Iberville* (Ottawa, 1937).

MACKAY, Douglas (revised to 1949 by Alice MacKay)—*The Honourable Company* (Toronto, 1949).

LA RONCIÈRE, C. de—*Histoire de la Marine Française* (Paris, 1909–32), Vol. VI.

CHAPTER XXI

TRADE, DIVIDENDS AND DISSENSIONS, 1688–1690

The Committee would not have expected any earlier news of their venture before 1689 even if everything had gone according to plan. They expected only the *John and Thomas*, Captain Edgcombe, a hired ship, to return that year. The others were all Company's ships and were to winter in the country, the *Churchill* and the *Yonge* at Albany and the *Dering* at York Fort, though she was to bring home the furs of the year if by any chance the *John and Thomas* should miscarry. Edgcombe with the *John and Thomas* in fact carried out his orders successfully and he had brought home the satisfactory cargo of 20,928 beaver from York Fort in November 1688. So the Committee appeared to have little to worry about.

But news that a French ship had arrived at La Rochelle from the Bottom of the Bay in November 1688 caused uneasiness and attempts were made to find out what had happened, and since the normal route for sending instructions to the Bay could have been interrupted, the Committee decided in November to send a duplicate copy of its letters through New York—the first instance of what came to be known as an overland express, an expedient which later became a fairly common feature of the Company's administrative system, and a further sign that Englishmen must have been gaining competence in inland travel.

The ship at La Rochelle would have been the *Soleil d'Afrique*, the fast French naval vessel which Iberville had sent off from Charlton Island in September 1688. But she could have told little of events in the north, for nothing of importance had happened before she left the Bay. In fact so composed did the situation appear that the Company declared its second dividend of fifty per cent., and there seemed little cause to doubt the wisdom of so generous a policy. The decision was taken on 11th July, 1688, when the Committee 'Considering the Money they have in Cash besides all engagements of the Companyes and the Trust that lyes upon them towards all the Members doe unanimously resolve to make a Divident of Fifty poundes per Cent.'

Here there were two elements worth comment, the size of the dividend and the emphasis on cash in hand. Yet only a few weeks

before the dividend meeting the Committee had been forced to borrow £300 for current expenses, and immediately after that meeting
the Governor and most of the Committee lent to the Company sums
equivalent to, or greater than, their dividends. Except to the King,
the dividend was not paid in cash, but in warrants drawn on Stephen
Evans the banker. This was normal enough—but the committee-
members surrendered their warrants to the Company. The King's
dividend was ordered to be paid in gold and as a gesture of loyalty
in those troubled days it was made payable in guineas instead of
pounds, and it was taken down to Windsor on 10th August, a time
when the Prince of Orange was daily receiving strong exhortations
to end the misgovernment in England, and when Churchill, Governor of the Company, had just written to protest his willingness to
serve him. Since France was one of the major sources of James's
strength, the dividend was accompanied by a petition that the truce
agreed with France in December 1687 might be properly observed.

There was, however, some inevitable delay, and although the
Deputy Governor of the Company seems to have taken the dividend
down to Windsor in person, as some sort of declaration of loyalty
to James, it was still not paid out in early October, when it was
offered instead to William, who had by then landed in Devon and
advanced to Exeter. William asked for the money to be paid in to
the Exchequer rather than to himself, so the Deputy Governor paid
only pounds instead of guineas, and got a receipt in the form of an
Exchequer tally. The fact that the dividend had been offered to
James would not have told against the Company in the Revolution
settlement, but the Committee was lucky in that the delay enabled
it to make payment to the new King with the same cash as had been
offered to the old one!

On the whole, despite the prominent part taken by Churchill in
the Revolution, the great political events passed the Company by,
and 1688 seemed a year of quiet prosperity in which the disasters
of the Bay were still undeveloped and in which, after the return of
the *John and Thomas*, the Committee felt so prosperous that they
turned to charity. They resolved, 'seeing God had blessed them in
the returne of their shipp the *John and Thomas* with a good cargoe,
that this Committee would think of Disposall of a summe of money
in such a Charitable manner as they shall think fitt'. Ultimately,
after satisfying several individual claims, they started a fund of £100
for pensions and gratuities for those who were wounded or maimed
in the Company's service, or for their widows and children.

But this apparent affluence cannot conceal the difficulties inevitable in the Company's practice of trading without adequate cash in hand. Those difficulties were emphasised when, on the heels of the decision to allocate a sum to charity and to pay the royal dividend to the new King, William III, Stephen Evans reluctantly informed the Committee that he, 'had more then ordinary Occasion for money at present'—for the West was in arms and the City was in difficulties —and he asked for the repayment of his outstanding debt. From his account it appears that the Company had been just about balanced in his books by May 1688, and that during the summer months he had received £1,837 10s. 0d. (most of it borrowed) and had paid out £7,096 6s. 2d., of which £5,100 was for dividend. The Company had therefore, in effect, borrowed the dividend almost *en bloc* from its banker! The Committee was only able to borrow a further £800 to hand over to Evans, and he got a further £2,800 banked with him as the result of the winter's fur sale, but he was still a substantial creditor on account of the dividend.

All the more interesting in the light of this financial problem is the fact that at this time rivalry with the French was forcing the Company into a more expensive shipping policy. Since Nixon's day the question of the 'great ship', hired and therefore forced to load in a hurry and start straight for home lest she should be caught in the ice and break the terms of her charter-party, had been debated by the Committee. On the whole they had continued to hire for the Atlantic bulk-carrying voyage and to build their own shallops and sloops for use in the Bay and for wintering with a crew of three or four hands. During the 1684 period of French rivalry, however, a large plan of building and buying ships which could carry the stores, goods and furs, across the Atlantic, and which could also be used as guard-ships, was started.

Such ships, being the Company's own property, could be kept wintering in the Bay to strengthen the posts there at far less cost than hired ships. The building of the *Hayes* yacht in 1680, with the decision to keep the *Rupert* for a second winter in the Bay, largely because of the 'force and the security shee may therefore afford', had set the Committee off on this policy. It was a policy which had to be kept flexible, but the little *Craven*, a pink of only forty tons built in 1682, fitted in well. So, as an interim measure after the loss of the *Rupert* at Nelson River in 1682, did the way in which 'some members of the Company' agreed to buy the *Success* in 1685 especially for the purpose of hiring her to the Company. Other similar arrangements were common at the time and it was not until 1687 that a determined ship-owning plan was embarked on. Then the pink

Edward and John of a hundred and twenty tons was bought and re-named the *Dering*, the frigate *Industry* of sixty tons was bought and re-named the *Huband*. A sign of the new problems inevitable in the ownership of shipping can be seen when the Committee decided not to keep the *Dering* idle in port at the end of her first voyage, but to look out for a profitable employment for her during the winter, 1687–8. Twenty years later they were to lose money in an attempt to ship coals from Newcastle to the south of England, and in 1687 they do not seem to have found any reasonable winter's use for their ships, nor indeed did they ever master this subsidiary problem of ship-owning and make their vessels work all the year round.

Nevertheless the need to have ships which could bring the furs home in case of need and which would add strength when they wintered in the Bay was such that in May 1687 the Committee resolved to buy a further ship of from thirty to fifty tons. This was not achieved in time for the voyage of that year, so in the following February (1688) the Committee agreed to the building of a hundred-ton frigate, to be ready by the end of April. When this ship, the *Churchill*, was launched early in May, a further ship, not to exceed fifty tons, was ordered; the work was to proceed although for the moment a price could not be agreed upon. This was the *Yonge* frigate.

The three ships captured by Iberville were therefore all the Company's own property, all newly built or reconditioned for the Arctic voyage, and between them cost a very considerable sum of money. The *Churchill* had cost £812 13s. 10d. for the hull and £501 0s. 6d. for stores and rigging; the *Yonge* £381 11s. 2d. for her hull and £235 1s. 3d. for stores and rigging, and the *Huband*, which Hamilton was to sell for a mere £100 in Limerick, had cost £140 and a subsequent bill of £423 for repairs and alterations. The ships, moreover, were the essential machinery for carrying out the Committee's policy of building the Company's own fleet and keeping the ships to winter in the Bay as guard-ships, and the *Hayes* sloop, also captured, had proved herself a handy vessel, capable of an exploring voyage or of making an Atlantic crossing. Of the whole number of ships which marked this phase of Company policy, therefore, Iberville's counteraction had left only the *Dering* and the *Albemarle*, both attached to York Fort, by the fall of 1689.

As yet, at the end of 1688, the Committee had no inkling of the disasters which this policy was to entail. Having ordered all the other ships to winter in the Bay, the members were well content with the return of the *John and Thomas* and they set to work to carry their ship-owning policy a stage further by ordering an ocean-going ship of a hundred and twenty to a hundred and forty tons, with a further small vessel of twenty to twenty-five tons for York Fort. Enquiries were made at provincial shipyards, at Shoreham and at Wivenhoe, but when the *Royal Hudson's Bay* frigate was eventually launched in March 1689 she had been built in a London yard. So too had the small vessel the *Northwest Fox*. Money had to be borrowed to pay for these ships; but in the early days of 1689 money could be got in London at three per cent.

The great ship and the small, the *Royal Hudson's Bay* and the *Northwest Fox*, were both given orders based on a most unrealistic vision of developments in the Bay. The *Royal Hudson's Bay* was to take her goods and her men—she had four new Blue Coat apprentices aboard—first to York Fort and then to the post which, the Committee hoped, Marsh had set up at Albany. The *Northwest Fox*, Captain Ford, was to go to York Fort, and was then to be sent by Governor Geyer to make a settlement to the northward of Churchill River. Royal commissions for the Governors were again sent out, deriving from the new King and Queen, and Thomas Walsh was also given the Company's commission as Chief of the post at New Severn. The Governors were told, since the Revolution in England had been followed by open war with France, that they were to capture the French posts, goods and vessels, to enter into alliances with the Indians, and to protect them from Indians led by Frenchmen.

In the hope that Marsh had already 'laid the Foundation of a happy Settlement' at Albany, the Committee now told him that in view of the great hazards of the voyage and the high cost of seamen's wages he should advance the Standard of Trade. Geyer was given similar instructions for York Fort, but both Governors were told to accomplish this according to their own discretion, and so as not to 'give any disgust' to the Indians. Geyer was also warned to be more careful in indenting for goods to be sent out to his post. Otherwise the Committee feared they would soon have ten years' supplies of some commodities in the country and none at all of others.

Brazil tobacco had been bought from Oporto in the summer of 1688 for the outfit of 1689, but perhaps the most interesting item of trade goods were the blankets sent to York Fort. It had been reported that the Indians preferred white cloth to the red and blue which had hitherto been shipped, so a trial shipment of three white blankets was now sent; they were cheaper, and when worn they were not so likely to frighten the game in the snow-covered landscape. Woollens were becoming more important, but the Company had not yet developed shipment of blankets to a point at which it could claim to be contributing to employment in the English clothing industry, it had not yet lighted on the distinctive coloured stripes of a later period, nor had it settled on one manufacturer for these goods, most of its custom going, as in this year, to John Rasen or Raysen, of Witney.

Enterprising and confident as the instructions for the ordinary trade at Albany and York Fort were, they were over-shadowed by the role assigned to the *Northwest Fox*. This little vessel, to be attached to York Fort, was to sail to the north of Churchill and settle a new post at the 'Great River' there. This river had been named the 'Deer River' by Geyer; it was to be re-named 'Dering River' in honour of the Deputy Governor of the Company. This was to be but part of a general expansion, for Geyer was told that 'wee would have you from tyme to tyme, to take all favourable Opertunityes still to make further and further discovery's', and the reasonable view was taken that the Standard of Trade at the new post should be only half of that obtaining at York Fort, so that its cheapness might give the new post a fair start.

At Dering River there was reported to be plenty of wood and water, and though Geyer had written that the 'Louzy Indians' had little beaver at Churchill he felt that a settlement at Dering River would bring down the 'Dogsides' (the Dogribs) to trade. The 'Dogsides' were reported to be a considerable nation, and Captain Ford was to sail as high up Dering River as possible, to build a post and to trade, and in the spring he was to send a canoe and some Englishmen to accompany the Indians, to find the Poet Indians (the Assinipoets of Athabaska) and to bring them down to trade. It would be most interesting if we could know whether the instruction that Englishmen were to venture up the river in a canoe was merely another example of the London Committee's remoteness from actuality on the Bay, or whether there really were Englishmen at this time who had mastered the delicate and strenuous art of canoe travel.

The instructions, in any case, were not delivered or put into effect, for the ships of 1689 never got out of the English Channel. About thirty leagues from the Scillies they met three French privateers. The *Northwest Fox* was taken 'or Rather yielded himself', but Edgcombe in the *Royal Hudson's Bay* fought valiantly for eight or nine hours, got away, and put back to Plymouth for repairs. Then, between the damage to his ship, desertions by his seamen when once they had got back to port, and lack of a convoy, he 'could not prevaile with the marriners to proceed'. So there was no shipment to the

Bay that year, 1689, and though the Company offered to ransom the *Northwest Fox* in Brest for £200, apparently she remained in French hands; Edgcombe was rewarded for his valour by the gift of a silver flagon weighing almost eighty ounces and costing £20.

The action of the French ships was to the Committee a sign that 'it pleased God who disposes all things at that time to frustrate our designs'; but it was strictly according to international law and might have been expected by the Committee, for open war had been declared against France. The Company alleged that the inroads of the French in Canada were one of the causes for the declaration of war, and the situation in Canada and the Bay was certainly affected by the change to open hostilities. William III was in such close touch with Churchill, and was so much the spear-head of a universal attack on the French, that he could be counted on for support of the Company in Canada.

Already, before the *Royal Hudson's Bay* and the *Northwest Fox* had convinced the Committee of the disapproval of the Deity and of the opposition of the French, they had begun to petition against the French Nation of Canada, the 'ill Neighbours of all mankind'. The petition, delivered by Churchill himself, was drawn up by the Committee on the 17th April, 1689, and was to set forth the old damages of the Company and to 'revive the Proceedings of this Company against the French'. It was heard in Council by William on 25th April, 1689, and was referred by him to the Lords of Trade and Plantations for report. There was as yet little that was new, for no information had come through; but the petition was highly topical in tone and appeal. Apart from their play upon the general threat of the French to all other nations, the Committee now harped upon the main strings of the Whig Protestant Succession. The fur trade was exalted as a source of customs revenue, as a support of navigation and commerce—as it might well be in view of the Committee's recent shipping policy—and as the rival of the Canada Company in France 'who manage the Beavor Trade there, Granted by that King to the Jesuits'. The Company asked that its Governors should be given Royal commissions, with a right to make alliances with the Indians and to give Letters of Marque to the Company's ships, empowering them to act as privateers.

The French privateers who took the *Northwest Fox* and who fought the *Royal Hudson's Bay* were therefore only acting as the Company itself had intended to do, and Edgcombe himself carried Letters of Marque. But the blow was severe, especially in that it cut the Committee off from its posts for a year in which great developments were expected. True, the outfit had not been a large one nor the expense heavy. Geyer had been told (if the letter had ever reached him) that few goods were being sent in view of the great cost of the 1688 outfit and since he had stated that he already had a three years' supply of trade-goods on hand at York Fort. Even so, the interruption was bound to be serious and to upset the confidence of the Company and the support which it could expect for its plans.

Enquiries into the possibilities of an offensive and defensive alliance with New York and New England, against the French, were also started, but apparently nothing came of this proposal. The occasion for this interest in New York and New England was probably a further letter from Edward Randolph to James Hayes, delivered in March 1689, describing the proceedings of the French during the 'late Truce'. Merchant information in the New World may well have put Randolph in a position to give Hayes some outline of the extent of Iberville's depredations, but the Committee could not be certain of the outcome of its great plans and expenditures of 1688 until the first-hand news brought by Hamilton and the crew of the *Huband* from Limerick in spring 1690, and the arrival of the *Dering* from York Fort in October 1689. Then, once more, the Committee could hardly believe the troubles which had befallen it. The news 'seemed hardly Credible at first, but proved too trew afterwards, for Bond and his mate, foolishly wandring to hunt Pateridges, were themselves caught Like woodecocks'.

The foolish capture of Bond and his men was not the only detail of which the Committee were informed. It became clear that the whole costly attempt to re-settle the Bottom of the Bay had simply fizzled out; worse, it had supplied Iberville with ships and tradegoods such as he could not get from his own *Compagnie*. For although Ste. Hélène had brought an overland expedition from Quebec in 1689, the ship sent from France to relieve and supply the French posts had been caught in the ice and had returned to Quebec. Moreover the English collapse at Albany had upset what little confidence the Indians might have felt in English ability and courage. York Fort, and perhaps its outposts, alone remained in English hands, and they would get no shipping this year.

Such considerations, too, had to be set against a realistic appreciation of the French attitude. The Company could not know that Frontenac was in 1688 planning to send the geographer Franquelin to establish the details of the lands whence their furs derived, so that the French might claim possession and discover an easier route to the Bay, both by land and sea. But they ruefully accepted the

I

evidence that there was no hope of an accommodation with the French, and that the Treaties of 1686 and 1687 'was onely intended for a Snare and is now wholly out of doors'.

Amidst such uneasiness and evil tidings it is again surprising to find the Company decreeing another dividend. This time it was twenty-five per cent.—a very substantial return, though perhaps disappointing after the fifty per cent. of the previous year. The declaration was not made until 11th September, 1689, and this time there was no grandiloquence about the cash in hand; dividends were not in need of so much explanation when they arrived two years running!

The strange thing about this dividend of 1689 was that although it came so late in the Company's year it was nevertheless declared during the doldrums when the news of the failure of the *Royal Hudson's Bay* and the capture of the *Northwest Fox* were known, when Randolph's letter of the proceedings of the French had been received and Hamilton and his men had probably got to Limerick, but when the *Dering* had not yet arrived in London to retrieve the situation with her considerable cargo. The large returns from York Fort then earned Governor Geyer a gratuity of £100 in addition to his salary and to £10 which he claimed Sir James Hayes had promised him, but they were not yet to hand when the dividend was declared in September 1689.

Not less remarkable than its timing is the fact that this dividend was paid through warrants on Thomas Glover, furrier and outstandingly the most important of the buyers of the Company's furs. Therein, in fact, lies the explanation of the whole dividend of 1689. In 1688 there had been the 20,000 skins brought from Hayes River for disposal in a London which was ripening for revolution and for trade to a Europe in which the French were selling their own furs and those which they had taken from the English in the Bottom of the Bay. The market was undoubtedly tricky, both for *coat* and for *parchment*, and the Committee were ready to make an agreement with the buyers beforehand that they should go through the motions of a sale of the *parchment* by auction provided the buyers would take it all at eight shillings a pound. But though the *parchment*, which would probably be largely destined for export, was sold, the *coat* beaver had stuck badly at the March sale in 1688 and something like 16,000 *coat* beaver of different kinds remained unsold—a situation which lent point to the Committee's plaints that beaver would not sell and to their exhortations that small furs, especially marten, be encouraged, for the importation of 1688 had also to be sold.

During the summer the old bogey of private trade to spoil the market rose again. This time it was Governor Geyer himself who was accused of smuggling quantities of skins from York Fort and seeking out a purchaser for them. Radisson was the source of the charge, but the accusation was overlooked and the Committee resolved 'to lay such an Obligation of Kindnesse and Confidence' upon Geyer as to engage his fidelity as well as his utmost industry for the future. He was given another gratuity of £100 and was also made Governor for the next three years. Still, the Committee were left with beaver on their hands and with rivals for an already glutted market.

A panic, throwing the furs on the market at this juncture, would have been fatal, but the Committee well understood the business of merchandising. For the sale of November 1688 only half of the remains of *coat* beaver was offered, and the price at which it was to be set up was enhanced to twelve shillings the pound. At one stage the Committee decided to sell in 'great lots' of eight hundred skins, a move which would have given the advantage to the bulk buyers, the big furriers. But after some debate they decided to sell in their usual lots of two hundred skins, a quantity within the reach of numbers of smaller men. They also tried to stimulate buying by announcing that they would not put out any more *coat* until the following March, and then not at a less upset price than eleven shillings the pound. It was a courageous attempt to keep conditions of sale normal and to retain some appearance of a seller's market. But it failed. In December 1688 the Committee noted that one furrier, Mr. Skinner, was the only buyer of *coat* beaver at the November sale, and he was offered all that remained at the price which he had paid, eleven shillings and twopence the pound. Such an offer to sell privately instead of by public auction immediately created a split within the Company, and roused suspicions of jobbery. A General Court in the following February (1689) called the Committee to book and ruled that all sales must be in public and by the candle, and that the Committee should have no power to make any sale by private contract unless specifically empowered so to do by a General Court. Having vindicated the principle, the General Court then immediately gave authority for the rule to be broken to get rid of the existent glut. But the way in which members of the Company were becoming involved in the Company's trade on their own accounts was indicated by the further rule that no member should 'pick or cull out any of the Company's goods before the sale', or should sell on his private account any goods acquired with the Company's money.

So instructed, the Committee put the furs up for auction in April

1689. But they played into the big export-buyers' hands by offering the *parchment* in lots of two thousand skins instead of two hundred. The *coat* beaver was still kept in seventy lots of two hundred each, but the *parchment* was offered in only six great lots. Again the result was extremely disappointing. None of the six great lots of *parchment* was sold, and in May the Committee used their special powers to enable any two members to sell it and the *coat* beaver if they could find a buyer; the sale, however, was to be confirmed by a General Court. By this private arrangement a sale was soon effected and all the *parchment* went at twelve shillings the pound, a shilling less than the upset price at the auction. The buyer was the great London furrier Thomas Glover, who paid £8,056 4s. 0d. It was his purchase which made the dividend of 1689 possible, and it was his cash which made the actual payments.

Thus encouraged, and with most of their back stock disposed of, the Committee felt justified in declaring the dividend of twenty-five per cent., payable in warrants on Thomas Glover himself. But although the Committee 'takeing notice of the late Considerable Sales by them made and duely weighing the Severall debts the Company owe Togeather with the present State of the Companyes Cash, doe finde that they Can well make a Divident of Twenty and Five poundes p.Cent and Leave a sufficient Summe in Cash to defray any Charge', the cash was not in fact there. A week later they were forced to make a rule that any 'debenture-holder' who required the repayment of his loan to the Company must give three months' notice, to enable the cash to be found, since 'they Cannot gratifye every one of their Creditors if they should all at one time require theire moneyes'.

The split within the Company which had been revealed by the problems of private sale or auction, and by the policy of sale by 'great lots' to the wholesalers or by small lots to the retailers, was serious. The meeting of February at which the decision was made to insist on sales by auction had witnessed an attempt to force the Committee's views through by the use of proxies. William Yonge had tried to use 'the late King's' three votes, as well as a dubious proxy for the Duke of Albemarle, whilst Sir Edward Dering, Deputy Governor, had also produced a proxy entitling him to vote on behalf of the Duke of Albemarle. Having made its rule in favour of sales entirely by auction, the General Court then proceeded to order that the Company's books must be balanced every year, and that the accounts must be presented to the annual General Court, to be held according to the Charter in November.

The powers of the Committee and of the Deputy Governor were further attacked in a resolution that elections should always be held at the General Court of November and that no Deputy Governor should be allowed to serve for more than two consecutive years, and no member of the Committee more than three consecutive years, while the committee-members were to resign in rotation, two each year. The Committee, as before, was to consist of seven ordinary members, plus a Deputy Governor and the Governor.

The troubles had arisen very largely over the difficulty in selling furs in the troubled London of 1688, but the split went deeper than that. There was undoubtedly a suspicion that the Deputy Governor and some members of the Committee had been guilty of jobbery. The acrimony arising from Sir James Hayes' departure from the Company had left a nasty taste, and so had the undignified departure of Onesiphorous Albin and the subsequent revelations of inadequate book-keeping. Suspicion and division were almost inevitable in the circumstances of the time, and the peculiarity of the rising struggle in the Company was due to two factors—it was largely conducted within the Committee itself, and it was dependent on the external circumstance that complaints against the Company were beginning to find voice in London furrier circles and even in Parliament.

The mouthpiece of the movement against the Committee and the Deputy Governor was Thomas Chambers, a shareholder and committee-man himself. For the moment he was defeated, for even the rule that sales must be made only by open auction had no sooner been passed than the practical difficulty of disposing of the furs had led to a temporary remission—a remission which had made possible the sale to Thomas Glover and hence the dividend of 1689. Apart from the restrictions on continuous tenure of office, the only sign of the growing hostility between Chambers and Deputy Governor Dering was the implied slight on the Deputy Governor to be seen in the rule that he must render account of the small sums which he dispensed on behalf of the Company. In itself such a rule is innocuous enough, but it shows deep disagreement, which was to come out in the next two years and to be ended only by the virtual expulsion of Thomas Chambers from the Company.

In the meantime the summer of 1689 had been passed in digesting the news both of Iberville's successes in the Bottom of the Bay and of the failure of the *Royal Hudson's Bay* and of the *Northwest Fox* to get out of the Channel. Some slight satisfaction was derived from the conclusion of the old case for the seizure of the *Charles* alias the *Expectation*, whose owners were still suing the Company in the

Court of King's Bench for wrongful seizure; the Company was now glad to settle out of court for a payment of £200 in full discharge of the case. Cash was tight, as usual, though in June 1689 the Committee managed to prolong a loan of £1,400, owed to a former member John Letten, who had died, so that the money had not to be produced. But members were forced to seek among themselves £500 'for the Companyes present occasions', getting the immediate accommodation from Stephen Evans until members of the Committee took up the loan.

These were temporary difficulties. The real problems were French rivalry and the glut of furs. During the summer, therefore, there were renewed petitions against the import into England of large quantities of fur and of beaver-wool from France and from Holland. And the instructions intended for the Bay in June 1689 bewailed the glut of *coat* beaver and underlined the need for alternative trades. *Parchment* was to be preferred to 'worn *coat*'; it was 'more vendable haveing a great quantity of *Coate* by us, which wee Cannott sell'. The return of the *Dering* from York Fort in 1689, with her cargo of peltry, therefore faced the Committee with the problem of disposing of this trade at a time when they had only just managed to clear stocks by deals which had aroused very considerable dissensions. They must have been almost glad that their attempt to recover the trade of the Bottom of the Bay had failed!

Having already promised that they would put up no more *coat* beaver until March 1690, the Committee now offered only the small furs and the *parchment*; the main item, to be offered in December 1689, was 7,200 *parchment* beaver in twenty lots (a compromise between the small lots of two hundred skins and the 'great lots' of the previous year). Largely as the result of the purchases of three furriers (Roger Arkinstall £2,869, William Skinner £1,448 and Richard Baker £952) all this *parchment* was sold, which must have been a great relief to the Committee.

In the midst of such problems, and perhaps because of a desire to stop a leakage of the discussions which were raging within the Committee, at this time the office of Secretary was abolished. The Committee decided that the 'Place and title of Secretary' was 'Chiefely in takeing the Minutes of the Committee and drawing of warrants for payment of moneys', and that this was an unnecessary office. Richard Banner was therefore discharged and William Potter, accountant, was appointed to act as Secretary in addition to his accountancy work. This was a reversion to the position as it had been under Onesiphorous Albin, but it brought no economy with it since

Potter was now paid £100 a year whereas the two men had each been paid only £50. It brought, however, some slight innovation in that the next meeting after the change began with the salutary practice of reading and approving the Minutes of the previous meeting.

But it is useless to try to put too fine a point of business efficiency according to modern methods upon the practices of the Company at this time. Clearly personal intervention and the mingling of private concerns with Company business was to be expected at all stages, and it is worth noting that although there were now official premises available at Scriveners' Hall off Cheapside, yet much of the business was done, and committee-meetings were even summoned at, the numerous coffee-houses with which London then abounded. Joe's Coffee House seems to have been a special favourite, and the sub-committee to provide the trade-goods in 1690 met there twice a week until it had discharged its task.

Iberville's peculiarly naval approach to the rivalry with the Company had by 1690 produced a strange situation in that he had begun to cause a serious shortage of competent ships' captains on the English side. Desertions and interloping had played their part, but by the end of 1689 the French of Quebec were able to report to Paris that they had captured eleven English pilots and that only 'le nommé Grimeton' (Michael Grimington) remained available for the English. He, it was said, had been pro-French when he was taken as a prisoner to France, and if he should be sent again to the Bottom of the Bay he would again be on the French side. This was an over-statement of the shortage of English pilots, though Grimington emphasises the French need. Described as an excellent seaman, he was taken to France so that he might be forced to teach arctic navigation to the French. The Committee succeeded in getting a protest made by the English ambassador, so Grimington was released and made his way to England; he had been mate to Captain Edgcombe in the newly-launched *Royal Hudson's Bay* in 1689 and for his valour in the action with the French privateers off the Scillies he had been awarded a silver tankard which, if it could be discovered now, would be a most valuable addition to the Company's collection of silver. He was to prove a loyal and ardent opponent of the French. Nevertheless ships' captains were a doubtful element and Geyer had to be warned that the captain of the captured *Northwest Fox*, Captain Ford, had 'revolted to the French Interest' and would probably be employed in some pro-French design, in which he might even sail the *Northwest Fox* herself into Nelson River.

Captains, however, were less of a problem in the struggle with

Iberville than were ships themselves. The Committee resolved early in 1690 that they would have to seek out a ship fit for use as a fire-ship. This would not be of any commercial use, its costs would be a heavy burden on the trade, and the desire for a purely warlike ship in addition to the cargo-vessels led the Committee into some curious manoeuvres, in which the lack of ship-owning experience of the Committee as a whole combines curiously with the participation of individual members as ship-owners.

First the Committee decided that the *Dering*, after her winter at York Fort, needed substantial repairs and alterations. She was to be made 'very defencible and a Square Sterne Shipp'. Apparently this was too much for the hull of the *Dering*, which had already been altered when the Company took her over as the *Edward and John*; for the Committee changed their mind and decided instead to turn her into the fire-ship, in which capacity she was called the *Prosperous* and was ordered to sail on the 1690 voyage under command of Michael Grimington. To fill the place of the old *Dering* as a cargo-ship the Committee bought a frigate, the *William* and re-named her the *Dering*, to sail in 1690 under Captain Young. The purchase of the *William* was carried through in the spring of 1690, and was one of those affairs in which members of the Committee may be seen trading with themselves in a dual capacity. Samuel Clarke, committee-man, played a large part in the negotiations and may have been a part-owner of the *William* before the Company bought her. He lent the Company half of the £700 purchase money, and he and his partner Edward West, the Company's Warehousekeeper promoted committee-man, lent the remaining £350. The third ship for the 1690 voyage was the *Royal Hudson's Bay*, again under Leonard Edgcombe. All three ships were the property of the Company; the two frigates were therefore under very positive orders to return to England that year, but the *Prosperous*, fire-ship, might winter in the Bay if necessary.

The oufit was adequate, the general tone of the letters and instructions strangely out of tune with the situation in the Bay, and far more dictated by events in Europe than by the achievements of Iberville and the failures of Marsh and Hamilton. The trade-goods showed confidence and strength; Brazil tobacco was still being bought in Portugal (through Samuel Clarke's trade connections) and there was also a 'Jointed Babie' which Geyer was to stand in his trade-room, to note the Indians' reactions and to send word whether they fancied such toys.

A definite note of urgency can, however, be heard in the Instructions. Geyer's request for an additional sloop for York Fort had to be refused, for men would not venture on such service. He was told that he ought to have fifty good hands at York Fort and a further twenty-five at New Severn, but that they could not be got and he must hope to recruit them from the ships' crews; the English labour market could produce only 'three actuall servants to abide with you'. Geyer himself was strongly urged not to think of retiring, in view of the war with France. He was given another gratuity of £100, while Walsh at New Severn was given £50. Geyer was virtually irreplaceable and the Committee felt that it was his 'Conduct and fidelity they can onely (or chiefly) rely upon in this time of a Publick warr'; they urged him 'with patience and Courage to abide it'. He was again pressed to try to adjust the Standard of Trade to rising costs 'which Tribles the Charge of former years', and to try to get the Indians to wear cloth instead of skins, so that on the one hand the demand for cloth would increase and on the other hand *coat* beaver would dwindle in supply and the Indians would produce *parchment*, the only commodity in demand 'for the trade is quite turned here in Europe'.

The post at Churchill does not figure in these instructions. The settlement of 1689 had made a fair start, and the Company had got about ten tons of blubber from it. But then lack of casks had interrupted the trade and 'an accident burnt downe Our house'. So, despite the purposefulness with which the Committee had set out its instructions in 1689, Churchill River had by 1690 proved a disappointment and the attention of both Governor Geyer and the London Committee was focused on New Severn, on Dering River, and on discovery and trade to the northward of Churchill. Geyer was therefore instructed to offer advances of pay, and gratuities, to any of the men who shewed forwardness in going upon discoveries, and in particular he was again urged to discover 'the River formerly called Buffelo now dering river, whence Considerable Traffick may bee expected from the Northerne Indians'.

Even before the ships and the Instructions had been sent off to the Bay in June 1690, great events had taken place in London. The disposal of the beaver of 1689, the obvious collusion with Glover and the great furriers, and the attempts to prevent beaver and beaver-wool entering England from the continent, had all produced opposition between the Company and the working hatters and feltmakers. Here the resistance was led and to a large extent organised by the Company of Feltmakers of the City of London, an organisation designed to regulate and control the use of furs, especially beaver-wool, in the making of felts and hats. The Feltmakers' Company had been set up in 1604, had been made into a Livery Company in 1650, and represented the views and cared for the interests of the employers and moneyed men in the felt-making industry rather than those of the artisans and journeymen of the trade. Such men resented the rising tendency of the Company to sell its furs by private bargain with the great furriers, and strongly urged retention of sale by small lots at public auction.

In the period of settlement after the 1688 Revolution, when the Company was sharing to the full in the general feeling that privileges which had arisen from the favour of the dispossessed Stuarts would now need the confirmation of Parliamentary grant, the dispute between the Company and the Feltmakers was argued out in Parliament. The first move seems to have come from the Company, with a decision in April that the Charter should be presented for confirmation by Parliament. The decision was the result of some previous thought, and the petition was already drawn up in the shape of a 'Case of the Company'. The Committee busied themselves very considerably over this important matter, for although it might be possible, if undesirable, to carry on the trade under the Charter as an act of the Royal authority, it would be most difficult to carry it on if an attempt were made to turn Royal authority into Parliamentary sanction and were to fail. An approach to Parliament must be successful, or it must be avoided.

Accordingly, the 'Case of the Company' was printed and distributed (as was the normal practice with Parliamentary business) with emphasis on the fact that the Charter gave right of dominion and propriety and so differed greatly from the charters of the East India Company or of the Royal African Company. The Deputy Governor was allowed a hundred guineas to spend at his discretion 'about their affaire in Parliament', while his opponent Thomas Chambers was also given £30 and £60 at different times. Chambers, however, was to render an account of his dealings and a sub-committee was set up to manage the business, with a promise that any expenses would be repaid. Sergeant Topsham was employed as legal advisor and was paid a fee of £30 and a gratuity of fifty guineas, and the proposed Bill was seen and approved by Sir John Sumers, the Solicitor General. With such care and attention, the Company's Bill moved rapidly through the various stages in the House and by the time that the Instructions were sent out to the Bay, towards the end of May 1690, the Committee were able to tell the Governors that the Charter had been confirmed in Parliament, 'Allowing our Lands and territories to be a Colonie belonging to the Crowne of England'. The result was 'that whatsoever was Eluded as Prerogative only before is now the Law of our Land and as Such to bee Enforced, which exceeds all Proclamations'.

This had not been achieved, however, without very considerable trouble both in Parliament and within the Company itself. The original petition of the Company, presented to the Commons on 28th April, 1690, asked for confirmation of the Charter on the grounds that the territory of Rupert's Land should be considered as one of His Majesty's plantations, which the Company had established and maintained at vast charges, at the cost of £150,000 damages done by the French, for which they could get no redress during the reign of James II, and at the risk of constant interruption from French and English interlopers. The Company then represented that 'such their Trade is not to be supported but by a Joint Stock'.

In reply the Feltmakers' Company put in a petition asking for a copy of the Charter so that they could formulate their objections to it, and declaring that the Company's monopoly would ruin the Russia trade and be a great hindrance to the whole trade of felt-making in this country. By the 'Russia trade' the feltmakers were probably meaning the import of beaver-wool from Russia, a commodity against which the Hudson's Bay Company protested but which was essential (either in a Russian or in an English style) for the feltmakers. The feltmakers were important critics, for although they suffered from dissensions within their Company and from a noticeable tendency of the masters to oppress their journeymen, they yet were one of the more successful means for forwarding the trade of this country at the expense of France and for profiting by the economic difficulties caused by Louis XIV's revocation of the Edict of Nantes. They furnished employment for the Huguenot refugee hatters who in their flight from France ruined the hat-making industry of that country and left the English hatters without rivals.

The Hudson's Bay Company's bill was nevertheless sent to a Committee which included all members of the Commons who were merchants, all who sat for the City of London, and all lawyers— those 'that are of the Long Robes'. Before it could become Statute other critics and rivals put in their pleas—first the owners of the *Expectation* again appeared, begging to be heard before the Charter was confirmed; then the merchants of New York and of New England pleaded that they would be discouraged by a bill for 'establishing a boundless Charter with sovereign Power, granted to the *Hudson's Bay* Company by King Charles the Second, upon false

Suggestions'. They claimed that the bill might prove 'very destructive to the Trade of England and the said Colonies'. Well supported though they were, these petitions were rejected and the Company's bill was passed by the Commons with a limitation to fourteen years' duration. An attempt to limit it to seven years was defeated, but when the bill went to the Lords, to be again subject to a Committee (on which Marlborough sat) and to face once more the petition from New York and New England, it was returned with an amendment limiting its duration to seven years, as had been proposed in the Commons. The Parliamentary sanction in which the Company now rejoiced therefore carried the severe limitation that it was effective for seven years only—a period so brief that it might well stimulate the Committee to increased activity, and to slightly speculative practices.

Moreover, this passage through the critical forum of Parliament had resulted in at least one public analysis of the Company, its claims, its constitution and its achievements. Perhaps the 'Impartial account of the present State of the Hudson's Bay Company' was the work of the feltmakers; perhaps it was produced by the New England merchants. It certainly spared no aspect of the Company. This printed 'account' described the Company as being composed of some thirty adventurers, with a capital of £10,000 of which only half had been paid in. Its merchandise, the 'account' alleged, consisted only of trifles and normally did not exceed £600 a year in value. Yet it had a boundless charter (this phrase is that used by the New England merchants in their petition to the Commons) for its inconsiderable trade, giving rights of jurisdiction and of making peace and war. These rights had been exercised against the owners of the *Expectation*. But the Company had made no new discoveries. The natives, said the 'account', were so timorous that there was no need for a joint-stock (for which the normal argument put forward was that permanent buildings, a steady policy, and arrangements for defence, were necessary in colonial trade), and the forts were in fact no better than pig-styes, made of squared pines rammed with moss to keep out the wind. The nakedness of the country was a better defence than any provided by the Company. Finally, the 'account' stated, this 'Diminutive Company' had presumed to ask Parliament to confirm its 'unprecedented boundless charter', which in effect gave the Company sovereign power.

Although these attacks were parried and the Statute was obtained, the achievement was mitigated by a clause of more direct topical interest even than the limitation to seven years' tenure of the privileges. The confirmation contained the significant proviso that 'the said Governor and Company shall make at least two public Sales of *Coat* Beaver in every year and not exceeding four and that they shall proportion the same into lots each of about one hundred pounds sterling but not exceeding two hundred pounds value. And that in the intervals of the public Sales the said Company may not sell *Coat* Beaver by private Contract at any lower price than it was set up at the last public Sale and that the *Coat* Beaver now in the Companies hands shall be liable to the same rules.'

This proviso did not affect *parchment* skins, which would mostly be bought for export to Russia and would go to the great furriers. Its aim was to maintain the interests of the English furriers and felters, who wanted modest supplies of *coat*. It came near to the desires of the feltmakers, and it also came very near to the deep and growing differences within the Company between Sir Edward Dering and Thomas Chambers. In the middle of June the Committee resolved to sell some of its furs and to put up twenty-six lots of *coat* beaver 'out of time' and eighteen lots 'in time' together with twenty-seven lots of *parchment*. The *parchment* was to be in larger lots than usual, of three hundred and sixty skins, offered at 12*s*. 6*d*. a pound. The *coat* was to be in normal lots but was to be set up at 11*s*. a pound. Before the sale, however, jobbery and the desire to get a buyer, between them, secured an arrangement with Thomas Glover, who agreed to buy a hundred lots of *coat* beaver—far more than the Committee had originally hoped to get rid of—at the reduced price of 8*s*. The sale was to be ostensibly by auction by the candle, and the Committee were sworn to secrecy, for sufficiently obvious reasons. Next day Thomas Chambers offered a better price than Glover— an additional £200 on the deal. He was rejected and protested vigorously, but the sale to Glover went through.

Such an agreed sale was of course contrary to the proviso of the Parliamentary confirmation of the Charter, and it is strange to find such a deal forced through against the wishes of a member of the Committee who knew all that was going on and had offered to make a slightly better deal himself. It is not, therefore, surprising that in August the Company at a General Court began to discuss the validity of the sale and Marlborough himself intervened to adjourn the Court for a week 'by Reason of the present heates'. He refused a plea that they continue the meeting, enjoined secrecy on all members, and so departed. The 'heates' had arisen because Chambers had produced a written accusation against Dering and the rest of the Committee.

The Committee stood together against this attack, and at their next meeting ordered that no member of the Committee should take any papers or copies of papers out of the counting-house, nor should any be shewn to any person without leave of the Deputy Governor. When the General Court of the Company met again on 8th August the Committee was ready for Chambers, although he made the first move by challenging the right of the Deputy Governor to call a Court. Marlborough was, perhaps wisely, absent on this occasion. The Charter was read through paragraph by paragraph, the Deputy Governor's right was acknowledged, and a new set of by-laws was set up confirming the Deputy Governor and a majority of the Committee in their right to call General Courts and ruling that such Courts should not in future be adjourned or dismissed without the consent of the majority of the Committee then present.

The Committee then moved into the attack. But Chambers refused to stay and hear the charge which had been prepared against him. His contempt was ordered to be entered in the Minutes, and the Court then decided that he had 'forfeited his Trust and misbehaved himselfe in his station'. He was therefore deprived of his membership of the Committee and branded as ineligible for any future election. After this his 'paper' was read, the rest of the Committee replied to each particular, and the Court voted *nemine contradicente* that his charges were frivolous and plainly malicious 'in that it was proved that he would have bought the goods in the verry same manner himselfe but was Rejected'. This was quite true, and it is not necessary to waste any sympathy over Chambers; the only serious point which he might have made was that he would have given £200 more than Glover. But as far as the major question of a corrupt bargain went, and as far as the claims of the small buyers were concerned, he was no better than his fellows. And he was probably neither so good a channel of distribution for the furs as Glover nor so satisfactory a buyer from the Company's point of view, for the sums involved were such as to dominate the Company's finances and would have ruined any but an expert and very wealthy furrier. Glover bought for £8,640 8s. 0d. in July 1690, and was still prepared to buy a further £5,841 12s. 10d. in August.

With such an influx of ready cash it is not to be wondered at that the General Court of 8th August, 1690, concluded with a vote of approval for the Deputy Governor and the Committee, since 'there needed noe other proofe of the prudence and good management of the Deputy Governor then the great benefitt the Company have Reaped since he hath been in the Chaire and that their Stock is now at Soe Considerable a Rate as 400 li. per Cent'. The Company was 'the only flourishing Company in the Kingdome', as a contemporary newsletter said.

In such circumstances three things were almost inevitable. Those who held stock would for the most part keep it and hope for a further rise; they did so, and although individuals such as Sir Edward Dering bought and sold freely during this period, the marked feature of the stock was that it was not 'active' even at the high price obtainable. Secondly, the credit of the Company would stand high in the London money-market; at this time loans were freely and easily made and would-be lenders pressed their cash on the Company, getting committee-men to secure preference for them. The Committee now was in a position to reply that it would remember the offers if it should have occasion for the money. There are examples of lenders refusing repayment, while members of the Committee themselves lent as freely in these good times as they had in the doubtful days. Dering, for example, secured for himself the privilege of lending the Company £1,500, as did Samuel Clarke for a like amount, whilst Samuel Cudworth, another member of the Committee, desired 'that the Company would accept of some moneys at Interest from a freind of his' and the Committee decided to oblige him by borrowing £1,000 from his friend, at the same time favouring the secretary-accountant's mother with a borrowing of £500. Glover, also, paid in his money for the fur sale promptly and had cleared himself with Stephen Evans as banker by the end of August.

Nevertheless the short-term needs of the trade were such that even in this period hurried loans and shortages of spot-cash make their appearance. Before the departure of the ships from Gravesend, in May 1690, the Committee were forced to borrow from the ships' captains to make adequate advance-payments to the crews, and to get a further £200 drawn from Stephen Evans hurriedly sent down to Gravesend by the tilt-boat; and in October a further £1,500 had to be borrowed from Evans on a three-months note-of-hand of the Deputy Governor.

These were temporary embarrassments, inevitable in merchandising unless large sums were to be kept idle pending such emergencies. They did not affect the general position, the temptation to deal actively in the shares, the ease of borrowing, or (the third result of the prosperity) an almost inevitable plan to take advantage of the position by increasing the stock of the Company. Such a project had been under discussion for some time, but nothing came of it until after a further successful sale. Having cleared most of its *coat beaver*, the Committee decided to put up twenty-seven lots of *parchment* in August 1690. The starting price was 10*s.* 4*d.* a pound, and it was all sold at 11*s.* 6*d.* Once more Thomas Glover was a large buyer, paying £5,841 12*s.* 10*d.* After this there followed a crucial meeting on 3rd September, 1690. Here the Committee reported that it had considered the doubling or trebling of the stock 'as hath been designed some years since, and practiced by an other Company with Extraordinary Success and Advantage'. The Company decided unanimously to treble, bringing the nominal value of its stock, on which it would have to pay interest, and which members could sell, up to £31,500. No call for extra money from members was made. The new stock was a gratis issue to existing holders. The Committee announced that they were 'desireous to make the Stocke of the Company as diffusive amongst their Majesties Subjects as possible, and more a Nationall Interest', and the new stock was therefore designed largely for 'unloading' on the public.

Apart from the gains which members would make from stock-sales, the recent passage of the Company's bill through Parliament had shewn that control by a small handful of some thirty shareholders was a source of weakness, and could prove a damaging charge. But the increase had yet to be justified on trading and financial grounds, and the Committee stated the reasons—that there were in the warehouses furs which exceeded in value the £10,500 stock issued; that the 1690 expedition was also equal in value to the stock issued and could be counted on to double its value in trade; that the two remaining posts at York Fort and New Severn were increasing their trade and could 'modestly' be expected to send home yearly returns worth £20,000; the posts, guns and other accoutrements, with prospects of new trade, were estimated at 'a considerable intrinsic value', and lastly the Company counted as an asset its hopes of a 'Verry Considerable Reparation and Satisfaction from the French' at the end of the war, a source from which it estimated it might get above £100,000.

This was, in fact, a reasonable estimate of the position, although hopes of reparations from the French were optimistic. Without that, the actual trading position was such as to justify optimism. The achievement of such a position on limited subscribed capital, with constant recourse to loans for working capital, was in itself remarkable, and there can be no serious doubt that the assets of the Company in 1690 were worth many times the par share value of £10,500. This had been accomplished at the same time as the English felt-

and hat-making industry had won dominance in Europe from the French, and by methods which meant that the Indians preferred trade with the English to trade with the French when they were able to exercise the preference. The achievement was remarkable although there was indeed much that had not been attempted, or had not been accomplished, and the position in the Bay revealed the predominance of the French.

The vast claims to promote English navigation, to forward a trade which would relieve unemployment or would contribute seriously to customs revenue or to great and important discoveries, were part of the stock-in-trade of the arguments with which English commercial and political life was riddled at the Revolution period. The East India and the Royal African Companies were subjected to much the same difficulties at this time; they were challenged by interlopers and were sued in the Admiralty Courts and then in Parliament when they captured their rivals and vindicated their charters; and they made much the same claims as the Hudson's Bay Company and sought similar Parliamentary confirmations of their privileges. The outstanding fact was that the Hudson's Bay Company had without any doubt established a new trade and had built up a substantial financial position with no worthwhile public support save the grant of a barren and practically unknown expanse of arctic lands and waters. This might not be an heroic achievement, perhaps not primarily a patriotic one. But it was useful. It was worth the minimum of public support, and it justified the proprietors in their confidence and, in the circumstances of the time, in their division of the spoils.

The rewards were not small. Having decided to treble the stock, the Company debated long over what dividend to pay on the new issue. They hovered between twenty-five per cent. or thirty-five per cent., but finally decided that their plans had been so obstructed by 'some Ill members, in crossing their Sales and other matters' that they could only pay twenty-five per cent. Even this apparently modest decision nevertheless meant that, for example, Radisson would find that the £200 of original stock which he had been allotted in 1684 would now become £600 worth; he received a dividend of £100 in 1688, a further dividend of £50 in 1689, and now in 1690 he would get a dividend of £125 on it.

Governor Marlborough, to take another example, was alleged to have bought £400 worth of stock in 1685. In return he received a fifty per cent. dividend in 1688 (£200), a further £100 dividend in 1689, £800 worth of new stock in 1690, and a twenty-five per cent.

dividend of £300 on his complete holding (now £1,200) in the same year—£600 in dividends and £800 in stock in a period of three years on an investment of £400. The sums involved were not large when compared with other deals in which Marlborough was involved; it is not clear what price he had to pay for his original holding in 1685, and it has been argued that the stock never really belonged to him but was throughout the property of William Yonge, used collusively to qualify Marlborough for election as Governor. There is no evidence for this, and it is in fact more probable that Yonge was the mouthpiece of Marlborough. Whatever the facts, if Marlborough got anything like the current price of £400 for a £100 share when he formally transferred his holding to William Yonge in December 1691, he must have sold for almost £5,000—a stimulating return on his investment, but one which could (and did) give rise to charges of stock-jobbing.

So great a triumph of the Committee and the Deputy Governor as was represented by this stock-trebling and the subsequent dividend reacted on the King as a shareholder, as upon any other. King William was paid a dividend of three hundred guineas—a slight error in accountancy in his favour since the royal holding had been £300, which had been trebled to £900, on which the twenty-five per cent. dividend should have been only £275. The gold was, however, accompanied by the plain hint that the fortunes of the Company were bound up with success against the French and a due care for its privileges. 'When your Majesties Just Armes shall have given repose to all Christendome, Wee also shall Enjoy our share of those great Benefitts, and doe not doubt but to appeare often with this golden frute in our hands.' So completely identified was the Company with the Protestant Succession that the deputation which waited on William with the dividend informed him that they prayed daily that 'in all your undertakings your Majestie may bee as victorious as Casesar, as Beloved as Titus and (after all) have the glorious Long Reigne and Peacefull end of Augustus'. In return for all of which William promised the Company such protection and favour in all their affairs as he could offer.

Secure at Court and in Parliament, and supported by the City, the Committee used the hour of triumph to confirm their power within the Company also. The Deputy Governor was awarded a piece of solid gold plate worth two hundred guineas as a sign of appreciation for his eminent care and pains in their concerns, and during the month of November 1690 the reaction even went so far as to alter the Minutes of previous meetings. It was resolved that the 'pretended protest' made on the previous 12th May should be 'unanimously oblitterated and made void and not to be entred into the faire minutes'—there is, of course, no record of the offending words, but the incident is part of the struggle caused by Thomas Chambers.

Further light on the sort of accusations which had been made, centring round the suspicion (obviously well-founded in Chambers' own case) that members were too interested in the fur trade on their personal accounts, is shed by a slightly later obliteration of a minute 'relating to the opening of Private Letters directed to the members of the Committee, which come home in the Companies Shippes'. The Company was now 'verry well Satisfyed of the Integrity and fidelity of the Severall members of this Committee'. Chambers himself was then deprived of the payments which he had earned as a committee-member, having been an 'Ill member' and done the Company great damage; his payments were paid into the charity fund for those who were wounded in the Company's service, and the Committee covered themselves by taking the right to fine, suspend from the Committee, or prevent the sale of the stock of an offending member. As the Committee gathered strength the rules for changing the Deputy Governor every two years, and for changing two of the committee-men every year, were revoked. Finally the basic problem was tackled on 20th November, 1690, by a resolution that it had been found prejudicial for the Company to be tied to sell always by auction since 'sometimes oppertunities of Advantage are Slipt for Contracts before a Generall Court cann be Called togeather, and that verry often Privacy in Transacting these agrements is of great Importance'. For a year, therefore, the Committee was given leave to sell either publicly or privately, as should seem best—this despite the fact that the Parliamentary confirmation of the Charter had insisted upon sales by auction.

BOOKS FOR REFERENCE

HUDSON'S BAY RECORD SOCIETY—Vols. XI, XX.

CHURCHILL, Winston S.—*Marlborough His Life and Times* (London, 1933–38), 4 vols.

CLARK, G. N.—*The Later Stuarts, 1660–1714* (Oxford, 1934).

ECHARD, L.—*History of the Revolution and the Establishment of England in the Year 1688* (London, 1725).

HAWKINS, J. H.—*History of the Worshipful Company of the Art or Mistery of Feltmakers of London* (London, 1917).

UNWIN, G.—*Industrial Organization in the Sixteenth and Seventeenth Centuries* (Oxford, 1904).

CHAPTER XXII

SALES, PROSPERITY, A NEW GOVERNOR, AND PLANS FOR RECOVERY, 1690–1692

The events of 1690 had proved the competence of the Committee, considered simply as merchants, and had resulted in an outstanding victory for them. Both in the internal debates of the Company and in the wider sphere of national and Parliamentary controversy they had defended themselves, and had been judged, first and foremost as merchants. Larger issues had indeed been introduced, but the touchstone had been the trade in beaver, and the result had been a verdict in favour of the Committee but with reservations both within the Company and in Parliament against a tendency for the Committee to abuse their control, especially in the matter of private sales to the greater furriers.

The triumph of the Committee was unmistakable. But it was not the end of the matter. Chambers himself was to re-appear, to face the Committee with the opinion of Sergeant Topsham (who had acted for the Company when its charter was before Parliament) that he could insist on being paid his Committee-attendance fees and could recover control of his stock, which the Committee had sold. He and others 'in an Indecent manner Rushed into the Committee Rome' in July 1691 and read out a paper abusing the Committee, and although he was allowed to dispose of his stock the question of his Committee-money lingered on. Nor were the Feltmakers' Company satisfied. In the following year they complained in Parliament that since the clauses in the renewed charter which dictated public sales carried no penalties, the Committee had freely broken these provisions. It was certainly true, from the evidence of the Company's own books, that private sales were essential features of the fur trade at this time.

In a market which was almost saturated, and from which much of the European outlet was cut off—as much by the difficulty and danger of shipping under war conditions as by direct embargo—public sales by auction would almost inevitably have exaggerated all the worst features of glut. Private sales, however, attractive as they might seem to the Committee in their troubles, proved also to have their drawbacks. In October 1690 the *Royal Hudson's Bay* came up the river to London with a fine cargo of 21,660 beaver. This was so large a consignment that it embarrassed even the customs officers, who refused to enter it all as one parcel; but to the Committee the cargo was doubly welcome since it was four-fifths *parchment* and only one fifth *coat*. Then followed Captain Young in the *Dering* (the converted *William*, now finishing her first voyage to the Bay) with a further 9,680 skins. The 'small skins', which would be used by the skinners as natural fur, not by the felters for 'wool', were put up for sale separately and sold well. Beaver, however, the mainstay of the trade, was a different problem. In January 1691 the Committee discovered that there were on hand over 23,000 *parchment* skins, which would make fifty-one lots. Even *parchment* was now beginning to hang on the Company's hands, though it was not quite so bad as *coat*. It was the 'want of Vent and a free Trade' which was held responsible, since *parchment* was still chiefly exported so that beaver-wool could be made from it.

In such conditions, and with such a quantity on hand, the Committee asked Thomas Glover to make an offer. His price was eight shillings a pound for the whole consignment. This the Committee thought 'but a verry meane price' and advised him to consult with his friends and improve on it. In the end, failing to get a good offer for private sale, they decided to put up for auction only half the quantity available and to start it at nine shillings and sixpence the pound. They sold only one lot of *parchment* and five lots of *coat*, and though the prices were reasonable the quantity sold was quite inadequate. The public had been given its chance to buy in the open market, and had waited for the Company to feel the effects of the dull market. The Company turned once more to Thomas Glover and sold to him the whole consignment offered for sale—about half the stock on hand—at his own price of eight shillings the pound. Glover then, probably with the intention of bringing the Committee to realise that there were alternative sources of supply available to him and the other furriers, informed the Committee, in October 1690, that there was a proposal afoot to get a Bill through Parliament to allow the shipment into this country of beaver from Holland on payment of a small duty. The project was scotched, and the Committee then offered to pay most of the costs of any seizures of beaver skins or beaver-wool which should be brought into this country contrary to the Navigation Acts, a problem which occupied much attention.

That the Company should be feeling the effects of a glutted market, at a time when it had only the furs of York Fort and its outpost New Severn as supply, is in itself an interesting comment on the charges made against its management of the trade, of restriction and monopoly, of lack of enterprise and ambition. A programme of expansion, for bringing yet more furs to the London market, had very little to recommend it when considered simply as a problem of merchandising. By ignoring the statutory limitations on its sales, by working in with Thomas Glover and his like, and by the kindly forbearance of its principal banker, the Company was able to manage its trade comfortably. But any further returns would be very hard to sell. Nevertheless, there was not at this time the shortage of ready money which had often been a feature of the Company's early history. Large sums—£1,000 and £2,000 on occasions—were both lent and repaid, and since Glover was prompt in his payments, the Company was so far from needing the support of Stephen Evans that it even felt able in June 1691 to make him a present of fifty guineas 'to Buy him a paire of coach horses'. In spite of all difficulties, the Company was obviously stable and prosperous. The Secretary-Treasurer's accounts were audited and the outstanding debt of £14 11s. 10d. was paid over to him, the Committee's powers of suspending any member for misbehaviour were continued indefinitely, and the right to sell privately was continued for a further year.

But though the financial position appeared to be more stable and promising than at any time so far in the history of the Company a reminder that its posts were subject to a most active and purposeful opposition came in the shape of news (which proved false) of the *Huband*, which was reported to have sailed over from Limerick to Falmouth. Other shipping problems were forced on the Committee's attention by the discovery that the *Dering*, formerly the *William*, was unfit for further service although it was only a year since the Company had bought her. But a syndicate of financiers, including Thomas Pitts, committee-man, let it be known that they were building a suitable ship, which the Committee agreed to hire for seven years. Attempts were then made to offer the *Dering* in part exchange, or to get her rigging transferred, and as this deal fell through the agreement to hire for seven years also fell through. The *Dering* was then to be put up for auction, starting at £850. An offer of £700 was received, but this the Committee refused, insisting on at least £950. Ultimately she was sold back to her original owner for £560. She had been bought for £700, stores had cost £627 13s. 6d. and shipwright's work £80 11s. 8d. The single voyage which she achieved finished with a Profit and Loss entry of £848 5s. 2d. loss.

Discouraged perhaps by such proof of the difficulties of owning ships, the Company then hired from Thomas Pitts and his friends the newly-built *Loyalty*, a ship of sixty crew, with twenty-four guns and four pederoes, and in view of its strength and newness the charge of £370 a year was probably as reasonable as could be hoped. At least the *Loyalty* gave the Committee all the advantages of using a ship built for the purpose without the costs and disadvantages which it had incurred in its purchase of the *William*.

With the fire-ship *Prosperous* still in the Bay, only the two ships, the *Royal Hudson's Bay* and the *Loyalty* were sent out in 1691. Their despatch from Gravesend caused a last-minute flurry for the Committee, for after all was ready and the ships had been despatched on the evening of 29th May, the members of the Committee at Gravesend heard that a ship had come in from Portugal with their long-awaited Brazil tobacco on board. They boarded the Portugal ship and spent all the next day putting their wares through the customs, and after a great deal of trouble got eight of their ten rolls of tobacco aboard a wherry and sent it down on the night tide to go aboard their ships.

This was not the only trouble which the Committee met in sending off the ships. Since open hostilities with the French had increased the dangers of service in the Bay and the chances of capture at sea, the seamen had required some sort of guarantee of a pension in case of injury, as had the landsmen when they got the opportunity. The expedition sent out under Marsh in 1689, to re-settle Albany, had despite its peaceable intention taken into account the chances of hostilities in a promise to the men that 'wee will take Care by way of Pension for such of them as haveing behaved themselves with Courage and fidelity shalbe wounded and the Wives and Children of those whoe shall happen to be Killed in our Service'. This the men found too vague and unsatisfactory. They wished to 'knowe your mindes in sending us for a Sacrifice for our Enemies and without any encouragement', and they asked both for stronger forces and for the same terms of pension as the King gave to his men. The Committee were able to tell the men that they had been 'before hand' and had already given instructions on this matter. The action between the *Hudson's Bay* and the French privateers off the Scillies in 1689 gave the Committee a chance to put their declarations into action, and there were two or three wounded men who claimed 'smart money' and one widow with two children to settle. The same demands were made, and the same terms offered, in 1690, and in 1691 the crews threatened mutiny at Gravesend and refused to take a general assurance from such members of the Committee as had come down the river to see the ships off. So the Committee were reluctantly forced to make a promise in writing to give the same terms of pension as the Crown forces enjoyed; the terms included both the Company's own ship, *Hudson's Bay*, and the hired ship, *Loyalty*, although there was some question whether the owners ought not rightly to have been responsible for the latter. That the seamen should have insisted on a written agreement may seem over-cautious, but the arrangement of the previous year, 1690, had been made in writing and there seemed no reason to relapse into a merely verbal statement that the Committee would 'pass their word and Reputation'.

Moreover, there was reason to suspect that as troubles multiplied the Committee might prove a harsh master. The men who had been captured at the Bottom of the Bay by Iberville in 1688–9 were for the most part back in England and asking for their pay, as were the wives of those who were still prisoners in France. They were persuaded to rely on the 'favour and kindness of the Committee' and not on their rights. Their accounts were then worked out and it was discovered that they had all been either fully paid or overpaid up to the date at which they had anchored at the Bottom of the Bay. The Committee therefore argued that since that time, as prisoners of the French, they had not been in the Company's employ, and giving them two pounds each as gratuity (almost two months' wages) ended their case. The treatment seems cavalier, and it probably caused a good deal of the semi-mutiny with which the ships' captains had to deal in 1691. But it was in accordance with the treatment which ordinary prisoners of war got from their employers in an age of mercenary soldiers.

'Smart money' and dangers from French hostilities were one source of trouble. Another was impressment and difficulty in getting and holding crews as soon as the war with France was on a regular footing. For the 1689 expedition Marlborough was asked to use his influence to get 'protection' for the Company's mariners; in 1690 he secured 'protection' for a hundred sailors a year, and the privilege was so important that the Committee thereupon presented their able Governor with a piece of plate of solid gold, value a hundred and fifty guineas. Other methods to man the ships, and to secure the men, were also tried. The Deputy Governor and Committee tried the effect of an official letter on a naval captain; at the same time they petitioned that in view of the importance of their trade they also might have powers of impressment, and they made good use of their personal influence. In 1689 they asked that they might recruit their seamen at beat of drum, but this apparently proved useless, and at the last moment before the ships sailed they were introduced to Captain Talmarsh, of the Royal Navy, who had hinted that he might spare some men and who showed the Committee a kind reception and assured them of his 'Civility'. He was 'very opertunely' dining aboard the *Northwest Fox* when two men threatened mutiny, and he dealt with the trouble by taking the recalcitrants aboard his ship and supplying two other men in their stead. Then, since he had Press Warrants but already had a full complement for his ship, 'the Deputy Governor wrought soe effectually with him' that he promised the Company's ships should sail with full crews. The Deputy Governor disbursed for the 'Immediate Service' of the Company thirty guineas at Gravesend on that occasion!

In 1691 there was no convenient Captain Talmarsh at hand, to help man the Company's ships with Press Warrants. The Company had felt the seriousness of the war shortage to such an extent that it even tried to get recruits from Scotland, but even so far north both seamen and landsmen were hard to be got. Some four or five were nevertheless brought from Scotland, and two of these were seized by a press-gang, together with others of the Company's recruits, in London. They were released by orders from the Admiralty, for the Company had sought protection for sixty men. The petition had been referred by the Council to the Lords of the Admiralty, and when the ships had safely sailed the Deputy Governor presented Lord Pembroke, First Commissioner of the Admiralty, with an 'Aume' of Rhine wine for his 'kindness showne to this Company'.

Between the tobacco, the 'smart money' protest, and the troubles over impressment, the ships' sailing at the end of May 1691 was something of a triumph for the Committee. Having accomplished so much in the successful despatch of the *Hudson's Bay* and the *Loyalty*, the Committee then turned to dispose of the remainder of the furs, predominantly *parchment* beaver, which the last bargain with Glover had left still on hand. This time they tried an alternative furrier, to arrange a private sale. Mr. Sands offered to strike a bargain if a suitable price could be agreed, but before settling with him the Committee turned to know what sort of price Glover would offer. Glover offered but a poor price—or so the Committee thought—but he was prepared to take the whole twenty-five lots of *parchment* whereas Sands wanted only four lots. So Glover got the whole consignment, including a black lot, at eight shillings the pound, a price which seemed low but which brought in the satisfactory sum of £5,929 12s. od.

The normal annual lull then ensued until, in October 1691, the *Loyalty* got back to Plymouth, in company with the *Prosperous* and the *Hudson's Bay*. The records give little further news of the *Loyalty* after her send-off from Gravesend, and she made only this one voyage for the Company. But the *Hudson's Bay* brought from Hayes River the useful cargo of 13,554 beaver, 120 otter and 70 lbs. castoreum. The bulk was still *parchment*, but *parchment* was now, with the European market suffering from war, almost as difficult to sell as *coat* beaver. This time the Committee relied upon open sale by auction, and all the furs which were offered went off at reasonable prices, the *coat* starting at nine shillings and sixpence. The total realised, and paid in by the end of February 1692, was £5,210 14s. 1d. Such a sale, carried through with no great difficulty, was to some extent helped by the closing of one alternative supply of furs. Helped by Glover himself, and with the co-operation of the customs officials, the Committee had secured the confiscation of a cargo of beaver which was being brought into the country from Holland. Thomas Glover's action in this matter may seem a little enigmatic, but he was deeply interested in preserving the Company's trade as a source of the furs which he shipped to Europe; he would not help any movement which reversed the flow and brought European furs into England, even at the cost of giving the Company a virtual monopoly of the London market.

From the Company's point of view such an open sale was most politic, for it just anticipated a further petition to Parliament from the Feltmakers' Company. Here the chief complaint was that the Company had neglected the statutory provision, incorporated in the Parliamentary confirmation of the Charter, requiring open sales. The open sale was therefore to the point, and with the Deputy Governor, Sir Edward Dering, disbursing fifty guineas for the 'Company's occasions' the Feltmakers' petition failed.

Yet money was getting tighter in London, and the preparation of the 1692 outfit found the Committee, despite the proceeds of the sale, faced with 'very Importunate' tradesmen, who had to rest content with the assurance that they should be paid in their turns, whilst one member of the Committee, Colonel Robert Lancashire, himself paid £600 for gunpowder to complete the cargo. To pay the seamen their advances in wages the Committee had to borrow locally at Gravesend at the last minute, and when the ships had been seen off, all members of the Committee were urged to scrape round among their friends to 'use their utmost Endeavers for the Raiseing of money in order to the payeing of the Tradesmens bills'. This was a complete reversal of the easy terms on which money had been available two years earlier, and it was fortunate for the Company that at this crisis in its affairs it had the firm support of its principal bankers.

Stephen Evans was by now so deeply committed to the Company that in the autumn of 1692 he was elected Governor in succession to Marlborough. Marlborough remained a very good friend of the Company in later years, but he had disposed of his complete holding of £1,200 stock and was not eligible for re-election in 1692. Beneath the surface there is some slight mystery attached to Marlborough's holding of stock in the Company, and it has been suggested that the stock belonged to William Yonge throughout, and was merely put in Marlborough's name in order to qualify him for election. Certainly Yonge habitually acted for Marlborough in routine matters of Company business, and ultimately it was to Yonge that Marlborough transferred both his original £400 of stock and the bonus of £800 in the new stock. The only evidence of actual possession, however, points in the opposite direction, since this purchase brought back Yonge into the Company's affairs once more (he had just completely sold out his own holding), and since it is on record that he held at least part of his newly acquired holding as Marlborough's nominee. There is, therefore, abundant evidence of close connection between Yonge and Marlborough; there is evidence that at least from 1692 onwards Yonge was to some extent 'put in' by Marlborough; but there is no evidence that at any time Marlborough was 'put in' by Yonge. Yonge was, however, an able and independent mouthpiece for Marlborough to have chosen. In the quarrels within the Committee which Thomas Chambers had provoked, he had demanded that the Charter should be read over clause by clause in order to convince himself that the Deputy Governor really had the powers which he then claimed, and he had denied Marlborough's right to adjourn a General Court of the Company. But Yonge was sturdily on the side of the Governor in the one dispute which Marlborough had with his Committee, over the treatment of Radisson. James II is alleged to have confided Radisson to the particular care of Marlborough, who in 1687 had secured from the Company an additional pension of £50 a year for his protégé 'till his Majesty shall putt him into some ymploy to that or better value'. This extra pension was still being paid by the Company in 1690, when the Committee decided to economise by cutting Radisson back to his original pension of £50 a year. The decision was maintained despite an appeal by Radisson and protests by William

Yonge as his chief supporter, but the Committee agreed to ask Marlborough's advice on the problem. They then took the rather harsh line of trying to exclude Radisson from the benefits of the stock-expansion of 1690 and ruled that he should have only his original pension of £50 a year and the benefit of £200 original stock according to his agreement. Neither Radisson nor William Yonge was content with this ruling, and they embarked on a Chancery suit which lasted for many years and which in the end brought a composition in Radisson's favour. In this matter Marlborough was without doubt in sympathy with Yonge's support of Radisson's claims, and the partly-collusive sale of his stock, by which Yonge was brought back into the Company's affairs, may well have been designed to some extent in order to secure Yonge's support and his evidence (for he had been deeply involved in the bringing back of Radisson in 1684) in this matter.

The difference over Radisson does not seem to have affected Marlborough's friendly relations with the rest of the Committee, or his interest in the Company. In all other matters save that of Radisson's pension he was most helpful and sympathetic. But towards the end of 1691 it was politic that the great lord should cease from active direction of the Company, for he was by then deeply under suspicion at Court and had even spent six weeks in the Tower. Ably though he had steered through the political and personal troubles of the Revolution, Marlborough had subsequently become the centre of the English malcontents who felt aggrieved at the promotion of Dutch soldiers and officials over the heads of Englishmen. He had been dismissed from all his offices, was suspected of carrying on some kind of correspondence with the exiled Stuarts, and took no active command in the war with France after 1691. The time was not far distant when William would write of him that 'I can say no more, than that I do not think it for the good of my service to entrust him with the command of my troops'. Officially Marlborough had transferred his shares in the Company to Yonge in December 1691, but he continued to take a friendly interest in the Company and he was even present at the General Court in November 1692, at which his successor was elected, though he took no part in the proceedings.

In place of the politically suspect Marlborough, that great and useful friend of the Company, Sir Stephen Evans, was elected Governor in 1692, and the merchant-member of Committee, Samuel Clarke was elected Deputy Governor in place of Sir Edward Dering, who by now was often too ill to attend to the business of the Company. In its money-crisis of 1692 the Company therefore had a great banker as its Governor and an active and successful merchant as its Deputy Governor. It could also call on the support of another great banker, John Sweetaple, newly-elected as a member of the Committee. John Sweetaple, later Sir John, had been one of the possible sources of the loans which the Committee sought in this year. He had been particularly mentioned by name when the members of the Committee had been urged to search round for help in the early summer, and he had proved friendly. By the time of the elections of November 1692 the Company was paying interest on £4,000 borrowed from Sweetaple (in addition to £3,200 borrowed elsewhere). He had produced the ready money to get the furs of the year past the customs, to pay off the seamen and to quiet the tradesmen. In return he received the bulk of the money from the sales of the furs, and for a period of about six years from 1692 he almost supplanted Stephen Evans as chief banker to the Company.

It was a time when friends in the City of London were essential, when the costs of the war were heavily felt in increased taxation, and when government loans had to be used to supplement taxes. With weak government credit and with rudimentary fiscal machinery, the cost of government loans at times rose to fourteen per cent., and private borrowers such as the Hudson's Bay Company had to compete for credit with this great rival in the form of an ill-organised National Debt. With Stephen Evans as Governor, Samuel Clarke as Deputy, and John Sweetaple on the Committee, the Company had done its best to deal with this chancey money-market.

The need for money in 1692 was vital, for the Company had decided to mount a large-scale expedition to recover its control of the Bay. During its prosperity and its troubles in the years 1690–2 the Company had not forgotten the threat which Iberville had revealed. Some signs of its reaction can be seen in the ordinary business of preparing the goods for export. The myth of the superiority of Dutch guns had been exploded, but there remained a suspicion that French woollens were more attractive to the Indians, small French goods such as a consignment of '200 horne Jewels' were experimented with, and brandy was without any doubt a valuable commodity which the circumstances of war made scarce in England. In 1692 the Company was able to buy a chance supply of Nantes brandy captured from the French and sold as prize goods. The ships' captains were refused a share in the purchase and the Governors were told to use any left from the needs of the posts for trade purposes.

The pressure of hostilities produced in 1692 projects of far greater weight than mere emulation in the preparation of trade-goods. The return of the prisoners taken by Iberville in 1688–9 had not only pointed up the indignation of the Committee at the way in which the Treaty of 1686 and the Truce of 1687 had been used to delude them, whilst the French undertook acts of warfare in a time of peace; it had also given detailed accounts of Iberville's activities and a more accurate estimate of the size of the opposition which had to be met. In particular, the narratives of Richard Smithsend, captain of the *Huband* and of James Miller, mate of the *Churchill*, gave the Committee a brief account of their own and the Company's misfortunes, and how they came to be taken by the French—an account which must have revealed that the dominating factors were the purposefulness and enterprise of Iberville and his Canadians contrasted with the ineptitude and lack of suspicion of the English.

Early in 1692, therefore, the Deputy Governor (still Sir Edward Dering) called an emergency meeting of the Committee to ask members' advice about a fresh attempt to settle the Bottom of the Bay. The meeting was held under an oath of secrecy, and after much debate the Committee decided to set forth an expedition not only to secure 'Fort Nelson' (York Fort) but also to recover Albany 'Provided they found things to answer their designed Intentions'. It was to be a large and expensive venture, with the *Royal Hudson's Bay*, the *Prosperous*, another ship of the size of the *Hudson's Bay* and two of a hundred tons, whereof one was to be a fire-ship. The proposal was approved within a week by a full Committee, protection was to be sought for two hundred seamen, guns were ordered to be made with all possible speed, a hundred and twenty barrels of gunpowder were bespoke with all expedition, and a small committee was set up to get shipping. Knowledgeable ships' captains with a record for courage and loyalty were not easy to find, and Leonard Edgcombe, with his sturdy conduct against the French privateers in the Channel to his credit, was secured by a gratuity whilst Michael Grimington was also re-employed.

In the end the expedition came to only four ships, not five—the *Royal Hudson's Bay*, the new *Dering*, the *Prosperous*, fire-ship, and the *Pery* frigate. All of these were the property of the Company. Without making any allowance for capital depreciation or even for interest on the cash locked up, or for sea-wages or insurance, for armaments or trade-goods, the expedition of 1692 cost the Company well over £9,000 for shipping alone, and it was a great accomplishment to have set it forth considering that the only capital ever paid in, despite the trebling of the stock, was still the original £10,500.

Edgcombe was given command of the brave new *Dering*,

Grimington was promoted to command the *Royal Hudson's Bay*, and two new men, Captain Cotesworth and Captain Baley, commanded the *Pery* and the *Prosperous*. But crews proved even more difficult than the Committee had anticipated, for the petition for protection of two hundred seamen from the press-gangs was often postponed and when at last it came before the Board of Trade and Plantations it met with a favourable reception but in view of the needs of the Navy it was only granted on condition that the Company should provide a hundred and fifty men aboard H.M.S. *Vanguard*. The Committee set to work diligently to fulfil the conditions, and fifty guineas were spent on the problem. Eventually some sort of crimp was brought into the business, for two members of the Committee reported that they had 'Treated with one about procureing of men for their Majesties Service and that they had a receipt for 20 men already'. But the Company's ships were still probably under-manned when they sailed from Gravesend, and the crews were cer-tainly not ideally chosen for their task. They had refused to go on board after taking their imprest money, demanding 'unreasonable sumes' for their 'Lying by in obscurity for the service of the Com-pany', and they were only got aboard their respective ships by the expenditure of £40, paid 'with good words and other methods used'. The 'other methods' were presumably the normal means for getting drunken sailors aboard an outward-bound ship, in the Royal Navy or in the merchant service. The men had, however, already been pro-mised pensions and compensation at least equivalent to anything which they might get from service in the navy, and since the Com-pany's ships carried Letters of Marque their chances of winning prize money by the capture of French merchant ships were fair.

All the same, the ships were subjected to the press-gangs when they arrived at Plymouth in their voyage down the Channel, and the expedition might have been crippled had it not been for the good offices of a naval captain there. He was later voted a piece of plate value ten guineas for his help, and Captain Edgcombe, the inter-mediary in the affair, was commissioned to discover what would be most pleasing to his wife. She preferred cash!

Hope stood high as the Committee brought this costly expedition up to the point of departure. This was the year of the decisive naval victory at La Hogue, and the Company's official letter to Governor Geyer at York Fort told him of the great victory over Tourville, with the corollary that 'we suppose that Mounsieur hath had a Cooling Care here in Europe from projecting any great attempts in America'. They hoped that peace would come in the new year, 'that

Arbitrary French King and disturber of all mankind being by the Almight hand of God by that time sufficiently Humbled'.

The war on land was in fact not going so well as the war at sea in this year; the attack on Dunkirk failed, the French took Namur and got possession of the whole line of the river Sambre, and William lost the battle of Steenkirk. The general English complaint was of too many Dutch officers; but the situation meant that the Company was able to recruit a couple of army officers to help in its operations in the Bay, and Captain Philip Parsons and Lieutenant Samuel Adams of the Independent Company of Foot were given Royal commissions for the purpose. Other servants, however, were not so easily got, and Governor Geyer was warned that 'Our Expresse Will and Pleasure is that for this one yeare you Suffer not one of our Servants to returne home, though wee desire you to recommend it to them in milde tearmes, that the Exigency of Our affaires are such that we cannot spare a man for this yeare'. Geyer himself had been persuaded to remain in charge at York Fort in the previous year. Then the Company had felt far less confident of the outcome of the war, 'God alone knowing on which side he shall please to cast the advantage of the scale'.

The particular danger which had been feared in 1691 had been that an attack on Port Royal and then on Quebec by Sir William Phipps and the New England colonists in 1690 would provoke revenge in the Bay. A further colonial irruption into French territory brought the New Englanders to Lachine. In these attacks Jolliet lost his ship, his wife and mother-in-law and ten to twelve thousand francsworth of trade-goods, and Iberville lost his brother Jacques, killed in battle. Personalities, as well as policy, were getting aligned for action in the Bay.

It is not probable that Iberville needed the urge of revenge against the New Englanders to spur him to further attacks on the Bay. He, and the French government behind him, had never ceased to plan the further advance of the *Compagnie du Nord* to complete control of the Bay. The posts captured in 1686 and 1689 had been accepted by the French government though the *Compagnie* was still not master of the situation in so far as it had been decreed that the beaver which it had taken to La Rochelle must pay the *Quart* in Canada, though the *Soleil d'Afrique* had sailed direct to France with the captured furs of 1689. Yet de Seignelay was urging the navy in 1689 to prepare a ship which could be sent to the Bay to get out the accumulated furs, succour the French posts and prevent the abandonment of the trade. So when Iberville arrived in Quebec in the autumn of 1689 he was well received and Denonville reported that he and the *Compagnie du Nord* had achieved marvels in a most extraordinary manner.

Iberville ruled at the Bottom of the Bay. But Nelson River still lay beyond his grasp, and without it his vision of French maritime control of the fur trade of the Bay could not be fulfilled. He had immediately put in a plan for the capture of York Fort, in which the *Compagnie* was to buy a ship of eighteen or twenty guns, which was to leave La Rochelle in March of 1690 and was to sail from Quebec to the Bay in May of that year. His proposals met approval, for they fitted in with other projects. It was suggested on good authority that although the amount of fur to be got from Nelson River might be disappointing, hopes were well warranted, and if Frenchmen could winter there they would be well on the way to discover the Straits of Annian and the North-west Passage.

Iberville, therefore, was back in the Bay again in 1690 with three ships, the *Ste. Anne*, the *St. François-Xavier* and the *Armes de la Compagnie*, with a commission as Governor of the posts in the Bay, and with a firm determination to capture the remaining English post at York. Governor Geyer (from whom no account of the affair survives) was on the alert and when Iberville approached the fort late in August 1690, he was spotted by the sentinel at the 'Outpost'. The alarm was given and Iberville was chased out of the river by a ship of thirty-six guns; this would probably have been the *Royal Hudson's Bay*, newly arrived from England with the *Dering* and the *Prosperous*. The English ship, however, ran aground on a falling tide and Iberville safely made his rendezvous with his consorts. Had Iberville succeeded in his project it would perhaps have been the end of the Hudson's Bay Company, for York Fort was its only serious post at this time.

The pioneer post in Churchill River had been burned down by accident in 1689 after a promising start with the whaling industry, and New Severn was in the gravest difficulties. That small outpost had met the full brunt of the disputes which had arisen between Geyer and Radisson—for it was Radisson who was responsible for the accusations of private trade and other misdemeanours which had been brought against Geyer. Samuel Missenden had been put in charge of this venture—a curious man with something of a continental background; his father lived in Hamburg. He had been sent as Chief to New Severn in 1685, but in 1687 had been persuaded by Radisson to desert his post and come home to testify against Geyer—'But what proofe he made and how rewarded is

K

notoriously knowne, for that hee was discarded the Company's service and never to be Imployed more'. Thomas Walsh replaced Missenden, and the new settlement to some extent recovered from its factious beginnings, so much so that in 1690 the Committee wrote that the settlement was of great importance (it was in fact the only post other than York Fort in their hands) and gave Walsh a gratuity of £50 for his zeal in trading a good cargo in 1689.

The approval of the Committee and the news of his gratuity could scarcely have reached Walsh in 1690 before Iberville, baulked by the watchfulness at York Fort, was upon him. Walsh had warning of the French threat from an Indian boy, and he and his men burned the post and took to the woods. Iberville took the beaver, which escaped destruction; but in September the accumulation of skins would not be heavy. Walsh and his men made their way, with some hardship, overland to York Fort. The Committee accepted the fact that the post was indefensible after the departure of the ships in 1690 and strongly approved Walsh's action in burning it down when threatened; a hand who suffered injury in helping to blow it up was given a reward of £10, and Walsh himself was strongly favoured and became Governor of York Fort itself on the retirement of Geyer in the next year.

The account of the affair submitted by the French Company alleged that Iberville found three 'great ships' and a fire-ship in Hayes River when he arrived. The Company, however, only sent out two ships and the *Prosperous* fire-ship in 1690. The French account also estimates the loss caused by the burning of New Severn at 100,000 *livres*—a loss which the English took very lightly and which never figured seriously in their claims against the French. The French Company was, however, soliciting royal help in its attacks on the English and would be apt to enhance its achievements. A royal ship of thirty-six guns and a loan of 30–40,000 *livres* was required to enable them to carry their plans to completion and to avoid the frustration which Iberville had felt when he was unable to put the last touch to his projects by destroying York Fort.

Iberville himself either wintered, 1690–1, in the Bay or, as he recounted (but his chronology is suspect), he returned to Quebec in the autumn of 1690 to find Phipps and the Boston fleet before the town and then, early in 1691, took an expedition to 'Coslard' (Schenectady) to repay the New England attack on Lachine. He was, in any case, commissioned in April 1691 to carry out the plans for the capture of York Fort with the aid of a royal ship which the French *Compagnie* had managed to get granted, but he was unable to proceed, being delayed until it was too late. So he sailed for France in November of 1691 and there found opinion, fostered by the former Governor Denonville, strongly in favour of naval support for an attack on the English posts. In February 1692, therefore, Iberville was given command of the royal ship the *Poli* for the capture of York Fort.

But although Iberville had emphasised that he must leave Quebec by the middle of July if he was to accomplish anything in the Bay, he was burdened with convoy duties as he crossed the Atlantic and was hindered by slow consorts and a late start, so that he did not even reach Quebec until 19th August (French style). The year was again too far gone for the proposed attack on York Fort to have any chance and he had been particularly ordered not to let the *Poli* winter in the Bay. But at a meeting held in Quebec early in September the members of the *Compagnie* were so insistent that Iberville detached the merchantman *Ste. Anne* to take goods and provisions to the French garrison which he had left in Albany while he went, on the orders of Frontenac (now once more Governor and no great lover of Iberville or his projects) to cruise off Boston and Manhattan.

This at least held promise of some action, and indeed of prizes; and Iberville so construed his instructions that, when he had decided he could achieve nothing off Acadia, he cruised down the New England coast, lurked outside Boston harbour, crossed the Atlantic and arrived in Rochefort in December 1692.

Iberville had, in many ways, made a most successful cruise. But he won no official approbation. Indeed, just as his failure to surprise York Fort in 1690 can now be seen as a failure to end the very existence of the Hudson's Bay Company, so his failure (this time certainly through no fault of his own), to take his man-of-war into the Bay can be seen as a major disaster for the French cause. This could not be realised by Iberville himself, by Governor Frontenac who had directed him away from the Bay, nor by Pontchartrain who had negatived the grant of the *Poli* by hampering Iberville with convoy duties. But Iberville was nevertheless coldly received in France. Had he been able to keep to the time-schedule which he had set forth, and arrive at Nelson River by 5th September, 1692, he would, with very little doubt, had been able to use his man-of-war to capture York Fort, the last post of any significance left in English hands. His late departure from France, his slow crossing of the Atlantic, and then his diversion away from the Bay, all conspired to leave York Fort unmolested and so to allow the small armada which the Company had prepared in 1692 for the recovery of its posts at the

Bottom of the Bay to enter on its task at leisure while York continued to supply the Company with the cargoes of furs on which it depended to give it that financial stability which was so necessary in those years.

At York Fort itself Geyer was still in command in 1692, with Walsh as second, both secure in the confidence of the Committee, rewarded by gratuities and taught by experience to be ever-watchful. Geyer had been anxious to retire from his command, but the Committee had put it to him that with the war at sea it was as dangerous to come home as to stay out, but much more dishonourable. So with a further £100 gratuity he stayed! He had planned to build a fresh post about eight miles higher up the river than the existing post, which was about a mile and a half from the mouth of the Hayes river, on its left bank, and the Committee approved of the plan but left it to Geyer to decide whether it would not better be left until the war was over. He delayed the move but concentrated on fortifying his post, which he reported in 1692 as completely fortified, and sent a plan which, as far as the Committee could understand it, left no doubt that the place should resist attack successfully.

The Committee was under no delusions about the French threat to York Fort, or the vital need to retain it; the trade hung by a thread in these years, and the realisation that the Committee appreciated this fact makes the confidence and expansiveness of its financial policy, the dividends and the increase of stock, all the more remarkable. Any policy which led to lack of support or to smaller and less effective outfits would have failed, for, the Committee well knew, the 'enraged and Subtill Enemy' was hovering round York Fort, 'Seeking how to devour Our last and best Stake Left'. Even for York, however, the Committee could not provide all that was demanded. Two years' supplies had indeed been sent out in 1690, in case the war should cut the supply line, and there was no intention to keep provisions short. But as costs rose there was increasing emphasis on hunting and the getting of country provisions for 'it must be a miracle of God's providence if some tyme or other a shipp doe not miscarry during this warr, which may putt you to hard shifts'. Guns, chisels, axes and other goods were carefully chosen according to patterns sent over by Geyer, and the war did not prevent the purchase and shipment of Brazil tobacco. Other goods, however, were hard to come by and Geyer was advised to be very careful in his trade of gun-flints and of brandy, since they were both French in origin.

On the whole, despite appreciation of the French threat, and of the vital need to retain York, the Committee was optimistic, even in an expansive mood. Geyer was to encourage his men by telling them that, with the hope of recovering the posts at the Bottom of the Bay, and with the fresh posts projected and the fullness and increase of trade from year to year (even with only York to draw from), there would surely be employment for all faithful and industrious servants. Here the accent was as much on new posts and increasing trade as on recovery of the Bottom of the Bay. Yet the fact that the Company could do very well with only the returns from York must have been a source of comfort; and it was put to the Committee in this year that since Radisson had won back possession of Nelson River for the Company in 1684, that post had produced furs to about the value of £100,000.

But York Fort alone was not the limit of the ambitions of the Company or of George Geyer. Churchill River was again to be opened up after the disastrous fire of 1689; casks for whale oil were sent out in 1691, the house was to be re-established and two 'Greenland shallops' (each twenty feet long and five feet six inches in the beam) were ordered and were sent out in pieces for the whale fishery. In addition to whale oil, the Committee hoped to make a serious trade in castoreum, a commodity of which small shipments had been coming home ever since 1687. The difficulty was to get either the traders or the Indians to take the castoreum seriously, but the Committee were hopeful of a trade of four or five thousand pounds a year if only the Indians could be induced to bring in the 'Beaver stones' which they habitually flung away, and Geyer was told to point out that 'every Beaver they kill hath them'. In fact the Committee laboured under the delusion that the castoreum came from the 'Beaver Codds', the 'gendering stones' of the beaver; but there was undoubtedly a vast quantity of the substance being wasted, and returns were slowly forced up over a period of years, an example of the difficulty of producing any response to market conditions in such a trade, and a part of a general attempt to find in minerals, drugs, whale oil or fins, sea-horse teeth or small furs, some alternative to beaver in the glutted market conditions of the time.

BOOKS FOR REFERENCE

HUDSON's BAY RECORD SOCIETY—Vols. VIII, IX, XX.

CHURCHILL, Winston S.—*Marlborough His Life and Times* (London, 1933–38), 4 vols.

CLARK, G. N.—*The Later Stuarts, 1660–1714* (Oxford, 1934).

NUTE, Grace Lee—*Caesars of the Wilderness* (New York, 1943).

TYRRELL, J. B. (ed.)—*Documents Relating to the Early History of Hudson Bay* (Toronto, The Champlain Society, 1931).

CHAPTER XXIII

HENRY KELSEY, 1690–1692

With all of its financial commitments in 1692, the Committee was heartened by the success of its first attempt at the policy which it knew, and had for long known, was the only true answer to the French. As early as the days of its first Bay-side Governor, Quaker Bayly, it had been realised that the only effective counter to French encirclement would be to send Englishmen, or at any rate employees of the Company, up to the head-waters of the rivers, to induce the Indians to come down to the Bay to trade.

The difficulty had always been that there were no Englishmen who were competent, either as 'Linguisters' or as canoemen, for such a journey. French renegades, including Radisson, were bound to be unreliable; native English would be infinitely better, but for its first fourteen years, up to the time of the first dividend in 1684, the Company had been working on so small and tenuous a scale that it took its servants as it could find them, and had no system for training up its own men for the peculiar tasks which they would have to perform. For the most part it required labourers and hands, men mature in bodily strength and with little to learn save the precautions necessary if they were to survive an arctic winter. The posts were so few in number, and they needed so small a complement of 'officers' that no special care was taken to supply them.

Yet the quality of the officers, and their unwillingness to serve for reasonably long engagements, proved a great handicap in the early years. Even when the trade and the posts were sufficiently established to give promise of long-term employment, for the book-keeping and managerial aspects of its posts the Company found it always difficult to find the right type of man. He had to be adequate in accountancy, able to read and understand the instructions sent out, to conduct the Indian trade and to maintain command over his servants, and perhaps to defend his post against the French. More would depend on character than on learning, but since the summer 'slooping' between posts was so important a part of the Company's business a knowledge of boat-sailing would be an advantage, and it is astonishing how many of the Company's officers came to be called 'Captain' as their periods of service wore on.

With the firm establishment of the Company's trade, therefore, the Committee began the practice of taking occasional apprentices, to train them in the peculiar difficulties of the business. Ten were on the books in the year 1684. They soon came to be drawn largely from the great foundation of Christ's Hospital in London, where boys were well grounded in writing and arithmetic, with a special entry into careers at sea available to them. Such educated poor boys were ideal for the Company, and 'Blue Coat Boys' began to make their appearance in the Company's books. They were all able to write fair hands and to cast accounts, and being young they would, the Committee hoped, 'easily attaine the Lingua' and so be able to travel with Indians. The Committee promised itself a regular supply of such apprentices.

Henry Kelsey was such an apprentice, though he did not come from Christ's Hospital. He was possibly a poor relation of the 'Captain Kelsey' who had supplied the Committee with a dinner in 1669, and who may himself be the same Thomas Kelsey who had invested £100 in the stock of the Company in 1679. Whatever his origins, Henry was taken on as an apprentice in 1684, and was a passenger outward on the *Lucy* in May of that year. He was then but fourteen years old, so that when he first attracted notice in 1687 he was still 'the Boy Henry Kelsey'. His achievement then was to have carried a winter packet of mail from the newly established York Factory in Hayes River to its subsidiary post at New Severn, a journey of about two hundred miles which had defeated a small party of Indians who had been sent with the packet earlier in the winter. The Committee therefore instructed Governor Geyer in 1688 that Kelsey should be one of the eight men to be sent to establish Churchill River 'because Wee are informed hee is a very active Lad Delighting much in Indians Compa. being never better pleased then when hee is Travelling amongst them'.

Kelsey was to grow into one of the greatest figures of the Hudson's Bay fur trade, distinguished alike by character, achievements and the expression of a clear-cut sense of purpose. For the moment, however, he was but an apprentice of seventeen years. His journey to New Severn was to be the prelude to an epic voyage into the interior, the first accomplished by a servant of the English Company, and both in its extent and in its consequences unique in the history of North America. But in 1688 this great voyage was not even projected. Kelsey therefore cannot cast the glow of his later achievements and his matured personality round the circumstances of 1688. But he must have given some hope of the kind of thing which an

English apprentice of the right sort, given an early introduction to life in the north, would make possible for the Company.

By 1690 he had given more substantial grounds for optimism, and for determined planning, for during the summer of 1689 he had been put ashore on the edge of the Barren Lands, according to the Committee's instructions. Churchill was a disappointing post, slow to attract Indians, and Kelsey travelled over two hundred miles in search of Indians to bring down to trade there and at York. He now first saw the musk-ox, which he was the first recorded white man to see and to describe, and after six weeks of desperate travel he was picked up at the mouth of the Churchill River by Captain Young in the *Dering*. It was in truth a 'brief, bitter little expedition', but it revealed a firm purpose to venture away from the shores of the Bay.

On his return to Churchill, Kelsey found it necessary to set out again to pick up some goods which he had left *en cache*. On his second return he found the Churchill post destroyed by fire and he was taken to York along with the rest of the small staff of the burned-out post, and found that his reputation for ability in handling Indians and for travelling with them was enormously enhanced. Although Governor Geyer only greeted him with the gruff acknowledgment that 'I had my labour for my travell', Kelsey had already accomplished much, especially in showing his own capabilities. The Indians round Churchill, among whom he had ventured, had at that time a reputation for being more treacherous than any other Indians in the country, and although Geyer never asked for any account of his experiences, he could not overlook the fact that Kelsey had gone among them in an attempt to bring them down to trade and had also shown that he was a more venturesome and determined traveller than his companion, who had been reluctant, scared of rivers and Eskimos alike, and openly telling Kelsey that he was a fool who was not sensible of the dangers.

Kelsey came pat to hand in 1690, when the Company was fully conscious of the importance of a friendly and progressive Indian policy both as an offset to the French and as a means of expanding its own trade. The reputation in which the Indians held the English had always been carefully fostered by fair treatment, but now in 1690 something more than fair usage was called for. The Company's reputation needed to be spread far afield in the interior. To accomplish this Kelsey set off from York Fort on 12th June, sent by Geyer but cheerfully undertaking the journey, to travel southwest to the Stone Indian country, the Assinipoets' lands. He intended to spend two years inland, and he was accompanied on his journey by the Captain of the Assinipoets. The Committee fully approved of the venture, hoped that the prospects held out to Kelsey would encourage other young men to undertake similar journeys, and promised Geyer that he should be well supplied with trade-goods to satisfy the 'Remote Indians' whom Kelsey was to bring down to trade.

Hastening over his journey (and over his account of it), Kelsey reached a point about six hundred miles south-west of York Fort by 10th July, probably near the present Pas on the Saskatchewan, but possibly on Lake Winnipeg or even on Cedar Lake. This he named Dering's Point and made of it a centre for his operations, of which the first was, in September, to bring the Assinipoets to a peace with the Crees. It was a peace which was soon broken, but it is of interest and importance as showing the constant burden of Kelsey's mission and also as showing that, whereas he found many of the Assinipoets still using wooden bows for hunting, yet their occasional contacts with the Company in visits to the Bay meant that they were now able to rout their enemies 'And with our English guns do make them fly'.

From Dering's Point Kelsey communicated with Governor Geyer, who sent him up a runlet (presumably of brandy) in the spring of 1691, with tobacco and other goods—clearly not enough for trade but enough to make him an acceptable ambassador, to persuade the Indians to make peace among themselves, to devote their energies to killing beaver and bringing them down to the Bay. The idea was that approved by the Committee in the following year, when Geyer was told to use such arguments in favour of peace and trade as might occur on the spur of the moment and to point out to the Indians that it did them no good to kill and destroy one another. If necessary Geyer was to tell them that he would trade no more powder or shot to the aggressors and so would expose them to their enemies.

Kelsey was not altogether successful in putting these arguments. He told his Indians (the Crees, Nayhathaways) that 'they must Imploy their time in Catching of beavour for that will be better liked on then killing their Enemies when they come to the factory neither was I sent there for to kill any Indians but to make peace with as many as I could'. But when their answer was 'What signified a peace with those Indians [the Naywatame Poets, the Gros Ventres] considering they knew not the use of Cannoes' he realised that he could effect nothing, and held his peace. So the Crees made their attack, and renewed it during the winter after Kelsey had once more made the peace. The result was that when Kelsey had once more wintered in the plains, probably with the Assiniboines (the Stone Indians or Mountain Poets as he called them) and set out to return to the Bay in 1692 the Gros Ventres sent word that they were afraid to accompany him as they had promised.

Nevertheless Kelsey returned to York Fort in 1692, having to some extent accomplished what he set out to do 'in keeping the Indians from warring one with another, that they may have the more time to look after their trade and bring larger quantity of Furrs and other Trade with them to the factory'. The Committee was well pleased and looked forward to continuing results in future years.

The Company's records contain very little on the details of the journey which Kelsey undertook though there are several mentions of Geyer's proposal to send him, and of his success, and Kelsey was warmly welcomed when he came back to London in 1694. But the Company either did not receive a copy of the account of the journey which Kelsey made or, more probably, the account was allowed to get into the hands of opponents of the Company. So the whole heroic venture could later be denied, or could be treated merely as the result of a headstrong boy playing truant in the woods instead of as a piece of deliberate policy.

This actually happened when the Company's Charter was challenged by Arthur Dobbs in 1749, and much strength was given to such a view of Kelsey's journey by the twin facts that the Company never claimed publicity for the journey and that, when challenged, it gave such a garbled version that the episode seemed slightly discreditable. It was not the Company's policy to allow information of its territories or of the exploits of its servants to become common knowledge. The habit of secrecy seems foolish and unnecessary now, but in the seventeenth century the probability of rivalry constantly emphasised the need to safeguard the knowledge of the navigation and the prospects of the Bay.

It was not until the twentieth century that an indisputable copy of Kelsey's journal, kept partly in prose and partly in verse, was discovered among the papers of Arthur Dobbs at Carrickfergus in North Ireland. The journal leaves much doubt as to the exact route which Kelsey followed, but it leaves no reasonable doubt that he reached the Saskatchewan and wintered on the prairies. That Dobbs, with a copy of Kelsey's Journal in his possession (perhaps abstracted from the Company's papers) should have suppressed it and put about the version of an adolescent flight from discipline, is merely an instance of the rancour with which he challenged the Company's position. His version gained credibility partly because the Company never put out its own version of the affair and partly because such a journey seemed out of phase with the general policy of the Company.

But in 1690-2 precisely the contrary was the case. In those years the financial strength of the Company was being most purposefully organised to resist the French challenge and to set forth the expedition for the recapture of the Bottom of the Bay, the Committee was strongly in favour of expansion to the northward, to Churchill and to 'Dering River', and the apprenticeship system was beginning to produce men who combined knowledge of the Bay with youthful vigour and some capacity for organisation.

Kelsey was the first product of that system, and although his journey stands out unique in the history of the exploration of North America, in the history of the Hudson's Bay Company it takes its place as the logical development of a policy which has hitherto been obscured by the glamour, and the controversy, surrounding the journey.

BOOKS FOR REFERENCE

BREBNER, J. B.—*The Explorers of North America 1492-1806* (second edition, London, 1955).

DOUGHTY, A. G. and MARTIN, C. (eds.), *The Kelsey Papers* (Ottawa, The Public Archives of Canada and the Public Record Office of Northern Ireland, 1929).

MACKAY, Douglas (revised to 1949 by Alice MacKay)—*The Honourable Company* (Toronto, 1949).

MORTON, Arthur S.—*A History of the Canadian West to 1870-71* (London, [1939]).

WHILLANS, J. W.—*First in the West. The Story of Henry Kelsey Discoverer of Canadian Prairies* (Edmonton, Alberta, 1955).

CHAPTER XXIV

JAMES KNIGHT RECAPTURES ALBANY, 1692–1693

As it made its decisions and its preparations for the great expedition of 1692 the Committee could not yet know how successful and enterprising Kelsey was to be. News of his return to York did not come to London until the ships of 1692 got back, but they knew of his confident departure and that he had got well on his way; they knew that Governor Geyer had made contact with him at Dering's Point by Indian messenger and had sent him supplies for making presents to Indians, and that their apprentice had survived his first winter living with the Indians.

From La Rochelle they had some rumours of the activities of Iberville and of the projected naval expedition to the Bay which he was trying to set on foot; and although they could not know of the delays which were to prevent him from attempting his plan in 1692, it was common knowledge that Frontenac as Governor of Canada was worried by the way in which the war was going. Prices were high in Canada and were rising out of control; the whole economy of the colony seemed to tremble out of balance, and the Governor was preoccupied with the inroads of the New England colonists to the south and did not wish to embark on fresh ventures to the north. Despite the threat of Iberville's preparations, the situation was heartening, and the interim report of Kelsey's journey added to the general picture.

If Kelsey, as the first apprentice to show the aptitudes which might be got by training for the Company's business, added to the confidence of the Committee, their main hope in 1692 (as for many years to come) lay rather in the old type of servant. In James Knight they had a shipwright, a craftsman trained in the rule-of-thumb technique of ship-design which placed him in a different class from the labourers and seamen who were the normal employees of the Company. He had behind him in 1692 almost twenty years of experience of life and trade in the Bay. He had gone on the early voyages and had, in his turn, served as shipwright, boatswain, landsman, trader and Deputy Governor. Not all of his relations with the Committee had been amicable, although he was one of the first traders whose knowledge had been used to help in the purchase of trade-goods.

Knight, however, was in 1692 as much an individualist as at any time in his career. Despite this—and Knight never attempted to disguise his opinions, especially as to his right to trade on his own account—he was picked to command the expedition of 1692 because of his experience and determination, as 'an Honest and discreet man from whose Prudent management wee promise Our selves great Successe', and he was given both a commission from the Crown and another from the Company. The commissions gave him power to make alliances with the Indians, and his Instructions bade him exercise humanity and justice; his chief Instruction, however, was to make an instant surprise attack on the French post at Albany.

Both in the negotiations before he set sail, and in the conduct of the 1692 expedition, Knight showed the defects of his qualities. His role, as always, was to bring the knowledge and experience of conditions in the Bay into relation with the directing power of the London Committee. That placed him in a position to make his own conditions and to go his own way with something of a truculent independence. Now he delayed acceptance of the command offered him, having 'severall Concernes of his owne' which demanded his attention. Then he started so late and progressed so slowly that it was a most fortunate chance for the Company that Iberville was held back that year, for Knight lost all chance of making the sort of surprise attack on Albany in 1692 which the Committee had in mind.

Whilst Captain Edgcombe in the *Dering* sailed direct to York Fort, delivered his cargo of trade-goods and the Committee's Instructions (which included information for Governor Geyer of Knight's expedition and plans) and got back to London again by November with a shipment of 24,236 beaver, and with an Indian boy, Knight decided that it was too late for a successful attack on Albany that fall and that his best plan was to winter the whole of his costly expedition in the Bay, so that he could attack early in the summer of 1693, before reinforcements could be got to the French post. He accordingly called at York Fort and then took the *Royal Hudson's Bay*, the *Prosperous*, and the *Pery* to the east coast of James Bay (the Eastmain) and to Gilpin's Island. There, during the winter, he met some trouble with the discipline of his crews, but he found that he could rely on his captains and was ready for action in 1693 when weather permitted.

During the winter it appeared at one time probable that the projected attack would prove needless after all. Knowing of Knight's plans, Governor Geyer wrote to him a warning letter from York

Fort, sending his message by Indian runner, to say that it was reported that the French had burned their posts at the Bottom of the
Bay and had set out overland for Canada. Later he was able to add
that they had found the journey impossible and had only got some
forty miles to the south from Albany. There was much truth in the
Indian rumours which Geyer thus passed on, for the non-appearance
of shipping or supplies from Canada had caused starvation and
mutiny among the French and over twenty of them had in fact set
out overland for Canada. But they had not burned their post; they
had left behind them a small garrison of eight men of whom five
set out on a hunting expedition. During their absence one of the
three left in charge (the armourer) ran amuck and murdered his two
companions, the surgeon and the Jesuit priest Dalmas, with singular
barbarity. The hunters seized him and put him in irons on their
return, but the result was that when Knight and his three ships
attacked on 2nd July, 1693, there were only six Frenchmen there,
including the demented armourer in irons. It was an almost ignominious end to such a project. After a brief resistance the five free
men escaped to the woods, leaving to Knight the post, the furs
accumulated, and the armourer in irons. Only two of the French
garrison ever reached Montreal.

Though cheaply won, it was still a great victory. It might easily
have been gained by a handful of men at a tenth of the cost, for the
secret of the success was the non-arrival of Iberville in 1692, and the
fact that the English came ahead of him in 1693, having wintered in
the Bay. But although a lesser force might have dispersed the small
and starving French garrison, and might have captured the booty
of over 31,000 beaver 'Traded by the French' it could neither have
re-established nor maintained the post.

The two escaping Frenchmen who reached Montreal brought the
news of the English success in the fall of 1693. Already succour
had been sent off by the French *Compagnie*; a flotilla of canoes had
been despatched in the spring of the year, but there is no further
news of them and probably they turned back on getting the news
that Albany had been retaken. There was still, however, some chance
that Knight and his men might have to fight to retain their conquests,
for Iberville and the *Compagnie de la Baie d'Hudson* fully realised the
importance of the Bottom of the Bay, and the way in which delays
and the lack of an adequate force had given the results of their
efforts to the English.

Early in 1693 Iberville had again been given command of the
Poli; and again he had been ordered to convoy some slow-sailing

merchantmen to Quebec. Then, with the frigate *L'Indiscret* and a vessel to be provided by the *Compagnie*, he was to carry out his long-agreed plan for an attack on York Fort with men-of-war. Calms, contrary winds and his convoy duties, held him back, as before in 1692, and he did not arrive in Quebec until 23rd July, 1693. That the French had surrendered Albany was not yet known, but when Frontenac called a meeting to debate the plan to sail for York Fort the decision was that Iberville would not have time to get into the Bay, complete his operation and get out again within the year, and that the Royal ships must return to France before winter. Even when this decision had been reached, Frontenac was in grave doubt during the summer of 1693. In August he decided that Iberville should take the frigate *L'Indiscret* and a small Boston ship, the *Mary Sara* which he had captured on his voyage from France, and should go to capture York Fort after all. But he then changed his mind.

In the meantime it was accepted that since no French ship had got to the Bay in 1691 or 1692 it was most important to get one through now, and the *Ste. Anne*, a ship belonging to the *Compagnie*, left Quebec, still in ignorance of Knight's success, in July 1693, with goods and provisions for the French garrison. On arrival she found herself engaged in a hot action with the English ships, and when it became clear that there were three well-armed vessels to oppose her where she had expected a friendly garrison, she made off to destroy the other French posts at Moose and Rupert, since they were no longer tenable with Albany in the hands of so powerful an English force, and was back in Quebec with her news by early November 1693.

The summer and fall had been taken up by Iberville in another commerce-raiding cruise off Newfoundland and the New England coast, from which he had returned to France by the end of the year. He then knew the measure, and the cause, of the English success in the Bay. He estimated the loss to the French at 200,000 *livres*, and he was convinced that if he had been allowed to sail to the Bay without concern for his wintering there with Royal ships he could have accomplished at York Fort what Knight had done at Albany. In this he revealed some of his less admirable qualities, for the changes in plan which had resulted in his cruising off Newfoundland in 1693 were in part of his own making. He had talked Frontenac into this Newfoundland venture, and he had insisted on the need for a second Royal ship in addition to *L'Indiscret* if his attack was to succeed. He had also used the interlude to get himself married. But although he may be partly to blame for the fatal delays, Iberville was as convinced as ever of the need for a sea-borne attack on York Fort, and as determined as ever to work for that purpose.

For the moment the English had snatched a great and cheap victory, and the Committee were jubilant. Almighty God had blessed and prospered them in recovering their just rights from the French; their expedition had been strong enough to stave off any counter-attack from the *Ste. Anne*; they brought home in 1693 the satisfactory total of 31,441 beaver 'traded by the French', and in their accounts they costed these furs at nothing.

It would have been almost too much to expect the whole operation to have gone without adverse comment. It was felt in London that with a little more local enterprise Geyer might have carried out what had proved to be so simple an exploit; and Michael Grimington was dismissed his ship for 'several omissions'—apparently he had not been sufficiently conscious of the barrier between commissioned and warrant officers on board his ship; and since he had himself started in the Company's service as an ordinary seaman who shall blame him? But the general mood was of sober and justifiable rejoicing, of which the proper counterpart was the gloom of the French.

In Canada Frontenac put the loss of French beaver at £50,000 and saw the whole affair as a proof that the English were better than the French at defending their colonies, sparing no expense and not doing things by halves, like the French merchants. Iberville's voyage, he rather smugly reported, would have been useless, since he had been too late and any shipping he took with him would have been liable to capture. Regardless of the fact that it was himself who had interposed to prevent it, he reported that the plan (Iberville's plan for a strong naval expedition) had been postponed for one reason or another for three years, and now the English success at Albany had ruined its chances. But Frontenac had other troubles; he found his Intendant impossible to work with, he feared a New England attack on Michilimackinac, and he complained bitterly of Jesuit misrepresentations of his régime, especially over the matter of permits to trade brandy to Indians.

Iberville was troubled by none of these things. They all fell into place, for him, as troubles of the Canadian colony which would to a large extent settle themselves when the great beaver trade of the Bay should be French by virtue of French possession of Nelson River, to be achieved by naval power; and in France he reiterated his conviction that even such success as the English had just won could be counteracted by the capture of Port Nelson. For this he had a clear and attractive plan, based on the loan of two ships from the French

Navy for limited periods, a thirty-six-gun ship to leave France in March 1694 and to be back in harbour again by November, and a twenty-gun ship to winter in the Bay and return in October 1695.

The essence of the whole affair was a realisation that the English Company's methods were correct in their approach and had proved effective in execution. Iberville was deeply and bitterly convinced of the correctness of his plan. But it was in essence no more than a copy of the Company's plan, which for the moment had brought complete dominance to the English.

BOOKS FOR REFERENCE

Hudson's Bay Record Society—Vol. XX.
Crouse, Nellis M.—*Lemoyne d'Iberville: Soldier of New France* (Ithaca, New York, 1954).
La Ronciere, C. de—*Histoire de la Marine Française* (Paris, 1909–32), Vol. VI.

CHAPTER XXV

LOANS, SALES IN EUROPE AND PROSPERITY WITHOUT DIVIDENDS, 1692–1695

Such success in the field would appear to have been cause for confidence at home. But in contrast with the high dividends and distribution of shares during the years when Iberville had triumphed over them, the members of the Committee found the period of their own success one of trouble and lack of dividend.

The first of their problems of these years was over Radisson. The extra pension which he had been granted until he should be found some employment under the Crown had been withdrawn in 1690 after it had run for three years, and he had been reduced to his original (1684) pension of £50 a year and the dividends on £200 of the original stock of the Company, increased to £600 by the bonus issue of 1690. Against this decision Radisson appealed, and he was given further consideration by the Committee. Marlborough felt some responsibility for Radisson's condition (which was such that he even seemed likely to have to 'shift for him selfe, & leave his wife great with Child & 4 Or 5 children more on the parrish'), and Marlborough's constant supporter in the Committee, William Yonge, submitted a long and detailed account of Radisson's services. Yonge maintained that all except the Deputy Governor, Sir Edward Dering, felt the strength of Radisson's case and that 'as he was the Imediate author of the Companies present prosperity, soe I myselfe was the first mover that induced him to it, & without me he had never come back to theire service, nay when I wrote to invite him, the Committee Ridiculed me for the attempt'. The Committee nevertheless remained obdurate—a sign of the dominance of the Deputy Governor—and early in 1693 resolved to do no more for Radisson; they reckoned that they had already given him 'such Large gratuities and guifts that hee has Received of the Company above £1000 in Eight years'—which is quite true, for such a reward means only a little over £100 a year.

The Committee might have acted more generously if there had been no lingering suspicions of the loyalty of this mercurial genius. But, apart from the question of loyalty, there was the fact that Radisson's constant lament was that Geyer at York Fort was incompetent, ignorant and corrupt, as against which the Committee recognised that Geyer, whatever his faults, had without doubt vastly increased the returns, so that York alone supported the whole trade of the Company, and produced dividends. In addition, there were straggling bits of evidence that Radisson might yet revert to the French service, despite his wife and children and his acceptance of English nationality. He was certainly approached by the French, and a letter to him from a certain M. Perry of La Rochelle came into the Deputy Governor's hands, whilst the French were considering the chance of getting hold of him in exchange for the English prisoners taken by de Troyes and Iberville.

Radisson himself was not definitely implicated in these moves, and he appealed against the Committee, bringing with him his father-in-law 'one Mr. Gwoodet'—the Godet who had been instrumental in bringing Radisson back to London in 1684. He was reduced so low that William Yonge even proposed a loan of £50 in November 1693, but he was not so low (or so lacking friends) that he could not begin an action in Chancery against the Company in the following June. The Committee retained Sir Thomas Powis, and at the same time William Yonge continued his efforts to get the Committee to make a reasonable settlement out of court.

The Company delayed a settlement both in Chancery and by private negotiation, largely on the ground that material witnesses were in the Bay and could not give their evidence. So the case dragged through 1695, but in June of that year Radisson got an order from Chancery for payment at least of his original £50 a year and in November he blocked a further attempt at adjournment. A General Court of the whole Company left the business to the Committee, to drop or continue as seemed best, and during January and February of 1696 the Committee (with Samuel Clarke as Deputy Governor in place of Sir Edward Dering) at last reached an agreement with Radisson and his two principal supporters, William Yonge and Richard Cradock. The Company 'condescended' to remit £50 which Radisson owed the Company and to pay him £150 in cash; in future they would pay him £100 a year pension except in years when they paid a dividend. In dividend years he would get dividends on his £200 of original stock but only £50 pension.

This, however, was not to be the end of the matter, for Radisson hoped also to get payment for the furs traded by the Frenchmen at 'Port Nelson' and brought by him into the Company's possession in 1684. He rejected the Company's offer and his Chancery suit was revived in November 1696, but he gained nothing thereby, for although he got judgment in January 1697, it was only for £100 a year pension, not for recompense for the furs. The Company began to pay him, in half-yearly instalments of £50 each, whilst a further payment of £320 18s. 0d. for costs was also paid over. But even this was not the end of the matter, for Radisson now began to prepare a petition to Parliament. It was however the basis for a workable arrangement, and the settlement is probably to be explained in part by the fact that by 1697 the Company again had need of Radisson's services, and particularly of his evidence.

The long, and as yet unfinished, trouble with Radisson revealed that the earlier schism within the Committee, and the differences between the Committee and the bulk of the stockholders, were by no means over. It becomes clear that there was a feeling that, as Deputy Governor, Sir Edward Dering was too masterful, and with his withdrawal the Radisson dispute quickly lost much of its bitterness. The troubles of 1690 had not finally ended, any more than the root problem of disposing of the furs had been solved. A motion in 1690 that each member of the Company should take an oath of fidelity had been turned down by a General Court, but later in the year new forms of oath had been devised for the Governor and for all officials, and in 1691 all servants of the Company had been required to swear (as Churchill had sworn on his election as Governor) that 'during a Joynt Stocke of the said Company (now established by Act of Parliament) I will neither directly nor Indirectly Trade to or from any Place within the Limits of their Charter for my Owne particular Account'. At the same time the servants in the Bay were warned to take no instructions save from the Deputy Governor and the Committee. In the next year, November 1692, the members of the Committee were required to swear that the stock which qualified them for the Committee was their own absolute property (the qualification for a vote in the General Court had been raised to £300 stock, and for the Committee or for Governor, Deputy Governor or committee-member, to £600 when the stock had been trebled in 1690). The requirement was abandoned almost as soon as it was introduced, a move which lends support to the suspicion that some members of the Committee, perhaps even Marlborough himself, did not really own the stock which stood in their names but were supplied with the requisite holding in order to get their voices in the Company's affairs.

The Committee, however, was not itself above disciplinary action. True, the amount of money to be distributed as 'Attendance money' was increased in 1693 from £200 to £300 in view of the Company's success against the French and the increase of trade; but members of the Committee were given only one hour's grace at each meeting, after which they were to lose their attendance money for that session, and it was not long before John Sweetaple (who could well forego the fee) was refused his money for late arrival. At the same time a special sub-committee was set up to meet twice weekly to deal with wages, a suitable oath for all stockholders was devised, a further attempt was made to get the petty cash properly accounted for, and the Secretary was instructed to get 'a Perticular Booke to keepe an account of cash paid and Received for the Company'.

At much the same time as these minor re-organisations in the Company's business methods were coming into effect, and as changes in the directing body were making themselves felt, the offices in which the Company's business was transacted began to become more constant. Coffee-houses still figured largely—seamen were engaged at the Amsterdam coffee-house, a ship was bought at Kidd's coffee-house, the *Dering* was put up for sale at the Marine coffee-house and Mr. Glover was interviewed about the sale of beaver at Vernon's. All of this meant a rather spontaneous approach to the problem in hand, and a lack of reference to previous correspondence or minutes, which would not normally be at hand as readily as they might be in a permanent office. At times there was reason for such a venue, as when in 1693 the Committee paid 'Mr. Loyd the Coffeman' (the founder of Lloyd's the marine insurance institution), £3 for intelligence of the Company's ships. But such occasions were rare; normally the use of a coffee-house for Company's business was a sign of loose organisation and it speaks of a tightening of system when, from 1692 onwards, the Company's own premises—still, until 1696, at Scriveners' Hall, off Cheapside—come more and more into use. The sub-committee to settle tradesmen's bills, for example, was to meet there as often as it liked.

The preparations for the 1693 voyage—undertaken of necessity whilst the results of Knight's venture were still unknown, when, indeed, he was still wintering on Gilpin's Island and had not yet attacked at all—were to put such a strain on the Committee that any extra efficiency would be welcome, and differences within the Committee were obviously to be avoided at all costs. Trade-goods presented little difficulty; Brazil tobacco was available from Oporto, bought there by the Company but shipped in a Portuguese ship and consigned to a Portuguese merchant in London to avoid some of the risks of capture at sea by the French. Payment was by bill of exchange, and an annual supply of sixteen to eighteen rolls of the tobacco cost the Company anything from a hundred to a hundred and thirty pounds. Alternative supplies and prices were available, and although shipment was not always punctual (that of 1693 arrived late) the Committee could still supply this important commodity in any quantity at a very reasonable cost. Guns, however, were not so satisfactory; the type and quality of gun for the Bay was under constant discussion, and although Dutch guns were no longer advocated, the English guns sent over in 1692 caused great complaints from the factories and the Committee resolved to take great care for the future, to take professional opinion on the subject and to employ a 'proof-master' to test all guns before they were shipped. Gunpowder, too, was a difficult store, dangerous to handle, liable to deteriorate if not kept dry and frequently turned over, and absolutely essential to the trade. Stocks of bad powder were steadily accumulating in the Bay, and by 1695 the Committee, spurred by a report from Knight on 'the badness of this Comodity', had to resolve to bring home and sell all back stocks and to start again.

Brandy was naturally a commodity most affected by the war, and the Committee warned its Governor both to keep careful account of expenditure and to husband supplies. The 'black market' price of French spirits had risen to twelve shillings the gallon! And although scarcity led to some spirits being distilled in England the Committee found this 'excessive deare' and doubted whether it would keep despite the protests of the distillers that it would keep for many years. In its instructions for both tobacco and spirits the Committee was beginning to favour a policy which became a strong feature of the Company's trade. Wages both on land and at sea were a major item of expenditure, and in shipping out more tobacco and more spirits (when available) the intention was that the Company might thereby 'lessen the extravagant wages of our servants', by encouraging them to spend at the Company's store.

Not only the wages but the maintenance of the servants seemed to the Committee a proper field for retrenchment. Here there was the undoubted fact that prices had risen in war conditions, but on the whole the short-term variations in food prices which the Company's purchases reveal (and there are innumerable entries on this subject) all point to the difficulties of catching the right moment for buying in a limited market rather than to serious changes. They reveal the tendency for prices to rise or fall, with such a purchaser, owing to the purchaser's notions of what market reaction is likely to be rather than owing to actual market conditions, and prices rise and fall considerably and rapidly more from the effect of the market opinion than from the actual state of supplies. In fact prices do not seem to have reacted to the war as violently as the Committee expected, for beef remained steady at 25s., pork rose only from 28s. to 33s., but other commodities showed no great movement except perhaps malt, which rose from 18s. 6d. a quarter in 1690 to 26s. a quarter in 1693.

Yet the fears of the Committee were active enough to bring stern instructions to the Bay. Geyer was again urged to frugality with the news that grains had doubled in price, beef and pork had risen fifty per cent., and the whole of Europe was in fear of dearth. He was, moreover, to destroy wolves and 'ravenous beasts', and to make hay and byres (as was Knight at Albany) since the Committee intended to send out cows, goats and pigs, which, they understood, survived in the similar climates of Finland and Lapland. The cattle were not sent in 1694—not indeed until the war was over—since it was held that they would be very vulnerable to raids. But garden produce and food crops were not held to be so threatened, and scythes, spades and garden seeds were shipped out, with a book of instructions, in both 1692 and 1693. The Committee was confident that, with a bank or hedge to keep the north-west wind off the gardens, they would thrive to perfection as easily as in any part of Sweden or Norway. Carrots, onions, mustard, turnips, lettuce, spinach, kidney beans, cabbage, radish were all to be tried, whilst various kinds of corn were also sent—wheat, barley, oats and pease. Great savings might be achieved, but the Committee thought that in any case the experiments should be made. 'Lett the event be what it will lett it be done'.

This was a policy which went back to the earliest days of the Company, to Radisson's goats and fowls. The object was in part to get fresh provisions and so to avoid scurvy, in part to save the costs of provisioning, and in part to be less dependent on Indian hunters and fishermen. Purchases of seeds had long been items in the accounts, and the policy was now vigorously pursued. Stephen Pitts was given a gratuity for industrious gardening in 1694, when York Fort reported on the 'refreshment' which the garden produced, and in 1698 Edward Williams of Cardigan, gardener, was employed and Knight at Albany was provided with four sows, one boar, seven goats, ten sheep, three hogs and three and a half dozen fowls. It had already been shewn that at Albany flax and barley could be grown, though wheat and hemp would not thrive.

Such attempts to grow provender were dictated by medical reasons, as well as by a desire to economise on European imports. The fresh foods had their medicinal value, and Geyer was at this time instructed that the Committee wanted a bottle or two of 'that Juyce that you tap out of the trees which you mixt with your drink when any one is troubled with the Scurvy'—an attempt to get the secret of Spruce beer as an anti-scorbutic which went with the despatch of cole seed to be boiled with the salted meat for the same purpose.

The costs and difficulties of preparing both provisions and trade-goods went together, and the counterpart of the urge for economy in provisions was an instruction to raise the Standard of Trade and to secure accuracy and economy in the indents for supplies. Geyer, in whom slipshod indents were a constant defect, had made no changes in the Standard of Trade in 1692 though ordered to do so in 1690, and was strongly urged to pass on the extra costs of war-time goods in 1693. Here the Committee, far removed from the personal problems involved, was dogmatic; 'if we would force the Indians they must give double the price or starve' they wrote to Geyer, whilst to Knight they were but little less severe. He was 'to make them beleve you must Leave the Countrey agine if you cannot gett those prices'.

The usual attempt to enlarge the run of commodities went with this urge to enhance the Standard of Trade. Whaling was, once more, to be pursued as a long-shore occupation. The men's wages remained a constant overhead charge whether they were fishing or sleeping, so they might as well fish; they would even do this for fun. The Committee thought no great skill was needed to harpoon the white whales when they followed the fish fry into the rivers, and they pointed out that Captain Young, though never in Greenland, had killed as many whales as the professional harpooner, who drew double wages. The Committee were managing to sell small consignments of whale oil without difficulty, and hoped for further supplies. Castoreum, too, received attention as an alternative to the still glutted beaver supplies, and Geyer was again urged to stimulate the Indians to bring in the 'Beaver Codds' and was told of the Russian method of preparing them by sun-drying.

Not all of the Committee's efforts were directed to economy and trade returns, however. In the confidence of victory they instructed Geyer that discovery was to be pushed forward. They had a 'longing desire' to find out Buffalo (Dering) River, and men were to be sent inland in search of turpentine and along-shore by sloop in search of 'sea-horse teeth' 'and soe yeare by yeare they must needs discover somthing more then hitherto we know'. Kelsey was back from his great journey inland; the Committee had the greatest hopes of the results of his pacifying policy, and he was re-engaged in 1694 after spending the winter in England. The Committee left no records of their reception of the young hero, but they were not in 1693–4 thinking of further deep penetration into the hinterland but of frequent and slight journeys to expand contacts nearer to the coast.

With hopes of the firm establishment of the Bay-side posts, with the care for local provender, and with the general confidence of the period, there drifts into the records something of that concept of Rupert's Land as a small colony which had been implicit in the Company from the start. Once more the evidence comes in the mention of clergy and women resident on the Bay. From the earliest records of its detailed instructions to its ships' captains, whether in its own employ or working under charter party for some other owner, the Company had always given its first instruction that the worship of Almighty God should be regularly observed on board. This remained a prominent part of such instructions. But towards the Indians the Company felt no missionary fervour, and although it becomes obvious from occasional notes that religious observances were a part of life in the posts, little provision was normally made for them. At times, as in 1682, homilies and books were sent out, but normally little was done. In 1693, however, Thomas Anderson was employed as a minister and was sent to York Fort. At the same time there is a hint that English women might share the rigours of a winter in the Bay, as Governor Sergeant and his 'parcell of women' (also accompanied by a priest) had shown in 1684–6. Early in 1694 the Company made an agreement 'with Captain Edgcombe's surgeon's wife, who was left last voyage at Yorke Fort' to pay £5 for a medicine chest. It is perhaps straining a strictly grammatical use of the language too far to insist that this can only mean that it was the woman, and not her husband, who had spent the winter at York. But that is certainly one meaning which can be put to the words; in fact it is the only correct meaning which should attach to them.

With all the optimism of these years, ships and seamen remained a sphere in which the Committee were, on the whole, not at home. Again in 1693 they tried purchase of a ship, and again they proved inept. The *Royal Mary* was bought in April 1693 for £3,000; she was re-christened the *Supply* and was then cleared of her copper-sheathing, well caulked, and given double bows with three-inch plank. This brought her cost up to £3,699, and she was ordered to set out on the 1693 expedition under command of Captain Simpson.

He, however, hung about the Pool of London instead of dropping down to Gravesend ready to sail when given his orders, and the Committee, keeping a watchful eye on its ships at Blackwall, dismissed him on the eve of sailing and sent the *Supply* out under command of Captain James Young. With her went the *Dering*, Captain Leonard Edgcombe. Both ships were bound for York Fort, but the *Supply* carried goods for Albany, to which she was to proceed when Geyer at York Fort had assured Captain Young that Albany was in English hands. The two ships were safely back in October, having touched at Baltimore in Ireland on their return journey and then come up-Channel to Plymouth. At the same time the *Prosperous* fire-ship, Captain Baley, and the *Royal Hudson's Bay*, Captain Grimington, got back to Plymouth, returning from their winter in the Bay and their part in Knight's recapture of Albany.

The Committee had so mismanaged the shipping as to leave no vessel in the Bay as a protection against a French counter-attack, and so as to have to pay off four crews at once and to dispose of four cargoes. The bill for wages came to over £3,000, and the newly-bought and reconditioned *Supply* proved, on her first voyage, unsatisfactory for the trade. The Committee at first decided to sell her at Lloyd's Coffee House, then to hire her out to the East India Company, then that the risks of the East India voyage would be too heavy. She was accordingly sold, to Captain Edgcombe himself, for £2,200; a heavy loss for one year's working.

In addition to their difficulties over shipping and sea-captains, the Committee also had to surmount the problem of getting seamen. Here some system of recruiting, especially in Scotland, begins to appear. Captain Simpson was called in to help, since he 'designed for Scotland' for his own personal reasons in early 1693. He was asked both to bring back some thick Scotch plaids as possible trade-goods and also to recruit some men 'who would serve the Company at Cheape wages'. They were to be between twenty and thirty years old, and any who had worked in the mines would be welcomed. Once more the Council was asked to secure the Company's men from the press-gangs and once more a naval captain lent his services, the Company paying naval wages until the men went on board the Company's ships and then 'satisfying the said Captain Bennet with an honorarium of £20'.

The result of all the preparations was that the Company found itself in 1693–4 in a promising but unbalanced position. The Bottom of the Bay had been recovered, the returns from York were better than ever, and Kelsey's journey bore promise of yet further argosies of canoes bringing furs from the Prairies and beyond, down the Nelson and Hayes rivers. But peltry was hard to sell in London in those years. So, although the Committee could not do less than praise and reward Geyer, who had achieved the returns from York Fort, yet it felt that change and some measure of blame must be insisted on. Geyer was welcomed home, was vindicated against Radisson's old charges of 'High Treason and wee know not what', was given a piece of plate of the value of £25 on top of his salary and the gratuities which he had received. But he was not sent back to the Bay. Thomas Walsh, whose chief claim to distinction was that he had burned down New Severn, succeeded in command of York Fort, but with a commission from the Company only, not from the Crown, and with an oblique reflection on Geyer in the note that the 'mismanered expressions' of the last letter home were imputed by the Committee entirely to the 'rudeness and selfe conceite of that single person that underwrote the same'.

But dismissing Geyer with thanks and a piece of plate could not really solve the troubles, which centred round the sale of the 1692 and 1693 cargoes and provision of outfits for the following years. Sweetaple was here a valuable friend of the Company, a useful member of the Committee, to which he had been elected in 1692. In November 1692 he lent to the Company the large sum of £4,000, a loan which was still unpaid in 1697 and which went far to meet the need for ready money. This was in addition to smaller loans for immediate needs, as when he made a deposit of £500 in security for payment of the customs on the 1692 shipment home. But Sweetaple's help alone was not enough, nor was he prepared to extend unlimited kindness to the Company; he was a vigorous supporter and user of the Bank of England in these its early days, and could not properly pass the bounds of strict commercial practice in his dealings with the Company. By shipping-time in 1694 the Committee were forced to admit that the Company had 'overdrawn Mr. Sweetaple several times' and to agree that he should be given three bonds, payable in a month, and should be settled with out of the first cash which came to hand.

Other loans also were necessary, and during the year from August 1693 to August 1694 the Company borrowed at different times sums which amounted to over £25,000. It must, of course, be emphasised that the Company did not necessarily owe so much at any one moment; some of the loans were clearly made in order to pay off debts which were due (as when £1,000 was borrowed in May 1694, to set forth the ships, and was repaid in June, obviously from the proceeds of a loan of £1,200 then contracted). It is difficult if not impossible to gauge the indebtedness of the Company at any particular date, but it is only too clear that the Committee were financing the trade almost entirely on credit, and that with Stephen Evans for the time being in a helpful but not very adventurous mood (probably watching the money-market carefully with the floating of the Bank of England on his mind) and with John Sweetaple in position as the principal banker for the Company, credit could only be got on strictly business terms.

It is interesting to note the sort of person who was at this time prepared to lend money at fixed interest and for limited time to such a Company, apart from the bankers. Constantine Vernatty who lent £1,000, was a retired captain of an East India Company's ship; John Moore, cheesemonger, speaks for himself. *Mrs.* Mary Datchelor, *Spinster*, seems something of an enigma according to modern usage, though the seventeenth-century 'Mistress' was often unmarried. Anne Killingworth, Lady Sadleir, Anne Gibbs, Ann Meese, Elizabeth Perryman, Mrs. Frances Potter and Mrs. Bridget Thompson all represent the need for a safe investment for the widows', as for the retired sea-captains', capital. Members of the Committee could be counted on to support their Company from time to time, as could employees and their relations; Samuel Clarke, Deputy Governor, lent £2,000; Thomas Pitts, committee-man, £1,500; John Nicholson, committee-man, £3,000 in 1693 and in 1694 £500; Colonel Robert Lancashire, committee-man, £500, and John Pery, committee-man, £1,000. Some few, such as Doctor Simon Welman, were just ordinary investors, but they were exceptions among the list of the Company's creditors, most of whom had some personal or trade connection with the Company. Some estimate of the real burden of such a policy can be judged from the amounts due in interest, under which heading the Company had to pay out £1,297 15s. 0d. from November 1693 to October 1694, and £1,706 6s. 0d. from October 1694 to October 1695. At six per cent. these payments represent a running debt of between £21,000 and £28,000.

The trade, however, was by now so firmly established that quite considerable sums had to be found from time to time, and there was no alternative to the loan for such purposes. The customs payments for beaver imported in February 1694, for example, came to £2,267 5s. 0d. The full trade costs at this time came to £53,754 for ten years' trade to Nelson River and to £44,519 for the ten years' trade to the Bottom of the Bay. Included in these figures were both

'Charges Ordinary'—(the costs of pilotage, heat and light, fresh provisions, smiths', glaziers' and plasterers' work, committee-money, rent, gratuities and porters' wages) and 'Charges Extra-ordinary' (the costs of taxation, wines, and the law suits and political processes in which the Company was engaged; 'Secret Service', which included bribery, counted large here). The 'Charges Ordinary' were split evenly, in the Company's accounting, between the two scenes of operations, and cost each £11,633 16s. 1d. for the ten years; but the 'Charges Extraordinary' £7,474 16s. 1d. were charged entirely to the attempts to recover the Bottom of the Bay. Such figures clearly are to some extent 'book-keeping' figures represent-ing a formal allocation of expenditures to certain items, but they give a fair enough picture of the over-all costs of operating the Company at this time. An annual expenditure averaging almost £10,000 is indicated.

Against this must be set the sales of beaver and other furs. The loans had their function in providing running cash for trade be-tween the sales, but they had to be justified by the amount of revenue produced by sales. Here it is interesting to note that the Company's furs were still sorted and 'lotted' previous to sale by ordinary fur-riers, not employed by the Company except for this purpose, who might themselves be bidders and buyers at the sale. In 1692, for example, the furs were 'lotted' by Mr. Arkinstall and Mr. Winkle, two London tradesmen. After the sorting came the touchy business of selling. In 1692 Mr. Byfield, a furrier who had in his time acted as sorter for the Company, asked for a private sale and then Thomas Glover also made his offer for private sale. He was ready to pay only six shillings and twopence the pound for *coat* and *parchment* together but would pay more for the *parchment* alone. The Committee re-solved that they would put everything to public auction and in April 1692 they sold all that they offered—ten lots of *coat* beaver at various prices; one lot of black beaver at eight shillings and eight pence the pound, and thirty lots of *parchment* at various prices; the total receipt was almost £8,000.

A contemporary 'Merchants' weekly remembrancer of the pre-sent money prices of their goods ashoar in London on Monday, July 11th, 1692' quotes the prices of Hudson Bay *coat* beaver at eight shillings the pound, and of *parchment* at the same price. Against this, the quotation for New England beaver in season was but six shillings, out of season five shillings, and staged four shillings; Maryland beaver in season fetched the same price as that of Hudson Bay, and Virginia beaver in season cost six shillings. The Company's beaver therefore stood well with the market, and the Committee had made a good sale, appealing to the general buyer against the great furriers. The sale of the previous February had brought in over £5,000. So with genuine revenue of over £12,000 for the year the Company was well placed to meet its costs, and its financial and trade policy must be held to be justified.

The market was, however, most uneasy. There was both the dispute with the feltmakers to be faced in its Parliamentary phase and a certain threat of rivalry from continental imports to be overcome. Here the Company enjoyed the good offices of the customs officers, who were ready to carry out their duty of confiscating any beaver not in the shipping of the country of origin, provided the Company would buy the confiscated goods at market price. In December 1692 one such consignment cost the Company £200. They had to pay the best price of eight shillings the pound, but at the same time as they were thus prepared to lose some profit in order to keep the London market free from competition they were making serious plans to invade the continental market to which, in fact, many of their furs had long gone.

The full ramifications of the European fur trade have not yet been traced through the international records of the European ports and toll systems. But from London alone enough evidence has survived to build up a fascinating pattern of international trade, in which the English furrier played a vital part and in which the raw commodities of his trade were the pelts brought from the shores of the Bay by the Hudson's Bay Company. Here the evidence is from the Port Books of London, in which the controllers and customs officers made records of all shipments into and out from the Port. There are gaps, but the picture can be discerned. Thomas Glover, for example, the great individual round whose ability the Company's trade at times revolved, disposed of some at least of his purchases by direct shipment to Russia. As early as 1675 he had shipped 2,000 beaver direct in one ship, whilst another furrier, D. Allen, had made a similar shipment.

The underlying fact that much of the Company's beaver annually found its way to the European market, to travel to Russia and there to be turned into beaver-wool and beaver trimmings, emerges from time to time both in the Company's records and in the customs accounts. Sales are made to such obviously European merchants as Otto Goertz and Jasper Vandenbusch; in 1685–6 Samuel Clarke (later Deputy Governor) paid £6 for forty small cub beaver with the purpose to 'Dress them and send them abroad in Forreign parts', and in 1692 with the same Samuel Clarke in the dominant position as Deputy Governor just vacated by Dering, the Committee took serious action.

In that year the *parchment* beaver was lotted into two qualities, that fit for the Russia trade and that fit for the 'Town' trade. The *coat* was to be similarly separated out. This order was indeed revoked, and after toying with offers for private purchase the Committee made a satisfactory public sale, as has been seen, but all of the problems, of private sale and of export, rose again in the autumn of 1692 when it became a question of marketing the returns of that year. Glover's bid for a bulk private purchase was again turned down but a concession to the large buyer was made in the size of the lots, which were from four to five hundred skins of *coat* and five hundred and twenty-five of *parchment*. Starting prices were low—five shilling the pound for *coat* and six shillings for *parchment*—but the sale brought in the satisfactory return of £8,670 3s. 5d. Here the great furriers were the important buyers, for export and for resale to the working skinners and felters. Glover only bought a little over a thousand pounds' worth, but his rival in trade Jacob Whiddon paid almost three thousand pounds, and there were several who approached his total. Roger Arkinstall, who had 'lotted' the previous year's furs, bought for £841; Richard Baker for £1,562 and Urban Hall (who lent the Company £1,000) for about £300, a sum equalled by the committee-man Colonel Robert Lancashire. They are all sums which challenge comparison with the difficulty with which the early members of the Company, however exalted their rank or vast their estates, had raised their first two or three hundred pounds for the venture only twenty years earlier.

The sale of May 1693 went equally well, and it was not until the Company had to dispose of the large number of skins taken from the French at Albany as well as its own returns that the problem became so acute as to lead to serious attempts to cut through the difficulties of the London market and to start independent trading to the continent. In November of 1693 the Company had 56,000 skins from York Fort and a further 36,000, largely of French origin, from Albany, to sell in addition to small furs including a very considerable number of marten. Not only was this more than twice a normally good year's supply, but the market was absolutely dead, beaver was a drug on the market, only two lots were sold on 9th May and none at all on 13th June, 1694.

That such difficulties were not peculiar to the English Company can be seen from the parallel troubles of the French. Frontenac's problems in deciding whether or not to unleash Iberville to capture the trade of Nelson River were in part due to his feeling that Canada was feeling the effects of a glut of beaver in 1693. A similar answer to the English solution suggested itself, and permission was given that Canadian furs should be shipped direct to Holland without touching at France. This, however, was vitiated by the influence of ship-brokers and insurance-agents, and while the French trade suffered these difficulties the English fur-market was stirred out of its doldrums in the summer of 1694 when Henry Summers, a furrier with whom the Company had had many previous dealings, came to the rescue and put the Company into direct contact with the Russian market. He offered to take all the cub beaver and one lot of black beaver, to pay seven shillings a pound, and to promise to export his whole purchase to Archangel. His offer was taken; he bought in all 10,300 skins and paid £2,618.

There is nothing like an active buyer for stimulating a market, and others were soon buying also; one, Jacob Whiddon, paid in £3,461 in June 1694. These sales gave the Company a fair supply of ready cash but they did not deal with the vast bulk of furs in the warehouse, and in the same month, June 1694, the Committee began direct export on its own account. To begin with, two casks containing five hundred skins were shipped to Amsterdam, consigned to trade connections, the Widow Castelayn and Isaac Simpkinson, for them to sell on behalf of the Company. Before the end of the year over 15,000 *parchment* and 3,500 *coat* skins had been shipped to Amsterdam; of these 500 *parchment* had been re-consigned to Archangel, where they were sold early in 1695. Hamburg was the other outlet to which the Company exported. About 12,500 *parchment* were sent there during 1694, of which 2,000 were reconsigned to Narva whilst the remainder stayed for sale. The route from Hamburg to Narva was overland *via* Lübeck; at Narva the Company had two agents, Messrs. Gabriel Dowker and Messrs. Robert Masters, for whom William Masters of London, merchant, went surety.

The furs thus shipped cleared the Company's warehouse and the London market. At the end of the year the Committee reported that all consignments had safely arrived and that some had been disposed of with good success. But in fact the venture proved a difficult business, and though attempts to export continued for many years they involved a good deal of correspondence and book-keeping. For although the Committee appeared to have made a favourable start with the four great ports of Amsterdam, Hamburg, Narva and Arch-

L

angel, from the start sales were slow, cash was hard to remit, agents hard to check, and the effect on the Company's accounts was largely due to the fact that when a shipment was made the beaver account was immediately credited with a sale at the price of seven shillings the pound—a fiction which brought in no actual hard cash and which ultimately had to be exposed and adjusted.

The 1694 venture into the European market was, in fact, a constructive attempt to reorganise the conditions on which sales depended but, as is so often the result, the chief consequence followed from a secondary issue. The European sales never provided a satisfactory market, never brought in worth-while sums. But they cleared much of the accumulated fur from the Company's stores and in consequence the London sales immediately took on a new air. A sale in November 1694 went well as a start to the disposal of the returns of that year, in which York Fort produced 46,000 skins and the Bottom of the Bay almost 16,000—another embarrassingly successful year's trade! Early in 1695 a successful attempt was made to get rid of all the old *parchment* left from 1693, and a further sale in March disposed of skins fit for the 'Towne Trade'. Henry Summers was the principal buyer at this time, buying for export, £3,000 or £4,000 at each sale, and the 1694 returns were for the most part uttered by this means and not by overseas sale direct by the Company.

It was not until early summer of 1695 that the Company began direct shipments again, with 7,000 for Amsterdam (where the first consignment, of 1694, had been sold in January 1695). The main effort in this direction went into pushing the furs from the entrepots of Hamburg and Amsterdam to the markets of Narva and Archangel, and the Company's agent at Hamburg, Charles Goodfellow, was induced by Samuel Clarke to go to Russia for two years on the Company's behalf. He was enjoined to be secret, for there were reports of a vast beaver trade capable of taking up to fifty or sixty thousand skins a year there, and he was to be given his expenses for two years and to be paid a commission on sales which the Company guaranteed to bring up to £200 a year. He was really a commercial traveller on commission for the Company.

The furs sent overseas in 1694 began to move eastwards to fit in with this project, and Archangel (where the five hundred skins of 1694 were already sold) got a further 4,750 from Hamburg and a like amount from Amsterdam whilst Narva got a further 5,000 from Hamburg, though no sale was effected at Narva until September 1695. Here Henry Summers was guarding his own interests and watching the possibilities of the Company entering into direct-sales rivalry with him as an export-furrier, for his clearing-purchase of all the remains of *parchment* in April 1695 was on condition that the Company should not export direct to Narva and should sell no further *parchment* except by public auction before the end of the year.

The outcome of this situation was that the Company had a more active London market but little more cash in hand. Its financial position, from the point of view of ready cash, can best be judged from John Sweetaple's account. He received £12,547 (including £5,750 on loan) between June and October 1693 and during that time paid out £10,687 (including some repayments of loans); between November 1693 and February 1694 he received £4,670 (including £2,950 borrowed) and paid out £8,462. At 15th February the position was that the Company owed him £4,000 on bond, a further £1,000 on short-term loan and an overdraft on running cash of £2,947 17s. 0d.—a total of £7,947 17s. 0d. During February and March he received £9,810 (largely from the fur sale) and paid out £6,509, so that the overdraft on running cash was wiped out by April 1694. During the summer period from April to November 1694 he received £5,011 but spent £11,122. Loans form part of these receipts, and repayments as they fall due form part of the expenditures. The over-all picture is of a company which, with loans, can just about meet current expenses as long as its banker will carry it over temporary shortages. There is no dividend, and no justification for one, despite the undeniable success in getting furs.

This situation comes out in occasional remarks in the Minutes, as when £1,000 had to be rapidly borrowed to deposit with the customs officers in October 1694. Care, too, arose from straitened circumstances; a series of old debts was cancelled when the Secretary reported that several of the creditors were already dead; and private trade came in for further censures, whilst imports of rival furs were pursued and the Governors of both York and of Albany were urged to find new commodities and to increase the proportion of small furs 'nothing being more vendable then small Furrs etc., for since we have Imported great quantity of Beaver it is a drugg and sells at a very low rate'.

The strange mixture of success in the Bay, shortage of cash at home, superfluity of beaver and insistence on completely reserving that trade, can be seen in the treatment accorded to James Knight when the news of his success at the Bottom of the Bay had been confirmed. His choice as second-in-command was Stephen Sinclair. But Sinclair had been under suspicion (like Geyer) since Radisson had attacked him; he was dismissed and Knight found Fullartine forced upon him as Deputy, though he was himself asked to stay on for a further year and was given power to appoint his successor and other officers. A parcel of beaver marked 'JK 1' was sold on his behalf and the money was, at his request, to be spent on a silver tankard for his son; but although this was not done all of Knight's other proceedings were approved of and the Committee unanimously voted him a gratuity of £500 (in accordance with their agreement before he sailed); yet 'for some reasons reserved to our selves' this gratuity was paid by a bond redeemable in six months, and in fact Knight lent this sum to the Company until 1701. Failure to pay him in cash was probably due in about equal parts to shortage of cash and to suspicion of Knight and private trade, or a mixture of the two.

Knight's success, however, could not be taken as final. The Committee was spending considerable sums on secret service money in 1694, and knew that Iberville was again actively pushing his plans for a naval attack on York Fort, and in June 1694 the Committee had once more begun to inspect its books and to draw up afresh an account of the damages sustained from the French. There seems to have been no particular urgency about this wish to estimate the claim against the French; it was part of a more general attempt to achieve a statement of the financial position. Here John Sweetaple— he became Sir John at the end of 1694—played his part, with the Committee meeting from day to day in order to draw up a balance which might be carried to the new books.

The attempt produced a revealing 'Profit and Loss' statement on the Company's shipping, of which the total loss was £5,826 17s. 5d. for ships (the *Huband*, the *Churchill*. the *Yonge* and the *Northwest Fox*) taken by the French and those (the *Dering* and the *Supply*) sold at a loss. Equally realistic an acceptance of the mistakes which had been made was shown in the way in which almost £2,000 was written off as bad debts; it was money owed by unsatisfactory servants, Thomas Walsh, Onesiphorous Albin, Andrew Hamilton, Captain Outlaw and Captain William Bond. Sweetaple himself drew back £2,000 of the £4,000 which he had lent to the Company, in September 1695, but between loans and fur sales he managed to keep the Company in running cash.

The attempt to strike a balance in the books, whilst it revealed some of the losses of the past, also revealed a summary of the state of the trade. From November 1684 to August 1695 it was reckoned that £72,163 1s. 4d. of beaver, at sales prices, had been got from the Bottom of the Bay and £60,461 3s. 6d. from Port Nelson; small furs added about a further £6,000 to these totals. Considering the inroads of de Troyes and Iberville, and that Hayes River had only been established in 1684, these figures speak well. They indicate an annual trade, taking one year with another, of the value of over £12,000. The figures included some fictitious sales of furs which had in fact only been transferred to the accounts of Amsterdam and Hamburg, and thence to Narva and Archangel, but even so they were basically most satisfactory, and it is most interesting to see the Committee arriving at much the same conclusion as a modern analysis of the figures leads to.

The satisfactory long-term trading position, however, did not prevent the immediate problems of the Company from being extremely onerous. There were many minor vexations. A cargo of beaver which had been seized late in 1694 proved to be the produce of the British colonies, and the customs officer had to be given a small douceur—a trifling matter, but irritating to a Committee under pressure; an attempt to widen the trade with the Baltic by importing tallow produced the meagre profit of £6 13s. 10d., and the experiment was not repeated; the ships' captains had to be made to hand in the logs of their voyages. More general was the difficulty that too many of the shareholders were engaged in selling their own goods to the Company for things to be easy; Samuel Shephard, a committee-man, sold the Company its spirits; Samuel Ongley, shareholder, sold it drapery and dry goods, William Atwill, shareholder and carpenter, did work for it, and many freely bought furs when the prices were right. Shipping too, was, as ever, troublesome; no ship was sent out in 1695, but the *Prosperous* was sent to Newcastle and on her way back to London she was wrecked; the bills for repairs to the *Hudson's Bay* since 1689 had come to almost double her original cost; the *Prosperous* was suspect and had to be 'viewed' with the object of further repairs, and a new sloop, the *Knight*, had to be ordered. On top of all this, Sir Stephen Evans, as Governor, proved to have very little time for the Company's business. The Committee waited on him in vain; and could only resolve to wait upon him again.

Even the currency proved a source of trouble. Guineas rose to the value of thirty shillings, then dropped to twenty-seven and then twenty-six shillings, and in the course of the year the Company had to accept an item for 'Loss on the guineas' of £1,674 17s. 6d.

None of these things would have mattered much if beaver had been selling well. But it was the fact that London would not buy which made the ventures into the Russian markets necessary and, since these ventures produced no ready cash as yet, led to the decision to send no ship in 1695. Henry Summers, the great export furrier, bought up to £3,200 in April, and Sweetaple received from sales almost £10,000 between January and June of 1695, and a further £6,900 in August and September, but heavy repayments of loans absorbed these sums almost as soon as they were available. True, that was no new thing for the Company, and things were not as bad as the Committee made out. There was indeed a considerable surplus of beaver (14,500) left in hand, almost the equivalent of a year's trade, and 25,350 had been locked up in the continental marts. This gave a poor and discouraging appearance to the sales, but the Committee had received worth-while sums in cash, more than enough to keep the trade flourishing.

Consequently, despite the gloomy tone of the letters and minutes, the year 1695 sees the early preparation of a handsome consignment of trade-goods for Albany—five hundred guns, 10,000 lbs. of duck shot and 10,000 lbs. of Bristol shot, 5,000 knives, 2,000 hatchets, 500 blankets and 700 yards of cloth, with caps, shirts, spoons, combs, tobacco pipes, gun-flints, beads and kettles in proportion. The tobacco admittedly was not to be the treasured Brazilian but English roll, but the Committee proposed to get French gun-flints despite the war; it was managing a difficult but well-established trade, one whose future now seemed secure and important though the immediate short-term embarrassments might preclude the payment of dividends.

CHAPTER XXVI

IBERVILLE CAPTURES YORK FORT, 1694-1695

The position of the Company in London and on the continental market depended in the last resort on possession of the posts from which furs could be traded. After Knight's success in the spring of 1693 the Committee had suffered to some extent from the glut induced by attempts to sell the furs captured from the French, but they had planned with confidence on the basis of holding their posts and had envisaged pushing northwards in search of new commodities and southwards in search of new fur-hunting Indians. Confidence was high and credit good.

But Iberville had certainly not accepted the recapture of the Bottom of the Bay as final, nor his own failure to take possession of Nelson River as anything but a temporary set-back. He was convinced, as ever, that the Nelson and Hayes were the overwhelming sources of good quality furs, and he estimated that whilst the Bottom of the Bay suffered from the defects of dangerous navigation (as Nixon had pointed out) but could be made to produce about 10,000 to 15,000 beaver a year, with Churchill capable of perhaps a further 10,000, the Hayes and Nelson rivers (the Ste. Thérèse and the Bourbon to him) could easily produce 60,000 if well supplied with trade goods. He therefore strenuously advocated in Paris a plan to annul the success of the English by an expedition to capture York Fort and rob them of the one post on which their trade had depended during the years when the French had possessed the Bottom of the Bay.

For this he would, he said, need two Royal ships, to sail for Quebec at latest on 20th March. He undertook to recruit eighty Canadians, who would be content with no wages so long as they were guaranteed a share of the booty, and he professed himself ready to find these men in food and drink, but not to pay them wages. Of the two ships for which he asked, he proposed that one, of thirty to thirty-six guns and with a crew of a hundred and thirty men, should play her part in the capture of the post and be back in France again by November 1694. The other ship, which he thought should be of twenty to twenty-two guns and a crew of sixty-five, should winter in Nelson River and should not return to Europe until October 1695.

To this proposal the Royal assent was obtained in March 1694; the French Navy was to provide two frigates with the greatest secrecy and the King was to share in the profits of the venture if the costs to Iberville and his associates were more than doubled by the booty. The detailed agreement which Iberville finally made in April gave him the two frigates which he wanted but bound him to recruit and to pay their crews. He was to have the booty to dispose of, and if he (and his associates) did not thereby derive at least twice the cost of the outfit they were to be allowed to retain the trade of the Nelson River up to July 1697.

Iberville therefore spent the early months of 1694 at La Rochelle, and was ready to put to sea by 10th May—six weeks or more later than the date which he had stipulated for departure. His plan had to be revised, and he now proposed to winter in Rupert River and blockade the English there, to move over and make himself master of York by March 1695; after which he would move to Albany in order to make war on the Iroquois from there. With this purpose he left Quebec on 8th–10th August, having taken on a hundred and ten Canadians for three years on terms of a share of the booty. Between them they were to divide a half share of the profits of the expedition, and each of them was to be allowed a hundred *livres* worth of goods to trade on his own account.

The prospects were good, in view of Iberville's previous exploits and skill, and the plan by now included a delay in the Bay after the capture of the posts, so that the British ships bringing the outfit for 1695 might also be captured. But the cost of recruiting and providing for so many Canadians—six Iroquois were recruited among the others—was clearly too heavy for Iberville, and the *Compagnie du Nord* (i.e. *de la Baie d'Hudson*) proposed to help at this stage on terms which were not unreasonable; after Iberville had captured the posts and had repaid himself, the *Compagnie* proposed to take over the posts and the trade in 1697. This Iberville refused, saying that he preferred not to negotiate with so many men. He said he would negotiate with a single proxy for the *Compagnie* and would arrange to pay them twelve and a half per cent. on their investment. At this stage the *Compagnie* pointed out that Iberville had no arrangement with Jean Oudiette, the original concessionaire who had taken over the rights, particularly that of the taxation of the fur trade, upon which the whole of the French-Canadian trade turned. But though the *Compagnie* refused him support, Iberville got the money which he wanted from private backers, who insisted on reserving their right to the trade in 1697.

Leaving Quebec with the *Poli* and the *Salamandre* under command about 10th August, 1694, Iberville was in the mouth of the Ste. Thérèse (the Hayes River) on about 24th September. The English post, York Fort, was re-designed and properly built by Geyer on the tongue of land which separated the mouth of the Hayes from the Nelson. Iberville landed a party of forty Canadians to reconnoitre the English position, and in the course of the subsequent skirmishes—for he did not attempt a frontal attack—Iberville lost his young brother Chateaugay, the third of the family to be killed in operations against the English.

Building their houses and berthing their ships, the French settled down to a similar harassing winter to that which had brought them success at Albany in 1689. But they did not have to wait until the spring. Iberville's batteries were ready to begin firing on the fort on 13th October, and on the 14th–15th Governor Walsh, unable to send his men forth in search of firewood and insufficiently supplied with it, sent to the French his terms for surrender. He stipulated (in Latin, as written by the priest Thomas Anderson) that he and his men should be allowed to retain their personal property, that they should be guaranteed transport to England or to France, and that after the Company's papers had been read by the French, and if necessary copied, they should be returned to English keeping.

Iberville was prepared to grant such terms and Walsh, as the Company asserted, 'basely surrendered to the French'. Walsh had under his command fifty-three men, including Philip Parsons, Captain of Soldiers and Deputy Governor, with the heavy armament of thirty-six cannon and six peteroes to defend his post. But the guerilla tactics of the French, cutting off the garrison from fuel, annulled the care and expense of the Committee, the shipping of heavy cannon across the Atlantic and the piling up of men and provisions. It was sheer improvidence on Walsh's part, for he had been re-stocked in August by the *Dering* and the *Hudson's Bay*, which had brought a normal assortment of trade-goods, including a supply of the prized Brazilian tobacco imported from Oporto. The Instructions which the ships brought contained no written warning of the danger hanging over York Fort, and the two ships made no attempt to remain in the country to act as block-ships. Yet the captains were alleged to have told Walsh, before they loaded up with 45,000 beaver and sailed for Albany late in August 1694, that spies in La Rochelle had reported that Iberville was coming. The Company had indeed spent a hundred guineas on secret service just before their ships left the Thames, and it is more than probable that their spies, as Iberville alleged, had brought reports of his preparations; the Committee certainly got news of a fleet of twenty-three privateers which put out from Dunkirk in June of that year and took out extra insurance against the capture of their ships homeward bound. Whatever the weight and certainty of the warning which he had received, Walsh was clearly at fault in that he had not laid in essential supplies to stand a siege; and he surrendered even before the siege had seriously started, on the day after the French batteries were completed. His terms dealt only with the personal property of himself and his men, and with the Company's papers; they contained no word of trade-goods or of skins, though they stipulated that the English should receive the same food and treatment as the French.

The English later complained (but not universally) of the treatment which Iberville gave them during the winter. Doubtless they suffered hardships; but Iberville himself lost twenty men from scurvy. The English, it was alleged, were promised the old post, Fox Hall, for a winter residence, but in fact all of them except Walsh and two or three others were turned into the woods to spend a dangerously exposed winter, during which some of them traded their bedding and other property to the French for food whilst others, including Henry Kelsey, were reduced to eating quickahatches (wolverenes) and other 'ravenous creatures'. One man, Thomas Jacobs, was alleged to have been tortured by Iberville's Indians to make him divulge the Company's affairs; he himself however refused to testify against the French. Walsh seems to have tired of the complaints of his men and to have left them to take up his own residence with the French. The English complaints are all reminiscent of the way in which Iberville had treated his prisoners at the Bottom of the Bay on his earlier expeditions, and probably his intention was to discourage the rank and file of the English from further service by the Bay. Whether he kept the letter of the articles of surrender is doubtful in so far as they promised equal treatment to French and English, though Walsh and some other Englishmen were prepared to swear that he had done so.

The ships had already taken the English furs to Albany and so to England, where they arrived in the Downs in October. But Iberville, with the Company's goods at his disposal, got the 1695 spring trade of about 45,000 skins. He then waited through the summer until 7th September in the hope of taking the English ships of the year with their cargoes of trade-goods, but luck was against him, for the glut of beaver on the London market had decided the Committee to send no shipment in 1695, and Iberville at last sailed for Quebec, leaving the Sieur de la Forest as commander of Fort Bourbon with a garrison of seventy Canadians and with Iberville's cousin Martigny as second-in-command. His voyage was so troubled by scurvy, however, that he changed course and made direct for France, to arrive at La Rochelle in October 1695. Then, though he sold the beaver which he had brought for 60,000 *livres*, he pleaded with success that he might be exempted from the clause in his agreement with the Crown whereby he should pay the wages of his crews.

The fact that the Company had decided to send no shipment to York Fort in 1695 because 'our warehouses were full of goods, and the marketts in London soe dull, wee could sell none' proved, as the Committee wrote, 'verry happy for had they gone to port Nelson in all probability wee should have lost them both, there being 2 french men of Warr there at that time'. But the lack of shipping meant also that the Committee had no news of Iberville's success in his long-cherished plan against York Fort until the English prisoners began to arrive home and to give their evidence. This news, however, came almost as soon as the Company's ships could have given it, for the captured men had been brought across the Atlantic in the old *Albemarle*, suffering heavily. Their treatment in the French prisons was too much for some of them, and at least four died in France. It was in November 1695 that the Deputy Governor of York, Captain Philip Parsons (who pledged his personal credit to get food and transport for the men, and to get them to this country), wrote to the Committee to give the first authentic news of the loss which they had suffered.

Later, the Committee estimated the cost of this feat of Iberville's in damage to the Company at £18,000. Already they had met, before they knew of this fresh disaster—indeed, before it had happened, in June 1694—to inspect their books and to reassess their claims against the French. But Iberville's last exploit had been achieved during a time of open war and could only be made the basis of a claim for damages if it could be proved that he had violated the terms upon which Governor Walsh had surrendered. To this point the Committee therefore turned. But collection of evidence against Iberville for breach of the terms of surrender proved difficult.

Ex-Governor Walsh refused to challenge the French. He said that Iberville and his men had kept the articles of surrender, and his affidavit was supported by Thomas Jacobs, mariner (who was alleged to have been tortured by having his fingers burned) and by Henry Pigot, a clockmaker who had found his way to the Bay, and

William Clarke, brewer. There was undoubtedly some hard swearing going on, and these men's mates said they were unwilling to give evidence for the Company which 'would not gratifie them for soe doeing' and that they boasted they were 'able to give the matter in dispute, for or Against the Company, as they pleased'. Walsh even called together some of those who had given evidence for the Company at 'The Crooked Billet' tavern in Billiter Lane and, having failed to persuade them to change their minds, departed saying 'Say or sweare what you will, my word shall goe further then all yours'. The sordid little interview in an East London bar speaks of the importance attached to the evidence of these men—and the Company was busy preparing its case for the next two years or more. It speaks, too, for the doubt which must remain about this episode; for in the end Philip Parsons, the Deputy Governor who had behaved well by all accounts, wrote to a French correspondent that he had in fact given evidence on behalf of the Company but that he might just as well have taken the opposite side.

Certainly the Committee had no intention of allowing any support to slip from it. When first-hand evidence could not be procured, then ale-house gossip was solemnly sworn to, and those who would not testify found their unguarded mutterings quoted against them. This, however, was all part of a long-term process, rather slowly undertaken as the Committee began to realise the extent of the damage done by Iberville and the need to prove that it was culpable damage which could be set against similar claims alleged by the French. For the French were also in a position to claim damages by the time that the justice of Iberville's treatment of Walsh and his men could be properly debated. This was due to the fact that the Committee's first reaction to the news of Iberville's long-delayed success at York Fort was, not to debate the justice of it, but to prepare an expedition to counteract it.

BOOKS FOR REFERENCE

Crouse, Nellis M.—*Lemoyne d'Iberville: Soldier of New France* (Ithaca, New York, 1954).

Frégault, G.—*Iberville le Conquérant* (Montreal, 1944).

Tyrrell, J. B. (ed.)—*Documents Relating to the Early History of Hudson Bay* (Toronto, The Champlain Society, 1931).

CHAPTER XXVII

THE RECAPTURE OF YORK FORT, 1696, AND ITS CONSEQUENCES

To undertake such a task as the recapture of York Fort and the trade of Nelson River in 1696 required particular determination. It was at a most unpropitious moment for the English Company that Iberville had at last accomplished his ambition—unpropitious but not quite fatal. He had indeed taken the post upon which he maintained that the whole of the English trade depended. But that contention was not so true in 1696 as it had been in 1692, for Knight had re-established the Bottom of the Bay and, in taking York Fort, Iberville had not driven the English out of the field. They now shewed a tenacity which argued as well for their sense as for their character.

This was, however, not a period in which such a company could expect unqualified support. The main effort against the French was on the continent, on the Dutch border so beloved of King William. Overseas ventures were secondary issues—as they proved when the war drew to a peace. The monopoly of such a chartered joint-stock company as the Hudson's Bay Company also roused criticism, and such companies were the subject of much discussion, both in Parliament and in the country. Of all this the French were well aware, and a French document summarises the losses sustained by English companies at this time from memorials to Parliament and extracts from Journals of the House of Lords. The East India Company had lost six ships, valued at a million and a half pounds; the Barbados Company had lost £138,000; the Africa Company £169,000; the Isles of Antilles Company £13,800; merchants of Pennsylvania £11,900 and Stephen Gardiner, interloper, £13,300. The Turkey Company was reduced to a solitary ketch.

The Hudson's Bay Company's losses do not figure in this list, but the statutory confirmation of the Charter, achieved in 1690, was due to run out in 1697 and the Committee knew that it must at all costs sue for a renewal. With Governor Stephen Evans and committeeman Colonel Pery sitting as Members of Parliament the Company could be sure of constant information, and Pery did in fact report back to the Committee on the discussion in Parliament. (This, incidentally, should not be taken as evidence of the political power

333

wielded by the Company, for Pery was a very insignificant member; and the opponents of the Company, especially Charles Boone the interloper, were well represented.) Here, in the matter of its Charter, the Company was for the moment, in 1696, merely watching and preparing for defensive action. Its main moves were far more positive, for it set to work to get official support for an attempt to recover its post in Hayes River without delay.

At this juncture the absorption of Governor Stephen Evans in his banking business proved a handicap for the Company. The state of war at sea was enough to warrant a firm appeal for convoy for the Company's ships; but the Company wanted more than that. The Committee sought a loan of two men-of-war to help undo Iberville's work. First a petition for convoy went before the Cabinet in February 1696; the Company was told that it could recruit ships' crews without fear of the press gangs in April, Letters of Marque for the Company's ships were sought in May, and at last the men-of-war *Bonaventure* and *Seaford* were allocated by the Admiralty to an attack on Hayes River early in June. They both proved short of men and of beer when the Committee visited them at Aldeburgh!

The Governor, as a man whose serious business was banking, can be forgiven for his absorption at this time, for the business world was in a turmoil in 1696 owing to weakness in the coinage. The Company was forced to refuse payment in bank-notes, to delay its sale and to drop its prices owing to shortage of acceptable money, and to pay its tradesmen in the only coin they would accept—old silver measured by weight and accounted at 5s. 2d. an ounce. There was no money in hand either to pay Radisson the pension due under his Chancery judgment or to settle the small bills due by the Company. The other great banker on whom the Committee relied, John Sweetaple, could not be expected to allow the Company to exceed ordinary commercial risks. He drew out the remainder of the £4,000 which he had advanced, refused a bill for £505, and announced that he wished to sell his stock 'but as yet he knew not the person to whome he should Transfer it'. He was too busy, and probably too worried with his own affairs, to attend punctually at the Committee-meetings, and was denied his Committee-money accordingly. As the year wore on the Committee were forced to write to the Company's agent at Amsterdam to ask him to try to raise £500 or £1,000 on the credit of the furs in his hands; in July they were seriously put to it to raise seven hundred guineas 'upon an urgent occasion and finding an absolute Necessity for Raiseing the same' to fit out the ships. They had no alternative but to borrow from themselves. It was a modest statement of their dilemma when they told their agent in Plymouth that 'in Truth Sir wee are verry much streitened for want of Pecunia'.

At such a time a proposal to move to better premises and to pull down and improve the small house in Culver Alley which the Company used in addition to Scriveners' Hall may seem unwarranted. But the Committee, having agreed to take over Sir John Fleet's house in Fenchurch Street on lease at £75 a year, moved in 'with as much frugality as possible' and with due care that none of the papers should be 'Imbeziled or Lost'. At the same time a proposal to pull down the small warehouse in Culver Alley and to rebuild it was accepted.

Nor was this the only sign of the incurable optimism and determination of the Company. The April 1696 sale had brought in 7,007½ guineas, at twenty-two shillings each, and £5 7s. 3d. in silver —together a most useful sum. But the July–August sale realised very little; only two lots of *coat* beaver out of twenty-four were sold, and no *parchment* out of sixty-nine lots. The hopes of a continental market had almost perforce to be revived, and the Committee entered with zest on the project once more. Over 9,000 skins were shipped to Amsterdam despite the fact that some 6,000 still lay there unsold; Archangel, where Charles Goodfellow had made a good sale of almost his whole previous consignment (8,744 *parchment* skins for £6,470) received a further 5,350 *parchment* during the year—and sold them well too. Narva was sent 2,462 skins. Hamburg once more was used as the entrepôt for Archangel but did no direct trade. As in previous years, these transactions cleared the London warehouses and figured in the books as sales-transfers of stock, but they brought no additions of immediate cash wherewith the Committee could furnish the expedition of 1696. Nevertheless the shipping of that year saw no stint either of men or of provisions and the whole enterprise was conceived in the most valiant terms.

The costs of this particular outfit are not clearly set out in the Ledgers, but the overwhelming item of £53,754 16s. 11d. charged to 'Voyages to Port Nelson' in November 1695 is the only entry between October 1694 and August 1697 under this head. It must be largely made up by the costs of the 1696 expedition; and when compared with the normal annual expenditure it gives some idea of the enormous costs of this year. If an allowance of almost £14,000 is made for the costs of 1695—a generous allowance when set against the costs of a normal year—then 1696 must have cost the Committee something in the region of £40,000. This was a sum about three times greater than a normal year cost, and about five times as great as the receipts of the year from fur sales. At its most conservative, the Company reckoned that it had spent £15,000 simply for the recovery of the post, apart from trade costs.

For the recapture of York Fort and the trade of the Nelson River the Company first equipped its own vessels the *Hudson's Bay* and the *Dering*. They were to sail to Nelson River with the two men-of-war, the *Bonaventure* and the *Seaford*. They were given a subordinate part in the plans for the capture of the post; but more to the point, perhaps, was the fact that the *Dering* carried in addition to her cargo eighteen casks of brandy to sweeten the captains and crews of the men-of-war for this task. The Committee later had reason to believe that the brandy had merely been sold to any member of the crews who had money to buy, instead of being distributed carefully and *gratis*, and had produced 'such a Mortallity which has never before happened in these voyages'.

Along with the expedition bound for York Fort went the new ship just launched, the *Knight* sloop, with orders for Albany. She was thirty-eight feet in the keel and fifteen feet four and a half inches in beam, a ship of about forty-seven tons, larger than James Knight had ordered but it was estimated that she might thereby be of some use to defend his post. She had cost £413 16s. 6d. She carried a request that Knight would stay in his command for a further year in view of the war, and his profit from private trade was returned to him with a gratuity to bring it up to £100 in value; his choice of John Fullartine as his deputy was accepted; his specimens of ores were proclaimed as probably holding great value 'because wee could have noe account of them from those who undertooke to make tryall of them', and his reasons for not advancing the Standard of Trade at Albany were accepted. He was sent no flax seed, which he had requested, since the Committee thought flax-growing required a technical knowledge which was not available. But otherwise he was plainly regarded as holding Albany and the Bottom of the Bay with the greatest competence and knowledge. He was given all he wanted, was approved in all respects and was thought of, as indeed he was, as the producer of the main volume of the furs until York Fort should be recaptured.

The preparation and manning of the other ships, however, took up the main attention of the Committee; the trading voyage to Albany was likely to prove the only source of furs for the year, but even that took second place. Recruits were sought from as far afield as Wales, where an employee was promised twenty shillings for every servant brought in. The other servants and seamen were encouraged by a letter from the Committee promising them satisfaction in case they should be killed or wounded, and the Captains' widows (if they should emerge as such) were promised quite substantial sums, £250 to the widow of Captain Baley of the *Hudson's Bay*, £200 to Captain Grimington's widow, and £150 to Captain Smithsend's widow. The men-of-war were supplied with beer, with an ox and with quite substantial douceurs for the warrant officers, the bombardiers and the gunners. Detailed plans were worked out, and the ships were seen off from Aldeburgh by the Committee early in June, after which no more was done until the arrival of the *Hudson's Bay* at Falmouth in early November.

No clear account of the actual events, in the course of which Iberville's master-stroke was reversed and York recaptured by the English, is available. Even Henry Kelsey, who had come to England after Walsh's surrender to Iberville and his own winter in the woods, in 1695, and who now went out again, kept only a meagre journal as far as the entrance to the Bay. Iberville maintained that his post was taken 'by capitulation'. The account of the priest Father Marest is perhaps the simplest and most straightforward; 'The English came and besieged us and took us prisoners'.

The English arrived on 2nd September, just two hours ahead of de Serigny, another brother of Iberville. He had brought two small ships from France, but finding the English in possession of the river, and in greater force, he left the post to defend itself and returned to France, losing one of his ships on the way. The English tried to land a party and began a fairly steady bombardment of the post, which was several times set on fire, and within three days the affair was over. The French were short of food and ammunition, they had seen their reinforcements from France sail away and leave them, and they surrendered on 5th September, 1696 (28th August, English style).

The Articles of Capitulation were to cause endless trouble, for the French maintained that they were not kept. The Company maintained that they were inadmissible, having been made by the naval officer Captain Allen, who had no authority to make terms; and that even if they were valid the French had forfeited all claim to honourable treatment because of the way in which Iberville had broken his terms of surrender to Governor Walsh and his men in 1695. The original Articles were certainly highly honourable. The French were to keep their colours flying until they marched out of the fort. They were then to march out with their arms, with their drum beating, their colours flying, their matches lighted at both ends and with a ball in their mouth (i.e. as though ready for action). They were to take with them two cannon which Iberville had brought from France and had left with them, and they were to keep the year's furs which had accumulated. They also stipulated that they and their goods should be taken to Newfoundland. Without such good terms they might not have surrendered—or at least not so easily. For Captain Allen had pointed out to them that he had driven away their reinforcements, and that they could not expect the like terms if he reduced them by assault.

Having got the post and the furs in his hands, Allen re-assessed the situation and informed the French commander Gabriel de la Forest that he could not transport him to Newfoundland, but that he might have the 'bomb-vessel', the *Knight*, to go wherever he wished. Allen also now denied the furs to the French, saying that they had been traded with English goods. He later offered a larger ship, the *Seaford*, man-of-war, as transport, but he did not relax over the furs. These consisted of 228 packets of *coat* beaver at eighty pounds each, 238 packets of 'dry' or *parchment* beaver at sixty pounds each, one packet of twenty-five pounds of the valuable black beaver, a packet of a hundred and forty marten, and an assortment of other furs. They were estimated as worth £13,519 9s. 3d.—a sum to which some slight addition was made on account of skins belonging to individual Frenchmen, some provisions, and the arms taken over. They were put aboard the man-of-war *Bonaventure* under Captain Allen's personal care.

The Company's men, Captain Grimington of the *Dering* and Captain Smithsend of the *Knight* said that they protested against the Articles from the start, and that Allen had only agreed with de la Forest instead of reducing him to complete surrender because he had a 'design to get the Goods into his own Possession'. Among the prisoners taken had been the English servant of de la Forest, John Lee, whom the Committee suspected of having remained in French service solely in order to betray York Fort to the French. He was brought to England, made his way up from Plymouth to London, and was there 'discoursed' by the Committee to see what they could get out of him. They got little but the information that during the past year the French had traded over 30,000 beaver at their post. Allen must therefore have got hold of almost all of the French returns; but that did not mean that the Company in its turn received anything like the amount under discussion.

On his way home Captain Allen in the *Bonaventure* fell in with a French privateer off the Scillies. It was reported that the Company's ships left him to fight it out by himself, and he got his ship free. But Allen himself was killed in the fight, and his young son brought the *Bonaventure* into Plymouth. In such circumstances it is not perhaps surprising that discipline should have been lax. Members of the crew were freely selling furs in Plymouth and the Committee was even moved to write to its ships' captains there to buy such furs at trifling prices if possible—at four shillings a pound for *coat* beaver and five shillings a pound for *parchment*. Among others, the ship's purser was reported to be selling the cargo, and over a thousand pound's worth of furs were reputed to be distributed among the burgesses and their wives.

The Committee did all that was possible to prevent such leakage. Already it was becoming probable that there would be a major dispute over the furs and the terms of surrender, and Captain Allen's death 'in the bed of honour' was thought to have saved him from danger both to his life and fortune for disobeying his orders. Both Grimington and Smithsend were warned by the Committee never to admit that they had assented to the granting of terms to the French. Eventually the Committee succeeded in getting permission for the captured furs to be transferred from the *Bonaventure* to the Company, the customs officers were prevailed on to confiscate some of those which had already been got ashore, and the Committee managed, with very great difficulty, to raise £500 to send to Plymouth for the expenses incurred. It is a sign of the general financial difficulties of the year, and of the lack of confidence in bills and bank-notes, that this sum was sent in cash by means of 'Mr. Morris the Carrier of Exeter'. When all was done, and the captured skins had been brought up to London, the Company claimed that it had rescued no more than a hundred and forty-nine skins in all—this, however, was a purposeful and obvious understatement, and it appears that the value of the skins so obtained and sold in London was about £7,000. The possession and sale of the captured skins was an urgent matter, but more important was the question whether they had been rightly taken or not—otherwise possession of them would prove a liability instead of an asset.

Whilst Captain Allen had secured all the skins aboard the *Bonaventure*, Michael Grimington had brought the French prisoners aboard the *Dering*. Gabriel de la Forest, the captured Governor, was clearly a most attractive Frenchman, who soon won a good deal of sympathy for his case once he had been let loose in England. There was, after all, much to be said for a man who had surrendered on terms which had been subsequently broken, and who had just suffered the inconveniences of an Atlantic crossing as a prisoner in so small a ship as the *Dering*. There was, too, at this time no lack of opposition to the Company and its privileges, and 'so many Englishmen solicited for the French Governor that he got a hearing before the Lords Commissioners of the Council of Trade'. This was achieved within a month or so of his landing, and by December 1696 the Company was faced with a claim for over £14,000.

Here, however, the Company found itself in a strong position, for the Secretary of the Council of Trade, under whom the affair was to be adjudged, was that Sir William Trumbull who had already done the Company such service as he could when he had been Ambassador to France in 1686. Now, when he was in what would be regarded, in modern terms, as a highly judicial and neutral post, he thought it reasonable that he should become an active member of the Company. Previously, as ambassador, he had been solicited by Marlborough to set forth the Company's case as strongly as possible; he had accepted some hospitality and some small presents, and his conduct could not be seriously criticised. Now, however, he became Governor of the Company in circumstances which cannot be explained away.

On 5th November, 1696—a date on which ultra-Protestant and anti-French feelings would be rife in England—Sir Stephen Evans transferred to Trumbull £600 of stock. Trumbull did not buy the stock. Two years later, when he had served his purpose, the stock was sold again and he made no claim to it or to the money arising from it, but then admitted that it had merely stood in his name but was 'the Company's Proper Stock'. In effect some members of the Committee, drawn by lot, bound themselves to Sir Francis Child, Lord Mayor and banker, for the payment of the money involved, and the stock was nominally held by Trumbull so as to make him eligible for election. Thus qualified, Trumbull was elected Governor at the General Court of 18th November, 1696. He attended in the afternoon, accompanied by several persons of quality, was told that it was customary for the Governor to take an oath, and took it, assuring the Committee of his zeal and fidelity.

Lest there should be any misconception as to the reason why he had thus been suddenly chosen, the Committee wrote to him early in December asking that he would patronise them with his presence when the Commissioners for the Council of Trade came to hear the case against the French for the possession of the furs taken at York Fort. So although de la Forest had secured much sympathy, and the Company reported that he could be seen daily on the Exchange, being made much of, the Company itself was by no means without support and could at least be certain of a friendly hearing. The Committee nevertheless was not easy about its case. It seemed likely that 'great trouble' would ensue and the Committee hoped to make it clear that any case for breach of the Articles of surrender would lie against the deceased Captain Allen, not against the Company.

Very shortly after his election as Governor of the Company, on 5th December, 1696, Trumbull began to fix a hearing for the case, and de la Forest put in copies of the Articles of Surrender and of the correspondence with Captain Allen at that time. At this stage the Company asked for delay, and denied Allen's right to make any such agreement, since it was plainly contrary to his instructions. Then after about a week's interval the Company began to assert that the treatment of Walsh and the other prisoners taken by Iberville in 1695 (for which numbers of affidavits were put into court as evidence) was adequate reason for any breach of the terms accorded to de la Forest. In January 1697 the Board heard both sides, with de la Forest claiming over £14,000 and the Company insisting that it had recovered but £7,000 worth of furs, largely traded with its own goods and small compensation for the £200,000 or more of damages which the French had at various times inflicted on the English. So the case proceeded, with expensive counsel briefed for the Company, and with the French Minister of the Marine protesting on behalf of de la Forest that the two cannon involved were the property of the French Crown.

Soon this affair became mixed and tangled with other issues, for de la Forest's support came largely from English rivals to the Company, and already a movement was on foot in the City which led to further Parliamentary proceedings within the year. Moreover, the preliminary discussions leading up to a peace with France were under way.

As early as May 1694 Matthew Prior had decided that 'France really desires a peace with us, though it chicanes a little in the way of asking it'. The 'chicane' had gone on until France made the first definite move in sending Callières (the same man who had persuaded Radisson back into the English allegiance in 1684) to Holland in the autumn of 1696. Then informal but constant diplomatic interchanges became possible, and it became merely a matter of time and the settlement of terms until the fighting should cease. By the time that the capture and recapture of York Fort were being debated in London, at the end of 1696, the terms of the Treaty of Ryswick were occupying the attention of the diplomats and the Company's affairs became merely a subordinate part of the general discussions on peace.

BOOK FOR REFERENCE

Jérémie, Nicolas—*Twenty Years of York Factory 1694–1714 Jeremie's Account of Hudson Strait and Bay*, translated from the French edition of 1720 with notes and introduction by R. Douglas and J. N. Wallace (Ottawa, 1926).

CHAPTER XXVIII

THE TREATY OF RYSWICK. IBERVILLE AGAIN CAPTURES YORK FORT. THE COMPANY SUFFERS BY THE PEACE. 1697

Although Sir William Trumbull had been elected Governor of the Company so that he should negotiate the settlement of the capture of York Fort and the disposal of the furs taken from de la Forest, he was also Secretary of State during the negotiations leading up to the Treaty of Ryswick. The Company could therefore be reasonably certain that its claims would not be ignored, and that it would not again be slighted in the peace. But William III was to a large extent his own Foreign Minister in dealing with the French; the professional diplomats under him were functionaries rather than directors of policy. In the event the terms agreed at Ryswick proved a bitter disappointment to the Company, who found that colonial matters in general, and the affairs of the Bay in particular, were completely subordinated to dynastic and European interests.

Rumours of the coming peace were current in London as early as July 1696, and definite negotiations were in hand during the summer and autumn. Secretary Trumbull was, quite legitimately, in constant correspondence with Matthew Prior to get details of the way in which negotiations were proceeding, but the tone of the whole affair was set in these early talks. French acknowledgment of William's title to the throne, exclusion of James from Paris, withdrawal of French support from him, and the establishment of a defensible system of barrier forts in the Netherlands, took the diplomats' attention; and of all these problems that of the royal title promised to give the most trouble.

In the preliminary terms, offered in January 1697, the Hudson Bay affair was not even mentioned, and although during March the French (conceiving that the post was in English hands since its capture by Captain Allen in the previous year) began to demand the return of York Fort (or Fort Bourbon) with compensation for breach of the Articles of Surrender, little attention was attached to the issue and it was only introduced into the negotiations as a means of evading Trumbull's influence. For the French were afraid that 'il sera difficile d'y parvenir par les voyes de justice ordinaire à cause de l'interest qu'y prend M. le Chevalier Trumbal'. Commerce and

343

colonies began to take their place among the subjects for discussion in June and July, but still Hudson Bay was not mentioned, and in August the French were beginning to think that a settlement of the boundary of Acadia, and the exchange of the French part of St. Christopher's and other islands in the West Indies for part of Newfoundland, would remove all causes of dispute with England. In fact, the English envoys were ready to be complaisant over these matters, for they were prepared to put colonial issues on one side with the formula that they should 'revert to the foot they were in at the beginning of the war, which we understand to be Your Majesty's pleasure'. A draft of terms proposed along these lines was sent to Mr. Secretary Trumbull in July, containing the vague phrase that 'Captured colonies in America and the West Indies [are] to revert to their rightful owners'.

Some of the lack of emphasis on the Bay was due to the fact that both the French and the English had fitted out strong expeditions for Nelson River; they knew that while diplomats were juggling with phrases something of importance was happening in the Bay. Neither side knew details of the other's move, though the Committee was able to warn Knight at Albany that the French had said that they would send from Canada in June and July of 1697 and would burn the factory in the Bottom of the Bay, and to tell Baley at York Fort that he was under similar threat. Here the report was that the French would send a ship or two with about a hundred and forty men, who would lie up in some harbour until the English ships had come home and would then 'streiten you for Wood' (the cause of Walsh's surrender) and so force the post to give in.

To counter any such move, the Company borrowed the *Hampshire* from the Royal Navy to act as convoy for its own vessels, and with such preparations in hand each side hoped that the news which would come from the Bay in the autumn of 1697 would give it such a superiority that any temporising diplomatic solution would be turned to its advantage by its success in arms. The positions of the two nations were not, however, quite parallel, for the English assumed that they held possession of the Nelson and their expedition was merely to reinforce the post there, whereas the French assumed that they had to recapture their position. So, while the English seem to have confidently ignored the Bay problem at this stage of the negotiations, the French plenipotentiaries were instructed that they must reject the British claims and must strongly oppose the British case.

That the French should have been more insistent than the British was not only because they thought their rivals were in actual possession but also because Frontenac had returned to Canada as Governor, and in 1696 had put in a strong report which must have had considerable influence. In it he maintained that the beaver trade was still, as always, the chief hope of a sturdy French colony in Canada, and that fears of the harm which it might do to settlement were ill-founded. The claim that it led to drunken Indians, he said, was exaggerated. There was indeed little order or intelligent administration in the fur trade, but the pleas that the beaver market was glutted were nonsense; the furs could easily be disposed of if the prices were right. The *habitans* were reluctant to plough more land; but there was already enough corn in Canada and too few beasts, and threats of wars kept people from agricultural settlement. Although he had just fitted out Iberville for an attack on Newfoundland, Frontenac thought that fishing would never prove the mainstay of the colony, at least not until supplies of salt were guaranteed and until peace with the English could be secured. So he reached his conclusion that the Indian trade was all that his colony could subsist on.

For Frontenac this meant primarily that the English must be kept away from trade at Michilimackinac. The French must assume the dominant role in the disputes between the Ottawas, the Hurons and the Iroquois, and must never allow these peoples to establish stable trade with the English. England could supply trade-goods at prices and in qualities which were out of the reach of the French and 'si les Sauvages jouissent une fois de Commerce de l'Anglois ils rompront pour tourjours avec les françois'.

But Frontenac's reasoned insistence on the importance of the fur trade to Canada was not tied only to the trade of Michilimackinac. As the terms of peace came under discussion they evoked a memorandum based on the fact that beaver from Hudson Bay were finer, better and more numerous, than those of Canada. Hence the Canadians had set up their post (in 1682) at Fort Bourbon. Assuming that the English still possessed this post in 1697, the memorandum demanded its restitution at the peace since it had been established by the French and had been captured only 'par le trahison des commandants'. Without such a restitution the English would be clear masters of the fur trade, since the skins of Canada would not sell in competition with those of the Bay.

The French plenipotentiaries at Ryswick were therefore instructed in this sense, although the trial of de la Forest and the interest of Sir William Trumbull to some extent confused the issue, in that it remained difficult to discuss the precise terms on which de la Forest had surrendered in 1696 because of the interest of Trumbull.

The result was that by early August, 1697, when the other problems were by way of getting agreed at Ryswick, French and English claims to the Nelson River still proved irreconcilable. Here the French, perhaps urged by Frontenac's insistence on the importance of the fur trade to Canada, took a far stronger ground than the English envoys, who were not even very clear as to their case. 'Nothing appears of much difficulty, only as to that of Hudson's Bay business' wrote Sir J. Williamson, and that, said this diplomat, was but a brawl (a 'braugle') of private interests of trading companies at bottom, on which the negotiators were 'left without the necessary informations of fact, much more without able and full proofs of what is said, as to the original right, upon which all will turn'.

The Committee had not failed to put forward the Company's claims. There is record that in May 1697 they sent a memorial of their case to the English plenipotentiaries on their departure for Holland, that they followed this up in August with a more general memorial on the English title to the Bay, and that they later submitted a reply to the French claims on this subject. Hearing that 'the Canada Company' had sent 'a Person' to Holland to present its claims, the Hudson's Bay Committee sent the Deputy Governor, Samuel Clarke, to the Hague, along with committee-man Colonel Pery and the Secretary.

The Hudson's Bay men, however, arrived too late and were told that it was 'an Agreement between His Majesty and the French King' that all places should be put in the same state as before the Breaking out of this Warr'. The utmost which they could obtain was a concession that French and English Commissioners should meet in England to adjust the affair between the English and French Companies.

So when eventually the temporising solution of a restoration of conquests was adopted, and the definitive Treaty was signed on 20th September, 1697, the Company found its affairs dealt with in cavalier fashion. By clause VII each monarch was to restore all countries, islands, forts and colonies, to the power which possessed them at the declaration of the war; and by clause VIII commissioners were to be appointed to settle the boundaries between Rupert's Land and Canada within six months. But the commissioners were tied to the agreement, specified in the Treaty, that 'the Possession of those Places which were taken by the French during the Peace that preceded this present War, and were retaken by the English during this War, shall be left to the French by virtue of the foregoing Article'.

This in effect gave to the French the right to Albany and the Bottom of the Bay by virtue of their capture by de Troyes in 1686 and despite its recapture by James Knight in 1693. Further, it was set down that the capitulation of the French at York Fort to Captain Allen in 1696 should be fully observed, that the merchandise then taken should be restored to the French and compensation paid for any which might not be recoverable, and that Governor de la Forest should be freed and returned to France. He, however, was already out of the story; the commissioners for the exchange of prisoners of war had decreed that he should be returned to France in August, but he had died in London in the same month.

Even the concession that commissioners should meet to discuss the complications involved therefore seemed to contain little hope that the Company could be satisfied by the Treaty of Ryswick. Governor Trumbull was 'pleased to give himselfe the Trouble' of explaining the treaty to the Committee, and advised a memorandum to the King. The Committee concluded that it was in a worse position than ever and 'That the French gott those Concessions into the Treaty of Peace by undue Suggestions and misinformations'. The arrangement in so far as it concerned the Bottom of the Bay they roundly characterised as based on 'an Egregious misinformation'. With their own Governor as Secretary of State (and certainly not above mingling his public and his private duties) the Committee could not have been better placed to get good terms than at this juncture, but they pleaded that they were 'the only sufferers by the peace', and they undoubtedly had no reason to congratulate themselves on the outcome.

But although Governor Trumbull had promised his help against the French, by late 1697 a peace which would be satisfactory in Europe was too badly needed for Hudson Bay business to hold up the settlement. The nation at war had suffered no less than the Company from the financial crises of these years, during which the King had been forced to accept guineas at a premium, his ministers had been forced to 'take pains' with bankers, merchants and goldsmiths, exhorting some and threatening others, and he had been reduced to the utmost straits by 1696. By that time there seemed no way of averting a mutiny among his troops unless credit could be got to produce the money to pay them, and William even threatened that he must abdicate and retire to the Indies.

In such a state, William could not be too particular over any point save French recognition of the Protestant Succession to the English Throne. This was a realism which was, on the whole, accepted. 'But what could His Majesty do?' asked one pamphleteer who decried the Treaty. 'We were weary of fighting, we were weary of paying, we were actually deserted by some of our allies and in danger of being deserted by more.' The Bay was therefore virtually abandoned in the Peace, and in the general satisfaction it was said that the only complaints heard against the terms of the Treaty were over the removal of James from Paris, and 'something about the Hudson's Bay company'. And if James Stuart could be got away from Paris, Villiers for one felt that he would be 'less concerned about the Hudson's Bay Company'.

Such an easy acceptance of the Treaty rose rather from the relief which it brought than from a close analysis of its terms. Anxiously though it had been sought, the Treaty in the event proved lasting and satisfactory neither in Europe nor in the New World. When its implications had been worked out it became clear that, although William had for the moment vindicated his claims to the English throne, the problem of the Spanish succession had not been settled, and the threat of world domination by the intolerant government of Louis XIV remained to trouble Protestant minds. The Partition Treaties, and ultimately the War of the Spanish Succession, were the almost inevitable results of Ryswick; and in the New World the Treaty brought even less of a settlement than in the Old. There, all remained open to dispute and to the arbitration of the commissioners, with their powers to settle boundaries and to arrange exchanges of territories to the mutual advantage of the two powers.

The joy over the Peace therefore soon evaporated. 'Let who will be gainers by it, *England* was none' wrote a pamphleteer. The need to abandon to the French the places which they had captured in times of peace rankled as one of the chief grievances here, and it was added (as the Company itself insisted) that 'This reflected the more Dishonour upon us, that the Injury done us in this Matter was one of the Causes of War insisted upon in their Majesties King *William* and Queen *Mary's* Declaration against the French King, dated the 7th day of May, 1689'.

The effect of the terms of the Treaty would indeed have been severe. But in fact the Treaty never operated in the Bay, its terms were never carried out. They should have given to the French the possession of the Bottom of the Bay, which James Knight had wrested from them, and they should have confirmed the English in the possession of York Fort, Hayes River, which had been in British hands at the outbreak of the war, and which Captain Allen's expedition had recaptured in 1696. But until the next major revision of possessions at the Treaty of Utrecht in 1713 the Company's trade depended on the Bottom of the Bay where, in defiance of the Treaty, Albany remained the only post in British hands, while the French, also in defiance of the Treaty, remained in enjoyment of their Fort Bourbon in Hayes River. This last situation, in particular, was something which could not have been expected (certainly not by the British) at the time the Treaty was signed.

Yet it was already in effect. The Treaty was signed on 20th September, 1697, and on the 2nd of that month (the 13th according to French style) the climax of the operation was reached when Iberville once more captured York Fort. Once more, as in 1686, he had vitiated the terms of an Anglo-French Treaty whilst those terms were in process of being drawn up.

Not anticipating the 'base surrender' of the French post after Iberville had left de la Forest in command in 1695, the French Navy had sent Iberville to a command off the coast of Acadia in 1696. There he cruised in the *Wesp* through the winter, capturing an English frigate and taking Fort Penkuit, and there he received orders for the second recapture of the post in Hayes River when the news of Captain Allen's success had reached Europe and stimulated the French to reply. His orders were, simply, to retake Fort Bourbon 'que les Anglais avaient pris l'année précédente par Capitulation'. They were dated 9th March, 1697, and they reached Iberville on the 18th May. He was to sail in the *Pélican*, of forty-six guns, and was to have under command the *Palmier*, the *Esquimo*, the *Wesp* and the *Profond*.

Of his voyage and the subsequent action there is only a brief account from the English point of view, and the most authoritative French account bears the marginal comment 'Je ne comprends pas', so involved is the narrative. With the four ships which had come from France to help Iberville came also the remains of the garrison which had surrendered in 1696, who had been transferred from England to France and so shipped out to join Iberville at Placentia; among them was Nicholas Jérémie, who later became Governor of the post, and whose account of his twenty years of Hudson Bay and Strait is one of the authorities for this period.

Iberville and his flotilla were soon in trouble; indeed they had already met trouble enough in their passage from La Rochelle, during which the *Wesp* and the *Palmier* had been in collision, scurvy had broken out, and all the ships had suffered from heavy seas. Sailing from Placentia on 8th July, they were in the ice by 25th, off

Hudson Strait. One ship, the *Esquimo*, seems to have sunk in the ice, and all the ships suffered, the *Palmier* particularly, as they were carried to and fro by the winds and currents in the ice-pack under the midnight sun. On 25th August the *Pélican*, despite great efforts to maintain contact, lost touch with her consorts in a fog, and when the fog lifted the *Profond* found herself in company not of the three French vessels but of three English ships!

These were the *Dering* and the *Hudson's Bay* (Company ships), and the *Hampshire*, a man-of-war borrowed to convoy them in view of rumours that a French counter-stroke in the Bay was imminent. A fire-ship, the *Owner's Love* was also prepared for the voyage, but nothing more is heard of her. The *Profond* ran into the ice to escape the English, but the *Dering* and the *Hudson's Bay* came up with her there and severely handled her. In the evening the powerful fifty-gun *Hampshire* came into the action, and eventually the English left the battered *Profond*, thinking she was bound to sink.

Iberville in the *Pélican*, in the meantime, had been carried clear of the ice into the Bay itself, and hoisting his topsails had reached Hayes River by 5th September. He anchored off the post and sent a party ashore. Next day the three English ships, whom he mistook at first for his French consorts, arrived. The *Hampshire* led the English into the attack 'in line' (presumably in line ahead), and the chances of a French reconquest of 'Port Nelson' seemed negligible, for the *Pélican* carried only forty-four guns whereas the *Hampshire* carried fifty-two, the *Dering* thirty and the *Hudson's Bay* thirty-two. The French had also suffered on the voyage; they had forty sick, and they were further weakened by the absence of the party which Iberville had sent ashore, so that they could muster only about a hundred and fifty men.

This was the sort of situation which called out the best qualities in Iberville. He made the *Hampshire* luff by running at her as if intending to board her, and then passed on down the line to cut the tackle of the *Dering*'s mainsail and largely disable her, and to give the *Hudson's Bay* the remainder of his broadside. The *Hampshire* put about to windward and came into action again, the three English ships using grape and musketry in attempts to dismast the Frenchman and to cause casualties in the crew. For two and a half hours the fight raged, and there were heavy casualties on both sides. Then the *Hampshire* tried to work up to windward of the *Pélican*, much of whose rigging had been destroyed, with the intention of coming down on the wind and ramming her, to end the fight. Iberville, however, foresaw the move and sailed a parallel course to windward.

During this manoeuvre appears one of the more dramatic episodes of the battle, dramatic enough in all conscience. For as Iberville and Captain Fletcher of the *Hampshire* sailed their damaged ships alongside each other each sent for a bumper of wine and, amid the fury of battle, pledged his opponent as a gallant foe.

This was Captain Fletcher's last act, for as the *Pélican* fired her broadside the *Hampshire* foundered with all hands. Iberville's account is dramatic in its brevity; 'I fired my broadside and sank her immediately, the vessel not passing onward three lengths'. But the whole account is written by the French in dramatic over-tones, whereas on analysis it proves that, ominous as this battle off the Hayes River was, and tense with drama as the participants must have been, it was not the scene of carnage and powder-blackened heroes which the French accounts make it. There were only seventeen casualties on the *Pélican*, of whom only one was killed. It is most unlikely that the *Pélican*'s guns could have sunk the *Hampshire* so swiftly. More probably she capsized; or her bottom may have dropped out. Most likely is the explanation that she touched on a shoal and capsized. For though Iberville reported that she sank, La Potherie, who was aboard with Iberville, wrote that she foundered under sail and that later the French anchored close to the wreck and found that she had stranded on a shoal.

At all events, the *Hampshire* was out of the action and the gallant Captain Fletcher was dead. The *Dering* fired another broadside and then turned and made her way out of the river. The *Hudson's Bay* surrendered and Iberville, against all the odds, was left master of the river, to reduce the post at leisure when his other ships should arrive.

His perils were not yet over, however. During the night the wind rose and both the *Pélican* and her prize the *Hudson's Bay* were driven ashore, striking on the flats at the mouth of Nelson River. The French crew got to land with difficulty, exhausted by their trials. The *Hudson's Bay* foundered in the storm, which had also brought to the Hayes River the missing three French ships, the *Wesp*, the *Profond* and the *Palmier*. Although the *Palmier* had lost her rudder they all came to a safe anchorage.

The English from York Fort skirmished effectively with the men who had landed from Iberville's ship, but the French worked up to the foot of the fort and demanded the surrender of two French and two Indians who had been left behind in the previous year when the English had taken the post. The garrison had been strengthened by some sailors who had got ashore from the *Hudson's Bay*, and its morale had been greatly strengthened by the authority of Captain Smithsend, especially as he was convinced that Iberville himself had been killed in the naval action. But the English were too inactive to prevent Iberville from landing mortars from his ships, setting up a battery and starting a bombardment of the fort. True, their cannon replied with an accuracy which won the admiration of the French, and they almost killed Iberville. They refused the first demand for surrender, but as the bombardment continued the Fort was surrounded and when it was obvious that an assault was imminent the Governor, Baley, sent the Reverend Mr. Morrison to discuss terms of surrender on the evening of 12th September (French style). His demand that the beaver should be reserved for the Hudson's Bay Company was unacceptable and Henry Kelsey, Deputy Governor, was sent with the next proposals, asking that the mortars and cannon of the post should be returned to England. This also was refused, and on 13th Governor Baley agreed on surrender, and the garrison marched out with the honours of war, with drums beating, muskets loaded, banner waving, match lighted, and with their arms and baggage. They were fifty-two men, including seventeen from the *Hudson's Bay*, and they yielded to Iberville £20,000 of skins, the produce of the year's trade, which should have been shipped home in the *Hudson's Bay*.

Leaving his brother de Serigny in command, with Jérémie as second, Iberville loaded the booty aboard his ships and was in France again by early in November. With typical Canadian confidence in the possibility of such a means of communication he had arranged to send news of his success in Port Nelson to Quebec by canoe, but nothing more is heard of this, and it is almost certain that he carried his own good news to France before it could have been known in Canada.

Once more the furs from the Bay were being shipped direct to Europe, without contributing to Canada, by Iberville and the *Compagnie du Nord*.

In Paris, Iberville found that the *Compagnie du Nord* was already negotiating for a permit to conduct the trade of Port Nelson when the English should have been driven out. The Crown was anxious to lease the post to the *Compagnie* on condition that it would promise to re-create the trade there, and that it would defray the costs of upkeep. For this commitment, the Canadian members of the *Compagnie* were not prepared; they maintained, probably with justice, that they had already invested all their available capital. So although the French members of the *Compagnie* seemed prepared to find money for the commitment, the offer was turned down with a plea that the *Compagnie* needed royal subvention and with a proviso that the end of the war would change the situation and make the offer more attractive.

This had happened while Iberville was crossing the Atlantic with a scurvy-stricken crew. His despatch, and his orders for the conduct of the garrison which he had left behind, were approved, and he was ordered to hand in an account of all the goods which he had taken, and to put them at the disposal of the Intendant of the Navy. For this of 1697 was a royal venture, not one such as that of 1694 in which royal ships were lent but the backing came from private finance.

Yet, since the *Compagnie du Nord* was holding back, Iberville made an arrangement with the Crown whereby he undertook to carry on the trade of Fort Bourbon, the name given to the French post, for two years. He was at the same time petitioning to be given the Governorship of Plaisance, to be given command of a ship, and to be sent on a voyage to Louisiana. These interests, particularly his activity in Louisiana, prevented him from further active participation in the Bay. But his concession of the trade at Fort Bourbon was leased to willing buyers so that the despondent note struck by his lieutenant La Potherie found no echoes. The latter, perhaps affected by the bitterness of his first voyage to the Arctic, felt that 'even though France should not hold these regions, the fur trade of Canada would not suffer; on the contrary it would improve. 'This superabundance of peltries from Hudson Bay can only work injury to the former if we keep up this fort, especially in time of peace. The merchants of Canada would in that case be obliged to sell their wares very cheap to the Indians. They are beginning to give up furs in France.'

The interest staked by Iberville meant that this view would not triumph; there were those who were prepared to risk causing a glut of furs in France for the sake of the chances of profits which the trade to Fort Bourbon afforded. There were those, too, who regarded the possession of this post as essential to Canada, as vindicated by the recent campaign and by the Treaty of Ryswick.

So when the boundary terms of the Treaty came to be discussed by the commissioners envisaged by the signatories, the rightful disposal of the post on Hayes River was, largely as a result of Iberville's action, a thorny point—so thorny, in fact, that no agreement was ever reached until the whole of the Ryswick concept was superseded, sixteen years later, by the Treaty of Utrecht. For those sixteen years

M

Iberville's magnificent naval action gave to France *de facto* possession of Port Nelson.

BOOKS FOR REFERENCE

COXE, W.—*Private and original correspondence of Charles Talbot, Duke of Shrewsbury* (London, 1821).

CROUSE, Nellis M.—*Lemoyne d'Iberville: Soldier of New France* (Ithaca, New York, 1954).

FRÉGAULT, G.—*Iberville le Conquérant* (Montreal, 1944).

LEGG, L. G. Wickham—*Matthew Prior* (Cambridge, 1921).

LEGG, L. G. Wickham (ed.)—*British Diplomatic Instructions 1689–1789 Volume II— France, 1689–1721* (London, The Royal Historical Society, 1925).

TYRRELL, J. B. (ed.)—*Documents Relating to the Early History of Hudson Bay* (Toronto, The Champlain Society, 1931).

CHAPTER XXIX

THE CHARTER FAILS; THE COMPANY CONDEMNED. 1697

The events in Hayes River in 1697 were, as it proved, to condition the whole period of the Treaty of Ryswick, in so far as the trade of the Bay was concerned. But they were not yet known in Europe at the time of the signature, although both sides must have known that some major change of balance would almost certainly result before the Treaty could be implemented. In all probability both were hoping that when the treaty should have been signed, and the situation on the ground should come to be reckoned up, they would be in a better position than their adversary had expected. Certainly the Hudson's Bay Company, with the *Hampshire* and two powerful Company ships engaged on the voyage, had no reason to anticipate that it would finish the year with the loss of the vital post which it had so recently re-captured.

Yet the Ryswick negotiations were carried on in conditions which gave the Company and its well-placed Governor but little advantage. For the difficulties over the furs captured from the French by Captain Allen, the articles of capitulation accorded to de la Forest, and the peculation of the furs at Plymouth, still hung round the Company and had reached the stage of Parliamentary proceedings just at the time when the negotiations for the Treaty were drawing to a close.

In January 1697 the Committee secured a sight of the recommendations which the Lords of Trade and Plantations had in mind, and found them 'very Partiall and many Materiall things for the Companies Advantage left out'. Then their good customer Mr. Glover appeared (with Lord Sidney) to support an Exchequer Bill which would have served as a direct precedent against the Company as far as de la Forest's furs were concerned. They challenged ownership of the furs taken by James Knight at Albany in 1693, alleging that they should have belonged to the Crown, and although the reference was only oblique to the case in hand over the recent capture of York, it caused further complications, led to the taking of Counsel's Opinion, the consultation of the Charter, and a certain element of dispute between the Company and those from whom it most needed support in 1697. The Company's case was that Albany had been built by the British, who were justified in recapturing it, and that the furs were entirely taken on land and therefore did not come under Admiralty jurisdiction as they might have done if they had been taken at sea.

With this additional cause of trouble raked up from the past, the Company had the present problem of the Treaty negotiations and the claims for York Fort furs, while within the year they would have to face Parliament and to ask for a renewal of the seven years' grant which they had received in the Parliamentary confirmation of their Charter in 1690. They also had to face the most immediate problem of maintaining solvency, for in 1694 even the great East India Company had forfeited its charter for failure to pay tax on its joint stock, and interloping designs were afoot. The Africa Company, too, was in trouble in those days, reporting to Parliament a loss of £400,000 and asking for permission to sell its posts, and the Company for the Discovery of New Trades (the Russia Company) was also resisting attempts to get its trade thrown open to the general public, and finally accepting a system of licences.

For the payment of its taxes the Company was put to sore straits. The Commissioners for taxation rated the Company at its own figure of £7,500, a figure which represented the value of goods 'both in the House as alsoe at the Water side'. This, however, did not mean that the Company had anything like that sum as cash in hand. The fur sale of January 1697 had not gone well; scarcity of money in the country had caused a delay and a drop in the upset price of the beaver to 8s. 2d. a pound for *coat* beaver and 8s. 8d. for *parchment*. Not all was sold even at those prices, and in May of that year the Committee was writing to its posts on the Bay (to Albany and York Fort) that there were about seventy thousand *coat* on hand which could not be sold. The traders were therefore to pay only half the price for *coat* that they paid for *parchment*, they were to take none that had not been worn for at least two years, were to keep it in the country so that the Indians might realise that it really was of little use, and were even to burn it before the Indians' eyes, fully to convince them.

This was doubtful policy even for the future; for the present it could do nothing to bring in money or to stimulate sales. The whole country was in the grip of war finance; to keep the fleet at sea the utmost the government could offer was to repay anyone who would advance the necessary money when funds should come to hand, and Parliament was inundated by petitions from the unemployed clothiers and woollen workers—many of them alleging that the East India Company was the cause of their troubles. The felting and hat-making industries suffered with the rest, and their troubles were enhanced by a change of fashion as the serving men of the country gave up the use of felt hats—or so the felters alleged.

A further sale in June 1697 took few furs off the Company's hands, and by November prices were dropping to 7s. for *parchment* and 8s. for *bright parchment*. By the following February they were mixing *bright coat* with the old furs and failing to sell them at 6s. 6d. the pound; they were down to 5s. the pound for *coat* 'out of time' and 6s. for *prime coat* by May 1698, and were by then trying to pay off a debt of £500 in the *old coat* beaver and, with eighty thousand *coat* by then unsaleable on their hands, they accepted an offer from Thomas Glover, acting for a friend, to take twelve thousand *parchment* at 6s. 0d. with the advantage of the drawback of the customs as long as he shipped them to Archangel via Hamburg.

Even this left great quantities, especially of *coat*, on hand, and it is not surprising that even in war conditions the Company continued its policy of direct shipment to the continent, especially as the agent at Amsterdam had at last managed to sell some of the *coat* shipped there. Continental sales, nevertheless, were not keeping pace with shipments, and by June of 1698 the Company had over twenty-two thousand *coat* lying at Amsterdam, while Hamburg had a similar quantity of *parchment*. Hamburg had shipped on about ten thousand *parchment* to Archangel in 1697, and in 1698 shipped a further twelve thousand; the 1697 shipment was well sold at Moscow, but that of 1698 was still on hand at the end of the year.

Such sales might give foreign currency to the Company, but they left about four years' returns on hand in Europe, and they did not bring the ready cash in England which the Company needed. The only valuable sales were being made in Moscow, and the produce had to be remitted in roubles to Hamburg en route for Amsterdam. This allowed the Company's envoys to Ryswick to draw on the Company's credit; but the difficulties of the exchanges led the Company to begin to dabble at this time in new trades, to try on the one hand to barter *cub* beaver for any goods vendible at Hamburg or Lubeck, and on the other hand to start shipping home hogs' bristles and Russian hides, tallow and beaver-wool, as well as the flax and hemp of which the Navy stood in such need. Here the Company was entering into competition with a small ring of naval contractors, but the initial cargoes, of 1697, seem to have been sold by auction without much trouble. But only about a thousand pounds seems to have been involved, and with the cost of the recapture of York in 1696 and of the *Hampshire* and her consorts in 1697 to pay for, the Company was in dire straits.

In March and May of 1697 the Committee had been unable to pay the wages of Thomas Walsh (for whom in any case they had no love) and they were forced to beg an extra six months' credit from their grocer and to pay him £60 on account before they could get provisions for the voyage of that year. At that time they could not even find £15 for rigging their ships, but they cashed a bank bill at a discount of over 20 per cent. for £175 instead of letting it mature 'having urgent ocasion for money' and 'invested' £50 of the money in six lottery tickets. They promised gratuities of £100 each to the captains who had taken part in the capture of York Fort in 1696— but they paid in paper redeemable in a year's time! By August the Secretary's cash balance was down to £29 in old money, and this was changed for £26 in pistoles or guineas and given, with a further £25 which had been borrowed, to the emissaries sent to Ryswick. By the end of the year the meagre remittances from the continent were being realised at discounts to pay the seamen, bills were being drawn on the Company's goods at Hamburg for the same purpose, and the men who had been in the *Hudson's Bay* when she was lost were firmly told that no wages were due to them, and they would get none; other servants were paid small portions of their dues in Exchequer bills. Against this must be set the fact that those who had been wounded in the *Dering* were awarded their 'smart money', the Committee taking care to find out what was paid in His Majesty's service and adopting the same scale as a standing rule for the future. But perhaps the precarious finances of the Company in 1697 and 1698 are best revealed when the banker Sir John Sweetaple sold so much of his stock that by May 1697 he had only £75 left and so voided his membership of the Committee.

These were most inauspicious circumstances in which to approach Parliament for a renewal of the Charter, even with Governor Sir William Trumbull ensconced as Principal Secretary of State and with Sir Stephen Evans sitting as a Member of Parliament and an almost automatic choice for any Parliamentary Committee dealing with trade. Another committee-man, Colonel Pery, also sat in the House and gave the Company up-to-date information of moves there. Yet such favour as the Company could find was little enough when set against the widespread distress and the need for peace with France.

The Charter, however, would run out if not renewed, so the Committee could not wait for propitious times but began to work for renewal as early as January 1697. Then, partly to strengthen the case against the French over the capture of York Fort by Captain

Allen, the Committee submitted a petition which, while amending the draft report of the Commissioners for Trade and Plantations on their dispute with de la Forest, also inserted the claim that the Company prosecuted a trade which was of great advantage to the whole nation because it began with the export of articles of British manufacture. Were the French allowed to dominate the beaver trade not only would this outlet for our manufactures cease but beaver would also rise in price. For, making a virtue of necessity, the Company was able to state that it sold beaver as low as seven shillings the pound, whereas when the French controlled the trade it had stood as high as forty shillings.

This all bore upon the Company's claim to be maintained in York Fort and to be vindicated against the French, from whom sums varying from a round £200,000 to a more meticulous £154,514 19s. 8d. were claimed—entirely for losses inflicted in time of peace and therefore not including the loss of the *Hudson's Bay* and the damage suffered by the *Dering*; with the last loss of York Fort (in which it was estimated that £18,000 of goods was involved and that the *Hudson's Bay* frigate had cost £2,556 19s. 4d.) the bill worked out to '£236,556 and upwards'.

As was almost inevitable, there was here a mingling of the justifications which the Company was advancing for its claims on York Fort with the reasons which it was preparing to put before Parliament for the renewal of the Charter. But the issues clarified as the year drew on. By May 1698 the Lords of Trade and Plantations had drawn up a summary narrative of the Allen capture of York, had considered the relevance of the Treaty of Ryswick to the problem of the possession of the post and of the furs, and had posed the two main questions at issue—did Captain Allen's instructions give him authority to grant terms of capitulation; and had the French in 1694 so broken their terms to Walsh and his men as to warrant English reprisals on de la Forest? The Company was by that time limiting its hopes to the intervention of the commissioners whom the Treaty of Ryswick had set up for the settlement of boundaries. So, although the French insisted that restoration of the furs should take first priority in any negotiations to implement the terms of Ryswick, and maintained that the breach of the terms of capitulation undermined the bases of civilised conduct, yet for the moment the affair was in abeyance and the realities of the situation were to be found in the Company's petition for convoy for its ships and for a royal commission for its Governor, coupled with its moves in Parliament for renewal of the Charter. Disputes over former incidents were not to

take precedence over plans for future trade, and in effect the possession of the furs of 1696 was as much a *fait accompli* in the English
favour as the possession of York Fort was in the French.

In readiness for the Parliamentary case, Secretary William Potter
took the precaution in June 1697 of checking over the published
copy of the Act of 1690 which confirmed the Company's Charter,
and comparing it with the original; he found it correct and got it
witnessed as a true copy. In March 1698, therefore, the Committee
was well primed to put its case to the Commons. The 'great quantities of woollen and other Manufactures' stood well to the fore, with
damages from the French coming second, while the grant for which
the Committee sought renewal was summarised. 'The substance of
the Act is to confirm the said Companys Charter and to enjoin them
to make certain Publick Sales yearly of Coat Beaver in moderate
Lots And in the Intervals of Publick Sales not to sell Coat Beaver by
Private Contract at any lower price than it was set up at the last
Publick Sale.' The need for a constant and organised trade, such as
only a permanent joint-stock could undertake, was reasonably put,
together with the success of the Company in developing its resources. 'Nor is the *Beavor* Trade to be Maintained or Improved by
a single or sudden Voyage of any Undertaker', claimed the *Case of
the Company*, 'but by the publick Charge of Fortified Forts and
Established Factories to abide there, with a constant Correspon-
dency with the Indians'. It was claimed that twenty years ago the fur
trade was 'not a penny benefit to the Kingdom', but it was now worth
£20,000 a year. The Company's Bill was presented to the Commons
on 3rd March, 1698, and was sent to a select committee, of which
Sir Stephen Evans was a member, on 11th.

At this stage Radisson once more intervened in the Company's
affairs. He had been called in to help the Committee in their case
against the French, and in the previous August a special coach had
even been sent to bring him to a meeting, at which he gave his version of the historical background of the contest between the French
and British. There were many points on which he alone could give
evidence on the three problems which were disturbing the Committee—English priority and title in the Bottom of the Bay and in
Port Nelson; the work accomplished by the Company under its
Charter; and the damages inflicted by the French, against which the
Fort Bourbon furs were to be set. He was sent to Sir Robert Jeffreys
to make a sworn affidavit of his evidence, which included a memorandum of Callière's orders to destroy the French post in the
Hayes River and a statement that he still had a copy of the letter

which Albanel had left for him at the Bottom of the Bay in 1672.

But although the Committee were well aware that Radisson would be 'verry usefull at this time as to the Affaires betwixt the French and this Company', and had tried to compose their differences with him, they had no resources with which to keep up payments due to him, and along with the Company's petition for renewal of the Charter the Select Committee of the Commons was also instructed to consider a petition from Radisson for the Company to be ordered to pay his dues. He alleged that he was now, in 1698, sixty-two years old, that he had four English-born children dependent on him, and that he had received no payments for the 'six actions' in the Company's stock which had been awarded him as a result of his Chancery suit against the Company.

At the least such a suit must reflect on the solvency of the Company and on its ability to perform the duties with which it claimed to be entrusted in carrying on its trade. Rightly so, for Radisson had turned to the Committee before he submitted his petition to Parliament, and in October 1697 had reminded members that there was £140 due to him, only to be told that though they were willing to do him what kindness they could, yet their circumstances would not permit them to pay him for the next twelve months. They did indeed borrow £100 for the specific purpose of paying it to him, but they could not clear their debt, and his action served to emphasise their lack of financial power at a most inopportune moment.

Radisson was not alone in his appeal to Parliament against the Company. On 12th March the Feltmakers' Company submitted a petition; on 19th the Skinners' Company put in its objections to the renewal of the Charter; on 28th the merchants trading between London and New York tabled their objections; and on 1st April the proprietors of the interloper *Expectation*, captured and wrecked by Nehemiah Walker in 1684, revived the old case in the form of a Parliamentary petition. It was alleged that the Company sold its exports so dear to the Indians that it got for sixpence beaver which it later sold for six shillings and that thereby it killed the Indian market for British goods and drove the Indians to the French.

Not only was the Company accused of mishandling this trade, but also of ruining the Russia trade. The Russia Company was at this time being subjected to attack in Parliament, and compromised by agreeing to allow non-members of the Company to trade under licence; the Hudson's Bay Company's direct trade with Russia could not therefore be attacked from the point of view of the Russia merchants. But the Feltmakers stated that the way of combing beaver-wool which had once been the monopoly of the Russians was now known in England and that cheaper and better felts, with more employment of Englishmen, would be achieved if the Company did not export to the continent. To this was added the claim that the best furs were sent to Russia and that the English felters were therefore tied to inferior furs while the Russia merchants were forced to buy furs suitable for their market from those exported to Holland, and so the New York and New England fur trade to London lost the chance of their custom. It was further urged that the Parliamentary grant of 1690 had merely been used by the Company as a means of stock-jobbing and that the dividend of that year and the three-fold increase of stock had been quite unwarranted by any improvement in trade and was due entirely to the grant of the Charter. Finally the whole concept of joint-stock companies was attacked, as a monopoly in themselves and as inefficient in practice; their trades had never flourished, whereas 'Open trades' such as those of the West Indies or Pennsylvania had greatly improved.

At about this time, too, appeared the printed *Impartial Account of the present state of the Hudson's Bay Company*. Here came an early appeal to one of the great reasons for attacks on the Company, for it was urged that not only had it not noticeably improved its trade, with twenty years of trade under the Charter behind it, but it had made no discoveries. The forts too—the Company had made a great point of the need for a joint-stock to maintain the permanent capital commitments of forts and trading posts—were described as no better than pig-styes 'being a few Pine-Trees, squared and laid one upon another, and rammed only with Moss, to keep out the Wind'. The Company was decried as consisting only of some thirty members, a diminutive company, without parallel, enjoying a position which enabled it to cramp industry and to discourage ingenuity, reducing the trade to proportions which made it of no significance to the nation, by virtue of a charter which granted sovereignty itself, a thing 'not consistent with the Wisdom of this Nation to grant', and which had been obtained under the specious pretext of discovering a North-west Passage.

There was much to invite comment in all of this, and it is surprising to find that the Committee allowed the Deputy Governor only the modest sum of twenty guineas 'towards the charges of reading the Company's bill in Parliament the second time'. Yet the bill certainly survived its second reading and went to a Committee of the whole House in May.

The Company had in the meantime strongly rebutted the accusations, stating that the price of skins had been steadily reduced, but that the Company was still over-stocked and had been forced to begin its system of export to Russia 'by the combination of the Skinners and other Persons against them', to ease itself of the great burden of *coat* beaver. The last shipment of 12,000 skins to Hamburg en route for Archangel had certainly been made for the sole reason that the Company had been unable to get what it considered a fair price from Thomas Glover and his friends, and it was able only too truly to say that the shipments left always enough stocks on hand to meet all demands for many years. Further, to carry the war into the enemy's country, the Company could truly state that beaver had never sold so cheaply as it then was, and that the high price of hats, which was driving them off the market, was due to the excessive charges of the feltmakers. As for direct shipment to the continent, the Committee argued that since any furs available in Holland had to come either from England or France, the Russia merchants always had their chance to buy on the English market.

At this stage the whole process of the pursuit of the very necessary renewal of the Charter disappears from view. The Company's bill went to a Committee of the whole House after its second reading on 14th May, and was then adjourned till 21st. But it was not then discussed, and it does not appear ever to have reached the House of Lords, still less to have received the Royal assent. Yet somehow the position had been settled; the Company was acknowledged as the sole proprietor of the lands in dispute. It was still involved in the dispute with the French over possession of York Fort—'a Place they call Fort Bourbon in the River St. Thereze, Places and names unknowne to Us, and wee believe to the best Geographers in the World', but safe-conducts, commissions, and convoy arrangements for the voyage were already in hand by the time that the Company's Bill disappeared from sight in the Committee stage of its treatment by the House of Commons.

Although officially the Company must henceforth either be considered as unchartered or as dependent once more on the original and purely royal grant, it met with full official approval and it does not seem to have hesitated in pushing forward its trade on this account. The silence alike of the Company's documents and of the national records on the fate of the bill obviously speaks for serious opposition and for the end of the attempt to renew the Company's Parliamentary status. But no explanation can be found for the sudden end of so spirited a move, and even Sir William Trumbull the

Governor does not seem to have given the Committee any reason why its plea should have been dropped.

The attempt to secure a Parliamentary renewal of the Charter ends in obscurity, but there can be no doubt that this represents an important defeat for the Company. It is true, of course, that the counter-petitions also sink from sight, but since the Company had begun the Parliamentary proceedings, and since the failure of its project left a marked weakness in the Company's position, the lack of conclusion must be counted as a defeat for the Company. It is unhistorical to treat the episode as a vindication of the Company's position against the opponents of the Charter because their cross-petitions also came to no issue. The Company had failed in an important matter, and had decided to accept its failure in silence.

For the moment the failure seemed to make but little difference; it was more important that only Albany remained to supply the furs on which all depended. But the lack of Parliamentary confirmation was to prove a weakness in future years, and it was perhaps of even greater significance that during this episode the Committee appear to have begun to suspect that the Company's papers and documents were being used to supply the information needed by its opponents. Consequently a policy of restricting information was started. Ships' captains were ordered to deliver in their logs immediately on their return to London, and a rule was made that no books or papers should be lent to any person without orders from the Committee. These were sensible precautions for a Company subject to so much criticism, but they confirmed the tendency to wrap the Bay trade in mystery, to make even the curious, still more the critical, depend on rumours supplied by enemies of the Company, and so to give weight to opposition by withholding information.

As a Company which had in its time held a Parliamentary grant but which had now been forced to relapse into dependence on Royal prerogative only, in a period when the prerogative carried little weight, the Company was henceforth vulnerable; and however sensible the arguments for secrecy may have appeared in 1698, the policy ultimately worked against the Company.

In the middle of all these troubles, the Committee could not overlook the claims of the French for the return of the furs captured by Captain Allen, or for compensation in lieu. While the French were disputing the basic right to the Bay, they were also demanding justice for de la Forest and the *Compagnie du Nord* as a necessary preliminary to the Peace, and their interpretation of the affair was eventually incorporated in the Peace itself with the proviso that the terms of capitulation accorded by Captain Allen must be observed, and that compensation for the furs must be paid.

The likeable de la Forest had died in London before this triumph for the French had been achieved, but even had he survived to add his personal claims to those of the French *Compagnie* it is not likely that the affair would have reached a settlement, for the English Company managed to delay and evade despite the lack of any official sympathy for its case.

Throughout the affair it is astonishing to see how much English opinion favoured the French claims. As soon as the facts were known, in November 1696, the Company had secured an order from the King in Council that the Admiralty should deliver to the Company the furs which the *Bonaventure* had brought to Plymouth and had sent three members of the Committee down to Plymouth to take charge. This was too simple a solution to be final, and in December the Lords of Trade began to interest themselves and the Company found that so many Englishmen were 'sollicitus for the French Governor' that there was every likelihood of great trouble.

The Company prepared its case to put before the Lords of Trade, with emphasis on Allen's sole responsibility and on the previous damages and the bad faith of which the French had been guilty. Governor Trumbull's serious attention was besought, and he was asked to be present when the Lords of Trade heard the case, 'for if the goods which are now come home should be taken out of our possession we may be frustrated of all our hopes and expectations of reparacion for damages done us at the Treaty of Peace, whenever it shall happen'. Trumbull lent his presence, but the Company found that notwithstanding its representations all was denied. Fearful that a decision on the lines which seemed to be likely would be a disastrous precedent, since it would be alleged at the Treaty of Peace that even in the height of the war the English had made restitution, the Company again entreated its Governor to intervene.

There for the moment the affair of de la Forest seems to have rested while the major considerations which dominated the Treaty took control and the French appeared to carry all before them. Had the terms of Ryswick been promptly carried out there is little doubt that the Company would have been forced to pay for the furs. But in May 1698 the Company was able to plead that the clause of the Treaty which insisted on restitution was bound up with the clause which set up the Commissioners for settling the dispute over the Bay and ordered them to report within six months. Since the French failed to appoint their Commissioners the Lords of Trade maintained, in support of the Company, that therefore no restitution on account of the captured furs was due. Here the Lords of Trade were beginning to consult the Company and adopt its claims in a way quite at variance with their apathy at the time of the Treaty.

The disputed beaver, valued at only five shillings the pound at a cash sale—though perhaps worth more if long credit could be given —had in the meantime been disposed of to the continent by the Company. But on the actual case for possession it could make but a weak claim since it proved impossible to get Walsh, who had been Governor of York at the surrender to Iberville in 1694, to make any kind of statement on behalf of the Company. On the contrary, he insisted that he and his men had received fair treatment, and he was the centre of a movement for intimidating those who were prepared to swear testimony which would support the Company's case. He was not the only man whom the Company wished to hold forth as the victim of gross abuse but who turned round and swore that he had no complaint, and it is not surprising that in June 1699 the Lords Justices gave judgment for the French and ordered the Company to make good the assessed value of the skins taken at York. But the value of the skins still remained to be determined, and in 1699 anti-pathy from some of its former employees mattered less to the Company than did the general feeling that another war with France was brewing up over the Spanish inheritance.

So the Company decided once more to petition the Crown, Trumbull protested against the assessment of the furs at £7,000, the 'State of the Case of the Company' was drawn up and submitted, and the Company professed that, whatever the justice of the verdict, it was utterly unable to pay such a sum owing to losses caused by French depredations. By this time it was true that the Company, as it alleged, had received no returns for two years, and that it could expect no trade for a further year. So, instead of pleading as formerly that the French furs were valueless in an overstocked market, it now claimed on compassionate grounds that they were 'some support to the declining Condition of this Company'.

The judgment against the Company in June 1699 followed on the heels of a diplomatic set-back when Secretary of State James Vernon handed to the Company two papers in April. One paper was a narrative of the Breach of Articles by Captain Allen in 1696; the other was an account of the furs brought home by him. But the answer put in by the Deputy Governor adequately stated the Company's case and again delayed action.

There the matter of the captured furs sinks into the ground.

Although the French later claimed that there was more due to them on this account than they had been paid (which presumes that some payment had actually been made) there is no record in the Company's documents that anything was ever paid. Certainly the Company was protesting to the utmost, and although the French were still insistent that restitution should take first priority when the commissioners to fulfil Ryswick should meet, they got little satisfaction. They protested that the confiscation of the furs contrary to the Articles of Capitulation was so odious that they could not imagine the English commissioners putting forward a defence of such conduct and they maintained that if restoration were not granted the whole basis of civilised conduct would be undermined. Thus goaded, the English administrators made some attempt to force the Company to clear the way for a general settlement. The Attorney General issued a Bill in September 1700 against the Company for payment of the £7,000 involved, but it is probably true that at that time the Company genuinely could not raise such a sum; in any case, it had no intention of doing so for this purpose. Counsel's opinion was taken, and once more the French claims were evaded, this time finally.

BOOKS FOR REFERENCE

Hudson's Bay Record Society—Vol. XX.

Ehrman, John—*The Navy in the War of William III 1689–1697. Its State and Direction* (Cambridge, 1953).

Willson, Beckles—*The Great Company (1667–1871)* (London, 1900), 2 vols.

CHAPTER XXX

ALBANY DURING THE WAR OF THE SPANISH SUCCESSION

Despite the unaccountable ending of the attempt to get a renewal of the Parliamentary confirmation of the Charter, the Company seems to have had no hesitation in keeping on with its preparations for trade under the terms of the Royal Charter to which it was now thrown back. The difficulties were financial rather than legal. The 1697 venture had brought back Michael Grimington in the *Dering* without having made contact with the English at York Fort, but Captain Man in the *Pery* had got to the Bottom of the Bay, and brought back from Albany James Knight and a cargo of skins which, at a formal cost of half-a-crown each, were estimated to be worth £5,569 18*s*. 10*d*. It was a good enough average cargo from the Bottom of the Bay, though the Committee reported the voyage not so successful as could have been wished.

The returned servants, however, could only be given a payment on account of their wages, and in order to get the beaver past the customs and available for sale the Committee had to fall back on the expedient of drawing lots among themselves, two luckless members going bail for the due payment and getting one per cent. on the six hundred pounds involved. After which, in April 1698, the Committee 'at last came to this resolution to borrow money upon their Beavor'. The solution seems to have been found when Captain John Nicholson, a member of the Committee, advanced £500, for which he was to receive 2,000 skins of *coat* beaver and 2,000 of *parchment* as security if he should not be repaid in ten weeks.

The London fur market was dead in 1698, and the Committee decided in June to take out the white beaver and the 'high seasoned skins' and to ship the rest off to the continent. Amsterdam was the entrepôt to which the shipments were made, and there the Deputy Governor Samuel Clarke and his son began to enter upon an active and involved business as agents for the Company. There, too, the Company managed to negotiate a bill for £500 on the security of its furs. As the year wore on a special clerk, John Paine, was appointed to keep the books of the foreign accounts. But they got into a sad mess all the same, perhaps because he could not keep the Deputy Governor in order; perhaps because this type of business involved a capacity which was not present in the members of the Committee. The new development involved the Company in correspondence with Bremen, Narva, Hamburg, Archangel, Amsterdam, Moscow and Leghorn, and produced in its time a many-sided series of transactions in bills of exchange. Although the method of book-keeping showed the furs brought home by the *Pery* as sold for £21,446 5s. 0d., cash was short, for almost £12,000 of this sum was due to a purely nominal sale to overseas agents, and sales in December 1698, and in March 1699, had brought in about £5,000 of the remainder, a contribution which would not be available for preparing the cargo in April and May of 1698. In these circumstances it is not surprising that a small economy should have been made in the purchase of Virginia tobacco; but the genuine Brazil commodity was also got from Oporto, and Colonel Pery went bond at the customs house for the dues. For the most part the credit upon which the cargo was prepared came from the tradesmen who supplied the trade-goods; they were still largely unpaid three years later.

Part of the difficulty at this time lay, without doubt, in the feeling that the members of the Committee themselves were not over-confident in the future of the Company; and Governor Trumbull was so much of an absentee figure-head that he was useful only when the Committee called upon him, and in himself gave no coherence or confidence. It is significant that the two great bankers, Sir Stephen Evans and Sir John Sweetaple, were both negligible lenders to the Company at this time. Although the money borrowed (at rates of interest varying from five to six per cent.) stood at about £15,000, yet the Company's weakness is in stark contrast with the strength of the East India Company. In June 1698 the East India Company agreed to lend £200,000 to the Government in return for a renewal of its charter—it may be that some such impossible condition was the reason why the Hudson's Bay Company desisted from its attempt at renewal, but this must be pure speculation. Of the vast sum promised by the East India Company, members of the Hudson's Bay Company advanced sums out of all proportion to those which they were prepared to advance for the fur trade; of known shareholders in the two companies Samuel Shephard advanced to the East India Company £1,500; Samuel Lethieullier £2,000 and Samuel Dashwood £3,000. John Merry advanced £1,000; Samuel Ongley £500, Thomas Lake £500 and Peter Hudson £1,000. Henry Kelsey was down for £2,000; but whether the explorer had a wealthy namesake, or where the Hudson's Bay employee could have got so large a sum are equally open questions.

It is clear that the Hudson's Bay men had money to invest but did not think it expedient to put large sums into the fur trade in 1698. It was a hand-to-mouth credit rather than major borrowing which saw the Company through its troubles; credit which left tradesmen unpaid and which was forced merely to agree to bail Captain Smithsend if his seamen should throw him into prison on account of unpaid wages.

Servants were almost as much of a problem as credit, and the Company had to pay out £10 to an agent for procuring men. But, although the Company was as strong as ever to 'Digg into the Bowells of the Earth' and was certain that its vast tract of land must contain some profitable mines, no miners were specially engaged in 1697. The two main personalities to go out again in the Company's service in 1698 were Henry Kelsey and James Knight, the latter to be once more Governor of Albany, with a Royal commission to support him. He was already owed £758 5s. 4d. for wages, in addition to bonds for a further £600 which he had lent to the Company, and he was able to make his own conditions for service. But as always he was suspected of private trade, and the Committee felt it necessary in his Instructions to promise that no tales from 'mercenary men' would be listened to.

Knight's Instructions were largely concerned with the need to prepare for further French attacks and for avoiding a further glut of *coat* beaver. He was to prepare to evacuate Albany if the French succeeded in their claim to be allotted the Bottom of the Bay in accordance with the terms of the Peace, while he was warned also that rumour indicated that a French man-of-war and two frigates were to be sent out—against which the Company petitioned for a convoy for its own shipping.

The trade in *coat* beaver was to be suppressed by all ways imaginable. Knight was even urged to burn some of it before the Indians' eyes, that they might be convinced how little he esteemed it, and he was to keep in the country such *coat* skins as he was forced to trade, instead of shipping them home, there to form a stock and to incur customs payments. He was if possible to raise the Standard of Trade, and he was to practise all economy in small matters such as the preservation of casks, the shipping home of sacks, cask headings and hoops, and of unserviceable goods and of men at high wages. He was also to press forward with any possible mines and with secondary trades in feathers, isinglass or castoreum (for which the Company now thought it had the Russian secret of preparation).

It was in the outcome a meagre enough outfit shipped in 1698.

It cost only a little over £3,000, and the Instructions of the year were equally uninspired, framed in view of the glut of beaver, the fear of French claims, and the general lack of confidence. Certainly the Company's credit was low, although its stock stood at a slight premium and the Company had itself to pay £672 for £600 worth of stock to give to James Knight against the £600 which he had lent on bond. Albany alone remained in the Company's hands, and it is evident that the complaints in Parliament of the meagre state of the fur trade found echoes within the Committee of the Company.

In the event it was to prove adequate that Albany should remain to the British, and that James Knight should have sufficient confidence in the Company to want to invest his savings in its stock. But Knight was sent out to command at Albany in 1698 in a far from confident mood. He was warned that there was a possibility that the negotiations with the French might result in the transfer of his post to them, and while the retention of a foothold in the fur trade was obviously essential, it was impossible to look to the future with any hope. The second loss of York was particularly discouraging; the brightest spot was that Captain Man in the *Pery* had failed to get to York in 1697, otherwise he would assuredly have fallen into the hands of the French. For the rest 'It had bin better wee had never regained it rather then to have lost it as wee did, but we must submitt to providence therein, as in all our Affaires'.

Albany for the moment remained, but even there the future was dark. All hands demanded a gratuity of twenty pounds (equivalent to about two years' wages) for staying out there in 1698, and the needs of the situation caused the Committee even to condone the otherwise unpardonable offence of private trade. Worse still, beaver were almost unsaleable in Europe, and had been so for many years. As far back as 1695 the Company had written that warehouses were full and markets dull; in 1697 they had over 70,000 *coat* beaver on hand, and in 1698 they warned Knight that the stock had risen to over 80,000. For four years running, the Committee recorded, it proved impossible to sell more than 12,500 skins, and the hardships endured at Albany (where shortage of provisions had almost ended the Company's hold) were equalled by the difficulties of the Committee.

The French seemed to have good reason to hope that, seeing no possible salvation, the English company might completely abandon the Bay. But although the revenue from sales had indeed fallen to about five thousand pounds a year, and Knight was sent out as Governor with the expectation that he would negotiate some sort of settlement of claims with the French 'to his content and our expectation', there was no sign at this dismal time that the Committee contemplated withdrawal. On the contrary, slight though the trading outfit was, the *Pery*, the *Dering*, and the *Knight* were all kept in active commission and the men who had earned their gratuities at Albany were told that never again should the Company's servants have to endure the like hardships.

But Knight served out his term at Albany and came home in the autumn of 1700 without any major change having occurred. The fear that the Commissioners might yet adjudge the Bottom of the Bay to the French still hung over the post, and no small ship had been sent out in 1699, as he had requested. There had been rumours and alarms, and the Indians had brought report of a wreck in the Bay. But both the *Dering* and the *Pery* made successful voyages, and Knight had kept the frigate named after himself in service, so it could only be assumed that the wreck must have been a French ship destined to set up a post at Moose. Knight had also been warned from London in 1699 that there was a rumour that an interloper had set out for the Bay, and the mysterious wreck might have been English; more probably, since no other evidence about it has survived, it was just the product of an Indian rumour. Whatever the substance, it did not upset James Knight or his trade, and the returns for 1699 were over 33,000 beaver from the one post alone, a most satisfactory trade, and more than enough for the London market.

Knight had without doubt rallied the post, had decided that it would offend the Indians to burn the *coat* beaver as he had been instructed, in order to convince them of the low esteem in which the Company held it, and had left to John Fullartine a post in whose continuance the Indians had confidence—which was the most important thing if they were to run the gauntlet of the French establishments and come down to trade at the Bay. But in 1700 there was a definite falling-off in trade, with the *Pery* bringing home only 19,000 beaver. Perhaps this was because the Company had sent out Virginia tobacco 'spun up' to imitate Brazil, but the Committee put the decline down to the 'stratagems of the French', and since two thousand pounds of choice Brazil had also been got from Lisbon it would be unwise to lay too much stress on the counterfeit. Governor Fullartine simply claimed that it had been an excessively hard winter.

Nevertheless the difficulty of selling the furs on hand decided the Committee not to send any ship at all in 1700; they considered Albany adequately provided, and that 'the badness of the market for beaver would not Answer our Charge'. The decision was based on the knowledge that the *Pery* was already in the Bay and available to bring home the furs, so that sales would not suffer (although the men might). But it left the Committee with the problem of finding some paying occupation for the *Dering*. After toying with the idea of using her in the salt trade they used her for shipping furs to Hamburg. The opportunity was not altogether lost, for the Admiralty asked the Committee to send out to the Bay an order for the trial of pirates, and the Committee took the chance to bleat that 'their sufferings in Hudson's Bay by the French, their disappointments and hard usage by the Articles of the Late peace, and the Present Discouragements they are under by being prosecuted by His Majesties Atturney Generall In A sute of Law, Lies so hard upon them, that they are not in a Capasity to send any shipp to Hudson's Bay this yeare'.

Still, however smart a rejoinder this might have been, trade dropped and it was not surprising that the returns for 1701 sank to below 15,000. Even this was something of an unwelcome addition to the stock of beaver. Marten were the prime demand of the fur dealers in London, and little else would sell. In consequence Fullartine was urged to encourage the trade in marten and other small furs, and the old alternatives to dependence on beaver, a search for minerals and exploitation of the isinglass of Slude River, were both stressed. As a step in these directions, the *Knight* frigate was to winter on the Eastmain at Slude River; there the trade in small furs might well be encouraged, while a professional miner, Gottlieb Augustus Lichteneger, was sent out with his tools, to 'make inspection into the Minerialls on the East Maine', though he was not actually to be set to work there until further orders, lest troublesome times should fall upon the Company. Gottlieb was a Saxon who had been taken to Canada as a prisoner of war by the French, and although the Committee seemed to feel both a confidence in his ability and a fear of his loyalty he remained innocuously in Albany and the Eastmain until his death in 1713 without accomplishing anything.

The fears of troubles which prevented the Saxon from being set to work on the Eastmain did not prevent Henry Kelsey from trading there. He had come to England after his capture at York Fort by Iberville in 1697 and had re-engaged for three years in 1698, being given an extra five pounds a year (to bring him up to £30) on the special recommendation of James Knight, who obviously had the highest regard for him. He must have worked in some fairly independent capacity, for he sent home separate journals; and it is most

probable that he had much to do with the loyalty to the English of
the Indians, for he was preparing a Cree Dictionary, which was sent
to England and was back in his hands in printed form in 1702. The
Committee had undertaken this pioneer work and sent it to him
'that you may the Better Instruct the young Ladds with you, in the
Indian Language'. Kelsey was now sent to trade on the Eastmain
and to winter there in the *Knight*, and the Committee fully approved
of the choice and promised itself a prosperous trade.

When Knight came home in 1700 Kelsey might well have been
made Governor instead of Fullartine, or perhaps Deputy Governor,
as the Committee realised, but he missed the appointment because he
was himself expected to come home. He would, however, profit by
the incentive which the Company now held out to its servants, to
encourage the taking of small furs. Any furs taken by private trapping by the Company's servants were to be handed in to the trade
room at the post by the last day of February—a well-chosen date,
after which the men would be wanted to start serious work in preparing the post for trade, and the Indians would soon be expected.
There would be little chance that furs got so early in the spring
could have been traded from Indians; they could only be the produce of the men's own activity during a period when they would get
very little to do around the post. The men's furs would then be
shipped home under separate marks and would be sold by the Company at its auctions, half of the sale-price going to the man concerned.
Those who concealed their furs and tried to sell them clandestinely
were to forfeit both the furs and all their wages. This was a reasonably shrewd move, though it did not prove finally satisfactory, for
Kelsey and most of the men whose contracts were out in 1701
needed more than the normal wages to induce them to remain in the
Bay at a time when the Committee was itself alleging that the French
were 'restless to ruin' the English and that the Company could 'noe
ways be Safe Unless Some Care be Taken by His Majestie for their
Security'. The Council at Albany, having heard an Indian report
that the French had set up a subsidiary post at New Severn, thought
it better to pay extra wages than to let good men go home. Kelsey
was put up to £50 a year, and others gained in similar ways.

Even in 1700 the proposed system for selling the small furs taken
by the men did not prove attractive, and in the next year it was modified so that they might keep the feathers which they got for themselves (they used them for bedding) though the Committee insisted
that the small furs must be sent home according to orders. Such a
concession was generous, for the feathers and small furs found a

market whereas beaver was 'a Very Drug' on the Committee's hands, and the Committee's hands were very full. The merits of open sales, private sales or bulk export to Europe, as well as the preparation of the outfit, all demanded attention. They had to meet twice a week at eight a.m., but all to little profit; they had managed to scrape up over £14,000 by the sales of 1699, but this fell to £10,000 in the next year and to less than £3,000 in 1702–3. So Fullartine was told to send home no beaver save perfect *parchment*, except as pieces. The pieces would not be liable for customs duties and so might well be stored in London till they found a sale; at least they would not tie up money in customs dues. Other skins except the *parchment* were to be stored at Albany until they were sent for. They had to be traded to keep the Indians loyal, and even alive; stored by the Bay they might get taken by the French, but the Committee had to keep costs to the minimum and could see no alternative. They did, however, go so far as to instruct Fullartine that staged skins, 'such as you call somer Beaver in the Northwest' should be cut up so that they might be brought home as pieces.

The possibility that the stocks of skins kept at Albany might be captured was a real danger in 1702, for war had been declared against France when it became clear that the Partition Treaties would not prevent Louis from claiming the Spanish Succession for his grandson. This was no surprise for the Company. In 1701 the Committee had put out enquiries on the continent to find out what French ships had set forth for the Bay, and they had warned Fullartine that, though at the moment we were at peace with the whole world, yet there was cause for apprehension lest, with the death of the Spanish King, war might break out with France and Spain. Apprehension, however, was not quite the same thing as the reality of open war, for the Company could now be certain that the rivalry at the Bottom of the Bay would be intensified as opportunity offered. The post was therefore to keep watch on a strictly military system, and trade with the 'upland Indians' was to be furthered by all means.

These instructions may in part owe their origin to the presence of James Knight on the Committee, bringing with him a realistic approach to the position of the isolated post at Albany. On his return to London in 1700 he had been given the £600 worth of stock which had stood in the name of Sir William Trumbull; the transfer was made in lieu of wages, and was appropriate in that Sir William ceased to be Governor—he must have been a great disappointment, for at few periods during its history did the Company wield less effec-

tive political power than during the important years in which it was
governed by this career-diplomat. Trumbull was replaced as Governor
by Sir Stephen Evans, and James Knight was forthwith elected to the
Committee. The concessions to private trapping, the wary approach
to the French, and the insistence on placating the upland Indians
were all such points of policy as Knight always urged, and the need
for precautions was further shewn by the order that the *Hudson's
Bay* should winter out as a guard-ship.

    This *Hudson's Bay* was a new ship of about a hundred and sixty
tons, which the Committee had ordered to be built in 1702 despite
the troubles and shortage of cash. They had sold the *Dering* for
£1,100 after inspection. At one time they also hoped to sell the
Pery, though in this they failed; she had made a 'long and tedious
voyage' home in 1701 and they would gladly have got rid of her.
The new *Hudson's Bay*, replacing the ship which Iberville had
wrecked at York, cost £926 17s. 4d. for building, to which the costs
of rigging and painting had to be added, so that the Committee must
have been out of pocket even taking the sale of the *Dering* into account. They valued the new ship at over £2,000, and all their hopes
for 1702 were concentrated in her. Fullartine was told that he must
bear in mind that she had been built purposely to oblige him, for
he had been emphatic in his demands, and navigation at Albany was
exceedingly difficult. The vital ship might so easily run aground
there that, in 1699, Grimington had been instructed not to take his
ship over the bar into the creek, and again in 1701 Fullartine had
been told that the *Pery* must unload 'without the Creeke' for fear
that she might be caught by a southerly wind and be unable to get
out into open water again before she became ice-bound and forced
to winter there.

    The Committee had taken the start of the war to heart, and had put
in a plea that, with only Albany on which to depend for trade, they saw
this post surrounded by the French, who came from Canada and
from Fort Bourbon, and who had now settled at New Severn; they
therefore asked for three men-of-war, a bomb-vessel and two hundred
soldiers, claiming that they could not be free from insults and encroachments as long as the French held any place on the Bay. At that
stage of the war however there was no force to be spared for such
an outlying sphere, and the Company turned to organise its own
defences. All that could be got from the government was the concession of a royal commission for Fullartine, whose office as Governor had so far lacked this authority. He had been paid as Governor
as far back as 1699, when Knight should have come home; in 1700

he was given a commission from the Company, and in 1701 an attempt was made to get such a commission from the Crown also. The attempt failed, but he was told that Counsel's Opinion had been taken and the ruling given that nothing was needed since a royal commission went by inference with that of the Company. But in time of war, and by the expenditure of £12 18s. 0d. the defect was remedied in 1702.

Although the Committee did their utmost, the government's need both for seamen and for landsmen was so great as to jeopardise the Company's position. Recruits were impossible to get even when the Company had promised to give the same compensation for death or injury as the Queen gave. After delaying in vain to get men, the ship of 1702 then had to wait further for the Russian convoy to take her up the North Sea. She did not sail till 21st July, still with an inadequate complement, and with orders to engage some ten or twelve stout young men at the Orkneys and to get some young black cattle if she should put in at any Scottish port. The year was now so far spent that it was assumed that the ship would not be able to return before winter, and Grimington was ordered to winter at Gilpin's Island. With bad weather and contrary winds, and being withal so late in the season, he did not make Gilpin's Island until late in September and it was January before Fullartine heard of his arrival, and February before a packet got through to Albany. The message was brought by Thomas Macklish, Junior, later to be Governor in the Bay for a long and formative period in the Company's history but in 1702 beginning his career as a young shipwright.

This non-arrival of a ship in the autumn of 1702 was a grave handicap to Fullartine, and when he gathered that there was a chance that he might get no ship at all in 1703 he wrote angrily off to tell the Committee that 'if the country will not defray the Charges of shipping Yearly it will soon not be worth the Keeping'. He had got down a great number of Indians to trade, many of them so Frenchified as to conduct their trade in the French tongue, and including one or two canoes of Ottawas, appearing at Albany for the first time. They brought good loads of the *parchment* beaver which he was still allowed to ship to London, and despite their heavy demands for powder, with which he was not very well supplied, he gave them the best treatment possible. The result was that when the *Hudson's Bay* came home in November 1703 she brought over forty thousand beaver. This was the trade of two years, of course, but it reflected Fullartine's zeal and skill. 'No man liveing without giving great distaste to the Indians can give less encouragement for the Coat Beaver than I do, and on the other hand I encorage the Parchment', he told the Committee.

Lest such returns should induce complacency in the Committee, Fullartine reported that the Indians consistently told him that the French had indeed set up a post at New Severn, but that it was occupied only in trade time and was little used, and that they were reported to have had a ship at Nelson River in 1702. A second ship was supposed to have been lost at sea, but the one which got to Fort Bourbon had wintered at the post, which had an abundance of goods and men and from which an attack on Albany was supposed to be threatened.

The dangers of such a situation made it difficult to carry out an important change in the Company's policy. To offset to some extent the cost of European provisions and the dependence on Indian hunters, the Committee had again taken up the policy of encouraging some sort of agriculture at its posts. By the time that war was declared Albany had a good herd of sheep and goats, and plans were afoot to send bulls and cows. In 1701 there was no room in the ship, but Fullartine was told to make hay in readiness for a shipment in 1702. Whether Grimington managed to get any Scottish cattle in that year is not clear; probably some evidence would have survived had he done so. In any case Fullartine was seriously wondering whether the whole project could be worth while. He then had a hundred and eight sheep and goats, but the goats were so small that one of his men could eat one a day, and although the sheep were not to be complained of, they throve 'indifferent well'. Moreover, the need for winter feed entailed heavy work and dispersion in the hayfields for his men at just the wrong time of year, the high summer when the Indians came in to trade and when a French attack might most be expected. His troubles were enhanced by the incapacity of his men. He sympathised with the Committee on the difficulties of getting recruits, but told them that what they had got were 'poor, Sorey, helpless fouls, and no ways fitting for the Countrey at this juncture'. There were indeed a few exceptions—perhaps the Orkneymen whom Grimington had recruited—and at a price ('the worst of them blowed at £20 a year') enough of the old hands were persuaded to renew their contracts.

But not all of those whom Fullartine would have wished to keep as a garrison would consent to stay. He was reduced to forty men, and among others Henry Kelsey came home in the *Hudson's Bay* in 1703; he had already been twice taken by the French in the course of his career and can have had little heart for a third such experience, especially since, in his position, he must have known only too well the indifferent quality of the men who would have to defend the post and the truth of Fullartine's warning that both food and powder were short. The men insisted on a ration of five pounds of flour a week, which was the amount which the Committee had ordered in 1684, when the ration was set at five pounds of flour and five pounds of meat a week. But Grimington's crew had eaten up eight casks of flour during the winter, and there was not enough in the country to honour the ration. So although Fullartine agreed to the demand he did not see how he would carry out his promise. Powder, too, was short; in accordance with his instructions Fullartine had raised the Standard of Trade for his blankets, but he had given full measure of powder, especially to the large bands of Frenchified Indians, and that 'sunk the powder', so that he had only seventeen barrels left when the *Hudson's Bay* sailed. No relief, and no extra strength, could be expected from the shipping at the post, for the *Hudson's Bay* was homewards bound and although the *Knight* was not to winter on the Eastmain she would help little at Albany; Fullartine had decided that the break-up of the river there was so unpredictable and dangerous that he must winter the ship at Gilpin's Island.

When to all these inevitable difficulties is added the firm expectation that there would be no ship from home in 1703 it is easy to understand the minds of those who decided to return with Grimington. Kelsey certainly was no coward to scramble home in fear of a French attack. But he had been out continuously since 1698, he had been passed over for promotion which the Committee admitted that he deserved, and although he must have been fully aware of the dangers threatening the post, home he came.

Fullartine's worst fears were realised, and even surpassed. Not only did he get no ship in 1703, but none was sent in 1704 either. As the Committee blandly explained, 'the Difficulties wee then Laboured under, Rendered the same altogether impracticable'. Since lack of shipping meant that there were no letters inwards or outwards for Albany for those years, and since the series of Journals preserved for that post does not begin until 1705, there is no knowing the details of the period except for the meagre information in the post's account books. A circumstantial account has been printed of an attack by the French, coming down the rivers, in 1704; but this account vouches no authority, it cannot be confirmed, and it is obviously inaccurate in that it names two different Governors for the post. Albany was certainly expecting an attack, and there had indeed been a proposal for such an attack with a force of twenty-five

Canadians, made in 1703 by the Sieur de Louvigny who had conducted an overland expedition in 1688, but the Intendant Champigny looked on de Louvigny as just another *coureur* trying to get round the restrictions, and nothing more is on record of the proposal. So while it is certainly possible that such an attack should have been made and should have been defeated, it cannot be accepted as having actually taken place, especially since the account bears a close similarity to accounts of a later authentic attack, in 1709.

The period is in fact one of which little can be known for certain. The threatened shortage of food seems to have been overcome, for on Christmas Day 1705 the issue to each mess of four men consisted of twenty pounds of flour, two pounds of bacon, eight pints of oatmeal, two pints of rice, two pounds of raisins, half a pound of currants, eight pounds of mutton, three fresh 'whavers' (wey-weys or geese) and two salt, a piece of salt beef, twelve partridges, four pounds of biscuit bread, two pounds of cheese, a pound and a half of butter, three pounds of suet and sixty fish—a reasonable bulk and variety for four men even if it had to last them a week!

The French attack, too, held off. So much can fairly be argued not only from the lack of evidence of such a venture and from the contradictions in the printed story, but also because the Albany Journals, when they begin in 1705, speak of an Indian who was at Port Nelson in winter, 1704, and who reported that the French then had two ships and an abundance of goods; his report was supplemented by a rumour from a man who was 'noted for a great Noose Munger', who said that an expedition which had set out to capture Albany had been forbidden passage by the Indians. Fullartine was sceptical of the whole story, but treated the Indians with respect in order to ensure their future co-operation. Such reports, made in 1705, would hardly have been noted without comment by a man who had himself met and beaten off the attack under discussion!

Apart from this, it can be stated that a very reasonable trade must have been achieved. When the *Hudson's Bay* next came to Albany in 1705, she was under command of Grimington's son, young Michael, who had been appointed in 1704. He was a less sure navigator than his father and, after almost wrecking his ship on the outward voyage, he also failed to get her clear of the river on the return journey before the ice set in. His late start was indeed partly due to his falling ill on board, but he also endangered his ship, and however explained it meant a year's delay. So when he brought the *Hudson's Bay* to London in late October 1706 he had the trade for three years aboard.

It amounted to over 50,000 beaver, and the annual trade of the post must have been in the neighbourhood of 16–17,000 skins, which was a very fair return from a post which had received no supplies for two of the three years, and which had started with serious deficiencies.

Young Grimington not only took a fresh supply of trade-goods but some new recruits—his father had put the Committee in touch with a crimp who was ready to 'procure servants' at the rate of twenty shillings a man—and some comforts for the men. This took the form of English roll tobacco. Fullartine had asked for Virginia leaf, but it took less room when rolled and so was shipped in that form; it was to be sold to the servants, but the Brazil roll which was also shipped was to be traded only to the Indians. The Committee had also instructed Fullartine to come home—he had requested it, being troubled with the gravel—and had appointed Anthony Beale to succeed him. Kelsey was in England, but he was again passed over although he was of much the same vintage as Beale as an apprentice to the Company and had accomplished infinitely more.

The new Governor soon gave proof of his quality, however. Fullartine handed over to him early in September 1705 and took his departure in the *Hudson's Bay*. But he then became involved in young Grimington's misfortunes. Starting dangerously late, the ship was run aground and they decided that it would be too dangerous to continue the voyage. Beale and his Council were therefore disconcerted to see the former Governor return within a fortnight of his departure, fated to spend another winter in the Bay and determined to take up his governorship again. Although Beale 'knew him to be given to passion' he stood up to Fullartine, insisted that the Company's commission placed responsibility for the post with himself, and packed Fullartine, Grimington and the ship's crew, off to winter at Gilpin's Island. He won his point both then and later, for after some delay the Committee voted him his Governor's salary for 'the yeare Captain Fullartine was forced to winter in Hudson's Bay— anno 1705'.

This contretemps merely underlined the dangerous difficulty of navigation in Albany River, for the *Knight* frigate was all this while stuck aground in the river at Bayly's Island, and when the spring brought an abundance of water in the river, it was held up by the ice still solid in the river-mouth, so that Beale feared a 'Dulage' flooding the plantation and had to make the necessary preparations.

The cattle, however, were thriving and providing fresh meat, and Beale had been sent a generous outfit. In the *Hudson's Bay's* cargo were four hundred gallons of rum—'English Spirits Distilled from Molasses'—and a supply of French gunpowder, which had a much higher reputation than the English. This was got by purchase of a prize cargo, for in 1704 a French ship bound for Canada, of about six hundred tons burthen, had been captured and the Committee had been able to buy fifty-six barrels of French powder, as well as French knives, hatchets and awls, which the Indians generally preferred. This had given them a chance to reverse a policy which Fullartine had advocated; in 1702 they had sent no hatchets or ice-chisels, since he insisted that it was better to make them at the post and got a second smith for that purpose. James Knight thought the price of the 'French prise pork' excessive, and the rest of the cargo was of English origin, at prices which compared favourably with those of the last outfit and still better with those of 1699; oatmeal which had cost eight shillings a bushel in 1699 and five shillings and sixpence in 1702 now cost only five shillings; bread which had cost sixteen shillings the hundredweight had dropped to ten shillings in 1702 and to nine shillings in 1705, and so through the whole range of provisions.

These things, however, did not take the edge off Beale's resentment at the way in which the Committee was treating its sole post. It had been 28th August before the ship had arrived at Albany—late enough to cause alarm—and even so Beale wrote that the Indians themselves were upbraiding him for the Company's niggardly outfit of one ship every two or three years. He said he had lost a great trade, especially in small furs, from the lack of goods in 1704, and he threatened that he would only stay to command if there would be a yearly ship, a proper commander for the *Knight*, and adequate men to defend the factory. It would also be far safer if the Company were to entrust the outfit to two small ships instead of to one great one. He concluded that continual disappointment had made all the men sick of the country; and he had only twenty-seven left when the *Hudson's Bay* sailed.

The Committee were not seriously alarmed at the non-return of the *Hudson's Bay* in 1705, assuming that it was due simply to her late arrival in the Bay. Preparations were early in hand for an outfit in 1706, and the *Pery* was prepared for the voyage, with orders to stay at the post and to work on the Eastmain. Here she was to be under the command of Henry Kelsey, now employed again. He had re-engaged in 1705, on terms which gave him £100 a year on his arrival in the country. This was equal to a Governor's salary, but Kelsey was not made Governor. He was to be Chief Trader at

Albany or at any other post where he served, was to act as mate on board ship, and was to have ten shillings a week 'Lying by money' until he sailed.

But the *Pery* was so late in arriving, on 1st October, that Kelsey was unable to take her on to the Eastmain. She had, in any case, damaged her rudder and run aground. Beale, no longer expecting a ship, had already unbent the *Knight's* sails and laid her up, so that there was no ship for the Eastmain. So Kelsey took a couple of hands and went off to spend the winter hunting, to keep out of the post and to save provisions. Other parties were likewise employed, examples of the way in which the English by this time could take such a way of life as natural. It was, however, a poor winter for such a venture; owing to lack of snow it was difficult to hunt and the post was plagued by an abundance of starved and cannibal Indians. The Indians, too, found that faulty guns led to starvation and they were disturbed to find summer beaver 'so much a Druge' that Beale was in constant fear of trouble with them. To end it all, spring came late at Albany, with fears that a sudden deluge would set everything afloat and perhaps jeopardise both ships. When the river broke up the two ships were indeed flung up a great way on land, and great efforts were needed to get the hunters in the marsh to safety.

The troubles of Beale and his small garrison were by no means over when the ships had been got afloat again and trade had started, though the *Pery's* rudder was repaired and she was sent home with the year's trade of 26,000 beaver. No ship was sent in 1707, despite Beale's desperate insistence on the need for at least one ship a year, and it was not until 1708 that ships were again sent out. This time the *Hudson's Bay* came accompanied by a new sloop of thirty tons, the *Eastmain*, designed to further the Slude River trade. They brought fifty men, and John Fullartine to relieve Beale as Governor. Kelsey, according to his contract, was to be Deputy Governor since Nathaniel Bishop was to go home along with Beale; he was to take the *Eastmain* to Slude River and to winter there with the special object of improving the trade in small furs.

At the same time it becomes clear that the Committee were almost in the dark as to the actual position in the Bay. For Fullartine was instructed that if he should find Albany captured by the French he should move to Moose and settle there. The Committee thought that if, instead, he made his post at Eastmain the trade of Eastmain would be drawn off by the French to Moose. The London gentry seem at least to have realised their limitations in this, for they openly told their Governor that 'wee Cannot be soe well able to Judg of oure Affaires in the Countrey, wee being soe farr absent, as you can Resideing there, therefore wee must Leave it to your discretion for the management of our Trade'.

As far as the French were concerned, Fullartine was to discover that the Committee were utterly at fault, and that at Albany the two years of silence had been passed in a peace disturbed only by Indian rumours which on the whole brought peace of mind rather than alarm. A canoe of Indians had come to Albany from Moose River in the summer of 1706, bringing 'a pretty many furs', and in the following March some Indians who had been at Port Nelson the previous year came in to trade and to report that the French had got no ship through for the past two years; they had seen a ship wandering in a rather lost fashion between Hayes River and New Severn, but she had not put into the French post. A little later a flotilla of canoes came from southwards up the river with reports that wars had broken out inland and that many Indians and many French had been killed. Then Beale had been told that the French at Port Nelson had withdrawn a little higher up the river, where they had built a good post; they still continued to trade at their old post, however, and a report of a new French post 'at a Lake a Little way up Moose River' proved to be a mere Indian story when Kelsey cross-questioned the Indians.

More stimulating was a report that the Moose River Indians brought, of many canoes of Indians and French gathering there, preparing to come to Albany and determined to burn the factory. As yet, by the time of Fullartine's arrival, this was but an unconfirmed Indian rumour over which a year had passed without fulfilment; but the general situation was such that a raid of this nature ought to be expected at any time, and there was plenty of reason to deter the English from following the Committee's advice and moving over to Moose, where a new post would be right in the path of a descent from Canada.

If the Committee were ignorant of affairs by the Bay, they knew their own business well enough, and Fullartine was warned that he must send home no coat beaver at all, 'noe not soe much as any peices'. A change in the customs administration had made useless the practice of cutting up the stage or summer beaver; every beaver had to pay a shilling and fourpence customs on entry into England, and that must have almost doubled the Company's outlay for each skin. It was better to keep the *coat* and *staged* skins in the country until the market mended, but *parchment* was still in demand and Fullartine was urged to send it home.

The summer of 1709 saw the French attack take place. A Canadian force of a hundred men worked its way down from the Ottawa River to Moose River, to the French post (St. Louis) there, with the intention of emulating the exploit of de Troyes and Iberville in 1686. Like that exploit, and so many of the French attacks on the Bay, this venture if successful would have presented the diplomats with a *fait accompli* as they discussed peace in Europe, for negotiations to settle the long-drawn-out war were just beginning. But although the French now had posts in the Bay at which they could re-form to launch their attack, they found the English ready and on watch. Early news of the French was brought by an Indian. The men were alert, disciplined and exercised in the use of their arms. Albany had been strengthened by the addition to its staff of a gunner at fifty pounds a year, and the Committee had sent out five mortars, five hundred shells for them, and sixty barrels of musket powder so that Fullartine was reasonably well prepared for the attack, especially since he had been told not to dissipate his forces in exploration until the war was over.

As the French came along-shore to land about seven miles from Albany, so as to work through the woods and effect surprise, they were seen, the alarm was rung, and they met a hot reception, leaving sixteen men dead while not a man was wounded in the post. The only casualties inflicted by the French were when they ambushed two Englishmen who were returning to the post. Fullartine's successful defence of Albany became a classic in the history of the Hudson's Bay Company and copies of his narrative were in later years sent out to the posts to show them how to do the like if they should be attacked (perhaps because by that time Fullartine had won a place on the Committee). But in itself the operation was negligible; the only lesson to be learned from it was that watchfulness paid.

After the one assault, seeing that they had lost all chance of surprise, the French did not repeat their attempt on Albany. They withdrew by the way they had come, and thereafter the threat from the French was over. But neither the Governor and his men nor the London Committee were to know as much, and watchfulness and preparations for defence continued to be essential. Indian loyalty too was a source of strength, and when four Mohawk chiefs were brought to London in 1710, asking for help from the English against the French, they were made much of in London, were given a 'collation' of dinner and wine by the Committee and gave them their first authentic account of the attack on Albany. As a result Fullartine was told that the Company should be ready to assist them at all times.

N

But although the Mohawks told of Fullartine's success the Committee still did not know the details, because no ship was sent out in 1709 owing to the 'great hazard and the heate of the warr'. Nevertheless Fullartine was voted twenty gallons of red port, and his officers the same quantity, for their successful defence of the post; Fullartine was later to get a gratuity of a hundred pounds for the same reason.

The French, however, seemed likely to come again. In 1711 an Indian came in from Moose River to report that the French and Indians were coming in the summer with a much stronger force than on the last occasion, and that they would not this time be repulsed but would undermine the factory and blow it up. That same summer, in May 1711, the Committee again told Fullartine that if the French should have taken Albany he was to go and settle at Moose —a repetition of the instructions of 1708 which argued ignorance equal to that reigning in 1708. But such rumours and misgivings were not necessary; Indians came in from Moose to trade at Albany in 1712 and 1713, and although the rumours of a French attack were repeated in 1713 (with reports of a ship to aid the assault and of wood-runners trading, but trading hard, at the head of Albany and Moose Rivers) yet the post was set at ease by the report of an Indian who had been at Nelson River in the summer of 1712. He assured the English that the French had neither goods nor provisions and (as was subsequently proved true) that the Indians had killed nine of them for offering violence to Indian women.

The trade of Albany, meanwhile, prospered though with some uneasiness over the governorship. Fullartine returned to England in the fall of 1711 and took his place on the Committee, the second Bay-side Governor to take a seat at the Board, to sit beside his predecessor James Knight and to bring reality into the discussions and the preparation of cargoes.

Knight had been engaged to succeed Fullartine as Governor, but his health was doubtful, so again Anthony Beale was appointed, and again Kelsey was passed over. He had met with some reproof over his interpretation of his position as Deputy Governor and had been told that no-one was to be equal to the Governor; even Kelsey as Deputy was definitely to be subordinate, to act under the Governor in his presence and to act by the Governor's orders in his absence. So, although Kelsey was congratulated on his efforts in instructing the apprentices, 'Especially in the Language that in time wee may send them to Travell', he was told to act with all mildness of temper, and the Governor was given a firm veto on any proposals which he might make. On Fullartine's return Kelsey wrote to say that the departing Governor had left him in command. But the Committee replied that Kelsey having formerly written to say that he 'designed home' they had sent out Beale. So for the third time Kelsey, now obviously disgruntled and apt to lose his temper, missed his promotion. He 'lay abroad' hunting his way through the winter rather than be cooped up in the post in such circumstances, and came home at his own request in 1712.

Notwithstanding this uneasiness, trade prospered. A rumour that the English had captured Canada in 1711 was indeed based on the fact that the invasion of General Hill was set forth in that year. The rumour proved more effective than the fact for, while the invasion failed, the rumour of its success drove large numbers of Indians to trade at Albany.

Shipping to bring home the returns was, however, difficult, for not only was the Company reluctant to venture on an Atlantic voyage in war-time but it was also trying to make some sort of profit on its shipping by engaging in the coal-trade, shipping coals from Newcastle to London and other southern ports. So in 1710 only the *Hudson's Bay* was sent out. She stayed the winter in the Bay, and when she came home in 1711 she brought the very satisfactory cargo of over fifty-one thousand beaver. This was, of course, two years' trade; and it also included some of the *coat* skins which had been set aside at Albany until the market should mend. For in 1710 the Committee had written that although beaver was still a drug on the market, especially the *coat*, yet twelve thousand of the best *coat* were to be sent home, the rest of that commodity being still kept at the post.

The known difficulties of navigation in the Bay, and of the approach to Albany, were then again manifested. When Beale went out as Governor he was almost shipwrecked, and the *Pery* on which he made the voyage was lost. After a long and tedious crossing of the Atlantic, he got to the mouth of Albany River on 20th September; but it was another six days before he could get up to the factory, and even then it was only by taking the ship's long-boat. One sloop-load of goods was got out from the ship, and the next news was that she had been grounded on a sand-bank (no extraordinary thing in Albany River), and that she had been pounded to pieces by a great tide and storm. Fortunately most of the goods were later salvaged, and even some of the ironwork, and the *Hudson's Bay* was available to bring home the accumulated furs. For although the Committee complained that it was difficult to sell beaver, the whole trade depended on a constant supply. The relaxation of the order to hold the *coat* skins in the country, which had been accepted in 1710 and carried out in the shipment home of 1711 was carried further in the orders of 1711, when Beale was told that he should send home all the accumulated skins except the *staged* (or summer) beaver, which was not worth the customs dues. A further fifty-one thousand skins were therefore shipped home in 1712.

Shipping, however, remained a constant preoccupation. In 1712 the *Knight* sloop was prepared for the Atlantic crossing, in case no ship should arrive, and the captain and crew of the wrecked *Pery* were put aboard her, together with Henry Kelsey. She was ready for the voyage by the first of August, and her crew went aboard. Then she grounded in the river until the 7th—an ominous experience for those who had seen the *Pery* suffer a like fate—but she got off and made the voyage home safely, arriving northabouts, via the Orkneys and the North Sea. Then the *Hudson's Bay* arrived at Albany, and trade was brisk. Three canoes of up-country Indians who were at the post when the ship came in spread the news inland, and so much did the status of the English and their post depend on regular ship-arrivals that in the following spring the Indians asked Beale that a great gun might be fired when a ship had come, so that the Indians might know that goods were plentiful.

The *Hudson's Bay* and the little *Knight* between them took home the fifty-one thousand skins returned to London in 1712. Such really magnificent returns from the one post go far to explain the manner in which the Company persisted in spite of the apparently insuperable difficulties of these war years, of which Oldmixon, writing in 1708, said that trade was dwindling to insignificance because there was no longer the demand for beaver which there had formerly been. But the difficulties in trading beaver in Europe were real enough, and they had their results by the Bay. More economic packing and shipping were called for, and Beale was instructed to sort and trim the *parchment* skins before despatching them, so as not to waste either shipping space or customs dues on useless parts of the skins, and to pack them tightly in parcels of eighty skins each. He complied, and he refused to trade out-of-season skins at all. The old urge to trade marten instead of beaver was kept up too. Here the outpost at East-main was a source of great hope, and the English servants also were encouraged to go trapping marten and small furs through the winters, as Kelsey and others had done. Beale started up the Eastmain trade again, since no sloop had gone in 1711, but it remained his opinion that the only way to stir up the trade in marten would be to trade brandy for them. Although his successor Thomas Macklish managed to send over eleven hundred marten which his own men had caught, he also traded brandy for them and thought it the best answer to the problem.

Other trades besides marten were urged. Some white rabbits' and hares' skins were to be sent home as an experiment, as were some musk-rat and some seal skins, and the business of prospecting for minerals was again to be put in hand. But the Saxon miner having died, Beale could do nothing in this matter.

Despite everything during these years, as ever, beaver remained the staple of the Company's trade, whatever its drawbacks; and a successful beaver trade depended on weather, on French rivalry, on satisfactory trade-goods, and on reasonable men to hold the posts and to handle the Indians on fair terms. With French rivalry visibly receding, and Frenchified Indians coming to Albany to trade, the Committee tried to recoup some of the extra cost of the trade goods which was inevitable in war-time by putting up the Standard of Trade. Governor Beale found it hard indeed to be urged on the one hand to treat the Indians kindly and to encourage them to come again to the English post, and on the other hand to raise the Standard by one beaver for each gun and on other goods in proportion. He protested, but he managed most of the order. He got the extra beaver for his guns, but he reported that it was impossible to drive up the Standard for broadcloth since it was so very narrow. Whether the Committee appreciated his pun enough to pardon his failure is not recorded.

This was taking advantage of the clear failure of the French as the War of the Spanish Succession drew to its conclusion, and the same factor must be invoked more and more to explain the stability and success of the trade at Albany. For despite the presence of James Knight and of John Fullartine on the Committee, towards the end of the war neither the goods nor the men seem to have been adequate in quantity or in quality.

Recruitment of 'Lusty young Labouring men, not married' in times of war, at rates of ten pounds for the first year, twelve for the second, fourteen and sixteen for the third and fourth, proved almost impossible even with a gratuity of a pound a man for the recruiting agent. No men were available to go out with Beale in 1711, and he reported that those sent in the previous year were simple fools, but not past learning. Seven were recruited at the Orkneys in 1712, and the garrison of the post was raised to forty-eight men in that year. But although there were a few good hands, the general quality was poor. Four were punished for thieving from the warehouse—they sought 'Nothing butt what was for the belly'—and four more were set to 'ride the wooden horse' for being drunken, fractious and disobedient.

Little more could be expected, for it was reported of them that many had never been more than two miles from the fort, and their diversions within the post were not inspiring. English dogs they must have had, for the burial of an Indian boy was recorded, alongside his dog, 'a little bitch one of our breed'. For the rest, 'Burn the Pope' was celebrated each year with an enthusiasm which cannot be understood by any save a Protestant Englishman, and the Queen's birthday, Christmas and the New Year, were honoured by extra rations and toasts, the flying of the colours, and salutes to the Governor with small arms. Other diversions from the narrow and enervating routine of life in the fort came with boat-building. Men were sent into the woods to look for 'Crucked timbars' to build a new boat, and she was successfully launched in 1713.

But it was a small and circumscribed community which kept the English flag flying at Albany; the astonishing thing is that there is so little record of fights, disputes or insubordination, and no record of crimes among the men themselves, such as stealing from one another. Much depended on the personality of the men, and with the example of Kelsey before them it would be surprising if none at all of the men ventured away from the post. Kelsey had done something towards organised teaching of Cree, so that the English might have at least that much capacity for voyaging, and others wintered out besides himself, hunting and mingling with the Indians in a way which was forbidden by the rules of the post. Two such strike a prophetic note (for both were due to make a name for themselves) when in 1711 Thomas Macklish, Junior, shipwright, and George Lisk 'went to Southard in a Cannow a Traping'.

Such individuals do much to mitigate the general impression of a garrison of unenterprising and stupid wage-earners, with no interests beyond their food and their warmth. But the balance must be kept true; the enterprising minority were a heartening leaven, but they were a minority only. The right type of apprentice was hard to find, although the Committee quite realised that its success in future years would depend on training its own employees. Even when the war was over the Governor had to be warned to take the greatest care of the apprentices, since 'there are few but are Wilde that offer their Service to us for that Employment'. A trickle of such trainees was nevertheless maintained.

If it cannot be held that the Committee, whatever care they may have taken, provided adequate hands for Albany, the same conclusion must be accepted for the trade-goods. An experiment was made in the shipment of rum for the trade. This spirit, so valuable in the fur trade of the New England colonies, and obtainable even in times of war from our own West Indies settlements, seems to have been tried as an alternative to brandy in 1706 and again in 1712, but there is no report of the reception with which it met and it did not bulk large in the trade. Tobacco continued to be the one staple of the trade in which the English, with their trade privileges in Portugal, had the pull over the French, and Brazil tobacco continued to be bought throughout the war although in 1708 it had to be supplemented by Virginia leaf and roll. The cost was not great, something in the neighbourhood of £10 a roll, and the quantity varied from four to thirteen rolls a year, but the expenditure of this small sum gave the English traders a great advantage since the Indians were so addicted to the Brazil weed; and the expedients to which the Committee were put to to get this tobacco are at once a proof of the importance which they attached to it and of the knowledge of European trade which, in their private capacities, the members of the Committee could put at the disposal of the Company. The 'Choice Brazeil Tobacco of the Sweetest Smell and of a Small Role about the size of a man's little finger' (the smallest it could be made, since the tobacco was traded by length, not by weight) was sought in Lisbon, in Hamburg, in Amsterdam and in London. Price did not matter; 'Note that wee desier the Best Tobacco therefore doe not Limit you in the Price' they wrote to Colonel Pery, who had talked with tobacco importers and had brought the information that the best small twist came from Pernambuco but that the Company had only bought Bahia twist which would not stand the delays necessitated by shipping. Pery, who had trade connections in Lisbon, normally bought the tobacco, but for purchases in Hamburg, Amsterdam or even Dunkirk Samuel Clarke, engaged in his own trade to those parts and with a son there resident, usually acted for the Company; and on occasions even the Governor, Stephen Evans, placed the order with London importers. The Committee were even prepared to buy twice their needs, in case one supply should be held up in delivery by the war, and their willingness to pay any price was not only due to their insistence on quality but also to the sheer necessity to get supplies. In 1708, for example, they bought an extra fifteen hundredweight at Dunkirk in case the Lisbon order might be delayed, and then a further thousand pounds

'Lett it cost what it will' so long as it could be got to London in time for shipment.

The Committee certainly realised the vital importance of Brazil tobacco and did their utmost to provide it to the traders—and succeeded in so doing. But other trade-goods failed lamentably. The best evidence for this is the letter which Beale wrote home when he took over from Fullartine in 1711. When he had seen the Committee in London he had been assured that they intended to man and maintain the post effectively, and he had been present and had seen and approved samples of the trade-goods as they were ordered. But he failed to get the servants he wanted when the *Pery* stopped at the Orkneys on the voyage out, and he found the goods lacking or not up to sample. He delivered an ultimatum to the Committee and insisted that either they must keep their promises or release him from the dangers and difficulties which lack of goods and men brought. Up-country the Indians were telling each other 'how wee be nessasiated for want of Goods', the steels and gun-flints on which so much depended were particularly poor in quality, and the supply of guns was quite inadequate. Next year the lesson was driven home; amid the general shortage he wrote of turning away sixteen canoes of Indians 'I have Nott one Gunn to trade with them Except I Run my flankers which I shall Nott'.

BOOKS FOR REFERENCE

INNIS, H. A.—*The Fur Trade in Canada* (Toronto, 1956).
OLDMIXON, J.—*The British Empire in America*...(London, 1741), 2 vols.
WILLSON, Beckles—*The Great Company* (*1667–1871*) (London, 1900), 2 vols.

CHAPTER XXXI

LONDON AND EUROPE DURING THE WAR

Even with all the difficulties attendant upon trading to a single and vulnerable post in times of open war, the Committee found that its returns were greater than normal market requirements. So much was this the case that the European market became a prime concern during these war years. The Committee had already, since 1694, had some experience of trying to sell its produce in Amsterdam, Archangel, Narva and Hamburg; on the whole the experience had not been too discouraging, and the practice became constant. Although Mr. Charles Goodfellow, the Company's factor in Russia, was specially enjoined to observe secrecy, the business must have been pretty well known in its general terms, for it served the great object of clearing the surpluses from the London market and also brought in quite substantial returns. In 1698, for example, the troubles which followed on the disappointments over the terms agreed at Ryswick were to some extent alleviated by £17,381 remitted from Amsterdam—and this was (apparently) a genuine remittance, not merely a 'book-record' of a sale caused by the transfer of the furs to the accounts of the factors. Certainly the Committee managed to draw bills against goods lying abroad, and so to get cash.

The money, however, was not always easily transmitted, and the Committee, easily took to the return trade, bringing timber, beaver-wool, yarn, hemp, and the Russian hides known as 'Juffs' back to English buyers. But even this trade was fraught with troubles. In particular it involved a double passage of the Sound, and a double payment of dues, for any trade brought from the Baltic. Here at least Governor Sir William Trumbull appears to have been of some use to the Company, to atone in a minor matter for his failure during the Ryswick negotiations. In 1697 a mixed cargo of goods belonging to the Company was on its way from Archangel on board a Swedish ship which put into Copenhagen. There ship and goods were arrested on pretence that they belonged to the city of Lubeck. But Trumbull's intervention proved successful, and the goods were restored though the Company had to pay heavily in customs dues to the Danes.

But the European market was changing in its demands. The Russian secret of combing the *parchment* so as to produce both

393

beaver-wool and a fine pelt had become known in western Europe by some time before 1698. Previous attempts to emulate the process in France and Holland had produced a commodity which the Committee had been able to exclude from England as detrimental to the Hudson's Bay Company and to the State of New York, since these skins had been treated 'by a fraudulent device to cut of the Beavor from the Pelt, and ymporting it under the Notion of Wool Custome Free'. Great quantities of such wool were alleged to be coming into the country, and the Skinners' Company joined with the Hudson's Bay men to protest. The Dutch part in the trade was, of course, purely that of middle-men, for by this time they had no direct access to beaver and had to obtain their supplies either from England or from France. But Dutch commercial skill was such that the Committee were forced to maintain constant watchfulness, and to secure the co-operation of the customs officers of London. Imports of this mock *beaver-wool* nevertheless continued even after the Feltmakers were prepared to state to Parliament (in 1698) that the true process as formerly practised in Russia was known here and was in fact done better than it had formerly been done by the Russians. Involved and full of overstatement as the official utterances both of the Company and of its opponents were on this subject, two things stood out clearly; one was that the increasing facility for making and using *beaver-wool* increased the demand for *parchment* skins upon which the process was worked and led to a decline in the demand for *coat*; the other was that despite this change in demand the Russian market remained important.

The insistence on *parchment* and the surfeit of *coat* were the constant themes of the Instructions to the Governors in the Bay at this time; they were Instructions well supported by the accounts of the sales, and they reached their climax in the order to keep the *coat*, which had to be traded in order to give the Indians goods for survival, in the store-room at Albany. But the fur trade could not easily or swiftly be adjusted to the changes in European tastes and techniques, and by the time Utrecht brought peace again—and for many years to come—the utmost the Company could do was to urge its traders to burn some of the *coat* before the Indians' eyes in order to convince them that it was valueless. But since the destination of the furs was almost incomprehensible to the Indians this achieved very little, and it was not a process on which the traders could embark freely for fear of 'giving disgust' to the Indians and upsetting the whole trade. So the *coat* continued to be traded and the ordinary commercial morality of buying to sell again on better terms was in this important matter inapplicable. The traders had to buy the *coat* so as to keep their Indians not only loyal but even alive.

The English furriers were under no such compulsion. They bought from the Company only such furs as they wanted, and at times they reduced the Committee to sore straits. In 1699, for example, the Company's warehousekeeper John Hawley, in partnership with one Thomas Zachary, offered to buy up fifteen thousand skins of the *coat* beaver at four shillings the pound. The Committee debated long over this low price and at last, considering that they had often put these skins up for auction without getting a bid, 'as also the Necessity of the Companies affaires Requiring Theire Spedy Raiseing of moneys, for dischargeing of severall sumes, which the Company are Threatned to be sued for', they accepted in the hope that in time the commodity might again come into general use (with a cheap sale to stimulate the market).

Such an incident brings forward again the problems of private sales as against public auctions. It also reveals that officials of the Company are taking an active part in the fur trade on their own account. That the warehousekeeper should have been prepared to buy to the extent of over nine hundred pounds may call for comment; but he was not the only one involved. The regular furriers bought as the market and the prices indicated. Some steady purchasers run right through the period, men like Thomas Byfield, Roger Arkinstall or Henry Sperling. Thomas Glover dropped out, and the other great mainstay of the early days, Henry Summers, died and had his business taken up by Godfrey Webster. Their deals are interesting; Richard Baker, for example, was buying to the tune of £1,200 in 1698; at times during the war he wanted only a few hundred pounds' worth to satisfy known customers, but as peace came in sight he was buying over £6,000 worth in 1712 and £3,000 worth in 1713. Almost equally important for the Company was the appearance, alongside of these steady supporters, of Samuel Clarke and John Nicholson on the Committee of the Company.

Clarke had first attracted attention as early as 1685. He had bought *parchment* to the value of almost a thousand pounds in the previous year, but in 1685 he bought a small consignment of forty pounds' worth of small beaver and cubs for export—a significant if small deal. He then pushed strongly for the expansion of the Company into the European market, became responsible for the sending of over £16,000 worth to Amsterdam by 1698, and was also engaged in bringing back to England the hemp and other Baltic produce which the Company imported in return. He was a substantial shareholder, but by no means a constant one; his holding was up to £3,000 by 1694, but was down to £700 by 1697. His knowledge of affairs in the Low Countries was such that he was one of the emissaries sent (too late to be any use) to prod the negotiators at the Treaty of Ryswick. His range was wide, and he engaged in shipments of woollens to Rotterdam, to Hamburg and to Virginia. The Committee used him freely to buy stores for the ships, to insure the cargoes, and to get the woollens, the guns and other articles for trade. He handled large sums for the Company and, except that the office had been abolished, he might almost have been called the Company's Treasurer.

Alongside this expert merchant—and certainly not less important, stood Captain John Nicholson. After serving on the Committee since 1693, in November 1701 he was elected Deputy Governor, for the Committee realised that he was a man on whom much might depend. It was accepted that, by means of a broker, he had bought all of the *coat* and *parchment* which the Company had put up for sale in May of that year, in addition to twenty thousand old *coat* 'out of time' or staged, i.e., summer skins. The terms were that he was not to sell these furs in Holland until nine months had elapsed, but that then the Company would give him the run of the Dutch market for the next eighteen months and of the English market for a year, until May 1702. The essence of the bargain was that Nicholson gave the Company over £8,000 of badly-needed cash and bonds, and that he was prepared to accept the delays and risks of marketing in Russia in return for a low price.

Other members of the Committee, and shareholders who were not on the Committee, can also be seen buying occasionally. James Knight, for example, bought over nine hundred pounds' worth of marten in 1706. But Clarke and Nicholson stand out pre-eminent in this respect. In so doing they mark the third phase in the management of the Company. The first phase was that of the courtiers and members of the Royal Society, with a small backing from City men, a period in which no great sums were involved and in which no dividends were paid. The second phase came with the changes following on the resignation of Shaftesbury and his followers, a phase marked by the domination of City men, by some dividends, increasing rivalry with the French, and by some elusive element of pro-Stuart Popery within the Committee. The third phase came with the growing importance of men who were actually engaged in the fur trade themselves. The presence on the Committee of James Knight and John Fullartine, with their knowledge of conditions at Albany, was matched by the presence of Clarke and Nicholson, with their knowledge of European markets.

Of the two men, Clarke pinned his faith to the Dutch market and Nicholson to the Baltic. Both outlets for beaver seemed to be badly needed by the Committee during the war years. But such was the close connection between the private ventures of the two men and the work which they did for the Company that both trading accounts ultimately got into a hopeless muddle, and it is not improbable that this could have been foreseen and that the ventures were only undertaken because the strong personalities, obvious knowledge and considerable fortunes, of these two committee-men coincided with difficult market conditions in London.

The Committee alleged, in a Parliamentary petition of 1698, that the cause of the beaver sticking in London was a combination of the skinners and other persons, which caused them to seek some means to 'ease themselves of their Burthen of Coat Beaver'. But the trouble continued too long for such a simple explanation to hold; it was part of war conditions, aggravated by the change in technique which made the *coat* unwanted in the west. Normally the *parchment* sold reasonably well, but even that was apt to stick at times and had to go for export; and whereas in 1700 and even as late as 1710, *parchment* was selling at five shillings the pound or better, by the end of the war it was down to something between three shillings and sixpence and four shillings the pound. Although the *parchment* had its uses in England and western Europe, so that the Russian market (either direct or reached through Holland) merely took off the surplus, there was now little use for the *coat* in the west, but Russia seemed still ready to absorb any quantity, provided the price was right.

The trade to Russia, however, was in a queer state and the Muscovy Company was in even more trouble than the Hudson's Bay Company when its charter came up for discussion in Parliament in 1697. The Hudson's Bay Company, so jealous of its own privileges, was ready to urge its friends to vote in Parliament that for the other comparable company anyone should qualify for admission merely by the payment of five pounds. This proposal failed, but when the Muscovy Company had been confirmed in its control, subject to allowing individuals to trade under licence, the Committee pressed the two Hudson's Bay members who were able to do so (Colonel Pery and Robert Nicholas) to take up their freedoms of that company. But even with two members of the Committee so well placed, two others actively engaged in the trade, and others (such as Knight and Fullartine) experienced and knowledgeable, the Company ran into trouble.

At Amsterdam the agent Isaac Simpkinson delayed remitting the sales-money to England under pretext that Samuel Clarke owed him money, and he refused to transfer his agency to another merchant until the Company had threatened to post him on the exchanges of London and Amsterdam. He was at last brought to book by the intervention of Clarke, but by 1710 the important Amsterdam trade was showing a loss instead of a profit, and the Committee decided to close that account.

In Russia also Charles Goodfellow caused much criticism by his bad accountancy, and even when his accounts were acceptable the money came through but slowly. An alternative to the direct employment of Goodfellow (who became Consul at Moscow) was tried in the use of the firm of Bland and English as agents. But although plans were laid to send out the Company's own ship the *Hudson's Bay* in 1707, to bring back a cargo of hemp, the Russia trade did not prosper. It was decided that there was little likelihood of advantage to be got by sending the *Hudson's Bay*, and the furs were disposed of, instead, to John Nicholson. At this time the Company's own shipments abroad went chiefly to Hamburg, but the Russian trade was still active and a very substantial cargo of over twenty-two thousand skins was shipped to Archangel. For Hamburg was more of a supply-depôt than anything else, and shipment was 'Chiefly done to Ease our markett'; there was little sale there and the use of *coat* to make hats 'in pelt' had largely been superseded there as elsewhere by the ease with which *beaver-wool* for felt could be got from *parchment*. From Hamburg the furs were shipped back to Amsterdam, where sales could still be made in 1709 and 1710 although there was danger of a glut and the agent had to be warned to let no-one know how much beaver he had by him. The French supply of furs to Holland had dried up by the end of 1709, so the Committee decided to keep its Amsterdam agency going despite falling prices since it provided an outlet for even the old *coat* beaver and allowed remittance in cash of the money of which the Committee stood so urgently in need. Early hopes that Amsterdam might even prove a means of selling English beaver to France were not fulfilled, but by 1711 Amsterdam had very nearly got rid of all the furs which had been accumulated at Hamburg.

The Russian trade had its own peculiar difficulties even after the agents had been called to book. The shipment of return commodities might indeed bring a double profit, but hogs-bristles, dressed hides, potash, tallow and yarn had to be marketed. This required knowledge and time, and the best market was not always in England. For a short time the Company found itself involved in a complicated trade routine in which furs were moved about from Hamburg to Narva or Archangel or Amsterdam. Russian hides were shipped as far afield as Leghorn, and substantial bills of exchange came from Hamburg although sales there were slight. But the two principal return commodities proved hard to master.

Hemp required special handling and used great shipping space for small weight, while it had to be sold in competition with a strongly organised ring of naval contractors, almost exclusively to the Royal Navy, which paid in Navy Bills due at a future date and liable to a discount if the holder were forced to sell for ready cash. *Beaver-wool* also was not easy to market, though at times it could be sold at the Company's auctions. It had to come by direct shipment from Archangel in order to escape a heavy customs payment, and one consignment came to London via Hamburg (thereby incurring customs) and was then shipped back to Hamburg again for sale. Moreover, the sale-price of the beaver did not always balance out well against the purchase price of the other commodities. So, what with delays and difficulties, the Company by 1709 was requesting that the debts of its Russian agents should not be invested in goods but should be remitted in sound bills of exchange. Potash, dressed hides or hemp were accepted as alternatives however, and so difficult was the business of remittances from Russia that a loss of over £700 was made by over-valuing the rouble, a loss of over a thousand pounds by shipping dressed hides to Hamburg, and smaller losses elsewhere. Special enquiries were made as to the possibilities of a barter trade, but the basic trouble was that the debts could not be collected in Russia.

By 1710 the Committee were writing to Messrs. Bland and English at Moscow to tell them that, far from improving on the trade of Goodfellow, they had merely accumulated further bad debts instead of good bills of exchange, and that the Russia trade had proved to be 'A Looseing account to all the Concerned'. The Company owed money to its agents, and the law of debt in Russia was such that it stirred the 'Truly Compassionate' hearts of the Committee. One man had been thrown into prison there, and both the person and the estate of the debtor were liable to distraint, 'by Imprisonment, or Sales of their Persons and families'. But the money could not be recovered, and by the end of 1711 the Committee was 'Sorry to understand there is soe Little Justice to be found in the Countrey. God Almighty Change the hearts of all men to doe that which is Right'.

The troubles over debt-collection and remittance of money were vastly increased by the methods which the Company adopted for the Russian trade. It was soon clear that the agents had muddled the Company's account with that of Captain John Nicholson, and for this the Committee was itself in part to blame, for it was too much to expect distant agents to distinguish over 'our goods, sent to your Place under Captain Nicholson's management' while in London it proved impossible to tell how much of the cash, or of the bad debts, should be ascribed to the one account or the other, especially when Nicholson himself died in 1710.

Nicholson had certainly bought and paid for considerable cargoes of furs at different times, as far as the normal practices of book-keeping would indicate. But even the apparently genuine purchase of over £8,000 worth in 1707 was later re-allocated 'Being for Beavor sent to Russia in his name anno 1707, and Charged to His account, when should have been charged to the voyage, it being the Companies effects sent Thither'. Since Nicholson had brought back much of the proceeds in the form of hemp and other goods, and had taken pay-ment in the form of Navy Bills, Transport Debentures and other post-dated securities, the business of sorting out the profits and losses became quite inextricable. So, although his widow was told that the account outstanding between the Russian agents and her late husband was really the Company's affair, by the end of 1713 the Committee came to a short solution by writing off some sixteen hundred pounds which, it alleged, the Nicholson estate owed.

Samuel Clarke, no longer Deputy Governor but an influential member of the Committee, had been to the fore in the attempt to straighten out the Russian accounts. But his own intervention in the trade to Amsterdam left that account in just as incomprehensible a state. The muddle had been revealed as early as 1703, but by 1714 it was still not cleared up. Important sums were involved; in 1703 the value in England of the beaver which he had shipped abroad was over £39,000, and he was refused any settlement and denied his payment for attendances at Committee-meetings until his state-ments were presented, while a loan of £1,000 which he had made to the Company was impounded and he was refused permission to sell his stock. But by 1713 the mystery was still demanding attention and the Committee was trying to get a clear statement before a new set of books should be begun. The accounts could not be put into a regular form until Clarke had submitted his returns, and although Clarke, old and nearly blind, wrote in the most affable terms offering arbitration, no decision could be reached. Here again the utmost which the Committee could accomplish was to berate the Amsterdam agents and to write off the deficit on the account.

So the difficult but stimulating attempt to trade direct to the continent ran through the war years, an attempt dependent on the knowledge that the *coat* beaver which could not be sold in London had its uses in Russia, and that the Russian market could be reached either through Holland or by direct shipment. It was a strange experiment, and one which reveals a very great deal of the structure and interests of the Company. Above all it was an experiment which, with its muddled accounts, bad debts, delayed payments and complex trade, nevertheless got the beaver moving and brought in cash and trade-goods.

ARTICLE FOR REFERENCE

RICH, E. E.—'Russia and the Colonial Fur Trade'. See *Economic History Review* (Cambridge, 1955), Vol. VII.

CHAPTER XXXII

THE FRENCH AT FORT BOURBON

Against all expectation, the troubles of the Hudson's Bay Company during the war years were not due to a shortage of beaver arising from the fact that they had only the Bottom of the Bay in their possession. On the contrary, whatever their complaints of their sufferings by the Terms of the Treaty of Ryswick, their main difficulty was to dispose of the embarrassing quantities of beaver which they obtained. The French, with Nelson and Hayes Rivers and their own post at Fort Bourbon in their possession, had for the first time an uninterrupted chance to get the magnificent furs of the 'Baie du Nord'; and yet the result of their enjoyment of this chance was that the French-Canadian fur trade finally and definitely ran itself out of the range of competition with the Hudson's Bay furs.

By the time that the war was over, and the Terms of the Treaty of Utrecht were under discussion (from 1709 to 1713) the French fur trade was hopelessly stagnant and the French hat trade had lost its export markets. The whole industry was overwhelmed by a dead-weight of surplus furs, accumulated over many years and for the most part rotten and unsaleable, and at the end of the war some attempt had to be made to set both the French fur trade and the French hatters' craft on their feet by imports from England—of English cloth for the fur trade and of English beaver for the hatters. This astonishing result from the period in which the French controlled the Nelson River trade goes far to explain the terms which the French were prepared to concede at the end of the war. But in itself so remarkable a failure requires explanation.

When French plans for the recapture of Nelson River were maturing in 1696 the basic trouble of the French system was already evident. At that time proposals were afoot to take the beaver trade of Canada out of the hands of the *fermier* of the Domaine d'Occident (at that time Louis Guigues) and to set up a new company of professional fur-merchants to handle the trade. But among other objections to the plan the chief was that such merchants would not take over the six hundred thousand or so of old skins which the *fermier* had on hand. The system of working the fur trade by means of the *fermier* and the *Compagnie du Nord* had produced a great mass of unsaleable skins even before Port Nelson was taken by Iberville, and it was to continue this process even more disastrously for the years during which Fort Bourbon lay in French hands.

The *ferme* itself had been held by Jean Oudiette for an annual payment of 350,000 *livres* from 1675 to 1685. He had therefore been forced to dispute with the *Compagnie du Nord* for the control of the furs which resulted from its capture of the Hudson's Bay expedition to Nelson River in 1682 and had ultimately compounded for shares in the *Compagnie*, in which he became the principal holder. His successor as *Fermier Général*, Jean Fauçonnet, held the *ferme* for two years only, until 1687, to be followed in rapid succession by Domergue and then by Louis Pointeau. The latter, when he handed over to Guigues in 1693, had amassed the dead-weight of 850,000 pounds of old beaver, which he passed on with the *ferme*.

The trouble was two-fold. The *fermier* farmed the whole revenues of the French West Indies as well as of Canada. The West Indies paid so well that financiers were prepared to stand a loss on Canada; and the prices of beaver at which the Canadians could sell to the *fermier* were so fixed that it was certain he would make such a loss. This, indeed, gave to the *habitan* a purchasing power in excess of the true value of his produce; to some extent it subsidised Canada at the expense of the West Indies. But it also led him to produce furs in such qualities and in such quantities that he ruined his own trade.

The price set at the start of Oudiette's *ferme* in 1675 had been four *livres* and ten *sous* the pound, whatever the quality of the beaver. The natural result was a spate of the *parchment* (*sec*) and the southern and summer furs which were most easily produced from Canada. In 1677 the prices were therefore adjusted, the *coat* (*gras* and *demi-gras*) going up to five *livres* and ten *sous* and the *sec* down to three *livres* and ten *sous*, with the intermediate grades at four *livres* and ten *sous*. The *fermier* was compelled, as part of his bargain, to buy all the furs brought to his warehouse at Quebec, within fixed times, at these prices. In return he got, apart from the payment of the *Quart* of beaver and other revenues, the monopoly of buying all the beaver of the colony for shipment to France.

The adjustment of prices imposed in 1677 failed to work a remedy. Fauçonnet left a surplus of over a hundred and thirty thousand pounds of beaver to his successor, and Domergue left over twice that amount. Faced with 'almost a million pounds' of such furs when he bought out Pointeau in 1693, Guigues insisted that the root trouble was that the *habitans* wanted four million *livres* of purchases in Europe when Europe only required three millions of their furs. So the *fermier* held the surplus furs and was forced to advance money to the *habitan* by the forced purchase of that doubtful security.

Guigues attempted two remedies. By a further revision of prices in 1695 he tried to make the production of *gras* more attractive; and he then also set to work to increase the consumption of beaver in France. He secured a crippling import duty on all foreign furs so as to give him the virtual monopoly of the French market and then he set about organising it. By buying the right to inspect all beaver hats in France—the Marque des Chapeaux—he got into his power the authority to insist on the manufacture of hats of pure beaver, without admixture of wool, rabbit fur or other impurities. Further, he then set up his own felting-shops in the Faubourg St. Antoine outside the city limits of Paris, used his authority to make the hatters declare the origins of their alleged beaver (much of which was either false or smuggled), and went a step further in the integration of the fur-felting industry by setting up a factory for hats, employing trained members of the Hatters' Company with their workmen, and made an arrangement with the retailers by which they would sell his hats for him.

Guigues' scheme cost him vast sums, and it failed because the retailers made more profit from fraudulent hats than from his true beavers, and so drove his goods off the market. He never seemed likely to push his wares into the export market of Spain and her colonies, and his efforts to stimulate French consumption left him with no capital or energy to take up the extra supplies which the enthusiasm of Iberville made available.

In fact, in 1696 the proposals made by a company of merchants to take over the fur trade from Guigues were based on the assumption that neither he nor anyone else would ever manage to dispose of the past accumulations, and that three-quarters of them would have to be burned. Those proposals came to nothing, and in 1697 Guigues renewed his control for a further twelve years. But he was not in a position either to bid for, or to welcome, the trade which Iberville had captured in that year.

Iberville, in re-taking Nelson River, had been acting as the direct emissary of the French Crown, not of the *Compagnie du Nord*, still less of the *fermier*, and when the victory had been won the disposition of the trade had still to be settled. The *Compagnie du Nord*, divided between French and Canadian interests with Oudiette holding the largest single share, was offered the right to control the trade of Fort Bourbon on condition that it repaid to the Crown the cost of Iberville's expedition. But the Canadian members, to whom the proposition was made, declined to commit the Company, though they hoped the King would maintain the post during the war and would hand it to them at the peace. In making this decision they brought out some essential features in the French problem. For they asserted that they could not possibly maintain the trade at Bourbon. Navigation in the Bay was too difficult and dangerous; they had no pilots or ships' masters, and the post was too far removed for them to be able to supply it overland from Canada. But if the Bottom of the Bay, or even Labrador, could be secured to them, they would undertake the trade there for the next twenty years. And from the Bottom of the Bay and their Canadian territories they could interrupt the passage of the Indians going down to trade in Nelson River.

These were old and fundamental reasons in the French mind. They were the matter-of-fact reasons which carried weight with the Canadian membership of the *Compagnie du Nord*. But if the French theorists and politicians would take the lead then the Canadians would take an eighth share in a new company formed to exploit the opportunity of Fort Bourbon.

A new company was in fact attempted, but although the members offered better contract prices for Canadian beaver than Guigues was prepared to accept (they offered the prices agreed in 1695 whereas Guigues wanted further differentials between the *gras* at six *livres* and the *veusl* and other varieties at three *livres* or less), Guigues got the contract. The trouble was that the 'Nouvelle Compagnie' did not amount to more than the five or six leading merchants of Canada, and that neither the Governor (Frontenac) nor the Intendant (Champigny) believed that they would keep their bargain and maintain the prices agreed in 1695. So, although there was still some room for manoeuvre in settling the prices, the administrators asked for support for Guigues and the certainty which he implied, since the discussions and uncertainty had already so upset the trade by 1698 that the *habitans* were afraid to trade for fear of a drop in price, and the Indians were becoming hostile.

Discussions over prices took the uncertainty through 1698, with the 'Nouvelle Compagnie' alleging that much of the accumulation of old furs would have to be burned and with the *habitans* and Guigues quite unable to agree over a proper price for the *sec*. The *habitans* in the end suggested that the *fermier's* monopoly should be ended and that they should form a company to pay him his *Quart* and a customs payment, after which they should be free to ship the furs to France themselves, and to get what price they could for them there. Guigues was ready to accept this offer, but the Intendant realised that the necessity was to give the *habitans* always greater purchasing power than his furs would produce on the open market, and intervened to plead that Guigues should be maintained in his monopoly, so that the *habitans* could buy goods and the Indians could be kept loyal.

But although Guigues added the manufacture of cloths, stockings and other garments of mixed beaver and other wools to his hat-factory, and sub-contracted his hatting industry to the brothers Coquelin, hatters, the sheer quantity of beaver beat him. Beaver was no good for cloth-making or knitting, and he could find no use for it. So, with merchants in Canada pressing for revision in prices, and ready to back their judgment, he was anxious to hand over. In 1699 he sub-let the *ferme* to Simon Prieur; but the amendments in prices had still not been adopted, so Prieur found that the unsaleable skins still poured in. The only real remedy was to stimulate consumption in France, but the alternative was to accept a take-over bid from the colonists themselves.

Convinced that what their staple trade needed was the devoted attention of a skilled merchant, the colonists agreed with a certain M. de Rhodes to act as their whole-time agent in selling beaver. They were then prepared to take over the whole accumulation which Guigues had piled up, including what he had in his turn taken over from Pointeau; but at the same time they wanted to control the whole of the *ferme*, including the *Quart* of beaver and the trade of Tadoussac. They were ready to agree to the payment of two hundred thousand *livres*, payable over a period of ten years, to settle for the old stock of skins.

It was at this stage that the trade from Fort Bourbon came into the arrangements. For Prieur alleged that the scale of prices to which he was tied was so much to the advantage of the *habitan* that both Acadia and Hudson Bay had joined in and had brought their furs to Quebec and sold them to him; he had been forced to buy over two hundred thousand pounds of beaver when he already had over four times that amount rotting in France, and he pleaded that trade to the Bay, and to Acadia, should be controlled since otherwise he would be overwhelmed. Also, he alleged, traders to the Bay would challenge the precarious economy of Quebec by wanting to ship direct to France, thereby increasing the glut of furs and adding nothing to the Canadian economy.

Not only the *Compagnie du Nord* had fought shy of the trade to Bourbon in 1697. The *fermier* and even the King himself had been scared by the expense involved in shipping and in maintaining the post. Frontenac estimated that the commitment would involve two ships, fifty sailors, a garrison of thirty men and officers, and in the end the trade had been offered to Iberville on condition that he paid the Canadians whom he had recruited for the capture, and cancelled his own claims. This meant finding the sums of thirty-five thousand and twenty-seven thousand *livres*. But Iberville, still being pressed to account for his expenditures, undertook the commitment on condition that he got the English goods which he had captured in the post, and that the grant ran to cover the trade of 1699. He was at this time in high demand since his services were needed for the enterprise of Florida, and he was able to set off the one venture against the other.

Odd though it may seem in face of the complaint that the *fermier* was in danger of being overwhelmed by the furs from Hudson Bay, Iberville was sure of his market, for the *fermier* was threatened by a glut of *sec* and Iberville was easily able to sell the fine *gras* which came from Bourbon. The estimates of the amounts involved vary greatly. The trade of 1697 was alleged to amount to over forty-four thousand *livres*; the correct figure should be forty-two thousand due on nineteen thousand nine hundred skins delivered by Iberville at La Rochelle. In 1698 he was alleged to have got forty-seven thousand skins, and in 1699 fifty thousand. By then it was still not clear that the French would either manage to retain the post or would wish to do so, for the rival claims of the Bottom of the Bay were being advanced. But it was certainly clear that the trade from Bourbon could be lucrative, needed to be controlled so as not to undermine the stability of the Canadian economy, and threatened the basis of the calculations upon which the *fermiers* undertook their responsibilities. The dangers were brought out by two enactments of 1700. In the one it was made permissible for Canadian fur returns, from the beginning of 1699, to be shipped to alien lands as well as to France, so long as the dues were properly paid. In the other the colony, as such, took over the whole of the beaver trade.

The need for access to the European market was clear, and the risks which the colony ran in undertaking its own marketing were seriously increased by these circumstances. Nevertheless the colony went ahead. Guigues could only hold to his bargain on the assumption that he could get the colonists forced to accept impossibly low rates for their beaver, and when his offer on prices had been rejected in 1699 he was content to sell to the colony the remaining ten years of his grant. The colonists were content to take over all his furs, including those in Holland, and those already consigned to Amsterdam or elsewhere. So long as they paid the due of the *Quart* in kind at Quebec they were to have freedom to ship their furs to France or to alien lands, and the *fermier* was not to sell his furs in competition with them.

Since the *fermier* had already agreed to sell all his furs to the colonists the last clause may seem unnecessary. But it was designed to safeguard the furs from Canada against competition with furs got from Fort Bourbon, which lay outside the scope of this take-over. There the legal situation was that de la Chesnay had sold his share in the *Compagnie du Nord* and of its rights to trade in the Bay to the *fermier* Oudiette. These rights, however, were only for twenty years from 1682, and they laid upon the *Compagnie* (and upon the *fermiers* as purchasers of a share in the *Compagnie*) the duty of defending the posts. Since the King had re-captured the posts in the Bay it was held that this duty had not been carried out and so all rights had lapsed and the King had the right to grant the trade there to whomsoever he willed; and he had actually granted it to Iberville, to trade in his own name. Iberville sold his Bay furs to the *fermier*, and in theory the latter remained free to continue buying even after he had sold his *ferme* of Canada to the colonists. The Bay trade therefore needed to be brought under the control of the colonists if they were not to find it a powerful rival.

Accordingly the colony, forming a *Compagnie de Canada* (sometimes called the *Compagnie du pays*, the *Compagnie des Castors* or the *Colonie de Canada en général*) for the purpose, not only undertook to carry on the beaver trade of Canada for the remaining ten years of the grant to Guigues but also made itself answerable for the costs of the trade to the Bay in a way which the *fermiers* had avoided. The *Compagnie du Nord* pleaded the costs which it had incurred in the past so that it might claim some compensation; but neither that *Compagnie* nor the *fermier* was anxious to undertake actual trade— merely to claim a compensation which was not forthcoming. The *Compagnie de Canada* entered upon its purchase with a cargo of goods shipped in 1700, the money having been put up by a group of Quebec merchants. The grant of the trade of the Bay had not then, in October 1700, been definitely granted to the *Compagnie de Canada* but that formal step was achieved in January 1701 and the Bourbon trade was then knit into the body of the fur trade of Canada.

The post which was then taken over was making substantial returns, but it was in an unpromising state. When he sailed for France at the end of autumn 1697 Iberville had left his brother de Serigny in charge of the captured post, more because the *Palmier*, which de Serigny commanded, had lost her rudder than because he had any experience as an Indian trader—for de Serigny's career had been almost exclusively that of a naval officer. Nevertheless the trade of the post was maintained (by the use of the trade-goods taken from the English) and the returns were sold to the *fermier* by Iberville at the high prices (five *livres* five *sous* the pound) for *gras* which had been set to discourage the normal preponderance of *sec* in the Canadian trade. In 1698 Iberville got a ship and sent out for the *Palmier* a spare rudder and some additional crew, for she was heavy to handle in the ice. De Serigny then handed over command of the post to his cousin and lieutenant Jean Baptiste Lemoyne, Sieur de Montigny, or de Martigny, and took the furs and the redundant Canadians to Quebec. He left a garrison of a sergeant and twenty men, with their officers, and a trading establishment of ten Canadians under the instructions of Nicholas Jérémie, lieutenant and interpreter, and later commander of the post.

The difficulty and cost of a sea-approach were still worrying the French, although there were those who maintained that apart from ice-floes navigation in Hudson Bay was no more difficult than elsewhere, and in 1699 the French were seriously pressing for an exchange of Fort Bourbon against the Bottom of the Bay. This went so far that orders were even drafted for de Serigny to sail once more to Nelson River, put all the French garrison and goods aboard his ship, and to hand the post over to the English, intact save for its arms. But the French government had not got the urgent appreciation of the time-table for sailing to the Bay which the London Committee felt. The order was too late, in the third week of June, and already Iberville had taken action. Assuming that it would then be too late for the English to send to the Bay, and therefore that his grant of the trade for 1699 would stand, he had sent off a small frigate with trade-goods in the second week of June.

The proposed cession of Bourbon in 1699 in any case came to nothing. Iberville's ship brought out the returns in 1700 and the *Compagnie de Canada*, taking over the fur trade from the *fermier* in that year, found that it had not only to find some thirty-three thousand *livres* of trade-goods to send a ship to Bourbon but also had to buy almost forty thousand *livres'* worth of beaver from Iberville and de Serigny. Moreover, the new company found that the post which Iberville handed over needed re-building and that rumours of an English plan to set up a post on Severn River (there is nothing of this in the Company's records) made it necessary to establish a subsidiary French post (Fort Phélipeaux) at Severn.

More serious even than these commitments was the fact that the new *compagnie*, after a year's working of its trade, could not see how any profit could possibly be got from the Bay trade. Setting the value of the furs against their cost in goods there was indeed a substantial profit; but when the high costs of marine insurance, the freightage on re-shipment to Amsterdam from La Rochelle, the wages of the servants in the post, and other expenses, had been reckoned, the furs from Bourbon in 1701 cost over a hundred thousand *livres*—and that was more than half of the total expenses of the *compagnie*. The new *compagnie*, with its vast mass of old furs taken over from the *fermiers* to dispose of in addition to the returns of the year, ruefully faced the facts that the *sec* would only sell in France or in Europe for less than the assessed cost price, and that the *gras* which had hitherto been so much in demand, and which was the main contribution of the Bay, would not sell at all. The reason for this last disillusionment was partly the decline of the French hat-making industry and in part, presumably, that in France as in England the spread from Russia of the hitherto secret method of combing the skins had led to an easier and better production of beaver-wool for felting, and so to a decline in the hatters' demands for the *gras*.

At any rate, the new *compagnie* could not afford to provide its own shipping, and in response to an urgent appeal for food, clothing and munitions, a naval vessel, the *Atalante*, was sent out in 1702. But it was selling the beaver, rather than getting it, which was the trouble, especially when the agreement by which the new *compagnie* had undertaken the trade bound it not to take advantage of the freedom to ship to anywhere in Europe but to consign all its furs to the Commissioners of the colony in France. An attempt to ship direct from Canada to Hamburg in 1702 caused trouble, and the furs were brought back to Amsterdam and there sold on behalf of the Commissioners.

By 1706 it had proved impossible even to get any shipping for the Bay, and the rest of the fur trade undertaken by the colony was also in a sad state. The yearly sales of beaver, despite the fact that the French were offering their *gras* at Amsterdam cheaper than the English, barely sufficed to pay the interest on the debts which had been incurred. The colony owed 33,000 *livres* cash, and in addition the letters of credit for which it had bought the beaver of 1703 rendered it liable to produce 132,000 *livres* by the end of the year. Further, the beaver of 1704 had been bought for 200,000 *livres* and that of 1705 for 139,000 in letters of credit; the merchants of Canada and La Rochelle had taken these letters of credit and had supplied goods to their value, and although the payment was not yet due it was inevitable. The attempts to find a market for the furs which kept piling up produced only two offers—one an offer to buy all the furs on hand in France for 950,000 *livres*, which could not be accepted since the debts as they stood amounted to over a million; (actually they stood at about two millions). The other was a more complex offer coming from Sieur Louis François Aubert, a French merchant resident at Amsterdam, the man who had acted as selling agent for the furs brought back from Hamburg to Amsterdam in 1702, and who appears to have been the chief intermediary in placing the French furs on the European market.

Aubert acted in conjunction with two French financiers, Jean Baptiste Neret and Jean Baptiste Gayot, and their syndicate was accepted. They took over 1,812,940 *livres* of the colony's debts, of which 1,033,431 *livres* were due to the firm of Dumolin and Mercier who had met the colony's letters of credit on condition that they acted as monopoly agents for the disposal of the furs. Against this debt was set the accumulation of old furs. But this, it was held, could not possibly be sold except over a period of at least six years. So Aubert, Neret and Gayot, stipulated for six years' interest on the sums which they would have to advance to pay off the debts of the colony, and they asked for six years' monopoly of the trade of the colony at the very low price of thirty-five *sous* the pound and settled for a compromise at forty *sous* the *gras* and thirty *sous* the *sec*— prices which were alleged to be lower than the buying price from the Indians. The colony was to deliver the furs at La Rochelle, but Aubert, Neret and Gayot, were to insure them on the voyage and were to pay for them even if they were wrecked. In view of the need for only a small quantity of good *gras*, this trade was to be restricted to an annual output of thirty thousand skins from Canada. But it was not made clear whether the *gras* which would come from Bourbon would be in addition to this quota, and the financiers bought all the furs lying at Bourbon awaiting transport, and the sole right to trade there for the six years from 1706 to 1711 inclusive.

The whole arrangement depended on the possibility of securing exemption for Aubert and his partners from the customs dues levied in France. But the agreement was accepted by the Council of Quebec in October 1706, and by the Conseil d'Etat in the following June, and went into force. It was too much to hope that this would bring satisfaction. The only novelty in it was that it brought Sieur Aubert of Amsterdam into control. That was indeed an important point, for he, perchance, might give that essential linkage between capacity to sell and necessity to buy which had hitherto been lacking. But although in 1709 the syndicate alleged that its 'fonds actifs' exceeded its 'debtes passives' by over a quarter of a million *livres*, the calculation was a dubious one, in which the mass of old beaver was counted as an asset, and in which there were 1,544,200 *livres* of the accumulated debts of the colony still to be paid off. In the next year they were pleading that they had so much *coat* on hand that they could accept no more, and were asking to be excused from their agreement to take up to thirty thousand *coat* skins a year. Against this it was claimed that the *habitans* had already traded on the basis of the arrangement of 1706, and it was finally agreed that for a fortnight all the *coat* which should be brought to the warehouse in Quebec must be bought at the agreed price, but the rest should be confiscated.

Even this arrangement, however, could not be made to work. When the great mass of old *coat* beaver which had to be disposed of was opened up the greater part of it was found to be rotten and useless, so that the syndicate had to plead to be allowed once more to buy the necessary quota of *coat* on the terms which had been agreed in 1706 (up to 30,000 skins a year at forty *sous* the pound). Then, perhaps because his finances could not stand the shock of writing off so large an asset, Sieur Aubert of Amsterdam went bankrupt. He left a debt of 360,000 *livres* incumbent on the syndicate, and the two remaining partners therefore found it quite impossible either to pay the debts incurred or to continue to trade. At this stage they called in again the firm of Dumolin, Mercier and Company, who had acted as agents for the colony and whom, to some extent, they had themselves bought out in the arrangement of 1706. On condition that this firm underwrote all the letters of credit which had been drawn against beaver from Canada, they were allowed to take the trade. Having satisfied themselves on these terms, Dumolin, Mercier and Company handed over the trade on the same terms to another financier, Philemon Cadet, in the summer of 1712.

So, as the peace conferences drew to a conclusion in 1712 and 1713, the vital fur trade of Canada was in the hands still of Neret and Gayot under the terms negotiated in 1706. By that agreement they had taken from the colony the duty of marketing the beaver which had been thrown upon the colony when it had acquired freedom of trade in 1699. But Neret and Gayot had been beaten by the trade. To escape from their liability to meet the letters of credit they had sub-let it to Cadet. They were in fact continued in their position, but they could make nothing of it for much of the Canadian fur was of poor quality and they were forced to pay the *habitans* more than the price at which they could sell the skins in Europe (they alleged twice as much). They had, too, a heavy bill for maritime insurance to pay, and while the *habitan* needed ready money when the skins were bought, the hatter needed credit when they were sold. At the peace in 1713 they reckoned they had lost over eight hundred thousand *livres* on the cost of shipping, and half as much again by the putrid beaver they had been forced to buy.

The whole trade was quite ruined. Neret and Gayot were indeed able to continue in their position, but they were not able to meet the letters of credit which had been drawn against them, and in 1717 the Deputy of the colony, the Deputy from La Rochelle, and other merchants involved, had to work out a solution. At the same time the Canadians were not getting adequate purchasing power and were accused of trading large quantities of furs to the English of the mainland colonies, who had the goods and the shipping which the Canadians needed. Lastly, the fur trade in France itself was near collapse. The glut of *coat* which had marked the years 1709–10 had been disastrously ended when the trade in *coat* had been held up so that the mass of old skins might be sold. As it became obvious that the great mass of furs was putrid it became equally clear that there was not even the means for giving the French hatter the proportion of *coat* (one-third) which he needed to mingle with the *parchment*. So France ended the war suffering once more from a surfeit of *parchment*.

For this Fort Bourbon, in war conditions, could offer no remedy though the post, as taken over by the colony in 1700, was driving a good trade. For it proved to be a liability rather than an asset, and it contributed to the glut of *coat* beaver which came to a head in 1709. Its difficulties are underlined by the fact that Neret and Gayot claimed that in addition to the other losses on their contract they had lost over two hundred thousand *livres* on the trade of Bourbon alone. Such excessive trading from Bourbon was achieved without any constant or generous contacts with the post. Shipments appear to have been spasmodic but fairly adequate up to 1707, when Jérémie (from whose narrative the information comes) went on leave to France. He spent the winter there, and recruited a fresh garrison to take back with him when he returned in 1708, having in the meantime been appointed Governor. His ship, however, failed to make Nelson River in 1708 and he was forced to winter at Placentia. Then, although he had only so short a journey to face, it was late in 1709 before he reached his post.

He found his garrison sadly distressed—as well it might be since no ship had got through for two years, but Jérémie's return, as commander, brought a knowledgeable and wise trader. Yet his period in command was utterly useless to the French trade since not a single ship got to him until the war was over. Indeed, his situation was made worse by the fact that although he only came on from Placentia in 1709, his ship arrived so late and so badly battered that she had to stay to winter. His garrison with this addition numbered eighty men, and although they ate 90,000 partridges and 25,000 hares during the winter, the inroads on European goods must still have been considerable. By 1712 he had not enough powder and shot to hunt game with guns, let alone to trade to the Indians, and a party which he sent out to hunt the caribou with the Indians found them suspicious and jealous. Seven of the French were massacred, and Fort Phélipeaux was pillaged by the starving Indians, so that the French spent the winter at Bourbon afraid to go out and hunt for the food which they so sadly needed.

The 'Compagnie de Castor' had sent out a ship in 1712, but it had failed to make the voyage, and so few were the competent Bay-pilots in France that in 1713 the Compagnie pleaded that the services of the same captain (Rousselot) might be allowed for a further attempt since he was the only French captain who knew the difficult navigation involved. Rousselot was not released for this purpose in 1713, but in that year at last Jérémie received a shipment, of delicacies and about eight thousand livres of trade-goods. Then, such was the capacity of Nelson River and so trade-starved were its Indians, that he traded over 120,000 livres of furs.

This came too late to save the French trade, and the purposeful bargaining of the English representatives at Utrecht secured the whole of the Bay to the English and so prevented such argosies from being repeated. So, to give the French hatters the gras which they needed, Neret and Gayot asked, and got, permission to import ten thousand pounds of gras from England or from Holland. Once the hatting industry had been put on its feet again with this supply, it was hoped that the furs from Canada would keep a constant traffic going. But even the Canadian trade needed revivifying in 1713, and for this Neret and Gayot had to ask permission to import three hundred pieces of English cloth. There was no other way to prevent the Indians from taking their furs to the traders from New York and Albany, for even the French took furs to the English in order to get cloth to trade for yet more furs.

The French hoped that once they had tied the Indians to trade with them by offering them genuine English cloths they would then be able to trade French cloths made in imitation. This was to prove a delusion, especially as the rum of the British West Indies became more and more a commodity of the New England fur trade as the eighteenth century ran its course. But even without rum, the doom of the French-Canadian fur trade was already written on the wall. During the years when the long-coveted trade of Nelson River lay in their hands their lack of ships and of skilled captains, their system of farming the trade, and their need to assess prices so that the Canadians might buy more goods than their beaver was worth, had all combined to ruin the trade. Some remedy might have been found if the trade from Bourbon could have been made to balance the preponderance of *sec*, or if an adequate market could have been found in France, subject to controls. But the unbalanced returns from Canada came to a France where the hatters were quite unable to accept delivery or to pay cash; the hard bargaining of the European market centred at Amsterdam could not be brought into line with the controlled prices at which the furs were bought in Quebec.

So although the beaver trade was to remain the principal (and most interesting) occupation of Canada for the remainder of the French régime, and French threats and French enterprise were to be held up against the Hudson's Bay Company, the trade was always henceforth (as it had been hitherto) out of balance. Neither in the marts of Europe nor in the Bay did the French ever again offer a serious economic rivalry to the Hudson's Bay men.

BOOKS FOR REFERENCE

INNIS. H. A.—*The Fur Trade in Canada* (Toronto, 1956).
JÉRÉMIE, Nicolas—*Twenty Years of York Facotry 1694–1714* ... edited by R. Douglas and J. N. Wallace (Ottawa, 1926).

CHAPTER XXXIII

THE TREATY OF UTRECHT; THE END OF A PERIOD

The protracted negotiations which led to the final agreement of the Treaty of Utrecht in March 1713 must, then, be seen against the facts of a fur trade in which the English Company was steadily meeting its liabilities, driving a trade which was profitable although the financial structure of the Company was such that no dividends were available, and was persistent in its claims. The French were everywhere weaker, with less easily substantiated claims to the posts from which they traded, and indeed with very grave reason to doubt whether those posts were, on a straight fur-trade analysis, of any advantage to France, finding it impossible either to market the annual catch of furs or to pay off the debts and letters of credit incurred in earlier years.

These factors would affect the negotiations in so far as conditions in the Bay and in the fur trade were known, and were allowed weight as against the major issues of the war, the immediate problems of Europe and of the Spanish Succession. And in contrast with the balance of interests when the terms of Ryswick had been signed in 1697, the affairs of Hudson Bay were both known and appreciated in 1713. From the point of view of both Whig and Tory parties, the War of the Spanish Succession had become a war for overseas possessions and for overseas trade. Despite some change of emphasis, the discussions of peace terms were not materially affected by changes in the structure of the British government, and by neither party were the Company's interests and claims so slighted and ignored as they had been at Ryswick, when William had decided that his interests in Europe dictated the acceptance of clause VIII. By this 'all Places should be put in the same state as before the Breaking out of this War', and so the French were given a *de jure* right to Albany and the Bottom of the Bay at just the time that Iberville gave them a *de facto* right to Fort Bourbon and the trade of Nelson River. Though from the Company's point of view one of the best things about the Treaty of Ryswick was that its terms were never enforced, yet it had a great effect on Company policy.

It was largely due to the otherwise useless Governor Trumbull that the Company owed the constant campaign against the terms of

Ryswick which ran throughout the years up to Utrecht. From the start in 1697 the Company placed its long-term claims to satisfactory boundaries and territorial rights higher than claims to pecuniary adjustment. This does not mean, however, that the claims to damages were allowed to lie dormant. The position was that adopted in its first memorandum, when the Company set out its claim to damages and added that though the bill might be disputed yet 'if we are not Intituled to a Specifick and a Numerical Satisfaction, Yet we may Claime an Equivalent in a full Restitution to all our Rights and Properties and a Just Secureing of us in them for the Future'. On that basis the Company's pretensions to Fort Nelson, its Deduction of Rights, its series of Memorials for Justifying its pretensions, its answers to the French memorials, observations, claims, assessments of damages and Memoranda to the Commissioners, began to flow in an endless stream.

The constant pressure meant that by the time terms of peace came again to be discussed no-one in authority could plead ignorance of the Company's claims, neither the Council nor the Lords of Trade, nor Matthew Prior and the other diplomatists. Among these Marlborough ranked high, and he kept the Company always in mind.

Negotiations for peace were started in 1709, with the Dutch conducting the discussions on behalf of the allies, and it soon became clear that the English were in no mood for compromise—which boded well for the Company and its claims. Not only were the Bourbons to renounce their claim to the Spanish throne, but Louis XIV himself was to drive out his grandson. Even these terms were not rejected out of hand by the French, and through March and April of 1709 the conferences continued, at Struense, at Woerden and at Bodegraven, with Marlborough and Eugene hardening their terms and with the French anxious above all things to prevent the campaign from starting again until they had had some respite.

During a brief visit to England by Marlborough there seemed to be some prospect that the Dutch might conclude a peace in his absence. But by May 1709 he was back at The Hague, with express orders to insist that the 'restitution' of Newfoundland must be one of the terms of any peace. To this the French agreed, and when the British added that Commissioners must also be appointed 'to finish the affair of Hudson's Bay' this stipulation also was accepted by the French.

This stipulation, of May 1709, was in itself of no binding force, for Commissioners had been agreed upon at Ryswick, and they had never arrived at any conclusion, still less satisfied the claims of the

o

English. It is most probable, in fact, that the English terms were much harder and more definite by this time, for Marlborough had been clearly instructed to tell the Dutch that Queen Anne would accept no peace which did not include in its terms the return of Hudson Bay. It is possible that the Dutch, anxious over the European situation and their own interests, toned down this intransigent demand before it was put to the French, but it is most unlikely that Marlborough, a loyal friend of the Company who had even attended Committee-meetings and offered advice after he had sold his stock, would have departed in any way from the full demand which he was instructed to make.

In any case, the instruction to Marlborough of 2nd May, 1709, shows that by then the Lords of Trade and the Privy Council had so far accepted the Company's case as to make no doubt of the need to insist upon restoration. This was a considerable achievement, and a great contrast to the apathy and ignorance of the statesmen at Ryswick, but it was not enough for the Committee. On 2nd May, the anniversary of the Company's Charter and the very day on which Marlborough received his instructions to insist on the Company's claims, two envoys from the Company sailed from Greenwich (in Marlborough's own convoy) to put the Company's case before the plenipotentiaries. They were Sir Bibye Lake (later Governor of the Company but in 1709 new to its affairs) and Captain John Merry, M.P. They had been appointed to this task at a General Court of the whole Company in April.

Bibye Lake and John Merry were back in London by November 1709, well satisfied with the outcome of their journey to Holland. But there is no evidence of what they managed to achieve there. The Committee sent them letters to present to Marlborough, and to his secretary, Adam Cardonell, and to his colleague Townshend. These letters, and the unofficial embassy, coincided in spirit with more official views, for Marlborough and Townshend were congratulated by the Council on their insistence that Newfoundland and Hudson Bay must be restored, and were again told 'that the Crown of England has an undoubted right to the whole Bay and Streights of Hudson; and therefore Her Majesty can never relinquish that claim, and does not doubt but your Excellencies will take the proper measures to obtain immediate satisfaction in that particular and not suffer it to be postponed till the General Treaty'.

Despite such firm insistence by the Council, and despite the presence of Bibye Lake and John Merry, the Hudson's Bay problem was not dealt with in the 'Preliminaries' to the Peace which were presented to the French in 1709; the West Indies were, and New-foundland was, and there was a clause for the restoration of all captured posts and land in the colonies—but no specific mention of the Bay. The omission led to a comment from Henry Boyle, Secretary of State, who told Townshend and Marlborough that 'though the restoring of Hudson's Bay is not an Article among the preliminarys, yet her Majesty's right to it is so evident and so fully set forth in the petition of that Company . . . that her Majesty will insist at the Treaty of Peace that this Kingdome shall have full satisfaction in that demand, and that all the places and Colonys possessed by the French in the Bay and Streights of Hudson be delivered up to the English'.

The 'Preliminaries' of 1709 were, in any case, rejected by Louis. But the episode had shown that the Company's petitions and memoranda had assured it of the support of the Council and of the Secretary of State, who were prepared to make the full surrender of all French posts in the Bay one of the basic conditions of peace. This could hardly be acceptable to the Dutch, or to those English statesmen or soldiers who placed heavy emphasis on Dutch support, and the Bay helped to produce a serious rift between the Dutch and the English. When discussions were resumed in 1710, at Geertruidenberg, Malplaquet had been won, but this did not necessarily mean that there would be more favourable consideration of the Company's case, for at Geertruidenberg negotiations were left entirely to the Dutch from fear that the French might drive a wedge between the allies.

Again the Company sent its representatives to the peace conference. The Committee had been forced to borrow money to pay the expenses of Bibye Lake and John Merry in 1709, but there seemed no doubt in their minds that at all costs they must prevent the sort of 'egregious misinformation' which had marred the Ryswick negotiations, and in February 1710 Bibye Lake was sent off to Holland again. This time he was accompanied by James Knight, now a member of the Committee and unique in that he combined the status of committee-member with first-hand knowledge of conditions in the Bay.

The French (in meeting a claim from the Dutch East India Company after Ryswick) had made the point that problems of this nature must be settled between the sovereigns, not between the companies concerned, so there could be no question of the Company's representatives entering into direct negotiations with the French. They could only stand behind the diplomats, provide them with information, and 'lobby' them, and since even Marlborough and Townshend were only standing behind the Dutch at Geertruidenberg, the Company's men were clearly not in a very strong position. But when Marlborough and Townshend were instructed to watch carefully to see that the Dutch did not neglect British interests they were also told of the Company's unofficial envoys. So, as it became probable that the Dutch would set aside British claims to secure their own terms for a European frontier, the Hudson Bay dispute came more into the picture and in May 1710 Townshend was instructed to insist that no clause should be accepted which would preclude the restoration of Newfoundland and Hudson Bay to the English, with redress for French encroachments in the past. Bibye Lake and James Knight were therefore able to report to their Committee that 'they were Assured by Mr. Cardonell and Mr. Walpole that all Hudson's Bay and Streights have been Demanded of the french by our Plenopotentaries and doubted not but the same would be granted'.

It was remarkable that at this juncture the Hudson's Bay men should have had such confidence in their claim to the whole Bay, for they had not been any more clear or consistent in their claims than the French. At Ryswick the French had claimed Nelson River (not knowing that in the meantime Iberville had captured it for them) and the English had vigorously rebutted the claim, protesting their confidence in their own right even to the extent of offering that if the French would submit to the same judgment they would renounce their claim if proved wrong by Civil Law and the Law of Nations.

The Company then alleged that, on a basis of strict legality, it should claim the whole of the Bay. But as time passed the Committee were prepared to be realistic and, if necessary, to accept terms. Boundary settlements which would leave the French as active rivals in the Bay were therefore under constant discussion, although the Committee alleged that the Company 'can no wayes be Safe from the Insults and Encroachments of the French, soe Long as they are Suffered to Remaine possessed of any Place in Hudson's Bay'.

This was an uncertainty which was echoed by the French approach. Essential as the prime *coat* beaver from Nelson River had always appeared to them, yet when they actually became possessed of it, it fitted in badly with the war-time circumstances of their trade. Torn between avarice and prudence, they could not make up their minds whether they wished to claim Nelson River at the peace or not. Some French-Canadians asserted that it was essential, others that it was dangerous and unnecessary. So the years of negotiation produced a series of projects in which both sides put forward unfaltering claims, and in which both sides also advocated compromise and an agreed boundary.

The most modest proposal which the Company put forward at this time was for a boundary line running north from Albany River on the West Main and north from Rupert River on the East Main. With a southern boundary at 53° this would give the Company a strip of territory with access to the Bottom of the Bay and to the coast of the East Main, but would give everything else to the French; and even the meagre strip to be left to the English would surely be subject to French pressure despite a proposed clause which would forbid French *coureurs de bois* from ever crossing the southern frontier.

This was an element in the problem which the French had always in mind, for the English had no counterpart to the wood-runners. While the English could smugly protest that 'it shall not be the fault of the Company of Hudson's Bay, if their Agents and those of the Company of Canada do not keep within their respective Bounds' (since they had no possibility of finding anyone capable of encroaching on the French preserves among their servants) for the French the problem was serious and difficult. Embarrassed though they were by the surfeit of beaver, they were nevertheless forced to think in terms of eliminating English competition both in the Indian trade and in the European markets. Their arguments therefore turned round the question whether, with Nelson River in their possession, they could cut off trade from the Bottom of the Bay by wood-runners, or whether the wood-runners would be more easily effective against Nelson River if that were surrendered and the Bottom of the Bay were in French hands.

The advantages of monopoly in this trade, and the capacity of the wood-runner to achieve it, were so fully realised by both sides that beneath the talk of boundaries and compromise both accepted that the French aim was 'de faire seuls le Commerce en pelleteries et d'en fournir a toutte l'Europe sanz apprehendre de concurrence', and that if left any foothold on the Bay they might well destroy the English trade. The boundary proposals therefore carried little conviction; their main purpose was to show how sensible and reasonable the English Company could be. Close behind lay the conviction that only the possession of the whole of the Bay would prove satisfactory. The argument had been put as early as 1701, when the Lords of Trade had told the House of Commons that the Company 'Represent that they can noe ways be Safe Unless Some care be taken by His Majesty for their Security', and the instructions to Marlborough

and Townshend in 1709 and 1710 are the result of the long programme undertaken by the Company to convince the official British
administration on this point.

Partly because in this matter the Company was advocating an expansion of imperial trade on lines which were common to both
Whigs and Tories, partly because the succession of memoranda had
produced a conviction in the administrators as well as in the politicians, the Company's claims were still strongly pressed after the
political changes of 1710 and 1711. The Sacheverell Trial, the decline of Queen Anne's confidence in the Whig Junta, the gaining of
a Tory majority in the House of Commons, and the replacement of
Sunderland by Dartmouth as Secretary of State, all left British policy
on Hudson Bay very largely unchanged. It is true that the Tories
followed a policy which was much more openly in favour of peace,
that they were more obviously suspicious of the Dutch and more
ready to negotiate separately than the Whigs had been. It is true,
too, that the Tories had a better-formulated and more active policy
of imperial trade, which must be defended by securing the Asiento
Contract for trade to the Spanish West Indies and by possession of
the outposts of Gibraltar, Port Mahon and Newfoundland. But on
Hudson Bay their policy was in direct line with that of their predecessors in office.

Eager to end 'the Whig war', the Tories sent Matthew Prior to
Paris in July 1710, having previously inspired the French to accept
the burden of initiating the discussions. Prior, poet and statesman,
had by 1710 a competent administrative career behind him. He
knew the stage of European diplomacy, and he knew the Hudson
Bay problem too, for he had been present at the negotiations at
Ryswick. He was ready if necessary to abandon the Dutch; but he
was not ready to abandon Hudson Bay or the Tory concept of imperial trade. So it is not surprising that when the discussions moved
from Paris to Whitehall in 1711, Hudson Bay should have been one
of the matters on which the British views were known. Although in
the brief text of the 'Preliminary Articles on the Part of France for
effecting a General Peace', which the French offered in October
1711, Hudson Bay was not mentioned, Louis had in fact instructed
his envoy to cede the Bay. He was much more concerned to protect
the French rights, to dry cod and to mend nets, in Newfoundland.

While the Tories thus accepted and publicised the Whig views
on the Company's claims they also conducted an enquiry into the
situation and, just as the talks in London were reaching a point at
which the diplomats decided to hold a general peace conference at

Utrecht, the Lords of Trade reported to Dartmouth, as Secretary of State, that the Company had a good right and just title to the whole Bay and Strait. This, therefore, was the instruction with which the British diplomats went to the final conferences at Utrecht, that these rights of the Company must be secured.

This was a time at which its long campaign of justification stood the Company in good stead. For while the politicians and diplomats were resolving to support its utmost claims, members of the Committee itself faltered. Discouraged by the long-drawn-out negotiations, they allowed Colonel John Nicholson, a former Deputy Governor, to make the startling and defeatist proposal that the French should rule the whole of North America north of a line drawn westwards from Montreal, while the English ruled all south of that line. The Hudson's Bay Company should be recompensed by a grant of all the land between Cape Breton Island and Cap Rosier in the St. Lawrence. This, said John Nicholson, would be a fair exchange since 'the Canadians having got their Indians from 'em will beat 'em out of that trade entirely'.

Such an offer of withdrawal came, it must be presumed, rather from the personal opinion of John Nicholson than from the considered debates of the Committee, for it is not mentioned in the Minute Books. But something of the kind must have been in their minds in the fall of 1711, when the failure of Colonel Hill's attack on Canada set back both the peace negotiations and the British hopes of dominance in North America. Yet there was no doubt that Hudson Bay ranked as one of England's irreducible demands when the conference met at Utrecht in January 1712. The formalities over, both sides submitted terms, on 5th March, which included cession of the Bay and Strait. Here the phrasing of the English 'demand' was more carefully and purposefully drafted than was that of the French 'cession'. The French merely offered to 'yield up entirely' ('ceder en leur entier') the Bay and the Strait, using the same term for handing over Acadia and St. Christopher's. The British demanded the 'cession' of Newfoundland, Acadia and St. Christopher's, but the 'restoration' of Hudson Bay. They also included a term that the boundary with Canada must be settled and kept, and that the French must reimburse the Hudson's Bay Company for all the damages inflicted in times of peace.

The Company's case, so often argued, was that the Bay had been discovered, and trade had been established there, by the English. The French, therefore, must not now be allowed to make an act of cession, for that would imply that the lands were French possessions and so would rule out the Company's claim for damages. It would, moreover, imply that up to the date of the Treaty and cession the English were trespassers on French soil. This was not a minor point on which the Company stood alone. The Lords of Trade urged that no act of simple cession should be allowed and that 'restoration' should be insisted on since the basis of the Company's title would thereby be confirmed, and since 'restoration' would also give the Company immediate enjoyment of its property without any further trouble.

This was a sign of the active care which the Tory diplomats were taking of Britain's overseas trade. But it was so fine a point of diplomatic phraseology that in the end it defeated its own purpose. True, the point was never challenged, was accepted by the French and was incorporated in the summary of terms which Queen Anne put before both Houses of Parliament in June 1712. *'France consents to restore to us the whole Bay and Streights of Hudson.'* Such opposition as was voiced by the Whig peers (including Marlborough) was a political gesture based upon the claim that we were deserting our allies. It was not due to criticism of the terms announced— certainly not to reluctance at accepting the 'restoration' of the Bay. Protests were in any case over-ruled and the negotiations went through to a successful conclusion in March 1713. The French did not challenge the concept of the 'restoration' of the Bay, and the general concept of the boundary which should be involved in such an agreement was that the boundary to the south should be marked by the watershed, with the lands covered by rivers falling into the St. Lawrence basin ascribed to New France.

The Treaty of Utrecht has been acclaimed as marking a new phase in Britain's colonial history since the key posts which were then ceded gave dominance in colonial trade, and the exhaustion of France and of Holland emphasised British supremacy, as did the grant of the Asiento contract. There is much truth in this view, and certainly the Tories outlined, and maintained, such a policy. Gibraltar and Minorca, and the other overseas posts, were needed as guarantees of the safety of our trade. The Hudson Bay affair stands on its own in this respect, for the Tories initiated nothing; they carried on the policy which had been laid down by the Whigs. It differs, too, in that it shews clearly the lasting effect upon policy of a persistent pressure group, shaping an 'official' policy as distinct from a party policy.

It was by creating such an 'official' policy rather than by lobbying at the conference itself that the Company achieved its purpose, for the diplomats received their instructions from the Council and the Secretary of State and were not open to personal persuasions on the spot. The Company, nevertheless, was unremitting in its attendance at the conferences from 1709 onwards. In October 1711 it had appointed Sir Bibye Lake, John Merry and the banker Sir Stephen Evans to represent its interests, and for the final phases (Evans having committed suicide) had nominated Captain Samuel Jones to act with Lake and Merry 'to treat and Agree with such person or persons as they shall think have, or may be Serviceable to the Company in this present Juncture'. Such assiduous attention to the diplomats earned the Company's men the title of the 'smug ancient gentlemen'. They carried the goodwill of the negotiators with them, but it must be doubtful if they influenced the major decision. Yet the Treaty gave them all that they had ever hoped for, and alike in London and at the Bottom of the Bay the Treaty was welcomed with unstinted enthusiasm. In London the Committee prepared a Humble Address to the Queen, to thank her for her great care and goodness. That supple diplomat, John Robinson, Bishop of Bristol (and later of London) was also formally thanked for the care he had taken of 'theire Affaire' at the Treaty. At Albany Fort Governor Beale and his men, though unable to understand the terms since the announcements were all 'written in france and none here could well understand them', were nevertheless convinced that the Treaty marked a great victory for the Company. They hoisted the flag, drank the Queen's health and fired eleven guns, then 'Drunk to our Masters' and fired nine guns.

But even before the summer of 1713 was out, events were to prove that the victory was not so complete and perfect as had been hoped. Despite the use of the word 'restore' the Company could not establish its rights in time to send a Governor and a trade cargo to Nelson River in 1713, and the assessment of damages and assignment of boundaries were to linger through another generation. Yet the Treaty did indeed mark a quite uncontrovertible recognition of a title which had been in dispute ever since the Company had revealed the wealth of the Bay. Damages and boundaries might remain unsettled, but this final recognition of the English title, never afterwards disputed, marks the end of the first phase in the history of the Company.

BOOKS FOR REFERENCE

Bourgeois, Émile—*Manuel historique de politique étrangère* (Paris, 1926).
The Compleat History of the Treaty of Utrecht . . . (London, 1715), 2 vols.

ARTICLES

Clark, G. N.—'War Trade and Trade War'. See *Economic History Review* (Cambridge, 1928).
Rich, E. E.—'The Hudson's Bay Company and the Treaty of Utrecht'. See *Cambridge Historical Journal* (Cambridge, 1955).

BOOK THREE

From Utrecht to Paris, 1713–1763

CHAPTER XXXIV

THE RESULTS OF THE TREATY OF UTRECHT. GOVERNOR JAMES KNIGHT

Gladly though the Committee acclaimed the Treaty of Utrecht, it brought neither immediate nor ultimate satisfaction. The immediate problem was to get the 1713 Outfit sent off in time to make the voyage and return the same year. Here the well-established rule was that the ships must leave the Thames by the end of May if they were to stand even a reasonable chance of completing the voyage, but although the Treaty had been signed in March of 1713, and the Hudson Bay clause had been inserted as a 'restitution' rather than as a 'cession' precisely in order that the Company might the more speedily enter upon its rights, the weeks dragged by without satisfaction.

It was 15th May before the Committee were even able to discuss the terms of the Treaty upon an official basis. Then James Knight was asked if he would undertake to be Governor of the posts which the French were to surrender, and he delivered his terms to the Committee in writing on 20th May. Knight wanted a salary of £400 a year, and a proportion of any new trade which he might develop. His mind was turning emphatically to minerals, of which he wanted ten per cent. of the profits, to whale-oil, sea-horse-teeth and musk, as well as to whale-bone and whale-fins. He insisted that he must be independent of the Committee, to decide where he should winter; and he insisted on his perquisites—a fur coat of any skins he might choose as long as they were not traded with the Company's goods, a beaver coat for his bed, and 'That what I gett of the French shall be for my owne use, as Presents when they draw out of the Countrey'. His uncompromising proposals were accepted and he was given as his Deputy Governor Henry Kelsey with a salary of £100 a year, plus allowance for a servant. But by 1713 Knight must have been well past seventy years old, and Kelsey's otherwise very modest proposals included the term that 'when he returns to

England, or in Case of his Death (which God forbid) I hope to succeed him'.

With two such commanders signed on, the Committee began to prepare shipping. The *Ormonde* was bought for £550 on 22nd May; she was a frigate of a hundred-and-ten tons burthen, and the Committee decided to re-name her the *Port Nelson* frigate. But as soon as they had docked her for inspection they were forced to conclude that she could not be got ready for use in 1713. This meant that only the *Hudson's Bay* frigate and the *Prosperous Hoy* would be available for the key voyage, to take over from the French and to show English shipping power again to the Indians of Nelson River. For the *Pery* (Captain Ward) had been damaged by grounding on a sand-bank on her arrival at Albany in 1711 and had then been 'quite destroyed' in the river in the course of the winter. This had left Governor Beale with the difficult task of getting some of his returns of 1712 home on the cranky old *Knight* frigate, which he had had heavy work to keep afloat until the frost sealed her leaks. He kept the old ship going, re-decked her in the spring of 1712, and sent her to England in company with the *Hudson's Bay* in that year. The crazy old craft made her voyage safely, but on arrival in the Thames she was sold as soon as the Committee had inspected her, for a mere £110. The Committee decided forthwith to build a ship of forty tons; the order was placed in March 1713, and the *Prosperous Hoy* was ready for the voyage by late May—a tribute to the speed with which the Thames-side dockyards could work in the eighteenth century. The *Hudson's Bay* had in the meantime been dry-docked, and so these two ships were ready for the voyage of 1713.

It was, however, 13th June before they could be got off from Gravesend, and even then so many details were still unsettled that neither Knight nor Kelsey could go with them. Nor had the discussions with the French reached a point at which the ships could carry instructions for the handing-over of the French posts. The Committee were making arrangements for an emergency meeting as late as 10th July, so that Kelsey might hurry across the Atlantic if the necessary documents could be got, but despite many efforts it was mid-August before the Company could secure, and could lock away in its chest, copies of the French orders to their Governors to yield the posts, together with Royal commissions to the Governor and the Deputy Governor.

The *Hudson's Bay* and the *Prosperous* had waited so long in the hope that Knight and Kelsey, with their commissions and their orders, might sail with them that it proved impossible for the ships to return within the year. The *Prosperous*, perhaps because she was built in such a hurry, proved a slow and 'leewardly' vessel, she sprang her mast in the Atlantic crossing, and she was so late in arriving at Albany that she was scarcely expected that year. Even so, when she arrived on 8th September, she had beaten the *Hudson's Bay*, which was quite despaired of.

The result of all these delays and mishaps was that the French were given a year's respite—and they took full advantage of it. Monsieur Jérémie, at Fort Bourbon, had received no support from France since 1708, and his Frenchmen had violently offended the Indians by their conduct on the caribou-hunt of 1712. Having lost seven of his men by an Indian massacre on the hunt, Jérémie was reduced to a garrison of only nine, including his chaplain, his surgeon and a boy. They were forced to abandon their subsidiary post at Fort Phélipeaux with eleven hundred pounds of gunpowder, and they spent the whole winter, 1712–13, in Fort Bourbon, not daring to go outside. They had no goods and their trade was at a standstill, with their Indians dying round them for lack of powder and shot—for the French also bore witness to the speed and completeness with which the Indians lost their skill with the bow and arrow and became utterly dependent on the white man's weapons for their hunts. But the respite of a year, resulting from the delay in implementing the terms of Utrecht, meant that in 1713 the French were able to send out a most welcome cargo of trade-goods, the first for five years, with which Jérémie was able to trade about 12,000 *livres* worth of furs by the time that James Knight came at last to take over the post from him in 1714.

This was not the only evil result from the delays of 1713. A further consequence of the need to winter the *Hudson's Bay* and the *Prosperous* at the Bottom of the Bay was that the Committee were forced to make new arrangements for shipping the Outfit for 1714 to the posts. The *Port Nelson* was ready for service by 1714 but a second ship was needed and the *Union*, a frigate of two hundred tons, was hired by charter-party. She carried ten guns and a crew of twenty men, and she was to make the voyage at a charge of £180 a month. For the Company the financial strain was severe, for there had been no returns in 1713—on the contrary, the fact that the two ships had wintered in the Bay meant that the captains and crews had to get pay and allowances for the whole year. Moreover the cargoes of 1712, brought by the *Knight* and the *Hudson's Bay*, had proved impossible to dispose of, furs being a drug upon a war-time market. So in 1713 the Committee still had some of its previous stock for sale.

Both in 1712 and again in 1713, in view of the difficult conditions, the Committee had been empowered to sell the furs either by auction or by private sale. An open sale in April 1713 went quite well for *coat* beaver; all the *parchment* then offered was also sold, and this was followed by a private sale of all the cub and prime *parchment* to Henry Sperling in June (a sale which brought in £1,729 8s. 7d. in cash by the end of July) and by a further sale of *parchment* to Sperling in November.

To offset such sales the Company had to make good a series of losses on the trade to Russia. This trade had since 1706–7 been conducted by Captain John Nicholson, whose handling of the trade had not been over-meticulous. By September 1713 his statement showed him as debtor for the large sum of £8,021 5s. 0d., and in 1710 Nicholson had so far reversed the normal process of the Company's trade as to 'sell' to the Company seventeen casks of *coat* beaver. This purchase was still on hand in 1713, when Deputy Governor Captain John Merry was instructed to sell it for the use of Madame Mary Nicholson, the Deputy Governor's widow. Henry Sperling was the buyer, but although the transaction brought a credit of £1,012 6s. 6d. to Nicholson's tangled account, it conflicted with the sale of the furs got by the Company's own trade, for one of the conditions of sale was a promise by the Company that no more furs would be offered in London until the following May or June. Even so, the Company had to write off as a bad debt the outstanding sum of £1,618 12s. 3d.

Still, the sales of 1713–14 produced over £8,000, and the Company's credit stood well—though substantial borrowing involved a proportionate payment in interest. Cash was tight and tradesmen had to wait for payment of their accounts even to the extent that a gunsmith to whom the Company owed £150 was imprisoned for debt by his own creditors. The tradesmen in general were told that they would be paid 'in proportion to what the Company can spare', and the Committee turned 'to endeavour to raise money for supplying the Companies present Occasions' in June 1714. The solution was to borrow, but the Committee could only raise £1,200 among themselves and they were glad to negotiate a further loan of £2,000 from Robert Sherard of Lincoln's Inn—probably an investment of a client's money. The shortage of cash was enhanced, too, by the fact that the Deputy Governor was allowed to borrow £500 of the money arising from the fur sales, and the Company preferred to invest in Exchequer Bills rather than to pay its tradesmen. However, with tradesmen willing to extend their credit, and with even the officers of the London customs house content to hold a bond for £500 issued by the Company as far back as 1696, the money for the Outfit of 1714 was got together.

Knight and Kelsey both suffered from the delay, the former in health and the latter in finance. In 1712 the Company had owed Kelsey about £200 for wages, and his wife had accepted the Company's bond for that sum. But after a year in London he had spent all his arrears and had borrowed a further £25. This debt the Company brought up to £100, and cancelled the whole sum as a gratuity in settlement of all claims and demands up to the date of sailing. The two men were each given a special allowance for fresh provisions on the voyage, not only because of their own merits and distinguished services but also because they were to have companions on board, for the French company arranged that it would pay freight charges and sent Monsieur Cullier and his Deputy over to London so that they might travel out to the Bay with Knight and Kelsey. At Fort Bourbon these two would arrange the hand-over of the French posts and would ship back the Frenchmen and their goods on the Company's ships.

With so much to arrange, the Committee did not manage to get the *Port Nelson* and the *Union* off from Gravesend until 6th July, 1714—about a fortnight too late for them to be quite certain that so important a voyage could be completed, out and back to London, within the year.

Along with his Commission from the Queen and his Commission from the Company, his copies of the French Instructions from Pontchartrain to the Governor of Canada and to the Governor of Fort Bourbon, Knight also took his Instructions from the Committee of the Hudson's Bay Company. As an important, and by now wealthy, member of the Committee he must have taken a prominent part in shaping those Instructions himself, and they show his own frame of mind. He was, first and foremost, to recover from the French the full possession of the whole of the 'Land and Territories Isles and forts Seas Bayes Rivers Creeks and Lakes Lying and being in the Streights and Bay of Hudson'. For this his Commissions from the Queen and from the Company were warranty. On taking possession of 'York Fort or Port Nelson' he was to warn his men of the disasters which had happened to the Company during his own memory 'through Cowerdize and neglect', and he was constantly to train his men to the use of arms. The French were to be allowed to remove their effects, and a list of their goods as they had stood at the return to Europe of the French ship in 1713 was sent out. Knight was empowered to buy any of the French goods which he wanted for trade—and he actually bought almost three hundred pounds' worth.

After the take-over from the French, emphasis was strongly on the development of new trade, in whale-oil and sea-horse teeth; and the discovery of minerals played an important part in the Instructions, as it undoubtedly did in Knight's mind. He took out with him a set of crucibles, melting-pots and borax, with which to try out any ores he might discover.

York Fort was to be Knight's residence as Governor, and Governor Beale was ordered to send up plank from Albany to help in the rebuilding which would be necessary there; for timber came more easily to hand at the Bottom of the Bay than in Nelson River. It was upon York Fort that the Company's main hopes and interests were concentrated, but though the Frenchman had made a good trade during the winter, Knight was by no means impressed with the state of the French buildings. Their house, he wrote, was 'not half so Good as our Cowhouse was in the Bottom of the Bay'. He had never set foot in such a confused place in his life before, with not a dry place to put his head in, and with the French houses (or huts) so ready to fall down that all he could do was to heap earth round them so as to keep his men warm through the winter. He had no hesitation in deciding to abandon the French site and to build anew.

Despite the good trade which Jérémie had made during the winter, Knight found that Hayes River was subject to many defects as a centre for trade. He arrived late in the fall, and he met a hard winter; then spring brought a thaw on the upper reaches of the river before the ice had cleared from the mouth. The result was a deluge of six fathoms of water; ice carried away one flanker from the post, tore to pieces a French brigantine and knocked down one side of the trade-house itself. There was two feet of water in the upper room of the house and Knight and his men were forced to leave the building and 'gette on Trees and Stages' in the woods to get some shelter. Few Indians came to trade, to complete the disappointment. They had been so long deluded by the French that many of them had gone to trade at Albany, and the massacre of Jérémie's men played its part in keeping the Indians away from York and boded ill for future trade.

These difficulties did not affect the decision to give priority to York when they became known to the London Committee; they certainly did not affect Knight's determination to concentrate upon York in 1714. Albany was indeed to be retained as a post, but both Governor Beale and his Deputy, Nathaniel Bishop, were recalled. Beale had by 1714 been thirty-five years in the Bay since he first arrived as an apprentice, and it was nine years since he first took command at Albany. In 1713 he had been warned by Indian rumour of the prospect of a French invasion overland from the south, directed against Moose and Albany, and his last winter in command had been spent in organising constant watches. When news reached him that a French ship had at last got through to Fort Bourbon he put in hand all preparations to withstand a siege. The *Prosperous Hoy*, when she at length reached him in 1713, brought no letters, for they were shipped on the *Hudson's Bay*; but her master brought news that peace had been signed, and Beale could relax a little. It was, however, Christmas Eve before he learned that the *Hudson's Bay* had arrived safely at Bayly's Island on the Eastmain, and before he got his Instructions and letters. In the meantime he had driven a fair trade, but had found it impossible to raise the Standard 'without Giveing the Natives a distaste' for the English since French opposition had crept so near that there was a French outpost established at the head of Albany and of Moose Rivers.

Beale was superseded by Richard Staunton at Albany, a man who had already served there as warehousekeeper, and who showed a real appreciation of the problems of the trade. In the circumstances of 1714, however, he was set a task which must have proved beyond the powers of the most experienced trader. This was to 'trade hard' with the Indians from the north so as to to drive them back to York Fort to trade, but to deal easily with the Indians from the south, from the west and from the Eastmain, so as to entice them away from the French opposition. In no case was Staunton to exceed the authorised Standard of Trade, and he was also strictly enjoined never to take any damaged skins, since they paid equal customs with prime furs and spoiled the lots at the sales. These complications at Albany made it obvious that Knight had to handle a series of inter-related problems rather than the simple resumption of the Nelson River trade. Apart from the problems of York and of Albany a further element was the rebuilding of the post at Churchill. These problems, even the rehabilitation of York Fort, outlasted Knight and marked the history of the Company for the entire fifty-years' period between the Treaty of Utrecht and the Treaty of Paris. These were the great problems which the Committee had to master,—the rehabilitation of York Fort, rivalry with the French at Albany, and development at Churchill—and these issues had all to be faced by Knight in the first year of his Governorship.

Both in its initial approach to these three problems of the eighteenth century and in its prolonged and determined efforts to solve them, the Company had always to manoeuvre so that the financial competence and confidence of the London committee-men could be geared to the ability of their servants to live, to trade and even to travel in the country.

At this stage in the Company's history, when the Treaty of Utrecht had given possession of the Bay-side posts, and the main policy of the Company was based on exploiting that possession, not on penetrating to the interior, it may seem out of place to include ability to travel among the qualities which went to formulate policy, for the Hudson's Bay men could not, as a general rule, travel inland with the Indians as the French did. Their métier was to trade fairly and regularly in their posts, so that the Indians would know for a certainty what welcome awaited them and would come annually to the shores of the Bay, ordering their lives in the period between visits in the certainty of the visit and of the trade which would accompany it. Here the contacts with the Gros Ventres and the Crees which Henry Kelsey had established stood the Company in good stead, and year by year a vast concourse of Indians come down the Saskatchewan to assemble at Lake Winnipeg, and brought their furs to the Bay once it had become common knowledge that the English, with regular and reliable shipments of goods, were firmly established there.

In general this was sound policy for the Company, and it was only abandoned with reluctance when a half-century of opposition had led to the conclusion that only by counter-penetration could the woodrunners be prevented from strangling the Bay posts (as Jolliet and succeeding generations of French Canadians had seen that they could do). When this had become clear, Englishmen were sent inland to dispute control of the headwaters of the rivers. This was indeed the logical outcome of the Utrecht terms, as had been appreciated at the time. 'These limitations are not otherwise advantageous or prejudicial to Great Britain', wrote Matthew Prior in 1710, 'than as we are both better or worse with the native Indians; and that the whole is a matter rather of industry than of dominion'. The fact that possession of the coast left the interior still open to dispute had been foreseen and accepted, but the Company had neither the men, the knowledge, the equipment in canoes, nor indeed the need, to prosecute that dispute with enterprise. Lacking the means to trade inland as the French did, it lacked also the urgent necessity to do so; for a thoroughly adequate trade was brought to the Bay by the Indians.

James Knight, however, was far from content merely to occupy the posts which he found. His Instructions of 1714 had bidden him to send home the Journals of voyages 'to all Places wether you Shall Send to make Discovereys', and this was a part of his duties which Knight had much at heart. In his first year at York, heavily beset by the troubles of that place, he sent one of his men, William Stewart, off in company with a 'Slave woman' to make peace between the Crees and the 'Northern Indians' (the Chipewyans) so that the latter might come down to the fort to trade. The Crees round York had driven the Chipewyans away from Churchill River on to the Barren Grounds, and Stewart's mission was to make peace and to persuade the Chipewyans to come down to trade despite the presence of the Crees. The 'Slave woman' was herself a Chipewyan who had been separated from her tribe during a raid; she proved an admirable interpreter and an enthusiastic advocate of Knight's policy. The remainder of Stewart's party consisted of Crees, persuaded to go into the Barrens and convince the Chipewyans that they could come down to the fort in safety. It was therefore most unfortunate that the first band of the Crees to meet with the Chipewyans should have fired on them and have killed nine. But Stewart and his woman overcame even this bad start. They made a peace, they explained the kinds of furs which the Company wished to trade, and how they were to be cleaned and cured, and they took back with them to York Fort ten young Chipewyans, to learn to speak Cree so that they might act as interpreters.

Stewart was away, travelling with his Indians, for almost a year. He claimed that he had travelled a thousand miles from York Fort, and he had probably in fact penetrated between seven and eight hundred miles in a north-westerly direction, crossing 'that Barren Desarts' and reaching the good country east of Slave River and south of Great Slave Lake. It was in itself a stupendous feat, it vastly enlarged the Company's horizons and ambitions, and it brought its trade-system into touch with the Great Slave Lake area. The year after his return, in 1717, Stewart was again sent out, this time to act as interpreter and to site a post on Churchill River.

Stewart's achievement was already both great in itself and great in its promise of vital development. He had 'endured great hardships in traveling to make peace amongst the northern Indians', for which he received a gratuity and a rise in salary, but despite his obvious merits and his value to the concern, he differed from his predecessor Henry Kelsey in that he showed no administrative skill, power of command or ability to shape a policy; and his later career is obscure.

The young Chipewyans whom Stewart brought down to help in

the expansion of a regular trade from York towards the Barren
Lands were balanced by an expansion in other directions. The Crees
reported rumours of Athabaska Lake and Athabaska River beyond
the head of Churchill River, and in 1715 they undertook a journey
(without white companions) which opened up a trade with Athabaska in which the Crees acted as middle-men. From the south-east,
too, the Mandans of the Red River area came all the way to York to
trade, lured by reports of the goods there to be got as presents or by
way of trade. But Knight's main enthusiasm, with all of this broaden-
ing of contacts to west and south-west, was still for expansion to the
north, with Churchill as a depot and with reports of a copper-mine
sited within reach of the sea as a great incentive. Here was a theme
which was to dominate policy for the next half-century, and apart
from sending Stewart to survey and prepare a post at Churchill,
Knight in 1718 also sent the apprentice Richard Norton 'to winter
with the Indians to divert 'em from going too warr, and to desire 'em
to go to trade at York Fort'.

Norton set out from Churchill in a canoe in July 1717. He travelled north to about sixty degrees and then 'took a great Sweep to
the Southward of the West' and met the 'Northern Indians' (the
Chipewyans again) whom he brought in to York to trade. The
details of the journey are obscure, but the hardships suffered by Norton are beyond doubt, as were the results. As late as 1750 it was reported that although he had been so young and 'unqualified for any
great matter', so that nothing remained in his memory save the
danger and terror which he underwent, yet he had established such a
peace to the north-west of Churchill as had not been broken by that
late date.

Such ventures by canoe and snow-shoe were pioneer attempts,
speaking much for the interpretation which Knight put upon the
Committee's Instructions—as for the courage and hardihood of the
men concerned. They did much to spread knowledge of the Company's trade in the far inland territories, but they aimed to bring the
Indians down to trade, not to take the Company's trade inland. In
this they were part of the normal policy of the Company, not a departure from it; and they involved only a very small number of
servants in the business of inland travel.

More widespread, and perhaps more important, was the day-to-
day travel on the waters of the Bay. The sloops and shallops attached
to each post were a vital and integral part of their equipment, and
the intercommunication which they allowed between posts, and
with the subsidiary outposts, was as important a part of the trans-

port system of the Hudson's Bay Company as was the ability to raft hay or wood, stones or provisions, or to lighter goods from ship to shore when the ships arrived from England. A very high proportion of the Company's officers proved themselves to be capable of handling a sloop on the waters of the Bay. Both Knight and Kelsey, for example, were good sloopers and were dubbed 'Captain'. But the full-time crews and captains of the sloops nevertheless tended to become a professional class, upon whom the trade depended—often in vain.

For the ventures northwards from York Fort and from Churchill, sloops and seamen became increasingly important as the century wore on. At the Bottom of the Bay the sloops were even more vital; for the posts at Albany, Rupert River and Eastmain were knit together by their water transport, and here there was already in existence the nucleus of that 'Southern Department', unified by transport, which took shape in distinction from the 'Northern Department' centred round York Fort. Eastmain in particular was dependent on its shipping, as it had been from its foundation at the start of the century, when the trade there had been conducted from the sloop sent from Albany. The need to send a sloop from Albany was not ended when a post was set up on the Eastmain, for the sloop was still sent not only with supplies of goods but also to act as a depot for the exploitation of the isinglass of Slude River.

Knight's régime was based on a very sound appreciation of these factors, and of the importance of shipping. But it was fated to start with a disaster which threatened to wreck his essential water-transport system, for the *Eastmain* sloop was lost at sea in October 1714, on a voyage from Albany to York Fort. She foundered in the ice off the mouth of Hayes River, and the crew blamed their captain for the wreck, alleging that he got caught in the ice only because he neglected his work, broached his cargo of liquor, and was perpetually drunk. The emergency called forth vigorous instructions from Governor Knight; a ship was forthwith to be sent from Albany to the Eastmain whatever the difficulties—'Loose not the EastMain Trade, but Encourage it all you Can', he wrote. With all his enthusiasms for spreading the trade of York inland and westwards, for establishing Churchill and using it as a base for exploring northwards and searching for the copper-mine, he still kept in mind the value of the Bottom of the Bay and the Eastmain, and the need of sloops to further the whole of the Company's affairs.

In such matters, as in the whole of his governorship, Knight expected, and got, full support from the London Committee. But he showed a sturdy independence and self-reliance, which verged upon truculence at times. 'I shall Observe and follow all such Orders as I Receive from you as farr as possible I cann', he wrote home in 1716, 'but it cannot be thought that you that are at that distance can see or know altogether how things goes here so well as I do that am upon the Spott altho' I do take all the care I can to give you what Information I am able that you may not be Ignorant of the State of this country but to tye me up to Close to follow your Instructions I think it will not be for your Advantage but if you please to give me a Little Lattitude. When I were in England I promis'd you I would do what lay in my Power to promote your Interests here which I have in no ways bean wanting as yett in performing of my Duty . . . there is no Man fitt to Serve you, that must be told his Business.'

Knight wrote under considerable stress in 1716, for he knew that the Committee suspected him of extravagance and of private trade, that some members thought he was in personal touch with his own friends on the Committee, that no-one in London had any worthwhile knowledge of the Bay, and that they did not even bother to read his Journals before sending him meticulous instructions for his day-to-day conduct of affairs. He had his own local troubles too. The rebuilding of York in a country where timber had to be brought from considerable distances proved a heavier tax on his resources than he had expected, and the Company caused great extra labour and worry by sending out pitch and oakum for the roof of the new house instead of the more expensive lead which he asked for. When he had pitched his roof three times it still leaked. 'Certainly never Man mett with more dissapointment and Obstructions by one Accident or Another to go on with Your business than I have done' he wrote after the winter of 1715–16, when he had also suffered from weakness in the knees, colds, gout, fever, ague—'All together and mauld me most desperately Ill'—at a time when the spring deluge had carried away everything, the medicines were all expended, and there was not even any cooked food to be had. 'I must have gone if Nature had not been very Strong' wrote the sturdy old man.

In addition to all of this, Knight suffered the humiliation of having to trade through the year without the help of a ship from England. The *Port Nelson* had not returned from the Bay in 1715 She and the *Prosperous Hoy* had both been driven out of Albany River before they had unloaded, and had lost all their boats in the storm. The *Port Nelson* was of too deep a draught to get snug into Albany River—she was, it should be remembered, on her first voyage since the Committee had bought her, a sign of their ineptitude in some matters—but the delays which followed made it necessary for her to winter at Albany. The Bottom of the Bay therefore sent no returns in 1715. Nor did Knight from York Fort, for whereas the *Port Nelson* wintered in the Bay the new *Hudson's Bay* never made port in that year. Captain Davis turned back when within fifteen miles of Hayes River, after beating about the Bay for three weeks. He was back in England in November and the Committee had to report that there was no trade home in that year; it was a grievous disappointment and the Committee found its remedy in discharging Captain Davis 'as he deserv'd'.

Knight had no remedy save abuse—'none but a Sott or a Madman would have done it'—and for him the failure of the ship was more than a grievous disappointment; it was a disaster, made all the more intolerable because the *Hudson's Bay* had been seen and heard from the shore, she had anchored in the mouth of the river and she would probably have come up to the post on the flood tide if Davis had only allowed her to drift. With few goods to trade, Knight had to ration the Indians, many of whom had come immense distances in response to his policy in sending William Stewart and the 'Slave woman' inland. Having no guns or ammunition to hunt with on their return journey, about a third were reported to have died of starvation as they went. Knight knew well the need to fortify a post in case of the ill-feeling which such a crisis of disappointment would provoke, and he had refused to embark on a whale fishery until he had got his buildings at York into some sort of defensible state, and indeed the frightened and disappointed Indians threatened to sack the place. Then when the Indians had at last been dispersed—those from the Saskatchewan stayed longest and suffered most severely—the Englishmen were faced with a difficult and dangerous winter. English provisions were exhausted despite the greatest care, and a new reliance upon hunting and country provisions, an ability to live upon the country, was perhaps the one good result from the sorry failure of Captain Davis.

The lack of a ship forced Knight to send his sloop to Albany for provisions, and it prevented him from sending to Churchill, as the 'Slave woman' had promised he would do and as he had 'Designed' for the summer of 1716. The delay gave all the more opportunity for inter-tribal jealousies to spring into activity, and in particular for the Crees of Nelson River to oppress the few Chipewyans who had followed William Stewart and the 'Slave woman' to the post. Knight sent the Chipewyans away from the post to hunt, but they were met and massacred by Eskimos at Churchill River. He was afraid to send out the invaluable 'Slave woman' who had accompanied Stewart across the Barrens but she died in the fort during the winter and it was with great difficulty that Knight secured another 'Northern slave woman' early in 1717, so that he could to some extent repair the evils caused by the delay and was ready to send the substitute out to take the place of the first woman interpreter, to meet at Churchill with the 'Northern Indians' who 'Promised her when she was their Last that they would gett a great deal of Copper to bring down against wee Settled at Churchill River and that their would be a great many their next Spring to look for us, if any of the Indians did make there Esscape from the Iskemays'.

Knight had early decided that a trade post to the north was a necessary adjunct to the posts at the Bottom of the Bay and in the Nelson-Hayes estuaries. As early as July 1715 he had written of his purpose to 'go to the Norward, where there is an absolute necessity of Settling a trade, which I believe and am Satisfied when once done, that all the Rest of the Country will be nothing in matter of Profitt, to what will be in a few years found there'.

Churchill River was the site upon which he picked for his outpost to the north. 'I was ever of the Opinion that the Northern country would be much for the Company's advantage to have a Settlement at Churchill River and I find I were not Misstaken.' The prospects of trade there had led Abraham into deserting the Company's service and setting out on his interloping voyage, and the same prospects had led the Company to persistent attempts to establish a post. Hopes of a white whale fishery and a consequent trade in oil were as much a motive as furs in the period 1686–9, the period between Abraham's report of a 'faire River' at Churchill and the abandonment of the small post which had been destroyed by a careless fire. About ten tons of blubber had been got in the year the post was destroyed, and the Company was anxious to open up the trade once more. But war and other difficulties had prevented action being taken and in the Company's petition of December 1711, which set the tone for the Hudson Bay discussions at Utrecht, it was asserted that Great Britain paid £26,000 a year for whalebone bought from Holland, Germany and France. The Company urged that it would set up a whale fishery which would increase the skill in navigation and the number of seamen available in times of war; it claimed that it had considerable experience in whaling and that this was a trade which should be reconquered from the French; and the French were certainly aware of the prospects of trade at Churchill, though they hoped for beaver rather than for whales. Iberville, knowing of the English post and its burning, had sent a party of Canadians to explore the river in 1696 and reported that the English could trade 10,000 beaver a year there, thus tapping the hinterland of the north and west even if they were deprived of the Nelson and Hayes rivers.

So, despite its tragic history in the failure of the early Danish settlement under Munck and the destruction of the English post, Knight turned to Churchill as the answer to his need for a post to the northward. The failure of the Danes was a lesson which he took into account; 'When the Dean Capt. Monk wintred at Churchill River he lost above 100 men by his not haveing time to build Winter setting in so Soon upon him'. Knight had a flattering report from Kelsey (who had been in the party which established the Company's post at Churchill in 1689) of the plentiful supply of game which could be got at Churchill. The information, it is true, proved unreliable and Knight was 'very much Deceived by Mr. Kelsey in his information of this Place'—but Kelsey had been but a young man when he had been at Churchill before. The plans for re-settlement were therefore laid with prudence. Having been held up by the failure of Captain Davis in 1716, Knight sent home a separate Indent for a new post at Churchill and proposed himself to go there as soon as the ice had cleared in 1717. Timber was to be cut and rafted to the site of the post before the ship arrived from England so as to avoid the fate of the Danish expedition, and the second 'Slave woman' and four of the 'Northern Indians' were to be sent up in the winter of 1716–17 to warn their countrymen that a trade post would be open in the next year.

The determination to settle at Churchill was pursued in detail. The ship from London, for example, was to sail direct for Churchill, and Knight sent home the necessary information to make navigation possible. This was all despite the known lack of timber and the general opinion that the dangers from the climate were increased because 'Them natives to the Norward are more Savage and brutelike than these and will drink blood and eat raw flesh and fish and loves it as well as some does Strong Drink'. Building at Churchill would be the 'Difficultest peice of Work as ere was done in this Country'.

The motive to overcome such defects was only in small part the desire to bring the furs of the Slave Lake and Athabaska areas down to the Bay. It was in great part the desire to exploit the great mine of copper to the northward, of which the Indians spoke and of which their accoutrements gave some evidence. Both Knight and the Committee were equally seized with the hopes of a paying mineral discovery. Knight sent home in 1716 a few bits of copper and pointed out that it had never been 'run' or smelted but was 'Naturally Virgin Copper' of which the country to the north was reputed to produce a great deal. He asked the price which such copper would fetch, what the customs dues would be, and said he hoped to purchase it so as to leave a clear profit of three hundred per cent. He showed, too, a sensible appreciation of the advantages of dealing in bulk; 'For it must be the Quantity thats sent home as must do your Bussiness and not too little purchased to Discourage the Indians from bringing at a Cheap rate'.

To these hopes and plans the Committee replied in 1717 by sending Captain Ward in the *Hudson's Bay* direct to Churchill River. They hoped that Knight would already have gone there from York Fort and that something of a post would be already settled, and in reply to Knight's request for 'a Man to take my place in Case I or My Deputy should do otherways than well that knows how to Mannage the Natives and that Understands the trade', and to his suggestion that Richard Staunton (whom they had just recalled from Albany) was such a man, they now sent Staunton out to Knight. His sending of William Stewart to the northward was approved and Stewart was given an increase in salary and a gratuity. If Knight thought it necessary, the *Hudson's Bay* was to winter at Churchill; but since seamen's wages were high the Committee hoped this would not be necessary. For the main pre-occupation, that of copper, the Committee sent the news that copper from the plantations paid no customs duty, and held out to Knight the hope that 'could you procure a Quantity either in Oare or otherwise, it would turn to a better accompt than Skins'.

Captain Ward was back in London by November 1717, to report that Knight himself was in a 'tolerable state of health' notwithstanding his illnesses of the previous winter and the fatigues of making the settlement. He had been prepared for a lack of timber, but he had been most disappointed to find that there was no suitable site for a post, and that the country was 'so bare that it affords neither fish nor flesh'. He had constructed a sloop at York Fort during the previous autumn and winter (the *Good Success*), and had sent William Stewart off as an advance-guard to Churchill, himself following early in July, accompanied by the *Prosperous Hoy* which had been brought up from Albany for the purpose. But the only possible site for a post at Churchill appeared to be 'Munck's Point' where the Danes had wintered and had died. The chief advantage of this position, which was without water or wood, and to which the ships could not make a close approach, was that it was defensible. Knight, alarmed by the numbers of Eskimos in the vicinity, got immediately to work to set up palisades commanded by four bastions, and it was in command of a defensible post that Captain Ward found him—and left him well supplied with provisions.

The Indians from the north came in to Churchill to trade and confirmed the rumours of a copper-mine, explaining that the copper was an alluvial deposit in the sand at the mouth of a great river—the Coppermine. Other, and even more dazzling, prospects began to open up, too. Already in his Journal for 1716 Knight had noted that the Indians from the north spoke of a 'yellow metal' to be got. The Committee had asked for samples, and though he could not yet comply with this request Knight could now be more explicit. The Indians, he said, came from 'the west Seas' and used this yellow metal in the same way as copper, wearing it for adornment. It was brought down by a great river which flowed out to the West Sea— by the Mackenzie.

With so much to work upon, Knight left Richard Staunton in charge at Churchill and returned to spend the winter 1717–18 at York Fort. There he convinced himself of the possibility of developing the gold and copper of which he had heard, and convinced himself, too, that although the Indians denied that there was any access by sea to the copper-mine or to the gold-mine rivers, yet such a route must exist. Between them, his views that the gold-mine could be reached by sea, and that it lay on a river which flowed to the West Sea, added up to a vision of the North-west Passage. Strongly convinced of the rightness of his information, he put Kelsey in charge of York Fort and left Staunton in command at Churchill and came home on the *Albany* frigate in 1718, to put his views before the Committee.

This was a course which quite met the approval of the Committee. Knight had warned them of his intention to return and they had sent him out eight dozen of wine to comfort him on his homeward voyage. They had confidence in Kelsey at least equal to their confidence in Knight; he had been in charge of York Fort in 1717 while Knight was setting up the post at Churchill, and the Committee then, though it approved of Knight's plans, had told Kelsey that should it please God that Knight 'should do otherwise than well, wee doubt not of your Prudent Care and Industry'. Now he was officially appointed Knight's successor with a salary of £200 a year, with a commission from the Crown as well as from the Company. He was given the choice whether to continue Staunton or to appoint someone else in charge at Churchill, and he was asked for his opinion about Churchill—'whether you think that place will Answer our Charge by bringing a new trade from the northward with the Usquemaies or others or by making a Quantity of Oyle: and whether it may not be a means to lessen the trade at York Fort, and be sure you give us your Candid thought upon this Subject'. The Committee were thus not averse from taking a check upon Knight, and a similar enquiry was sent to Staunton, with particular emphasis on the question whether the trade of Churchill would come down to York Fort if the Company spared itself the cost of the extra post.

The Committee had some minor differences with Knight, too— he was suspect of some extravagance in his use of provisions, and although he was ready to take advantage of the bargains to be got when the Indians were 'all in a Hurry' and so to get an 'Overpluss' of furs, he had insisted that this was not the time to raise the Standard of Trade. He thought, too, that although the English market was sated with *coat* beaver he could not follow the Committee's instruction and convince the Indians that he wanted no more *coat* by burning it before their faces. Rumour would fly fast, and such an action would merely convince the Indians that he did not want to trade at all and would undo much of his efforts to bring them in from the north and west. He continued therefore to buy the *coat* although he promised that he would sort the pieces from the whole skins and would in future trade no more summer beaver. He had been instructed to send home only a third of his beaver as *coat*, the rest to be *parchment*, and to keep the remainder of the *coat* in the country; and although he was told that badgers, rabbits and musk rats were not worth paying customs on, he was strongly encouraged to build up a trade in martens, for which there seemed an insatiable market, not even spoiled by the fact that the French shipped 28,000 martens from Canada in 1716.

This trade in small furs, especially in martens, Knight not only encouraged; he took a personal share in it, and quite openly shipped home the furs which he had caught. Here the distinction was between furs which the Company's servants got by trading and those which they got by trapping. Knight had a past history of persistent private trade. Now he was beginning private trapping, and although the Company sold his furs at the Company's sale and credited Mrs. Knight with £52 2s. 9d. the Committee cannot have been well pleased with the example set by the Governor, and wrote to Kelsey that they had certain information that the ships of 1718 had brought home great quantities of private furs, as well martens as others.

Even his private trapping was, however, a minor complaint against Knight. On broad lines he commanded the confidence of the Committee and he sat among them as a member, the first man to bring actual experience of the Bay to the Committee-meetings in London and to talk there, explaining his views as an equal, not as a hired servant. During the winter of 1718–19 he silenced whatever opposition the Committee held and won full support for his plans for a sea-voyage, of discovery and of gold- and copper-seeking.

The result of Knight's winter in London was, in the first place, that the Committee was firmly persuaded not to abandon the new post at Churchill. It was accepted that the site had very grave defects, especially in that it involved almost complete reliance upon England for provisions. This was dangerous not only because the English garrison would be left starving if the ship failed to make the voyage —longer and more difficult than that to York or to the Bottom of the Bay—but also because the Indians could thus easily become a source of weakness instead of strength. Already in 1718 they had to be persuaded to leave the post 'least by their Stay they should prove Burthensome and So Starve themselves and us, this place being so bare that it affords neither Fish nor flesh'. Nevertheless the Committee decided that there were good hopes of the post, and they decided now to call it Prince of Wales Fort. Accordingly, on the arrival of the *Hudson's Bay* Captain Ward went ashore, formally proclaimed British sovereignty and named the fort on 17th August, 1719. Perhaps a more practical sign of determination, Kelsey was empowered to consign to Churchill whatever seemed necessary to him, regardless of the original destination of the goods.

Along with the *Hudson's Bay* two other ships left London in early June 1719. They were the *Albany* frigate—a ship specially built of shallow draught for the Bottom of the Bay when the *Port Nelson* had demonstrated the need for such a ship in 1715—and the *Discovery* sloop, a new vessel built during the winter. This was a small ship of about forty tons, costing £180, ordered in December 1718 and ready by May 1719. The *Albany* and the *Discovery* were not to be considered as part of the normal trade outfit of the year. They were forbidden to come into any post or to trade at any place where a settlement had already been made south of 64° except under stress of weather. They were to make their rendezvous at Resolution Island at the mouth of Hudson Strait, and were then to explore to the north of 64°. The captains, David Vaughan of the *Discovery* and George Berley of the *Albany*, were placed under Knight's orders except in so far as their position as ship's masters forbade it in the navigation of their ships. But if by evil chance Knight should die upon the voyage they were to carry out the projected exploration and, in particular, were to 'find out the Straights of Anian, and to make what Discoveries you possibly can, and to obtain all sorts of Trade and Commerce . . . Especially to find out the Gold and Copper Mines if possible'. They were to be most careful not to get frozen in, and having found the Strait (the North-west Passage) they were to be sure to observe the height to which the tide rose and the point of the compass from which the flood came.

The mixture of renewed search for the North-west Passage, of expansion of trade, and of search for precious metals, was of Knight's own brewing. It was a mixture in the authentic tradition of British development overseas, and Knight's instructions did not differ materially from those to his ships' captains. They were instructions which clearly represented Knight's personal views, and to him must be ascribed a great deal of the Company's new enthusiasm for such a project. The instructions had been hammered out after a series of meetings between Knight and a sub-committee. He negotiated as an equal, for he had himself been a committee-man and a large shareholder (though he sold all his stock), and eventually an 'agreement' between him and the Committee was duly sealed and locked away in the Company's chest. Knight was in fact given the full credit for the expedition which, the Committee wrote, was fitted out 'upon your Application to us', and he was in this venture rather in the position of an independent venturer than a normal servant of the Company.

In all probability the old man could in any case have had but few more years of active or influential life left in him when he set out in 1719. His own death was even to some extent anticipated by the Committee and would not in itself have altered policy. Yet not only Knight but both his ships and all of their crews perished on the voyage. They vanished in the waste of arctic waters. Nothing was immediately known of their fate; they simply did not return to any post, and gloom and despair settled on the garrisons.

This major tragedy ended for more than a generation the attempts to expand to the northward or to seek the Passage upon which the Company was beginning to embark in 1719. The loss of Knight's convictions and driving force must be taken into account here, but more important was the hardening of the Committee's opposition to such ventures. The financial loss was reckoned at between seven and eight thousand pounds, the equivalent of a year's trade; but it was not so much the financial loss as the renewed appreciation of the hazards which led the Committee to frown upon exploratory ventures unless they were closely and obviously connected with the maintenance and the enlargement of trade.

This did not mean that the Committee refused to countenance or to finance voyages of exploration or expansion—merely that they did so with caution and without that enthusiasm and persistence which, until Knight's disaster, seemed to promise an era of 'expansion to the Northward'. It was, indeed, a small expedition northward from Churchill which turned the uneasiness at Knight's failure to return into the certainty that a major disaster had taken place. In 1721 the Committee sent the *Whalebone* sloop out to Churchill, to make a rapid voyage north to $62\frac{1}{2}°$ and return to Churchill to winter, so that in 1722 she might go north again and perfect her discovery. Captain Scroggs set off from Churchill in the *Whalebone* in June 1722, taking with him Richard Norton as interpreter, and hoping chiefly to explore the coast and to find the copper-mine. He was back and anchored in the Churchill River on 25th July, reporting that he had been where the *Albany* and the *Discovery* sloop were both wrecked 'and he doth affirm that Every Man was killed by the Eskemoes'.

No full report of Scroggs' voyage has survived, but the gloom and discouragement which followed his report are palpable even at this distance of time. Later research has made it most probable that Knight's party was seriously weakened before the Eskimos fell upon it. But this could not be known at the time, and Scroggs' report bore down upon the Committee in London and upon the posts by the Bay with all the weight of utter failure accompanied by disaster, by complete massacre, and perhaps even by cannibalism.

BOOKS FOR REFERENCE

BARROW, John—*A chronological history of Voyages into the Arctic Regions; undertaken chiefly for the purpose of discovering a North-east, North-west, or Polar Passage between the Atlantic and Pacific: from the earliest periods of Scandinavian Navigation, to the departure of the recent expeditions, under the orders of Captains Ross and Buchan* (London, 1818).

COATS, Captain W.—*The Geography of Hudson's Bay: being the Remarks of Captain W. Coats, in many voyages to that locality, between the years 1727 and 1751* edited by John Barrow (London, The Hakluyt Society, 1852).

KNIGHT, Captain James—*The Founding of Churchill Being the Journal of Captain James Knight, Governor-in-Chief in Hudson Bay, from the 14th of July to the 13th of September, 1717* edited by J. F. Kenney (London, 1932).

MORTON, Arthur S.—*A History of the Canadian West to 1870–71* (London, 1939).

CHAPTER XXXV

GOVERNOR MACKLISH AND STABILISATION
AT YORK FORT

The shock of Knight's disaster diverted the Committee's interest away from exploration to the fur trade (especially in martens and other small furs), to the establishment of a whale fishery, and to mineral workings. In all of these directions Churchill was the spring-board of the Company's efforts. There Henry Kelsey had taken responsibility, as Governor of York Fort, when Knight sailed to England in 1718. He was under some suspicion, probably of private trade, but the Committee seem to have been strongly in his favour and sent him out a list of the charges and of the names of his accusers, to enable him to justify himself. Knight had ended his career at York by quarrelling with Kelsey, but the new Governor had for long been closely associated with Knight, and had been the source of Knight's information about the gold-mine—for his knowledge of Cree, and probably of other Indian tongues, was outstanding—and his plans and proposals brought no great innovation or reaction.

In 1719 Kelsey himself left York Fort to visit Churchill. There in June he loaded up the two sloops *Success* and *Prosperous* and sailed north to trade, to explore, and to seek the copper-mine. In 1720 he repeated this procedure, sending Captain Hancock only, in the *Prosperous*. Hancock was back by 3rd July, reporting that he had met 'great mortality' and had made no trade. This was discouraging, but not conclusive. In 1721 Richard Norton, whom Knight had sent off in 1718 and who had come back to Churchill in 1720, set off in the spring with an Indian lad and came back to the post in June. He brought with him a band of eighty 'Northern Indians' and two 'Copper Indians' who said they had seen the mine and knew the country. One of them was prepared to sail north in the sloop; and it was becoming clear that sea transport would be necessary if the copper, once discovered, was ever to be properly developed. Richard Staunton noted in his Journal for Churchill that the two Copper Indians whom Norton brought in had been unable to bring any quantity of the metal and that 'I have Done all I can to finde a way to come by water in Cannoes through the Countrey and not to come Creeping by Land'. The Indians all insisted that there was a great quantity of

448

copper to be got, but that the mine was a great distance to the north.

Kelsey had other troubles on his hands besides the search for copper. Behind the scenes was the problem of Knight's fate. The Northern Indians in 1721 reported that Copper Indians had met white men in 1720 and had traded a great deal of iron from them. This might have been Knight; but by 1721 the Committee were quite at a loss and were even writing to ask Kelsey whether Knight could have fared so badly as to have come to winter at York.

The reason why the Committee thought it possible that Kelsey should know about Knight was that no news at all, and no returns, had come home from Churchill or York Fort in 1719. The *Hudson's Bay*, Captain Richard Ward, had been sent to Churchill in 1719, to drop some of her cargo there, pick up the returns and reports and proceed to York Fort. The previous year, in 1718, the *Hudson's Bay* had met with 'Disaster going out of the river' on leaving York Fort for England but had then been successfully refitted by Kelsey. In 1719 the disaster was complete. The ship was lost, 'cast away' in the river, though some of her cargo and equipment were saved. The captain and crew got safely back to the post and refused the offer of 'a hoy' (the *Prosperous*) to sail to England. Kelsey therefore had to feed and house them through the winter until ship-time in 1720, when they were brought home as passengers in the *Hannah*. Captain and crew, on their return, claimed wages for the whole period of their absence from England; the Company claimed they had been kept in idleness for thirteen months since the wreck, refused to pay them except to the date of the wreck, and prepared to defend its case. In the meantime Kelsey had the captain and crew to deal with, and seamen wintering were always an incitement to idleness, discontent, debauchery and private trade, as Governor Nixon had discovered. Kelsey also had to face a reprimand for having to some extent caused the wreck. He was ordered to buoy the channel of the Hayes River, so that the ships could in future come safely up to Five Fathom Hole, and so that the Governor of the fort need no longer go right out to sea to meet the ship.

At the same time, by the *Hannah* in 1721, Kelsey was told that Churchill was to be considered still as an outpost of York Fort, so that he could 'draw down' trade-goods from Churchill if he wished, and Richard Staunton was recalled from Churchill, to be replaced by Nathaniel Bishop, an 'Old Servant' of the Company who had served through the war years at Albany. Kelsey's control of Churchill was thereby confirmed, and he was also encouraged to develop the possibilities which the Committee saw in that post. The *Whalebone* sloop was sent, as has been seen, under command of Captain Scroggs, for the purpose of exploring the coast to the northward. She was to remain out and the *Prosperous* was to be sent home.

Kelsey, after the failure of Hancock in the *Prosperous* in 1720, had worked out a scheme, typical of the man, whereby he himself should sail north and should 'winter to Northward' in 1721. This the Committee, already alarmed over Knight but as yet not knowing his fate, refused to sanction. They insisted that such a plan involved the hazard of his life and that in any case he could make as much discovery, both of whales and of other commodities, if he sailed from Churchill in June as if he wintered away. At the same time the Committee noted that 'the Person Capt. Knight sent upon a discovery' (Richard Norton) had returned to Churchill and expressed a hope of 'better encouragement' in the search for copper. So Kelsey was instructed to persist in the northern voyages and the search for whales and copper in 1721, although his enthusiasm was curbed.

In fact, Kelsey anticipated and duplicated the Company's plans. While the *Whalebone* was sent out for the purpose he took the *Prosperous* from York to Churchill, arrived there early in July 1721 and immediately set out again to the northward. He took with him Richard Norton as 'Lingister', and one of the Northern Indians who promised to take him to the copper-mine. But he was back at Churchill by 16th August and had returned to York by 10th September, having had no opportunity to 'goe the Lenght of the Copper So that theire is no farther Discovery made then formerly'.

Kelsey was called home in 1722, and the Committee then faced the fact that both of the men upon whom they had relied to reinvigorate their trade in 1714 were useful no more. Knight, they knew by the report of Scroggs, was dead; Kelsey had arrived in London with these tidings, recalled by the Committee after an eight years' spell of duty, the termination of thirty-eight years in the Company's service. The reasons for his recall are nowhere apparent; he was merely 'called home having been eight years out'. The ardours of his service would perhaps have made him, at fifty-two or fifty-three, already an old man—certainly ripe for recall. But it seems a pity that the Company's books contain no record of any expression of gratitude to this magnificent employee at the end of his long service. Probably he parted from the Company under a recurrent suspicion that the charges laid against him in 1719 had some foundation, for the Company was not an ungenerous master, and although Henry Kelsey was allowed merely to disappear from the Company's books, *ex gratia* payments were made to his widow for some years after his death.

Kelsey was replaced at York Fort by Thomas Macklish, or McLeish, the younger of two Company servants of the same name, uncle and nephew; both were ship's carpenters by trade and both had served for long periods at Albany. They were employed there together as early as 1699, and the younger man was reputed to be better than his uncle. They had both lasted out the war years at Albany, and both were recalled in 1713, but the younger Macklish was then sent out to Albany in 1715, to be Chief Trader there under Knight's command. He replaced Richard Staunton and in many ways that was typical of his career; for Staunton was enterprising and assertive while Macklish was cautious and conservative. Staunton was recalled because he claimed a rise in pay which the Committee would not concede, and he remained in England until Knight sent for him to take command of the new post at Churchill; he stood for Churchill and the desire to explore and expand. But Macklish at Albany had shown a dour competence which contrasted strongly with the imaginative enterprise of Knight, Kelsey, and to a lesser extent of Staunton; his promotion to command at York may be taken as a symptom of the trend in the Company's policy which the recall of Kelsey indicated. It was not that Macklish was unenterprising or even that he could not travel or did not believe in travel. He had been paid a gratuity as far back as 1706 for his 'Extraordinary Service' in travelling from Albany to Gilpin's Island and back, he had made a canoe-journey to the south, trapping furs, and his period in command at Albany shows that he had a very clear view of the need to extend the Company's trade.

This, however, was a view of expansion in which direct rivalry with the French wood-runners was an immediate spur and at the same time a limiting factor. Any move which did not have rivalry with the French as an immediate object was to him extravagant, but any move which could be shewn to have direct relation to that policy was sure of his energetic support. In this, of course, the circumstances of Albany and of Churchill differed greatly. Knight's policy of expansion had been phrased against the threat of French competition in the upper reaches of the Churchill and Nelson rivers and he had, for example, defended his refusal to burn *coat* beaver by saying it would drive the Indians to trade with the French—'that's to the french wood Runners which are Settled in that lake they call the Sea Lake near our western Indians'. But although Knight said his Indians could do this as easily as they could go to the French from the Bottom of the Bay, the Sea Lake to which he alluded was Lake Winnipeg, the distances involved were vastly greater than those at

Albany, and the comparison was really out of place. For whereas the French had to travel, and to transport their trade-goods, well over a thousand miles to intercept the Indians at Lake Winnipeg, an expansion which only took place during the succeeding half-century, it was but five hundred miles or so from Quebec or Montreal to the headwaters of the rivers on whose trade Albany depended, and the route was already well known and to some extent settled.

Already during the discussions which had preceded the signing of the Treaty of Utrecht the French had decided that they could threaten the English trade at Albany by wood-runners from the South, as Jolliet had argued that they might easily do. The threat was built up as soon as the Treaty was settled. By 1714 the English Company was complaining that the French had started a settlement and built two houses seven days' paddling up the Albany River, and thenceforth French rivalry at Albany and the neighbouring rivers increased steadily. But although the French were ready to trade at the headwaters of the rivers and to save the Indians from making the journey to the Bay, the English still held great advantages. Chief among these was the marked superiority of their trade-goods, especially of the cloth and of the tobacco. It was, indeed, accepted that the inferiority of the French trade-goods was the reason why the French had to transport them inland. If the Indians were forced to travel to get their requirements, they would go to the best market, to the Bay and not to Montreal. The purchase of English cloth was therefore, for the French, a corollary of the policy of expansion into the interior, of the maintenance of a post at Michilimackinac and of developing the network of the *Postes du Nord*. So although the English traders complained that their cloth had been stretched and torn till they were ashamed of it, and the Company shipped as little cloth as possible 'nothing being got by the same', it remained a great attraction.

Even more attractive was the Brazil tobacco which the English managed to buy in Lisbon and to ship out almost every year, war or peace. It was accepted that Brazil tobacco was 'a Bewitching Weed amongst all the Natives, and as for the English Roll they do not care for it'. Buying direct through its agent in Portugal, the Company waited yearly till the ships had arrived from Brazil and then bought the 'newest sort and sweet sented', the twist to be the smallest possible 'no thicker than a man's little finger, it being to be sold by measuer, and not by weight'. At times the system broke down; in 1717 drought in Brazil made tobacco so scarce and dear that little was shipped, and in 1718 it was reported as quite unobtainable at a time when even English tobacco was very dear. At times, too, a dry and powdery roll of tobacco found its way into the consignment. Then the Company's servants were either forbidden to buy tobacco or allowed only such as was 'so damaged that it will not trade with the Indians'. Such contretemps were, however, exceptional and even then they might be overcome by a chance purchase of the 'Bewitching Weed' at Hamburg or in Holland—as happened in 1715. But when the year's supplies of tobacco really were scarce (as in 1715 despite the purchase in Holland), then the Indians were likely to desert the English posts. They might be in danger of going to the French; or they might waste their time in wandering between the English posts in the hope of finding better supplies and perhaps a lower Standard of Trade. Thus, for example, the tobacco shortage of 1715 brought from the Committee a strong warning that York Fort must be careful not to attract to itself the trade of Albany. Under Knight and Kelsey the newly-recovered Nelson River trade was being nursed and expanded; but the Committee rightly insisted that French rivalry was more threatening at Albany.

This rivalry with the French at the Bottom of the Bay was never far from the Committee's mind. In the years after Utrecht it was a rivalry to be met by good trade to attract the 'Upland Indians' from the south, and by developing a subsidiary post on the Eastmain, to push the trade among the Indians of the north and east, in the direction of Labrador. This was, on the whole, a conservative policy, defensive rather than enterprising, and depending on competitive trade. The ebb and flow is registered in such incidents as the arrival of forty canoes of 'French Indians' at Albany in 1717, and their satisfied departure with a promise to return in 1718. For that year the Company sent out a present of a fine cloth and a laced hat for the Indian captain. But in error they also supplied Albany only with coarse powder suitable for cannon and with no fine powder, on which the lives of the Indians would depend during their winter hunting. So the 'French Indians' refused to trade, and Thomas Macklish lost another round in the slow fight which he was waging at Albany.

On the Eastmain he was less on the defensive. Here there was a long tradition of expansion from Albany, in which Macklish himself had taken at times an active part. The endless attempts to develop a trade in isinglass, or slude, centred round Slude River on the Eastmain; during the war years the habit had grown of sending a sloop to winter on the Eastmain and, for example, in 1708 Kelsey had been sent to winter with the *Eastmain* sloop so as to encourage and develop a trade in small furs. The difficulties of conducting such a trade were greatly increased by the need to work from a ship instead of from an established post. A post would cost extra wages and provisions, but it would also give the Indians a sense of permanent contact which was invaluable in bringing them down to trade. Consequently although the Committee were careful to keep Albany possessed of a sloop for this purpose—the *Diligence* was sent out for the Eastmain trade in 1717 for example, when the *Eastmain* sloop and the *Prosperous Hoy* were both ordered up to York Fort to take part in expansion to the northward there—yet plans for a post were also accepted. Some sort of house was undoubtedly in existence as a warehouse for the ship and Macklish, exercising his proper craft by building a small sloop and two longboats for the trade, strongly urged that a new house, more commodious for the trade, should be built. This the Committee accepted in 1719, at the same time as it accepted Macklish's proposal to rebuild Albany factory itself at Bayly's Island, since the existing post at Albany on the mainland was in disrepair.

Macklish therefore was not entirely averse from new posts or a policy of expansion, but he was eminently careful; and it was with the careful Macklish that the Committee replaced Knight and Kelsey in command at York Fort and at Churchill. His tenacity at Albany had been invaluable, but it had been the tenacity of a trader rather than of an explorer or adventurer. He had there rivalled the French, not by pushing up the rivers to meet them in the hinterland but by 'trading larger', by varying the Standard of Trade so as to give the Indians a better bargain. Thus he had managed to secure a 'Benjaman's portion' of the Indians' furs. But, as he explained to the Committee, he got the trade because the Indians came 'not out off more Love to us then to the French but purely upon account that we give them near twice the Value for their Furrs'. He had obviously been a successful trader at Albany despite the difficulties of his period in command, for the post's returns immediately declined under his successor Joseph Myatt. Rivalry with the French had made the Indians 'so Politicke in their way in trade, so as they are not to be Dealt by as formerly', and the trade-goods with which Myatt was supplied were, so he wrote, so defective that 'Never was any Man so upbraided . . . by all the Natives, Especially by those that borders near the french'.

Myatt had a difficult staff to manage, too. There were slanderous reports of irregularities and debaucheries, such as to disgust and terrify the Indians and to drive them away from trading at Albany. In addition to spoiling the Company's servants and causing a great scandal to religion in general, events at Albany as soon as Macklish had gone certainly drove away the Indians—it was hoped they had followed Macklish to York. The sort of men employed, and successfully managed by Macklish, may be judged from the fact that in 1719 the Committee complained to him of a very great quantity of martens and some very fine 'Wishocks' which had been brought from Albany and sold to the furriers for several hundred pounds before the Company could be ready with its sale.

It was inevitable—and was, indeed, probably intended—that a man with Macklish's character, background and career, would react to the problems of York Fort, Churchill, exploration to the north and penetration to the south, in a way quite different from the ways of the dead Knight or the dismissed Kelsey. There was certainly an element of 'departmentalism' about his first approach to his new command. Under him Albany had been made virtually independent of York; it was nominally under the command of Knight or of Kelsey but its trade and accounts were kept 'independant' and Albany was ordered only to supply the northern posts with trade-goods or provisions in the direst emergency. The beginnings of something like rivalry between a Northern and a Southern Department of the Company's territories can be seen in the situation, and it was almost with a feeling of rivalry that Macklish took over at York. The buildings erected by Knight and Kelsey called for his first comment. They needed much gravel, and timber retaining-walls behind which the gravel might be packed, to keep them out of the bog; and the buildings themselves, wrote Macklish, were worse than a Scotch or an Irish hut. The worst labourer at Albany had better quarters than the Governor at York.

Even so, Macklish readily admitted from the start that York was a place of greater profit than Albany; and he so far conceded the danger from the French (which could not be overlooked when it had been so recently proved) as to order six gun carriages for his one-ton guns. The potential wealth of York, however, seemed to Macklish to be quite independent of Churchill, and his acceptance of the trading possibilities of York did not carry him on to accept the need for Churchill. In his first year at York he shipped home the very satisfactory returns of 36,275 Made-Beaver, and he reported that he could increase or decrease the quantity at will—'Itt layes wholly in our power to make that trade greatt or small'. To him the only question at issue was whether the trade should be conducted from York or from Churchill. He had sent home over a thousand martens from Churchill and saw prospects of increasing that trade, but he had been forced to send beef and bacon over from York since the fishery

at Churchill had failed, and his deep conviction was that Churchill
would never repay the cost of the ship and of the men which it entailed. Most of the fur trade carried on at Churchill was only 'A
Robbing of this place' (York Fort) and he exercised his authority to
shew the truth of his opinion by an order that Churchill should trade
at the same Standard of Trade as York. Given no better prices for
their furs at Churchill, he was confident the Indians would come to
York. Something of a personal note creeps into his report that all the
Indians 'so much talk of by Capt. Knight and his hangers on does
not exceed 200 famileys', and it is clear that Macklish blew cold upon
the enthusiasm for Churchill.

Part of Macklish's mistrust of Churchill must be attributed to the
fact that he did not share the enthusiasm of the hunt for precious
metals but was completely engrossed in the fur trade. Earlier, when
he had been at Albany, he had suffered much from Knight's eager
gullibility, passed to him as orders from the London Committee.
Knight had reported a white metal like dull pewter on the second
island north from Cape Jones, heavy yellow rocks on three 'broken
shattered islands' to the west and again at Cape Hope, a variety of
coloured stones at Lancashire Island, and a score of other 'finds', all
of which Macklish was ordered to follow up. Nothing came of any
of these ventures, save that Macklish took command of York and
Churchill in no mood to be much of a treasure-seeker.

The London Committee, however, were still enthusiastic. Kelsey
had reported in his last year, in 1721, that the copper-mine lay to the
north and east of Cary's Swan Nest, and he had been told to encourage the Eskimos to bring as much copper as they could. Kelsey
had been working on Eskimo rumour, which reported a river by Sir
Biby's Island (Bibby Island) running up to where the copper could
be got, but even Kelsey was beginning to be a little doubtful about
the copper and hoped for an improvement in trade from that *or from
some other commodity*. The Indians from the north were to be encouraged too, as well as the Eskimos. Bishop at Churchill was to
question the 'Red Iron Indians' about their mineral deposits and was
to continue the quest for copper. But Bishop proved a disciple of
Macklish rather than of Knight, and in 1724 his successor Richard
Norton (the boy whom Knight had sent to winter with the Indians to
the northward) reported that no Copper Indians had come to Churchill since they had been so much discouraged by Bishop. Norton
had 'done my Endeavour to fetch up the Great Discouragement' the
Indians had suffered, and he hoped they would come again in future
years. But although he had sent off an Indian to bring samples of the

copper, he yet had to write that the Indian had 'resolved me there was no such thing as a Passage to them it being all a frozen Sea where they are. He said itt was such a Distance off that he Could not Traveil their in less than 3 Winters time; and he thought he could do more good in gathering the Indians together to gett furrs'.

With even Norton faltering and placing furs before copper, Macklish supported this letter from Churchill almost in triumph. He checked, however, and allowed for a return journey also. Whereas Norton (whose whole career was to be ruined by his inability to manage accounts and letters) gave the impression that the Indian required three years merely to reach the copper-mine, Macklish wrote that 'They have placed the Mine so far as they cannot goe *and come* in less than three years'. With such discouragement even the London Committee gave up, and in 1725 Macklish was told that the mine appeared to be at such a distance that a trade in copper would come to little. So ended one phase of the expansive policy which Knight and Kelsey had brought to the Company in the years succeeding Utrecht, the search for the copper-mine, which might well have led the Company to the mouth of the Coppermine River half a century before Samuel Hearne reached the Arctic by that route.

The impetus was dying off in other ways too. Discovery to the northward went together with the search for copper, and that also (with its lingering desire to find a North-west Passage) was practically abandoned by 1725. A sloop continued to be sent north on a summer trading voyage, but this was comparatively unadventurous routine, following the pattern set by Kelsey and by Captain Scroggs, and the end of the attempts at discovery was marked when in 1725 the *Whalebone* was ordered home and Richard Norton at Churchill was warned not to allow young John Butler to travel with the Northern Indians (as his father wanted him to do) in order to learn the language. No one was to be absent from duty on 'such pretence', and this was emphasised as a positive order. The mood of reaction, the triumph of the steady trader Macklish over the visionary enthusiasm of Knight and Kelsey, was not seriously modified by the fact that Macklish was told to give encouragement to the 'upland Indians' from the south so as to increase trade, for this was quite a different, more passive, policy than Knight's enthusiasm to push north.

With all of this recession, horizons had nevertheless been enlarged, interests and enthusiasms had been aroused—and the post in Churchill River remained. This was one matter in which Macklish did not triumph. Perhaps it is just another example of the effect of inanimate possessions in shaping policy; the simple existence of the

Churchill River post led to a policy of maintaining it. Perhaps the Committee felt for Knight and his ideas a loyalty which they did not feel was logical enough to commit to paper. At all events Macklish's plea that York Fort could well conduct the trade which went to Churchill, saving the cost and the responsibility of a post, was overruled. Probably the reason was the simple mercantile consideration that the Committee were determined to encourage Churchill to the utmost 'being unwilling to run so great a Hazard upon Ship both out and home for two Factories'. A third major post, in addition to Albany and York, would greatly lessen the chance of a barren year.

But since the hazards, apart from those of warfare and capture by the French, were chiefly run at sea, the logic of this reasoning entailed that shipment to each of the posts should be in a separate vessel. This was the course adopted. Macklish had begun by treating Churchill strictly as a subsidiary of York, sending it a generous outfit, supplying it with provisions and dictating its policy. This was proper enough in view of the early difficulties at Churchill, the lack of wood even for fires, the need to raft it from a distance, and the scarcity of provisions there. The trade of Churchill, too, was slight and unsatisfactory during these years. Following on their 'discouragement' by Bishop, in 1724 the Churchill Indians were attacked by the 'Southern upland Indians' and robbed on their way to the fort. But Norton, with the London Committee's approval, made presents and gave encouragement both to the southern and to the northern Indians, and there were hopes of a better trade in 1725—especially in martens. But in 1725 trade was again poor, the martens and small furs being especially disappointing, and in addition the pinnace, so important for rafting wood and providing transport for the post, was lost.

This was all the more disappointing since it seemed to bear out Macklish's contention that a post at Churchill would never cover its costs. He reported the failures almost with satisfaction. The Committee, however, stuck to their intention; Macklish was smartly told to harp less on Churchill and to see that York's trade came up to his expectations. He was moreover ordered not to send to Churchill since the Committee would supply that post by an independent ship, and Churchill began thereby to be given something of independence from York.

It was significant that the status of Churchill should be marked by the sending of an independent ship, for shipping in those days went far to indicate the Company's policy. Yet ships could not be entirely controlled by policy. They had their own hazards, and this was an unfortunate period where shipping was concerned, for in August

1724 Captain Coats ran the *Mary* frigate (one of the two ships of that year) aground on Weston's Islands, homeward bound from Albany. Most of the furs were lost; the passengers and crew 'with much hazard came to Albany Fort in their Boates' and remained there a whole year consuming provisions.

To some extent the loss of the *Mary* was offset by the *Whalebone*. This magnificent little sloop was reported as 'fit to go to any part of the world'. She had been sent to Churchill by Macklish in 1724, together with the frame of another sloop, the *Marten* (though Macklish thought they would probably only knock the *Marten* together as they had done the *Success* 'after the first year Ready to goe to Pieces'), and the *Whalebone* had remained at Churchill to help with whaling but not to undertake the annual northern trade voyage; she was in reserve to cross the Atlantic if needed. In 1725 the *Whalebone* was therefore available for an Atlantic voyage. She was, moreover, deteriorating fast on the shallow moorings and flat shore at Churchill. So the Committee ordered her home. She was to be sent out again 'when there is any prospect of her doing us any service in a Discovery or otherways'. The return of the *Whalebone* in 1725 therefore marks the abandonment by the Committee of the policy of exploration to the northward. True, it was accompanied by a promise of renewed support at a later date, and Norton was told to send in a yearly report of 'any Discovery or Matter to the Nor'ward or else where, for the Companies Interest or Advantage . . . and we shall make due improvement thereof'.

More significant than this saving clause in the Committee's instructions was the fact that the separate ship sent to Churchill (to mark the Committee's determination to continue with that post and to separate it to some extent from York) was the *Hannah*, under command of Captain Middleton. Christopher Middleton had spent several years at sea before he first sailed in the Hudson's Bay Company's employ in 1721. He then went as second mate in the *Hannah* to York Factory, and there agreed to transfer as mate to the *Whalebone*, which had just arrived from England to prosecute the northern discovery, and which sailed to winter at Churchill before going north in summer 1722. Middleton's task was to 'draw the Land and make Observations', and during the winter he taught the elements of navigation to several members of the crew. But he also aroused the deep hostility of Captain Scroggs of the *Whalebone*, who refused to take him when he set off in 1722. Scroggs said he would answer to the Committee for his dismissal of Middleton, but the reasons have nowhere been set down. So Middleton was left behind when the *Whalebone* sailed north. He passed the summer of 1722 whaling at Churchill, and diligently examined his pupils when they came back from their voyage with the tragic news of Knight's failure, of the remains of the *Albany* and the *Discovery*, and of the dangers of seeking a North-west Passage.

Middleton was in due course brought home, and continued in the Company's employ. Captain Scroggs' indictment, whatever it was, did not affect the Committee, and in 1725 Middleton was given command of the *Hannah*—significantly enough in preference to Henry Kelsey, who also applied for the post. He was an intellectual sailor, deeply and effectively studious of the problems of northern navigation, later to become a Fellow of the Royal Society and to read many papers to that learned body. Already by 1725 he was collecting information and analysing it scientifically, and in the spring of 1726 he published in the *Philosophical Transactions* of the Royal Society his 'New and Exact TABLE Collected from Several Observations, taken in four Voyages to *Hudson's Bay* . . . . Shewing the Variation of the *Magnetical Needle* . . . from the Years 1721, to 1725'. He was to take a prominent and most reputable part in the further search for a North-west Passage, and it was a pregnant chance which brought him to the command of the *Hannah*, bound independently for Churchill in 1725. In the decision to maintain that post, in the determination to free it from Macklish's jealousy, the Committee, urged by trading considerations, paid but lip-service to the concept of further discovery to the northward. But in retaining Christopher Middleton in their service they kept, and gave great opportunities to, a purposeful and well-equipped (if subsequently unfortunate) explorer.

BOOKS FOR REFERENCE

KNIGHT, Captain James—*The Founding of Churchill* . . . edited by J. F. Kenney (London, 1932).

RICH, E. E. and JOHNSON, A. M. (eds.)—*James Isham's Observations on Hudsons Bay, 1743 and Notes and Observations on a Book entitled* A Voyage to Hudsons Bay in the Dobbs Galley, 1749 (Toronto, The Champlain Society, 1949 and London, The Hudson's Bay Record Society, 1949), Vol. XII.

CHAPTER XXXVI

SIR BIBYE LAKE, PROSPERITY AND THE BUBBLE

The dozen or so years after Utrecht, during which the enthusiasm for precious metals, for discovery to the northward and for whale-oil and small furs as an alternative to beaver, had waxed and declined, were inevitably affected by the financial position of the Company. But financial considerations worked only in reverse, for the years of purpose and enthusiasm were years of great financial difficulty while those of inactivity and reaction were years controlled by a London Committee which was distributing a steady annual dividend for the first time in the history of the Company.

As it emerged from the War of the Spanish Succession the Company was, at least on paper, close to bankruptcy. It had been carried through the war years largely by the backing of Sir Stephen Evans, the banker who had been elected Governor in 1700 in succession to Sir William Trumbull. He did not pay sedulous attention to the Company's business (in fact he only made three appearances at Committee-meetings during the year 1702–3 and only nine during the year 1703–4) but he made substantial cash advances when they were badly needed.

In particular Evans underwrote the Company's ventures into the Russian trade and its attempts to obtain payment for its furs by importing hemp and selling it to the harassed Lords of the Admiralty. The difficulty of obtaining payment from Russian purchasers was such that by 1711 the Company was in despair, and whether by barter or by purchase, the Company was already implicated in the shipment of Russian commodities before 1711. Hemp in particular had seemed an attractive speculation, especially in times of war, but there was only one major purchaser for hemp in England, the Commissioners of Her Majesty's Navy; and the Commissioners normally bought only from a small ring of reputable contractors. So even in war-time the Company showed some boldness in attempting to import and to sell Russian hemp. They had tried the hemp trade in a small way—about a hundred pounds—as far back as 1697, when they supplied the rope-makers with hemp to make ropes for the Company's ships, tried to pay the rope-makers' bills in hemp, and were finally happy to get rid of their purchase at public auction.

461

In 1702 hemp was attempted far more seriously. Samuel Clarke, as Deputy Governor in 1701, was largely responsible. He was always an enthusiast for direct trade with the continent and with Clarke as Deputy Governor, and Evans as Governor, the Committee in 1701 shipped home from Archangel seventy-six bundles of hemp. This was a 'considerable quantity', and was insured for £2,000. About forty-two tons of this hemp (seventy bundles) were successfully sold to the Commissioners of the Navy by Samuel Clarke. But it had not been an easy bargain; at first the Navy refused to buy and Clarke tried to find a market on the continent, then the Navy bought for thirty-three shillings a hundredweight, but paid by a *Navy Bill*. The Company needed cash, and the *Navy Bill* was discounted at 9½ per cent. by the Governor, Sir Stephen Evans, so that the Company lost £132 10s. 0d. of the £1,394 14s. 8d. realised by the hemp.

This was to prove a constant difficulty with the hemp trade, but one in which Stephen Evans was able to be most useful to the Company. He was steadily enlarging his holding, and he held £3,700 of stock in 1701 and £4,200 in 1703. He was prepared not only to lend thousands of pounds against the security of a *Navy Bill* (he advanced £2,200 on this security in 1703, and comparable sums in subsequent years); he was also ready to lend smaller sums to meet urgent demands. Thus in February 1703, the Company having 'Urgent Occasion' for cash to pay its tradesmen, Evans advanced £200, to be repaid from the sale of the hemp of that year. In October of the same year he advanced £500 to pay the customs on the returns of the year from the Bay, and he was constantly supplying the ready cash which the Company needed.

With Evans and Samuel Clarke in support, and with John Nicholson, Deputy Governor in succession to Clarke, also personally involved, the trade to Russia continued, and shipments of hemp became regular, despite the fact that the Tsar began to tax the export in 1702. By the end of 1703 the Company had shipped a hundred and seventy-one bundles direct from Archangel and a further fifty from Amsterdam. All save twenty had been sold to the Navy, and sales amounted to over £4,000. Once established, the Company was able to sell constantly to the government; in 1709, for example, Woolwich bought for over £4,264—but by that time war finance was beginning to tell, and the rate of discount on a *Navy Bill* was 26 per cent. so that even such substantial remittances, equal to the produce of a successful fur sale, were not adequate for the needs of the Company, and borrowing both by direct loan and by delayed payment for goods and wages was still an essential feature of the Company's trade.

In this there was nothing new. Such borrowing had always been the practice of the Company, and it was almost an inevitable corollary of the small amount of the subscribed stock. What was new, and important, was that during the war years and the Governorship of Sir Stephen Evans a more modern and legal practice was adopted. Instead of loans of a quasi-debenture nature, definite Debentures were now issued. Thus, for example in 1700 the Deputy Governor (Samuel Clarke), Colonel Pery and Samuel Pitts, Committee-men, subscribed £300 for the payment of customs on the in-coming furs and the Minutes record that the 'said Bond was taken up by Debentures' which were cancelled when cash became available in February 1701. The use of the term 'Debentures' is significant, but from the point of view of business history it is perhaps unfortunate that this first example should so speedily have been ended, for the contribution of the debenture shareholder is that he lends his money at a comparatively low fixed interest without power to demand its repayment. Thus the ordinary shareholder and the management can increase their working capital at known cost and without risk of embarrassment by sudden demands for repayment. The use of the term 'Debentures' in 1701 must therefore not be over-emphasised. More important developments were continuing without such outward marks. Of these one was the Company's own rule in 1689, that repayment of loans could not be claimed without three months' notice. The other was the rising custom of stamping the Company's bonds for loans (according to Act of Parliament) and the steady substitution, from 1697 onwards, of such stamped 'Bonds of the New form' for the old contracts of loan. Between the Company's ruling and the statutory requirement, loans became more and more permanent, and of the nature of true debentures.

One such long-term loan brought in its train a law suit which clarified and strengthened the Company's position. In the period when the Company's credit stood high and many were anxious to lend money, around 1692, Thomas Pitts had introduced many investors to the Committee, and he had himself lent £1,500. He lent other sums at different times, and although in 1692 he gave notice that he wished to be repaid £1,000, when he died the Company was still in his debt to the extent of £1,500. Since this was vouched for by the new formal stamped bonds, not by the note of hand of one of the Committee, his heirs had a good case against the Company. They sued in the Court of the Exchequer in 1701, and the Committee responded by refusing permission for them to sell their stock in the Company and by ruling that they must pay 'all the unnecessary costs occasioned by the Law suit'. But they then closed the case by agreeing to pay £500 down in cash and a further £1,000 in six months provided the brothers Pitt would pay £5 costs and discontinue the suit. Such a conclusion brought a little clarity into the debenture problem since it showed that the Company as a corporation was liable for such loans rather than the individual who negotiated the business. The converse, that the Company as a body had rights over the trade carried on its name by members, was proved by a subsequent suit. Here the Company sued its former Governor, Sir Stephen Evans.

The difficulties of the war years, and constant reliance upon borrowed money, had resulted in payments for furs sold by the Company being made in the bonds issued by the Company. Despite its need for cash, the Company could not well refuse to accept its own script in payment; and the way in which such bonds circulated and acted as a sort of currency may be judged from the record that in 1713 John Knight of the London customs house presented a bond for £500 which had been made payable to Sir Jeffrey Jeffreyes as far back as 1696, and which had come into Knight's possession after passing through several hands. Payment in its own bonds was, of course, but one step removed from the Company's habit of paying off the bonds as a first call on the cash received at the sales. But it left the problem of finding ready cash even more difficult than before.

It was the tradesmen who suffered most from the lack of ready money. Almost £1,000 of unpaid bills was carried over from 1702 to 1703. The hemp and beaver sales of that year allowed considerable payments to be made, but in 1704 the Committee could only go so far as to agree that the Company pay all its tradesmen's bills 'so furr as the Present Cash will Permitt'. A special loan of £500 was negotiated in 1705 to pay the tradesmen, but they were only paid in full for the goods supplied in 1705 after the sales of 1707 had brought in the money. Even allowing two years or more for payment, the Company still left many accounts outstanding, and by 1708 it was reduced to the last desperate expedient of borrowing in order to pay interest on previous loans. The grocers, ironmongers and ships' chandlers were by now anxious and clamorous, but could only be promised payment if the furs sold for ready money, not for bonds already issued. The Company was soon forced to urge its agent in Amsterdam to send over all the money he had available from sales—or if the furs were 'not sold for money wee crave leave to draw upon you 5 or 6 hundred pounds at usance'. There were substantial arrears of pay due to servants also; William Dolbey the warehousekeeper was owed £750 by 1707, Anthony Beale Governor of Albany was owed £600 and Nathaniel Bishop his Deputy £200, John Fullartine £500, the younger Thomas Macklish £100. Even Radisson's 'Salary' was £50 in arrears in 1709, and was to be paid 'Ass money comes in'.

Great efforts were necessary to raise the money for immediate payments, of which the most essential was the customs payment on the incoming furs. Money was tight in London, and the Committee could not always raise funds at the statutory rate of six per cent. In 1708 they had to allow a one per cent. premium in addition, and they had to be content to borrow at one month's call instead of the six months which would have given them time to sell their furs. The same terms were offered in 1709, and the whole Committee were then recommended to set to work to procure money upon the security of the *Navy Bills* with which the Company had been paid for its hemp. A special General Court of the whole Company, called to meet the crisis in 1709, set up a committee of three Adventurers and two Committee-men to inspect and report on the affairs of the Company. The details of their report have not survived. It is possible, indeed probable, that they were unable to unravel the maze into which the Company's accounts had fallen, and that everything else in the accounts was overshadowed by the alleged asset of about £100,000 damages claimed from the French. It is, however, a strong indication of the plight of the Company that the Committee should have allowed ordinary adventurers not only to sit upon, but to outnumber themselves in such a committee of enquiry. This was a result of a rear-guard action by the Committee, who had answered the first request for a 'True State of the Company at this Juncture' in November 1708 by proclaiming that any adventurer could certainly inspect the books. They had then reluctantly ordered the Secretary to produce a 'State of the Companys Concernes', and only when that was thrown out had they succumbed, called a Special General Court and accepted the special committee then set up.

Part of the reason why the Company's accounts presented such a problem at this time was that the officials were constantly mingling their own private trade with that of the Company. To some extent this was a general and almost inevitable feature of the trade. The business man who supplied goods or hired a ship to the Company, the financier who under-wrote the ships' insurances and who made (or refused) loans, might well be a member of the Committee or even Governor of the Company, as long as he declared his interest. But three members of the Committee had gone far past these limits by

1708. Samuel Clarke, former Deputy Governor, was at one time virtually conducting the trade to and from Amsterdam in his own name but on behalf of the Company; John Nicholson, Deputy Governor, was doing the same for the direct trade with Russia; and the Governor, Sir Stephen Evans had begun to implicate the Company in the finance of discounting bills and was about to launch it into an insurance project.

In all of this, private and Company goods and money were separable only with the greatest difficulty. Samuel Clarke's management of the Russia trade produced an endless muddle, but Nicholson's accounts do not seem to have caused so much trouble, perhaps because they covered fewer years. Yet the special sub-committee of 1709 found an error of £318 9s. 11d. in his account, and he owed the Company at that time over £1,300, which he repaid by selling back some *coat* beaver which he had bought for export. He then handed over *Navy Bills* to the value of £4,264 which he had got from managing the hemp trade and was 'sitting on', and paid the further debt which he owed to the Company, £998 16s. 11d. by delivering to the Secretary an Irish Transport Debenture for £997 16s. 7d. Even so, when his account was finally balanced in 1713 the Committee had to write off the balance of £1,618 12s. 3d.

Sir Stephen Evans' venture was more easily kept in a separate account. In the depth of the depression of the Company's affairs, while the special sub-committee was trying to draw up a statement of the accounts, a certain Andrew Valentine submitted 'A Proposall for the advaintage of the Company'. This was considered, approved by the Committee in June 1710, and ordered to be put into execution as soon as possible, counsel's opinion having been taken from Sir Edward Northey. The only points divulged to the General Court of the Company concerned the terms on which Valentine should work, but did not state his business. He was to work from six to eight hours a day, Sundays excepted; and he was to get one-fifth of the clear profits from his proposal for life, or if he died within fourteen years his executor was to get one-tenth up to the end of the fourteen years. But as for the business itself 'at Present it was not Thought Convenient to divulge the Same' and the General Court was perforce content to leave the matter to the Governor and Committee.

The counting house in the yard of the Company's house was therefore fitted up for Valentine, he was given £10 and a promise of a further £5 for his preliminary expenses, and he was told to print his prospectus as soon as possible. He opened his office in August 1710 and it then transpired that his business, conducted by him for the Company, was a form of insurance for helping apprentices to set themselves up in trade when they had completed their training. The Company was chiefly required to provide premises and to lend its name, so as to encourage the apprentices to trust Valentine. Almost from the beginning the venture was extended to marriages, and in both forms Valentine's office became something in the nature of a 'Christmas Club' in which small regular payments were made by the members and from time to time a share-out would be voted, producing small capital sums which would help some of the young people to set up in business or as householders.

By October 1711 Valentine required larger premises, and in November he paid over to the Committee a 'dividend' of £500, which was put into the Profit and Loss Account. But already he was leading the Committee to adopt the fatally easy fallacy of the insurance agent, paying out the premiums on new business as dividends on previous investments. The minutes and the accounts of his business were kept separately and the details have not survived. But there could be only one end to such practices. Within six months, in May 1712, the Committee was waiting on the Attorney General to procure his favour in relation to Valentine's office, and Valentine was ordered to take down the board over his door and not to undertake any further business without orders from the Committee.

The Attorney General promised his good offices, and the Company agreed to see the matter through, for the existing policies must be paid out as they matured. For this the Company issued two bonds, for £500 and for £100, and agreed to pay this money to Valentine as he should have need of it; in fact it doled out sums of about £70 to him as his 'Dividends' for marriages or apprentices became due. In all the Company had to find over £900 to get clear of the affair, but it recovered and cancelled its guarantee of the business; and it took double security for its advances to Valentine, and further paid him not in cash but in claims against Sir Stephen Evans.

Evans and his partner William Hall had in the meantime gone bankrupt. He had a strangely speculative type of business, and one of his chief activities was to accept 'insurances', which were valuable to merchants but pure gambles to him (unless he had inside information), on the course of the war—insurances against such contingencies as 'That Namur will be captured by the fourteenth of the month'. So far was he by this time from financing the Company that in January 1712 the Committee successfully proved before the Commissioners in the Guildhall that the Company had a claim against its Governor for £844 3s. 3d. They recovered only £11 1s. of this, payment being made at the rate of threepence in the pound.

Evans then committed suicide. But his business with the Company was not yet done, for the trustees of his property on behalf of his creditors naturally wished to include his holding of Hudson's Bay stock among his assets. The Committee agreed to give them details of his share-holdings and transfers, but they checked their bye-law 'Relateing to the Stoping of Such Persons Stock where it shall Apeare any person is Indebted to the Company', and refused to allow the trustees to sell the stock. This action was challenged in 1716, and the trustees were then told of the Company's power to make bye-laws under the Charter, and of the effect that they would not allow the sale or transfer of Evans' stock until his debt to the Company had been paid in full.

Valentine, set to recover the money which he needed from the estate of his former patron, was deeply involved in this conflict, and Evans' successor as Governor, Sir Bibye Lake, was left a free hand to direct Valentine, the Company agreeing to pay up to £20 of any legal expenses in which the defence of Stephen Evans' debt to the Company might involve Valentine. The affair gathered momentum when in 1719 the trustees discovered that Evans' holding was not the mere £500 of stock which then stood in his own name. He had been mistaken in thinking he was bankrupt, and among other assets was a further holding of £3,574 ostensibly held by Thomas Lake (father of Governor Sir Bibye) but really in trust for Evans. In 1720 the trustees sued the Company in Chancery, Valentine was called into full consultation by the Committee, and the losses on his insurance project were charged against Evans.

The decision was eventually given in favour of the Company, which thereby covered itself for its losses on the insurance venture, gained protection against members of the Committee (or other shareholders) who conducted its business, and achieved a power which was the counterpart of the responsibility which it bore for the acts of individual members of the Committee. In all of this the Company was not only battling its way through the financial difficulties of the war years; it was also drawing sensibly closer the bonds which united it as a joint-stock corporation, and the verdict which it obtained in 1720 ranks as an important step in the evolution of the legal concept of a joint-stock company. But in its progress towards such consolidation the Company had passed through years of the greatest financial difficulty. Those were the very years in which it was called upon to finance Knight and Kelsey, the resettlement of York, the building of Churchill, and 'Discovery to the Northwards'.

In spite of the financial difficulties of the war years (during which the Company was not alone in its troubles) the shipments outwards were continued, and as peace approached the Company's affairs began to seem more prosperous. In 1710 the arrears of Committee-money, going back to 1706, were paid off after the ship had been successfully despatched, and in 1713 the Committee again ventured to pay themselves for their services during the previous two years. By one means or another the voyage of 1710 was fitted out at a cost of almost £15,000, and the 1711 voyage cost almost £14,000; that of 1712 dropped to about £7,500. By this time, too, the Committee were paying bills up to date, and although some servants accepted bonds in lieu of payment (Henry Kelsey for example) and some tradesmen were still protesting the details of their old accounts, the whole business was wearing a more prosperous and organised air. There was no last-minute search for cash to pay the customs; the Secretary was given £1,200 and was instructed to get the cargo admitted, and the Committee could even afford a gratuity to Governor John Fullartine of Albany—though it was grateful when he accepted a bond instead of cash!

Three causes were chiefly responsible for this comparative stability—the disputes over the estate of Sir Stephen Evans had brought Samuel Jones, as one of the trustees, into contact with the Company, and he brought with him both wisdom and wealth. It was he, for example, who lent the £2,000 needed for customs and other charges in 1712. He was elected to the Committee, where he served long and well, and he eventually became Deputy Governor from 1729 to 1735.

The second reason for stability was that Sir Bibye Lake was elected Governor in succession to Sir Stephen Evans, and he brought to the Company a close attention to business which it had not hitherto enjoyed. He was the first Governor for whom the Hudson's Bay Company was his major interest; for his predecessors had been courtiers, princes, politicians, diplomatists, generals and bankers—never primarily Hudson's Bay men. Sir Bibye Lake was primarily, almost exclusively, a Hudson's Bay man and an able, astute, and knowing one too! A member of the Middle Temple, he had got his first £1,000 worth of Hudson's Bay stock as early as 1709. He was probably only twenty-five years old then, and he 'bought' (for it is possible that no cash changed hands) from his father Thomas Lake, also a Templer, and Deputy Governor of the Company in the year 1710–1711. The elder Lake was deeply involved with Sir Stephen Evans and was alleged to have held much of his Hudson's Bay stock as the deputy of Sir Stephen, so it is quite probable that Sir Bibye's first holding of Hudson's Bay stock was part of the concealed assets of the banker. He successfully claimed a baronetcy vacated by the death of an uncle, and although he had serious interests both as a member of the Temple and as a Sub-Governor of the Royal African Company, from the start of his career he devoted most of his very genuine talents to the Hudson's Bay Company. He was sent to Holland to represent the Company at an early stage in the peace negotiations (in 1709 when he can have been but little more than twenty-five) and he must have been under thirty when he was elected Governor in 1712. He was to hold that post until 1743, an eventful and lengthy tenure which earned him the respectful title of 'The perpetual Governor'. His shrewd and tactful guidance undoubtedly counted for much even in the early years of his authority; and he knew the ways of both the Court and the City so well as to be an invaluable asset in the period of post-war speculation.

Samuel Jones and Bibye Lake counted for much, especially in combination. But important as personalities are, neither of these men could really have retrieved the fortunes of the Company without a third factor. This was the simple commercial factor that furs were selling well. The great furriers, buying largely for export, were the key to this situation. The revival started in 1711, when one man, Richard Baker, bought £12,482 14s. 4d. worth of furs between February and May. This in itself was enough to bring an air of enthusiasm and hope into the Company's affairs; and there were others, such as Henry Sperling whose purchases enabled the arrears of Committee-money for 1711 and 1712 to be paid.

The period covered by Knight, Kelsey, 'Discovery to the Northward', the search for copper and the founding of Churchill, is therefore one of rising confidence and moderate prosperity, based on competent administration and an active market. As the new administration gathered knowledge and competence the prosperity increased; it was, indeed, a period of a general rise in prosperity and confidence between the end of the war and the bursting of the South Sea Bubble, and the Hudson's Bay Company, with Bibye Lake as Governor, shared in the upward move. The *coat* beaver account for 1717 showed a profit of over £5,000; for 1718 it showed a profit of over £8,000, with over 10,000 skins 'resting' unsold. The trade in *parchment* beaver showed less profits—a mere £1,930 in 1719 for example—but as in 1720 and 1721 the market fluctuated and profits on *coat* beaver fell to about £2,000, those on *parchment* rose to £6,000 odd in 1721 and 1722.

Though the Committee were striving to develop secondary products, and in particular were busy encouraging the trade in martens and other small furs which 'never Lye on hand as Beavor doth', beaver was still the mainstay of the Company's trade. And beaver was producing a very satisfactory return. Consequently in 1718 the payment of dividends was resumed. This was not unexpected. In May of that year, when the annual letter was sent to Macklish, he was told that the Committee were 'in hopes the Company may in time reap some Benefitt for their Cost and Labour, Who have not received one penny Dividend almost these thirty yeares'. When the *Mary* arrived safe with the returns of 1718 from Albany on 16th October, therefore, the Committee resolved to wait no longer, and on 24th October a dividend of ten per cent. was voted 'Takeing into Consideration the State of the Company both as to theire Cash as Likewise to theire Effects both at home and abroad, And that it has pleased God one of theire Shipps is already arrived with a good Cargoe and May Expect this yeare two more from Hudson's Bay'.

Sir Bibye had brought the Company out of the barren years. The first dividend since 1690, the fifth to be paid in fifty years of trading, was ten per cent. only, a modest yield compared with the fifty per cent., twenty-five per cent. and bonus issue of stock, which had marked the previous periods of prosperity. But whereas the great dividends of the past had been few and scattered, this dividend of 1718 was the first of a long unbroken series. Not until the French again sailed into the Bay, and La Pérouse captured York Fort in 1782, did the shareholders again pass a year without a dividend. Sir Bibye had brought the Company into a period of over sixty years of uninterrupted prosperity.

The list of stockholders to whom the dividend was paid is a revealing contrast to the list of early Adventurers. The King's Most Excellent Majesty still heads the list; but George I never took any of the active personal interest in the Company which the Stuarts had shown. There are no Adventurers who could in any way be called courtiers; the nearest approach to that courtly adventurous spirit which had launched the Company and secured the Charter is the persistence of Robert Boyle's small interest, now in the hands of his executors, on which a mere £5 dividend was paid. For the rest, the small body of thirty-five shareholders were either widows, and executors of deceased shareholders, or City men who often took an active part in the fur trade or in cognate trades. William Dolbey the Warehousekeeper, for example, traded actively in furs and was paid a dividend of £50 for his share in the Company; John Butterfield supplied the groceries for the Company and his executrix received a £60 dividend. John Nicholson had managed the trade to Russia, and his executrix received £155 6s. 0d. The biggest payment, £418 8s. 0d. went to the executors of Thomas Lake. The second largest, £160, went to his son, the Governor, Sir Bibye Lake.

Some few less active, perhaps more disinterested, shareholders there were. But it is clear that the Company had by 1718 become a Company of active, commercial men, backed by a small number of inactive shareholders. Here Sir Bibye Lake was not only the largest living shareholder at the time of the dividend, he was also the embodiment of the change in management. He was largely responsible, too, for the dividend itself. So, at least, the Committee thought and they put on record their 'opinion that the same was oweing to the good management of the Governor Sir Bibye Lake, and for that Reason did unanimously vote the Thankes of this Court'.

Sir Bibye's part in securing the dividend must seem to modern eyes slight, for the fur sales were the basic reason, and here he could have done little beyond insisting upon the end of the semi-private trading which had delivered the furs for Europe into the hands of Samuel Clarke and of John Nicholson, and upon normally accurate and responsible accountancy. In two other matters, however, he had played a prominent and successful part. He had taken over the dubious and uncertain, largely reluctant, policy of investing in government bonds which had developed from the acceptance of payment for hemp in *Navy Bills*, and had organised it into a far-sighted and successful investment policy. And he had pushed the negotiations with France to such purpose that although no satisfactory settlement had yet been achieved, yet confidence in the Company and in the vindication of its claims stood high.

Under Sir Bibye's guidance the Company developed into a successful banking and finance corporation. Since these were the years during which post-war confidence, especially confidence in the future of English overseas trade, was building up to the South Sea Bubble, it was most fortunate that the Company had at its head a man who knew how to take advantage of the easy and confident money-market which could be found in London. His approach to such matters may be seen from the minutes of the first meeting over which he presided—that of 21st November, 1712, just before he was elected Governor. The Company then borrowed £2,060 from Captain Samuel Jones, promising payment after the spring sale of 1713. With this borrowed money sixteen Exchequer bills of £100 each and three Bank of England notes, value £350, were bought. These notes were locked away in the Company's chest to mature. Bibye Lake's Committee was from the first engaged in the banker's business of investing borrowed money, and throughout his Governorship it continued that policy, with investments in government securities, East India stock, South Sea stock, land and trade.

In the early years of Sir Bibye's Governorship such borrowings and investments were conducted against a background of an acute shortage of cash to carry on the trade. In 1713 the Company found that its difficulties had been enhanced by doubtful loans to the extent of more than £4,500, a fact which meant that in 1714 the Governor and Committee had to be urged 'to Endeavour to Raise Moneys for Supplying the Companies present ocasions'. Even with improvement in sales of the Company's furs, the day-to-day working capital of the Company remained (as it had always been) a capital raised by loans and debentures, not from the stockholders or from ploughing back the profits of the trade. There was nothing remarkable, therefore, when the Company issued debenture bonds for £4,000 in 1716. The bonds were to bear no interest, but they were negotiated at a discount of £6 5s. 0d. per cent., which amounted to much the same thing. It was of a piece with the policy and practice of the new Governor that the bulk of the money so borrowed should have been 'laid out' in investments, and further that he himself should have been a principal borrower.

Exactly how the Company benefited from these transactions it is difficult to discover, for the Committee appears systematically to have lent at a lower rate than it borrowed at! Thus the bonds of October 1716 were issued in September at a discount of $6\frac{1}{4}$ per cent. and were payable in full in December, so that the Company paid the full discount for three months' use of the money—the equivalent of an interest charge of 25 per cent. per annum. But in June 1717, £3,000 was laid out at a mere 5 per cent., and Bibye Lake himself had in the meantime borrowed from the Company £3,200 at 4 per cent. The folly of such a procedure was realised when in December the Committee decided to reduce the rate on the Company's bonds to 5 per cent. and to pay off all bond-holders who insisted on the previously-agreed 6 per cent. But even this left the Company making no gain from most of its investments and losing on its loan to the Governor.

The picture becomes even more obscure and suspect when in April 1718 the Committee resolved to bring the loan to the Governor up to £7,000 'as moneys Come in'. The loan was for six months, but was renewable (as was common practice), and the interest was a mere 3 per cent. per annum. The security given was 'certaine Lands in Lincolnshire and Essex'; for legal reasons the money was ostensibly advanced by Captain John Merry, Deputy Governor, but he signed an instrument acknowledging that the money was only his in trust 'his Name being made Use of for that purpose, But is the Proper Moneys Belonging to the Company'. The transaction is the more extraordinary because the Company was immediately forced to borrow money at 5 per cent.

But success had undoubtedly attended on Sir Bibye, and the loan to him was closely followed by the dividend of October 1718—a dividend declared in consideration of 'the State of the Company both as to theire Cash as likewise to theire Effects'.

Difficult though it may be to see where the Company profited in Sir Bibye's transactions, there is no doubt that the air of efficient thoroughness which he brought with him enhanced the reputation both of the Company and of its Governor. Shortage of cash ceased to worry the Committee. The dividend of 10 per cent. in 1718 was followed by one of 6 per cent. in 1719, and then in 1720 the Governor came before the Company with proposals which shewed the scope and the competence of his financial power. These were the days in which the rising confidence of the investing public, which had produced a steady period of prosperity in the City since 1711 (with only two temporary set-backs in 1714 and 1715) resulted in the spate of financial projects known as the South Sea Bubble. The high point of prosperity came in 1718 and 1719, and the resumption of dividends by the Company fits in well with the general picture.

In the crescendo of investment England was not alone. John Law's schemes in France had much in common with the South Sea scheme in England, and even surpassed it in the way in which the Scots financier aimed to fuse into one concern the whole of French overseas trade. At the basis of the developments in both countries lay a belief in the 'Fund of Credit', a belief that trade could be financed by credit based upon cash which had already been loaned to government. The result of this was that trading and manufacturing companies had no working capital with which to finance their operations, nothing but government bonds for funds advanced and very largely dissipated in wars. Such a method of providing alleged 'capital' really gave nothing but credit on the basis of government scrip as a pseudo-capital, and the credit was needed to borrow further sums of actual cash from the general public, with which the merchants' commercial operations might be financed. In this there was nothing out of phase with the financial history of the Hudson's Bay Company, which had spent its exiguous subscribed capital in acquiring possession of the posts which were its chief fixed asset, against which its credit was staked and upon the security of which it raised its working capital by 'debenture bonds' or loans which differed from such bonds only in their lack of formal status.

But although the Hudson's Bay Company was at home with the general principles of the 'Fund of Credit' method of financing overseas commerce, it was most reluctant, even under Governor Bibye Lake, to carry such principles to their logical and dangerous conclusion. For one thing, the Committee still kept the nominal capital small. As late as 1717 the nominal capital still stood at only £31,500 (to which it had been raised by the trebling of the stock in 1690), whereas the other three companies for overseas trade stood, the South Sea Company at £10,000,000, the United East India Company at £3,194,080, and the Royal African Company at about £450,000.

It is true that much of the vast alleged capital of these other Companies (especially the South Sea Company) represented nothing but loans to the government; and therein lies the second distinguishing feature of the Hudson's Bay Company. Its small capital contained no fictitious element due to loans to government. Such government bonds as the Committee held from time to time were due either to the fact that the Company's hemp had been paid for by a postdated *Navy Bill* or to the fact that the Committee had deliberately bought the government's paper as an investment—perhaps because it was at an attractive discount, perhaps because it yielded an attractive interest.

Governor Sir Bibye certainly knew what was going on in the City during the Bubble period; for the Royal African Company, of which he was Deputy Governor, had perfected a system whereby dividends were paid out of increased subscriptions paid in by the shareholders themselves! This iniquity was effectively cancelled by the re-organisation of the African Company in 1708, when Bibye was just beginning his active career in the City. The Governor had, moreover, the great opportunity and experience of being in Paris on the Company's business in 1719, a time when English financiers were entranced by the immense speculation which marked the climax and failure of Law's schemes. For Law's *Compagnie des Indes* consolidated French tropical trade and the French fiscal system in a way which abused the 'Fund of Credit' system so as to lead inevitably to inflation, and Paris in 1719 became 'the Mecca of the speculators of

Europe', and many English and Scots financiers were among them. Though ostensibly on Company's business, to settle the boundary with Canada, Sir Bibye probably speculated a little. He certainly learned much, and when he returned to a London which was lagging about six months behind Paris in reaching the climax of the boom, he set to work to develop the possibilities of the Hudson's Bay Company.

At that time, early in 1720, the South Sea Company and the Bank of England were both putting forward proposals for funding the as-yet unfunded portion of the National Debt to the extent of about thirty-one million pounds, while other companies were also being floated in considerable numbers and with capitals absurdly large by comparison with that of the Hudson's Bay Company. In January 1720, new capital issues amounted to £6,000,000; in February not only was there the proposal to convert the national debt of £31,000,000 into South Sea stock but new capital issues totalled at least an equal sum. A wave of speculation was developing in London; the new companies of February each proposed capitals averaging about a million pounds; by June two millions was more normal, and during the single week ending 11th June new capital issues came to £224,000,000. Share prices were rising too; South Sea stock advanced over six hundred per cent. in five weeks in May and June, after rising over two hundred per cent. from January to May, while the Royal African Company showed an even greater increase during the early period. On the whole, however, speculation took the form of new promotions and issues rather than of buying and selling existing stocks.

In any case, the small sum involved in the capital of the Hudson's Bay Company was in the hands of a very limited number of interested 'Adventurers' and dealings in the shares were never active even in such a boom. Sir Bibye, however, found no difficulty in persuading this small band of stockholders that they should profit, and their Company should be enlarged, by the ease with which new shares could be uttered in London in 1720. On 19th August, 1720, he laid before the Committee a proposal for enlarging the stock, with a view to carrying on a more extensive trade—a proposal which was unanimously approved. A General Court was to be called, the proposition was to be printed in the *Daily Courant*, and in the meantime the Governor was empowered to pay up to £1,000 'to such person or persons he shall thinke fitt for their Greate services done the Company without any account to be given for the same'—perhaps a reference to the recent negotiations with France, perhaps 'groundbait' for the proposed flotation. Governor Sir Bibye told the General Court that the Committee found the stock of the Company too small to enlarge the trade and to make it 'more a National Interest', and he was given a unanimous vote of confidence and asked to work out the problem with the Committee. Within the week, on 29th August, 1720, the Committee had made their decision.

The basis of the resolution was the conviction that 'according to the best account and Calculation that Can be made of the Company's Quick and dead Stock and Lands' they amounted to £94,500 at a moderate valuation. This was conservative enough, though there had been no time to make more than a hasty estimate. The actual figure adopted bore obvious reference to the proposals in hand and was clearly not meant to represent accurately the Company's financial position; it did not include the vast claims (£100,000) for damages against the French. The proposal was that the existing proprietors should have the nominal value of their shares enlarged so as to represent more fairly the stock which they owned. The first resolution was, therefore, that the 'Present stock' should be 'enlarged' from £31,500 to £94,500; the second resolution followed, that each proprietor should receive three shares of £100 for every such share which he held, free of charges.

So far the proposal was quite defensible in view of the assets of the Company. It would give the proprietors more shares to sell, if they wished; but it would not add to the trading capital of the Company. The third resolution of the Committee was, therefore, that new stock should be 'engrafted' on to the enlarged old stock at the rate of three new shares for each old one. This would mean a new issue of £283,500, would bring the stock up to £378,000, and altogether would entail a twelve-fold increase of the stock of the Company.

Only existing proprietors were to be allowed to subscribe for the new 'engrafted' stocks and so to reap the benefits of the bull market which they would almost certainly meet on the London Exchange. The new shares were to be issued in September 1720, they were to be issued at par, and subscribers were to pay ten per cent. every three months until they were fully paid—so that proprietors could get control of blocks of the new shares, and sell them if they rose in value, on initial payment of only a tenth of their par price. The details were worked out briefly and effectively. Payments would be forfeited if later instalments were not duly paid; a 'proper Instrument' for the project was to be prepared and sealed; the Governor's holding must be increased to £1,800, and a vote at the General Court must be given only to those who held £900. The Transfer

Book must be shut for a month to prevent hurried purchases by those who wished to qualify for the new subscription; and the ledgers and transfer books of the new and old stocks must be kept separately.

The Committee approved these resolutions unanimously, and next day (30th August) they were put before a General Court of the Company. Here also they were approved, as was a draft of the form for subscription which the Governor produced, and a 'Preamble' for the subscription. A few days later, at a Committee meeting, Governor Sir Bibye explained the great trouble which Captain John Merry, Deputy Governor, had taken over the new subscription. The Deputy Governor was forthwith voted a gratuity of two hundred guineas, while the Governor himself was presented with five hundred guineas as a token of gratitude for his services both in going to Europe and in other matters.

The stringency with which the Committee proposed to limit the new subscription to existing stockholders then caused a small crop of investors who claimed that they held stock but had not formally registered it with the Company or taken their oath to the Company. At the end of a week, by 6th September, the new subscription had brought in £2,359 12s. 0d. in cash, and further sums were coming in daily. These, of course, were only the first cash instalments paid for the new stock, and represented ten times that amount of stock taken up.

So the Committee worked through September and October of 1720, with an indifferent fur sale to bring them back to their real business, and with a report of the loss of the *Hudson's Bay* frigate to depress them. But far more serious depression was already haunting them. Their projects had been launched very late on a falling market, and it was probably only because new subscriptions were restricted to existing stockholders that the issue succeeded so well in September and October of 1720, for the general boom had reached its climax in the last week of June; after that date collapse can now be seen to have been inevitable, whether the innumerable companies went forward and uttered yet more shares so as to get cash to trade, or whether they stood still and awaited the full payment for shares already issued. Credit was grossly overstrained, and the practice of allocating new shares against a small down-payment had produced a gigantic inflation. The market was steadied during July, but there was an undercurrent of serious selling-out of stocks and in August, just before the Hudson's Bay scheme was launched, a new issue of South Sea stock ominously went to a discount.

The Hudson's Bay scheme, in these circumstances, derived its support from its appeal to its own stockholders. It was helped, too, by the clear position of the Company as a chartered corporation, for in August the South Sea directors tried to divert the dwindling investments away from new ventures by prosecuting four new companies for contravention of the 'Bubble Act' of 1718. The new ventures had offered shares for public subscription, and though without a charter, had acted as companies. The South Sea Company won three of its four cases, and the Bubble was pricked. Credit, which had soared universally, collapsed equally generally. The Hudson's Bay proprietors might to some extent be immune, and their loyalty to an undoubtedly chartered body which was *not* offering shares for public subscription carried them far. But the astonishing thing is that, in view of the time at which it was launched, the scheme achieved anything. South Sea stock slid from £850 to £390 between 20th August and 19th September, it touched £180 before the end of that month, and the last fortnight of September saw the 'Nemesis of bad finance' descend upon London. Credit was unobtainable; it was unfashionable not to be a bankrupt, and although the period of panic selling was soon over, deep depression ruled and the price of stocks crept slowly down—South Sea declined from £1,050 in June to £121 in December and Bibye Lake's interest in the Royal African Company slid from £200 a share to £45 in the same period.

Though the Hudson's Bay Company was immune from most of the troubles of the collapse there could be no doubt that it was not a suitable time to proceed with the sale of its new stock. In November 1720, therefore, the Governor faced a General Court and explained that 'the Posture of Affaires in Generall being much Altered' since the new scheme had been adopted at the end of August, the Committee had decided to proceed no further. The trebling of the stock by the bonus issue to stockholders was to stand; henceforth the 'Old Stock' of the Company would be reckoned as £94,500. But the sale of the new 'Engrafted Stock' was to be halted. Each stockholder who had subscribed his initial payment for the new stock was to have 'the same made stock', but there the matter was to rest. The General Court unanimously approved this proposal, and proceeded forthwith to re-elect Sir Bibye as Governor. The failure of the scheme had done nothing to damage his prestige in the Company, and disappointed though the proprietors might be at missing the boom, this was a period when they must have been intensely grateful to have missed the slump also.

The final episode came in December 1720, when the Committee

took into consideration the 'Present Scarcity of moneys, and deadness of Publick Credit' and decided that subscribers would prefer not to pay the remaining instalments on the new stock which had been assigned to them. They were to be given stock up to three times the amount of the actual payments which they had so far made and were to be released from further payments. The second payment of a tenth of the value of the new issue was almost due to be paid, and the subscribers must have welcomed this amnesty. Members who had not yet made any payment but who still wished to enlarge their holding were given up to the end of the next quarter, 25th March, to take advantage of this modified proposal. A General Court approved the reversal of policy unanimously, the Company's seal was taken off the 'Instrument' for the new subscription, and so the 'Bubble' episode closed for the Company.

What with the bonus issue and the new purchases of stock under the modified terms, the capital of the Company stood from 1720 onwards at £103,950, of which £3,150 represented actual new cash paid in to the trading reserves as subscriptions for the new shares. The new cash in hand was most welcome, especially in the circumstances of 1720–1; the capital of the Company had fortunately not been increased beyond a point at which the trade could pay a dividend on it, and the good fortune of the Company was demonstrated when in June 1721 a dividend of five per cent. on the stock of £103,950 was declared.

BOOKS FOR REFERENCE

HUDSON's BAY RECORD SOCIETY—Vol. XII.

EHRMAN, John—*The Navy in the War of William III 1689–1697* ... (Cambridge, 1953).

SCOTT, W. R.—*The Constitution and Finance of English, Scottish and Irish Joint-Stock Companies to 1720* (Cambridge, 1910–12), 3 vols.

CHAPTER XXXVII

THE FUR TRADE, LIFE BY THE BAY, AND FRENCH RIVALRY TO 1730

The fortunate ineptitude with which the Governor and Committee mis-timed their Bubble proposals was to some extent due to pre-occupation with French affairs, for Sir Bibye was in Paris on Company's business at the height of the boom. The terms agreed upon at Utrecht had made it seem necessary for such an envoy to be sent to Paris, for the Company was still unsatisfied. After the Treaty had been made public the Company lost no time in preparing its statement of damages due to the English under the eleventh article of the Treaty. The books as far back as 1681 were combed for details, a sub-committee was set up, to meet daily and then, when it had presented an interim report in August 1713, to meet twice a week. So by the time of the General Court on 20th November, 1713, the Governor was ready with a bill for damages, drawn out with great care and amounting to 'near One Hundred Thousand Pound'.

This, to be sure, included interest and even interest on estimated profits which might have been made. The loss of the *Rupert* in 1682, for example, was charged at £3,760 14s. 11d., and interest on that sum at £7,013 9s. 10d.; the trade-goods taken by de Troyes in 1686 were charged at cost at £5,562 12s. 0d. to which was added their 'value by Standard of Trade', £17,550. Interest on the combined sum was claimed at £37,339 8s. 6d. This single item therefore swelled an original loss of goods which cost less than £6,000 to a claim for over £60,000. But even this bill was for loss of ships and goods only; the capture of the posts themselves was not included, and the Committee may even have thought they were being moderate. For as early as 1706, and again in 1711, the claim had been rated as high as £108,514, and during the La Forest case in 1696 the Committee had estimated the losses at over £200,000.

There was, however, but little chance of recovering any such sum from the French, for they also had a plausible tale of damages suffered from the English. As long ago as 1699 they had been able to bring their total to 200,000 *livres*, to which they added a further 300,000 *livres* for ships taken at sea during the war. Not all of this damage was attributed to the Hudson's Bay Company (whose exploits were, indeed, meagre); but the Hudson's Bay bill was brought to 400,000 *livres* by 1714, and their losses, by whatever agency, left the French quite unable to pay any recompense to the English Company.

The whole of the French fur trade, and with it the economic life of Canada, was by 1713 in such a state that even if responsibility for the English claims could have been allocated among the numerous participants, nowhere was there ability to pay. Three factors stood out clearly. First, the European market was glutted to such an extent that the Deputy for La Rochelle (the city whose merchants were most deeply involved in the Canada trade) had even proposed to a Council of Commerce that no recovery would be possible unless half of the accumulated stocks of beaver were taken out and burned. Second, this glutted market was served by financiers who were not allowed to trade in accordance with their natural practice of buying only such quantities, at such prices, as the market would stand. Prices and qualities were set by ordinance and agreement, so that there was a premium on *gros cuir* and *bardeau*, with thick heavy skins and little fur, at a time when even the best *castor gras* from the Bay could not be sold. Third, the competition against the English, to secure the furs from the Indians, was one in which the French were handicapped by their routes and by their goods.

This last factor was one round which an endless argument centred —but the case put by knowledgeable traders was that the French posts to the south, Detroit and Frontenac, caused an annual loss and brought only low-grade furs; the posts in the Bay were almost impossible to maintain by sea without government help; and the furs shewed the truth of the contention that the trade could never flourish until the Indians had been instructed and disciplined. As things stood, the French had to give enhanced prices for any furs, however bad, brought in by the Indians, for fear they should go to the English. Albany, Manhattan and New York were as important as York Fort; and the Indians ruled the rival markets. As early as 1704 an assembly of the Sable, Ottawa, Huron and Salteaux tribes met a Council of French administrators at Lake Erie with the declaration that they would go where they wished with their furs—'Cette terre n'est pas à vous, elle est à Nous et nous la quitterons pour aller où bon nous semblera'. The declaration was pointed by a reference to the French lack of trade-goods, and de Vaudreuil drew from it the typical French answer to this problem of the Indian trade. The Indians, he said, would not come to Montreal to trade if the French ceased to send inland; 'Quand ces sauvages seront obligez d'aller chercher bien loing ce qui leur est necessaire ils iront toujours où est le bon marché, au lieu que s'ils trouvoient leurs besoins sous leurs maines ils les prendroient à quelque prix qu'ils fussent'. De Vaudreuil was therefore convinced that the French must continue to voyage inland and take the trade to the Indians, a conviction which he still maintained in the discussions of 1720 and 1721; and he also advocated that the French should overcome some of their disadvantages by buying cloth for the Indian trade from England.

These almost irreconcilable difficulties of the French fur trade, with their ultimate quandary of maintaining a lien on the Indians in the face of a glut of furs, had played their part in delaying the settlement of boundaries at Utrecht. For the *castor gras* of the Nelson River trade, prime in quality though it might be, was only needed in limited amounts by the French hatters and so the French diplomats were left without clear instructions whether to insist on the retention of Fort Bourbon or to let it go to the English. The result had been that other considerations, in particular the English determination on this point, had triumphed and Monsieur Jérémie had been ordered to cede his post to Governor Knight. But the settlement of a permanent and satisfactory frontier between Canada and Rupert's Land had proved as difficult and impossible as any agreement upon damages.

The negotiations which followed the Treaty of Utrecht were conducted by the British diplomats in full consultation with the Company. In April 1714 Bolingbroke was supplied with a memorandum on the Company's case and its claim for damages, set off against the French schedule of goods left behind at Fort Bourbon, and he presented the problem to the Council. The matter went to the Lords of Trade and Plantations, and the Committee of the Company were asked to appear before their Lordships and give their views. So in August 1714 a fully-prepared memorandum of the previous discussions on boundaries and damages, with a map, was submitted. With little real hope of getting damages from the French, the Committee were perhaps more sanguine over a boundary settlement. Here the English claim was for a line running from Cape Perdrix or Grimington's Island, at $58\frac{1}{2}°$ on the east coast of Labrador, cutting the Labrador peninsula in two until it came to Lake Mistassini (Lake Mistoseny or Misessinke), running through the Lake until it came to 49°, and so westwards along the 49th parallel.

The Lords of Trade and Plantations pressed for the nomination of French commissioners to agree on the details of the Utrecht settlement and Bolingbroke showed his personal interest in the matter, asking for a progress report in August 1714. But by then the Company had further complicated the issue by claiming part of the freight of the *Union* frigate, which had brought the French goods and men from Bourbon, and James Knight's purchases of stores and goods from Governor Jérémie had also to be taken into the account. The Company was still pressing for a settlement in May 1715; but, as was later recorded, it was never able to bring the settlement of the boundary to a final conclusion, nor did it ever receive any compensation for damages.

From 1715 to 1719 the matter rested, with the main interest of the Company devoted to Knight's projects in the Bay, to French encroachments down the rivers, and to the financial developments which marked the governorship of Sir Bibye Lake. But in 1719, as the bubble of speculation was swelling both in England and in France, the regulation and organisation of overseas trade became an insistent matter of government concern, especially for the projects of Richard Law in France. In his plans a *Compagnie D'Occident* was to co-ordinate and dominate French colonial trade to all parts of the world, and a settlement of the Canadian frontier was much to be desired as a preliminary to the scheme's operation. The move for a settlement therefore became equally welcome to both sides, and in July 1719 the Company was told that the Lords of Trade and Plantations were to send Colonel Bladen as their envoy to Paris to try to settle the claims for damages and for a boundary.

The Committee thereupon called in a lawyer, Jeremy Dummer, to manage the matter, and accepted his memorial, which Governor Sir Bibye then carried to Colonel Bladen. He was kindly received both by Colonel Bladen and by the Lords of Trade and Plantations, and the latter suggested that he should go with the colonel to Paris. This was a suggestion which the Committee accepted gladly, giving the Governor a gratuity of two hundred guineas and offering to pay his expenses 'without any farther account to be given of the same'. So Lake took Jeremy Dummer with him to Paris, and there spent most of the month of November 1719 in bolstering the English diplomats in their discussions with the French. He was not back in London again until towards the end of December, and then had only to report that he had found an 'Aversion in the French to comply with the Article of Utricht, Particularly in that Part which relates to pay moneys for former Damages done us'. He, and Colonel Bladen, had steadily put forward the former notions of a boundary which would keep the French to the south of the 49th parallel except in Labrador (where the line would run up to cut the east coast at Cape Perdrix at 59°) and they added to the long-term proposal a definite and pointed complaint against French encroachment since Utrecht in Albany River, where the wood-runners were cutting the Indians off from the Bottom of the Bay.

Nothing was accomplished in Paris, and the expectation of a suitable settlement with the French had nothing to contribute towards that confidence in Sir Bibye which carried him through the Bubble crisis. In fact, French feeling was steadily hardening against the surrender of the Bay in its entirety which had been conceded at Utrecht, and by the time of the mission to Paris of Colonel Bladen and Governor Sir Bibye the expansionist colonial element was again a force in French councils, so that both La Mothe Cadillac and Dulhut could argue that the English insistence on 'restitution' instead of 'cession' in the Hudson's Bay clauses of the Treaty of Utrecht restricted the English claims to lands which had actually been in the *rightful* possession of the English. This would mean either that the problem of right should be taken back to the status at the Treaty of Breda (as Cadillac claimed) or that the old questions of first entry to the Bay should be re-examined—which, the French held, could lead only to the conclusion that the French were first at Nelson River, the English first at the Bottom of the Bay. Therefore the 'restitution' would apply only to the Bottom of the Bay and the boundary would have to be drawn so as to limit the English to the coast even there. This would be a line somewhere between Lake Nemiskau and the old Fort Charles, Rupert River, and it would follow the coast round the Eastmain and to the west, leaving Moose to the English and Abitibi to the French, who would also get Nelson River and all to the west of it.

This argument that the English should be confined to a narrow coastal strip was based on an acknowledgment that the value of such a strip depended on sharing the Indians of the interior with the French posts, so that the latter would in effect be able to strangle the English trade. It was the old concept of Louis Jolliet, urged by his successors; and it proved as unacceptable to the English in 1719 as it had been thirty years earlier. The Committee which had survived the Bubble crisis was therefore forced to realise that amicable settlement with the French was not to be expected, and that the only effective argument was possession.

The fact that Governor Sir Bibye was in Paris during the exciting months of October and November 1719 probably explains why the Hudson's Bay Company was so slow in launching its Bubble project, for without him there was much competence but little initiative in the Committee. So it is at least arguable that although the claims against the French brought no repayment and no settled frontier they nevertheless brought the great boon of an escape from Bubble finance. Had the project of August 1720 been launched only a few months earlier it must have gone so far as to make withdrawal impossible, and the Company must inevitably have lost the reputation, and the borrowing capacity, of a sound and conservative concern; this was, by the eighteenth century, one of its main assets. As things stood, the chief mark of the succeeding period, from 1720 to 1730, was the staid prosperity of the Company's trade. Here there were several aspects to the business, but first stood the fact that the returns of furs were magnificent and that they were easily and steadily absorbed by the London market. A certain amount of financial speculation added to the prosperity, and it is notable that during this period the Company has, for the first time, surpluses to invest and is able to pay off all its 'bonds'.

In the fur returns beaver still held pride of place though the attempt to stimulate the hunting of martens persisted. The Company's servants were encouraged, as they had been by James Knight, to hunt for small skins and were promised that if they declared their furs and sent them home openly they should be allowed half of the sale price when the Company had disposed of them at its sales. This was a promise seriously kept, and officers and men alike were credited with the sums which their furs realised and the idea was even carried so far that on occasions the Committee gave an extra gratuity because a man had been so 'tied to Company's business that he cannot get out trapping'. But in 1729 a new approach to the problem of small furs was tried with the order that, instead of sending their trappings home for sale, the servants should sell them direct at the factory, the price offered being a quart of brandy and a half-pound of sugar for two martens. The old system had certainly produced some abuses and some difficulties; James Knight's private trappings had been a constant irritant, Kelsey's troubles at the end of his career were almost certainly connected in some way with accusations that he had connived at private trade, and there were accusations that furs worth hundreds of pounds were privately sold in London before the Company could be ready with its sale, and that the warehousekeeper at York took the Company's best skins and substituted his own poor ones, stole brandy to buy skins from the Indians, and falsified his accounts.

The martens had undoubtedly sold well during the war years, producing an annual profit of about £2,000 with very little delay, and they continued so to do down to the 1720's. The profit on martens in 1720, for example, was £2,767 13s., and in 1721 £2,623 15s. 7d., and the Committee anxiously spurred the trade in small furs which 'never Lye on hand as Beavor doth'. But other small furs made but little profit; white foxes were not worth sending home since three were worth only one ordinary fox, and they were to be traded only at four or five to a beaver even if they were well furred and not matted. Martens were, in any case, a trade which fluctuated from year to year, and they showed the difficulty of adapting the fur trade to the European market. From York, for example, there was but a poor trade in 1725, but in 1726 the 'Upland Indians' were encouraged by their treatment the previous year and brought in over two thousand. York and Nelson River were, however, badly placed for marten-hunting, and Macklish wrote in 1728 that two-thirds of the natives never saw a marten in their country; the York martens came only from the home Indians, hunting round the post, and from the 'Great Plain Indians', the 'Poets' from the far Saskatchewan. There were years in which the returns of martens compensated for slight returns in beaver, as in 1732; and sometimes the profit exceeded £3,000 in a year, as in 1723–4. But on the whole it appears that the utmost that could be said for such a trade was that it was an attractive and profitable side-line, for a profit even of £3,000 a year would not have sufficed for the Company as it stood in the 1720's, with its increased capital and increasing commitments. The same is true of the other 'small trades', in goose quills, feathers, foxes, wolverenes, and even in whale-oil; here also the stimulus of giving a quart of brandy for every white whale caught at Churchill was tried, but the returns were negligible—four and a half tons in 1722, one and a half tons in 1723 and but little more in 1724.

Indeed the Committee, for all the talk of the difficulty of selling beaver, never seriously tried to replace it by other trades at this time. Despite pressure from the French wood-runners inland from Albany, and despite a promise made to the Indians to entice them down to trade at the British post, the Committee insisted that martens must only be traded at the rate of three to a beaver; the French, it was alleged, did indeed trade them at the rate of one to a beaver, but they took thirty beaver for a gun as against the rate of ten to a gun which the Company allowed. This would mean that the general standard of the Company's trade would be so comparatively generous that the 'better pennyworths' would secure a fair share of the normal trade, especially in beaver, but that they traded on equal terms with the

French for martens at thirty to the gun and so almost deliberately yielded that trade to them.

The different approach to the beaver trade, in which reiterated assurances that it was a drug on the market went with a firm determination to drive a hard trade and to challenge the French, was an expression of market conditions in Europe. There beaver was, by reason of its comparative cheapness and plenty, no longer a luxury fur but one for which there existed a wide market for common consumption. Especially was this the case in England, where the Company was able to assure Parliament that the Russian secret of combing the beaver-wool from the pelt had been introduced into this country, so that beaver-wool was more plentiful and cheap than it had ever been and the making of hats had become a flourishing trade.

The sated markets of the war period were quite rapidly stabilised. Even in 1712 the Company had been able to dispose of most of its stocks, though at low prices—three shillings and fourpence for fine *parchment* and four shillings and eightpence for *coat*. In 1713 and 1714 a series of small private sales (partly to William Dolbey, the Company's warehousekeeper) led up to larger transactions with the great merchant Henry Sperling, buying for export. But in November 1714 the Company still had on hand over 20,000 *parchment*; the *coat* was almost cleared out by November, in the sales which had followed the return of the ships of that year. Prices however were rising to about eight shillings the pound for *coat* and about six shillings for *parchment*. The Committee therefore decided to keep substantial reserves for the London market instead of shipping them to Europe, and the whole stock was cleared by April 1715. In that year fears of the consequences of the 1715 rebellion caused special orders to be made for the ships to come home west-about for fear of trouble in Scotland; but Captain Davis failed to make his landfall in the Bay and brought no returns. This roused Knight's anger but left the market largely unaffected, since although the *parchment* was selling briskly in 1715 the *coat* was sticking, and there were about 26,000 skins on hand when the ships of 1716 brought the returns of two years and threatened something of a glut again. Stocks then mustered over 64,000 *parchment* and over 41,000 *coat*, but only about 6,000 of the *coat* were unsold during the November sale, and these were cleared by June 1717, while the vast bulk of over 62,000 *parchment* was cleared by April of that year.

Then followed a series of years in which increasing returns were regularly sold within the year of their shipment; the 46,000 *parch-*

ment got in 1717 were all sold by April 1718; 40,000 received in 1718 were sold at steady prices between six and seven shillings the pound by the autumn of 1719, and so on. The returns rose as York Fort got into steady production and Churchill produced its quota. *Parchment* numbered 47,000 in 1720, 51,000 in 1721, and with a setback in 1724 continued to top the 50,000 mark with York producing about 40,000 skins a year. *Coat* was still discouraged, as it had been for many years; it fetched a better price per skin but the big market was for the *parchment* from which beaver-wool might be combed. Returns in *coat* ranged between 7,000 odd skins in 1718 and 22,000 odd in 1722; they averaged about 10,000 skins a year and sales reached just about that amount, rising to over 20,000 to dispose of the big shipment of 1722.

Here can be seen the solid base of the prosperity of the Company, with revenue from sales bringing in anything from £20,000 to £30,000 a year and hovering round £27,000. The element of profit contained in such sales receipts is extremely difficult to estimate, for the skins sold were the product of goods shipped and of expenses incurred over a number of years. The system adopted by the Company was to enter the skins at an arbitrary estimated cost which hardly varied from year to year; normally the 'book-cost' was from two shillings and threepence to two shillings and sixpence a pound though on occasions (as in 1685) it was as low as one shilling and sixpence. Against this estimated cost was set the actual price fetched by the furs at the sales, to yield an estimated profit for each shipment when the whole consignment had been disposed of. The method had many defects, not least that of starting from an arbitrary cost price which bore little relation to the constant changes in the trade. It also meant that in many years the result was a combination of cash profit plus furs in hand. An easier way to arrive at the trading position would probably have been to strike an annual balance of trading costs versus cash received from sales. On such a basis the Company during these post-war years would have been making a profit of about £10,000 a year.

The result was that, instead of being a borrower, the Company became an investor. In 1701 for example, and again in 1706, it had been forced to borrow to pay the customs on its furs; in 1709 it had been forced to accept almost forced sale of its skins in Amsterdam, at a price 'miserably Low beyond Expectation' in its need for 'Present Moneys', and the whole of its trade up to the Treaty of Utrecht was conducted against a background of bonds, debts and debentures. In contrast with this the steady payment of dividends from

1718 onwards is backed by constant evidence of real prosperity. Not only is Governor Sir Bibye able to borrow (£400 in November 1714, £500 in December, £2,000 in May 1715, £3,000 in May 1723); he is also allowed to anticipate his 'attendance-money' for work on the Committee. Others shared the prosperity too. Gratuities were regularly given to the secretary, to the warehousekeeper and to other servants, and in 1726 the General Court of the Company took into account the 'great Trouble and Care the Governour, Deputy Governour and Committee have taken' and voted to the Governor a regular stipend of £150 a year, with £125 to the Deputy Governor and £75 to each Committee-man. This was increased to £200 for the Governor, £150 for the Deputy and £100 for the Committee-men in 1729, and it is obvious that such payments are not merely a method for sharing the profits but are a recognition that the Company's affairs demand the constant attention of the officials.

Even the King shared the general prosperity. Although members who wished to partake of the new stock projected in 1720 should have made their initial payment of ten per cent. to the bankers Atwill and Hammond by 25th March, 1721, those who had omitted to take the chance were allowed till the end of June. This in effect allowed the Company to take up a little more capital, and it allowed members who had been frightened at the time, but who realised later that the Company was one of the few concerns which had come safely through the Bubble, to put in a little more money. His Majesty, however, could not be expected to act as an ordinary stockholder, and so the General Court assumed that he had paid his due of £90 (ten per cent. of his holding of £900, which represented his original share of £300 trebled in 1690). He was thenceforth paid his dividends on a holding of £2,970, which represented his previous £900, plus the assumed payment of £90, all trebled. On such a holding the ten per cent. dividend of these years came almost to the total value of the investment (assumed in the case of the Crown) of less than half a century ago.

Nor was this all. In addition to the loans made to the Governor, the Committee found themselves faced with the problem of investing an accumulated surplus and so forced to play the part of active investors on the London Exchange. The loan of £3,000 made to the Governor in May 1723 was made on the security of a holding of South Sea stock which the Committee soon decided to sell, so that the transaction really amounted to an investment in South Sea stock by the Company. Later transactions were more direct, although the legal difficulties in the way of direct investment in annuities (which were the favoured investment) by a joint-stock company made it necessary that stocks should be held in the names of individual members of the Committee. In January 1724 £3,000 of South Sea annuities were bought in the names of Captain John Merry and Captain Samuel Jones while John Merry also held £6,000 worth of annuities on behalf of the Company. By 1732 the cash in hand was reckoned at £17,129 and the investment of £10,000 in East India stocks was decided on. A last loan of £11,000 to the Governor at 3 per cent., to buy an estate in Derbyshire, was a tribute alike to his financial activity and to the affluence to which he and his Committee had brought the Company.

Stable and prosperous though the Company undoubtedly was in the years between 1714 and 1730, it was not without its troubles. Expansion to the northward, the search for the copper-mine, attempts at whaling and other new sources of trade, the establishment of Churchill and the steady encroachment of the French, all gave constant cause for anxiety and demanded the closest attention to business.

Here there was much which had to be done in England, and the Committee did all that was possible there. But much also depended upon the servants by the Bay-side, and when peace brought some improvement in the type of man available this was more than welcome. During the war Governor Fullartine had been forced to complain that the Company sent out 'poor Sorry helpless souls and no ways fitting for the Country'; and the old servants, knowing the pinch in which the Company was placed, were able to demand increased wages, going at times so high as to insist on being paid as much as the seamen! The worst of them 'blowed att £20 a year', and most of them got about £30 a year. The strength of the 1720–30 servants lay, of course, in the officers, and here predominance lay with the tradesman, apprentice, or even ordinary servant, who had been promoted up to command.

Thomas Macklish the promoted shipwright who had started his service as a young man under the guidance of his uncle, and who had at least twenty years of service behind him when he was promoted from the command of Albany to York in 1722, was in the tradition of Knight and Kelsey although he differed from them on policy. His influence, both in driving a steady trade at York and in discriminating against Churchill, was important but not continuous. He was 'seriously indisposed' in 1722, and he came home at his own request in 1726, to go out again as Governor of 'the Bay and Streights of Hudson in America' in 1727. 'Captain' Anthony Beale was another such, although he did not have a craft in his hands. He had been apprenticed to the Company in 1678, one of the first to be taken, and he had a wealth of experience of life in the Bay. He had acted as Governor of Albany in 1705 when Governor Fullartine had 'designed for home' to cure his stone and gravel and had been unable conscientiously to press Kelsey to stay since the latter also needed a period at home to recover his health. Beale had stood out against Fullartine despite his 'great passion', and he showed similar strength of purpose throughout his career. He had been second in command at York in 1721, was made Governor when Macklish returned home in 1726, and went to Churchill in 1727. There he subdued the disorders which had arisen, and there he remained in command until he came home at his own request in 1731.

But the officers had their defects as well as their virtues. The disorders at Churchill arose from the one-sided brilliance of another former apprentice, Richard Norton. He had made a great reputation early in life by his voyages to the northward with Indians, and he had undoubtedly suffered greatly in his travels—perhaps enough to blunt his wits and certainly enough to accentuate a natural defect; it was said that he had suffered so much that he could hardly remember the details. He had been made Trader at Churchill in 1723 and had succeeded to the command there within the year. But with all his knowledge of Indians he proved unfit to manage the post. Trade was small, consumption of provisions was high. Yet the men complained of their rations, and in 1727 Norton was brought back to York to be instructed 'in the nature and method of our Trade' by Macklish. He seemed pleased with the change, but although he was again given command at Churchill in 1731 when Beale came home he proved for the rest of his career unable to get his 'affectionate kindness' for the Indians into conformity with the Company's system.

Deprived of the sober influence of Macklish, Albany produced in modified form the difficulties which Norton had allowed at Churchill. Joseph Myatt, a former carpenter in the Company's service, was made Chief in 1722 when Macklish moved to York, and the appointment was followed by an immediate decline in trade which led to fears of mismanagement. Myatt was therefore placed under Richard Staunton, but Staunton stood by him and maintained that he had been slandered by the malicious, so that Myatt was promised that he should not lose financially and that he would probably get back his command on Staunton's retirement (as he did in 1726). The incident shows the difficulties of finding suitable officers from among the tradesmen in the fur trade, but there had been more serious features in the reports of trouble at Albany. There was the report, later thrown up against the Company as a sign of its repressive attitude towards the Indians, that an Indian boy was taken into the trading-house, was instructed in Christianity and was taught to read. Staunton, after enquiry, reported that the Indian boy was in no way concerned with trade 'and as for Mr. Myats instructing him to write and reade, I doe ashure you thatt he thoughte noe harme'. The kindly act was nevertheless a direct breach of instructions. From 1719 onwards Governors had been constantly warned not to allow the Indians into the trading room, not to teach them to read or write 'or otherwise admitted to prye into any of the Company's affairs', and the incident at Albany brought a reiteration of these orders to all posts.

In truth the Company was in something of a quandary where its relations with the Indians were concerned. Its main policy remained, as it had been under Knight and Kelsey, to prevent Indian wars and to direct the Indians to hunting instead. Such a policy necessitated constant attention. It was in a way a civilising mission. True, the chief motive was to increase the supplies of furs; but the impact of the ordinary trading habits of western peoples on an uncivilised race has as deep and lasting an effect as the more self-conscious changes in habits and cultures advocated by priests and educationalists. Certainly in this matter the Hudson's Bay men can be clearly distinguished from the Dutch settlers of Orange and Manhattan, who supplied the Iroquois with the fire-arms which made that tribe the tyrants of the American plains; and from the French, who from the earliest days of Samuel Champlain had adopted a policy of participating in Indian wars in order to spread their influence and authority. Knight, Kelsey, Norton, Beale and Macklish—one after another they tried their utmost to implement that policy which the Committee had so fully approved. 'The Preservation of Peace amongst them is of the utmost Importance and Therefore Desire in a particular Manner that you will be very Diligent in every Method that may any ways Tend to prolong it.' The task of the peacemaker, however, was not always easy, especially when the example of the French in leading the Indians to war gave rise to an expectation that the English might do likewise. Norton was bluntly asked 'whether they must Stand Still and be knockt on the head Like Doggs or fight in their one Difence or noe by Reason we had ordered them not to warr with any Native'. Macklish offered generous supplies of tobacco, brandy and powder, to enable peace to be made with the 'Poits' (reputed to be led by the French) but found his efforts spurned. Yet the efforts continued, strongly backed by London.

The incident of the Indian boy at Albany, and the reiterated orders not to allow Indians into the posts, undoubtedly reveal a fear that the servants of the Company might 'go native'. Here an analysis of the motives at work reveals a quaint mixture of moral reprobation and of commercial caution.

The North American Indian had, within one generation of contact with the fur trader, become so utterly dependent on European fire-arms for hunting that the Company was fully justified in claiming (as it did in 1726 for example) that 'many thousand Families of the Natives for want of the supply they Annually receive from us, of Guns, Powder, and Shott, wherewith they kill the Beavor, Buffalo and several other Beasts of that Country, the Flesh whereof is their food, will by the disappointment of the not arrival of the said ships, be starved before the next Year'. The same dependence on European supplies had been noted by the French when they were in possession of Nelson River, and their Governor Jérémie left a tragic account of the starvation, cannibalism and infanticide, caused by his lack of trading-goods, 'for they had lost their skill with the bow since Europeans had supplied them with fire-arms'. Lack of snow could also interrupt winter hunting, unseasonable weather could ruin the partridge or the goose hunts on which so much depended, the buffalo or the deer might fail or the fisheries prove barren. Even when well equipped, the Indian and his family could only survive each successive winter by a miracle of endurance, skill and hereditary capacity. His trading journeys to the Company's posts were brief exciting interludes dominated by his need to return to his hunting grounds before the rivers froze.

But there had also arisen a considerable body of Indians dependent on the posts in a different manner, 'home-guard' Indians who hunted in spring and fall to provide geese and partridges for the English to live on. These more permanent hangers-on were a corollary of the Company's endless complaints of the consumption of European provisions. The shipments of garden seeds, of pigs, sheep, goats and cows, were parts of this policy of cutting down dependence on European food. But although their gardens and their cattle brought great pleasure to the factors they made little serious impression on the food situation. Perhaps the turnips and the cabbages lessened the incidence of scurvy, but juniper beer was probably more effective even in this. Carrots, peas and beans could also be grown, especially at Albany, but as a supplement to European fare it was the great goose and partridge hunts, and fishing, upon which the Governors relied. Fourteen thousand fish laid down at Albany by the end of October was a meagre catch, the 'worst year ever', and threatened a winter of short allowances since the ration was three fish a man a day. But yet Governor Fullartine hoped he might feed fish to his men on three days a week during the winter, whereas in a still worse year, when only twelve thousand were laid down, he could only look forward to one day's fish diet in each week until the spring hunts brought the wild-fowl again. Similar quantities of birds were required—three thousand geese to last Albany through summer until fall brought the birds to the marshes once more.

It was the 'home-guard' Indians who conducted the hunts, not the Europeans. For a whole generation yet to come the European servants were unable to hunt for their own food; so much so that the Indians told the English they had not one man could kill a goose, and as late as 1750 the Indians were able to threaten to starve the posts by refusing to hunt. Such a policy of dependence on the hunting of the 'home-guards' brought close and constant contacts with them. For they almost necessarily remained within reasonable distance of the posts throughout the winter. Consequently during a hard winter they came into the post expecting food. They also brought in an occasional deer which was a welcome addition to the winter fare of the Englishmen.

The Company accepted its responsibility for this relationship, and oatmeal was a regular part of the annual shipment, designed specifically to feed the Indians in cases of need. They were consistently fed and cared for in sickness at all posts, though there were occasions when food was so short that the Indians had to be sent away— as at Churchill in 1721, when Richard Norton had to be sent out to live in a tent, and when almost thirty Indians, old and young, were 'lying upon the factory', eating European food 'Under a pretence they are all Snow blind', and a further party of sixteen Indians was sent away to hunt, for fear they would starve both themselves and the English.

Such a realistic approach was essential if the Indians were to be forced to fend for themselves. Otherwise they would become idle dependants, progressively less and less capable of supporting themselves and of getting furs; and such habits would soon spread from the 'home-guards' to the hunting tribes up the rivers. Even the Indians from north of Churchill, whom the Company was particularly anxious to encourage, were sent away because they brought no furs. The Company 'did not desire their Company Eampty handed'.

With all of its care to prevent the growth of utter and idle dependence, the Company could not prevent the development of the type

Indian described as 'thouse hungary Dogges that are nevar from the facthory'. Dependence on them for the goose and partridge hunts entailed the obligation to feed them through the winter and to keep them both loyal and fit for hunting. To encourage the more distant indians to travel in search of furs, too, the Hudson's Bay men developed a habit of allowing them to leave their old, their young, and some of their women, at the posts whilst the hunt lasted. In some sort this practice served as a permanent bond, to bring the Indians past the French cordon to trade at the Bay. It resulted in some Indian children growing up under the constant influence of the post, and it resulted almost inevitably in a certain number of Indian women becoming attached to the posts, and to individual servants.

Such women were at best liable to be fed 'on the strength' of the post; more probably they led to peculation of drink and clothing; and certainly they introduced an element of indiscipline. Again the problem produced a mixture of morals and materialism—best exemplified when the Committee reluctantly admitted that it could not control the relations of Richard Norton (then Chief at Churchill) with his Indian woman and her family, but that in no circumstances was the Company to be put to any extra charge. When they felt they could, they took an even stronger line, ordering that no women be allowed to live in the factories and instructing the Chiefs 'to hinder as much as Possible the detestable Sin of Whoring, which we are informed is practised in the Factory [Albany] notwithstanding what we have so often ordered'. These almost inevitable consequences of the persistence of the English posts, and of the enforced celibacy of the servants, together with the growing familiarity of the English and the Indians, began to produce a small number of English half-breed children. The English half-breeds never became so numerous or so important as the French *métis*, but they included some remarkable characters and they cannot be ignored in the history of the Company, for they mark a stage in the acclimatisation of their English fathers.

The strictures on Albany contained not only reproofs for allowing an Indian boy to be brought up in the post, but also reports of 'irregularities and debaucheries, disgusting and terrifying the Natives from coming to trade', and ruining and spoiling the servants. Myatt's reputation in this matter was vindicated, but subsequent years saw the steady weeding out of the undesirable men from Albany. Four were sent home in 1726, for example, as 'turbulent Sottish men', including one mariner who was 'so monsterous Wicked and Disobediant' that he was certain to corrupt others if he remained.

Myatt maintained, probably with justice, that the complaints of his own conduct came from those who had done what they pleased under Staunton's command; he himself had punished the chief transgressors, but three men had died of 'Excessive hard Drinking' and the rest thought it the 'greatest Mortification in the World' that he should try to keep them sober. The Londoners in particular were so well acquainted with the debaucheries of town life that he despaired of ever reclaiming them. The labourers recruited for Albany in 1726 were 'Sotts to a man'.

In such a quandary the Company relied upon three factors—the characters of the officers, scarcity of brandy, and recruitment from the Orkneys.

Since the officers wrote, or at least signed, the letters home it is difficult to ascertain their real characters, but the chances are that the officers were more discreet, but little different from the men. Myatt himself died of a 'Gout in his stomach' in 1730—which might give rise to some suspicion. And Thomas Bird, Chief at Albany in 1739, not only left his accounts in a hopeless muddle but died as a result of drink. His successor Rowland Waggoner, to whom Myatt had given the character of one of the best servants he ever saw, died within a year of his appointment, also of drink. His successor Joseph Isbister proved to be a man, long practised in the fur trade, of great strength and independence of mind (he later denied even the London Committee's right to interfere with his command) who set to work to check the irregularities and to overcome 'that height of Insolence that threatens to Demolish all forms of Government'.

The officers were, in fact, typical products of the artisan class in England at the beginning of the eighteenth century, and from most of them any heroic insistence upon continence or sobriety was not to be expected. Discipline of an arbitrary kind they might insist on. But they were not bred to command; for the most part they were promoted servants. Their rule would normally be fair and sensible but neither far-sighted nor high-principled. An evaluation of life in the posts should not be too harsh, nor should the solace of the bottle be easily condemned on moral grounds. Life, especially for the officers, was solitary and depressing, with long periods of enforced idleness. Despair, loneliness, and indifference must each in turn have attacked the posts by the Bay every winter, and chronic ailments which modern medical skill could diagnose and cure could then only be suffered. Stone, gravel, 'pains in the breast', difficulty in breathing, even the 'Gout in the Stomach', all spoke of long periods of chronic ill-health and constant pain, for which only one anodyne was known or available—the bottle.

Nor were conditions constantly evil. Albany seems to have got into a particularly bad mood at this time, but complaints from York or Churchill are very few, and even at Albany it is clear that occasional debauches colour the whole picture. The Committee's remedy lay in restricting supplies of liquor. Small beer was brewed at the posts from malt sent out; some 'ordinary' beer was also sent out ready brewed, and a small quantity of strong beer for use on the voyage and for an occasional issue at the post. Beer caused no trouble; nor did the gifts of wine sent to allow the Chief to entertain at his table. But brandy had to be shipped in considerable quantities, especially where (as at Albany) French opposition was serious. The Indians would expect a gift of a dram, a pipe of tobacco and perhaps some prunes (of which they were most fond) at the start of trade, but such gifts made it difficult to require strict accounts for the quantity shipped or to stop pilfering. The Indians would often take payment for their furs largely in brandy if it was available, and at trade-time the posts would require to maintain the strictest watchfulness to guard against attacks and fights. The temptation for the men of the post to share in the drinking at trade-time was strong; and it met with constant warning and remonstrance.

Illicit shipments of brandy from England, sent to the men by their friends and relations, were a separate and more important danger than access to the trade-brandy. Here the Committee should have been in a strong position since it controlled all shipping but, despite constant reiteration and a system of sealed consignments working in with rewards to informers the brandy still found its way to the servants. Yet although servants were from time to time convicted of writing home for brandy and other goods for private trade, and seizures were sometimes made and were sometimes evaded, such a source of temptation could only supply fairly brief debauches, and the Company could be secure in the knowledge that, on the whole, the men had no other shop save the Company's store.

Precautions to discipline the men, and to restrict their access to brandy and to women were, however, at best palliatives. The real remedy, as the Committee realised, lay in choosing such men as required no discipline. With this in view as an alternative to the unsatisfactory Londoners, the Company at this time began seriously and steadily to follow a policy of recruitment in the Orkneys. Scotland had already been tried as a source of labour, but apart from the difficulties involved by distance it is probable that the latent Jacobitism of the Highlanders at this time would make them suspect to such a Committee as ruled the Hudson's Bay Company. Certainly the attempts to recruit Scots were dropped. The use of the Orkney-men, however, developed to such importance in the history of the Company that it would be easy to exaggerate the conviction and pur-pose with which the system was started. In practice a great deal of the argument in favour of the Orkneys seems to have sprung simply from expediency, from the fact that if the ships sailed from London before the necessary complement of men had been recruited, then the Orkneys were the best port of call at which the deficiency might be made good.

Local connections, however, supplemented this reason for using Orkneymen, and as early as 1708 the Committee had written in January to 'Mr. Grimsay at the Orkneys' to instruct him to recruit twelve or fourteen servants, lusty young men between twenty and thirty years of age, of whom two were to be tailors. The move was made as a result of consultation with the ships' captains, and they and outgoing officers played their parts in recruitment, working in with local agents who received instructions to get the men ready in expectation of the ships' arrival.

Bred as crofters and fishermen in the far north, used to the cold and hunger of their own homesteads, and with their native hardihood unimpaired by evil living in the slums of England's towns, the Orkneymen proved admirable servants in the Bay. True, they had their defects. They got a reputation for a dour lack of enterprise in contrast with the more spectacular French Canadians; but they were loyal, and capable of enduring great hardships. Myatt at Albany, for example, wrote home that he welcomed the Orkney recruits of 1726, though those engaged as seamen seemed to know very little of the matter. By that time their reputation stood so well, and the system had so far become common practice, that in the following year the ships' captains were simply told that the Company had been dis-appointed at the last moment by several servants who had contracted to sail; the ships were therefore to call at the Orkneys and to recruit the necessary number. So the system continued, with a valuable and sobering addition to the sources of recruitment open to the Com-pany and with a possibility, too, of getting cattle which might be transported and thrive, or at least survive, by the Bay. Hardy Shet-land sheep and cows were taken even to Churchill as early as 1732; and they throve there although Richard Norton had 'bad success' with a horse from the islands.

The steadiness and the comparative sobriety of the Orkneymen

were invaluable; but steady and sober trade could not for ever maintain itself in the face of rising French opposition, and it was French
opposition which set the tone of the Company's development in the
Bay during the period following on the diplomatic victory at Utrecht.
From 1713 to about 1730 the French moves were cause for uneasiness but not for alarm. But during these years the scene was set for
the more purposeful rivalry of the next generation. Although the
Hudson's Bay men were on the whole tied both by their own inclination and by the Committee's policy to defensive measures, yet
they were acquiring a knowledge of the country and habits of living
in the Arctic which were to stand them in good stead when, in the
next generation, the opposition from Canada made more active
resistance necessary.

From the start it became clear that the surrender of the Bay at
Utrecht would not bring the end of French opposition. The French
claim to Lake Mistassini had been maintained in the negotiations
following after the signing of the Treaty, and their possession of the
trade of Nemiskau River had not been seriously disputed. More important was the fact that they carried into effect their contention that
the boundary should run from Lake Mistassini to Lake Superior,
thereby giving themselves control of the Moose and Albany Rivers
and their tributaries.

In this territory trade, under the control of the *Compagnie des
Habitans*, working in with the financiers Neret, Gayot and Company,
was carried on by a system of licences or *congés*. These *congés* are in
themselves modest enough signs that the French fur trade still suffered from a glut of furs, for there was only a single canoe licensed
for this area in 1720, followed by two in 1722 and again in 1723, and
by four in 1724. But there were more illicit traders out among the
Indians than there were *congés* issued, and in any case the sheer fact
that there was competition, an alternative market to which the
Indian might take his furs, mattered more than the extent of that
competition.

As soon as the trade began to pick up a pattern again after the
signing of the Peace, therefore, French rivalry on the upper waters
of the rivers leading down to Albany began to figure in the Company's
correspondence. The French were cited by Albany from 1715 onwards as the reason for a decline in the returns of that post. They
were reported to have built two houses up the river, in the midst of
Indians who habitually came down to trade at the English post and,
to emphasise the fact that the value of their rivalry did not depend
on their numbers, they would 'seldom spare for cost when a bargain

is to be got'; so the English were forced also to adopt uneconomical methods of trade and to decide that now was the time to 'oblige' the Indians. The French were without doubt 'treacherous neighbours' at Albany, but their trade had not the organisation or capital behind it which should have made it a serious long-term rival. In fact, the Indians said that the French traded hard and that the English gave better value for all furs except cats; and in 1717 the English even traded cats with about forty canoes of 'French Indians' whose captain promised to come again in 1718, and kept his promise.

In this rivalry the trade-goods and the trading habits of the English brought them a fair proportion of the furs—enough certainly for the London market to absorb, and enough to produce the dividends of these years. But French competition threatened consequences which, in view of the Indian character and habits, could not be estimated. Threats and rumours could divert the Indians and could ruin the trade of a post even when some among them fully realised the importance of keeping both sets of white men in play. They had, for example, flocked to Albany in 1712 in consequence of the rumour that the English had then captured Canada. In similar vein they were easily persuaded to desert Albany in 1725 when no ship arrived there and when the French wood-runners spread a rumour that 'severall hundreds of the Indians which are theire freinds will come and kill us with the Indians which traide with us'. This sort of threat was a constant feature of the trade both now and later, and it was common both to the French a few days up-river from Albany and to those coming to the great plains and lakes to the south and the west of Churchill.

Wide as the French threat spread, it was Albany which was the post worst placed to face such an opposition. There, in the winter of 1728, the men were kept on constant and exhausting watch because of a rumour that the French had engaged large bands of Mohawks to pillage the post. Some opponents were indeed seen during that summer, but the winter passed without incident and in the next year the Governor, Joseph Adams, was surprised (for he knew nothing of the affair) to learn that the Mohawks had indeed prepared to attack but had been deterred by the fact that one of their number had been shot by a guard. As a result of the rising tension the defences were checked over; the post was reported to be in a better posture for defence than at any time for twenty years, the carriages for the guns in the flankers were renewed, the English went about their trade confident against anything but a surprise attack—

and partly for these reasons the trade increased by 1730 to an 'Extra-ordinary Good Cargoe'.

Nevertheless Albany, like the other posts by the Bay, demanded the constant attention of the Committee and of its own men to the maintenance and improvement of its fabric. The post to which the English had clung during the war was badly placed on the east bank of Albany River on a 'back creek' formed by a group of islands. In 1721 the Committee decided to remove the post to Bayly's Island off the west bank of the river, where Governor Bayly had built his early post. Here the sloop could come alongside the post; but the ship from England could still not get up the river far enough. It was a 'usall' thing for the ship to ground in the river and Governor Macklish, as a shipwright, was loud in his demands for a ship which could both cross the Atlantic and sail up Albany River (for which a draught of eight and a half feet or less was necessary). Even then adverse winds might well keep the ship out of the river and so delay the vital unloading and loading programme. The *Albany*, appro-priately named since she was specially built for that post at Macklish's request, delighted him and he promised that she would be able to load and unload in six days. But even she was held up by fog and wind at the river's mouth for six days on her maiden voyage. Albany was, in fact, still facing the same problems as Governor Nixon had faced, problems posed by the unchanged facts of deluges, fogs, tides and winds, to which the only answer was that the ship from England must run some risk at the Bottom of the Bay at any depot save Charlton Island. There she would need two sloops to discharge her cargo, but the advantages over Albany or any other post might be worth the cost.

This was a re-assessment of the situation which was urged, but was not yet accepted, in 1720. Timber was reasonably plentiful near Albany, and the rebuilding of that post was pressed on. By 1722 the new building was reported as complete and 'in a good posture of defence'. But the fact that the ice at the river mouth held up the spring break-up led to an annual danger of a deluge, so that the great guns were mounted and sited at first in the flankers to the post and then, after a 'very rude Deluge' in 1722, in a separate battery commanding the river bank. Even so, despite the report that all was complete and ready, the re-building and re-fortification proved a constant strain. At the end of the period 1713–30, when a new urgency in the French rivalry brought a fresh assessment of the defences of the post, the Council at Albany reported that the gun-carriages were once more in need of repair and that time would not permit the 'Great House' to be taken down and built again.

While Albany was thus dominated during the period 1713–30 by the conditions imposed by French rivalry in the upper reaches of the rivers, the rest of the Bottom of the Bay was no less influenced by the same conditions. Here trade came in two streams—from Moose River and from the Eastmain—both vulnerable to the French, for when the Treaty of Utrecht confirmed the British in possession of the Bottom of the Bay, no immediate effort was made to stabilise either of these sources of trade by the establishment of a new post. Albany, alone, conducted a trade which was adequate for London's demands and it was even feared that the increases which were expected from development at York and Churchill might prove an embarrassment. The earlier posts at Moose and on Rupert River were therefore not renewed until French rivalry made the possibility of a glut of furs less important than the maintenance of the English position. This, however, did not mean that these sources of trade were neglected, merely that they were not thought to warrant a separate establishment. The Eastmain trade, formerly conducted from the post at Rupert River and later to develop to north and east into the Labrador trade, was conducted in the early years of the eighteenth century by sending out a sloop from Albany, to trade and sometimes to winter at Slude River, and as Macklish took control at Albany the habit of trading by sloop to the Slude River was steadily pursued and a high proportion of martens in the Eastmain returns was most gratifying to the Committee.

This was a policy in which everything depended on the sloop, as did so much in the Bay during these years. But there were years when the sloops were inadequate. In 1715, for example, the Eastmain voyage had to be abandoned because Governor Knight at York lost his sloop in an 'excessive storm of wind' and commandeered the only available sloop from the reluctant Macklish at Albany. Next year Macklish himself built a sloop, the *Albany*—'a fine floaty Vessell and Sails well'—on purpose so that he might continue the Eastmain trade, but by 1721 the *Albany* was so leaky as to be useless and the Committee then sent out a new sloop from England so that the Eastmain trade might continue.

By that time new ideas were beginning to take hold. Even when the sloops were adequate the Eastmain trade was in danger, for it was well known that most of the Indians who traded there came from the south, not from the north or east, and they were therefore very liable to be intercepted by the French traders. In 1722 Joseph

Myatt, Master at Albany, who had in his time served on the sloop sent to trade at Eastmain, sent home a plan for a more regular post to be built at the mouth of Slude River. He went to winter there on the *Beaver* sloop in 1723–4, and during that time he completed building his 'factory' there and brought in a good trade. Next winter he also spent at Eastmain, and prospered although he was ill for most of the time. His post undoubtedly gave more security to the British than the sloop had afforded, but was more important for the confidence which it gave to the Indians as against French threats; it stabilised the trade and made it clear that the English would return from year to year in a way which the visits of the sloop could not achieve. For although the post at Slude River still continued to be dependent on the goods brought yearly from Albany in the sloop, and the needs of Albany still dominated the situation, the great change lay in the decision to keep the post open through the winter. After the ship from England had unloaded at Albany the sloop would take the consignment of goods to Slude River and would winter there with her crew, then in early summer the sloop would bring the Eastmain returns to Albany, leaving at most a couple of men at Slude River, and would so arrange her journey as to arrive at Albany in time to be able to help unload the ship from England and to get the furs from Eastmain checked, packed and ready for shipment.

Significant as it was as a sign of the Company's willingness to set up an outpost where French rivalry made it desirable, the Eastmain post did not differ in essentials from the previous system of trading from the sloop, with just a small storehouse ashore. For ten months of the year the sloop was the main source of strength, and the sloop captain normally commanded the post. But the sense of continuity which the post gave was of great value, and Eastmain prospered, with a 'good trade' in 1727, a 'tolerable trade' in 1728 and an 'extraordinary trade' in 1729–30. This was despite the undoubted advantages enjoyed by the French, who were 'with the Indians in the place where they catch the furs', and who also spread assiduous rumours that they were about to descend and destroy the small and badly-defended post.

The re-establishment of a post at Moose River, the other auxiliary to the trade of Albany, was undertaken on a quite different scale. Here also the trade came from the south and was subject to French rivalry. But whereas the post at Eastmain was built in order to secure a trade which was additional to that of Albany itself, that at Moose was designed merely to secure trade which, it was argued, would otherwise come to the main post. Here again it was the much-abused Joseph Myatt who put forward the proposal, having had personal experience of the difficulties caused because Albany was the only post at the Bottom of the Bay. The Moose River Indians had to come along the shore to get to Albany, and they held that journey in particular dread. Not only were they averse from sea-travel in canoes, but they were always liable to be taken right out to sea in a strong ebb or in a storm, and in summer they could catch neither fish nor fowl in the course of the journey. Myatt himself had seen them suffering so badly from hunger as they came along the shore that they had been forced to stew up their beaver skins on the beach. It was therefore comparatively easy for the French to entice the Moose Indians away from Albany while they closed in on Moose River from the south and the west, and Myatt readily fell in with an Indian petition that a post should be re-settled at Moose. This he advocated even though he recognised from the start that it might well draw trade from Albany.

In 1727, therefore, Myatt sent his sloop-captain, Mr. Bevan, to survey Moose River and to find a site for a post, while the Committee considered his proposal and came to a decision. Bevan finished his survey of the river in an Indian canoe (in itself a sign of the in-creasing competence and adaptability of the Hudson's Bay men), and reported that it was a fine river with a good channel and that he had found the site of the old Hudson's Bay post on an island in the river. The Committee also reached a decision—that the post was 'of absolute Necessity'—and agreed to send out a new sloop, the *Moose*, to serve the post, to send out a draft and model for the building, and extra hands for the job. Captain Christopher Middleton, rehabili-tated in the good graces of the Committee since the affair of Captain Scroggs and the *Whalebone*, and well qualified by his scientific in-terests and his knowledge of surveying, was to explain the Com-mittee's views; but the exact site of the post was to be left to the decision of the Council at Albany, of which Middleton would be a member while his ship was at the post. In fact the Committee hoped that both Myatt and Middleton would be able to go to Moose to settle on the site, and they tentatively suggested that it might be in 'the Place where the Old Factory formerly stood'.

These decisions were taken in December 1729, reinforced by Myatt's continued urgings. 'All the Ill propertys that I am capable of Judgeing, that Attends it, is It's being in the Mouth of an Enemy' he wrote in 1729, 'for if all be true that is reported, the French have a small Settlement not far from it'. Accordingly in 1730 bricks and mortar and the new sloop were sent out, and Middleton drew a plan of a fort with six bastions. This the Committee approved, though on second thoughts it was reduced to four bastions. Middleton was to leave his ship, the *Hudson's Bay*, at Charlton Island and was to proceed in the sloop to Moose River, with a general authority to choose the site and to supervise the problems which the new post would raise for the management at Albany, while from Albany itself were sent Thomas Render to take command of the new sloop, John Jewer the carpenter to direct the building operations, and John Bricker because he was well qualified in the language. Joseph Adams (then Master at Albany in succession to Myatt) was ready to send more hands to help in the building of the post, but he felt that the chief need was for a competent Chief, and he implored the Committee to send a suitable man out from England.

So the re-building of Moose Fort, 'in the Mouth of an Enemy', was begun in the summer of 1730 as a means of preventing French encroachments and making the English trade more attractive. Though the bricks sent from England arrived broken, no brickmaker was sent to remedy the defect by making local bricks. Yet the building advanced. It was sited for defence, and the garrison was considered in terms of defence, thirty men being asked for in place of the twenty allotted. But no Chief was sent out in 1731, and authority sat ill on the shoulders of the sloop-master Thomas Render. He provoked the men to refuse their duty and Adams had to go to Moose from Albany to pacify the post in the fall of 1731. He then transferred Bevan from command of the *Beaver* sloop and the new post on the Eastmain to Moose, and in 1732 Middleton reported the post to be in 'good forwardness' and the Indians desirous of trade, a report borne out by the carpenter John Jewer, who announced that he had made good progress and who was sent some lead sheeting to complete his roofs.

As soon as the Moose post was established, the safety of the river and the anchorage (by comparison with the dangers of Albany) led to a decision to ship direct from England to Moose, and thence by sloop to Albany instead of the other way round. So the revived post quickly took an important place in the Company's design for trade. But in origin and first purpose it was intended to be no more than a defensive reply to the danger from French encirclement.

At York and at Churchill the threat from the French lay further off than at the Bottom of the Bay. But it was just as real a threat, was part of the same problem, and had much the same general consequences. Knight had early written of the rivalry of the French near the 'Great Lake' of Winnipeg—with pardonable vagueness and exaggeration but with real appreciation of the problem. In the same vein Macklish wrote from York in 1728 that 'Now is the time to obliege the Natives before the French Draw them to their Settlement'. His nearest rivals were 'four Days paddling from the Great Lake that feeds this River', somewhere north of Lake Winnipeg, and his troubles were not only the normal trade rivalry, the bringing of brandy into the trade, and fears of attacks on his post by the French, but also fears that the French would stir up the *Poets* (the Assiniboines) to attack the trading Indians of the English posts. Nor were the French content merely to urge the *Poets* on to war. While the English steadily pursued their traditional policy of preaching peace to the Indians, and even of offering trade-goods which might pacify the *Poets*, Macklish reported that 'several of the french goes Yearly with the *Poits* to Warr with most of our Indians here', and in 1729 he recounted that three hundred and fifty canoes of his 'Upland Indians' had fled at the mere rumour that the *Poets* were led on the war-path by eight Frenchmen.

As at the Bottom of the Bay, the circumstances of these years led the Company to review the buildings at York with an eye to defence. From 1723 onwards the buildings which Knight had put up there were re-modelled. A 'Mason and a Bricklayer in one Person' who had helped to build a fort in Newfoundland was sent to build, or at least to face, the two bastions with stone as a defence against fire-arms, six 'great guns' were mounted, and the buildings were in the process improved and made more healthy. By 1729 Macklish was confident that York was safe against any land-attack by small arms or by Indians, despite the local shortage of good building timber. The post remained, however, in his opinion, the worst contrived post in the country 'both in respect of Defence and Conveniency', and though he thought it would not actually fall down for some years he was convinced that the local building materials made it impossible at York to build a post which would survive an attack by ships.

The re-building and defence work undertaken at Albany, at Moose and at York, was in evidence also at Churchill, for Churchill lay under much the same threat as York; the French posts in the area of Lake Winnipeg were at the strategic centre of the trade. In 1720 Governor Knight had outfitted an Indian to travel inland by Churchill River to Lake Missinipi—in some ways a counterpart to his sending of William Stewart to the Barrens. The Indian went lame and achieved nothing, but the rumour spread inland. Three canoes of Indians who had taken four months to travel down the rivers from Lake Missinipi got to Churchill to trade, and in the following year forty canoes of Missinipi Indians came into Churchill from 'the Great Water that lieth at the head of this River'.

That these Missinipi Indians should come to trade at Churchill speaks for the difficulties which the French were throwing in the way of trade. It speaks also for the unity of the northern trade system, and its problems. Indian report had rapidly spread the news that the English had adjusted their Standard of Trade so as to stimulate their new post at Churchill; Knight and Kelsey had begun to 'trade larger' there than was allowed at other posts, and in the end the Standard had to be raised at Churchill in order to restore some of the trade to York.

The Missinipi Indians who wished to trade to Churchill were clearly open to the French, and the normal trade of that post, apart from its aspirations to the northwards, would come from the Barren Lands and perhaps from the Saskatchewan prairies. Such a trade was in the gravest danger, as may be judged from the 1731 report that three canoes of French wood-runners, on their return from Canada in that year, had gone 'into the great Lake, to the most noted Places where the Indians resorts, and what with threatening to Proclaime Warr against them Provided they Came to trade here, likewise to Encourage their Common enemys the Poetts to break the Peace with them', wrought great damage. They turned the Indians from the English 'not for their being more kindly used by the French but Intirely out of Fear'. So, little as Macklish might support Churchill as a base for northern adventures in which he did not believe, and strongly as he maintained that the normal trade of Churchill might more cheaply be conducted from York, he nevertheless showed himself ready to treat Churchill as an outpost against the French to the south and west. He was therefore prepared to divert food and trade-goods, and even Indians, there. True, such care broke down under stress, and Macklish always regarded York as the senior and more important post. When, for example, the trade-goods designed for York were lost in the *Mary* in 1727 he felt no compunction about taking part of the shipment intended for Churchill, and when he again sent to Churchill for goods in 1730 he was disconcerted to be told that Churchill was virtually an independent command, and he asked for a firm ruling on that point.

Urged and controlled by the Committee, even Macklish never seriously tried to interrupt the progress at Churchill, and there the danger of French rivalry produced a far different answer from that at the Bottom of the Bay. At Albany and the dependent posts at the Bottom of the Bay timber was reasonably abundant, and the danger from the French lay in an overland attack from Indians or wood-runners, not in heavy attack by shipping. Wooden defences were therefore both possible and adequate. At Churchill wood, even for burning, was difficult and distant, and the danger from the French lay in a sea-borne attack with heavy ships' guns, not in an overland approach across the great barren wastes to the south and west. So great was the scarcity of wood that firewood had to be rafted and ferried from considerable distances, and by 1730 the Committee were seriously thinking about plans to abandon the place where Governor Knight had built, and were assembling materials to build afresh in a more proper and convenient place.

The Committee decided on 'Eskimay Point', where the post would command the entrance to Churchill River, and in 1731 they sent out masons and other craftsmen, with plans and a model for the post, together with barges and punts, cattle and horses, so that a stone fort might be pushed forward as fast as possible. Lime, it was reported, could be made at Churchill and so a stone fort seemed possible where lack of wood and the nature of the French threat made the more easy and normal wooden structure inappropriate.

So, despite the fact that Knight's foundation of Churchill was part of a policy of expansion, the permanent post begun in 1731 falls into the ordinary scope of the Company's defensive plans. The siting of the post was well within any interpretation of the boundaries which had been discussed at Utrecht or later, and once the Committee had made their decision they never relaxed in their determination to build a permanent and defensible post. The first stone fort in the Arctic, accepted as the post-Utrecht period ends in 1730, was the logical culmination of the Committee's resolve to resist French threats and to defend their rights against European attacks, especially from the sea. In this defensive attitude it was of a piece with the reconstruction at Albany and York, and with the building at Moose and Eastmain.

During the post-war period from 1713 to 1730 the rivalry of French and English by the Bay had been persistent but lacking in incident. It was a rivalry in which the English turned steadily to the construction of defensively-sited posts designed to secure the minimum trade-areas in which the treaty had confirmed them, while the French skirmished through the woods and went far to accomplish their traditional design of intercepting the trading Indians as they went to the English posts. The English company had behind it the great advantage that the London market proved able to absorb all the furs which its expanding trade could produce, while the French found themselves hampered by the needs of the colony of Canada, the system of tax-farming, a declining hat-making industry, and dependence on the Dutch for access to the wider markets of Europe and of Russia. But the state of the European market did not dictate the terms on which the rivalry for furs was conducted. Though at base this was an economic strife, in which a solvent fur trade was the first necessity, other interests dominated the contestants, especially the French, and the economics of the struggle faded into the background.

To some extent this was due to the personal and national interests which were involved. To some extent it was inevitable in such a rivalry, in which the economics of competition demand that survival must be achieved at whatever cost. But to a great extent the terms of the rivalry were dictated by the nature and the desires of the Indians, who did not in this matter differ greatly from any other primitive people brought into contact with the productive capacity and resources of Europe, with its apparently illogical requirements, its rivalries and its passions. Slowly realising that the Europeans had come far to trade and that they could not afford to go back profitless, the Indians brought to the fur trade an element which was at least as important as the national habits and background of either the French or the British, and which set the pattern in which those European factors reacted in North America.

The Indian attitude to the trade was complex and to some extent self-contradictory. But it was none-the-less a real factor in the trade. They showed the first natural reaction of savages in trade-contacts with Europeans in that in their initial dealings they placed but little value on their wares, which to them were superfluous. There was no thrift, and little sense of value, in them, and being used to regard the peltry which the Europeans wanted as surplus commodities and to want European goods only as luxuries, they were not disposed to exert themselves provided they could satisfy their immediate needs. Sophistication came early, as the Indian became dependent on the trade-gun instead of on the bow and arrow, and as iron goods became a part of his life. But with his habits and characteristics the Indian, even when he had become dependent on European trade, could normally be stirred to extra endeavour by his desire for luxuries for immediate consumption rather than by his basic needs. It was the Europeans who, on the whole, worried about keeping the Indians alive and capable of hunting through the winter, not the Indians themselves.

This picture of a wildly improvident Indian, regardless of tribe, circumstances or personal character, must clearly be taken as a very broad generalisation, subject to a multitude of exceptions. But as a broad generalisation it was true of the eighteenth-century Indian, and it produced two results, both of which favoured the French approach to the fur trade. It meant that an unsophisticated Indian, as yet unused to trade with Europeans, traded on far easier terms than those with years of experience, and so lured the trader further and further afield to make touch with new tribes. And it meant that even when habits of trade and of dependence on European goods had grown up, goods for immediate consumption were more in demand than those for survival or the furtherance of future trade. An adventurous and flexible approach therefore had much to commend it. The English from Albany reported of their Indians, after a generation of trade with them, that 'The Indians don't mind little measure providing they can live and have but little Trouble', and the French system and habits fitted in admirably with this attitude. They kept a far less rigid Standard of Trade than the English company imposed on its traders, and consequently they could trade well when chances offered and could attract Indians to trade by offering bargains for one kind of furs or in one kind of trade-goods, relying on Indian character to deliver the rest of the trade to them when once the Indian had been lured into making contact. For example, they rated marten skins much higher than the English did, and thus got many Indians to trade with them; and in their own way they used brandy more freely. The French, it was reported, actually traded very little brandy. But they gave it away quite generously, making presents of enough to attract the Indians to come to them, to make them drunk and less careful in their bargains.

While these factors favoured the French approach, their system also has its defects. Even if the Indians went the whole long journey to Montreal with their furs, they could get there only a woollen cloth which was generally accepted as inferior to that of the English, and iron-ware and guns which were also less attractive. If, as was more habitual, they traded at the upland posts to which the licensed canoes brought the French wares, they found that the weight and bulkiness in transport meant that woollens, guns and iron-ware, were in short supply and dear as well as suffering from the alleged defects of French manufacture (though there were times when the Hudson's Bay men told their Committee that the French goods were vastly superior).

The result was that over a period of years a system developed whereby it became possible for the Indians to trade the prime furs of their catch for light goods and luxuries to the French at their inland posts, and then to bring down the remains, or such portion of their prime furs as they had hidden or as the French offered poor prices for, to the Bay. There they would trade for the guns and shot, the cloth, iron-work and the heavier and larger blankets which the English alone could supply. So, within the conditions imposed by his own mentality and habits, the Indian dominated the fur-trade rivalry of the 1713–30 period and enjoyed a seller's market. From the Bay inland spread a net-work of Indians, traders who constantly took English goods up the rivers. The use of European goods was known far beyond the actual contacts of European traders, European influence spreading through Indians who developed and practised the function of the middleman. This meant that the policy adopted by the English company tended to place their trade in the hands of these intermediaries. The attempts to draw down the upland Indians to the Bay were slow to take effect for this reason, while the Indian accustomed to trade became lazy, preferring to trade up in the country rather than to hunt, and grew 'so Nice and Difficul in the way of Trade that I admire to see it'.

Generous treatment of the trading Indians, and in particular the giving of presents, was therefore encouraged. Trade-goods were carefully scrutinised and checked, and shipments of brandy became regular features of the Company's trade, for in 1716 Macklish had reported from Albany that 'Brandy is a Rare Commoditee, for I can have more Done towards promotting the Trade in small furrs for 2 Gall of Brandy, then for 40 Beaver in Any other sortt of Goods in the Factory, Itt is become so bewitching a Liquor Amongst all the Indians Especially Amongst Those that Trades with the French'. Brandy was, however, not easily got in England, and as late as 1746 the general letter from Albany reported it as 'hot fiery stuff and very disagreeable to taste'.

The merits of their heavy goods, and the charm of Brazil tobacco, together with their fair and long-term treatment of the Indians, offered the best English reply to French tactics based on knowledge of the Indian character, brandy, and a grip on the strategic Lake Winnipeg area. Winnipeg, however, was but the furthest outpost area in a fur-trade war which embroiled the whole of the eastern side of the north American continent. Since Utrecht the English mainland colonists had pushed north and west in pursuit of the Indian trade. The business of supplying English woollens from New York to the French fur-traders was forbidden (as was all trade between New England and New France) in 1720, and the establishment of a post at Oswego on Lake Ontario in 1722 marked a determined encroachment by the colonists on the French trade. The alignment of the West Indies with the English mainland settlements ensured that the outward expansion of the New England fur trade could be helped by rum as freely as the French could use brandy, and the post at Oswego flourished and soon proved a formidable rival to the French posts at Niagara and Fort Frontenac. The French countered by the construction of a series of posts—at Niagara to contest the Lake Ontario trade, at Detroit to contest Lake Huron and Lake Michigan, and at Fort Vincennes to contest the trade of Lake Michigan and the Mississippi. Their organisation of the *postes du nord* was part of the same counter-offensive, though indeed the project of cutting off the Indians from access to the Bay had been fully discussed and accepted long before Utrecht was signed.

The threat under which the Company's posts traded during the years up to 1730 was therefore part of a wider rivalry in which the New England traders, the government of Canada, the missionaries and geographers obsessed by the concept of the Western Sea, and the French fur-traders themselves, were all involved. The determination to protect overseas trade on a colonial basis which the Tory government had shown during the Utrecht negotiations persisted into the peace period, and it was clear throughout that European rivalries could very easily spread to the colonies. The Company's rivalry with the French was therefore rightly accepted as a serious problem which demanded constant attention, and government and public opinion alike demanded that the Company should be eager and active.

So far, in fact, was the English company from that apathy and indifference with which it has been charged that it seems to have allowed its policy to be deflected out of all proportion to the threat on its own flank. In this period the *postes du nord* cannot themselves have attracted any significant volume of trade, for in 1723 only three canoes were licensed for Kaministikwia and one for Nipigon; in 1724 and again in 1725 only one canoe went to Kaministikwia, and in 1728 a further three. When the situation is considered in the light of the serious threat which the New Englanders were bringing against the French from the south, of the small quantities and the inferior quality of the goods taken inland to interrupt the Bay trade, and of the steady prosperity of the English company, the traders and the Committee seem to have been much too alert to see danger where there was none.

But the scene was played against the memory of de Troyes and Iberville, and against an uneasy European background. War was

R

imminent at any moment, and the wood-runners might indeed attack the posts or stir up the Indians. These things were therefore accepted, with their corollary of the need for active defence, from the time of the first return of the English to their restored posts in 1713. Small-arms drill, reminders of the disasters due to cowardice and neglect, the employment of qualified gunners, were all parts of the response. When in 1720 war with Spain broke out the Committee feared that France might soon join the Spaniards and take the opportunity to attack the posts by the Bay, and in view of the French ambitions which had just been revealed by the failure of the 1719 attempt to settle a boundary and by the noticeable encirclement of Albany this was a reasonable fear. The ships' captains were therefore instructed to make certain that the posts were not in enemy hands before they brought their ships within range of the shore guns, and a system of pre-arranged signals from shore to land was adopted for that purpose.

There were, then, present in the situation before 1730 all the elements of a direct rivalry between French and English for control of the Bay fur trade, and each side had set out the main features of its policy. But as yet the French were but distant and meagre opponents; the *postes du nord* existed but were not actively exploited, and the English were building and consolidating, while the Indians still interposed as a buffer between the two, bearing rumours from the one to the other and exploiting the situation as best they could. Neither side had produced a vigorous policy of active opposition.

BOOKS FOR REFERENCE

GIRAUD, Marcel—*Le Métis Canadien. Son role dans l'histoire des provinces de l'Ouest* (Paris, 1945).

INNIS, H. A.—*The Fur Trade in Canada* (Toronto, 1956).

LAWSON, Murray G.—*Fur: A Study in English Mercantilism, 1700–1775* (Toronto, University of Toronto Studies, History and Economics Series, 1943), Vol. IX.

MORTON, Arthur S.—*A History of the Canadian West to 1870–71* (London, 1939).

CHAPTER XXXVIII

FRENCH EXPANSION TO THE PRAIRIES UNDER DE LA VÉRENDRYE

The changes beginning in 1730 were largely the results of the impact of fresh and vigorous personalities. The French threat took on a new vigour and to some extent a new direction under the influence of Pierre Gaultier de Varennes, Sieur de la Vérendrye, and his sons; and partly as a result of the French successes, English opposition to the Company developed a new purpose with the personality of Arthur Dobbs. Of the two men de la Vérendrye comes first both in point of time and of causation, for the English opposition was spurred by fears that under his leadership the French might achieve their ambitions, and Arthur Dobbs and his fellows certainly avouched the French successes as proof of the need for a more active policy than the Company pursued.

The *postes du nord* as they existed before the advent of de la Vérendrye were part of what might be called the static rivalry of the French and the English. They underlined the purpose rather than the accomplishment of French ambitions; they were indeed a potential threat to the trade of the Bay, but as yet their achievement was negligible. Since 1713 the French had maintained a post at Kaministikwia on Lake Superior, and in 1717 this outpost was transformed into a strong fort. This was a result of a plan propounded in the previous year by de Vaudreuil, Governor, and Bégon, Intendant, of Canada. In their memorandum plans to interrupt trade to the English posts by the Bay intermingled with the traditional French search for the Western Sea. The known route from Lake Superior to Rainy Lake and so to Lake of the Woods was set out and thence a route was reported to 'the Sea of the West'. This was in fact the Winnipeg River route to Lake Winnipeg. The original memorandum was followed up by a proposal to press towards the 'Sea of the West' by building posts at Kaministikwia, Rainy Lake and Lake of the Woods, with interest divided between exploration to seek the 'Sea of the West' and the establishment of fur-posts which would draw the Indians away from Hudson Bay. The ultimate decision, given in 1718, was that the three posts should be built but must be paid for from their own trade in furs. Further exploration, however, would be paid for by the King.

So planned, the *postes du nord* won significant support. From Kaministikwia an outpost was established at Rainy Lake in 1718, and it was this outpost which lay behind the interruption of trade reported in 1722 at York Fort. From Rainy Lake the French hoped to get access to the *castor gras*, the *coat*, which their hatters needed, and to the other fine furs of which their loss of Fort Bourbon had deprived them. The post was a clear rival to Hudson Bay, but the French found that trade at Rainy Lake and Kaministikwia was as seriously interrupted by Indian wars as was that at the posts on the Bay. The French could no more prevent the Sioux from attacking the Crees and the Assiniboines, the former located near Kaministikwia and the latter enticed in to trade, than the English could prevent them from attacking those going down to trade at the Bay. The Crees and the Assiniboines, like the English, accused the French of arming the Sioux and of stirring them up to war, and Kaministikwia's trade suffered and the post remained a fort from which the *coureurs* might set forth rather than an active centre of trade to which furs would flow and where Indian information on the 'Sea of the West' would accumulate, while the post at Rainy Lake, if it could be so called, was occupied but casually.

Then interest in the search of the 'Sea of the West' dominated the scene with the determination to establish Fort Beauharnois among the Sioux Indians, at Lake Pepin on the Mississippi. This was largely a missionary venture, established in the hope that the missionaries would get such information from the Sioux as would make the search swift and certain when it was resumed. The route to Fort Beauharnois, however, lay through the lands of the turbulent Renards, and in 1730–1 they forced the temporary abandonment of the post. In 1731, therefore, after crushing the Renards, the French again occupied Fort Beauharnois, ready to resume their search for the 'Sea of the West', anxious to open new beaver territories to counterbalance the expansion towards Lake Ontario of the fur-traders from New England, and led by de la Vérendrye.

De la Vérendrye had been engaged in the fur trade at his estate on the River St. Maurice since he returned to Canada after fighting in the War of the Spanish Succession—during which he was seriously wounded and was captured at Malplaquet. In 1727 he had secured appointment as Commandant of the *postes du nord*, on the northern shore of Lake Superior, by which time Kaministikwia figured as the central *poste du nord*, with outposts at Nipigon and Michipicoten, whilst it was also the bridgehead for the expansion westwards to Rainy Lake and Lake of the Woods. So de la Vérendrye, and Kaministikwia his headquarters, commanded the intertwined French efforts—the effort to drive westwards through Rainy Lake and Lake of the Woods towards Lake Winnipeg and the 'Sea of the West' with which the French confused that lake; and the effort to spread north from Nipigon towards the Bottom of the Bay. The move westwards threatened the hinterland of York and Churchill; the move northwards threatened the trade of Albany, Moose and Eastmain; and in both directions the English became aware of a fresh urgency as de la Vérendrye got control.

By this time it had been accepted that Fort Beauharnois on the Mississippi, though re-occupied, would not help the search for the 'Sea of the West', and de la Vérendrye put forward a proposal, remarkable in its suppression of much that was commonly known, advocating the establishment of a post on Lake Winnipeg from which he would lead the further search for the 'Sea of the West'. This amounted to a firm proposal that the French should occupy the area between Lake Superior and Lake Winnipeg. It was clearly designed to anticipate English moves and to bring the French to new sources of fur, but for policy it was put forward as a necessary step in the search for the 'Sea of the West'.

His proposal received the support of Governor Beauharnois, who allowed him to set out in 1731 with fifty men and one priest to establish a post on Lake of the Woods with no more than a decent reference to the 'Sea of the West' but with the firm purpose of establishing a trade and diverting the Indians from Hudson Bay. De la Vérendrye approached his expedition from much the same point of view, with apparent enthusiasm for further exploration but with purposeful regard for the fur trade; he asked to be confirmed in his command of the *postes du nord*, so as to use them as entrepôts for his further ventures and as a means of raising money and of contracting with merchants and *voyageurs* for supplies of goods and transport in return for permits to trade.

Mutiny halted de la Vérendrye at the Grand Portage on Lake Superior in 1731, and he wintered at Kaministikwia, sending La Jemeraye, his nephew and second-in-command, to build a new post, Fort Pierre, at Rainy Lake. Indian wars, especially by the Sioux and Saulteurs against the Monsonis, the Assiniboines and the Crees, made La Jemeraye's first winter an unprofitable one, but it must be doubtful whether in any case he would have reaped a large trade in his first year, when the news of his post had not yet spread. The post, however, was set up and in 1732 de la Vérendrye came up to Fort Pierre on Rainy Lake, intent on pushing forward to make a new establishment at Lake of the Woods, from which Lake Winnipeg might be explored. He managed to build a substantial post, Fort Charles, well fortified, with a chapel and several houses, at Lake of the Woods, but it was spring again before he sent forward a party under his eldest son (he had three of his four sons with him) and La Jemeraye to summon the Indians from Lake Winnipeg to come in to trade at Fort Charles.

In all of this de la Vérendrye had shown great ability, although so far was he from bringing nearer the discovery of the 'Sea of the West' that his approach to Lake Winnipeg led to acceptance of the conclusion that the 'Sea of the West' must be further on, probably to the south, to be reached by the rivers Assiniboine and Missouri, since Lake Winnipeg drained north towards Hudson Bay. He had, however, shown great power to dominate the Indians, even to the extent of preventing many of their wars (except against the Sioux of the Plains). He himself had penetrated far and his *coureurs* had still further widened the sphere of French influence.

It was therefore inevitable that the Hudson's Bay men, and in a different way the British public and government, should become conscious of the new vigour and purpose of the French moves in Canada. For the move to the north and west was not the only sign of French activity; a stone fort had been set up at Niagara in 1726, Fort Vincennes was erected in 1727 to check the Indian trade of Lake Michigan and the Mississippi, and in 1731 a fort was built at Crown Point. To the south the trade rivalry of the English colonists was being opposed by a ring of forts. In the north and west the *coureur du bois* was spreading out from de la Vérendrye's posts, trading guns and brandy, leading the Sioux to attack the Crees, the Assiniboines and other trading Indians. And de la Vérendrye himself was advancing his posts further towards the focal point. From Fort St. Charles at Lake of the Woods he sent his second son Pierre to choose a site for a post near the mouth of Red River and in 1734 Fort Maurepas was built there by René Cartier while de la Vérendrye went to Montreal, Pierre explored much of Lake Winnipeg, and a Fort Rouge was built at the mouth of the Assiniboine; these were indeed but slight and temporary buildings, but they clearly marked the fact that de la Vérendrye had opened up durable communications between Montreal, Lake Superior and Lake Winnipeg. He was, moreover, already moving on past Lake Winnipeg; and in so doing he was to some extent stirred by Indian rumours which seemed to promise success at last in the search for the 'Sea of the West'.

But he was at the same time bound even more firmly to the fur trade, for the official encouragement to search for the 'Sea of the West' rather than to trade furs had not been accompanied by an official grant in aid, and the Montreal merchants must still be depended upon for finance. Maurepas as Minister of Marine and Colonies fully approved of the progress made, but ruled that 'Sa Majesté est cependant toujours dans les dispositions de ne point entrer dans aucune dépense par raport à cette entreprise', in 1734 as again in 1735. De la Vérendrye was therefore reduced to getting goods on credit from the Montreal merchants in 1734, and in 1735 he even farmed out the posts, which he had created, to the merchants.

In this de la Vérendrye was curiously caught in the dilemma of trying to reconcile the search for the 'Sea of the West' with the pursuit of furs. He was to some extent driven by the French government's insistence that he should press on with exploration at his own cost, so that whether in actual truth the fur trade was his primary interest or not (and there has been much discussion on this point), he was in any case forced to put it in the forefront of his plans in 1735 even when officially divorcing himself from active participation, in order to get materials for the exploration to which he was ordered.

De la Vérendrye was unable to get as far as Fort Maurepas on Red River in 1735, and in 1736 he had to face deep personal tragedy. His nephew and invaluable second-in-command, La Jemeraye, had died in May 1736 near Lake of the Woods, and then a strong party of twenty-one men in three canoes, led by the priest Aulneau and de la Vérendrye's eldest son, had been massacred on an island in Lake of the Woods by the Sioux of the Prairies. The Monsonis, Crees and Assiniboines, were eager to join the bereaved father in avenging his son, but he dissuaded them and in a visit to Montreal in 1737 laid serious plans for further exploration. His project was to work from the Assiniboine south towards the 'Riviere des Mandans, qu'on croit être le Missouri' and to reach the Mandans and their river he would, he suspected, have to cross the height of land from the valley of the Assiniboine.

As early as 1735 La Jemeraye had sent in news derived from the Assiniboines of the 'Ouachipouennes' (Mandans), a tribe of fair men, with beards, who built forts and drawbridges and lived in permanent and fortified villages along the banks of a river which flowed west-south-west and led to land at the mouth of their river occupied by men who used iron tools and claimed to be of the same stock as the French. La Jemeraye had it in mind to journey to the 'Ouachipouennes' in 1736, and de la Vérendrye on his return from Montreal in that year instructed his eldest son, as he sent him to Fort Maurepas, 'As soon as supplies arrive to leave with six Frenchmen and forty or fifty Assiniboin in order to reconnoitre the Ouachipouennes, now called Konatheattes, a race of men white in colour and civilised, who till the soil and live in forts and houses'. Shortage of trade-goods, fears that the Crees, Assiniboines and Monsonis, might make war on the Sioux to avenge the massacre of the Lake of the Woods, and the reluctance of his Frenchmen, kept de la Vérendrye at Fort Charles through the winter, but he spent his time collecting information about the great river of the Ouachipouennes and was convinced that it ran not westwards but southwards, to discharge (as he thought) into the Pacific Ocean. He had in fact been given a confused picture of the connection of the Saskatchewan and Nelson Rivers, of Cumberland Lake and the routes to Churchill and York Fort, as well as of the Red River and the Missouri flowing southwards and of the Rocky Mountains, sadly out of place, as the height of land. Although he still wrote of his purpose to explore he also exhorted the Indians to hunt beaver and to desist from going down to trade with the English, and in 1737 instead of pushing west and south he returned to Quebec to negotiate fresh supplies from the merchants.

All of this confirmed Maurepas in his suspicion 'that the beaver trade had more to do than anything else with the Sieur de la Vérendrye's Western Sea expedition', and de la Vérendrye was called severely to task and told that he must keep his promise to reach the Ouachipouennes in 1738 or else be recalled. Then, with all his posts and privileges at stake, de la Vérendrye showed his merits as a *voyageur*. He left one of his sons in command at Fort Charles, Lake of the Woods, and made his way to the Forks of the Assiniboine where he harangued the Indians against trading with the English and travelled up the river to the portage leading to Lake Manitoba. Here he built Fort La Reine in 'the road by which the Assiniboine go to the English', near the site of the present Portage la Prairie on the Assiniboine. With twenty chosen men, two of his sons and two traders, he then set off from Fort La Reine on 16th October, 1738, to travel overland on foot to the Mandan village. Accompanied from the start by twenty-five Assiniboines, he finished his journey on 3rd December, escorted by about six hundred Assiniboines and a party of thirty Mandans who had come to meet him.

He found that the Mandan villages were indeed orderly and well built, but much of the reports proved ill-founded; they were not white men, and they could give no real information about the 'Sea of the West' or the route thither. So de la Vérendrye struggled back to

Fort La Reine early in 1739, a sick and disappointed man. His visit to the Mandans was not fruitless, however; it led to further exploration and to a very considerable French advance.

More prosaic but more fruitful was the result that the explorer satisfied his critics and was prolonged in command of his posts, and that he turned from the Mandans and the Missouri to the Saskatchewan as the best approach to the 'Sea of the West'—as it was also to the furs of the north. On his return from the Mandans in the spring of 1739 de la Vérendrye had sent off his son, the Chevalier, to explore the rivers which fell into Lake Winnipeg, especially the Blanche River, or Saskatchewan. He was also to try to prevent the savages from going to the English by encouraging them to look for a French establishment in the near future. In April 1739 de la Vérendrye heard that the Assiniboines were assembling at the 'Lake of the Prairies' (Lake Manitoba), making canoes in readiness for their annual voyage to the Bay to trade with the English. He managed to intercept a party of sixty, and traded their beaver, and his reports leave no room for doubt of his zeal to interrupt the beaver trade to the Bay, despite the fact that he was at this time officially giving all his attention to exploration. The mission of the young Chevalier to explore the Saskatchewan was therefore part of a comprehensive and threatening plan, and it was followed by other ventures.

The trading side of his commitments certainly required de la Vérendrye's attention, for the men at Fort Maurepas and at Fort La Reine were short of food, and they had no goods to trade with the Indians. It was true that a party, left with the Mandans, brought news of Indians who had come in from the south and west, riding horses and bringing accounts of white Christian people there, dwelling beside the sea. So zeal for the Western Sea was revived. But first de la Vérendrye must bolster up his dubious credit, for his furs had been seized for debt, his supplies were costly and inadequate, and a special journey to Montreal and Quebec in 1740–1 only brought him back with a meagre outfit for exploration at the cost of pledging the future of his fur trade. His return journey in 1741 was marked by his failure to prevent the Monsonis and the Crees from going to war with the Sioux, and to deal with these dangers he decided himself to stay at Fort La Reine and to send his sons on the search for the Western Sea.

The exploration was delayed until April 1742, and during the winter of waiting de la Vérendrye sent his son Pierre to build Fort Dauphin on Lake Dauphin (Lac des Prairies as he called it), and it was probably at this time that the young man also built the first Fort Bourbon where the Saskatchewan flows from Cedar Lake to Lake Winnipeg. Then in the spring his two sons, Louis-Joseph and François, set off from Fort La Reine with only two companions, to go first to the Mandan villages once more and then, from July 1742 to March 1743, to wander in a south-westerly direction from the Mandan villages across the Bad Lands of the Little Missouri in search of the 'Horse Indians', who had visited the Mandans with their talk of white people living near the sea. The Frenchmen thought they had reached the 'Mountains of Bright Stones', the Rockies, beyond which lay the Pacific, and it is possible that they had done so. They were certainly in the country of the dreaded Snake tribe, and over two months later, during which time they had been working their way back towards the Missouri, they buried a leaden plate which has since been discovered and which fixes their position on 30th March, 1743, as at Pierre, South Dakota. It must therefore remain as a possibility that in January 1743 they were at the foot of the Rockies.

Uncertain as many aspects of this journey must remain, it is clear that the Chevalier and his brother crossed the prairies, and clear that they convinced themselves and their father that exploration north and west would be more fruitful. In this direction, therefore, they turned and it is evident from a map based on information supplied by de la Vérendrye and his sons that by 1750 the Saskatchewan had been explored up to the Forks and that the connection with Hudson Bay was accepted, since the Rivière des Cristinaux was shown running north from the Saskatchewan to an English fort by the sea—a representation of Churchill River and Fort. The Bourbon River was also shown, running north from Lake Bourbon (Cedar Lake) to York Fort, and a French post called Fort Bourbon was shown on the south shore of Lake Bourbon near where the 'Rivière aux Biches' (Red Deer River) flows into the Lake; this post was established in 1748 and de la Vérendrye described it in 1749, in his last public letter, as 'on the lower course of *Rivière aux Biches*, the last one of all the forts I have established'. So de la Vérendrye's posts dominated the focal area of Lake Winnipeg, Lake Manitoba and Lake Winnipegosis; and he was turning his attention more and more to the Saskatchewan.

This, however, brought little satisfaction to Maurepas, who could only suggest in 1742 that de la Vérendrye's enterprise might go faster if some suitable officer were associated with him in command of the exploration, and perhaps if one of his sons also were replaced by another officer. Such officers were to be paid by de la Vérendrye himself! Against this order Governor Beauharnois protected de la Vérendrye on the ground that the posts were not well enough established and the enterprise was loaded with at least fifty thousand *livres* of debt. Forts Dauphin and Maurepas, also, had been abandoned in 1742 and the Indians had gone down to trade at the Bay. It would in any case be easier to carry out the changes in 1744, when de la Vérendrye had asked to retire on grounds of ill-health. So he was in 1744 relieved in command of the posts of the west by Nicolas-Joseph de Noyelles, who had experience of Indian warfare, had commanded at Detroit, and whose ability to deal with the western Indians was thought adequate 'pour les maintenir en paix avec les Sioux et les engager à troubler les Anglois'.

Beauharnois, however, still defended de la Vérendrye strongly, maintaining both that he had secured for France large quantities of peltries from which the English formerly profited and that he had himself made very little profit thereby. The explorer himself submitted a summary of his achievements, and together they elicited even from Maurepas the long-desired Captaincy of a Company of artillery for de la Vérendrye, in 1745. His achievement was indeed great and was emphasised by the failure of others, and when in the following year de Noyelles asked to be relieved it was again de la Vérendrye who was proposed to command the posts of the Western Sea. In 1749 he received the appointment, together with a Cross of St. Louis for himself and an ensign's command for two of his sons.

For de la Vérendrye recognition came too late. He planned to set out in 1750 'to continue the establishment of posts and the exploration of the West, which for several years have been interrupted', but he died at Montreal in December 1749, worn out by his labours but yet eager, at the age of sixty, to set out afresh. His son immediately applied for command of the posts of the west and put forward the plan which the father had in mind. This was to set out from Fort Bourbon (Cedar Lake) in spring 1751 and to penetrate up the Saskatchewan to the height of land in the mountains. It would take two years to reach the Rockies from Montreal, even in good weather, but there the Chevalier de la Vérendrye would build a post.

At last the French had accepted the route which was to lead them to the Rockies—beyond which lay the 'Sea of the West'. Ease of travel by canoe and the ability to use the Cree tongue all the way to the Rockies were accepted as arguments which placed the Saskatchewan route above the Missouri. It was a pregnant change of approach, formulated by the hard experience of de la Vérendrye and

his family. But de la Vérendrye was dead, his worth at last acknowledged by the award of the Cross of St. Louis, and his sons were not
allowed to carry out the plan which they had put forward. Instead,
an officer of marines, Jacques Repentiquy de Saint Pierre, was given
command of the western posts, and he refused the services of the
sons of de la Vérendrye. Saint Pierre sent a party up to The Pas on
the Saskatchewan in 1750, with orders to follow the river up to the
mountains in the spring. A French party certainly set out in 1751
from The Pas, and returned with an account of a journey of over
seven hundred miles up the river. But whether they took the North
or the South Branch of the Saskatchewan, and whether they built
their post, Fort La Jonquière, at the foot of the Rockies (as Saint
Pierre said) or in the prairies south of the present city of Edmonton,
is still open to question. Indeed, Saint Pierre's post may not even
have been so far up the Saskatchewan, perhaps even below the Forks
of the River.

Fort La Jonquière was in any case destroyed by Indians in 1752
and Saint Pierre's successor in command of the posts of the west,
Louis Chapt, Chevalier de la Corne, built a more lasting settlement,
possibly on the site of La Jonquière, just below the Forks of the River
in 1753. Fort la Corne, or Fort St. Louis des Prairies as this post
was called, remained an effective trade post, and shows how even
the ineffective successors of de la Vérendrye continued and completed
the work which he and his sons had begun, accepting the Saskatchewan rather than the Missouri and therefore pressing always into
the territories which dominated the lakes and the headwaters of the
rivers which flowed into the Bay. Fort la Corne completed the chain
of posts running from St. Pierre on Rainy Lake, Fort St. Charles on
Lake of the Woods, Fort Maurepas at the mouth of Winnipeg River,
Fort La Reine at the portage from the Assiniboine to Lake Manitoba, Fort Dauphin on Mossy River, flowing out of Lake Dauphin
into Lake Winnipegosis, to Fort Bourbon on Cedar Lake facing
the mouth of the Saskatchewan, and The Pas (Paskoyac) blocking
the Indians of the Saskatchewan off from the Bay.

Between them these posts made Rainy Lake and Lake of the
Woods into French inland seas and diverted much of the furs of the
Assiniboine and the Saskatchewan from Hudson Bay to the St.
Lawrence. De la Vérendrye and his sons had always been clear that
such a diversion of fur was an essential part of their task, and many
times they exhorted their Indians not to go to trade with the English.
Maurepas and the French government too, heavily though they in-
dicted the explorer and his family for giving beaver priority over

exploration, nevertheless insisted, unfairly as it seems to us, that furs must bear the costs of exploration, and the Hudson Bay trade was inevitably affected.

But the threat shifted in emphasis, and the English got no relief when de la Vérendrye's family was passed over. On the contrary; the newcomers turned against the English as the cause of all their troubles. De La Vérendrye's successors were in everything less purposeful than he; they complained of the hardships of the routes whereas he merely protested that such journeys took time; they protested at the food whereas he merely explained that such ventures must be carefully prepared. It was therefore in character that whilst de la Vérendrye was constantly working to cut off the furs from the English, his successors complained that the posts of the west could never flourish as long as the English remained by the Bay. Again, de la Vérendrye and his family showed genius in winning the loyalty of the Crees, the Monsonis and the Assiniboines, though later generations maintained that they had spoiled the Indians and had set standards of gift-giving and of trade which could not be maintained. His successors, however, found it impossible to keep the peace among the Indians; Fort La Reine was almost inundated by them, further exploration was made impossible by Indian wars, and for this the reason given was that the Indians would always remain turbulent and independent as long as they had English posts at the Bay to which they could trade.

The English would probably have been surprised to learn that the effects of their posts were felt so far inland. For although the official policy of the Hudson's Bay Committee was always to preach peace among the Indians and to give presents and encourage far-coming Indians so as to 'draw them down to trade', they had but little confidence in the success of such a policy during de la Vérendrye's régime. On the contrary, they were always obsessed by the fact that they were acting on the defensive and that the French were constantly drawing nearer and nearer to the Bay, cutting the Indians off from trade. Part of the explanation of this is to be found in the financial machinations to which de la Vérendrye was driven. Forced to pay for exploration from the profits of the trade at his posts, he had no option but to sub-contract the trade with merchants at Quebec and Montreal in return for supplies and money. At times, as for example from 1735 to 1738, he was even forced to contract away the whole trade, taking no part himself—and even so he landed himself in law-suits, which he hated! In consequence, the trade of the French posts was carried on by a system of licences which gave much of the actual Indian trade to the adventurous, and often unscrupulous, *coureurs de bois*, who spread French influence far in advance of the actual posts which had been founded.

Much fur was indeed brought to the main French posts and there traded, and though the conduct of such trade differed greatly from that at the Hudson Bay posts in that there was more ceremony, more festivity, and more danger of an outbreak, the essential economic fact remained the same—the Indians brought their furs in to trade at the post, as they did at the Bay-side. This, however, was but one branch of the French trade whereas it was all, or almost all, of the Bay-side trade. The French *coureur en dérouinnes* also travelled around among the Indians, sometimes set up a small and insecure post (to shelter him from the weather rather than from the Indians) and traded with the Indians 'in the woods and in their habitations'. It was this outer ring of skirmishers which brought home to the English the advances made by the French, and made them seem always on the defensive. It also brought the trade into a new perspective, placing it upon a footing in which the European sought out the Indian to trade with him instead of leaving it to the Indian to bring in the furs to the posts. Thereby the dominant position was ceded to the Indians; at base they were acknowledged as the controlling party in the trade. In the bargaining they were the sought-after party; and although they weakened their position by becoming utterly dependent on European goods, yet the move to seek out the Indians for trade instead of bringing them in to the posts marks a definite cession. Prices of furs rose accordingly, partly by absorbing increased costs of transport, partly by the addition of presents to the actual standard of trade, and in the last analysis by competitive buying.

The Company's officers were fully aware of this encroachment on their trade and, bound by a rigid 'Standard', found it hard to meet competition. The wood-runners were avouched as the reason for a decline in the returns from York Fort in 1732; and the report from Churchill supported the contention that York was suffering from a defection of the Indians 'that borders near the french'. In the same year a wandering Frenchman with his 'slave' (his squaw) turned up at Albany Fort itself. Joseph Delestre had been book-keeper at Fort Bourbon when the French were in possession of the Nelson River. He came unarmed to Albany under pretext of recovering debts due from Indians, and Joseph Adams could think of no reason to detain him. But there were reports of other Frenchmen also, of two settlements up the river and of a third being built only four days' journey from the fort. The Committee in 1733 ordered that no such *coureur* was to be admitted within the factory gates or allowed to talk to the servants. All lawful means were to be used to make them depart and the Committee were to be kept full informed of any French moves. So Delestre was even more cautiously treated when he returned to Albany in 1733 and found his way also to the newly-re-established post at Moose.

The Committee not only ordered the French to be kept away from the posts; they also ordered all shrubs to be cleared away for a distance of half a mile from the defences, while the men were to be lodged in the flankers, and the fortifications were to be improved. So real were the fears of a French invasion in force. For Delestre was not the only Frenchman who haunted the English posts in those years. A 'Monsieur Guillet', governor of a 'factory' consisting of two 'natural Frenchmen' and some wood-runners, sent in a tempting and placatory letter to William Bevan at Moose. Bevan was loyal, and recalcitrant, and the Committee fully approved of his attitude though they were reluctantly convinced that the Company had no power to prevent the French from settling on the upper rivers and intercepting the trade.

The only remedy, as before, was to treat the Indians kindly and to give them good value. Here the quality of the English goods was a great asset, and the sturdy Macklish at York, feeling that the masters at Moose had been 'Endued with Uncommon patience to Suffer themselves to be abused under their Noses so grossly' felt that he could even get trade from near the French post. The Indians, however, complained that the French forced them to trade and that they could only get to the English posts by stealth. On the whole they were pleased with English goods, but the French gunpowder seems to have been genuinely superior and their cloth, knives, and hatchets were also desired by the Indians—so much so that the Committee ordered samples of the French goods to be sent home with explanations of the qualities which the Indians found attractive. Whether trading with the French or the English, the Indians craved guns, powder, Brazil tobacco and brandy, and except for brandy the samples left the Committee convinced of the excellence of their own wares and mystified by the Indians' liking for the French goods. In this they were right, for it was not the quality of the French wares which led the Indians to the wood-runners; it was the fact that the wood-runners came to them. They told the Indians they would visit all the English posts 'and will Intercept the Trade by force if they Cannot have it otherwise'. Moreover they traded by winter as well as in the spring and autumn and, all things considered, it remained true that it was not smallpox or Indian wars which cut the Company's trade—'But its the french that is our chiefest Obstical, they encreasing more than ever'.

This 'yearly Increase into the Hart of your Honours Trade Inland' went far to justify Maurepas' suspicions of de la Vérendrye. To some extent he and his posts were opening up fresh beaver country, trading with Indians who had hitherto found beaver so plentiful that they clothed themselves in the skins in winter and then in spring, when they would be the *castor gras* which the French needed, threw them away 'faute de commerce'. To some extent de la Vérendrye was getting beaver from Indians who had never previously bothered with it. The Assiniboines of the Assiniboine River, for example, were described by the Crees as 'people who did not know how to kill beaver, and whose only clothing was buffalo skin, a thing we did not require'; they had never seen the French and did not know how to trade. But much of the fur which from 1730 to 1763 found its way through the French posts to Montreal and Quebec came from trade which would otherwise have swelled the returns of the Hudson's Bay posts.

Apart from the trade of the *coureurs* and of the merchants to whom he issued licences, de la Vérendrye himself conducted a very considerable trade, so large as to cast suspicion on the pleas of debt and poverty with which his official correspondence is interspersed. In 1734 he sent out two hundred and seventy-five packages of furs in eleven canoes. Six hundred packages were made up at Fort Maurepas alone in 1735, and in that year the posts of the west between them produced nearly a hundred thousand good skins. That was the year in which de la Vérendrye was forced to cede the trade to the merchants on a system of licences, but the quantity of fur was nevertheless very considerable. The Indians were trading with both French and English and were shewing considerable commercial sense in so doing, for it was commonly reported by the English factors that at times they only got such skins as the French rejected, and that the Indians traded the light and valuable skins with the French (who would not be burdened with heavy skins of no more value than the light ones) and that they then brought the heavy skins down to the English. So far did the facts of the transport system dominate the situation that there were definite reports that the French posts of the west were, by the time of de la Vérendrye's death, supplied with their heavy goods (especially the iron-ware which was so difficult in the canoes and on the portages) by Indians who had traded them from the Hudson Bay posts and carried them inland. But even with the limitation that the French could supply few heavy trade-goods and preferred not to take the heavy skins, their trade flourished, it achieved something like stability after about 1745, and it deeply affected the Hudson Bay trade.

The returns from York Fort, for example, had been worked up to 47,000 'Made-beaver' in 1730 and to 52,000 in 1731. They dropped to 37,000 in 1732, and stayed even lower (at about 32,000) for a ten-year period. At the end of that time, with relapses in 1744 and 1746 which were definitely ascribed to Indian wars, the York returns climbed back almost to the 40,000 level—but that was still about 20 per cent. less than they had been before de la Vérendrye came into the posts of the west.

In considering such figures we must bear in mind that other factors were at work besides the French. At Albany, for example, though the presence of the *coureurs* was accepted as 'the very probable' reason why the returns fell off from 1732 onwards, the establishment of the subsidiary posts of Moose and Eastmain must also have affected the trade of the parent factory. And York's decline from the 'very great Trade' of 1731 must be seen against the fact that Churchill's returns in 1732 were bigger than for many years, probably because Macklish had sent the Port Nelson Indians to trade at Churchill instead of at York. On the other hand, it was explicitly stated that York was in that year disappointed by the non-arrival of Indians 'that borders near the French', and Churchill's trade rose only by about eight thousand skins, from 7,455 to 15,378, whilst York's returns fell by fifteen thousand. In fact Churchill's trade shewed little more than the normal increase to be expected at a new post until 1737, when the York Fort Indians heard of the loss of the outward-bound ship and brought their trade to Churchill. It was the argument that York and Churchill between them produced very little more than York alone had formerly produced which called forth comments on the vast charge and expense of Churchill, for to the end of the period the returns from York alone in 1731 were never exceeded by the two posts combined.

It was, however, not only by way of direct diminution of its returns that the Hudson's Bay Company felt the French opposition. On the whole, adequate supplies of furs came to London. It was in the need to establish new and costly posts, the need to spend money on fortifications and on men to man them, the need to make presents and to grant credit to Indians and to accept even unsatisfactory furs from them, that the costs of trading were enhanced. And when the furs had been got to London they had to be sold at a price necessarily affected by the influx of French skins into the European market. Increased buying prices and decreased selling prices were the almost inevitable results of such a competition as the French made necessary.

For the English company, fortunately, the competition for the European market was not very important during these years. The English hat-making industry flourished. A generation earlier, exports of English-made beaver hats had been small and spasmodic, and to some extent balanced by imports of coarser hats—two dozen beavers and a dozen half-beavers to Jamaica, three dozen half-beavers to Bilbao, three dozen beavers to Barbados, three dozen beavers and three dozen felts to Calais as against eight dozen coarse trimmed hair hats, four felt hats, twenty-seven dozen Bast hats from Ostend and 2,700 Bast hats from Rotterdam, with thirty-five dozen 'Shaven Hats' from Flanders. But by the 1730's a steady export industry had developed. Exports, formerly by dozens but now by hundreds, of beaver and half-beaver hats to the British West Indies were an important feature of the trade. Equally important was the trade to Spain and Portugal and so to their colonies. From a total export figure of £44,000 in 1700 (perhaps a bad year to choose, for the Company then had only the furs from Albany, and the French were satiating the European market) English exports in furs rose to over £263,000 by 1750. Of this trade more than eighty-five per cent. was due to exports of beaver hats, and about forty-five per cent. of the exports went to Spain and Portugal.

Direct exports to the Spanish West Indies formed an insignificant part of these shipments, for Spain jealously excluded other countries from trade with her colonies. But the annual 'Flotas' and galley convoys in which the trade from Spain to the New World was organised took out such heavy consignments as to make the Spanish colonies the great market—a market, too, from which the returns were in bullion. This fact placed the hat trade alongside the slave trade as a method by which the other countries of Europe might invade the trading preserves of the Spanish Empire. The fur trade played its part in dispersing the wealth of the Indies, without which it was held that Spain would be one of the poorest and weakest kingdoms in Europe. The French covetously estimated that the annual shipment of hats to the Spanish colonies amounted to ten or twelve thousand beavers and four or five thousand half-beavers, absorbing about four hundred and fifty thousand pounds of skins. But the French industry was in such quandaries, reduced even to getting hat-makers from England, that much of the market was inevitably lost to France.

Yet the trade was acclaimed as vital, both because it provided an outlet for the furs of Canada and because it opened up 'un des plus considerables retours des Indes'. For exactly the same reasons, because it gave access to the wealth of the Indies and because it disposed of an important colonial product, the English trade assumed an importance out of proportion to its volume. It must be accepted that the fur trade, including the imports from the New England colonies (which normally produced a very substantial proportion, between a third and a half of the total imports of raw furs) accounted during the eighteenth century for less than one-half per cent. of the total value of English imports, while exports of raw fur accounted for less than one-quarter per cent. and exports of hats to less than one-and-one-quarter per cent. of the total exports, even when shipments to the British mainland colonies, to the British West Indies, to the East Indies, Russia, Italy, the Guinea coast, Germany, Holland, Flanders and even to France herself had been added to the bulk trade to Spain, Portugal and their colonies. Even so, negligible though it might be on a percentage basis, the export English hatmaking industry was netting returns of over £137,000 by 1725, £153,000 by 1730 and £263,000 by 1750, and these were sums which denoted a prosperous and important industry. Although the outports offered substantial competition to London in the export of the baser felt hats, the beaver hat exports went almost exclusively from London, and so the Hudson's Bay Committee was assured at the same time of an active and lively London market for its furs, of criticism and complaints of its qualities and prices, and yet of support from a prosperous and important local industry when supplies of beaver seemed to be threatened.

BOOKS FOR REFERENCE

BREBNER, J. B.—*The Explorers of North America 1492–1806* (London, 1955).

BURPEE, Lawrence J.—*The Search for the Western Sea. The story of the exploration of north-western America* (Toronto, 1908).

BURPEE, Lawrence J. (ed.)—*Journals and Letters of Pierre Gaultier de Varennes de la Vérendrye and his sons. With correspondence between the Governors of Canada and the French Court, touching the search for the Western Sea* (Toronto, The Champlain Society, 1927).

CROUSE, Nellis M.—*La Vérendrye Fur Trader and Explorer* (Toronto, 1956).

GIRAUD, Marcel—*Le Métis Canadien* (Paris, 1945).

INNIS, H. A.—*The Fur Trade in Canada* (Toronto, 1956).
LAWSON, Murray G.—*Fur: A Study in English Mercantilism, 1700–1775* (Toronto, 1943).
MORTON, Arthur S.—*A History of the Canadian West to 1870–71* (London, 1939).

ARTICLE

MORTON, Arthur S.—'La Vérendrye: Commandant, Fur-trader, and Explorer.' See *The Canadian Historical Review* (Toronto, 1928), Vol. IX.

CHAPTER XXXIX

THE SLEEP BY THE FROZEN SEA

While de la Vérendrye, his sons and their successors, were spreading the French posts up the Saskatchewan and in the hinterland of the Company's posts, the Hudson's Bay men were tied to the shores of the Bay for a variety of reasons. The Committee's policy was based on a tradition in which contact with sea-going vessels and the enticement of the Indian to bring his furs down the rivers to trade was fundamental, adequate furs for the Company's markets were got by these means, and neither employees nor equipment were suited for a policy of expansion into the interior. Indeed, with memories of Iberville to spur them on, the Committee's natural reaction to the French activity was to concentrate on preparations to beat off a maritime attack.

Easily explained and in many ways defensible though such a policy might be, it attracted little admiration when compared with the splendid exploits of the French, and it soon came under heavy criticism. Such criticism seems all the more warranted when it is considered that even in the preparation of their posts to resist attack by ships the Committee seemed to have failed. The outstanding example of this policy was, of course, the building of the great stone fort at Churchill, begun in 1731. For at Churchill the constant pressure to complete the fortification had achieved some peculiar results by 1741. The Committee had given firm support in all aspects of this task. Extra men had been recruited. The labourers when possible were got from the Orkneys, but the masons came from the Cotswolds, used to the rough work of squaring stone and building cottages, not to the ornamental work which was the only craft known to many English masons by the eighteenth century. A quarry had been opened, a lime-kiln built in 1731, and the site at Eskimo Point, six miles from the old Factory House, fully approved. An indent for either a hundred and nine men with two teams of cattle or for eighty-four men and four teams, so that the crew of four masons could always be kept supplied with stone, and would find their foundations dug and laid, was not fully met, but bulls and cows and horses were sent out and even when, as in 1733, lack of shipping cut the indents for other posts, Churchill was not skimped. The fear was that a sea-borne attack might be launched, and Eskimo Point was chosen because it commanded the bay at the back of Cape Merry so that not even the smallest boat could land. The heavy work of hauling the stone needed for such fortifications needed horses and cattle, and the existence of horses and cattle led to dependence on imported grain and locally-made hay, so that the whole economy of the little post became unduly complicated and, for example, the team of oxen had to be killed when the loss of the *Hudson's Bay* in 1736 meant that no grain was available. The cattle also involved problems of shipping space, of veterinary skill, and of appropriate harness.

Richard Norton proved in many ways a wayward and headstrong Chief for such a post, but he pressed on enthusiastically with building, even to the extent of providing most of the timber from a local source of which, as he boasted, he alone knew. His reports of work accomplished were always optimistic, and by the time he came home at his own request in 1741 (after successfully resisting an attempt to undermine him by Thomas Bird) he was able to report that the ramparts of the four bastions had been raised to a height of ten feet and that four curtains connected the ramparts, each filled with gravel, with board runways for the guns and with a parapet five feet high pierced by forty-eight gun-ports. A defended gateway commanded the approach from the river, and inside the fortifications had been built a large factory-house, floored and roofed by 1741. There were also a kitchen, smith's shop, brew house, bake house, provision shed, and a great powder magazine whose walls were five feet thick and whose roof was a six feet thick stone vault. It should have been all 'sufficient bumb Proof', as the proud Norton reported it, and with eighteen cannon in position out of the total of thirty-six indented for, it seemed more than adequate.

True, Churchill's trade could hardly be accepted as firmly established; it slumped to 10,907 'Made-beaver' in 1740 and was subject to even more 'Accidents' than the trade of the other posts, and both Norton and other members of his council were strongly suspected of making over-generous presents to Indians (a modest present of a pipe, some tobacco and perhaps some prunes or 'toys' was a normal compliment of trade). In return the Indians made presents of furs, and the 'pernicious system' which resulted diminished the Company's returns and roused the Committee's suspicions.

The dangers of war, however, meant that the military strength of Churchill looked likely to stabilise the trade. For York Fort could not possibly resist any attack. 'If Every man was made of Steel or brass what Could we do with a formidable Enemy by Sea, in a wooden house that will make good tuch wood, our barricadoes or outworks a handfull of men may Shove down with their Shoulders' wrote Governor James Isham. He therefore suggested using the sloops to take the York furs to the protection of the stone fort at Churchill in the spring, there to await the arrival of the ships from England, and when he himself had been transferred to the command of Churchill on Norton's retirement he set on foot a scheme to transfer not only the furs but also the Indians and the actual trade from York to Churchill. It was a scheme which the Committee approved, and Isham and his Council were confident that the trade might be so diverted without difficulty.

But at Churchill the fortification was by no means so complete and successful as Isham had been told. The last year of Norton's command had in fact seen a frenzied effort to make the post fit for the war which had actually broken out, but despite his self-satisfaction Norton reported in 1740 that the post was in no posture for defence, and he proposed not to send the sloop on its northern voyage for a year so as to get on more rapidly with the building. He pressed on with building to such purpose that he even engaged several Indians as builders' labourers, but it is not, perhaps, surprising that the year's work under such conditions, although it enabled Norton to put in a glowing progress-report, left his successor far from satisfied. Part of the walls had already fallen down, and another thirty-foot length of rampart fell during Isham's first year in command. The walls were not thick enough to carry the parapet, and for the most part they were neither bedded with mortar nor were the stones bonded together. The interior wall of the curtain had to be moved eight feet so as to give that much extra width on the parapet, the flankers had to be moved, and it transpired that even the boasted magazine was damp and suspect. Much though it had expended, the Company found that when the War of Jenkins' Ear broke out in 1739, to merge into the War of the Austrian Succession and to involve open hostilities with France in 1740, Churchill was not defensible. Even with the danger of actual war to spur them on, the Committee could accomplish little. The cannon sent out in 1743 could not be landed at Cape Merry, and in 1744 the *Seahorse* took a further six twenty-four-pounder guns for the battery there. This was a matter which caused considerable delay and acrimony, and it was 1749 before the Committee declared themselves satisfied with this battery, at which a garrison of twelve men had to be maintained throughout the period of open water.

Richard Norton's defects as an accountant and administrator go far to explain the failure at Churchill. He was, however, a great traveller, and he had the confidence of his Indians. So, in a different way, did his successor in command, for though James Isham was not himself an adventurous soul, he nevertheless had considerable sympathy with the explorers. He had begun his service as a 'writer' at York in 1732 under the tutelage of Macklish. Gaining a reputation as a very sober young man, he made rapid improvement, was on the Council at York by 1735, and was Chief there in 1737. He represented the book-keeper's approach to life and trade by the Bay, a promoted clerk who never ventured to become a traveller with Indians, or even a sloop-master. He was not enthralled with life at York, and wondered whether he ought not to return to England in 1737, but having accepted command he set to work to improve and strengthen the Company's position and to vindicate the authority and responsibility of the post to which he had been promoted. He sent home detailed and sensible criticisms of the trade-goods with which he was supplied—the beads were too large, the cloth too narrow, kettles too small, the powder weak and foul—and he defended the practices of the traders, especially in making presents to the Indians and in watering the trade brandy. He proved himself a stern disciplinarian, purging York of drunkards (though his successor in command did not agree that he had done so) but sending home sympathetic character-studies of most of his men. For a promoted clerk he ran into much trouble because of his careless and inaccurate accounts and indents, and his trade returns shewed poorly when compared with those of previous years. He found the post at York in very poor repair, and he came into sharp contact with the Committee since he maintained that the existing site at York was too marshy to support the stone building which the circumstances called for. He was ultimately proved right, and under his successor the Committee endorsed his view, but in 1741 he was over-ruled and, protesting his willingness to defend York to the last if called upon, and fully aware of the French threat, he was transferred to Churchill.

Predominant though Churchill undoubtedly was in the plans for fortifying the Company's posts, the building of the great stone fort was pursued alongside plans for the other posts, which were by no means neglected. A new plan was adopted for Albany to make it more defensible and to allow the removal of all trees, shrubs and other cover to a depth of half a mile from the fort. The heavy guns sent out for Albany's defence did not, however, meet with the approval of Richard Staunton as Chief. He placed his reliance upon small arms and a clear field of fire and sent the guns home as useless, pointing out that despite their boasts (and their high salaries) the gunners of York had not prevented Iberville from bringing his ship right up above the factory in 1694. The cannon were sent back to Albany on the eve of the outbreak of war in 1739. The Committee wondered 'even with astonishment' that Staunton should have considered them useful only for show and should have returned them, and cannon continued to be sent to all the posts (with a result that two different qualities of gunpowder had to be kept). But even the Committee realised that valuable as the brass pieces might be to impress the Indians or to use as signal guns, they involved the maintenance of costly and idle specialists, and that French strength on land and weakness at sea made it probable that any attack would come overland and the cannon would be useless.

Descriptive accounts of Fullartine's defence of Albany in 1709 were therefore sent to all posts, with reiterated instructions, year by year, to keep the men sober, exercised in their small arms, disciplined and watchful, and to keep the field of fire round the posts clear of cover. These instructions went to York and Churchill as well as to the Bottom of the Bay, but the Committee realised that, lacking in ships though the French might be, any attack on those two posts would have to come from the sea. A system of signals for incoming ships was therefore arranged, the buoys which alone made navigation possible near the posts were only left in position when the ship from England was expected or present, all strange ships were to be fired on, rewards and pensions were promised to those who conducted themselves valiantly—or to their widows and orphans!—and the defences were vigorously reinforced. At York Thomas White managed to convince the Committee (as Isham had not) that the old post could not satisfactorily be repaired; there was no adequate foundation for any stone building on the site chosen by Knight in 1714, so in 1740 White began to build a new post two hundred yards lower down the river. Two years later, however, he reverted to the old site, bringing the footings in by ten feet. Timber was scarce and distant from the site, as it had always been at York and Churchill, yet good progress was made and the main house was finished and lead-roofed in 1743, leaving a curtain wall and a row of stockades still to be erected. For this the masons, and the stone, were drafted to York from Churchill in 1744.

The complements of all posts were increased; to Churchill went an engineer, Captain Robert Evinson, to train the men and to lay the cannon so as to command the river-mouth. To York went a ship, the *Seahorse*, with fifty men, to stay in the country and act as a garrison and mobile defence—this despite the cost and the well-acknowledged difficulties of provisions, discipline and private trade, which always occurred when a ship wintered in the Bay and upset the normal routine. She was to stay at York till 15th September, then to leave twenty men there and go to winter at Churchill.

The interludes of peace did not mitigate the French threat or in any way lighten the burden and cost of vigilance, to leave the Company free for experiment and expansion. For the French had been known to take the Company's posts in times of peace; they were 'Slie Sutle and artfull to perfaction', and their very existence made relaxation impossible.

Along with the commitments of defence, the Committee had to study the trade of their posts. Here again was a further argument against the setting up of inland posts, for unless they were so far inland as to make transport and upkeep difficult, costly and dangerous, they would merely draw off the trade of the Bay-side posts. Therefore unless the trade was already effectively interrupted by the French, so that upland posts would compete with the French instead of with the Bay, there was no case for them. The first move therefore must be to organise and develop the trade of the Bay-side posts, but the Committee was trading under difficulties, for war conditions and the troubles of the London market caused serious defects in the trade-goods. The sugar of 1737 was the worst that ever came from London; no blue cloth was sent to Albany in 1737 and the vitally important nets and lines of 1736 were made from 'Damnified Hemp'; goods were entered on the bill of lading which could not be found on arrival, others were sent but not entered. Tobacco was normally good but even that was in some years impossibly rotten. The gunpowder was a constant source of recrimination between the traders and the Committee, the traders urging more careful manufacture and purchase and the Committee insisting on dry storage, constant turning over, and sale of old stocks first.

The correspondence books make it clear that the traders had cause for complaint but that the Committee were open to suggestions and criticism (as when 'Toys' were sent out, and brass stoppers for tobacco-pipes at Isham's suggestion); Sub-Committees were appointed to prepare cargoes and they gave much thought and time to their business, meeting three times a week when necessary. The defects in the trade-goods were sometimes due to natural causes—as when the year's crop of Brazil tobacco was of poor quality—but at times they were due to defective workmanship, as when the ironwork proved bad, hatchets and files full of flaws, cloth shrunken and of poor quality at the centre of the roll despite the Committee's care. Some things there were in which the Committee proved inattentive, particularly in 1737 when the Secretary Thomas Bird was ill. But the general impression is one of a Committee laying out its money with care and consideration, if with little imagination; and the correspondence on the subject of trading-goods must always be read against the picture of factors and committee-men sparring not ill-naturedly for position. Both sides to the contest left openings—the traders by careless packaging, extravagant expenditure and improvident indenting, and the Committee by an occasional shipment of poor goods and by a slightly unrealistic approach.

Both traders and Committee, however, fully accepted the fact that they must organise and supply the trade of their posts on the assumption that the Indian trade had become competitive. The trouble was that the competition varied from post to post. This called for some flexibility in the Company's Standard of Trade, but variations in the 'Standard' between one post and another would certainly produce the result that over a period of years the Indians would flock to the easier post; and a competition between the posts would merely run up the cost of furs but would not increase or improve the supply.

The period is therefore marked by acceptance of French rivalry and by constant efforts to discover their Standard of Trade and the quality of their goods. This proved difficult, for the wood-runners who were the Company's closest rivals allowed themselves considerable latitude and traded according to circumstances rather than according to a fixed standard. The information, too, could only be got from Indians whose advantage it was to bid up the white rivals. So though reports were indeed sent home, it was accepted that any information on French trading methods was not completely reliable and that the Indians were so perfidious that no two would agree on a tariff save for the fact that the French always traded a marten as equal to a beaver whereas the English still insisted on trading three martens for one beaver. To give a lasting impression of the English resources as well as to allow of close examination, a 'French Indian' was sent to London from York in 1743; but strict orders were issued to prevent other Indians who might spy on the Company's trade from getting access to the posts, and the Committee were firm in saying that no more were to be sent to England.

Despite the steady market for beaver which was provided by the flourishing English hat industry, the Committee showed a constant desire to find alternatives. The possibility of a white-whale fishery from York was again taken up in 1740 and 1742, the endless attempts to get the Indians to bring in castoreum persisted (still in vain), and the hopeful search for minerals went on. In this matter the Committee shewed some perhaps unwarranted suspicion of their servants, for they refused to send crucibles to Moose and rejected Isham's request for some phosphorus in 1743. Isham only wanted the phosphorus to 'amuse' the Indians, but the Committee wanted all trying out of the ores to be done in England. Neither close supervision nor a promise of gratuities produced any precious, or even semiprecious, metals though Isham reported a mine near Churchill and Albany sent home what it hoped would be silver ore.

A further long-standing, if secondary, problem which occupied much of the Committee's attention at this time was that of encouraging the use of country provisions instead of the increasingly expensive, and less satisfactory, European food. For years the Committee had tried to encourage an interest in botany and in gardening, and from 1733 onwards the surgeons and traders were made responsible for sending home samples of the local plants (Isham sent four boxes-full from York in 1737 and again in 1738). But though some pretence at enthusiasm was shown, the traders on the whole seem to have thought, with Thomas White of York, that their 'Time and thoughts' were 'Sufficiently Employed in what is more conducive'. It was White, too, who most roundly expressed the general apathy over gardening. He had not been brought up to tillage and professed himself an indifferent judge in those matters; and though some servants held that useful crops could be grown, especially at Moose and Albany, he maintained that it was June before seed could be sown, that the soil was infertile, even the pine-wood was full of knots, and the whole of Rupert's Land was for him 'a barren country'. Isham was perhaps a little more accommodating, but even he could only report that he had managed to grow turnips and 'salad' but that no corn would grow, and though barley and oats had come to an ear they had never ripened. The Committee, however, continued their urgings, sent out seed, and hoped to cut the bill for provisions.

Though the Committee strove in vain to foster any enthusiasm for gardening in such a climate, their efforts to develop local supplies of fresh meat were better rewarded. Deer were plentiful at times, but though the Committee shipped over good Bay salt, the venison would not take salt and so must be eaten fresh. The result was that during the great deer drives, when upwards of a thousand might be killed by one tribe, there was a surfeit, but 'in a month afterwards shall not Gett a Deer for Love or money', except for the tongues. It was 'a Very uncertain place for the English mens Living'. Geese and partridges, on the other hand, could not only be got in great quantities but could also be salted, and eaten through the winter. Churchill in particular was well placed for the white geese, which rested on the marshes there for about three weeks in May on their way north and for about six weeks in August and September on their way south. Further south, where white geese were scarce, blue geese were plentiful; Albany in particular depended on the success of the spring and fall hunts. York, on the other hand, could be very unlucky, and while, for example in 1742, Churchill salted 3,800 from the spring hunt and Albany got almost the same (3,736), York got less than 300. But although thousands were salted down, the normal ration was half a goose a man a day for six days a week, so that seven hundred geese would only last the twenty-four men of Moose for ten weeks.

Partridges were a valuable supplement to geese, and Isham considered them the chief winter provision for the English at Churchill in some years, when he expended four hundred a week for eight months out of the twelve. Rabbits and hares could also be got throughout the winter. But in all of these hunts the English were as yet completely dependent on their 'home-guard' Indians, 'those Indians that Keep's constant attendance to the factory's in the Seasons', as Isham called them. The Committee urged that this dependence should be broken, but the reluctance and incompetence of the English are clear. By 1747 all posts were still being reproved for their dependence on Indians. Churchill was specially instructed to send Englishmen out with the Indians on the goose-hunts, 'that being so material an article', while Albany replied that English servants were already used for fishing and for partridge hunting but that the Indians must be depended on for geese. English servants were, however, sent out with the Indians to learn how to kill geese. From the *Observations on Hudson's Bay* which Isham wrote at Churchill there seems no good reason why the English servants should not have been successful food-hunters. The hunts took place near to the posts, the gun was the weapon, not the bow and arrow, and though some stalking was at times required the normal method was to shoot from behind a breast-high butt made of brushwood. And Isham noted that 'these Natives are good Mark's men with their Gun, tho not to Compare to Some of our own Country men'.

The true reasons for dependence on the Indians, once the Committee had broken through the apathy, and the easy reliance on imported food and Indian hunters, were serious. A high proportion of the English servants were artisans or labourers who would normally enjoy 'taking a gun for a walk' but who would not take kindly to anything like a specialised appointment and responsibility as post-hunter; something more nearly akin to casual poaching would be their notion of fun, and many of them were town-bred (though that did not involve a complete divorce from country-side skills and pleasures in the eighteenth century). This, however, was a factor which could be controlled and overcome, and when the other reasons for dependence on Indians had been settled, by the end of the century, the posts were in fact able to produce an adequate supply of English servants who would spend weeks at the goose-tents and would provide amply for their posts.

But the Committee could not so easily remedy the other conditions —which were that the goose-hunts took place during trade-time when the plantations round the posts were full of Indians and security reasons forbade the dispersal of English servants to the marshes; and that the 'home-guard' Indians resented the attempt to replace them by Englishmen. Both of these conditions were aspects of the general uncertainty of the English position, and though the posts might agree to choose out men 'with an Inclination to a Gun and Inure them to Hunting and fishing' they could neither face any general dis-satisfaction of the Indians nor spare men in adequate numbers for the hunts until their position was more secure. That meant, in effect, until the French threat had been minimised and finally removed from the Bay. Indeed, the French threat led to emphasis on the need to ship out adequate provisions from England, for in case of war the Indians would all be frightened away by the wood-runners 'who are half French and Naturalized to them'.

Dependence upon the 'home guards' and upon imported provisions might nevertheless have been considerably lessened if either officers or men had been more enterprising. But during the war period of the eighteenth century it is not surprising that overseas service under the Company should have been indifferently performed. Press-gangs and prize-money between them made service in the Navy both difficult to evade and more attractive than in peacetime. Recruitment for the Company was bound to suffer, and both officers and men declined in quality. Consequently, if the officers had much more experience and served for longer periods than in the early years of the establishment of the Company's trade, yet they had their serious failings, and the men even more so. James Isham, for example, emerges from his writings as an interested and lively person, attractive and sympathetic, but though the Committee accepted most of his views and supported him in major matters, they did not find him an ideal Chief as far as the ordinary trade, development and defence, of his post were concerned. The trade returns did indeed increase, from almost eleven thousand Made-beaver in 1740 to almost seventeen thousand in 1742 and to eighteen thousand and five hundred in 1743. A 'mine' was discovered and samples of the ore were sent home (it proved useless), and Isham shewed himself interested, active, and able to keep on good terms with the Indians. But he was sick of the gout and a 'Great Cold', scarcely able to walk and 'Very full of Pain'. His management called for a certain amount of almost routine reproof from the Committee; his general letter home was not written out in paragraphs in the prescribed manner, his packages home did not always tally with his bill of lading, and he indented for goods which the Committee thought unnecessary and at times extravagant—and he was far more seriously and purposefully criticised by his successor in command.

In all of this Isham was better than the average post-master upon whom the Committee had to base plans—slightly better than average but not exceptional. In one respect, indeed, he compared favourably, for while the other Chiefs had followed the lead of James Duffield at Moose and had embarked on a forthright contest with the ships' captains, Isham had remained silent, and so escaped the rebuke which fell upon the other Chiefs. The immediate origin of the quarrel was obviously some personal rancour between Duffield and Captain Coats; Duffield prided himself on the reformation which he had brought about at Moose, the transformation of the post from a 'weak Defenceless nasty hole, into a Strong and regular Fort', and on the collection of the best cargo ever known from Moose in 1744. He had also built a schooner at the post, and he was not prepared to accept the opinion of the ship's captain as to the best place to lay up his sloop for the winter; he even protested against the standing order that the captains must be members of the Council while their ships were at the posts. He, and Isbister at Albany who was with him in this matter, were strongly ordered to conform or to resign, and Duffield was told to lay the sloop higher up the river, where Coats said, and not to extol his knowledge; the two Chiefs were to do their duties as became faithful servants and to leave the captains to their proper tasks.

Though this storm passed over Isham's head, when he was called home in 1745, partly at his own request and partly to be questioned, he found his whole period of management at Churchill impugned. His command went to the censorious Robert Pilgrim, who found on arrival that Isham had left behind a Council which was only too ready to disavow his management. 'As Mr. Isham has been Resolved to Act wholly and Soly of himself and in himself, we humbly hope you will Excuse Our Answer to another Man's failing', they wrote home; and Pilgrim welcomed their mood. He in his turn was to cause trouble and complaints because he treated the Indians so harshly that they would not hunt for the post and so his men suffered from lack of fresh meat. But before he was sent to Moose in 1749, there also to 'discourage immoderate Drinking and Private Trade', he had built up quite a damning case against Isham for conniving at the 'Suttling and Trafficking Fellows' who pestered the management; and even when he had left Churchill he wrote in a report on it as a place 'where there has been so Epidemical a Corruption and Deeply Rooted by examples of those who ought to have known better'.

Pilgrim had the bitter censoriousness of the secret drinker. He condemned Churchill and Albany alike, and his predecessor at both places. At Albany he was even so disgusted at the 'Horrid Impious Actions (which would make a Wright Reverand Tremble)' that he asked to be excused the impiety of reading Divine Service to such rascals. But when he in his turn had succumbed to the climate and to his vices the very fair-minded Thomas White, who succeeded him, replied in answer to a direct enquiry that 'Mr. Pilgrim being dead having very little to say of his general good Character We beg to be excused entring into his bad one'. Pilgrim's condemnation of Isham and of Churchill need not necessarily be taken too seriously. But on the other hand there is no reason to believe that the Committee's long struggle against drunkenness, insubordination and private trade, had changed the general texture of life by the Bay. Occasional seizures of spirits, reiterations of the rules for sealing up all spirits on board the ships, and from time to time exemplary punishments, all make it clear that conditions by the Bay, the type of man and the type of officer who could be recruited and the background of life in England from which they stepped, between them made the persistence of the old conditions inevitable. Indeed, the very Captain Coats on whose behalf the Committee had fought the traders was himself soon dismissed for trading very considerable quantities of brandy.

Brandy was, and was to remain, one of the Company's great problems. While rum from the West Indies had become one of the staples for the expanding fur trade of the New England settlers, the Hudson's Bay men had not relied to any great extent upon liquor. This was partly due to the fact that they were trading to Indians whose first contacts had normally been with the French, and who had therefore become accustomed to brandy. The English competition progressed by offering better value in heavy goods, especially in cloth and iron-ware, which suited the pattern of the English trade with its bulk shipment to the posts by the Bay. Competition by offering brandy which would have to be got from France, which could become difficult or impossible to obtain in war-time, and which was admirably adapted for the French system of carrying the goods inland to trade, was not to be encouraged. Nevertheless shipments of brandy to the English posts became regular—a hundred and eighty-eight gallons to Hayes Island, a hundred and twenty-five to Albany and a hundred and twenty-six to 'Port Nelson', as early as 1682 for example.

French brandy, however, was difficult to get, and attempts were made to substitute 'English brandy', especially for sale to the servants. This 'English brandy' appears to have been a raw sort of gin, and was not popular. Governor Fullartine, for example, preferred to be allowed whisky, 'usquebaugh', in 1702. Yet the trade brandy must have remained the English 'Gin-type' of drink or something close akin to it, for it was bought at a steady price of about four shillings a gallon from 1689 through to 1710 (and perhaps later) whereas the brandy sent to the Governors and ships' captains cost fourteen shillings a gallon. Later, in 1735, the prices agreed with the Company's dealers were two shillings and threepence a gallon for rum ('molasses spirit'), seven shillings and sixpence a gallon for French brandy, and two shillings a gallon for 'Clove water'. On the simple evidence of price, therefore, it must have been a raw spirit which the Company used for its trade, either to Indians or to its own servants. Though the Company used large quantities of such cheap spirits, a thousand gallons of 'fine spirits' at three shillings and ninepence a gallon in 1708, for example, and used a tincture, and later molasses, to colour the 'English brandy' and make it look like the French, yet the Committee hoped that such large supplies would be traded only 'with that Moderation as may preserve Sobriety which may prevent any Ill Consequences'. They even went so far as to warn their Governor to 'Trade as Little Brandy as possible to the Indians, wee being Informed it has Destroyed severall of them'.

This was expecting too much, especially in the face of French competition. Isham was convinced that it would mean the end of the trade in small furs (which the French tempted the Indians to leave inland before bringing their beaver to the Bay) if brandy were aban-

s

doned, although he recorded that 'I think, as others has, itts a pitty they was allow'd to taste of that Bewitching spirit calld Brandy, or any other Spiritious Liquor's—which has been the Ruing of a Great many Indians, and the Chief Cause of their Ludness and bad way's they are now given to'.

The trading of spirits to the Indians was but one part of the Company's troubles. Close akin to it was the problem of allowing spirits to the Company's servants and, as a corollary, of taking the risk that they would either ruin their own health and morals or would trade the liquor to the Indians in rivalry with the Company. Both of these things happened, and caused prolonged correspondence and disagreement. Nor were the 'hands' alone suspect on these counts. The officers, and even the Governors, were at times called to account, and ships' captains were always under suspicion.

Allowances to officers were always generous, and had been so ever since Governor Nixon had complained of his inability to maintain a suitable table. Governor Fullartine was allowed forty gallons of spirits for his outward voyage to the Bay in 1708; Thomas Macklish was then allowed to take fifty gallons in addition to his allowance. But private shipments of spirits were not always so openly acknowledged or permitted. So many were the illicit consignments, so necessary was the connivance either of the captain or of someone on ship-board, that the Committee took to sending a list of the permitted shipments and of sealing the licensed liquors with red tape. All else was contraband and was to be confiscated. The hunt for private trade continued through the period, with both officers and men under suspicion and with the ships' captains never clear of charges of connivance. Some hundreds of gallons of spirits were illicitly shipped each year, and the Committee could not escape the conclusion that 'if there was to be no receivers there would Sertainly be no thift'. Even Macklish was called on to explain how he had come by the furs which he shipped home, and the Committee never got rid of a suspicion that some of the furs shipped by servants were traded for the Company's own spirits, for the system of making presents to the Indians rendered close accountancy impossible, and the custom of watering the brandy gave an equal latitude to the trader.

The Committee's care probably curbed the shipments of spirits, and probably cut down the volume of private trade, but one of the last episodes of this period was the dismissal of Captain William Coats for illicit shipment of brandy and other goods. He traded over two hundred gallons in one year at Albany, and had run a similar trade at Moose, York, and even at the new little post of Richmond.

It was therefore to be expected that at times both traders and men would be suspect of drunkenness, and that discipline, trade, and defensive precautions would all suffer alike. But the sots were without doubt a minority, otherwise nothing could have been accomplished, and reports on the men vary considerably. At one end stands Isham's description of York Fort in 1738—'No Gang of men Can behave soberer, than has been here'. At the other end stands Thomas Carr, who was sent home first from Churchill and then from Moose, but who contrived to be re-employed and sent to Moose again; a vile man, said Chief Factor Richard Staunton in 1738 'and his Brother John Smith as he calls him, and I wish they do not both goe up Holbourn Hill in a Cart'.

This aspect of the Company's problems was brought right to the forefront in the years 1736–40, for on Christmas Day, 1735, the new post at Moose, from which the Committee hoped so much, was destroyed by fire in the space of two hours. The fire originated in the cook-house, and the Committee learned for the first time—and deplored—that there were two cook-houses at Moose. But it soon became apparent that the fire worked such complete destruction because at least some of the men were 'in liquor'. Richard Staunton, sent out to take command of the new post on which the Committee immediately decided (in which the powder-room was to be kept distant from the cook-house, and in which there was to be only one cook-house), confirmed this view. Everyone at the post, according to him, must have been 'Stupified or else some one man would a Endeavour'd before the flames broak out, to a found from whence that Smoak Should proceed for so many hours together'. 'Drunkness and Debochery' were the causes of all the misfortunes. Bevan as post-master, he said, had been made a tool of by the men, even the apprentices had been 'deboched', and vice and ignorance predominated 'to a monsterous degree of wickedness both amongst the English and Indians'. The Indians brought their women into the post and thereby gained influence over the English, and themselves learned 'much villainy'. It was a bitter indictment of a situation which shamed Staunton and undermined the health of Governor Macklish.

The Committee in London regretfully admitted that the tragedy was due to the 'Wickednesse, Extravagance, and Carelessness of our People there', and when the fire was followed by the loss of five men in a boating tragedy the instructions to the other posts bore the mark of the lesson. The Chiefs were to keep their men from excess in drinking and were to punish it severely. The report that Thomas Bird had disgraced his command at Albany, and had died of the consequences, produced a decision in 1740 to send all the trade-goods indented for by that post except two hundred gallons of brandy; the system of sealing up the shipments of spirits was reinforced, and the ships' captains were firmly ordered to ensure that none of their crew carried out any spirits for the men by the Bay.

Preparations for defence of the existing posts and for a more careful and thorough development of the trade certainly dominated the Committee's thoughts during the War of the Austrian Succession. But there are signs, too, that members were open to new ideas and alive to the need for expansion of their influence and for active rivalry with the French. Here development of trade on the Eastmain, and so inland to Labrador, seemed to be the most promising opening. In 1740 the Committee began to pursue a line of thought which had been started by the establishment of the permanent post at Slude River, and had written to ask for information about a 'Large Lake a hundred Leagues in Compass Joined to two other Lakes of vast Circumference the Northern Parts whereof are frequented by the Esquemaies and the Southern Part inhabited by some of your trading Indians'. The great lake was reputed to be near latitude 60°. This was in answer to a proposal from Joseph Isbister at Albany, and he was told he might send a sloop on a voyage of discovery to find an entrance from the coast provided she kept clear of the ice on the Eastmain coast and kept to the west of Mansfield Island and all other islands until she made Cape Henrietta Maria. It was important not to hazard one of the sloops on which so much depended.

The ships' captains were questioned, and reported that they knew of no such opening, and in 1741 Isbister was urged first to check his Indian reports and to send north in the fall to explore the coast if possible. Again in 1742 he was urged to explore northwards from Slude River, but the Council at Albany insisted that Isbister, with his personal knowledge of the Eastmain, should accompany the expedition and that the sloops were in too bad a condition. So in 1743, with the new *Eastmain* sloop available, the Committee again returned to the project, and in 1744 two sloops, the *Eastmain* from Albany and the *Phoenix* from Moose, at last undertook the voyage. They were ordered to go as far north as 60°, but they were back at Moose by mid-August having only gone as far as 57°.

Though the sloop-masters then reported that they had discovered the lakes and rivers mentioned by Isbister, yet the voyage was really of little value, for both the Committee and the Chiefs concluded that they had not gone far enough and that they 'pretty well know the Coasts as far as they have been already'. The traders were by this time convinced that such a project needed more support than they could give with the resources at their disposal. Like provision-hunting or gardening, such a voyage needed to be fitted in at the busiest time of the year, and by open water the sloops were needed at Moose and Albany to buoy the channels and to load and unload the ship from England; they ought not, therefore, to go on a voyage until after the ship had sailed for home. Moreover the sloop hands, and even their masters, were often 'unhandy men', and the emphasis on Joseph Isbister, who could not leave his post at Albany, merely underlined one weakness in the proposals. The 'unskillfulness and insufficiency of those persons nominated' made them very doubtful of the success of the expeditions, but sure of the prejudice to their own trades. The Committee, too, realised the dangers and shared the disappointments, and so in 1744 the northern expeditions to the Eastmain and Labrador were postponed 'till peaceable times'.

In these decisions and ventures it was the London Committee which reviewed the evidence and the prospects, and whose verdict controlled the situation. In sum the Committee decided after consideration and experiment that there was neither need nor opportunity for a change of policy which would bring a radical expansion of trade. But in one direction the French threat led a trader by the Bay to undertake local action, subsequently accepted by the Committee, which marked a significant departure from the Company's accepted policy. Henley House was established on the individual initiative of Joseph Isbister, Master of Albany.

It was in 1743 that Isbister reported that the Albany trade had fallen off because a party of three hardy *pedlars* (an early use of this term in the Company's documents) had set up a post at 'Shea a Mattawan, the Great meetting place that all Indians must pass to Come to this factory'. They had 'choused out of their goods' about thirty canoes of Indians who were coming down to trade at Albany.

Isbister had but fourteen men and an apprentice under his command at Albany, with a further seven and an Eskimo boy on the sloop. He had had very great trouble with discipline and could rely on no one but himself; even his second-in-command, George Spence, was lazy and comfort-loving, several of his men were insubordinate and 'addicted to Licker', he classified his mutinous sloop's crew together as 'Stockton rabble', and on one occasion when he decided to thrash one of his hands for drunkenness and sleeping while on watch, followed by insolence and an assault upon himself, he could get none of his tradesmen or labourers to assist by tying the man to the stove-rails to receive his punishment. Troubled by a constant pain in his side, so busy that he was quite unable to attend his own private traps, Isbister had passed an unquiet winter, struggling for order and mastery against the legacy of Captain William Coats and his illicit brandy, 'who is the instrument of all confusion and irregularities and Can in one day overset the best of reformations'. In spring 1743, as the river broke up he had suffered a greater 'Deluge' than any Indian could remember, with water seven feet deep on the plantation and a foot deep inside the house itself; he had lost thereby all the timber which he had prepared for a sadly-needed re-building of the house, and he found that, sick as he was, he himself could work twice as fast at house-building with an axe as the English-trained house-carpenter, the 'mearest blockhead I ever saw', whose best occupation was making a set of stairs. Isbister came through the winter, determined but exhausted, to face a summer trade in which the French opposition had taken on a new colour. The defects of some of his trade-goods, and the flaws in the official Standard of Trade were emphasised by the defects of his system of communications.

There were two serious factors in the situation as Isbister faced it. One was that the upland Indians who brought down to Albany a share of the furs of the lakes and forests of the interior all came from the westward (as he understood the course of the river), which made them easy to intercept at the junction where the western branch of Albany River flowed into the main stream. Therefore the Indian report that the French had completed their trade and hurried off to Canada so that they might return betimes in the fall and build a more permanent house at the strategic river-junction seemed to imply a permanent threat to Albany's trade with the uplanders. Secondly, it had never been known before for even the 'Home Indians' of Albany to trade with the French; the opposition was on the doorstep and the Indians came to Albany with only some few indifferent martens to trade for a drunken bout. They were already supplied and clothed, and Isbister could report that the French cloth was undoubtedly of worse quality than the English, but that it was better laced to make it attractive to the Indians.

Isbister realised that he had not strength to capture the French on their return and send them to England, as he might have done since the two countries were then at war. So, after consulting his unhelpful second-in-command, he decided that the only thing to do was to go inland and build 'a little factory-house' such as he had already built at Eastmain. He reached this important decision on 7th May, 1743, and in so doing he realised that although for the moment it was a decision which affected Albany alone, the fundamentals were common to all the Bay-side posts and the decision, with its change of policy, should apply to 'all the rivers where our factories are settled on'.

The problem was an old one. Albany was particularly vulnerable to French interception, and the alternative methods of combating it had long been under discussion. As long ago as 1702 Governor Fullartine (whose success in repulsing a French attack Isbister celebrated with a pail of punch to his men) had been told that the Committee did not think it convenient to embark upon a new settlement during the war, and he had been told to counter the French and to bring down the Ottawas and other upland Indians by spreading reports of the great supplies of goods which he had available for trade. This, with emphasis on fair treatment for the Indians, remained the Company's policy, reiterated from London and accepted by the Chiefs and their Councils. It was no light matter for Isbister to strike out afresh and, without permission from London or even discussion of his project, to embark upon a new policy.

He himself led his party inland, having previously sent his apprentice, the incorrigible 'boy John Dingley' up to the deserted French encampment to confirm the Indian reports. 'That miscreated boy' had almost set the post on fire and had committed most possible crimes, including the theft of a considerable consignment of trade-goods; he even committed such 'Detesteableness of Crime' as made Isbister's 'haire Stand on eand to read', but yet he was capable of setting off in company with four Indians and of bringing back a very sensible and helpful report.

Isbister set off on 4th June, taking with him eight of his fourteen hands. The English were in six canoes, and they were accompanied by ten canoes of Indians. They took with them a vast quantity of lumber so that a house could be built with speed, and they found the journey a novel and exhausting experience. But Isbister looked to the future and hoped that 'time and Experience may render it more Easey to us and that the present fatigues will redound to the Company's intrest and our Credit'. The experience further convinced him that the Company must venture inland, for he noted ruefully that 'I do not wonder now why the Natives do not Come Downe to the Sea Side in greater Numbers'.

Choosing a site on the north side of the river about five miles above the French encampment, Isbister reviewed the situation and, estimating that he was about a hundred and twenty miles from Albany, decided that this would be too far for the Company's servants,

'Comonly old before they Come into this Countrey and . . . intirely Unhandy in Cannoes and unfitt for this way of life'. At this point, however, one of his Indian captains told him 'that we ought to be more industrous and go up the Country as the French do'. The Indians promised to hunt for the English and, thus encouraged, Isbister decided to persist in 'this Uncomon atempt I mean for us English factors but not for the French'.

He saw the foundations of the house laid and then returned (in three days' travel) to Albany. By mid-July the boy Dingley came down to report that the house was built and the roof was going on, and William Isbister from Moose was appointed master and sent up with seven canoes in which were two small carriage-guns and a small selection of goods for winter trade. For even Joseph Isbister had not fully accepted the concept of an inland trading post. He proposed an establishment of only six men, and the function of the post was both to prevent the Indians from getting enticed during the winter and from being intercepted in the summer. The object was to persuade and encourage the Indians to take their trade down to Albany, not to conduct a trade at Henley. The strategic siting of the post was therefore important. The French had posted themselves at 'the very part that all Cannoes must pass that Come Down to Albany Fort'; no Indian could avoid them, 'the situation of those 2 Arms of our River [the Albany] being such that a small party of Men are enabled to block up this part of our River'. Isbister had therefore gone past the site of the French post and built his house a little further up-stream, on the north bank of the Albany, where it had a good prospect of both branches of the river.

Faced with the choice of accepting this innovation or of withdrawing the six men left at Henley, and so of acknowledging complete defeat on this front, the London Committee not only approved the local initiative but increased the establishment. It was, however, emphasised that the object was defence rather than trade; the post was to prevent the French from hindering the Indians as they came down to trade at Albany, and its function and position were underlined in the instructions (interesting in the light of future events) that in case the post should be in danger of capture by the French it must be destroyed, the cannon must be spiked and the house blown up.

The 'showing of the Flag' which Isbister had accomplished at Henley produced results in an improvement of Albany's returns in 1744. The building was then finished and William Isbister, left in charge, was instructed to make the post as defensible as possible, but the consequences of such an innovation proved to be complicated and doubtful. Within a year George Howie was complaining from Moose that Henley was intercepting trade which would otherwise have come down, quietly and inexpensively, to his post, and the London Committee agreed that, despite the improvement at Albany, the new post had 'hurt the Company's trade'. Albany, as might be expected, was strongly in favour of the new post when the Committee reviewed the situation in 1746, but the Committee noted from the Albany Journal that the French were reported to have built afresh a little up-stream of Henley and to have secured a good trade. They therefore wrote that Henley 'has hitherto been of very little use to us, if it has or is likely to be of any advantage desire You will fully explain the same to us, How and in what Manner, We are or may be Benefited by it'.

The reassessment seemed all the more necessary because in high summer of 1745, the time when a French threat was most to be feared, William Isbister had forsaken his post and indulged himself in a visit to Albany. He was refused the gratuity which he asked for, was reprimanded and sent back to his duty. Even Joseph Isbister was forced to admit that Henley was incompatible with exploration on the Eastmain, but in reply to the Committee's query he argued that without Henley the whole trade of Albany would have been intercepted, and urged that the report of the new French post was only Indian rumour, to be taken in conjunction with the Indian request that Henley should be supplied so as to carry on both a winter and a summer trade. The Committee, however, decided in 1747 that it was 'now pretty plain that Henley House has been of little or no Service to the Company'.

Even with so reasonable an analysis of the situation to support condemnation and withdrawal, the Committee nevertheless persisted in keeping the post going. But they refused to allow trade there all the year round since they thought that the killing of summer beaver would thereby be encouraged. Henley House therefore persisted, an inland post hedged round with limitations and subject to many misgivings, an attempt to winter with the Indians without diverting trade from the Bay. Reluctant as the Committee might be, they had accepted a departure from their policy of complete dependence on sloops and on posts by the shores of the Bay.

But with the significant exception of Henley House the London Committee, despite the serious consideration of projects for expansion to the south, to the north, and to the north-west, had by 1744 reverted to its policy of keeping its posts only by the shores of the

Bay. This was a policy soon to be attacked as a 'sleep by the frozen sea'. But it was actually a policy which involved the Company in constant watchfulness, for the defects of the English servants, the threats of the French and the weaknesses of the Indians, were all alike fully realised and accepted as the bases of policy and as the determinants of the kind of posts to be built and maintained. The care with which the Committee analysed the documents sent home by their servants in the Bay shewed that the apparent apathy was based upon knowledge and the acceptance of facts. Given certain limitations of personnel and of facilities, the Committee chose a policy which took those limitations into account, and emphasised the construction of strong posts by the Bay and rigorous care for defence.

The war years were a period in which the Company had to face bitter and persistent challenges in the English press and in Parliament. For the Committee the dominating fact was always that they must be prepared to defend their trade in conditions of open war. They had seen the Company's claims ignored at Ryswick, had seen them accepted at Utrecht. But neither the Ryswick surrender nor the Utrecht triumph had made any difference in the Bay, nor had the non-fulfilment of the terms of the treaties affected the relations between England and France. The Company was on its own. Despite the attention paid to colonial trade by the ministries of eighteenth-century England and the high importance which had been attached to the trade of Hudson Bay at the Treaty of Utrecht, the French threats to that trade were not among the causes of the wars of the middle years of the eighteenth century. These were European wars projected on to a colonial field in North America, the West Indies or the East Indies; and Hudson Bay was clearly a most subordinate problem in the minds of the statesmen. Yet the War of the Austrian Succession from 1739 to 1748 and the Seven Years' War from 1756 to 1763 left the Company's posts in Hudson Bay open to legitimate attack and so almost as much concerned with problems of defence as with an increase in trade, especially if the latter could only be achieved by establishing highly vulnerable posts in the interior to the southward. But while the Company was thus forced on the defensive, the French were a constant menace, 'industriously intercepting' the traffic of the upland Indians to the Bay; and part of the appeal to public and parliamentary opinion against the Company depended on the need for 'making Settlements, higher up the Rivers in better Climates, and by that Means securing that Country and Trade from the *French*'.

BOOKS FOR REFERENCE

HUDSON'S BAY RECORD SOCIETY—Vol. XII.

KNIGHT, Captain James—*The Founding of Churchill* ... edited by J. F. Kenney (London, 1932).

MORTON, Arthur S.—*A History of the Canadian West to 1870–71* (London, 1939).

Report from the Committee, Appointed to enquire into the State and Condition of the Countries adjoining to Hudson's Bay, and of the Trade carried on there (London, 1749).

ROBSON, Joseph—*An Account of Six Years Residence in Hudson's-Bay. From 1733 to 1736, and 1744 to 1747* (London, 1752).

CHAPTER XL

ARTHUR DOBBS AND THE NORTH-WEST PASSAGE

In themselves the Committee's policy in London and their policy by the Bay were sound and reasonable. Their first care was to secure the posts, their second to organise and regulate the trade to fit the demands of the London market and the opportunities of European sales, their third to train and manage their servants, and their fourth to expand inland when these other considerations made it necessary and possible. These were, of course, all constant problems, and they were not dealt with in any sort of order but, for the most part, as inter-related issues. The Committee's management of such a complex and threatening situation had to be conducted on the assumption that no help could be expected from government unless such help was thought justifiable for major reasons of state, and in the certainty that the trade would be subject to interruption whenever diplomacy led to a crisis in the relations of England and France.

It says much for the Committee that they so managed affairs as to satisfy the London fur-market and so as to produce a steady run of dividends, year by year. But something more was needed in response to the spectacular advance of the French into the interior, an advance which seemed to promise that they would take possession of the vast areas of North America while we remained within sight of tidal water, tied to the coast. The very success of the Committee in trade at such a time naturally evoked complaint of lack of enterprise and, in the end, a challenge to the Charter.

Here the lead was taken by the pertinacious Ulsterman, Arthur Dobbs. Comfortably well-off, he was High Sheriff of the County of Antrim from 1720 onwards and a member of the Irish House of Commons from 1721 to 1730. His interest in trade, especially trade on an imperial basis, led to an 'Essay on the Trade and Imports of Ireland' which served as some sort of introduction to Sir Robert Walpole, then Prime Minister. Dobbs was also deeply interested in the scientific aspects of northern exploration, as Robert Boyle had formerly been, and in the history of attempts to discover a North-west passage to the Pacific. He was sufficiently well esteemed to be appointed Engineer-in-chief and Surveyor-general in Ireland, and his zeal and knowledge were such that he was able to get together an 'abstract' of all the journals of the explorers of Hudson

Bay, from which he concluded that a practicable North-west passage existed and should be found and utilised. His interest at this stage was predominantly academic, but he presented his abstract to Colonel Bladen, one of the Commissioners for Trade and Plantations, with the intention that the South Sea Company should prosecute a search for the passage.

The Commissioners did nothing, and Dobbs' project seemed to have fallen through when in 1733 he visited London and submitted it to Sir Charles Wager, First Lord of the Admiralty. Wager introduced him to Samuel Jones, Deputy Governor of the Hudson's Bay Company, but Jones was too deeply imbued with the traditional policy of the Company—and perhaps too much dominated by Governor Sir Bibye Lake—to give much support to Dobbs. He gave an account of the ill success of Knight's expedition to find the 'Straits of Annian' with the *Albany* and the *Discovery*, and gave the Company's conclusion that exploration by sea north from Churchill would prove profitless. Had a passage been possible, Samuel Jones thought that the Company would have discovered it.

The extent of the privileges and powers conferred by the Company's Charter was not generally known in 1733. Indeed, the Committee had always been jealous of divulging the actual terms of the Charter and had even gone so far as to order that any member of the Committee who possessed a copy must keep it secret. Dobbs, however, had his curiosity whetted by what he had learned in his talks with the Deputy Governor; and it must also be remembered that de la Vérendrye was just at this time pushing out towards Lake Winnipeg, and that French circles were full of talk of the approach to that 'Sea of the West' which filled Dobbs' mind. There were those in the French camp who were convinced that the chief reason why Hudson Bay had been demanded at Utrecht was because the English wanted it as an approach to the passage—'c'est apparement pour la cherche à loisir et pour empescher les autres nations de la chercher qu'ils ont obligé la france de leur ceder le Detroit et la Baie d'Hudson sous la paix d'Utrecht'. Dobbs concluded that the Hudson's Bay men were, by treaty and charter, in control of the avenue to the passage upon which his mind turned. He was not such a man as to allow them to remain in unquestioned control, especially in view of what he considered their firmly inactive policy. In 1735 he managed to get permission to peruse the copy of the Charter which the Plantation Office held, and he convinced himself that the Company's privileges had been granted in such terms that the Company alone would derive benefit from any discoveries which might be made.

With this conviction that the Company alone stood to profit from the discovery of a passage, Dobbs secured an introduction to Governor Sir Bibye Lake, and despite the Governor's reluctance to repeat the failure of Knight's expedition (which he said had cost the Company between £7,000 and £8,000), Dobbs persuaded him that it would be enough in the first instance to instruct the sloops which were available at Churchill to make a summer voyage north to Roe's Welcome. There an observation of the tides would give all the data necessary for a conclusion as to whether a passage existed or not.

Such a plan in fact involved no great departure from projects which the Committee already had in hand. True, their Governor at Churchill had been pre-occupied with building since the Committee had decided to build a fort at Eskimo Point in 1731, and Richard Norton as Chief had been loaded with administrative and planning duties which were foreign to his nature and to some extent beyond his capacity. The complement of men had been increased to twenty-four, a draft plan had been sent out from London, and the management of Churchill had been made independent of York. But, though Norton's talents lay in an ability to win the confidence of Indians, even he found it difficult to reconcile the quarrels of the southern and northern Indians who came to trade at Churchill, and still more difficult to increase and stabilise the trade with the northern Indians, who came from so far 'that it is 2 or 3 years between there Coming to the Factory'. Between trade with the Indians and building against the French, Norton and his men were more than fully occupied, even when the complement was raised to sixty-four in 1733. So 'exploration to the Northward' had degenerated into the collection of information from the northern Indians combined with occasional slooping voyages in pursuit of summer trade, such as Henry Kelsey had originated. But even within these limitations it appeared that Dobbs might be satisfied.

It was the slooping voyages to which he turned, and which the Committee also had in mind. In 1732 a new sloop, the *Moose River*, was sent out to the post of that name, with orders that the old *Moose River* sloop was to be re-named the *Churchill* and sent to Fort Prince of Wales. Churchill was at this time getting a very fair share of the use of the available sloops, for the *Albany* sloop was sent thither loaded with timber and other building material from Albany while the *Marten* sloop and the *Musquash* were also stationed there. It was therefore no novelty when, in March 1735, clearly under the influence of Arthur Dobbs' ideas, and perhaps in direct response to his appeal to Governor Sir Bibye Lake, the Hudson's Bay Company set up a Sub-Committee to deal with instructions and proposals for a discovery expedition. After which the 1735 General Instructions to Churchill, sent by the annual ships in May of that year, contained orders that Churchill should send a sloop north the following year, in 1736. This, however, was to be something at once greater and smaller than Dobbs had proposed. Whereas he aimed at the magnificent prize of a passage, but asked only that observations of the tides might be made, the Company projected a new settlement, but it sought trade rather than discovery. In the orders it was arranged that the ship from England in 1736 should accompany the sloop northwards and that eight or ten families of Indians should be taken to help found a post and to persuade the Northern Indians to hunt for whale-fins, ivory, oil, and furs.

In 1736 the Committee, having already warned Churchill of their intention, again considered the matter from a historical point of view. The journals and accounts of previous attempts were reviewed at a Committee-meeting in March 1736, and in the Instructions of that year the *Churchill* sloop was again ordered north on a discovery (to sail in 1737). The previous orders for a voyage in 1736 by ship and sloop to found a post were cancelled, and the orders now were that in 1737 the *Churchill* sloop with twelve men, and the *Musquash* with six men and three or four 'Home Indians' should sail (without the ship) direct to Roe's Welcome. There they would find a bay or harbour in which they might lie secure and conduct their trade. They were to treat the Indians well, encourage them to hunt, especially whales and seals, and to promise that the sloops would come back to trade again in the following year. The sloops were also to make observations (though the trees and soil and the likelihood of minerals and of furs received more attention than the tides!), and the ship to England was to wait at Churchill until as late as 10th September in the hope that it might bring home the journals of the expedition.

It was as well that in 1736 the Committee revised and re-affirmed its orders for 1737, for no sloop went north in 1736 since the *Hudson's Bay*, outward bound to York Factory, was lost in the ice on 3rd July. There was barely time to save the crew, and all the cargo was lost. Captain Spurrell, in the *Mary* consigned to Churchill, brought home the returns from York, and although the rumours of shortage at York caused some migration of trade from that post, Macklish was in fact able to supply his trade through the winter with no shortage save in Brazil tobacco. But this was accomplished by borrowing from Churchill as well as by using up the reserves stored at York; the *Churchill* sloop could not be sent north in 1736 because she had to be ferrying goods between the two posts, and Norton reported that by the time she was available it was too late to do anything before the spring of 1737. He would then send the sloops up the west coast from Churchill to Roe's Welcome, as ordered, after which they would proceed to Pistol Bay to meet the ship from England.

The *Churchill* and the *Musquash* therefore sailed from Fort Prince of Wales on 4th July, 1737. Their departure anticipated the arrival of the ship from England, and Captain Coats in the *Mary*, bound for Churchill, carried a variant of the Instructions for the expedition, ordering the sloops to trade at the bay near Roe's Welcome (Pistol Bay) until the ship joined them there, and then to sail north as far as possible. The *Mary* was to sail direct to Whalebone Cove in Pistol Bay, latitude 62° 14' or thereabouts, as soon as she had passed Hudson Strait. So the Committee intended to press forward with a voyage of discovery, not merely to trade within known limits; and the careful writing of ships' logs, with exact observation of the strength and direction of tides, was insisted upon. These were signs that the Committee were alive to the possibility of the thesis which Arthur Dobbs had propounded. The North-west passage was in their minds.

Other possibilities also were, perhaps more realistically, envisaged. Two sets of instruments for boring into the earth and drawing up a soil-sample were sent out from London, and the expedition was instructed to use them whenever a landfall was made 'to see what the Earth was and whether there was any likelyhood of a Mine'. The borers may have been taken north in 1737, but they were not used. This, however, was a comparatively slight disappointment, for the 1737 expedition proved a complete failure. Captain Napper of the *Churchill* died at Whale Cove on 7th August; his mate brought the *Churchill* safe back to the fort, but she parted company from the *Musquash* on the way, and the two little vessels must each have made an anxious journey. The trade, too, was negligible and the prospects forbidding. They had found the coast perilous, with no navigable rivers, no woods, and the trade 'trifling and Inconsiderable'. Between them they brought only about a hundredweight of whalebone, three barrels of blubber and about twenty pounds of 'ivory'.

The Council at Churchill could see no encouragement in this to risk a further expedition in 1738, but since the sloops' captains had followed their instructions, and had promised that the ships would come again to trade in 1738, the Churchill Council was ordered to send one sloop to Pistol Bay in 1738, to drive what trade it could and to try to persuade the 'Indians' to come south to trade at the fort. Bringing Eskimos down to the fort was, however, soon accepted as a dangerous practice, liable to drive away the trade of the Indians with whom the Eskimos were constantly at feud; the English, too, neither understood nor trusted the Eskimos in their early contacts with them. So in 1739 the policy of drawing the Eskimos to trade at Churchill was abandoned. Each year a sloop was to be fitted out, ready to trade to Pistol Bay, in June and July, but that was all that was to be attempted.

Such orders merely represent an effort to consolidate and enlarge the trading prospects which the expeditions had disclosed. As far as discovery and a North-west passage were concerned, the Company was completely disillusioned and confirmed in its opinions. The sloops had not found 'any the least Appearance of a Passage', as Governor Sir Bibye told Arthur Dobbs. He added that he had already been blamed for running the Company into so much expense, and excused himself from further demands. Dobbs, however, was not prepared to accept such a conclusion, and it is from the failure of the 1737 voyage in the *Churchill* and *Musquash* that his quarrel with the Company dates. He easily convinced himself that the Company had been trifling with him and had merely sent out a routine trading expedition, with no trained observers and with no serious intention of searching for the passage. In this view he was supported by Captain Christopher Middleton, though Middleton could see the Company's point of view, appreciated the difficulty of the task, and lacked the rancour which was developing in Dobbs.

Middleton had advanced greatly in the Company's esteem since he had been rejected as mate of the *Whalebone* by Captain Scroggs and left behind at York in 1722 while the 'Discovery to the Norward' of that year fizzled out. He had been appointed to command the *Hannah* in 1725 and had continued thereafter year by year to command one of the Company's ships to the Bay. He therefore had behind him a wealth of experience in arctic navigation, and his original enthusiasm for scientific survey had never faltered. In 1722 he had closely questioned the members of Scroggs' crew on their return from the north, and had later published for the Royal Society a table of variations of the magnetic needle. When the Committee decided to build a post at Moose in 1730 it was Middleton who was entrusted with the plans and the surveying of a site. He was also called upon to help re-design and fortify the post at Albany.

It was at this period, in 1735, that Middleton had become acquainted with Dobbs, for the Royal Society paper on the variation of the magnetic needle convinced the Irishman that Middleton combined scientific knowledge and practical experience to a unique degree. Middleton was consulted by the Committee during their enquiry into the history of expeditions in search of the passage, and he incurred some displeasure by giving too candid a criticism of Scroggs' voyage, declaring himself convinced of the passage, and offering to go and find it. His offer was rejected, but Sir Bibye Lake authorised Middleton to divulge to Dobbs the plans for sending the sloops north from Churchill. Up to 1737, therefore, there seems to have been nothing to conceal, with a general enthusiasm and interest shared by the Company, Middleton (who became a Fellow of the Royal Society early in 1736), and Dobbs.

In 1737 Middleton commanded the new ship *Hudson's Bay* on its voyage to Churchill, where he formed his own first-hand opinion of the two sloops as they came back in August with their disappointing news. It was an opinion which fitted in with, and perhaps inspired, the suspicions which were forming in Dobbs' mind. 'In my Opinion', Middleton wrote to Dobbs on his return to London in November 1737, 'the People on board were not duly qualified for such an Undertaking. They prosecuted their Voyage no farther than the Latit. 62° ¼ North, and returned without making any new or useful Discovery'. He further suggested that he and Dobbs should meet in London, and added the disingenuous request that Dobbs would be 'so good as to conceal any Intelligence I may have an Opportunity to give you from Time to Time of this Affair'.

Middleton was, without any doubt, supplying Dobbs at this time with copies—perhaps even with the originals—of the Company's records of former voyages of discovery to the northward. His own knowledge, and the opportunities which he enjoyed, were great. 'I have perused all the Company's Journals about the Discovery, as well as all others I was able to procure, whether in Print or Manuscript, from the year 1615 down to the present time. My inclination has led me that Way these many Years—I wintered at *Churchill* for this purpose in 1721' he wrote, and added 'Of all this I furnished Mr. D—— with the most exact and particular Account I was able to give him'. His interest, like that of Dobbs, was concentrated on discovery, not on a trade rivalry 'For I had no Notion that any Information which Mr. Dobbs might receive from me, could possibly interfere with the Trade of the Company'. Here lies the most probable explanation for the disappearance of the detailed account of Scroggs' voyage in the *Whalebone* in 1722, and for the discovery of Henry Kelsey's Journal among Dobbs' private papers; they probably went from Middleton to Dobbs and never came back to the Company.

Dobbs, convinced by the perusal of such journals that the Company had never been more than half-hearted in its search for a passage, and officially informed that in any case the Company would now make no further attempt, suggested to Middleton that they should try to get the Admiralty to undertake an exploration. Middleton was interested, but his living depended on the Company. He was reluctant to quit good employment and anxious not to be dismissed. He commanded the *Hudson's Bay* in her voyage to Moose in 1738, to Churchill in 1739, and again to Moose in 1740. He was nevertheless most attracted by the thought of an Admiralty expedition for pure discovery, and he promised Dobbs his help in making enquiries and observations to further the search.

Such activity could not go unnoticed, and Middleton began to arouse the suspicions of the Committee. 'What the Company intend to do hereafter I am entirely a Stranger to as they keep every thing a Secret' he told his enquirer, with the warning that 'from some Questions I have been lately asked, I found they seem suspicious of my corresponding with you. To remove which Jealousy, I returned such Answers as perhaps I should not have done had I been independant of them'.

The Committee were not suspicious of Middleton alone. In the general atmosphere of criticism which Dobbs and de la Vérendrye between them had engendered, the old passion for secrecy burst out afresh. This, it must be remembered, was the period in which Anson's voyage round the world started (in 1740) as some sort of counter to the discoveries of Bering 'toiling slowly and painfully across the vast, dreary wastes of Siberia' towards the same goal of an East-west passage. The Hudson's Bay Company could not remain aloof at such a time; York was ordered to open up trade with the western Indians who lived to the north and east of the 'great Lake called Assiniopolis'; an Eskimo was brought from Moose to London (where he died) so that the Committee could get information about the Eastmain and Hudson Strait. The house at Slude River was re-built and then plans were discussed for removing it so as to be better sited for forwarding trade to the north and east, opening up the interior of Labrador; and a lively interest in Labrador remained although this project was dropped. At Churchill also, though the outbreak of war in 1739 meant that everything was subordinated to the re-building of the fort, Norton was reproved in 1741 for not sending his sloop north for 'making new discoverys and Improving our

Trade'. There was a general feeling, among those interested, that something great in the way of arctic discovery and trade lay just round the corner. The Company was bound to be implicated, to watch potential rivals with jealousy and suspicion, and to try to keep its knowledge and experience for its exclusive use.

Middleton, together with all the Company's employees, therefore began to feel a fresh stringency in the attempts to prevent valuable knowledge from being divulged. The censorship of correspondence between England and employees in the Bay had long been a part of the Company's struggle to prevent private trade. The Governor of Albany, Joseph Adams, had been called on to deny that he had begun to send home memoranda and papers in 1731. He had avowed that he was innocent and would suppress such a practice, and the Letters Outward had capped the incident by a firm veto on any correspondence relating to the Company's affairs except with the Committee. In 1738 a new point was put on the veto, obviously aimed directly at Dobbs and indirectly at Middleton, by orders that no letters, writings or journals might be communicated, and in the following year this was repeated, with special instructions to the ships' captains that they were on no account whatsoever to communicate any of the Company's affairs or to deliver any writing or journal of their voyages to any person whatsoever, except to the Committee.

In view of their thinly-veiled suspicions, the Governor and Committee were probably neither surprised nor disappointed to find that Middleton had left their service in 1741. He did, however, depart rather hurriedly—so hurriedly as to upset the shipping plans for the year. Since war with Spain (the War of Jenkins' Ear) had broken out in 1739 the chance of a command in the Navy for Middleton had been brighter, and though he accepted the fact that the war would involve a postponement of discovery expeditions he thought that successful service would give him an advantage when the project was resumed. Dobbs supported him, and in 1740 Middleton had several interviews with the First Lord of the Admiralty, Sir Charles Wager. Unwilling to relinquish his Hudson's Bay employment until another command was certain, in March 1741 he allowed himself to be nominated once more to command the *Hudson's Bay*. But within a week he resigned, telling the Committee he had accepted a commission in the King's service.

The *Hudson's Bay* had to be taken out of the shipping arrangements for the year, and the *Seahorse* alone sailed to Churchill and then to York, while the *Mary* went to Moose and Albany. This was not the only cause for uneasiness. In April a General Court of the whole Company was called, to be told by the Governor that Middleton was sailing in command of an expedition for discovery to the north-west, 'to find out a Passage to the South Sea, China and the East Indies'.

The stockholders left it with the Committee to hinder any encroachments on the Company's trade, property or privileges, and the Committee certainly did their best to prevent the projected Admiralty expedition from impinging on the Company's preserves. At first they would only agree that Middleton and his men should call on their factories in cases of the utmost extremity, and gave no instructions that they should be allowed to winter at the posts; they even went so far as to ask the Admiralty to forbid Middleton to winter in any of their harbours, except in distress, and that he should be restrained from injuring their trade. Under pressure, they protested that they did not mean to hinder or oppose the expedition, and although still apprehensive of the harm he might do them they ordered their posts to give him such assistance as they could. The Company in this matter was not in direct contact with Middleton, who only received from the Admiralty a copy of the orders which had been sent to the factors on the eve of his setting sail from Galleon's Reach in the Thames. These orders still stopped short at giving assistance if he were 'brought into real Distress and Danger of his Life or Loss of his Ship'.

In command of His Majesty's bomb-vessel the *Furnace*, with the sloop *Discovery* in convoy, Middleton sailed from the Thames early in June 1741. His previous experience, and the normal practice of the Company in this matter, can have left him in no doubt that he would have to winter in the Bay before embarking on his discovery, and as soon as he had negotiated the Strait and arrived at Cary's Swan Nest he held a Council which accepted this foregone conclusion. To reinforce his own experience he had with him William Moor, his former mate in the *Hudson's Bay*, as commander of the *Discovery*, and Edward Thompson who had been surgeon and member of the Council at Moose for three years. Such men, like Middleton, knew that they had little choice, and although their orders were to respect, and even to protect, the Company's ships and posts, and they knew that the Company's orders to posts did not fully cover them, they made for Churchill and arrived there on 8th August.

The Governor of Churchill upon whom Middleton proposed to call for help according to the equivocal orders from the London Committee was James Isham, newly ordered to relinquish his command at York and to supersede Richard Norton at Churchill. He left York with a genuine sense of the urgency of the danger from the French, for he had just been informed of a French post of thirty men, barely four hundred miles inland, and had even received an offer to share the trade from the French post-master—an offer which he ignored. At Churchill he was to find the urgency if anything increased, for trade from the Saskatchewan to that post was interrupted both by Indian wars and by the French, and the buildings were neither so sound nor so far forward as had been reported. Isham had little to spare for anything but the fortifications and the trade of his new post, for which he opened up a quarry on the site of the old factory and got trucks for transport, six more cannon, and indented for men and horses to speed the work.

Middleton and his crews could hardly have expected a warm welcome from a man in such a position, especially when the orders from the Committee had only spoken of help if they should be in danger or real distress. Yet his previous acquaintance with Isham led Middleton to regard him as a friend, and he was not disappointed. He was not, however, met on arrival by Isham himself, for the new Governor did not arrive at his post until two days after Middleton. He had waited at York for the arrival of his successor from England, Thomas White; and from Thomas White he had received a verbatim summary of the Committee's views on the Middleton expedition. White had been in London during the discussions and had been sent out without any written instructions for York, though the Committee had promised them to him. Isham therefore knew that at the last moment some sort of agreement had been arranged between Middleton and the Company. Dobbs later said that the Company had offered a bribe of £5,000 and that though Middleton had refused the money he had agreed not to harm the Company. In return (and this much is certain) the Company issued supplementary orders to tell Churchill to afford the best assistance possible.

So although the temporary Governor at Churchill, Robert Pilgrim, met Middleton most warily, and even fired a shot across his bows, when Isham arrived two days later the explorers were made as comfortable as was possible. They were accommodated in James Knight's old post, about six miles upstream from the new fort, and Isham provided food and winter clothing and recruited Indians to hunt for food. The ships were drawn up out of the water, the explorers and the Company's men settled side by side, and both Middleton and Isham later incurred censure for being too cooperative, for the London Committee had particular reasons for wishing to keep both the Indians and the Englishmen at the Company's posts isolated from such independent expeditions as Middleton led.

Even the Company's own ships' captains and crews provoked comparisons as to terms of service and wages, standards of food and drink and conduct. They often provoked crises of discipline, challenged and defied the Governor and his authority, introduced excessive alcohol to the posts, and facilitated private trade. If the Company's own ships could produce such problems, how much more were Middleton and his independent command to be dreaded! Moreover, Middleton had a doubtful reputation in the matter of strong drink even when he was in the Company's service. In 1738 he had brought out as his ship's carpenter one, John Booth, who had been the only man sent home for evil conduct in 1737, and had allowed him ashore (to corrupt the Company's servants) despite the protests of the Chief at Moose. He had also shown strong sympathy for Bevan and the men who had allowed Moose to burn down, and had refused to sign Richard Staunton's adverse report. It was therefore not surprising that he should fall foul of Isham on this and kindred matters.

Yet Isham certainly did all that was reasonable to make Middleton and his men comfortable for the winter—even to the extent of making some of his own men winter in the woods. Middleton, for his part, made it clear that he would do everything in his power to protect the one thing which seemed vital to Isham, the Company's trade. He forbade the expedition men to have any clandestine dealings with Indians and he confiscated a selection of trade-goods which he discovered on board his ships. Since it was his own suggestion which had caused the trade-goods to be shipped, his action here caused much recrimination. It had been Middleton (so both he and Dobbs agreed) who in the first disappointment at the failure of the *Churchill* and the *Musquash* in 1737 had suggested that the Company's Charter might be challenged, especially since its confirmation by Parliament had not been renewed. If the Charter could be overthrown, he suggested that further discovery might be financed by a group of merchants outside the Company, provided they could have freedom to trade in the Bay. Acting on this hint, Arthur Dobbs put up the money to get a legal opinion and was told by the Attorney General that despite the Charter the Company had no right to an exclusive trade; '*every Merchant in* England *has an equal right to trade there*'. It was therefore as part of a firm policy, in which zeal for discovery had reached a climax in a challenge to the Charter and to the right of exclusive trade, that the trade-goods had been shipped on the *Discovery*.

Middleton's confiscation of the goods and his veto on trade marked an important divergence from the policy agreed with Dobbs, and inevitably provoked bitter comment. Even though Dobbs maintained that he had no share in the goods, he asserted that such an attempt to trade would have been quite legal, and he later accused Middleton of twisting the last-minute Admiralty instructions to protect the Company's trade and shipping so as to cover all his 'Favours and complaisance' to the Company. Middleton, for his part, admitted that the Governor and Committee had recommended the protection of their trade to him, and said he thought it a natural and reasonable request. Further, when they had allowed him to winter at Churchill, he thought it would be a 'mean and base Return for their Hospitality, as well as the highest Ingratitude' to plunder their trade by allowing his expedition to trade with the natives. So, however much future recrimination might be implicit in his veto, he at least gave James Isham full co-operation on the subject of trade and even allowed him to send a watcher on board the ships during trade time. The two men had interests in common, too. They made astral observations together, and while Middleton put together a scientific paper on the 'Effects of Cold', Isham drafted a more random series of 'Observations on Hudson's Bay'.

But while Isham had both work and provisions for his men, Middleton was short of both. His men suffered heavily both from scurvy and from frostbite; by the end of winter he had lost eleven men from scurvy and several others were sadly stricken. One had been drowned, one had died a natural death, and many had lost their toes or had otherwise suffered. They led a 'most miserable slavish life', which broke their spirits despite the efforts of the two commanders, and they emerged such 'poor scorbutick Creatures' that they could scarcely man their ships. Middleton tried to alleviate their hardships by putting the men to work, especially the artificers, carpenters and armourers, whom he lent to the fort; and by a certain amount of marching and drilling. 'Gunpowder Treason' was marked by a fireworks display, but Middleton also brightened this and all other occasions by a distribution of alcohol which was vastly in excess of anything the Company's men could hope for. His normal issue on festival days was thirty gallons of brandy for brewing punch, and at their best such days concluded 'with all possible demonstrations of joy, to the great pleasure and satisfaction of the natives'. On less fortunate occasions Middleton must have helped to undermine his men's health, and he certainly created a problem of discipline for Isham. The Christmas celebrations, for example, lasted from twelve to fourteen days and Middleton decided to give his men 'strong beer and brandy every day all the time'. The English beer was all expended by Christmas Eve, after which the brandy was accompanied by 'spruce beer'. The latter concoction was the local specific against scurvy, and it might normally have been beneficial because of its infusion from freshly-gathered spruce leaves. But in company with so much spirits, and riding on a diet of 'hard tack' (for it was a hard winter and the hunters could get but little fresh meat) it did not save Middleton's men.

The lavish use of alcohol lay at the root of most of Middleton's own troubles, and of his differences with Isham. It prostrated his men, it provoked difficult comparisons with the Company's rules and practices, and it provided Middleton with a means of making good his losses at the Company's expense. Such temptations came upon Isham and his men at a particularly difficult time in the winter of 1741–2, and Isham can easily be forgiven for resenting the uses to which Middleton put his lavish supplies of drink. For owing to drunkenness Isham lost his tailor, normally a sober young man, killed by the cold when lost within a quarter-mile of his tent, and he had to dig a grave for one of his Indians frozen to death 'being a little in Liquor'. During the period of extra rations at Christmas three of Isham's men got so drunk that they had to be arrested in their own interests. They wanted to go and 'sleep by the river'. One of them was put in irons for abusing Isham's second-in-command. He broke out, was caught and was given twelve lashes by Isham. The other two escaped to the woods and were not caught for four days. Then they were given twenty lashes each, as a warning to the rest of the men.

Throughout the winter Isham had to combat the actual effects of the spirits brought to his post by Middleton, the subversive spirit which Middleton's dispensations raised, and the fact that Middleton had no scruple about recruiting his crews from among Isham's men 'with Liquor, fine words and preferment'. He actually got five of them, including two sailors, to sail with him when spring brought open water; they forfeited their wages from the Company and they caused bitter correspondence and recrimination with Isham, whose outspoken remonstrances are a sign of the difficulty in which he found himself placed.

Apart from this problem of drink and recruitment the two commanders seem to have spent the winter helpfully and with mutual respect. Isham lent the post's longboats to the expedition, and the expedition men repaired them; he provided cloth for winter clothing and he recruited Indian hunters to get them fresh meat. He even persuaded two northern Indians to go with the expedition and Middleton in his turn, having made up his complement, forbade his lieutenant to recruit a third Indian who was essential to the post because he acted as an interpreter. On balance it seems clear that, with different objects in view, both men behaved sensibly and with reasonable regard for the other's problems, and Isham was close to the mark when he wrote that Middleton had both been 'very serviceable to your Honours Interest' and a 'very troublesome guess'.

They had some quite serious disputes, even on the eve of the departure of the expedition, and Isham was heartily glad to be rid of the explorers; but with genuine and simple goodwill he added his 'whom God Send Safe' to his note that the *Furnace* and the *Discovery* had set sail on 30th June, 1742.

Even when reinforced by Isham's men and with the two Indians aboard, Middleton's ships were in a sorry state to undertake Arctic exploration. He had 'not three seamen among the whole number of private men', and most of his crews were 'a set of rogues' who (he wrote) for the most part deserved hanging before they ever signed on with him. They had already caused him trouble and had broken and plundered every cask aboard, and now they were so sick and weak, with half of them 'so taken with the Scurvy, that they have been uncapable of doing Duty', that even including his officers he 'had not above five or six Men in a Watch able to go aloft to hand or reef a Sail'. His officers too were so badly qualified that he had told Isham it would be possible for him to make the voyage without a man on board knowing whether there was such a passage as he sought or not. Except for his Lieutenant and the two Masters he had no-one who could even tell in what part of the world he had been— an apparently innocuous remark which was later held against him.

All depended on his own vigilance and ability, and it says much for his competence that he took his crazy craft as far north as 66°. He entered the inlet which had been his objective and, deciding that it was not a sea-passage, christened it *Wager River* after the First Lord of the Admiralty. Disappointed here, he concluded that there was no such passage as he sought. 'Undoubtedly' he reported 'there is no Hope of a Passage to encourage any further Trial between Churchill and so far as we have gone; and if there be any further to the northward, it must be impossible for the Ice, and the Narrowness of any such Outlet, in 67° or 68° of Latitude, it cannot be clear of Ice one

Week in a Year, and many Years, as I apprehend, not clear at all'. When, eventually in 1821, Lieutenant William Parry passed through Frozen Strait to Repulse Bay he proved the truth of Middleton's conviction that there is no strait on the shore of Hudson Bay leading to a passage, and Parry then wrote that 'Above all, the accuracy of Captain Middleton is manifest upon the point most strenuously argued against him'.

Middleton safely brought his ships back to England, to reach the Thames in October 1742. His return brought considerable publicity, and the Hudson's Bay Company, for the first time in its career, found itself in the limelight. His paper to the Royal Society on 'The Extraordinary Degrees and Surprising Effects of COLD in Hudson's Bay' was read very shortly after his return to London and won for him the Society's prize gold medal for the year, while two articles in the form of letters describing the experiences, by a gentleman-observer who had been aboard, John Lanrick, were published in the *Gentleman's Magazine*, and Middleton and the Company found themselves in the centre of a pamphlet-war typical of eighteenth-century London.

For Middleton's conclusion that he had been mistaken, and that *Wager River* was not a passage to the Western Ocean—further, that no such passage existed—did not convince Arthur Dobbs. When he had taken time to digest the report, and to listen to accounts of the way in which Middleton had adjusted his differences with Isham, had forbidden trade to the expedition, and had respected the Company's position and attitude, Dobbs concluded that there could be only one explanation. Middleton must have been bribed by the Company.

So, after a period of amicable correspondence in which he reluctantly agreed that it would be vain to continue the search for a passage, and concluded that the only safe way to the Western Ocean lay by the Nelson or the Churchill River, Dobbs again developed his attack upon the Company. This route to the interior and then westwards could only be pursued by laying open the trade and dissolving the Company as far as that was necessary, and then making settlements higher up upon these rivers. He still thought that Middleton's enthusiasm for the passage would carry him on into a clear challenge to the Company and its Charter, asked his opinion of the climate, and told him of his plans; 'I shall make no doubt of ingaging the Merchants to join us in opening that Trade, and settling those Countries'. Trade and inland settlement were now to be the preliminaries to the passage.

In this Middleton could not follow Dobbs. He had shown himself careful of the Company's trade, and eager though his scientific interest in the passage was, he was not anxious to take part in a merchants' attack upon that trade; in any case he felt convinced that even if the Charter were abolished the trade would soon be absorbed by a few private merchants. Disappointed, and angry that Middleton had already protected the trade, Dobbs accused him of being bought by the Company, and the Admiralty called upon Middleton to answer the charge and kept him ashore as a sign of disapproval. Middleton's *Vindication* in 1743 was the first publication in the ensuing pamphlet-war, to be followed by Dobbs' *Remarks upon Capt. Middleton's Defence*, Middleton's *Reply to the Remarks of Arthur Dobbs*, Dobbs' *Account of the Countries adjoining to Hudson's Bay*, and Coat's *The Geography of Hudson's Bay*.

As controversy rose, the chance conversations and unpremeditated actions of the whole episode were bitterly recalled and analysed. Dobbs convinced himself that Middleton was ready to perjure himself about the passage in order to leave the Company undisturbed in its trade, while Middleton saw Dobbs getting more convinced that the trade must be invaded and asserted that Dobbs must have had 'the Advantage of private Trade at Heart' from the beginning, and had been prevented by himself from 'diving into the Profits of the Hudson's Bay Trade'. At the Court of Enquiry which the Admiralty ultimately held, Dobbs was defeated and Middleton was vindicated—but he was not given another command until 1745.

Dobbs derived his enthusiasm in part from his own inner conviction and from his rising hostility to the Company, in part from the narrative of Joseph la France, a renegade *coureur de bois* who had given him an account of the strategic importance of the Lake Winnipeg area as a place of assembly from which the upland Indians began their annual journey down to the Bay—unless they were intercepted at the French posts. La France had himself made the journey from Lake Winnipeg to York Fort, and he knew the route which he described and spoke with authority and persuasion. He advocated that the English Standard of Trade must be lowered so as to entice the Indians from the French, and that the English must build posts in the interior.

But the essence of the Company's policy was that there were serious arguments against building posts in the interior. It was not simply a question of changing a defensive policy for an active one; there were factors involved which could not be changed so easily, if at all. In this view, opposed to Dobbs and la France, the investigation into the Middleton voyage confirmed the Committee; they stood firmly by their traditional argument that it was an utterly different proposition to bring a canoe-load of furs downstream to the Bay from that of working upstream with a load of trade-goods. It was therefore beside the point to argue that because Indians could bring furs down to the Bay the Company could establish inland posts. Quite apart from the responsibility of supplying and defending such posts, the Company had not the *voyageurs* to get the goods inland.

Much discussion and experiment was to be needed before an inland transport system which could be worked by the ordinary English hands was arrived at, but for the initial discussions on inland settlements it was assumed as a prime necessity that the birch-bark canoe, the vehicle evolved by the Indians and adapted by the French, was essential. The English, as yet unable even to hunt for themselves, could certainly not travel by canoe—at least not in sufficient numbers. Middleton had finally condemned any attempt to settle inland because he knew that out of over a hundred men employed by the Company not five could venture in a canoe, 'they are so apt to overturn and drown them'.

Both Isham and Middleton (and probably most of those who knew anything of the Bay at first hand) were convinced that sloops provided an admirable means of transporting goods along the coasts of the Bay, but that nothing much could be accomplished towards inland settlement until the French had been driven from the interior. Trade would follow the flag, and until British rule had preceded them the Committee were not prepared to add the burden of an extended defence of communications to the cost of transport.

It was not merely apathy but deep conviction, and acceptance of limitations of equipment which arose from habits of trade, which dictated the Company's policy. The establishment of inland posts was a problem upon which both Isham and Middleton confirmed the Company in its accepted policy, and upon which Dobbs and la France developed a further attack based on charges of apathy and neglect. It was, however, a problem which lay at a tangent to the original purpose of the Dobbs-Middleton-Admiralty expedition, which had been exploration to the northward from Churchill and the search for a North-west passage. To this original purpose the Committee tried to fasten attention; they were eager to discover in what ways Middleton's expedition would react upon the general interest in a North-west passage, and in what ways it should cause a reassessment of the Company's policy for northern exploration in general and for a search for the passage in particular. For the moment they were reasonably certain that 'In all appearance any such design is totally laid aside for the future'. But they gave much serious thought to the problems involved and to the threat to their trade which, with Arthur Dobbs developing his new line of thought, appeared imminent. Isham's Journal of the events of the winter was carefully read through, and many critical notes were scored in the margin; there was clearly some suspicion that he had been too friendly to Middleton, and the presents exchanged by the two men caused much discussion. But in the end the Committee approved his conduct while telling him to question closely two Indians whom Middleton had taken north with him and had set ashore before sailing for England. While seeking all information themselves, they reiterated their veto on the spread of news outside the Company; all ships' captains were again ordered not to deliver any writing or Journal save to the Company, and they were to search all trunks and boxes to discover such reports, and were to affix a notice to their mainmast warning their crews of the veto.

For the rest, the Committee knew that the sloop would sail north from Churchill each year, and they tried once more to bring the far northern Indians south to trade at the fort. Isham replied that this was impossible; there was not an Indian in the country who could carry such an invitation north, and in any case the distance was too great and the Indians were not good at travelling in canoes along the bleak shores of the Bay. Those who had gone with Middleton had seen only the deep bay and the one river in addition to a number of small rivers and creeks. So, although Isham judged that there must be woods to the north because of the number of martens, wolves and wolverene which were brought in to trade, the Committee decided that nothing spectacular would be achieved in that direction, that Middleton was right in saying that even if a passage existed it would be impossible to navigate, and that the only defensible policy was to continue with the annual slooping voyage from Churchill.

With so much basic agreement between the Company and its detractors the difference was that, whereas the critics alleged that French opposition ought to drive the Company to expand into the interior, the Committee were convinced that this was good reason for refusing to do anything of the sort. The normal routine which came nearest to a voyage of discovery which would disarm the critics was, of course, the annual sloop-trading voyage north from Churchill. The *Churchill* sloop had gone north in company with Middleton in 1742, but had not gone so far as he and had returned to the post when he had sailed for England. She went again in 1743 and brought back a fair trade 'having made an Intollerable Good Voiage', but in 1744 the news of war with France led to orders that such 'Northern Expeditions' must 'be suspended till peaceable times'. Exploration to the north, like penetration to the south and west, was weighed against hard facts, and especially against costs, and returns in trade.

It is quite clear from all of this that neither the Committee nor the traders were at all likely to overlook French rivalry as the conditioning factor in the trade. Had there been any such danger, Arthur Dobbs was at hand to emphasise the point: 'the *French* giving them Goods at a cheaper Rate than the Company, all the Eastern and Southern Trade is in a manner lost to the French, and a considerable Part of the Southwestern Trade, they scarce preserving the Trade at *York* Fort and *Churchill* River to themselves'. By supplying woollens, iron tools, guns, powder and shot at what he vaguely called 'reasonable Rates', Dobbs held that the profit from the trade could be raised from £40,000 a year to £100,000.

On the whole, the Hudson's Bay Committee would probably have admitted that they were not adequately securing 'that Country' against the French. They never made such a straightforward admission, but the basis of much of their argument against inland posts was that they were impossible until the country had already been secured, so there was a tacit admission of the charge. But the Committee would nevertheless have maintained (and did in fact maintain) that Dobbs' second objective, securing the trade against the French, was already being pursued by the best and most effective means available. The Company's own trading results proved this in that they supplied the London market with adequate but not excessive quantities of fur, at prices lower than had ever been known, which profited the Company, kept the Indian co-operative, and enabled the English hat-making industry to take a share in the export trade.

Yet this competent balance in trade was in many ways the strongest argument against the Company in a time of such strong national rivalries for trade and for empire as the mid-eighteenth century. Certainly the combination of prosperity with apparent lethargy gave Arthur Dobbs strong grounds for attack, and he used the arguments to such effect that he got support from 'many generous and public spirited Persons' and in January 1745 a petition was presented in the House of Commons asking for Parliamentary help in the further search for a North-west passage. The petition used the old arguments about opening up new countries to provide an export market for British manufactures and to improve the commerce and navigation of the country, and it was referred to a committee containing all the merchants in the House and all the members for sea ports. In March a Committee of the Whole House resolved that the discovery of a passage would be of great benefit and advantage to the trade of the kingdom and that a public reward should be given to anyone who discovered the passage. The resultant bill received the Royal assent in May 1745, when the reward was fixed at twenty thousand pounds. The expedient of offering a reward was one which allowed the government to show support without incurring any expense or responsibility unless and until the project should prove successful.

Thereupon a public subscription list was opened to procure the £10,000 which was thought necessary to set out an expedition, and Dobbs got together (and dominated) a committee of subscribers which called itself the 'North West Committee'. Under his leadership the 'North West Committee' purchased two ships, the *Dobbs* galley, a hundred and eighty tons, and the *California*, a hundred and forty tons. Costs soon began to exceed the public subscriptions, but Dobbs drove his Committee on to equip the ships at their own private expense. Knowledge of arctic navigation was so limited that the 'North West Committee' had to recruit former employees of the Hudson's Bay Company for ships' captains. Command of the *Dobbs* galley was given to William Moor, who had been employed by the Company since he was a boy, had risen to be Chief Mate in the Company's ships and had sailed with Middleton (who was his cousin) in command of the *Discovery* in 1741. The *California* was commanded by Francis Smith, who had served in the Bay from 1738 onwards in command of the sloop *Churchill*, conducting the annual voyage north to Pistol Bay for trade and discovery.

For the Committee of the Hudson's Bay Company it was disconcerting to find that even in Parliament the conclusions reached by Middleton were not accepted as final. There was nothing secret about the 'North West Committee', nor about Arthur Dobbs' challenge to the Company, and the House of Commons in its discussions called upon the Company to produce the Journals kept by Scroggs, Smith, Crow and Napper in their voyages northwards. The Hudson's Bay Committee therefore followed Dobbs' machinations with some anxiety, and were instructed by a General Court of the Company in March 1745 to take all care to hinder any encroachment on the Company's trade, property or privileges. Proceedings in Parliament were closely scrutinised, and the Committee at least achieved the concession that the bill offering the reward for the discovery should contain a clause safeguarding the Company's trade. Moreover, Middleton's successful vindication of the conduct of his expedition meant that official support could not reasonably be given to this further project. The most which Dobbs achieved was that the reward should be offered; but to gain the reward he and his supporters had to venture and to succeed as private individuals. They could not get semi-official support from the Admiralty and intervention with the Company, such as Middleton's expedition had enjoyed although, in general terms, all subjects of the King were to render assistance. Yet the Company's ships' captains were instructed in 1747 to give the expedition, if in distress, all reasonable succour consistent with the safety of their own ships. They were at the same time carefully informed of the clause in the Act of Parliament which prevented the 'Discoverers' from infringing on the Company's trade.

With this much to comfort them, the Hudson's Bay Committee nevertheless turned to a closer review of the Middleton episode, and particularly of the accounts of the winter spent at Churchill, and it was at this time that James Isham was recalled to London for questioning, in September 1745. The Minutes of the Committee carry no references to his interviews, and the comments written into his journal of 1741–2 make it clear that the Committee suspected he had been too friendly and helpful to the expedition; but Isham, like Middleton, vindicated his conduct. He sailed in the ships of 1746 to take command at York, a post for which the existing governor, Thomas White, had recommended him with a diffidence due to the chance that the Committee might not approve.

In the state of tension which ruled in 1746 shipping needed convoy even in the North Sea, creeping up the coast from the Thames to Yarmouth and thence to Newcastle and the Orkneys, and it was the irony of fate that the Company's ships and the explorers should have proceeded up the North Sea together and at the Orkneys should have been placed under the protection of Middleton, now in Admiralty employment and in command of the sloop *Shark*.

The hostilities with France also led the Hudson's Bay Company to renew its instructions for defence of its posts against any strange ships which could not give the agreed signals on arrival, and to cancel the northern voyages for the year. The utmost defensive strength was to be concentrated at the posts, and not only were the sloops held back from exploration but in addition the *Seahorse* was sent out as an extra vessel to act as a garrison and the men were promised rewards for their valour and pensions for their wounds should the French attack. In the event, these precautions were put into action against

T

the explorers, not against the French. For this there was some justification, for Moor and Smith, ostensibly seeking the North-west
passage, were rivals of the Company. They had been told by their
'North West Committee' that they were to trade with any Eskimos
whom they met in the Bay, and were to do so at a better standard
than that of the Company.

Both the Hudson's Bay Committee and Isham were quite convinced, though they could not know Dobbs' orders to his captains,
that the sending out of a second expedition after Middleton's failure
could only mean that Dobbs was either impervious to conviction or
that he was only interested in trade, not in discovery. In either case
he and his ships deserved little help, and Isham certainly did not feel
inclined to stretch a point in their favour. When, after an unhappy
voyage since parting with their convoy, the explorers limped into
Hayes River, Isham was already there to greet them and he did it
according to the letter of his instructions, taking up the buoys and
beacons and shotting his guns.

The explorers, with no winter clothing, had decided to winter at
York in order to set forth in the spring. But Isham from the start
showed his determination not to be put out by their demands on his
hospitality, and it was only under cover of their commissions as
privateers that the explorers were able to make any claim upon him.
He then sent round to the other posts on the Bay to procure a copy
of the Act of Parliament offering a reward for the discovery of the
passage, so that he might extract a promise that the fourth clause,
protecting the Company's trade, would be observed. After that he
had as little to do with the explorers as possible, advising them
against some of their more perversely ignorant and dangerous plans,
helping to provide winter clothing and some sort of housing in log-
tents, but seldom emerging from his aloof truculence.

This was all the more sensible of him because the officers of the
expedition, whom Isham quartered in a separate establishment at
'Montague House', quarrelled endlessly among themselves—so
much so that Smith sought asylum with Isham after two months in
which he had not spoken to Moor. He even left his wife behind him
when he came away. Isham was able to remain on reasonable terms
with Smith, but with Moor and with the super-cargo Henry Ellis
(sent to make notes and sketches, and the author of *A Voyage to
Hudson's-Bay, by the Dobbs Galley and California*) he could barely remain civil. He had, however, learned much from his experiences with
Middleton, and though he had difficulty in preventing the expedition from making contact with the Indians, with the possibility that

trade might ensue, he met no trouble from the debauching of his men, either by liquor or by promises.

The winter passed without major incident—two parties of Englishmen (with one Englishwoman, Mrs. Smith) dragging out the days within gunshot of each other but allowing themselves only the minimum of formal communication in the midst of the frozen wastes. The incident produced two revealing accounts of the conditions of life at York, one from 'the Clerk of the California' and one from Henry Ellis. Of the two, Ellis's *Voyage to Hudson's-Bay* was without doubt the better written, but it was based on so superficial a knowledge of the Bay and was so partisan in its many attacks on the Company and its officers that Isham's 'Notes and Observations on a Book *entitled* a Voyage to Hudsons Bay in the Dobbs Galley etc. 1746 and 1747 *Wrote by* Henry Ellis' opened with a trenchant condemnation. 'I observe', wrote Isham, 'its a common Rule with some persons that writes a history of Voyages etc for want of a proper and just Subject to make a complete Book; the Enlarge upon things which is neither consistant with truth, Justice, nor honour'. Isham's strictures were those of a man who really knew the country, the trade and the people, incensed by the superficial ease of Ellis's writing and by the attacks upon his own rather churlish conduct and on the Company which he served.

At the heart of his reaction lay a conviction that the policy of keeping to posts by the Bay-side was best in the existing circumstances. Ellis impugned the policy, but Isham got to the root of the matter when he argued that inland settlements could only rob York and Churchill of their trade 'unless the French was Dislodged from the Great Lake or Little sea so call'd'. Arguing that the Indians brought their women and children down to trade at the cost of freight in the canoe ('for its a sure Observation when women and children appears in their cannoes, you Depend upon their having but few goods'), Isham reasoned that the supply of furs was controlled partly by the natural periodic plenty and scarcity of beaver, and partly by the Indians' desire for goods; not by ease of transport. For the Indians could, and did, easily step up the transport-capacity by leaving their families behind when the other circumstances varied. His conclusion 'if all men Depend upon a Good Cargo' therefore brings the basic problem of trade policy to the rule-of-thumb test of the practical and experienced trader and adds greatly to a lively appreciation of the actual human conditions. In the last analysis the supply could only be increased by driving out the French, or perhaps by lowering the Standard of Trade.

Ellis's account stung partly because his descriptions of natural phenomena roused the natural historian in Isham, partly because Isham felt that 'Whowsomever, so mean, or illiterate this person makes the Reader to beleive of us factor's in Hudsons Bay, we are capable of answering of him; in a truer and more Reasonable Stile than he is capable off &c'.

To the editor of the 'Chronological History of Voyages into the Arctic Regions', however, Ellis's account was 'a plain, unaffected, intelligible narrative' whereas the other, *An Account of a Voyage For the Discovery of a North-West Passage by Hudson's Streights, to the Western and Southern Ocean of America*, he attributed to 'the Clerk of the California, whose name was Drage' and described it as 'a pedantic disputatious, dogmatical performance'. Isham would have disagreed as completely with this censure as he would with the praise of Ellis, for the *Account of a Voyage* at least acknowledged those things which he had done to help the expedition, and it was more concerned to give an account of what had actually happened than to speculate, and to criticise the Company and its traders for their character and policy. To him the *Account of a Voyage* was slightly the better work; 'As to mr Dragg's Last Book, itt wou'd be only a Repitition of the same thing over again, I therefore do not think it Reasonable to make any Remarks upon itt, more than I can but Observe he is more perticular as to truth then the aforemention'd Author's'.

Such recriminations merely underline the conclusion that the expedition had found in Isham nothing more than the truculent underling of a concern which was dedicated to the unimaginative neglect of great opportunities, while he had found them perverse, ignorant and ill-equipped exponents of views which he knew to be wrong. This was the background to Isham's second winter as a reluctant host to an exploring party, and there can be little room for surprise that he saw them off in June 1747 with more goodwill than he had shown at any time during the winter.

Even the perversity of Ellis, Moor, Smith and Drage, however, could not discover a passage. The reports of the expedition might perhaps have been less critical and bitter if they had concluded with success instead of failure. But 'our hitherto imagined Strait ended in two small unnavigable Rivers', concluded Henry Ellis of the venture into Wager Inlet. He, indeed, thought there were reasonable indications that the passage might lie to the northward, in Repulse Bay, but he was over-ruled in his suggestion that the expedition should proceed there and obtain convincing evidence.

So the expedition really achieved nothing, and the report, on their return to London in October 1747 was received by Arthur Dobbs with the verdict that they had been 'defeated in their Expectations, by the Timidity, ill Conduct, or bad Inclinations, of some of the Commanders and Council'. The existence of a passage was still unproved, and the expedition, apart from the personal animosities which had boiled up, was at loggerheads on that point. While Henry Ellis was convinced that another expedition, properly conducted, would get conclusive proof of the passage, the Clerk of the *California* was equally emphatic that no single piece of evidence supported the argument for a passage; even he, however, agreed that this did not positively prove the non-existence of the passage. This was practically a repetition of the results of Middleton's expedition, and Dobbs met it in much the same way.

His rancour turned against the Company. His determination to challenge its position hardened, and he sought Counsel's opinion on the chartered claim to an exclusive trade. His legal advisers told him that his 'North West Committee', because of its enterprise and the costs which it had so far incurred, had acquired a position rather like that of the Adventurers of 1668 before they were incorporated into the Hudson's Bay Company by Royal Charter. This was support enough to encourage Dobbs to petition the King in Council, asking that the 'North West Committee', in its turn, might now be incorporated into a company which should be granted all the lands which it might settle or discover, with the right of exclusive trade to those lands for a period of years. He had quite an effective case based on the attractive prospects of fresh dominions and a new trade; it was well put and powerfully supported, and Dobbs' petition went forward to the Committee of the Privy Council in January 1748 and was submitted to the Attorney General and the Solicitor General in February.

The petition was such as to be well within the competence of these high legal officers, for it was not concerned with geographical data, tide measurements and arguments for or against a passage, but simply with the legal validity of the Company's Charter. Dobbs pleaded that the Charter was illegal because it did not specify the territories concerned and also because the Company had not fulfilled its terms, had not searched for the passage, had not settled its lands or set up a colony, and had even connived at French encroachment whilst opposing British settlement.

Dobbs had his case prepared, and a series of supporting affidavits filed, before he presented his petition. The Company could not mobilise its defence so speedily. The traders' reports for 1747 and 1748 left the comforting conclusion that the expedition had not impinged upon the Company's trade, and the Committee had begun to relax when Dobbs' petition again upset them. Then, in March 1748, a General Court of the whole Company took note of Dobbs' petition and instructed the Committee to prepare a case against it. But although evidence could be organised from some London furriers, from the ships' captains, and from some of the traders (Joseph Isbister, Thomas White, George Howie and Richard Ford) who happened to be in England, no effective case could be prepared without Isham, and he was still at York and could not possibly be brought home before the fall of the year. With the Law Officers of the Crown hesitant and advising a test-case to ascertain the validity of the Charter and to a large extent supporting the Company on the ground that its apparent lethargy was inevitable from the nature and circumstances of the case, the Company was able to work for delay whilst it sent for Isham to be its key-witness.

So when Isham arrived once more in London in October 1748 it looked as though the Company was secure in its privileges until Dobbs or some other person fitted out an interloping venture which would lead the Company to take legal action and so produce the necessary test-case. For such a course, however, it was impossible to raise money from the public. So Dobbs, with the Privy Council confirming the Law Officers' interim rejection of his petition, turned from the Council to Parliament. He prepared a petition that trade to the Bay might be thrown open and a new company incorporated (the two were really incompatible) and canvassed the great trading centres of London, Glasgow, Liverpool and Bristol for support.

This petition was never presented to Parliament, for the merchants wanted to be assured that it would be effectively supported before they would sign, and when Dobbs submitted his proposal to a prominent politician renowned for his opposition to illegal monopolies he was disconcerted to be told that it appeared that the Company 'had done their utmost in extending the Trade, that it could not be further extended, that by opening the Trade, and others embarking in it, might ruin their Trade, and the Whole be lost, and that it would be hard to attack the Company's property'. To Dobbs this merely meant that his great parliamentarian had an unexpected 'Prepossession in favour of the *Hudson*'s Bay Company'; but it was enough to scare away any merchant support from his petition.

At this stage, at the end of 1748, even Arthur Dobbs, after eighteen years of 'trouble and attendance', gave up and left the field to the Company and to 'some more happy Adventurer'. But first he published, in 1749, his *Short view of the Countries and Trade carried on by the Company in Hudson's Bay*, and his *Short Narrative and Justification of the Proceedings of the Committee appointed by the Adventurers to prosecute the Discovery of the Passage to the Western Ocean of America*.

It was as yet by no means obvious that Dobbs had withdrawn from the contest, and in any case, although Dobbs undoubtedly felt a unique personal hostility in his attacks on the Company he had both roused a general interest in the affairs of Rupert's Land and had published a great deal more information (not always accurate) about the fur trade than had hitherto been available. England in 1749, too, was hostile to monopolies and charters, especially when the privileged companies were reputed to be inefficient. The Parliamentary sessions of 1749 saw much discussion of trade matters, of measures to protect the linen, the cotton, the woollen, the iron trades. There was a clear feeling for stimulating trade and opening markets, and the Royal African Company in particular came under steady attack. In such an atmosphere the Hudson's Bay Company could hardly hope to rest immune, and in March 1749 the House of Commons set up a Committee to enquire into the state and conditions of the countries adjoining Hudson Bay, and the trade conducted there. The 'Right the Company of Adventurers trading into *Hudson's Bay* pretend to have, by Charter to the Property of the Lands and exclusive Trade of those Countries' was also to be the subject of the enquiry. This meant that the Company, its Charter, its trade, its territories and its pretensions, were to be the subject of a full Parliamentary report.

The Parliamentary Enquiry of 1749 was pushed forward in the House with some urgency, for there were many petitions from all over the country, dropping Dobbs' proposal for a rival chartered company but praying that the trade might be thrown open—petitions common in their form and requirements but varying in origin from the Merchant Venturers of Bristol (who were by now merely a municipal oligarchy not concerned with trade as such) to the town council of Kendal, who had no connection with the fur trade. The appointed Committee set to work to collect evidence and immediately ran up against the fact that so little was known about conditions in the Bay that witnesses indulged in blatant exaggeration, and sometimes in falsehood; John Longland, for example, a former shipwright in the employ of the Company who was giving evidence in favour of the petition, was committed to the custody of the Sergeant at Arms for prevarication.

The Hudson's Bay Company, whose Committee had been instructed to watch all these proceedings, was called upon to present its evidence, and the Report was printed on 26th April and was presented to the Commons sitting as a Committee of the Whole House on 1st May, 1749. The Company also presented a petition embodying its case on the same day—and within a week the episode was over. The House, considering the Report of its Committee, the evidence of witnesses on both sides and the petition of the Company, decided that there was no case for annulling the Charter, throwing the trade open, or interfering with the Company.

This was to prove the end of the chapter. No other attempt to dispute the Company's Charter was in fact to come from England, and its privileges were destined to remain unchallenged as long as the basic condition of the 1749 Report lasted. This basic condition was that the French held Canada and the focal areas of the lakes whence the Indians came down to trade by the Bay. The Company's system was vindicated 'unless the french was Dislodged from the Great Lake or Little Sea so call'd: which is not practicible whilst Canada is in their possession'. The evidence was that, from Kelsey onwards, the Company had kept in mind the possibility of penetrating south into the hinterland and north towards a passage if such existed, but that expansion in both directions was limited by practical and climatic difficulties which the opponents of the Company had grossly underestimated. Captain George Spurrell, with many years' experience of sailing to the Bay behind him, had told the House of Commons Committee that much of the evidence adduced by Dobbs was lies, that he knew there was no North-west passage between 51° and 61°, and that, even if one should exist, it could not possibly be navigable. That was the considered and responsible view of the men of 1749 about the passage, and Isham's view that inland posts would not repay the extra cost of carriage also carried the day, especially since he (in his evidence on 4th May, 1749) had been prepared to concede that such posts might well conduct a very respectable trade.

This outcome, however, could not be anticipated by the Company in 1749, for already twice within the decade they had assumed that the fallacies of their critics had been adequately exposed, only to find the criticisms and the counter-projects persist with weighty backing. London was full of rumours that an expedition to trade in the Bay was to be sent out for the express purpose of provoking a prosecution from the Company and so securing the test-case and the legal verdict which the Law Officers of the Crown had recommended. So

York Fort was ordered in 1749 to build a hut at Flamborough Head, higher up than the factory in Hayes River, and to keep six men there until the rivers froze and it was too late for the Indians to travel down to trade with interlopers. The Committee feared that it would be Dobbs himself who would lead such an expedition. In 1749 all posts were therefore ordered to treat any expedition to discover a passage with civility if it should be in distress, but to take all precautions to ensure that there were no contacts with Indians, and no trade. They were, for this purpose, to prevent the explorers, if they came, from going higher up the rivers than the posts—a point of policy upon which Isham had tried to insist with the *Dobbs* and *California*. In 1750 four cannon were sent to strengthen Flamborough House —described as 'Hope post, on Hayes Island over against Flamborough Head'—the complement of men at York was brought up from thirty-two to forty men, and James Isham was sent out to take command of the Flamborough post.

Important and helpful as Isham's evidence had been, and fully as he had vindicated both his conduct and the Company's policy, he had not been restored to one of the Company's major posts. John Newton, his successor when he had been recalled to give his evidence, was to remain in command at York and Isham was to serve under him. But it was an important appointment to which Isham was sent. His instructions were elaborate and forceful; the Company was apprehensive in 1750 that 'our antagonists the Bristol and Liverpool Merchants in conjunction with some Londoners that attacked the Company in Parliament' were fitting out an expedition for Nelson River, and Isham was told to cut down the beacon, take up the buoys, carry out all the routine precautions and, if this should still fail to keep the interlopers out of the river, he was to go yet further up-stream and make a settlement at Steel River in order to prevent them from getting contact with Indians. As things turned out, Newton drowned himself while swimming, and Isham took command at York. Flamborough House was completed and was placed under the command of Samuel Skrimshire, an unsteady man, lazy and unfit for forwarding any business. But it was never intended to be a separate trading establishment, and Skrimshire had certain merits; he enjoyed travelling and he was one of the very few servants of the Company who were competent in the Cree tongue.

The interlopers, however, did not appear 'notwithstanding the Various Reports and Schemes that have been spread abroad to amuse the world', and by 1753 the Company decided that Flamborough House did not even serve the purpose of supplying fresh provisions for York, and gave Isham permission to close down the outpost unless interlopers should actually appear.

Now past his prime and hampered by gout, Isham settled down at York to end his career. The threat from Dobbs, and the urge to seek a North-west passage, were both over and Isham's serious duties lay in running his post and in opposing the French. 'We have nothing more at Heart', wrote the Committee to Isbister at Churchill, 'than the Preservation of our Factorys, the Security of our People and the Encrease of our Trade'. Defence rather than attack, security rather than penetration to the lakes and plains, were the Company's watchwords still.

BOOKS FOR REFERENCE

HUDSON'S BAY RECORD SOCIETY—Vol. XII.

BREBNER, J. B.—*The Explorers of North America 1492–1806* (London, 1955).

BURPEE, Lawrence J.—*The Search for the Western Sea* (Toronto, 1908).

CLARKE, Desmond—*Arthur Dobbs Esquire 1689–1765 Surveyor-General of Ireland Prospector and Governor of North Carolina* (London, 1957).

CLERK OF THE *CALIFORNIA—An Account of a Voyage for the Discovery of a North-West Passage by* Hudson's *Streights, to the Western and Southern Ocean of America* (London, 1748–49), 2 vols.

COATS, Captain W.—*The Geography of Hudson's Bay* . . . edited by John Barrow (London, The Hakluyt Society, 1852).

DOBBS, Arthur—*Remarks upon Capt.* Middleton's *Defence* (London, 1744).

ELLIS, Henry—*A Voyage to Hudson's-Bay by the* Dobbs Galley *and* California, *In the Years 1746 and 1747, For Discovering a North West Passage* (London, 1748).

MIDDLETON, C.—*A Vindication of the Conduct of Captain* Christopher Middleton (London, 1743).

Parliamentary Report 1749.

CHAPTER XLI

LIFE AND TRADE BY THE BAY

The period until the end of the Seven Years' War, in which the Company was left to enjoy its privileges without challenge from English rivals, was a period in which its operations were more fully the subject of public discussion and speculation than had been possible at any previous time. The twenty years' defence of its rights had inevitably torn aside the shroud of secrecy in which the Company had hitherto managed to conceal its operations, and although much of the information available in 1750 was wildly partisan and inaccurate, the controversy had also made available a satisfying selection of real facts.

For the previous lack of knowledge the Company was entirely to blame. In part this may be ascribed to lack of care, in part to over-carefulness. The lack of care is manifest in the revelation that although from the beginning the traders and ships' captains were instructed in the keeping of journals and logs, no care was taken to preserve them, or the letters sent home from the posts. The accounts of the posts are available from 1692 onwards, but though they contain occasional letters and notes they lack the human touch, and until 1701, when the Letters Inwards from Albany begin to be filed, and 1705–6, when the Journals of the same post begin, there is no method of getting an insight into conditions of life and trade in the Company's posts save by occasional records such as Nixon's Report or appeals to the Government, or by reading into the Committee's resolutions, replies and shipments outwards, the conditions which called for such action. The over-carefulness, whereby the Company further emphasised the general lack of information on affairs in the Bay, is shewn in its policy of restricting publication of information.

This aspect of the Company's policy was clearly brought out during the Dobbs' episode and the Parliamentary enquiry. A system for censoring letters from the Bay was an established part of the attempt to suppress the twin evils of private trade and of illicit shipments of goods. With it went a series of injunctions 'that none of our Servants do send any Intelligence to, or Carry on any Correspondence with any Person whatsoever in London or else where relating to the affairs of the Company', and the Captains were ordered to search all personal luggage afresh when they had brought their ships to the Thames. Middleton, in his *Reply*, had remarked upon this and had guessed at the reason: 'I believe the Company think it their Interest rather to prevent than to forward new Discoveries in that Part of the World, and for that Reason they will not suffer any of our Journals to be made Public'. Neither the Minutes nor the Letters of the Company give any inkling of this motive, but probably Middleton was not far from the truth in his guess. In any case, the fact is sufficiently evident. Arthur Dobbs knew it, and denounced it. He found great difficulty in trying to ascertain the facts—a difficulty which he partly overcame by getting Middleton to 'borrow' the Company's documents for him to read.

The result was that when Dobbs attempted to enlighten the public he was open to castigation from those few who were in a position to detect the lack of first-hand knowledge. Captain Coats, for example, was no great friend of the Company which eventually discharged him, and he summarised Dobbs' 'State of the Countries' as a valiant and industrious attempt to piece the evidence together— 'Such as it is, 'tis the only publick description of that country'. But even Coats found it based on contemptible inaccuracy. 'What Mr. Dobbs has thought fitt to call a discription of Hudson's Bay, is so erronious, so superficial, and so trifling, in almost every circumstance . . . that when it first appeared it was matter of astonishment to all those who may be supposed to be competent judges.'

The authentic evidence produced during the Parliamentary enquiry of 1749 changed this situation by the publication of many documents from the Company's archives—actual figures of the trade over a period of years, and evidence from such experienced Bay-dwellers as Isham, White and Isbister. But Parliamentary Reports were as unattractive reading in 1750 as in 1950, and the general public got its impression rather from the partisan pamphlet literature than from the judicious report. It was therefore almost inevitable that such an impression should be critical, for the Company still muzzled the Company's friends while fresh support was forthcoming for the attackers.

This came from Joseph Robson, a mason who had been sent out to the Bay in 1733 to help build the great stone fort at Churchill. Though originally engaged for only three years, he had re-engaged for a second three-year contract in 1745 and did not come home finally until 1748, by which time he had acquired a knowledge of York as well as of Churchill, and was acting as supervisor and surveyor of buildings rather than as a working mason. He was a severe critic of the Company and gave evidence against it in the enquiry of

1749, alleging in particular that its establishments (even the stone-work) were not durable, that penetration southwards up the rivers was easy, that corn could be grown as far north as York, and that a colony could be founded and maintained but for the Company's obstruction. Then, among the other publications which accompanied the *Report* of the Committee of the House of Commons, Robson published his *Account of Six Years Residence in Hudson's Bay* in 1752. Much of his book, like his evidence before the Committee, bore obvious signs of personal experience and knowledge. In particular, his descriptions of the posts and his maps and plans were detailed and accurate, and with so much that was accurate and circumstantial it was easy to carry much which was false and tendentious. In his book Robson coined the phrase 'Sleep by the Frozen Sea' to describe the Company's policy of not penetrating up the rivers, and he gave garbled versions of such attempts at penetration as the Company had made; and he carried conviction. His description of Henry Kelsey as a boy who had run away because he had been beaten, not as the willing apprentice encouraged by his Governor and rewarded by London, for example, was accepted until the recent discovery of Kelsey's own account of his journey made Robson's bias indisputable.

But in the 1750's Robson and the other opponents of the Company carried the day for lack of any attempt to state the Company's case and policy. When Malachi Postlethwayte published the first edition of his *Universal Dictionary of Trade and Commerce* in 1751 he could do no more than utter a warning; 'if there are any falsehoods and mis-representations contained therein, only to injure the Company, and no way serve the public, let the author answer for them, for the public can only depend on the reports of those who have been in these countries'. Postlethwayte could but base his account almost entirely on extracts from Robson.

Examination of the documents which the Company did not choose to disclose to the public leaves it still open to doubt whether the Company was not at that time justified in its major policy, the so-called 'Sleep by the Frozen Sea', in the conditions and with the men, knowledge and capital, available in 1750. It is easy to judge from a modern knowledge of the wealth of the prairies that penetration up the rivers would have been sound policy. But eighteenth-century England's population stood at only about eight millions, and there was little urge to find colonies for emigration, while English agriculture was booming and was firmly entrenched as a social bulwark, as a sound investment, and as a prop of the national economy. On balance in these years England was an exporter of grains, not an importer; and even if the potential agricultural wealth of the prairies had been known there would have been few who would have coveted it as an accession to the imperial economy. The American colonies, after all, were still within the Empire and there was no reason to think that the Canadian prairies would be in any way more desirable or easier of access than the hinterland of the sea-board colonies of America, which as yet had barely begun to spread inland. In fact when the Seven Years' War was over and a victorious British government was faced with the choice of retaining or of returning Canada, the decision proved difficult, and Canada might well have been restored to the French. There was little serious feeling in favour of extending Rupert's Land into a colony of settlement.

Criticism came from those who wished to enlarge the fur trade, and to participate in it; and whereas the discussions at the Treaty of Paris give ample evidence of the lack of desire for Canada, the verdict of Adam Smith (surely no friend of chartered companies!) a decade later shows the accepted view of the fur trade of those who had no ambitions to share in it. The Hudson's Bay Company was in 1779 the only chartered corporation for which the author of the *Wealth of Nations* was prepared to admit any justification. With all its defects, he thought such an organisation appropriate for the barren and inhospitable territories of Rupert's Land. Where even Adam Smith could see reason in the Company and its policy, there must at least be room to doubt that the attacks against it derived their force more from a wish to share in the supposed profits of the fur trade than from the more public-spirited reasons which were so often avouched.

In such circumstances the Company's policy would certainly be defensible; for although the potential capacity of the fur trade was one of the matters upon which the 1749 Report was least informative enough transpired to make it very doubtful whether any serious increase in supplies of furs would be worth while. Robson and the other witnesses who thought that the trade might profitably and easily be expanded were ignorant of the business of marketing the furs; even so, they all agreed that the Company always traded all the furs which the Indians brought and that it was virtually unknown for an Indian to be sent away with a refusal. The question was whether more furs or better furs (especially the martens which went to the French) could be got either by a more attractive Standard of Trade or by posts inland. Here the 'evidence' became pure supposition. Witnesses aired their views as to the way in which the Indians might react to such policies and Mr. John Hardman, Merchant of

Liverpool, gave the Committee a brief summary of the classical thesis of the eighteenth-century merchant seeking a colonial market. 'Being asked, Whether the *Indians* would be prevailed upon to kill more Beasts than to purchase Necessaries for themselves for a Year? he said, He did not doubt but that they would, in order to dispose of them to their Neighbours; that at present, perhaps, if they were to kill Furs enough to supply them with Necessaries for Two Years, they would not come down to trade; but if they were once made sensible of the Conveniency of having some Property, they would then desire to carry on a Trade, and supply their Neighbours; for that the Witness did not apprehend, that all the *Indian* Nations came down to trade; that this Notion of Property would increase; though it would not increase their real Necessities, yet it would furnish them with imaginary Wants.' Here was the commonplace, rarely expressed so succinctly, of the market-seeking European merchant. And it is true that a European notion of Property has generally been developed and has proved the basis of trade.

Such generalities, like many of the proposals to liberate and expand the trade, derived not from close knowledge of the fur trade but (as one witness agreed) from 'Conversations in the World, and the general Notion of things'. But how to market such increased returns, if they could be got, was another question. Here the facts of the existing market mattered, and were elicited. In general even the hostile witnesses conceded that the Company understood its business; the question was whether its interests and those of a nation in search of an expanding market for its manufactures, especially for its woollens, were identical. To demonstrate that the trade was so organised and exploited as to tie in with the market for furs the Company put in tabulated statements of its shipments outwards, its returns, its costs and its sales over a period of ten years, and it put forward Henry Sperling to give evidence. He was the son of the Henry Sperling who had been so intrumental in linking the Company with the European market in its early years, and he testified that he was a fur merchant and a stockholder of the Company with twenty-eight years' experience behind him. The Company's furs, he said, were unquestionably the best in quality which the European market could get; though the French furs were seldom damaged, those from Hudson's Bay always sold best, and the difference in price was generally about one-third. He was in close touch with the French situation, and got regular yearly reports of the French shipments to La Rochelle, for he had always been engaged in the export trade. With this knowledge and experience, he found that the European market, in which Russia still played an important part, fluctuated with circumstances. He had known furs to lie for as long as a year awaiting sale, largely because of a change in fashion; and much depended upon the price. This, he alleged, particularly applied to the Russia trade, where five times the quantity might be disposed of if the prices were lower.

Sperling's evidence 'That the Company understand their own Interest, and, in general, deal in Commodities that turn to the best Advantage', and 'that he questioned whether they could employ double the Stock, because he apprehends no more Goods can be got', reflected the conviction of a man who, though he was a stockholder, professed no knowledge of the Company's management of its affairs. He was made use of to show that the quantity produced was about as much as the market could absorb without producing conditions which would favour the buyers and reduce prices. For 'when a great quantity of any Species is imported, it lowers the Price'—a maxim avouched by Sperling to which John Tomlinson, merchant of London supplied the corollary in his admission that opening the trade and allowing competition would probably raise the prices paid to the Indians—at least to start with. Though the experience of the next half-century was to prove the contrary, and was to shew that the market could absorb furs vastly in excess of those produced by the Company, yet the Company convinced the House of Commons that its practices were all that prevented excessive quantities of furs being produced at exorbitant prices, quantities which could only be sold at low prices.

There remained, however, the aspects upon which Sperling had not commented, the costs and profits of the trade. Here none but the Committee knew the real facts, and 'general conversation' kept London merchants agog with rumours that the annual exports amounted to about four or five thousand pounds' worth of manufactures, against which could be set imports worth from thirty to forty thousand pounds—figures which by the magic of controversy were used to support allegations of a profit of from one thousand to two thousand per cent., regardless of transport and other costs!

In defence of its Charter, the Company provided some real data, and the Customs House added supporting information. For ten years from 1739 to 1748 the Company priced its exports at £52,464 5s. 10d. a yearly average of £5,246 8s.; they ranged from £6,736 0s. 9d. in 1744 down to £4,007 16s. 10d. in 1742. As a check on this, the Customs House accounts 'cast up by fixed and standing Estimates, and not at the real Cost' from 1736 to 1746 showed values of £40,240 1s. 1d. for the ten years. Fluctuations in actual prices, as against the fixed estimates of the Customs House, ensure that the two lists do not vary from year to year according to any fixed ratio. But the evidence of the Company's documents now available makes it clear that the Company's figures were substantially accurate, and that the Customs figures were based upon a conventional range of alleged prices which gave to the export merchant an advantage of about twenty-five per cent. in assessing the values of cargo for duty. Some articles, too, were exempt from export duty.

In addition to the total costs of goods shipped out, the Company also reported that the trading-goods by themselves for the ten years 1739–48 amounted to £36,741 11s. 5d. The remaining £15,722 odd would be for stores, provisions, building equipment and clothing. Such costs were ignored by those anxious chiefly to prove that the Company exported negligible quantities of British manufactures, but they had to be taken into consideration in any attempt to assess profits as against costs. Further, the Company sent in its figures for 'Charges attending the carrying-on the Hudson's Bay Company's Trade', shewing that these far exceeded the cost of goods. For the ten years under discussion charges had amounted to £157,432 14s. 4d., a yearly average of £15,743 5s. 5d. So charges and trade-goods alone averaged £19,417 8s. 6d., and the annual average of the export of goods not for trade added a further £1,572 5s. 6d., bringing average total costs to £20,989 14s. 0d. a year.

Against these costs the Company set its actual revenue, item by item, for the fur sales from 1739 to 1748. In each of three years 1739–40, 1744–5 and 1747–8, the sales just topped £30,000. The total for the ten years was £273,542 14s. 10d., an annual average of £27,354 5s. 6d., and an annual average of profit of £6,364 11s. 6d., or a little over thirty per cent. on outlay. This was indeed a handsome enough trade for the proprietors, taking one year with another, and fully warranted the steady payment of dividends and the accumulation of funds in the East India Company and other investments. But the figures by no means justified the general City feeling that the Company was making such profits (from one to two thousand per cent.) that the trade must be thrown open. Nor did they justify the suspicion that the Company was trading with the Indians on such hard terms as either to rouse indignation or to scare away the Indians to better markets with the French.

To complete the picture the Company published a detailed copy of its Standard of Trade. This list was drawn up so as to shew a slight advance in price over the Bottom of the Bay at both York and

Churchill—an advance justified perhaps by the increased cost of transport and by the extra charges of building and maintaining those posts by comparison with Moose and Albany, but due chiefly to the lack of active French competition. The advance, however, is less justifiable when considered against the facts that the Indians had longer journeys to make to get to Churchill and York, and that their furs were normally in better condition at those more northern posts. The difference between the two pairs of posts was adjusted by the Company so as not to make it worth while for Indians to desert one post for the other. A pound of Brazil tobacco, for example, was traded for a beaver at Albany and Moose whereas the Indians of York and Churchill got only three-quarters of a pound for a beaver.

Amid the diversity of goods shipped for trade, tobacco, cloth, duffels, flannel and blankets, guns of varying lengths, and gun-powder were the most important items. The guns cost, one year with another and taking one gunsmith with another, about a guinea each for a three-foot gun, and they entailed the maintenance of an armourer at each of the posts, and of a 'proof-master' in London; for although the Indians easily became entirely dependent on guns, they were not always adept at handling and maintaining them. Enoch Alsop, who had been employed as armourer at Moose, told the House of Commons Committee that 'the Musquets furnished them by the Company, are worth above 20 Shillings apiece; that they frequently burst, not from the Fault of the Gun, but by overcharging, or from Snow getting into the Muzzle'. For such guns the standard of trade stood at ten beaver at Albany and Moose, and fourteen at York and Churchill. There were good profits here, for ten beaver would sell in London for about fifty-five shillings; but by the time the costs of trade, and of maintaining the posts, had been added to the cost of the gun, the Company could not be suspected seriously of exploiting the Indians. Certainly there was nothing revealed which approached a profit of two thousand per cent. (as Robson and his friends suggested), nor anything like the habit of stacking the skins up to the height of the gun, as other detractors have alleged.

The official Standard of Trade, however, reflected the attitude of the London Committee, and was not necessarily common practice in the posts by the Bay. The revelations of the Dobbs episode and the 1749 Report not only make possible a reconstruction of life by the Bay but also an analysis of the points upon which the 'Bay-governors' (as Robson called them) differed from the London Committee. On the whole, Robson's contention was that the London Committee was well-meaning, but that it placed too much reliance upon the Governors, who often misled it. He felt strongly and bit-terly on this point, having quarrelled with Norton and then with Isham. But Robson was not the only one whose evidence tended in this direction; Matthew Sergeant told the Parliamentary Committee that the Factors often advised the Company badly because they en-joyed fixed salaries, and there is ample evidence, both for this period and for earlier and later times, that the relationship between the official Standard and the actual trade was fluid and nebulous.

One of the points upon which the Company differed from Richard Norton had been the 'Overplus of Trade'. This was a system by which the traders had early learned how to mitigate the inflexibility of the 'Standard', and by 1750 the system had become clear, both to the Company and to later historians who read the Company's docu-ments. The evidence was that the Governors kept the Standard of Trade as a purely token basis for their accounts with the Company: the actual trade was carried on at the best rate which the Indians would tolerate. There was nothing necessarily dishonest in this, for the Governors spent most of the 'Overplus' which they got from 'improving' the Standard on making presents to the Indians, and at times in granting them credit. Such a system of trade would leave little mark in the official accounts and letters upon which a history of the Company must, for the most part, be based. Indeed, Richard Norton told the Committee that the 'Overplus' obtained by watering the Indians' brandy was his own perquisite and refused to divulge it. This the Committee rated 'one of the most unreasonable answers that was ever sent from a servant to his Masters', and they got from Richard Staunton, Master of Moose, the information which they wanted. The Indians, Staunton said, knew the official 'Standard' for twine, blankets, guns, files, tobacco and cloth, so there was no over-plus to be got except in brandy, powder, and the less important articles of trade. This information was given only for Moose, in 1738, and there is no reason to believe that Staunton's report ap-plied to other posts or other times.

But the general impression is that the Governors all had their own methods of 'improving' the 'Standard'. Richard White, basing his evidence chiefly on seven years' service as clerk at Albany (though he had also been second-in-command at Churchill for ten years) told the Parliamentary Committee that 'some of their Governors have their Measure for Powder too short, and don't fill even that short Measure above half full; that the Profits gained by this Method are distinguished by the Name of the Overplus trade, which signifies the Number of Skins which are gained more than are paid for, on the footing of the Standard; that the Company know of this Practice, for that the Witness himself kept accounts of it for Seven Years; and either the Governor, or the Company, take all the Profits of the Overplus trade'. The Parliamentary Committee got a further insight into this system from Christopher Bannister, for twenty-two years an armourer in the Bay, who said the Company used the Indians badly, that they did not give a sufficient price for the furs, and that he himself had been ordered to shorten the measure for powder, 'which ought to be a Pound, and within these 10 Years has been reduced an Ounce or two'.

The Parliamentary Committee suspected the evidence of the *coureur de bois*, Joseph la France, whom Arthur Dobbs produced to show that penetration up the rivers was possible and desirable and that the Company's methods and standards could easily be improved. La France was dead by the time evidence was taken, and his views were expounded by Dobbs on the basis of 'minutes' made at a series of interviews with the *coureur*. The originals even of the minutes had been destroyed by Dobbs, and the Parliamentary Committee was clearly in justifiable doubt as to how far la France's evidence, as printed by Dobbs, was from first-hand experience, from rumours reported by la France, or even from views put into the *coureur*'s mouth by Dobbs. On the 'Overplus Trade', however, la France was quite detailed and categorical. During a visit to York in 1742, he said, the Indians had got much less than the settled 'Standard' for their furs—a pound of gunpowder for four beavers (instead of for one), a fathom of tobacco for seven beaver instead of for one, and one pound of shot instead of four or five pounds for a beaver. To support this, the Indian Chief described by James Isham in his 'Observations' warned the trader that 'the powder being short measure and bad, I say!' he should 'tell your Servants to fill the measure and not to put their finger's within the Brim', and he complained of the cloth-yard with a plea that the 'old measures' should be brought into use again.

Elusive as the 'Overplus' trade must almost necessarily be, it was by no means a novelty even in the Company's accounts. There was enough evidence during the Arthur Dobbs affair to raise grave doubt about it, and Joseph Robson (as might be expected) castigated it as 'big with iniquity'. From within the posts themselves came rumblings of the disquiet caused by the system. For example, in 1744 Thomas Mitchell, a man new to the Bay, was sent from Albany to trade at Slude River on the Eastmain with two Standards of Trade to observe, one from the Company and one from Joseph

Isbister. He called down a torrent of abuse upon his head by appealing for advice to James Duffield at Moose and the episode reveals
both the undoubted existence of the Double Standard, and the fact
that the Committee was aware of it. For Isbister sent the whole correspondence home to the Committee. Not only was the Committee
aware of the system; it made no serious or successful effort to stop it.
As late as 1772 the new but experienced Master of Moose, Eusebius
Kitchin (he had previously served as a surgeon) set to work to revive
the trade of that post and, among other abuses, attacked the system
of the Double Standard. The Indians, he said, had been driven away
by 'sleight of hand'; the yardstick by which cloth was measured was
three-and-a-half inches short, the powder-measure was too small, and
in most articles of trade the Indian was tricked.

The revelation of the Double Standard of Trade, and of the consequent 'Overplus', brought to light much that went on within the
posts. The Masters, it becomes clear, normally remained aloof from
their men, disciplined them strongly—at times harshly—and did
their utmost to prevent them from mingling with the Indians,
especially at times of trade. The men, clad in beaver 'Toggys', found
the weather not impossible; some of them even said they preferred
the climate to that of England and that they would gladly settle in
the Bay. Their main work was as labourers or 'hands', to bring down
wood and fodder to the post, to handle cargo at ship-time and furs at
trade-time, to collect and stow the stones which ballasted the ships
for their homeward journey (the furs being so much less weighty
than the general cargo outwards) and to play their part in the in-
cessant work of building and of reconstruction which the posts
demanded, whether they were wooden or stone-built. Some little gardening at the Bottom of the Bay can be detected; and some hay-
making and animal care at Churchill and at Albany took up a few
days in the year. But on the whole the men were occupied to keep
the posts in fair repair, and at a pinch to defend them. The craftsmen—tailors, carpenters, armourers, blacksmiths—the clerks and
the sloopers normally did not stray from their trades, and craftsmen
such as masons, bricklayers or gunners were specially recruited as
circumstances warranted.

All, including the officers' servants, the ships' crews and their
boys, were given the minimum opportunity of becoming familiar
with the Indians. This was an aspect of life by the Bay which was
reserved for the officers, their interpreters, and the apprentices. The
French had long ago said (before de Troyes raided the Bay) that the
English were so aloof from the Indians that they traded with them

only through a hole in the wall. But James Isham's 'Observations' and other descriptions of trade-time give a very different picture—of calumets, and speeches and 'a little brandy to make us drunk', with the plantation of the post full of Indians. Yet Robson still told the Parliamentary Committee that the actual trade was done 'through a window or hole', while Isham's 'Observations on the Trader and a Gang of Indians' starts its serious business with the Englishman saying 'Come and trade', to which the Indian replies 'Open the window', and the Englishman answers 'The window is open'. The trade concludes with 'Have you done', to which the Indian replies 'Yes, you may shut the window', and in his guileless way Isham fully confirms that, however free might be the reception of the Indians on the plantation, the trade was still conducted with the greatest lack of confidence, 'through a hole in the Wall'.

For this the reason was partly that the Indians must be kept from a free and easy access to the Company's goods, partly that the trade must be formalised and dignified. The visit to the post must be made a memorable event, and conferences, presents and the exchange of compliments and decorations, all played their part. Leading Indians were fitted out with 'Captain's' accoutrements of feathered hats and laced coats, sometimes of scarlet, so as to tie them and their followers to the Company from whom they derived such honours. Nor were empty honours the only things bestowed upon the Indians; the habit of supplying them with oatmeal and other provisions during their lean times had grown and hardened. Normally it affected the 'Home Indians' who hunted for the posts rather than the uplanders who only came down to trade, but a really bad winter, with little snow and difficult hunting, could bring even the uplanders down to seek food. In spring 1731, for example, there were two or three hundred Indians starving and 'lying upon' Albany. This was a matter in which the Committee found it difficult to draw a line between sense and sensibility. In general the starved Indians were to be kindly treated, fed and recuperated, and then sent to hunt for their sustenance at the first opportunity, 'that they may not eat the bread of idleness'.

Refusal to allow idle and malingering Indians to pass their winters at the posts instead of hunting did not imply that the Company aimed to exploit or ill-treat them. On the contrary, the Letters Outwards of this period are full of instructions to the traders to treat the Indians well and fairly. They were to 'use them very civilly Especially the leading Indians, and at all times to Trade upon an Equal Foundation'. Kind and civil usage was to encourage the Indians and to contrast with the ill-treatment of the French from Canada; and when the Committee suspected that Indians had been abused or robbed the Instructions gave the traders no respite. Along with this went reiteration of the old policy of persuading the Indians to hunt beaver instead of making war upon each other, or, indeed, upon the Eskimos. Obviously the actual treatment of the Indians must have varied from post to post, with the character and views of the Governors, but even the hostile witnesses admitted that abuses were due to evasion of orders, not to the orders themselves, and while Richard White recorded that he had known harsh Governors who had beaten and starved the Indians, Matthew Sergeant said he had never seen a sober Indian beaten.

But though the Committee always ordered that the Indians must get fair and humane treatment, there were four points on which they insisted that the Governors must never relax. Drunk or sober, in trade-time or in winter, the Indians were never to be allowed in the trade-room, and in time of trade they were not even to be allowed into the factory but were to be kept out on the plantation. Secondly, in time of trade the hands were not to be allowed to go out from the factory and talk to the Indians on the plantation 'for feare of any Surprize, and to prevent all private Trade'. Thirdly, the Governors were to persist in training their European hands in hunting, despite the fact that the 'Home Indians' resented this. Fourthly, the Governors were to set their faces against the development of 'Trust' or 'Credit'.

How far credit was really an innovation is open to doubt, for there are signs that some credit was an essential feature of the Indian trade from the start. But in the mid-eighteenth century the Committee began to inveigh against it as an innovation, introduced to tie the 'Home Indians', 'as a bridle to bring them more dependent on the Settlement for our necessary Subsistence'. In 1741 the order not to 'Trust' the Indians was laid down as a standing rule for all future conduct of the trade, and enquiries at that time gave the impression that the credit system was only recently developed to any importance, that it was largely confined to Moose and Albany and the Indians who could go to the French to trade, and that it worried the traders as much as the Committee. Richard Staunton reported from Moose in 1738 that he had been three times Commander and had never left a single skin of debt on his departure; but the custom of Moose and Albany, he discovered, was to trust the Indians for hundreds of skins' worth of goods. The Indians ran debts at both posts, and in bad years could easily go to the French, and so the Company lost both the Indian and the goods. Moreover, when the Indian had made but a poor hunt and could not pay his debt, he was very liable to desert to the French, and Staunton thought the credit system a 'ready way of Selling of an Indian to the French'.

Sometimes, however, credit could obviously be a great encouragement to trade; indeed in some form or other it became essential as a means of carrying the improvident Indians through a bad season in a fit state to hunt through the winter. The policy was therefore relaxed from one of utter condemnation to attempts to confine the system to the provision of the necessities of life, especially to hunting equipment. But in practice the thing inevitably came to depend on the sense and humanity of the trader; an Indian who had spent his trade on brandy and was then given credit for powder and shot was, in effect, given credit for the brandy. Isham and his contemporaries certainly used the system, and his dialogues contain such phrases as 'my canoe mate Brought my goods did you not see him', to which the trader answers 'I did see him he Brought your Debt'; or the Indian, being told he is in debt for five beaver in martens (i.e. fifteen martens) and ten *parchment* beaver and replying sadly 'what must I trade my beaver is all gone'.

Essential as it clearly was, the credit system was difficult to adjust, and depended on the trader's insight into his Indians' characters (as all credit trade must always depend) and could produce chaos—as when Henry Pollexfen the elder took command at Moose in 1757. He found that his predecessor had left Indian debts to the extent of over eight hundred beaver. The Indians had gone to the French, or to the post at Eastmain, and had got the notion that the debt was a personal matter between the departed trader and themselves. They had therefore kept away until the ship had taken him to England and had thought thereby to evade their debt. Even so, Pollexfen was convinced that credit was a great encouragement to the trade of Moose, and he used his authority to entice the Indians back to the post by forgiving part of the debts and granting some judicious advances.

Robson denied that he had ever seen an Indian given credit, even for necessaries, but there can be no doubt at all that the 'Trusting' of Indians was a normal and important part of the trade. His statement cannot be accepted as evidence of anything more than his own limited experience, if that; for the granting of credit, like the Overplus Trade, was clearly one of those matters officially forbidden but generally connived at, and in which the Committee hoped to mitigate the disadvantages by securing goodwill and common practice between its posts. For this reason, as for others, the Committee encouraged the Governors to maintain a correspondence with each other, and many of the letters which passed between the posts at this period are preserved with the other correspondence. Most of such letters, lacking the set form prescribed for the letters home to London, are friendly rambling affairs which reveal the Governors' pre-occupation with the immediate problems of provisions, shipping, the weather and the Indians. Urgency sometimes intrudes, especially when French competition is under discussion, and there is much of local significance, as when a sloop is due to be sent from one post to another. But in general such correspondence was easy-going, friendly, unco-ordinated and respectful.

Yet from time to time, as trade dwindled, the Governors suspected their neighbour of 'enticing' Indians out of their normal routes. In particular the early and amicable determination, dictated from London, to divert the Indians from York to Churchill as a place of greater safety was soon abandoned, and Robert Pilgrim from Churchill expressed himself most forcibly on the 'detestable practice' whereby 'the Indians are in Generall Brib'd and Inticed in an Extraordinary manner to go to York Fort Nay even those Western Indians which have frequented this Place for Years are Tamper'd with'. To this Thomas White replied that he had done nothing to entice the Indians, but that it was probable that Pilgrim had not only lost the trust of his English servants but had also estranged the minds of the Indians! It was Pilgrim also who roused a storm of competition between Moose and Albany.

The attractions of one post over another could never be ruled out, especially when the flexibility of the Double Standard of Trade, and the presents and credit which that Double Standard made possible, added to the purely personal merits and demerits of the traders. The Committee strongly and persistently discouraged enticement, but it could never make all posts equally attractive, and in the last resort it was the Indians who took their skins to the most attractive market. They could not be actively discouraged and sent away with their goods, for they would almost certainly go straight to the French. 'The truth is they are a free people, and will go where they find best usage.'

The ability to make presents to the Indians which the 'Bay-governors' derived from the Double Standard of Trade raised a further serious problem. As a means to check private trade with the Indians, as well as to encourage servants to get used to the country and to learn to hunt, the Committee had agreed to allow the men to set their own traps, provided the furs so obtained were openly produced and sent home to be sold with those of the Company. The sale price was then divided between the Company and the servant and, with some misgivings, the Committee had tolerated this system from the governorship of James Knight onwards. But when it became apparent that the Governors habitually made presents of the Company's 'overplus' goods to the Indians it became a matter of doubt whether the furs which the Indians in their turn gave to the Governors ought not to be regarded as, in fact, the result of trade, a sort of gift-exchange. So whenever a Governor's alleged private trapping became sizeable, the Committee required an assurance that he had actually trapped all the furs himself and had not received them in exchange for presents, or even in gratitude for dispensing the Company's medicines to the Indians. The Committee firmly refused to believe that one man could trap a hundred pounds' worth of furs in a year in addition to his ordinary duties, and they were probably right in this.

In the end, in 1751, 'lying out a Trapping' was completely forbidden at Albany, as it had been previously in individual cases, in order to prevent the abuses. But private trade could not be prevented, for the sloop-masters, the ships' captains and the crews, were the essential personnel for the prevention of private trade, and they were so difficult to control that the abuse persisted even when the ships' captains were promised twenty per cent. of any confiscated furs. Do what they would, the Governors could not prevent the men from getting at the Indians before they had traded, nor the ships' captains from trading in martens and small furs; they hid their contraband trade in holes in the cliffs and rocks outside the fort, and the officers found it impossible to prevent the trade utterly.

Of a piece with the difficulties of private trapping and private trade was that of hunting and provision-seeking. There is little evidence at this time that fish was regarded as a potential food in any quantity; as late as 1767 Moose reported that 'We did Endeavour last Winter to catch Fish in Netts under the Ice, but could not succeed'. And although it is true that garden-produce occupied much of the time of the Parliamentary enquiry yet the evidence was chiefly in favour of the argument that if the Company established posts up-country the milder climate would give increased fertility. While crops and fish were negligible, however, hunting was much insisted upon, both by the Company's friends and its critics, and the Europeans were beginning to show signs of becoming 'such experienced Artists in Hunting and Fishing' as to be independent of the Indian hunters.

The men were ordered to be well fed, and the evidence reveals that they drew their rations and cooked and consumed them for themselves in small groups or messes, usually of four men, much on the same lines as a naval mess. Normally there was little fear of starvation, the posts would carry over a year's supplies of European provisions, and the problem was one of a balanced diet, of economy, and of independence of the Indian hunters. Though troubles occasionally arose over short rations, as at Churchill under Robert Pilgrim, it was admitted that the one man who was alleged to have died of starvation had got the same allowance as the rest; and the allowance was six pounds of flour a week and a daily allowance of flesh or cheese, some days three-quarters of a goose each, with pease and small beer, some days three partridges with pease, some days about three pounds of venison. These were not starvation allowances. Pork and European fare came as extras, and feasts and holidays were marked by issues of food as well as of liquor. But here again some latitude had to be left to the Governors, who seem to have used it sensibly, especially when the goose and partridge hunts came off. At times, indeed they were so lavish with their livestock as to run into censure—as when six pigs and four kids were killed in one day at Churchill, or when the bull was killed and eaten there on the 'extream idle Plea' that hay was short.

In general it was geese and partridges which formed the main supplement to European fare; and by this time they substantially reduced the costs of provisions and furnished the major part of the sustenance for the posts. Venison was a valuable supplement but, as Isham noted, it meant that the English (like the Indians) lived sometimes like princes and sometimes like beggars. It was either a feast or a famine as far as fresh meat went, for the venison tainted before it was cool enough to be salted in the summer, and so had to be eaten fresh. The 'perdigious Variety of fowls', on the other hand, were often 'Extrodinary good Eating fresh or Salt . . . and is the cheif of our Diet'. At Churchill Isham recorded that he had expended four hundred partridges a week for eight months out of the twelve, and they were equally important (though not always so dependable) at the other posts. At Albany English proficiency in hunting for the pot had been greatly improved by the introduction of a net for taking partridges—a great economy in powder and shot, and a technique which gave the English an advantage over the Indians. In 1744, when the Indians were coming in starving and the birds were wild and difficult, the English were netting from thirty to forty birds a day. The net was sent to the other posts, with detailed instructions for use; but it seems to have taken many years to be successful except under the eye of its inventor.

Whether in hunting for food, in trapping furs round the post, in getting wood for building or for burning, or simply in meeting on the plantation, the men certainly got ample opportunities of mingling with the Indians, and even of trading with them despite all rules to the contrary. Yet the Committee still wished to keep the Indians apart from the Europeans and numerous witnesses were rightly emphatic that the Company made no attempt to civilise the Indians, nor even to Christianise them. The Committee, it is true, revealed a definitely Christian influence in its instructions; regular religious services were to be held on board the Company's ships and in the posts, and Bibles, prayer-books and books of homilies were sent to the Bay. But this was for the European servants only. Even the 'Home Indians' were not civilised or admitted to be converted, and the story of the Indian boy who had been taught to write at Albany lingered on among the Company's servants as an example of the policy pursued. Such indifference called for serious comment, but it was the almost inevitable result of the Company's fur-trading approach, for the Indian could only be civilised or effectively Christianised if he were weaned from his nomadic ways. It is a commonplace of missionary history that Christianity is sloughed off as the convert reverts to nomadism, and Richard White told the Parliamentary Committee that civilising the Indians could not be 'an easy Matter to be attained, since it would be necessary in that case to bring them up to Labour from their Youth'; and, of course, an Indian brought up to labour was lost to the fur trade.

But while the men could be prevented from teaching the Indians to read or write, or to speak English, and there are many complaints that the Governors punished their men for 'intercourse' in its ordinary social sense, it becomes clear that 'intercourse' in its sexual sense was becoming increasingly common. The Committee had set its face against Indian women in the early days, partly on moral grounds but with more conviction on the grounds of danger and of expense. The French were an example here, but an example of warning also. Nevertheless it was almost inevitable that intercourse should have grown, for even Richard White recorded that 'the Indians were a sensible People, and agree their Women should be made use of', and Isham found the Indian women 'very frisky when Young' and 'Lud from their cradle, being prone to all manner of Vices;— Maidens are Very rare to be found at 13 or 14 Years, and I believe may Safely say none at 15 Years'. The English half-breed was therefore becoming a feature of life at the posts, and domestic ties to some extent explained the willingness with which men spent year after year at the posts, willingly renewed their engagements, and volunteered to settle there if the Company's Charter were overthrown.

Isham wrote of the half-breeds that 'those Indians that has had copulation with the English, has Brought forth into the world as fine Children as one wou'd Desire to behold', and added that he would 'Venture to say without any Disgrace to —— that they are pretty Numerious'. Robson reported that the Indians were 'not very susceptible of the tender passions; for an Indian will gladly lend his wife to an Englishman for a bottle of brandy' and the cynical promiscuity which tended to develop came to a head when in 1755 it was alleged (but not proved) that the English who were sent to settle inland at Henley House were advised to keep no women in the post but 'If his passion was strong, with a pint of Brandy at any time to any Nasty Bunter would assuage that grief'. Such behaviour was almost inevitable when active men were quartered for long periods among those with the concepts and habits of the Indians. More excusable and formative was the habit of permanent co-habitation, and it was this which accounted for most of the half-breeds who became an important feature of the Company's rule.

How far down the scale the habit spread it is difficult to determine, but certainly a high proportion of the Governors of this period had their Indian women—despite an English wife and family. Most of the half-breeds, it was said, were Governors' sons. Here, as in so much else, James Isham is a well-authenticated example. He was most solicitous about his English wife and daughter, and pestered the Company for home-leave in order to take care of them. But the 'Governor's woman' caught the attention of the officers of the *Dobbs* and the *California* during their winter at York, and his second tour of duty there, beginning in 1750, was on condition that 'you do not harbour or Entertain any Indian Woman or Women in our Factory or permit others under you to do so'. He left all his property to his half-breed son Charles, who became an apprentice to the Company and developed into a respected and valuable trader, for he had both the loyalty and affection of the Indians and an English background and education. Richard White knew of no attempt made to educate children in the Bay 'except those of *Englishmen*, who are generally the Governor's Sons', but the Governors were not the only fathers of half-breed families, and the system whereby the men were allowed to buy from the Company's store in advance against their wages leaves evidence of the way in which English servants bought goods and food sometimes to the full extent of their wages for the year. This was a dangerous practice when carried to this extreme, especially when some kinds of goods were in short supply for normal trade purposes; and men who were completely 'spent-up' but burdened with an Indian woman wanting English provender and bits of finery were bothersome and hard to discipline. The Committee's ruling against advances to the full extent of wages, however, only drew back the reply that men who drew for their families said that if they could not have as much as they thought necessary for their support, especially as it was due, they would be obliged to leave the posts and seek a subsistence elsewhere.

Such an ultimatum would, of course, be equally *à propos* for the English families for whom the men drew advances in London—advances which the Committee always checked and tried to keep from exceeding half the wages due. In either case the system of advances reflects upon the way in which the men by the Bay were isolated from their English background, deprived by the very nature of their service, and by the impossibility of forming anything like a colony, of any chance of normal family life. One or two of the witnesses before the Parliamentary Committee did indeed assert their willingness to go and settle by the Bay, but the Company's documents at this time contain no instance of a servant or an officer proposing, under any terms, to retire from the service but yet to live in the country. Occasional men climbed the fences and went off to the Indian tents by night, absented themselves from the factories and threatened to go off and live in the country; but there is no record of any man attempting to live independent of the Company.

The men, like the Committee, accepted at heart the conviction that life by the Bay was not possible on anything approaching the terms of a normal colonist. Even Robson agreed that at the Bottom of the Bay the fur trade must be the basis of a livelihood. That involved shipments and supplies from England. Those who alleged that they were prepared to settle or to go into trade in Rupert's Land based their convictions on the fact that real stone forts with heavy defensive armaments were not necessary; but they agreed that something in the nature of posts or block-houses, rather than free and uncontrolled settlement, was certainly needed.

So, although there was something of a protestant crusade, almost a puritanical complacency, about the moral precepts which the Committee sent to the Governors, the inhibitions of life by the Bay were generally accepted in principle even when they were evaded in practice. Conditions varied considerably with the Governors. A martinet could cause as much trouble as a sluggard, and some of the Governors, from their own accounts, were in the worst tradition of the sea-service from which they derived their example. Placed as they were, the Governors had to ensure that 'Command must be Carried or else There would Not be any living'; they often had to reduce 'a mutinous and turbulent set of people into a due Subjection and a sense of their Duty', and to prevent and discourage even 'dumb insolence' and idleness. Punishments sometimes took the form of fines and stop-pages of pay, especially for drunkenness, private trade and affliction with the 'Fowle Disease' (in which case the surgeon, despite protests by the Committee, got a month of the victim's pay to teach him to be more careful!). Sometimes the men received a formal thrashing or were put in irons—perhaps sent home. At times the Governor's temper simply gave way, not always with good results. At Albany Joseph Isbister knocked down a man and broke his leg for 'caballing' and refusing to go to bed on Christmas Day at the appointed time; on another occasion he chased a man through the post and out of the gate for refusing his duty. It is not an edifying spectacle, but at least Isbister reduced his men to 'Capettolate', as did Isham and most of the disciplinarians. But arbitrary punishment could be dangerous, as when Henry Pollexfen resented being told that it was not a man's job to come and ask for work. He 'desired him not to be saucy nor to give me any ill language' and 'gave him a little blow with my hand upon the head'. In return he was struck in the face and knocked off the joist upon which he was standing, to fall heavily to the ground five feet below. The mutineer was put in irons and sent home, which seems a little vindictive, for other servants, drunken, abusive or incompetent, were given great latitude by their officers.

Such incidents, however handled, were to be expected in such circumstances; it would have been cause for very serious comment if they had not occurred from time to time. The powers of discipline and punishment were derived from the penal clauses in the Company's Charter and were conferred on the Governors by their Commissions. So when a disgruntled servant threatened to sue a Governor for damages, as the surgeon Pearson threatened to sue Pollexfen for five hundred pounds, the Governor clutched his Commission as his legal warranty and refused to part with it. The punishments, deeply though they may offend twentieth-century minds, were not cruel or severe when viewed against the keel-hauling or thrashing round the fleet by which discipline was at that time preserved in the Navy, the floggings in the Army, the punishments which an unreformed legal system freely administered in British courts of law, or

the discipline to which the Committee-men themselves had submitted at their schools. This is not to defend the system; merely to
insist that heavy corporal punishment was a normal concomitant of
discipline in the eighteenth century. The Company, in any case,
throughout set its face firmly against vindictive and cruel punishment; it tried to insist that the men should be well fed, well found and
well treated, and it firmly resisted arbitrary authority. From any
point of view it was better to send home the 'most Abusive, likewise
Drunkards, Swearers and neglectors of their Dutys', as well as the
occasional 'unsociable and untractable Lunatick man', rather than to
embark upon endless punishments; and that is what the Governors
did. It called forth comment that the Committee never took proceedings against such men in the English courts. Such a course of
action never seems even to have been contemplated, and so the
records carry no account of the reasons, whether this sprang 'from a
mistaken lenity, or for some secret reasons'.

In any case, too much can easily be made of the troublesome and
harsh side of life by the Bay. There are, indeed, occasional instances
of an officer being struck by a servant, more cases of duty being refused, and more of insolence, idleness or debauchery. But there is no
case in which these men, with arms in their hands, the woods at their
backs and sloops at their disposal, ever engaged in anything which
could in any sense be described as mutiny.

So continuous and significant a record of (comparatively) good
conduct must be attributed to the fact that, obvious as were the matters on which Governors and men were liable to differ, the Governors
had for the most part had experience of the men's messes before they
took command; and they had the full support of the Committee in
doing as much as possible to alleviate the weary boredom of routine,
except in times when constant attention was needed to forestall an
expected attack from the French. Some of the hands could certainly
read, though not all, and the consignments of books are evidence of
care, alongside of which must be put the organised diversions of the
post. These would not be anything like the games which a modern
enquirer would expect, for ball-games would be quite out of place
and were not even popular in England in the eighteenth century.
Countrymen's sports, the hunt, coursing hares, fishing, perhaps
cock-fighting, were the diversions of the English at this time. But
they find no place in the journals of the posts, though given a legitimate occasion the Governors were willing to stage a diversion. The
Queen's birthday, Christmas and the New Year, the anniversary of
the Company's Charter, and above all (in an Anglican tradition

which then meant much) 'Hang the Pope' on the fifth of November, were often celebrated with holidays, extra rations of food and of drink, perhaps a bonfire and perhaps a contest of 'shooting at a mark'.

Even so, the utmost which could reasonably be expected was quiescence, a sort of apathetic indifference in which the men's attention was absorbed by problems of food and drink, and their energies taken up by regular and routine labour. The sort of conditions which were necessary for the sober running of the posts made it almost inevitable that the enthusiasm and 'spontaneité' which characterised the French should be but little in evidence. They were, in fact, strongly discouraged; the old and experienced Governors were keenly conscious of the wish of the younger men to make experiments and, instructed from London that 'We have nothing more at Heart than the Preservation of our Factorys, the Security of our People and the Encrease of our Trade', they in turn ordered their subordinates to 'follow your instructions for Trading *attempt no new Methods*'.

BOOKS FOR REFERENCE

HUDSON'S BAY RECORD SOCIETY—Vol. XII.

DOBBS, Arthur—*An Account of the Countries adjoining to Hudson's Bay, in the North-west Part of America* (London, 1744).

GIRAUD, Marcel—*Le Métis Canadien* (Paris, 1945).

ROBSON, Joseph—*An Account of Six Years Residence in Hudson's-Bay* (London, 1752).

U

CHAPTER XLII

ATTEMPTS AT EXPLORATION AND EXPANSION

When the Dobbs-Middleton-Isham episode was over, there was an acknowledged need for development. By 1750 the Company's posts, with their 'Home Indians', their hunting and their winter packets of letters between the posts, were almost living off the country in a way which would have seemed quite impossible a generation earlier. But Henley House was the only attempt yet made to settle inland, and projects for opening up the Eastmain coast and for exploring northward, and perhaps westward, from Churchill were all too easily laid on one side.

True, Henley House persisted despite the conviction that it was more effective in intercepting Indians who would otherwise come down to Moose and Albany than in diverting them from the French. It was dependent for provisions on Albany and was not attractive to the men, who at times refused to go there; but it seems to have been well built, looked 'far more dreadful than Eastmain' with gun-posts all round it, and had the general appearance of a 'little Castle'. Certainly in its early years the outpost seems to have performed its proper function. The leading Indian who had persuaded Joseph Isbister to build at Henley himself continued dutifully to come down and trade at Albany, a small trade of only about a thousand skins was got at Henley, and this was reported to come from 'foreign Indians' and the 'western guards' who formerly went to the French. The Indians therefore reported that the French were 'putt to their Shifts' to live during the winter, and that they were reduced to vague threats that they and the 'Nodways' were coming to destroy the English posts.

Henley, however, despite so promising a start, revealed the serious difficulties in the way of siting inland posts. Apart from the insoluble question of setting the charges of the post against declines in the returns from Moose and Albany on the one hand and the need to combat the French at whatever cost on the other, there was the fact that the English, as yet, did not know how to supply, or to communicate with, such a post. The Indians had originally promised to hunt for the small English garrison, but within a year it became clear that the close rivalry with the French left the Indians in command of the situation. They would trade all their goods for brandy, and above all they would not supply provisions except for brandy. For over a century this habit of the Indians, of exploiting inland rivalry and the Europeans' dependence for food in order to demand brandy in trade, remained a constant feature. But when Henley House first brought the practice to the attention of the Hudson's Bay Company it proved disconcerting.

This was the more so because, although Henley was only about a hundred and fifty miles by water from Albany, the Hudson's Bay men were inexpert in inland travel. The remedy to the provisions problem was to send up part of the goose and partridge hunts, salted in casks, along with European provisions from Albany, for the shore-marshes were the ideal places for such hunting, yielding incomparably better returns than spasmodic hunting in the interior. In addition, the Indians had to be prevented from becoming provision-hunters on a brandy basis for Henley and had to be kept to habits of fur-hunting on a normal trade basis for Moose and Albany. Provender therefore, as well as trade-goods, had to be got inland, against the current and over the 'Great Falls' of the river.

For this purpose the Hudson's Bay men first took systematically to the use of canoes. The 1749 Parliamentary Report had elicited a good selection of evidence about canoes; some witnesses had spoken of large canoes which would carry twenty or thirty men, with luggage, which they said would go up the rivers, and of 'small Birch Canoes, from 18 to 25 Feet long, and from One to Two Feet broad' in which the furs were brought down to the Bay. The first class mentioned would be quite large canoes, and it is open to doubt whether the witnesses were reliable on this point, for one of the arguments in favour of the setting up of inland posts was that the Indian canoes held only a couple of men and perhaps two or three packs of furs, which was but a small portion of the furs which would be available if the freight-load of a canoe were not a limiting factor. Isham said that eighteen feet in the keel was the longest for an Indian canoe, and when he came to describe the manufacture of a canoe he said they had four thwarts, one at each end and two in the middle, with room for one person to sit 'between' each thwart—which could mean a crew of three, or at most five, according as Isham is interpreted, but certainly not of twenty or thirty. Isham, however, supplemented his own knowledge by relying on the description of the Frenchman Lahontan, and the latter allowed for infinite varieties in size, running from ten feet to twenty-eight in length, and holding from two people up to fourteen. The larger canoes, Lahontan added, were used for warfare rather than for commerce, and when used for transporting provisions or merchandise were commonly manned by only three men.

Large or small, the canoe was difficult to manage and easily over-set; but it was considered the only possible means of transport to the interior. So when Albany began to undertake systematic transportation up-river to Henley, canoes had to be used. Middleton had reported that not five of the Company's servants were capable of venturing in a canoe. But the miscreant apprentice Dingley was sent off with Indians in a canoe to see what the French post at Henley meant, and when the first consignment of stores and provisions was sent, in June 1743, it went in four canoes, three small ones and 'one Great that I had made for this purpose'. Further supplies also went by canoe, and by September 1744 Isbister had two large and two small canoes of his own in commission. The large canoes had been built to his own design, and had cost him a gallon of brandy each to build. It is to be supposed they were made from birch-bark and this would be possible at Albany although at York or Churchill, as Isham wrote, no birch could be found within sixty or eighty miles of the sea-shore. It was probably of these two 'Great Canoes' that the Parliamentary witnesses wrote, for one of them spoke of his own journey to Henley, with the men towing the canoes.

Already there was talk of using flat-bottomed boats, which would carry a greater weight than the canoes and could negotiate the shallows and the rapids. In 1746 Isbister built a boat at Albany which, he argued, would enable Henley to be kept supplied without the help of Indians, and in the following years boats, which the English servants could manage, largely replaced canoes on this route. But for the pioneer work, the first journeys inland even with provisions and supplies, it is quite clear that the Company's servants had turned to, and had mastered, the canoe at least to the extent of being able to penetrate up the rivers with the assistance of Indians.

Even with this vital problem solved, Henley nevertheless proved a most difficult and dangerous innovation. The Committee, unconvinced of its trade value, was yet glad to learn that the post was in a defensible state and ordered that it should be kept so despite the peace with France. Joseph Isbister from Albany ordered the master to discourage the trapping of summer furs, told him to trade only when winter had fully set in—otherwise the Indians were to be sent down to Albany unless French rivals were in the vicinity—and to get what information he could of the North and South Branches of the Albany river. Particular care was to be taken to ensure the defence of the post, and the rules for keeping the Indians under control were severe; never more than one Indian at a time was to be allowed in the house, and the English were not to disperse in the woods while wooding or hunting. Then, in 1751, William Isbister was recalled for 'sottishness and ill Conduct', to be succeeded by William Lamb, for whom the previous instructions were enlarged and repeated, with a special caution against negligence and too great a love of liquor.

The warnings were necessary, but were not heeded. On 20th October, 1754, Lamb with twelve men arrived back at his post after a visit to Albany. Seven of these had merely been sent to help with transport. They were not intended to winter with him and he sent them back and settled down with his five hands. The next that was heard from the post was in the following March, when a band of Indians arrived at Albany to report that in February they had found Henley House broken open and abandoned. They concluded that the English had been 'deluded out of the place of defence' by treacherous Indians whom the French had sent. Suspicion soon began to fasten upon 'Wappisis alias Woudby', the *Captain* of the 'Home Indians' of Albany, and as the story became clear it marked the ineptitude of relations with such closely dependent Indians as the 'Home Indians' had become. Woudby, 'the Old Pirate' was put in irons at Albany, and ultimately he confessed that, assisted by his two sons, one son-in-law and two upland Indians, he had murdered the master and all the men. It was a tragedy of over-familiarity, and laxness combined with exploitation. The Master, it was later asserted, had followed the practice rather than the precept of the Governor of Albany and had two women 'at Bed and Board' all through the winter; the other English also 'Keeped there Woman'. The Indian men claimed their share of the victuals and other comforts, and were angered at not getting the freedom of the factory, either at Henley or at Albany. They chose a time when the English were carelessly dispersed, killed them, and took and pillaged the post.

After a formal trial, at which all the English at Albany were present, Woudby, his sons and his son-in-law, were hanged. Joseph Isbister was deeply mortified at this end to his own personal project, and though there were strong feelings that women had proved the destruction of people, goods and trade, he felt convinced (perhaps because he wished so to feel) that not women but the French were the cause of the massacre. The Indians, he decided, had left the post standing instead of destroying it so that it might be there for the French to take over, and he therefore sent a party of Indians inland with orders to burn the buildings and prevent them from falling into French hands. It was a strong decision, especially as it was already apparent that the large number of upland Indians who had shared in the spoil of the post would not dare to come in to trade either at

Albany or at Moose, and that the trade of both those posts would suffer.

The Committee in London were deeply upset by the melancholy news, and notwithstanding their earlier mistrust of the post, resented the decision to burn it. Forthwith the complement of men at Albany was increased to forty, so that Henley could be set up again. But the ship of 1756 was late in arriving at Albany, the essential provisions had not been prepared, and although the Committee had ordered forty men only twenty-four could be mustered, of whom some were so alarmed on hearing of the massacre that they were ready to pay five pounds for a passage back to England. In any case, eight of these were needed to raft home Albany's winter firewood, so that if twelve were sent inland to Henley there would only be four left to guard Albany. So the Committee's orders, and the fiery offer of George Rushworth to go inland and so rout the French as not to 'leave one french log upon this River', were alike set aside.

It was 1757 before an expedition could be prepared, strengthened by two volunteers from the sloop and three from the ships' company; for the others it proved necessary to ask the Committee to send out a sawyer and the necessary hands explicitly bound by contract to go inland, since the ordinary hands of Moose and Albany dreaded the thought. The boats then led to abandonment of the plan, for there was not enough water in the river to carry them up; but in 1758 more effective preparations were made and George Clark, carpenter, was appointed master of the proposed post, to take up his duties in the spring of 1759. So when, on 1st September, 1759, Clark reported that he had built a 'Square House' on the old site, commanding both branches of the river, it seemed as if the Company's first inland post was indeed re-established, to represent both a change of policy in the Committee and an active determination and adjustment to circumstances by the men. But little more than a fortnight later, on 17th September, George Clark was dead. A body of Indians, or of Frenchmen disguised as Indians and mingling with them, attacked the post, shot Clark dead and wounded another man. The remaining two Hudson's Bay men defended the house till dark, then escaped, leaving their wounded companion with some Indian women, and walked down river until they met the boats coming up with more supplies.

The immediate support which might have righted this second disaster was not forthcoming. England was engaged in the Seven Years' War, French attacks were perfectly legitimate and were to be expected, and neither at Moose nor at Albany was there any enthusiasm for the outpost. The two bases had troubles enough of their own to add to the fact that the French, who were undoubtedly involved in this attack on Henley, threatened to attack Albany and so drove off a great deal of trade. Moreover, Joseph Isbister was no longer in command at Albany, to meet the threat with his deep confidence in Henley. Ill-health had threatened to drive him home as early as 1744, but he had only removed to Churchill from 1748 to 1753 and had then come back to Albany. There he had dealt with the massacre of 1755, but in the following year he was relieved by Robert Temple, who found the Albany buildings in good repair (except the east curtain, which he began to reconstruct) but disapproved of the policy of an inland post. Temple never hoped much from Henley, he felt that it robbed Albany of trade, and he feared that every fresh venture would be met by fresh disaster.

The unwillingness and inability of Albany to venture again to Henley was more than equalled at Moose. There also Robert Temple had made his influence felt, when he had been sent from Albany in 1751 to take temporary command during the illness of Robert Pilgrim. He had found the trade of the post in decline; it had dropped to only a little more than four thousand beaver in 1751, and he could do but little to revive it. The buildings too had been allowed to decay till the post looked like an old deserted building which had not been inhabited for several years. Much of this was ascribed to Pilgrim's illness, and to the 'Supineness inactivity and (to give it no worse Name) the Negligence' of which he had been guilty, and to the 'sottishness and idle behaviour of his men'. A steady programme of rebuilding at Moose had to be undertaken, with the proviso that no green wood should be used, and this occupied all the attention of the masters. It was a programme which was closely affected by events inland, as for example when building was held up in 1755 because of the massacre at Henley; and in its turn the complete absorption of Moose in its own problems meant that no men, provisions or enthusiasm, were left over to supplement Albany's lack of enthusiasm for Henley. Re-building was still the obsession at Moose in 1757 and 1758. But there were other problems too, for trade was not recovering and Moose's returns were down to twelve hundred beaver in 1756. The decline was due to the fact that the home Indians were starved while the 'French Pedlars increase and come into the rivers and stop the Uplanders in their way'.

So, twice destroyed, the Company's pioneer inland post lapsed. It had still not been re-built by 1763, when peace with France and the cession of Canada to Great Britain brought short-lived hopes of an end to opposition from the Canadians. But that year the Council of Albany voted against re-settlement at Henley both on the ground that Canadian opposition should now cease and because re-building would demand men and building materials which could ill be spared.

Despite the unwillingness of Albany and Moose servants to venture inland, and the difficulties revealed at Henley, the Committee had come round to a conviction that, in its own time and for its own purposes, it should pursue a policy of expansion. Here the long-standing ambition was to open up the Eastmain coast. This was an ambition which carried back to the 1730's, to the days when Middleton had sent home an Eskimo boy who would be useful in opening up a trade in Hudson Strait, and when Joseph Isbister had persuaded the Committee to build a new house up Slude River.

Although there were current rumours of great rivers, and of a system of three great lakes in the interior which would make it possible for the Company to open up a large trade with the centre of the Labrador peninsula, it was then agreed in 1739 that, for the time being at least, it was not advisable to move from Slude River. The small house there (which served as a model for Henley) therefore remained the extent of the Company's commitment on the Eastmain for many years; it was supplied and to some extent provisioned from Albany, and its master was a subordinate trader with perhaps two or three men under his command, who took his orders from the Governor of Albany. Contact between Albany and the outpost was by sloop, but winter 'expresses' by Indians or even by English servants, and sledge loads of blankets or other goods when required and available, were also interchanged.

It was not until the Arthur Dobbs' episode began to stir the Company that a more serious interest was roused in the Eastmain, for Dobbs had in mind not only a search for a North-west Passage and further trade with the interior, but also the possibility of exploration and mineral development on the Eastmain, and of a trade in whale-oil, sea-horse teeth and seal-skins with the Eskimos of Hudson Strait. None of these possibilities had been overlooked by the Company. But navigation through Hudson Strait was usually the most difficult and dangerous part of the voyage, being also the most northerly; icebergs there were frequent, fogs were normal, and the coast was treacherous. Ships' captains were regularly instructed, and encouraged on a percentage basis, to trade with any Eskimos whom they might encounter in their passage. But they were not to go out of their course to seek them, and they were never to allow them on board their ships. If the coast, and the Eskimo trade, and the interior, were to be opened up, that must be done by sloopers from the Bottom of the Bay, not by the ships in transit.

But the Bottom of the Bay had the rivalry of the French and the establishment of Henley to absorb its attention. 'As for my part I am disabled from Carring on any work by this Henly', wrote Joseph Isbister in 1744. Yet although he insisted that he was unable to support Henley with provisions, or to man it for defence, that he had no hands to get his winter firewood home, and that his goose-hunt was late and had failed, so that there could be 'no pretending to send the sloops on a discovery', nevertheless an expedition was sent in 1744.

At Moose James Duffield had set to work to build the *Phoenix*, a handsome sloop (Isbister called her a schooner and wanted her called the *Albany*) which was launched in May 1744. Something was needed, for of the available sloops the *Moose* was almost out of action; she needed a new 'gripe' for her stern, her boat would not 'swim', her masts and rigging were rotten, and her bowsprit and sails carried away so that she almost lost the complete returns of the Eastmain trade. The *Diligence* had had to be broken up as unserviceable. The *Beaver*, too, was 'Bolt sick and Nail sick in every part'. As long ago as 1735 the Committee had been warned that she would founder if she ever touched bottom, and since the Eastmain trade and the prompt loading and despatch of the ships for England depended on the sloops, there could be no exploration until the slooping situation eased. But the *Phoenix* was sent a set of sails from England, and she was sailed up from Moose to Albany in June 1744. There, in accordance with previous arrangements, Isbister had prepared the provisions and supplies for an expedition. He sailed her back to Moose Fort, where the decrepit *Moose* sloop joined him. They were weatherbound in Moose River for a valuable week, from 20th to 26th June, but they then sailed to Charlton Island. At Stratton Island they met the *Eastmain* sloop and transferred the Eastmain returns from her to the *Moose*, so that Isbister could sail the *Moose* back to Albany while the *Phoenix* and the *Eastmain* went on a voyage of discovery.

The *Moose* barely got her furs to Albany under a jury rig, but the *Phoenix* and the *Eastmain* arrived safely on 14th August. Though their voyage has its importance in revealing the initiative and capacity of the Governors, the ability to build the *Phoenix*, to provision and organise the expedition on a co-operative basis, and to time it so as to make the best use of the shipping, to get the returns in furs all ready for the ship from England and to get the buoys and beacons set and other normal slooping duties accomplished, yet it achieved little in the way of discovery. Apparently the two sloops went as far north as the entrance to 'Wenepegg Gulf' in latitude 56° 30', and then returned to the Bottom of the Bay, unimpressed by anything they had seen.

But the project was neither forgotten nor neglected. In 1747 the *Eastmain* and the *Moose* were ordered to set out on a trading voyage along the Eastmain coast in the spring of 1748. They were to go as far as Cape Digges, in latitude 63°, and from the point at which the 1744 voyage had ceased they were to make observations and explore the coast thoroughly. It is as a commentary on this voyage and its predecessor that the evidence given to the Parliamentary Committee of 1749 must be judged, with indifferently qualified witnesses saying that the Eastmain trade was carried on by a sloop which wintered at Slude River with a crew of eight, that there was no intercourse with the Indians between Slude River and Cape Digges, though furs and timber abounded there, and that valuable ore had been got from the coast. On the last point the evidence became more matter-of-fact and less speculative, and there was first-hand witness that the 1744 voyage had brought back from the 'Labrador Coast' samples of ore which yielded both silver and lead. The samples had been brought back on the personal initiative of Captain Thomas Mitchell, who had no particular instructions to look for minerals, and the Company had decided not to attempt further development of minerals on the East-main. But the rumours which deck-hands spread led to much jealousy of the Company's Charter, and to at least one abortive project for an interloping expedition aimed at the mineral resources of the East-main.

In fact, the Company was not so indifferent to the prospects of fur-trading, timber development, or mining, on the Eastmain as its detractors would have held—though it took a realistic view of the difficulties and dangers. The 1748 orders were followed up in 1749, when John Ball of Cardigan was asked to recruit seven labourers from Britain's lead-mines, to stay five years in the Bay at a wage of £10 a year. He only managed to get three, from Cardigan and Montgomery. At the same time Thomas Mitchell, late master of the *Eastmain* sloop, who had discovered and brought back the original samples of ore, was ordered to take the new sloop *Success* and to choose a site for a post on the Eastmain coast anywhere between 59° and 56½° north. He was then to load up a cargo of ore, take it to Albany and return with the miners to Slude River, telling the Indians there that in 1750 he would build a new post far to the north, to which they should take their trade. In the spring of 1750, therefore, he was to sail from Slude River to Albany, pick up that post's carpenters and an assortment of trade-goods, and go north to establish his new post. He was for this purpose to take the *Eastmain* sloop, but the *Success* was to accompany him, to stay with him for twenty-four days, and then to go south to Slude River. The ship from England was to call in at the new post on her homeward voyage, to load ore instead of stones as ballast; and if she did not shew up Mitchell was to return to Albany before winter set in.

Attention was not entirely concentrated on minerals, for Mitchell was ordered to trade with Indians from Cape Digges down as far as latitude $58\frac{1}{2}°$, or even to the great Gulf of Hazard in $56\frac{1}{2}°$—anything further south would have meant competition with Slude River —and was encouraged to get whalebone, whale-oil, and furs. But the ores were much to the fore, and forty per cent. gratuities were promised to those engaged if the venture proved profitable.

Even with such inducements the rather elaborate but carefully-thought-out plan went wrong. Albany set the carpenters to work during the winter of 1749–50 to pre-fabricate a frame house for the Gulf of Hazard since the evidence was that no local wood was available there, and the two sloops set out on 20th June and had the house, Richmond House, built by 25th July. The site chosen for Richmond was on an island in Winipeke Bay, Gulf of Hazard. But already the situation was discouraging, for the Master of Albany had reported that Thomas Mitchell was not to be trusted; he had in hand a proposal which would rob the Company of the best returns. Mitchell had, however, sent in both a cargo of ore and a report as a result of his 1749 voyage. The ore weighed fifteen tons, but whereas the Committee had expected lead, they got only sulphur and low-grade brass. This disappointment was emphasised by Mitchell's report, for he wrote that he had explored the coast in clear weather from Cape Digges southwards and had found no river or creek in which a ship might find shelter after passing Sir Thomas Smith's Sound. There was, he wrote, no bush nor brake, and hardly a living thing, on the whole coast until he came to Richmond. Against this, he reported that his post had many Eskimos to the north and many Indians to the east and south, so there were fair prospects of trade. There was, too, fine fishing and hunting although wood must come from the Bottom of the Bay; and in his search for minerals he thought he had found a copper deposit.

The more promising Richmond appeared, the more dangerous it was to have a man like Mitchell in command. He sent no ore home in 1750, and he was recalled and replaced by John Potts in that year. Potts found that the three miners had been sent to Little Whale

River and had been given the impression that the mine was a chimera and the new settlement a joke; they were very much their own masters at a distance from the post, and they proved 'disorderly and intolerably idle'. He sent them home before their contracted time, but he found the whole little settlement lifeless and dispirited. The Indians assured him that wolves, foxes, otters, wolverene and deer could be got, but that the country produced few beaver or martens. Yet he saw that the Indians who frequented a lake at the head of Whale River were always clothed in beaver, so he hoped he might bring them to trade. He was ordered to abandon the useless mine which Mitchell had started at Little Whale River and to search nearer home, round Winipeke Bay and on the south shore of the Gulf of Hazard; emphasis was on mineral development, with hopes of lead, silver and copper, and on defence, for which he was sent eight pieces of cannon.

Potts seems to have met with the approval of the Committee, but his returns from Richmond in 1751 amounted only to 'a very few Furrs and skins, a trifling quantity of Lead Ore and a bag of Patridge Feathers the whole of which are so inconsiderable' that he feared heavy censure. The time-table for the use of the sloops and for a call from the homeward-bound ship was working out quite well, and this proved essential. Yet Richmond was in a dismal situation, with no timber available and no partridges or other hunting, despite the cheerful early reports. It was entirely dependent for subsistence on Moose and Albany, in a way in which the first posts had been dependent upon England, and the Company's concepts had so changed that although it had formerly seemed natural that posts should be dependent on English provisions, it now called for remark that they should be dependent on each other for country produce. Potts was reproved for such dependence; but he, like the other traders, was by now certain that it was beyond dispute that Richmond could never 'answer the expense'.

Disappointed though the Committee might be, they were not prepared to decide that the post would never pay expenses until it had tried every possible method. An adventurous man, George Humble, was therefore ordered to be sent up-country to draw the Indians down to trade at Richmond. 'Let his Journey be Eastward, from whence we have the greatest Expectancy' wrote the Committee, and in 1753 Potts was severely taken to task because his returns seemed so insignificant that it did not seem possible that he had seriously tried to secure a trade, nor had he sent Humble inland.

The Committee's determination was in part fixed by the interest which the Lords of Trade shewed in Labrador; for in 1752 a proposal that a company should be formed to trade to Labrador had stirred their Lordships to send an enquiry as to the state of the Company's property on the Labrador Coast and the Company had formed a Sub-Committee to draw up an answer. The Committee vouched the Charter as a title to the land, and explained the Company's recent attempts to develop its property. Ten thousand pounds had been spent in setting up the post, and men had been ordered to penetrate into the country. But this was a barren tract of land, with few inhabitants, few beaver, few furs of any kind, and but little merchandise. Any proposal to trade to Labrador could, they said, only be meant as an oblique challenge to the Charter, for the prospects of trade could not possibly warrant such a venture.

It would seem strange that the Company itself should persist in the face of so much discouragement. But two factors, apart from the fact that Richmond represented a considerable investment, told in its favour. First, Joseph Isbister, now Chief at Churchill, gave encouraging reports derived from his early experience on the Eastmain that the Nascopie Indians never traded with either the English or the French but that they might be enticed down to trade by neighbouring Indians. It proved difficult to get the coastal Indians to go in pursuit of the Nascopies, but in December 1754 an Indian was sent off, spurred in part by a credit of twenty beaver and in part by a threat to cut his ears off! He was back in the following July with twelve Nascopies. But they had already sent all their furs east for trade, and in any case they reported that although they got plenty of martens there were no beaver in their country. Potts sent the Nascopies back to the interior with handsome presents to the value of a hundred and sixty beaver and they promised to come to trade at Richmond in the future, not to go east to the Atlantic coast; but although further Indians were sent inland as emissaries, the Nascopie Indians did not bring in any reasonable trade, and by 1755 the Committee was still at a loss to know whether any worth-while furs might be got from Labrador.

The second factor which determined the Committee to continue with Richmond was the hope of whale-fishing, which was strongly in mind at this time. From about 1746 to 1749 hopes of getting white whales had been, in the main, pinned to York. A special sloop, the *Whale* sloop, was sent there, and although the Committee thought no special skill was needed to get a white whale, a harpooner was also sent. It was not until 1752 that it was decided he could never catch enough whales to pay his wages, for the whales at York were very 'shy', and he was withdrawn. York was in future to get its whales by encouraging the Indians with payment in brandy. So from about 1749 whaling enthusiasm was concentrated on Churchill, where many white whales were reported to come into the river. There also two harpooners were sent—father and son at wages of £25 a year, plus £1 for every ton of oil got. No one at Churchill had any knowledge of the process of separating the blubber, and there were no cisterns for the work, but the quantity was not such as to make cisterns necessary. In 1749 the harpooner was hard at work all summer to produce only twelve casks of boiled oil, and no blubber was left. When, therefore, Richmond Fort reported in 1752 that the Little Whale River was full of white whales, the solution of the post's trade seemed obvious.

The methods of whaling at Little Whale River, as described by Potts, were quite fantastic. After the flood tide had brought the herds of whale into the mouth of the river, the Indians swarmed into the water and splashed and shouted to prevent them going out on the ebb tide. Then, as the river fell, the great sea-beasts were left stranded on the shore, and the Indians killed them at leisure. Even so, Potts found it difficult to get the hunt pursued. The Indians would do nothing 'unless I dayly make them Drunk'. They took pay in tobacco or in brandy, and he found it necessary to hold back part of the payment until the season was over so as to keep them from wandering off. To make their human barrier across the mouth of the river they needed great numbers of Indians, and he found it necessary to promise a bottle of brandy each to forty families whether they actually killed or not, in addition to payment for the carcasses. An attempt to use a net in place of the human drovers worked for only three days before the force of the outward surge of whales and water broke the net. The fishery was therefore dependent upon a massed effort by the Indians, and even when whales were plentiful good returns could not be depended on, for the Committee in London was strongly reminded that conditions of labour were dictated by an utterly different economic background from that of England. 'Whales are to be kill'd by Indians, and they are a People that can't nor won't be Commanded.'

Costly and degrading though the whale industry of the Eastmain might be, it was nevertheless attractive, and in 1753 a summer post was set up at Little Whale River, to rank as a subordinate outpost of Richmond and to serve for the whaling only, though small parties might be sent during winter or spring to tend the stores left there, to prepare for the summer season, and to give an impression of permanence and of friendliness. The Indians, as they had been from the start of the settlement, were perfectly friendly to the English and though irresponsible were only too eager to become completely dependent, but the Eskimos were still something of an enigma to the English, and were a terror to the Indians. They haunted the outpost at Little Whale River, shadowing the men on their journeys, disappearing from view with their sledges or leaping into their kayaks and paddling away to Knapp's Island off the coast. It was therefore an encouraging sign when in January 1754 young Henry Pollexfen, in charge of a small party at Little Whale River, reported that he had managed to fraternise with some Eskimos from Knapp's Island, who had been fed and given small presents. Others had come to the post and although 'Chimo' was about the only word understood by both sides, there seemed obvious goodwill and two Eskimos were taken to visit Potts at Richmond.

Watchfulness was relaxed in the face of such signs of friendliness, and early in February all the men at Little Whale River left the hut about their various duties, leaving only the apprentice boy Matthew Warden in charge. They returned to find the hut plundered of everything, including some fire-arms, and the boy carried away by the Eskimos. The men made all speed for Richmond, where there was a strong force of twenty men—albeit some of them were of little use, like the tailor of whom it was written that 'the Reason of his being Constantly Employ'd to brew, is because he has not Courage to Fire a Gun'. Potts closed the gates and put his post on guard. The fate of the poor boy hung heavy over the men, and thirteen of them volunteered to make an expedition to search for him, but Potts decided that they could not pursue the Eskimos to the islands, and that anything in the nature of a sortie might cause the boy to be murdered.

Within a few days a party of Eskimos appeared at Richmond and, after a suspicious interlude followed by the friendly cry of 'Chimo', three of them were enticed into the post. There Potts seized them and, with dramatic mime, tried to indicate that he would hold them hostages for the safe return of the boy. Marching his men in constant succession past his prisoners to give the impression of a great garrison, he hoped to impress them. He then released one of the three to convey the message which he flattered himself he had made him understand, and settled down to watch his two hostages and to hope. The two Eskimos seemed stoically indifferent until, in the middle of the night, they suddenly seized some arms which (against orders) stood in the guard-room within their reach and began to use them as bludgeons to fight for their freedom. Knowing the weapons to be loaded, and fearing for their lives, the Hudson's Bay men shot both the hostages. They still hoped that the boy might be brought to the post for exchange, and that they might trick the Eskimos. But Matthew Warden was already dead. He had been killed soon after his capture, within two hundred yards of Whale River house.

The whole story is a sickening narrative of ineptitude and suspicion. The initial act of treachery was without any doubt that of the Eskimos, and the tragedy brings the Company's normal relations with the Indians, whatever their defects, into strong contrast with this unhappy affair. It makes clear the mutual dependence of the Company and the Indians in contrast with the suspicion and the dangers of trade with the Eskimos, for after the tragedy Potts could neither get the Indians to hunt nor to kill whales; they were with the whites, against the Eskimos. The whole trade of the post was at a standstill and all were dependent on English provisions, which would not last the summer. Potts was in favour of abandoning Richmond completely, and pending an order to do so he asked for more provisions from Moose and Albany. The *Moose* sloop was sent to succour him, and the post remained, but in 1756 it was dismantled and re-built at Whale River since the whale fishery predominated in its trade and there could be no question of setting up a second vulnerable out-post; the Indians, too, had requested the removal.

But suspicion of the Eskimos, failure of the mines and lack of fur returns, had already sealed the fate of this first attempt by the Company to penetrate, and to win the trade of, the coast and the interior of Labrador. Effort had been purposeful and persistent until failure was inescapable, but the men in charge were never so sanguine as the Committee. Potts had reported in 1752 his fears that the post 'never will turn to your Honours Satisfaction', and in 1756 Henry Pollexfen Junior wrote that he was convinced that Richmond could never get a trade save at the cost of Eastmain; he 'could if dying Receive the Sacrament that not the Value of one hundred Pounds worth of Furs has been gained to your honours advantage the whole six Years this Factory has been built'. So in 1759 the Committee yielded. The post was burned so that all the iron could easily be got from the ashes, and in August Richmond was abandoned. The Company had suffered a genuine defeat. It had quite failed to get the Nascopie Indians to hunt in order to trade for English goods. The failure was due to fear of the Eskimos, which kept the Indians from hunting, and to the whale-fishery which gave them all the tobacco and brandy (and other goods) which they wanted.

The failure at Richmond left the Company in 1759 where it had stood in 1749, with no post between Cape Digges and Slude River —and the Eastmain post at Slude River was in such a broken-down state by 1762 that a programme of complete re-building had to be undertaken.

While the failures of Henley and Richmond absorbed the expanding energies of the two posts at the Bottom of the Bay, the northern posts also took their share in attempts to found new houses. With the end of the *Dobbs'* and *California*'s attempt to find a passage, general English interest in that project wilted, and it was the New World which next ventured in that direction, with an expedition from Philadelphia in 1753 and 1754. But Churchill was almost inalienably devoted to northern slooping voyages even after the Company felt that the passage itself was a dead issue. The *Churchill* sloop was therefore ordered north on a voyage of trade and discovery for 1749, to go along the west coast to Bibby Island, Seal River, Knapp's Bay, Pistol Bay and Whale Cove, then to sail round Cape Fullerton and discover as far north as possible. Joseph Isbister, Governor at Albany, was promised a share of the trade for himself 'to Excite you to push it on to the utmost extent', for the sloop had first to sail from Churchill to the Bottom of the Bay and back. She provided adequate commentary on the difficulty of tying shipping to an exact time-table in arctic conditions by arriving at Churchill so late in 1749 that the voyage had to be postponed till 1750; the delay was contributed to by the misfortune of the *Mary*, damaged on her arrival from England in Churchill River, and the episode admirably shews the chain-reaction of delays in this trade. But the interlude gave the Committee a chance to modify the instructions, with an order to attempt trade with the Eskimos, and to repeat that the *Churchill* must on no account be prevented from going north in 1750, and in every succeeding year. Then in 1751 the *New Churchill* sloop was sent out for the purpose, 'the Strongest that ever was sent into the Country', and her master was held to his task of advancing trade to the northward by the Committee's knowledge that he had been guilty of a private trade in martens. Even so the returns were not encouraging; but the Committee were convinced that this was because of the poverty of the Indians and urged that the sloop should go further afield, if possible as far as Wager Bay.

The men at Churchill were in agreement with the Committee on this. The basic troubles over the building of the post were largely ended when the secondary battery had been sited and erected at Cape Merry (a point upon which the Committee insisted despite the objections of James Isham as Governor, of his successor Robert Pilgrim and of Robert Evinson, the military engineer sent out to site the guns). The battery was finished in 1749, and the Committee ordered the guns to be kept constantly manned during the time of open water. But when peace with France reduced the danger, the complement of Churchill was reduced to forty-two men, and the Committee's instructions began to dwell less upon defence and more upon trade, exploration, provisions and the use of cattle, especially upon the need to use deer for haulage instead of demanding a constant succession of horses. The building of a wharf, the construction of a crane, re-building and repairing the post and the battery, provided routine duties. But trade remained small although an extra six men were allotted to Churchill in 1751. Some of the difficulty was ascribed to the 'natural aversion' which the Indians felt for Churchill, some to the blandishments (strongly denied) of the masters of York, and some to the 'many illicit practices' amounting to an 'Epidemical Corruption' which were tolerated at Churchill.

The notion that all was not well with the management of Churchill began to gather weight as Ferdinand Jacobs rose to importance there. He had gone to the post in 1732 as an apprentice, and had continued in steady employment there, a 'Diligent Sober Young Man' keeping the books and helping to manage the trade. In 1740 he was made Deputy Chief, and in 1752 he began to command the post. Except for the year 1759–60, when he came to England on leave, he remained in command at Churchill until he was transferred to York in 1762. But it was as Deputy Chief that he began to inveigh against the practices of the Governors under whom he served, and their predecessors. He undoubtedly had an unrivalled knowledge of the business of the post and of the fur trade in general, including the evasive issues of the Double Standard of Trade, the Overplus, Credit, and the way in which presents to Indians dovetailed in with the alleged private trapping of the Governors. In 1756 he was himself called upon to prove that a suspiciously large parcel of otters which he said he had trapped was in fact the produce of his own hunting and not the outcome of presents (of the Company's goods) which he had made to Indians. He then protested his length of service and skill in the trade—twenty-four years' service and never once home, and now in command of a post which gave more trouble and fatigue than any two in the service. It was an impressive record, in itself a sign of the technical skill upon which the Company could now rely; and it qualified Jacobs to hold opinions on policy as well as on detail.

Much of Jacob's energy was absorbed in building, as seemed inevitable at Churchill, despite the cost and time which building in stone had involved. By 1754 he had completed the south-west curtain, put up the pediment of the gate, pulled down the south-east flank of the west bastion and re-built it to the height of the base of the parapet, 'which Part of the Building is very Strong Regular and well Built and makes the Front of the Factory appear grand and Beautifull and I will venture to say will Stand to the End of Many Ages'. He set to work on the task himself, and in 1757 he reported that he hoped to complete the whole of the south-west square of the fort except about thirty feet of the rampart wall of the curtain which had been done by Isbister and which would stand for many centuries. That year he had finished fifty-nine feet of the interior wall of the south-west curtain, up to a height of twelve feet; and though he complained that it was arduous work for himself and one mason yet he boasted that better work was never done.

Though Jacobs complied with the standing instructions to send the sloop north from Churchill every summer, his long experience led him to urge as early as 1752 (his first year in command) that little would ever be achieved in the way of discovery as long as only one sloop was sent and the commander shewed no more ardour and diligence than had gone into recent voyages. But the Committee were not purposeless in sending the annual voyage north. In 1753 Jacobs was told (as he already knew from Indian report) that between latitude 61° and 64° there was a river called *Kish-stack-ewen*, which ran a considerable way up into the country. He was to send the sloop to explore the river, and he revised the sloop's instructions and impressed upon the Committee that he 'heartily wished a full discovery'.

But although Jacobs was quite certain that the river existed, year after year the sloop failed to find it and instructions to find and explore the *Kish-stack-ewen* had to be repeated, both from London and from Jacobs. It was not until 1760 that anything certain emerged, with the report that 'The Straight but I think more Properly River being found to the Northward, for a Description and Account of which, I refer you to the Sloop Masters Account is a Lucky Event'. Captain Christopher, in the *Churchill* sloop, had found the river and had sailed a hundred miles up it, returning with the conviction that this was a river, not a strait, but that even so it offered great hopes of being able to carry the Company's trade into the heart of the country. He had in fact sailed into Chesterfield's, or Bowden's Inlet, which he called the Grand River.

Christopher was ordered to press further on up the 'river' in 1761, and in 1762 Jacobs sent both the *Churchill* sloop and the *Strivewell* cutter under command of Moses Norton. The cutter was to push on when the way became impossible for the sloop, and Norton managed to penetrate two hundred and thirty miles up the inlet, until he came to an end in a lake or bay, with no outlet to the west. Next year the sloop was sent to explore an inlet near Whale Cove, which it found to be a kind of bay, full of ridges and shoal water. The search was still on, and in 1764 another opening on the north-west side of Marble Island was to be searched. But there was no urgent enthusiasm to search for a passage which always eluded the search, once the *Kish-stack-ewen* had been explored.

Here also, therefore, as at Henley and at Richmond, the Company had shewn considerable enterprise and determination during the post-Dobbs period, and had ultimately met with a disappointment which was all the more real because here also it was accompanied by a falling-off in trade. But it was neither the building programme nor the probing of the coast northwards which was held responsible for the decline in Churchill's trade. The causes alleged were always wars among the Indians, lack of trade-goods, and the counter-attractions of York. The small trade in the years 1755, 1757 and 1758, in particular, was explained by the non-arrival of the Indians from Athabaska—a sign of the way in which the Company's trade at Churchill had begun to draw down the Chipewyan Indians from Lake Athabaska—and Jacobs proposed as a remedy to send William Grover 'into the Countrey with a Carefull Indian' in the summer of 1759 when the Chipewyans came down again and could accompany the Englishman on his journey.

Jacobs, like most servants of the Company, and the Committee itself, had always entertained some such notion of inland voyages, and in his first proposal on the subject, in 1753, he had recommended that James Irwin should be retained in the service since he was 'very necessary in going *Patrooner* to the woods'. This was a use of words which revealed a transition from the French technique of sending a *bourgeois* inland, to command and lead an expedition, but shews the influence of the Dutch fur trade of New York and Albany in transferring the Dutch term for the French concept to the English fur trade. No report of these proposed journeys survives, and Grover subsequently proved himself a most indifferent traveller. But Churchill's trade recovered to over 13,000 beaver in 1762 and to over 29,000 in 1763, largely because a band from a new tribe who had never seen either a European or a factory came down to trade in

1761. Jacobs traded 'largely' with them and maintained the upward trend of his returns. The Company's trade was expanding towards those fur preserves from which the successors of de la Vérendrye drew the furs which made Montreal wealthy.

BOOKS FOR REFERENCE

HUDSON'S BAY RECORD SOCIETY—Vol. XII.
GIRAUD, Marcel—*Le Métis Canadien* (Paris, 1945).
MORTON, Arthur S.—*A History of the Canadian West to 1870–71* (London, 1939).

CHAPTER XLIII

THE COMPANY PENETRATES TO THE PRAIRIES; HENDAY, SMITH AND WAGGONER

While the opening of new trade and the loyalty of the distant Chipewyans from Athabaska marked the revival of the returns from Churchill, so that normal trade got predominance over discovery to the northward, York Factory began to take the lead in serious and successful exploration. This was perhaps the more remarkable because the achievements (which were quite outstanding) were fostered, directed and organised, by James Isham, who held firm and well-grounded views on the limitations of any policy of expansion into the interior.

True, Isham had already had the task of setting up the outpost at Flamborough House. But Flamborough had been built so near to the main factory at York that it cannot be considered as an attempt at expansion; it was a purely defensive outpost, designed to forestall the interlopers whom the Committee feared in 1749. The house was built by 1750, but as the urgency of the opposition diminished the need for such a post declined, and by 1753 Isham was told that he might shut down Flamborough House if he wished.

Freed from this responsibility, he was able to give his attention to other problems, and in particular to a review of his convictions about inland posts. At the time when he gave his evidence before the 1749 Parliamentary Committee he had been quite convinced that inland posts were not practicable. The rivers, he said, were so full of shoals that boats could not get inland with reasonable cargoes of goods, no corn could be grown as far as he knew, and the Indians would, in any case, rather starve than turn to farming. So the problem of feeding such a post seemed insuperable unless provisions were to be carried inland (as at Henley) or unless Indians were to be diverted from hunting furs to get food. Moreover such inland posts could only secure trade by diverting it from the posts in the Bay, and they would not have behind them the marshes which enabled the Bay-side posts to procure so much of their food from the goose and partridge hunts. Nelson River, in any case, was particularly inappropriate as a means of access 'being above 40 miles up that River, full of intricate Sholes, and Narrow channels, with Deep falls'.

But although Isham was convinced that inland posts were impracticable—certainly until the French had been driven from control of the Lake Winnipeg area—he was equally convinced that it was folly not to send emissaries inland to make peace and to draw down the Indians to trade. He even conceded at an early stage of his career that inland posts might follow such voyages and he put forward an argument for a small post at the Cumberland Lake junction of the routes to York and to Churchill, which would serve for York in much the same capacity as Henley served for Albany. Greater experience of the difficulties of inland transport convinced him that such a post would need to be at least a hundred miles inland to do any good, and at that distance the costs and difficulties of transport would begin to mount. With so many factors balancing in his mind, Isham was not set against penetration inland; indeed he held it an error to 'sitt quiet and unconcern'd while the french as an old saying, not only Beats the Bush but run's away with the Hair also'. He was sure that there were men who, with suitable encouragement, would venture inland either to bring the Indians down to trade 'or to give such a Discription of the Country that a Settlement might be made their'. So great was Isham's faith in the value of sending overland voyagers of the Kelsey type that he thought the best way of opening up the Coppermine territory would be by sending 'two Experienc'd men that is of a healthy Constitution' overland on that quest; he proved to have a sound grasp of the problem here, for within a generation the mouth of the Coppermine had been investigated by just such a traveller as he had envisaged.

During his latter days in command at York, Isham found his instructions from London entirely in keeping with these mature convictions. He was told first to get together all available information about the hinterland of York, and he was then to choose a suitable man to send far inland with presents to the Indians. When in 1753 he sent home a proposal for a post up Severn River, reporting that the French had a settlement there, he was told to send the sloop first, and if the French were in possession to decide on a place to build. But when the sloop-master's journal was sent home the Committee felt disappointed and reproved Isham for accepting Indian rumour of a French house when none existed. His survey was deemed inadequate, and it appeared that the Severn became impassable except for small canoes within a few days' journey from its mouth. Isham himself reported that it dwindled to a 'trivial Brooke' before it got inland 'parallel to Henley House' and there was good reason to doubt its value as an axis for trade. Yet the Committee so far accorded with Isham's main desire to set up what may be called a 'defence and blandishment' post on the same lines as Henley that they accorded permission for a log tent at Severn while the river was open. They were against a serious trading post, which they regarded as an 'Artifice of the Natives, who doubtless to save themselves a little Trouble, would have us make a Settlement on allmost every River that Runs into the Bay', but though investigation revealed that the Severn was navigable to the Company's ships only twelve miles up from its mouth, the Committee nevertheless, in 1756, accepted Isham's pressure and conceded permission for a house with ten men.

The Severn post, in fact, opened a new approach to the lands of the Crees. It was so convenient that it soon became obvious that the Indians would frequent it as long as the Company maintained a trade there, and complaints were soon on hand from Albany that the Indians who used to trade at Albany were now content with Severn. So, despite an inauspicious start and apathy from the London Committee, the post there persisted.

But at the time more importance was attached to another of Isham's proposals. While he was suggesting the establishment of Severn he was telling the Committee (once more) that 'if a proper Person were sent a great way up into the Country with presents to the Indians it may be a means of drawing down many of the Natives to Trade'. The Committee were in a mood to neglect no opportunity to extend their trade and interests, and Isham was told to choose any suitable man and to send him inland. He chose Anthony Henday.

Henday was described as a bold and enterprising man, who volunteered for this task. His background was not particularly auspicious, for he had only been recruited in 1750, an outlawed smuggler from the Isle of Wight who was paid ten pounds a year as a labourer and net-maker. But he had already shown his capacity for travel with Indians, for he had been used by Isham to collect the data on distances from York which the Committee required. With a party of Indians he had walked on the ice up the Hayes River to Fox River, up the Fox and on to Split Lake, thence down the Nelson to its mouth and so home to York Fort. Isham duly reported the distances involved, with the suggestion that an additional post might be built at the Lower Fork of Nelson River. This was in February and March of 1754, and in June of the same year Henday was sent inland once more. He was to keep one trusty Indian as a constant companion, and was to travel with a band of Cree Indians who were returning from trade and who promised to take him to their own country, the Saskatchewan, and then to pass him on to the Earchithinues. These people, members of the Blackfeet, had not yet come down to trade by the Bay—they had not mastered the use of the canoe—and Henday was to make presents to them, as to all others whom he met, and to encourage them to catch beaver and to bring them down to the Bay.

Henday and his companions went by the route which he had already travelled on foot, up the Hayes to the Fox River; then, however, they took the southern branch of the Fox and so, by a route which subsequently dropped out of use, and which is difficult to check from his Journal, across from the Hayes River to the Nelson, to Cross Lake and so up to Moose Lake on the Lower Saskatchewan, which he reached on 16th July, 1754. Henday paddled through Moose Lake to the Saskatchewan and westwards, plagued with mosquitoes, to turn south on the Birch River and enter Saskeram Lake. He left Saskeram Lake by the Carrot River and after two days' paddling left the canoes and marched south-west-by-south to find 'our Indian Families in a starving condition'. His interest in the Indians and their families, and their acceptance of him, was undoubtedly facilitated by the fact that by this time he had settled down with what he described as his 'bed-fellow' from among the Indians with whom he was travelling. She performed all the normal functions of a squaw for him, and very greatly assisted his journey. But she does not appear in the official copy of Henday's Journal which Isham sent home, for the Chief Factor had personal reason to know the Committee's views about co-habitation with Indian women, and had only been confirmed in command at York in 1751 on condition that he neither kept Indian women in the post himself nor permitted others to do so. Henday's 'bed-fellow' therefore does not figure in the official copy of his Journal; but he could not have lived and travelled as an Indian nor, in all probability, could he have gained acceptance as he did, without her help.

Once on the prairies, journeying south-west-by-west, Henday and his companions soon assuaged their hunger; they killed many red deer, and though Henday found the flesh coarse and not to be compared with moose, yet it was a great relief from the fish diet on which they had subsisted so far. They turned west to strike the South Branch of the Saskatchewan a little to the north of the modern Saskatoon, crossing the river in canoes which the Indians made of willow and covered with parchment moose skins. Then, moving north-west from the South Branch over level prairie land, Henday picked up traces of the 'Archthinese Natives' whom he had come to seek, and then struck the North Branch of the Saskatchewan near the Elbow, where the river turns north-east. He followed the course of the river for twelve days, of which two were taken up in feasting with a band of Assinipoet (Assiniboine) Indians, and one in resting. In his nine days of walking across the 'Muscuty plains' beside the North Branch, hunting as he went, Henday reckoned he had covered just a hundred miles. Despite the plenty of game, he wrote at the beginning of September that 'we are yet above 400 in number, two thirds of whom live chiefly on fruit'. The buffalo had taken 'the route upwards', following the river north-west, which was the reason why, although two of them had come into his camp on horseback, the main body of the 'Archthinue Natives' was proving so hard to find.

As Henday turned away west and south-west from the course of the North Branch on 5th September (somewhere in the region of the modern Battleford) he met a band of Eagle Indians, remarkable for the fact that the men went entirely naked; they had never previously traded with any European but he persuaded them to hunt furs and to take them down to the Bay. For a week he travelled west-south-west across the prairie, his feet swollen but otherwise in perfect health, his greatest hardship the warmth of the weather.

Now Henday reported finding buffalo for the first time. His first experience was to find a dead beast, left by the Archthinue; his second was to kill a bull and to find it 'nothing but skin and bone'. Then the Indians killed three, and the next day (13th September) the party was in among the herds 'grazing like English Cattle'. They killed seven that day, and next day Henday went hunting with the Indians 'all armed with Bows and Arrows killed seven, fine sport. We beat them about, lodging twenty arrows in one beast. So expert are the Natives, that they will take the arrows out of them when they are foaming and raging with pain, and tearing the ground up with their feet and horns until they fall down'. Next day they found 'the Buffalo so numerous obliged to make them sheer out of our way', with packs of wolves hovering round to pick the carcasses which the Indians left; for in such plenty the Indians often took only the tongue and left the carcass. Henday himself was 'well stock with tongues'.

Henday's gifts were not literary, and the first English description of a buffalo hunt does nothing to impress upon the reader the stupendous wealth which confronted him. The comparatively easy living which he had enjoyed since striking the Saskatchewan had probably dulled his appreciation of even the coarser pleasures which the buffalo brought, and it is only from later descriptions that it is possible to imagine the plenty, and the slaughter, among which Henday moved. The first Englishman, in all probability the first white man, to see the buffalo hunt, does nothing to rouse the imagination. He does, however, make it clear that the hunt was with bows and arrows only, ammunition being scarce and costly, and so he reveals the possibilities of the frantic waste of the great wealth of the buffalo which later came when the hunt was made with guns, and when the fur trade provided a market for the pemmican which could be made from the hunt. For even with bows and arrows, and hunting for their own immediate subsistence, the Indians killed great numbers 'only taking what they choosed to carry'.

So Henday journeyed through September, in a general direction south-west-by-west. He bought a horse to carry his provisions, and he saw several wild horses. Still in the 'Muscuty Plains', he wrote that 'I cannot describe the fineness of the Weather, and the pleasant country I am now in'.

It was the 1st October, about sixty miles (by his reckoning) short of the Red Deer River of Alberta, that he made serious contact with the Archthinues, a term applied to the four equestrian tribes, the Gros Ventres, the Blackfeet, Bloods and Piegans (the last two being sub-groups of the Blackfeet). Seven tents of the Bloods came to Henday's camp 'the men all mounted on Horse-back, with Bows and Arrows, and bone spears and darts'. After exchanging gifts, the Indians rode off to join their main body, and Henday travelled on, sometimes through 'Buffalo in great droves', in a south-west-by-westerly direction until 14th October, by which time he had reached a point somewhere west of the present town of Balermo.

Here he met the main body of the Blackfeet, assembled under their Great Leader. It was an imposing sight—about two hundred tents pitched in two rows, the Leader's tent large enough to hold fifty people. Henday was welcomed, the grand pipes were smoked in complete silence, and then buffalo meat was served and talk began. But neither at the feast nor on the next morning could Henday impress on the Leader the advantages to be gained by trade with the Bay. They had their horses, fine tractable animals, on which they hunted the buffalo with bows and arrows. They never lacked food, but they had been told that those who traded at the Bay were often starved on the journey (as Henday privately admitted in his Journal). Moreover, they had no knowledge of canoes, and the sum of the conversation was that the Leader said it was a long way, and his young men could neither travel in canoes nor be without buffalo meat; to which Henday replied that it could easily be accomplished if the Blackfeet could gain acquaintance with a canoe, and 'could eat Fish, which they never do'.

Before parting from the Blackfeet, Henday went to see them hunt the buffalo on horseback. He found them most expert, able to drop a buffalo with one or two arrows. For himself, he was fully occupied in managing his horse!

The Blackfeet then moved away to the west, promising to see Henday again in the spring. Some of the 'Assinipoets' moved north, while Henday and his party moved west-south-west, with the women beginning to work up beaver garments ready for the winter. Gentle frosts and snow had already begun to come upon them, and Henday was astonished to find his Indians so improvident that they preferred to kill buffalo, and a few beaver for feasting, instead of laying in a store of beaver for clothing. They wandered in a desultory manner, with many days on which they 'travelled none', but they got out of the 'Muscuty Plains' on 29th October, getting into a level kind of tall woods and plenty of creeks, after which they began to turn more northwards. Henday reached his farthest point westwards on 21st November, when he was about in latitude 51° 50′ North and longitude 114° West. He was almost certainly within sight of the Rockies, though his Journal does not mention the fact; but beaver and otters were plentiful, and there were several days of drumming, dancing and feasting.

As Henday began his return journey, gently wandering south-south-east, the Indians began to disperse, and by 4th December his party consisted only of himself, two men, five women and four children. The Indians had neither powder nor shot, and were utterly dependent on Henday. Beaver, however, could be got by breaking open the beaver-houses, without expenditure of shot, so that Henday had no qualms about husbanding his resources.

The party turned east and then north-east, catching their last glimpse of the Rockies on 24th December, and moved slowly in the direction of the North Branch of the Saskatchewan for a couple of months. They reached the river on 3rd March, and travelled north-east on the ice for a couple of days. The water was then already beginning to flow over the ice, and by 7th March Henday's Indians were vigorously at work collecting materials for canoe-building, while other bands were working alongside of them and just downstream. It was a time of feasting and dancing once more, and Henday found opportunities to solicit several bands to avoid the French and trade at the Bay with the English. Moose, buffalo and bear were killed, and the weeks passed happily. Henday gave away his horse on 8th April; on 20th he saw the Indians conduct their traditional Dog-feast, and on 23rd he displayed his flag in honour of St. George and explained the ceremony to the Indians. That day the ice in the river broke up. Geese and swans were flying north, and Henday killed a swan with his bow and arrow. The mosquitoes came, stinging without mercy to spoil the idyll, but on 28th April Henday at last embarked for York Factory in his canoe and paddled thirty-four miles down-stream in company with twenty canoes of Assiniboines.

As the North Branch of the Saskatchewan bore him down-stream, Henday found his flotilla of canoes steadily augmented until by the time he reached the French trade-post Fort la Corne, on 23rd May, he had over sixty canoes in company. The Blackfeet had kept their promise, and met him en route; but, wrote Henday, 'I did my Endeavour to get some of them down to the Fort; but all in vain'. They did, however, trade furs—wolves, beaver and foxes—with the Indians who were going down to the Bay, and even with Henday himself, so much so that in all Henday's sixty-odd canoes there was scarce a gun, kettle, hatchet or knife left.

A further disappointment which awaited Henday was that he proved unable to get his flotilla safely past the French traders, who supplied the Indians liberally with brandy and water, and traded over a thousand prime winter skins before Henday could get them under way for York once more. The experience was repeated at the lower French post at Basquia, and though Henday increased his strength to seventy canoes he had obviously lost a great and valuable trade to the French. He was now reduced once more to a fish diet, which he found insipid without salt (having expended the last of his stock), but he made his way without serious incident by the same route as he had used in his outward journey, till 'on the 20th day of this month of june we arrived at the fort, where we were kindly received'.

It was a prosaic end to a prosaic narrative. But the achievement completely outshines the narrative in which it is told. In just under a year this Englishman, with only four years' experience of the country, had travelled over a thousand miles alone with his Indians to the foot of the Rockies, had wintered there with them, and had safely returned. He was able to speak French, but the Committee had doubted his ability to measure his journey at all accurately, and he seems to have been such a man as was capable of doing and of feeling far more than he could commit to paper—so much so that the Committee confidently assumed that it was Isham who drafted his Journal. Even so, Henday's matter-of-fact narrative repays detailed study, for he was a shrewd observer and in his own cryptic way he got his thoughts on paper.

To the Company at that time his most important revelation was the way in which de la Vérendrye and his sons had driven the French trade westwards from Lake Winnipeg and had sited their posts on the Saskatchewan so as to intercept the trade coming to the Bay. Hitherto such information had come only from Indian rumour, not to be completely trusted since the Indians had such an obvious interest in getting the Company to set up inland posts. But after Henday's return there could be no doubt of the strategic siting of the French posts 'the Real proof of which' said Isham 'is plain by the Acct. of Capn Henday's Journey'.

Even the detailed and important evidence which Henday brought, however, did nothing to change the Committee's attitude or intentions. Henday had been sent inland to persuade the Blackfeet to keep the peace, to hunt furs and to bring them down to York. He never pretended to any success in this, but after studying his Journal the Committee merely repeated their conclusion that settlement inland was impossible 'because only within 4 days travel from York Fort the River Ceases to be Navigable for anything but the smallest canoes'. They were determined to encourage everything with the least shadow of a chance of increasing their trade, but they would not build inland up the Nelson River. This was indeed a negative conclusion for a great deal of very positive evidence, all of which should have led to a different decision.

Henday had been forced to pass the French both in going and in coming, and on each occasion his remarks are most stimulating. He had no idea what sort of welcome he might expect from the French, and in writing back to York just before he arrived at their first house on his outward voyage he had, with a forthright simple generosity which well became him, said that 'if the French should shoot me, I have nothing to lay to Your Hon Charge'. He was at that juncture still ten days' travel from the French post at Basquia (The Pas) on the Saskatchewan (the post built by the younger Vérendrye in 1748) and when he arrived there on 22nd July he was pleasantly surprised at the kind and friendly treatment accorded him by the two Frenchmen left in possession while their companions and their master (de la Corne) took the furs down to Montreal. He soon found that the Assiniboines of the vicinity were 'strongly attached to the French interest' and, though friendly enough, saw no reason why they should make the journey to York.

His experience with the French on his return journey was far more illuminating, for then he saw them during trade-time, and his conclusion was that although during his wanderings, especially at the rendezvous where canoes were made on the North Branch of the

Saskatchewan, many Indians 'in the French interest' had accepted his presents and had promised not to trade with the French, yet they could not hold to their resolution. Paddling downstream, he came first to the French outpost of La Corne, founded a year previously, in 1753, about ten miles below the Forks, and then to the main post at Basquia, which he had passed on his way inland. There was at some time a further outpost between these two posts (for the French outposts were slightly-built houses, easily abandoned) but Henday does not mention it. His conclusion, after seeing the French engaged in trade, was that 'It is surprising to observe what an influence the French have over the Natives', and that 'The French talk Several Languages to perfection: they have the advantage of us in every shape; and if they had Brazile tobacco, which they have not, would entirely cut off our trade'.

Watching in impotence while the French traded, Henday decided that many of his Indians would part with all they had if only they could persuade the French to take their heavy furs. But the French would take nothing but prime winter furs, and when trade was over Henday noted that several of his Assiniboines then gave the heavy furs, left on their hands because they were refused by the French, to some of their friends with instructions on the trade they were to drive at York.

This interesting transaction was the last stage in the fur-trading system of the hinterland which Henday revealed. The Assiniboines and Crees who came to York were, when his Journal is pointedly analysed, the 'factors' of those who refused to come. As he wandered over the Muscuty Plains and among the creeks and woods at the foot of the Rockies Henday had tried in vain to get his companions to hunt for furs. They met him with knowing looks and, though they idly refused to hunt except for food, they promised that when the time came to start back for York they would have all the furs they wanted. His own band were not the only Indians in that far distant land 'who yearly visited our Settlements'; Hudson Bay goods were known there—as were the hardships of the journey—and Henday soon came to realise that the bulk of the furs brought to the Bay were not caught by those who brought them. Those enterprising intermediaries (with whom he was himself travelling) were able to spend an idle winter, drumming, feasting and dancing, hunting only for the pot, because they brought inland from the Bay the ironware and guns which enabled them to buy furs in the spring. His surmise proved correct (indeed it was more than a surmise, for his squaw had told him of the practice) and he himself conducted a very profitable trade. Old axes, guns, knives, powder and shot—all were traded, and Henday grasped and reported the fact that this intermediate trade in European goods was an added argument for direct contact between the Company and the hunting Indians, whether they were Blackfeet or Assiniboines. Those Indians who came down to trade had promised Isham that they would add their persuasions to Henday's. But 'they never opened their mouths' when the problem came up for discussion, and Henday grasped the reason, 'for if they could be brought down to trade, the others would be obliged to trap their own Furs: which at present two thirds of them do not'.

When such a revelation of the middleman Indian, able to refrain from fur-hunting, is added to the first-hand evidence of the way in which the French took the prime furs and left the heavy stuff to go down to the Bay, often in charge of an Indian factor, and to the reasoned refusal of the Blackfeet to make the long journey, it becomes obvious that Henday's contribution to the logical argument for penetration to the interior was as important as his contribution to the knowledge of routes and methods for such penetration. This, however, was a contribution which was not so quickly assessed and accepted as his achievement in travelling. That was something which immediately appealed. The Committee were 'much pleas'd' to hear of his journey, and hoped that others would be encouraged to do the same. He was given a gratuity of £20—and though that may seem little enough for the feat which he had accomplished, it was a bonus payment of two years' wages for him.

The Committee's reading of Henday's Journal as a proof of the folly of building up the Nelson River was not a sign of any intransigent determination not to go inland. It was rather a sign of the genuine reason which they avouched for that decision—an acceptance of the serious defects of the Hayes and the Nelson rivers as routes to the interior. Elsewhere, in places where this did not apply, the menace of the *coureurs de bois,* and of the small outposts from which they circulated, caused a different reaction, particularly at the Bottom of the Bay. There the *coureurs* continued to intercept the Company's trade despite the founding of Henley House. They were reported to have built a log house above the English, and although that proved to be only an Indian rumour, Albany's trade was industriously 'intercepted', and the Committee prepared to resist by setting up an enquiry on the French Standard of Trade and the quality of their goods. French prices seemed high—twenty-five, thirty or even forty beaver for a gun were reported, and six for a yard of cloth—but there seemed to be two great points in favour of the

French. They actually traded no brandy ('a hot fiery stuff and very disagreeable to taste', said the Albany report), but they gave away enough to make the Indians drunk, and then traded their other goods; and they had their goods and their posts in places where the Indians caught the furs, and so saved them a tedious journey.

There was nothing new in any of this, but it was as well that the Committee should again be reminded of the basic conditions of their trade. The conclusions were accepted. Henley was maintained despite the two disasters there, and at the time of Henday's Journal (which came hard on the heels of the massacre of 1755) the Committee had even resolved to build yet further inland. Henley had apparently done something, but not enough; the French were reported to have carried off a great cargo in 1754 and to dominate every waterway leading to the Bay. Four canoes of them had got from the North Branch of the river above Henley to within a hundred miles of York Fort—and the Committee were also aware that war with France might break out at any moment.

The actual announcement of the outbreak of the Seven Years' War was sent out to the Bay as a postscript to the Instructions of 1756. The Master at Albany had been instructed in 1755 that he must send further inland to counter the French, to build a log-tent, or perhaps even a strong house like Henley, to prevent the Indians from being molested, as far above Henley as Henley was above Albany. His strength was brought up to forty-two men for the purpose, but the project fell through because of the murder of William Lamb and his five companions at Henley in January, 1755. So the Committee's proposals to take a counter-offensive from the Bottom of the Bay came to nothing. Moose and Albany remained on the defensive, pleading that 'nothing prevents the increase of your Trade in these Parts but Our great Enemys the French'. But the determination to maintain Henley, and the proposal to go even further inland, show that the decision not to follow up Henday's voyage with a settlement was not due to lethargy but to a realistic appreciation of transport difficulties.

Even at York, Henday's return in 1755 was by no means the end of the matter. Within a week, on 28th June, he was sent off again, with a white companion, William Grover, 'to gain the forreign Indians down to trade'. But they were back at the fort by 2nd July, for Grover proved unequal to the journey, 'being Jaded by the time they got 10 Mile up Steel River'. That ended any further exploration from York for 1755; and Henday himself had begun to feel the results of his travels, for in 1756 he refused an engagement for three years at twenty pounds a year 'saying He hath not Been wright well since His last Expedition'. However, he went inland again in 1756, instructed by Isham (despite the Committee's conviction that the only way to enlarge the trade of York was to *bring down* the natives to trade, and that there was no chance of settling up the Hayes or Nelson) 'to take a true and Exact acct. of the place he entemates, for a Settlement, computed 500 miles up'. His sickness was something more than an excuse to evade a contract, for he returned to York on account of sickness, and during the winter he accepted an engagement for five years, with a bonus of one year's wages (£20) at the end of the period. (Henday, incidentally, saved almost all his pay, and at the end of his time, when he came home in 1762, he drew £112 15*s.* 9*d.* of the £120 which he had earned—which perhaps provides some evidence to support Andrew Graham's statement that he left the Company's service because he was abused by the ships' companies for not buying luxuries from them.) In the winter of 1758 he was sent to winter out from York Fort at Ship River—an increasingly common practice and in itself indicative of the way in which the English were learning to live in the country—and he fell so ill 'of a cold' there that the Chief (Humphrey Marten, during Isham's absence in England) got seriously worried and sent a party of men to bring him home in March. He was then employed about the post as a net-maker and fisherman, and in June 1759 he went inland again to the Blackfeet country on the borders of the Rockies.

This time Henday had with him a nameless Frenchman who had drifted down to York in the summer of 1758 and whom Humphrey Marten had treated well since he was mindful that the French of the interior had acted kindly towards Henday. He also had some Blackfeet, for his early journey had produced the result that in 1758 five canoes of 'Bloody Indians' had come down to trade. With him, too, went another Englishman, Joseph Smith. No journal of the expedition has survived, but the Frenchman soon returned to York, lame, while the English went on with the Indians. They returned in June 1760 once more after an absence of a year all but a week, in company with sixty-one canoes.

For Joseph Smith this was not his first voyage to the interior, though it was his longest. He had even more experience of this way of travelling and of living than Henday, for in 1756 he had gone inland from York with Joseph Waggoner as his companion, travelling with a band of Swan River Indians. Smith's Journal survives, but its crude and cryptic English makes impossible any attempt to follow him accurately. It appears most probable that they went up Hayes

River and so over to Cross Lake, then up East River and so to Lake Winnipeg, 'Wineapeck Sockahagan', which they reached on 22nd September. They seem, in fact, to have followed the route which the *coureur* Joseph la France had described to Arthur Dobbs and the Parliamentary Committee of 1749. From Lake Winnipeg they travelled to the Saskatchewan, and left their canoes on 18th October. Then they came to the French post on Cedar Lake (Fort Bourbon) at the end of October, and found it empty. Moving south and south-east they came to 'the hills' and found them 'very lofty' on 11th November, and they spent the winter wandering, hunting, feasting and resting, beside the Assiniboine.

Here they met Frenchmen, first two, then six, who were also wintering with the Indians. The French had no powder to trade, and (perhaps for this reason) the Indians took kindly to the English, even those who had never heard of the Hudson's Bay Company. So much so that they threatened to retaliate when the French muttered that they would kill the English. The tribes which Smith and Waggoner were in search of were bent on the war-path and had no goods to trade, but the Englishmen 'lay by' from mid-December to mid-February, and then worked their way back to Swan River ('Soon Cipie' in their Journal) in March 1757. There they built canoes and, after witnessing the same sort of 'brandy trade' at Fort Bourbon as Henday had seen on the Saskatchewan, they set out for York Fort, going down by way of Oxford and Knee Lakes.

Smith and Waggoner had penetrated well south of Lake Winnipeg and had cut into the French system in much the same way as Henday, but well to the east of his incursion into the 'Muscuty Plains' of the upper Saskatchewan. This was more pioneer work, and in fact it opened up a route from York to Playgreen Lake and so to Lake Winnipeg and the Saskatchewan, Sturgeon-weir River, and the Churchill in one direction, to the Assiniboine and Red River in another. But although the Indians had told the English of a rumour that a post was planned for Little Playgreen Lake, no such post was established. The route, however, was not allowed to lapse because no post was founded. 'The two Josephs'—as Isham affectionately called them—were sent back inland in June 1757, after a bare week at York. This time they went through Lake Winnipegosis to Manitoba Lake and so across country to the Assiniboine. Here 'in the Baren grownd', they met the Sinipoets (the Assiniboines) and saw a new method of killing the buffalo. 'Ther was a pound as the maed to kill the boffler in and that day wandey [Wednesday] ther was 67 cam in at onese.' On another day eighty-six were killed in a pound, and at this stage it is perhaps not surprising that the travellers 'lay by' for many days together. In the spring they again made their canoes on Swan River, and worked their way down to York, to arrive on 30th June at the head of a flotilla of fifty-seven canoes.

Isham (returned from England) now sent an English servant Isaac Batt and an 'Esquimay Boy' George Potts (Isham's personal servant and probably the half-breed son of John Potts the surgeon who had commanded at Richmond) inland with the Sturgeon River Indians whom 'the 2 Josephs' had brought down. Smith himself also went inland again in 1758, and again he found that the French had no powder to trade; they had indeed brought 'sum backer' but it was 'veary bad' and certainly not to be compared to the Brazil twist tobacco which the English supplied.

Henday, therefore, was by no means the only servant of the Company with valuable experience of inland travel by the time of his second journey inland; in fact Smith was if anything more experienced than he, and the French in the interior were being faced with serious competition. The war, too, had begun to cut French supplies to Canada, and to cut even more severely the English cloths upon which they relied for the Indian trade. True, Wolfe had not yet captured Quebec, and in June 1758 Indians had told Isham that the French inland had received a letter from Canada with a 'recruit of 10 Frenchmen'. The 'Year of Victories' had not dawned and even after Pitt's resounding triumphs and the conquest of Canada the small garrison of York was kept on the alert by a report that the French would attack by land and sea in the fall of 1759. Yet French confidence and purpose were faltering and if the ultimate struggle for possession still seemed undecided, Isham was nevertheless able to write in July 1758 that 'I now by Experiance find a great advance in trade' by sending inland expeditions. His trade had increased despite a steady and alarming mortality among his 'Home Indians'; in 1756 only thirteen canoes of Sturgeon Indians had come to trade, in 1757 thirty-nine canoes came, and in 1758 they were fifty-seven. Isham hoped that the increase would continue, and in fact Batt and Potts in 1759 brought down forty-four, to be followed by twenty more the next day and by a further fifteen a week later—a total of seventy-nine canoes. The trade of York rose steadily from 21,000 Made-beaver in 1754 to 27,000 in 1756 and 33,642 in 1760.

The French trade suffered, but their threat was still a real one. Of Severn River Humphrey Marten wrote in May 1759 that 'I may be thought Impertinent for what I am going to Say, yet I am Sure it proceeds from an honest heart, which is, if that there is not speedily

Some Method taken to Secure Severn River from the Encroachments of the French, a very Great Loss in trade must Necessarily follow'. That year, however, saw the French hold on the upland Indians weakened. Joseph Smith returned from his journey to the Assiniboines with the news that the Indians had broken open and plundered the French house—presumably Fort Bourbon on Cedar Lake—while from Churchill came similar heartening news as Henday and Smith set out once more for the Blackfeet.

Churchill had not taken a very active part in the English thrust to the interior. York under Isham and his successors Andrew Graham and Humphrey Marten (for Isham died on 13th April, 1761) took the lead and produced Henday and the 'school' of Hudson's Bay winterers. It is the more remarkable that Churchill should take so little a part, for although Henday himself, Joseph Smith and Isaac Batt were English, it is certain that George Potts was at least half 'Eskomay', while Joseph Waggoner was probably the half-breed son of the former Governor Rowland Waggoner. Close alliance with the Indians was a necessary condition of success, the increasing number of half-breeds in the Company's employment was a great advantage, and in this respect, Churchill should have stood supreme, for in 1759 Ferdinand Jacobs handed over the post to Moses Norton. This man, who was later to gain a most unenviable reputation, is described as a full-blooded Indian, and one who combined in himself the worst characteristics of both the English and the Indian races. He first appears on the Company's books as an apprentice to one of the ships' captains, and it is most probable that he was the half-breed son of Richard Norton, former Governor of Churchill, who certainly had some Indian children. For the moment, in 1759, Moses Norton only held command at Churchill for a year, until Jacobs returned. But he had been Second for some years, and it says much for the preoccupations of the post that his influence was not felt earlier and more strongly. For 1758 was a year in which no trade came to Churchill from the Athabaska Indians, and Norton soon took steps to follow York's lead in going inland to fetch trade. William Grover was the man to hand for the purpose; he had been too poor a traveller to go with Henday in 1755 and had spoiled that project, but he was a former apprentice and a useful and willing man. Moved to Churchill in 1756, he served in many capacities, was always regarded as the most likely man to send inland, and in 1759 was actually sent off by Moses Norton. Once more, however, Grover failed. He was back at Churchill within three days of his departure; the 'very Honest Good Leading Indian' with whom he had set out fell sick twenty-four

miles up the river, Grover came back for help, and found on his return that the Indian had recovered and gone off without him!

Norton had not put all his trust in the ill-fated Grover. He had
also sent inland a handsome present of tobacco, brandy and other
things, by the hand of a near relation of a 'Spanncible [responsible]
Leading Indian' who had not been down to Churchill for several
years, and was reported to be trading inland with the French. To his
delight the renegade came down to trade in 1760, bringing three or
four strangers with him. It was not only Norton's gifts which had
wrought the change. The French had not gone into their house in
1759, but had merely sent some of their Indians to spread rumours
that the reason for their non-arrival was that they had fought a 'Skir-
mish' with the English and won a victory. Norton had, of course, no
information as yet of Wolfe's victory, but he sturdily insisted that
this must be 'a great Falsity'.

News that the French had not gone to their far inland posts therefore came down to both York and Churchill in 1759; and the results
were to be seen in the trade returns, as in the fact that new Indians
began to come in to trade—though Churchill was disappointed in
this. News came of eight Indians of a different tribe from any that
traded at Churchill, who had started out for Churchill but had turned
back on account of one of the 'Southern Indians' falling lame.

So far the difficulties of the war-beset French had coincided with
the efforts of the Company's servants. The latter did not cease in
1759. In that year George Potts and Isaac Batt were sent back into
the Sturgeon Indians' country, again after a very brief interlude at
York. In 1760 Batt seems to have done nothing very notable, but
Potts again went inland. This, however, was a disappointing voyage,
for he came down to York in June 1761, bringing no trade with him;
his Indian leader had died and he had been unable to keep the Indians to their hunting. Potts was immediately sent inland again 'Not
being a fitt person to Entertain amongst English Men, having 3 bad
properties, Drinking, pilfering, Swearing and Accustomed formerly
to go Over our Works'—that is, to consort with the Indians and
their women.

Joseph Waggoner, meantime, had also continued to bring down
the 'Upland Indians' to the Bay; he went in with the 'Uplanders' in
1760, and in 1761 he brought down sixty-five canoes to trade. He
also brought news that though he had passed two French houses
inland, there was not a Frenchman to be seen. At the same time
Humphrey Marten at York got seven canoes of Indians down to
trade, with the news that 'the french left Basquea in the Fall and none

of them has been Seen this Winter as usual'. York had previously been alarmed by a report that the Indians were all deserting Albany because they said that the French had captured one English post, 'which if true must be Moose or Eastmain Forts'. In fact it was neither. This was merely an Indian rumour; the truth lay in the reports brought from inland by Waggoner and the Indians. The French had deserted their upland posts and not only Canada but the hinterland of the fur trade right to the Rockies lay in British hands.

BOOKS FOR REFERENCE

HUDSON's BAY RECORD SOCIETY—Vol. XII.

BREBNER, J. B.—*The Explorers of North America 1492–1806* (London, 1955).

BURPEE, Lawrence J.—*The Search for the Western Sea* (Toronto, 1908).

HENDAY, Anthony—'York Factory to the Blackfeet Country. The Journal of Anthony Hendry, 1754–55', edited by Lawrence J. Burpee (*Transactions of the Royal Society of Canada*, Third Series, Vol. I, Section II (Ottawa, 1907).

ARTICLE

WILSON, Clifford—'Across the Prairies two centuries ago'. See *The Canadian Historical Association Report for 1954–1955* (Ottawa, 1955).

CHAPTER XLIV

TRADE, INVESTMENT AND THE PEACE OF PARIS

The victory on the Heights of Abraham left the French of the interior without direction, organisation, or (perhaps more important, for they were outspoken individualists) trade goods or markets. The military events for the rest of the war, until the Peace in 1763, therefore offered no threat that the French fur trade might recover its power to menace the posts by the Bay. But the natural advantages of routes, knowledge and contacts with the Indians, had not ceased; they had merely passed into English hands.

Already by 1761 the fur-traders from New England and the south, who had been as much concerned as the Hudson's Bay men over their own trade rivalry with the French, had begun to work from Montreal. They had begun to find the advantages of the river-and-lake approach to the fur lands of the north and west, a source of better furs than they had been able to get from the south and east of the continent. By that year Moose was feeling the new form of competition, and its Master was writing that his trade was being encroached from the south and south-east by 'Interlopers who will be more Destructive to our Trade than the French was'. For 'The French were in a manner Settled, Their Trade fixt, Their Standard moderate and themselves under particular regulations and restrictions, which I doubt is not the Case now'. The new rivals were, he said, alluring the Indians to their posts by considerable presents and by trading upon easier terms than their neighbours. He feared that trade would soon become nothing but an auction which would be 'carried by them who bids most'; such wild competition would entail the ruin of many, and the survivors would then have to contract their standard of trade, and would thereby lose the Indians.

There was something very shrewdly prophetic in this early analysis of the new rivalry from Montreal, and something clear and cogent in the argument, also put forward by Pollexfen from Moose in 1761, that the rout of the French did not mean that the Company could relax in its care or in any way alter its standard of trade. The Indians would be most adversely affected by any attempt to cut the 'Standard', for their minds did not work according to normal European thought on trade matters. 'When they have been once used to a

648

Custom, there is no breaking it with Safety'; if they had got used to receiving a yard of tobacco for a beaver they would prefer to trade where they only got a foot rather than abate by six inches the price to the trader who habitually gave them a yard.

Pollexfen at Moose was not alone in his warnings that relaxation and a drop in the 'Standard' were not to be thought of, and the Company can have seen little hope that the victories and the imminence of peace would bring any great relief. But there seemed very little of which the Committee could complain, little which called for remedy in the last years of the war. Shipments home, and sales in London, enabled the Committee to maintain dividends throughout the war, and the prosperity of Sir Bibye's period as Governor was continued under his successors, Benjamin Pitt, Governor from 1743 to 1746, Thomas Knapp from 1746 to 1750, and Bibye's son, Sir Atwell Lake, Governor from 1750 to 1760. The dividend did, indeed, fall as low as seven per cent. in 1749 and 1750, but neither the Company nor the City was ever in any doubt about the stability and the prosperity of the trade.

In view of the opportunities for investment which the period offered, and the skilled way in which Sir Bibye had started the Company on a policy of investment, it would have been cause for remark if the Committee had always had sufficient mobile cash in hand to meet all its expenses. There were, in fact, occasions even during this period when ready cash to meet immediate demands had to be raised by short-term loans—as for example in 1750, when Secretary Hayes wrote to the Deputy Governor, John Merry, to warn him that there would be immediate need for about £4,000 when the ships arrived and to ask him to extend his loan outstanding until some South Sea Annuities held by the Company could be sold. But the notable feature of the Company's financial history during this period is that it always had very substantial sums invested. The picture of the Company struggling along on short-term loans and debenture borrowings up to 1713 is most emphatically reversed.

With this went a steady and most business-like approach to the Company's affairs, with a complete revision of the By-laws in 1739, regular weekly meetings of the Committee every Wednesday, and close and constant attention to the trade in all its aspects. With Sir Bibye himself, for example, the Committee's relations were always cordial, if not deferential, and he was certainly always given accommodation when he could give reasonable security; he was at times allowed to borrow even up to the extent of £22,000. But in 1738 the Company took out a Chancery injunction against him, to prevent him from selling the £12,222 stock which stood in his name. In a similarly business-like vein from 1745 onwards the accounts for the ships are kept in a new and more sensible way. Formerly all expenses were added to the cost of the ship, year by year; the result was that as the ship got older and more worthless she stood at ever-increasing sums in the books. From 1745 onwards the value of the ship was written down by a proportion each year until she had been brought to a nominal figure.

Ships, and wages to their crews, still played an important part in the Company's annual expenditure. With furs selling well, revenue from trade ran at an annual level somewhere between £22,000 and £30,000, rising towards the end of the period. The annual payments ran at something below this level—at £22,948 in 1728 for example —so that what with the unexpended balances on the year's trade and the interest from sums invested, the Company's capital steadily increased. Each year, after payment of dividend, the cash balance left with the Secretary amounted to something between three and five thousand pounds, and it is not, therefore, surprising to find that the Company becomes a quite substantial investor in the more staid stocks.

Apart from advances to Sir Bibye and other members of the Company against security, there were three main types of investment made by the Committee—in the South Sea Company, in the East India Company and in the Bank of England. All were easily negotiable, and the Company bought and sold freely, moved by considerations which, could they be discovered, would throw much light on the London investment market from year to year but which do not affect the history of the Company as such. For example, in February 1732 the sum of £10,000 in Bank notes was locked away as cash available; by June the Secretary had paid the bills of the year, amounting to £19,215 19s. 3d., and all that was left in the chest was £3,000 in Bank notes and Sir Bibye's bond for £2,129 15s. 7d. This, however, was in itself a very satisfactory balance after the payment of the accounts, and when the sales had added their quota of over £25,000 in cash, in the following June the Committee found itself with £22,067 7s. 6d. to invest, having just recently bought £10,000 (nominal) of East India bonds at a slight premium. A further £10,000 of East India bonds was therefore bought in October 1733, the holding in South Sea annuities was brought up to the round figure of £1,000, and in November of that year the Committee took stock of its script locked away in the chest and found it had £7,300 in Bank notes, £2,700 in gold, the £1,000 of South Sea annuities, and a hundred East India bonds each worth £100—a holding of something over £20,000 nominal value, with dividends and debts all paid.

Such investments were at that particular juncture perhaps a little more than the Company could afford, and the securities were not all held until they matured. In October of the same year, 1734, thirty of the East India bonds (on which a dividend had in the meantime been paid) were kept out of the chest for realisation, and a little later twenty of them were sold, to be re-purchased after the fur-sale of November had brought the Company into funds again. At about the same time begins a habit of investing in Bank of England stocks; £2,000 was laid out in 'Bank circulation' in February 1734, and a further £3,000 shortly afterwards. The details of the investments do not matter from the point of view of the history of the Company; the essential thing was that the Company had become an investor instead of a borrower.

During Sir Bibye's régime the total of investment was kept at about the level of £20,000; in 1737, for example, the stock-taking revealed that the balance consisted of £1,279 at the bankers (William Atwill and Company), £1,572 5s. in Bank Circulation stock (a token payment for ten times the value), £11,248 in East India Bonds, £1,167 10s. in Old South Sea Annuities, £3,082 4s. 8d. in Exchequer Tallies and Orders, and £3,080 2s. 8d. still due on Sir Bibye's mortgage for his estate in Derbyshire. There were also, of course, the assets of the posts and ships, the stocks of goods and furs, the house and warehouse in London, and that unsubstantial asset (if it can be so called) the 'Account of the French Nation' for damages in time of peace.

From 1746 onwards the series of 'Balance Books' began to be kept. Here the balance of stocks in hand, ships, posts, remainders and other assets, was set out every half year against debts and dividends due. Forts and fortifications were reckoned as an asset of £100,000. The debt due from the French Nation was counted as an asset of £100,543 13s. 9d. and in 1746 the first balance showed a total of £255,121 14s. 1d., which meant that the mobile assets of the Company amounted to about £50,000 at that date. The system was vitiated by the practice of reckoning the value of the posts from the 'Value of goods remaining and exported' so that the insignificant post of Richmond with heavy remains in hand stood at £18,579 18s. 6d. while Albany, having few remains, stood at only £904 in 1757. But it gave a fair indication of the constant stock-taking and of the increasing investments of the Company.

This was continuous prosperity, and the fact that the investments rose steadily in value through the century is evidence that the war years did little to upset the Company's trade. At the balancing of the books in July 1745 investments stood at £34,852 6s. 6d., in addition to which there was cash in the iron chest to the value of £700 and cash in the Secretary's hands to the value of £1,065 12s. 0d.—a total of £36,617 18s. 6d. By July 1756, at the start of the Seven Years' War, investments had risen to £46,000, and the cash in reserve stood at over £2,000. By the end of the war, in July 1763, investments were of the nominal value of £59,000 (Consols had been bought at a discount), cash in hand stood at £5,959 3s. 3d. and cash in the chest, which was soon invested in Exchequer Bills, easily negotiable but bearing 4 per cent. interest, stood at over £16,000. The habit of tucking away surplus cash in Exchequer Bills became the regular practice of the Committee; it brought in as much as £300 a year in some years, but normally it was used as a lock-up for money between the end of the November sale and the payment of tradesmen's bills in the following June, and brought in a little over £100 for the six months period. By 1769 (the end of a ledger) the wartime prosperity had continued into the peace period and the investments of the Company stood at £89,000 nominal value, in addition to £773 cash; the Company's assets, all told and including the claims against the French, were reckoned at £340,365 13s. 7d.

This was a remarkable achievement, and was certainly the basis for the Company's survival during the difficult period which the Peace ushered in. It meant that the Company which had emerged at Utrecht dependent on the connivance of a bankrupt Governor, who was also a banker, for the cash to meet its tradesmen had become a substantial corporation, with a well-chosen and solid portfolio of investments and with a substantial backing in the City which gave it stability to overcome even the most strenuous opposition. Of its investments by this date £30,000 was in East India Bonds and a further £3,000 in East India annuities; £10,000 was in Old South Sea Annuities, and £46,000 was in various forms of Bank of England stock (£20,000 in Consols; £20,000 in 3 per cent. Reduced Annuities and £6,000 in the 1756, $3\frac{1}{2}$ per cent. Annuities). Even with the prevailing low rate of 3 per cent. yield, this meant that, with its gains from Exchequer Bills added to its dividends, the Company was getting about £3,000 a year from its investments. The intangible aspects of financial stability were even more important than this revenue; the approach of the Company to its own finances and to the City, and the reaction of the City to the Company, were factors which conditioned the developments of the next half-century.

The period of the peace negotiations gave warning that the times to come would not be easy for the Company despite this phenomenal growth in its wealth. The war period had been one in which, quite apart from the Dobbs attack on the Company, there had been a marked feeling throughout the prosperous cities of Great Britain against such chartered companies as were successfully exploiting their privileges, and even stronger feeling against those who were neglecting their opportunities. The Journals of the House of Commons and of the House of Lords during this period contain innumerable petitions from tradesmen and merchants of London and the provincial cities praying for the annulment or modification of the chartered privileges, and especially for modification of the great companies—the East India Company, the Royal African Company, and the Hudson's Bay Company.

The extent to which this general feeling against chartered companies could affect a particular issue is shewn by the fact that at the time of the consideration of the Company's affairs by the Committee of the House of Commons, in March 1749, petitions came in from all over the country, often from areas which had not the slightest concern with the fur trade—from London, Yarmouth, Stockport, Wolverhampton, Shrewsbury, Leeds, Hull, Liverpool, Carlisle, Newcastle-under-Lyme, Clitheroe, Manchester, Halifax, Nottingham, Birmingham, Derby, Lancaster, Wakefield, Macclesfield, Wigan, Ripon, Appleby, Whitehaven, Preston, Kendal, and from the Merchant Venturers of Bristol. The petitions were often couched in identical terms, and they shew the common background of merchant interest and organisation working through a system of pressure-groups in the House of Commons, rather than serious interest in the fur trade or in the North-west passage. The attempt to establish a rival company for development of the trade of the Labrador coast, in 1752, was of a piece with such a general challenge to chartered rights. Still more indicative of the general attitude was the fact that although the Labrador syndicate of that year challenged the Hudson's Bay Company's rights on the double ground that the coast from Belle Isle to Hudson Strait was not included in the Company's Charter and that the Charter had not been renewed in Parliament, yet they sought just such an exclusive grant of trade for themselves. The Lords of Trade and Plantations spoke the normal language on this subject when they replied that, as to an exclusive grant of trade 'the experience of the many inconveniencies attending such grants more particularly in the case of the Hudson's Bay Company, makes it a matter at least of great doubt and difficulty'. Chartered rights were not popular; but they were useful, and their holders were men of weight and influence.

So the Company maintained its rights to the trade of the Eastmain, as it had maintained its Charter against the challenge of Arthur Dobbs. But the transfer of sovereignty over Canada to the British Crown in 1763 at the Treaty of Paris completely changed the situation. Already the rights of settled colonists to trade with the Indians had been upheld against company rights. In 1737 the settlers of South Carolina had maintained that despite the Act of the Government of Georgia, they had the right to trade with the Indians of their vicinity; their case was that the Crown alone could not grant an exclusive trade and that therefore only such charters as had been confirmed in Parliament were valid. For this argument the Royal African Company was put forward as a company whose privileges had been taken away because they had not been confirmed by Parliament, while the East India Company was vouched as a company fully justified because it had been confirmed by Parliament. The Hudson's Bay Company was in jeopardy.

While the position of chartered companies as a constitutional anomaly was thus under discussion, the actual extent of the lands covered by the Charter was also open to dispute and was the cause of some anxiety. Following hard on the heels of the Dobbs affair and the vindication of the Company, in 1750 came a request that the Company should define its claims. This, like the challenge to chartered rights, was not a particular attack on the Company but was part of a wider attempt to define limits and claims on the American continent, especially in view of the encroachments of the French. A commission had been set up in 1749 to settle boundaries, and all Governors of British colonies were asked to submit maps and the best descriptions available of the limits of their territories; the Hudson's Bay Company was included among the others. Here the Company inevitably threw back to the discussions of 1719, in which it had tried to establish a southern boundary with the French in fulfilment of the terms granted by the Treaty of Utrecht. A memorial and a map were submitted in October 1750, the Company's case was included among the others discussed in Paris during the negotiations which followed the Treaty of Aix-la-Chapelle, and the boundaries were argued from 1750 to 1753. But with Governor Shirley of Massachusetts in a dominant position, interest was devoted to settling a boundary for Acadia and Nova Scotia, and enthusiasm gathered round the problem of the return of Louisburg to France rather than round a move to vindicate claims to unchartered areas in the north.

These were years in which the Company was so far from securing its southern frontier that it could with justice inform the commissioners that though the French had 'never offered to navigate in the Bay, nor made any settlements on the coast, or carried on any trade there' since Utrecht, yet they had raised an opposition by means of 'Inland interloping settlements' and by wood-runners. In answer the Company had erected its own defensive posts at Moose, Henley and Flamborough (Richmond and Severn were not as yet in action in 1750). At the same time the opportunity was not lost to enlighten the administration on the facts of the fur trade and to protest in advance the validity of the Company's policy of trading from posts on the shore, rather than of sending inland and establishing posts analogous to those of the French. The Indians, they told the commissioners, were 'altogether a Wandering People' who lived by hunting and had no agriculture; they traded where they would, and they were in the habit of carrying goods inland not only for their own consumption but also to dispose of them among other natives there 'which it is apprehended is better performed by them than could be done by Europeans, as the Rivers that Run into the Bay admit of no Navigation for Ships or other Vessels of Burthen at any considerable distance up the same'.

There was nothing new or original in this, but it is interesting to see the conviction with which the Committee reiterated to government the wisdom and knowledge with which the traders filled their letters. Such views were not so irrelevant in a memorandum to the Lords of Trade and Plantations in 1750 as might appear, for they were parts of the defence of the Company's policy against British rivals, and the challenge of 1749 was still in men's minds.

As against the French, nothing was achieved in these years. But British rivals were held at bay, and the Company was left to carry out its own policy of opposition to the wood-runners—upheld even in its claims to Labrador. After the failure of the Labrador challenge of 1752 the next episode came with a further enquiry from the Lords of Trade in 1755. To this also the Company replied as it had replied to all such enquiries since Utrecht, with a desire for a boundary to the south from Cape Perdrix to Lake Mistassini and so westwards along the 49th parallel.

The capture of Quebec and the other victories of 1759 did not bring to an end hostilities in Canada; it was not until Montreal had been taken in the following year that the Company's servants in their voyages to the interior began to find that the wood-runners were withdrawing, although Jean Baptiste Larlee had come into York as early as 1759, and had been taken into the Company's employ, and in 1760 Albany had written of the capture of Quebec as 'a National Advantage' which would be 'a means of enlarging the Trade of Your Honours Settlements'. The Year of Victories did, however, initiate a series of negotiations for a peace, and though changes of monarch and changes of minister, with the chances of politics and the fortunes of war, delayed the end of hostilities until 1763, the rest of the war was fought out against a background of constant nego- tiation. With the accession of George III and the rise of Bute to political power, Pitt could not maintain his control of the war and the negotiations, and he resigned, to be succeeded as Secretary of State by Egremont in 1761. He was, however, well in the saddle when moves for a peace were started, and the Lords of Trade sent on to him a copy of the memorial which the Company submitted in December 1759, claiming full satisfaction for damages and stating its boundary claims as they had stood since Utrecht.

The Company had chosen well in soliciting Pitt's favour, for not only was he the outstanding political personality but his general con- cepts of imperial trade and of ousting the French from the American continent placed him on the Company's side. He was, too, the Great Commoner, the friend of the City; and he looked to the Treaty of Utrecht with almost the same regard as the Company. To him 'The Treaty of Utrecht, which was an indelible stain on the last genera- tion, is become the unattainable desire of the present'. It was his opposition to a premature peace which drove him to retirement in October 1761. But it was the news that plenipotentiaries had been nominated to discuss terms of peace which led the Company to seek his protection in April of that year. Under the form of a petition to the King, the Company put forward a memorandum of its claims against the French, of the damages received, and of the long history of the abortive attempts to settle a southern boundary. At any peace, the Company asked that its claims might also be considered and settled. At the same time the Committee asked for an interview with Pitt himself and, learning that he was unwell and could not see them, sent him a copy of the petition, with a covering note regretting his indisposition and the lack of a chance to put the Company's case to him.

Pitt was indeed vitally interested in the problems of North America, determined to oust the French from the trade of that continent. But since he was equally determined to have nothing to do with peace negotiations at that juncture, he was unable to lend any support to the Company since he would only hold office on condition that no opportunity to serve the Company's interest, no negotiations for a peace, were accepted. In the event, peace negotiations were continued, and Pitt surrendered the seals in October; the Company found its memorandum and petition taken up by Lord Egremont, who had succeeded him as Secretary of State. The Committee were given an appointment with Egremont in September 1762, but there is no evidence that the case of the Company bulked at all large in the propositions for discussion with the French. The major issue as far as North America was concerned was whether Canada should be retained or should be returned to the French, or whether Guadeloupe (or later almost all of the French West Indies) should be taken instead. As British naval success in the West Indies went alongside of the peace negotiations the original problem suffered a shift of emphasis, and it became clear that the Canada *versus* Guadeloupe issue had reached a stage at which it was almost certain that the terms of peace would give Britain both Canada and some portion of the French West Indies—but not necessarily Guadeloupe.

If Canada was destined to remain in British hands, the boundary of the Hudson's Bay territories to the south would be a purely domestic problem, as between two British territories. It could therefore be settled at leisure—or perhaps not settled—and there is no need to wonder that the Company and its claims appear to have taken but little of the care of the statesmen who were negotiating the peace. True, such neglect argued a willingness to overlook the claim for damages and to rest content with the certainty that the boundary problem would be capable of settlement. But responsibility for damages would by now be impossible to attribute to any specific French body, the sums had been swollen by compound interest out of all relation to the original losses or to any capacity to pay, and it is more than doubtful if even the Committee of the Company at this time seriously hoped that the 'Account of the French Nation' would ever be paid. The large sum outstanding was written off without comment in the early years of the peace.

The Company and its claims therefore held no major place in the minds of the statesmen who negotiated the peace. They were dominated by other interests, by the possibility that possession of Canada might, or might not, react on the wavering loyalty and economic balance of the southern British colonies, and by the mercantilist obsessions with the West Indies, with sugar and with navigation. It was not until a month after the definitive terms had been signed with France that Egremont turned, in March 1763, once more to the Company, to ask for a statement on the limits of the Company's claims in Labrador.

With almost a century of trade behind it, the Company was in a strong position by 1763. It was a position of strength based upon its sound and staid internal balance, however, rather than a position of power based upon its political importance, the volume of its trade or the personalities involved. With few exceptions this had been typical of the first century of its life.

When the first group of courtier-statesmen who predominated among the founder-members of the Company had given way to the City men in the crisis of 1679, the Company had seen the last of great national personalities. The only exception to this was Marlborough; otherwise its Committee and its Governors were reputable, solvent and shrewd, but not such men as to sway the nation. Of a piece was the Company's position in national politics and in the national economy.

The Dobbs episode had raised quite a flutter over the Company's position, its trade and its Charter. But even at that time the Royal African Company and the East India Company had occupied more, and more serious, attention. With two or perhaps three ships a year engaged, with exports in the neighbourhood of £20,000 a year and imports and fur sales of about £30,000, the Company was an insignificant element in the national economy, and when it attracted interest it was on account of the potential value of its trade, not on account of the actual achievement.

The Company's position even in the fur trade fitted in with this background. So much is talked of monopoly, both by the Company and by its rivals, that it is natural to assume that the Company had a monopoly of the London fur-market, and perhaps even of that of Europe. But this was never true. Throughout this century the London furriers derived quantities of beaver from the mainland American colonies which fell very little short of those got from Hudson Bay. The quality of the Bay furs put them in a class apart, but that was a distinction which lost its edge as the century wore on and the ability to make beaver-wool from any kind of skin made the *parchment* and even the summer skins almost as useful as the fine quality *coat*. So in London the prices fetched by the Company's furs were prices reached in competition with important shipments from Boston and New York, from Virginia and Maryland too. When, as was normally the case, much of the fur was destined for the markets of

Europe, the prices fetched were set against the state of the European trade and so the Company's furs were in competition with those produced, under conditions of great political stimulation, from Canada. So although the 'exclusive trade' of Hudson Bay and its adjacent territories undoubtedly gave the Company a highly favoured position, it was not such a monopoly as enabled it to hold the British furrier or hatter to ransom. England had furs enough, and to spare. They had to sell on a competitive market, and the Company's favoured position for production had never given it a monopoly for selling.

The Charter had indeed been challenged, but although the Law Officers of the Crown had wished that the challenge might be brought to the decision of a test case at law, the point at issue remained still open. The question was whether a Royal Charter needed Parliamentary confirmation to secure validity. But since the challenges came from would-be rivals in the field of production, not from victims of a sales-monopoly, no great public feeling was ever involved and the Company emerged unscathed. The Charter was still valid, if disputed.

But although the Company and its Charter survived the challenges, its relations with Government and with government officials never reached a point of cordiality, let alone of connivance. Since the day when James Duke of York, as Governor, had refused to sign the Company's letters, official support for the Company had been cold and reluctant except during the negotiations for the Treaty of Utrecht. It is significant that no damages were ever recovered from the French and that the 'Account of the French Nation' in the end had to write off a loss of over a hundred thousand pounds. No boundary with the French was ever settled, and even as Britain came victoriously up to the Treaty of Paris the Company's claims were still being steadily and purposefully put on one side. This, also, was typical of the century which had passed, for throughout that period the Company had been able to count on the vague benevolence of Government rather than upon any active and purposeful interest. Even when the indifference which led to the Treaty of Ryswick had been replaced by the firm policy of the Utrecht period the change had come with a general change in government policy, not with pressure for the Company as such. In fact, the concept of the Company as a great corporation of lobbyists, secure in the backing of well-placed politicians, is as far from the truth as is the concept of a Company monopolising the London fur-market.

Yet the Company had in fact preserved its Charter, had enlarged its trade, extended its operations to the prairies, and built up a stable and satisfactory chest of investments. All of this had been done upon the original capital of something less than £10,000 paid in, to which the only addition had been made in the few thousands actually subscribed during the Bubble period—a total of perhaps £12,000 in actual investment by the proprietors. For the rest, the working funds had come from judicious borrowing, and the accumulation of capital had come from remarkable restraint in the payment of dividends and from steady accumulation of undistributed profits.

Up to 1763 the accumulation of the profits of this quiet, well-ordered, and by no means spectacular company had been its best policy. It was perhaps a slightly inexplicable policy, for the purpose of such considerable investments could not easily be foreseen; but it was a policy which accorded well with the unobtrusive sanity which marked most of the Company's proceedings. It was a policy, too, which was to prove invaluable in the new conditions which came with the British conquest of Canada.

The second half of the eighteenth century saw the complete victory of the British in the struggle for overseas possessions. In the basic command of the seas, in the possession of strategic points for the protection of colonial trade, and in both India and America (the two major theatres of colonial war) the French had been decisively beaten. In the West Indies too, victory had gone to the British and disposal of the spoils lay in their hands. But already new ideas were at work, and trade upon a basis of freedom, rather than a system of rule interwoven with chartered corporations, was gaining an increasing hold upon men's minds. As yet such ideas were not applied to the American colonies; indeed they were not clearly formulated or expressed for our old colonial possessions, since habits of thought, machinery for administration, and an established routine of trade, all made for formalism and conservatism there. But for the newly-conquered possession of Canada there was no such background; the new régime made possible an alliance between the enterprising French *voyageur* and the enterprising English merchant. This was to prove a formidable combination, and the Company had to face it at the level of purely business competition for furs and for markets. The Charter lay in the background, unchallenged but by no means indisputable, as it had lain for half a century. The Company was well-connected, liable to be called upon at the highest political level but unable to sway discussions at that level, as it had been for half a century. But the strength of the Company lay not in its privileged status nor in its nearness to government, but in the sound financial and trading position which it had built up in the competitive trade of the London fur-market. In the half-century which followed after the conquest of Canada privileges and influence counted for even less than previously. It was as well that the Company had built up its strength and its balances by sound trade, for the ensuing era of free-trade from Canada left it nothing else on which to rely.

BOOKS FOR REFERENCE

Cambridge History of the British Empire (Cambridge, 1929), Vol. I.
Cambridge History of the British Empire (Cambridge, 1930), Vol. VI.
EGERTON, H. E.—*Short History of British Colonial Policy* (London, 1897).
HARLOW, V. T.—*The Founding of the Second British Empire, 1763–93* (London, 1952).
MORTON, Arthur S.—*A History of the Canadian West to 1870–71* (London, 1939).
PARES, R.—*War and Trade in the West Indies, 1739–63* (Oxford, 1936).

ARTICLE

GRANT, W. L.—'Canada versus Guadeloupe, an Episode of the Seven Years' War'. See *American Historical Review*, Vol. XVII, pp. 735–43.

INDEX

INDEX

15

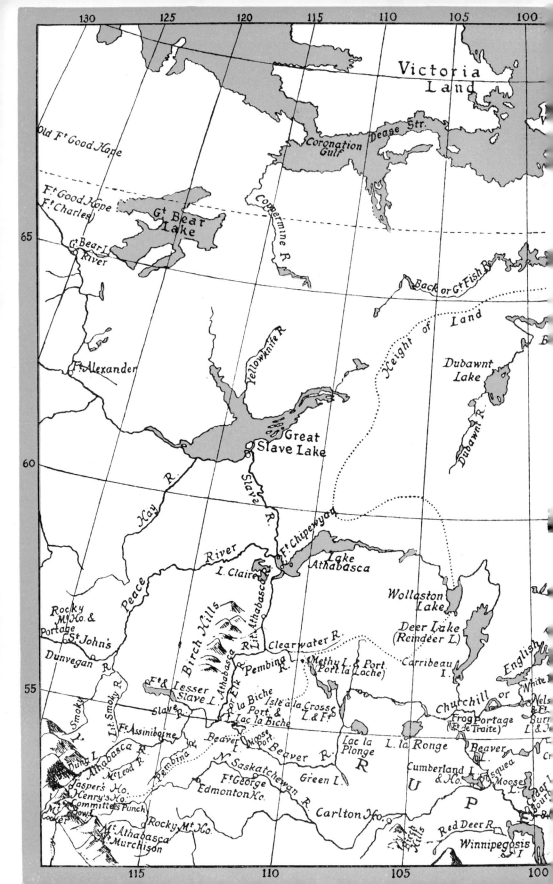